THE SHIPS AND AIRCRAFT OF THE U.S. FLEET

THE SHIPS AND AIRCRAFT OF THE U.S. FLEET

TWELFTH EDITION

BY NORMAN POLMAR

NAVAL INSTITUTE PRESS
ANNAPOLIS, MARYLAND

To My Parents,
Dave and Ida

.

Contents

Preface

This twelfth edition of *The Ships and Aircraft of the U.S. Fleet* describes the U.S. Navy of the early 1980s. This edition continues the effort begun in the eleventh edition, to provide a new order of coverage of the U.S. Fleet. The breadth and depth of data on the Fleet —its ships, aircraft, weapons, electronics, organization, and personnel—are greater than available in any other single volume.

Increased emphasis has been given in this edition to the coverage of naval aviation and electronics, two vital aspects of modern fleets. In addition, an expanded strike and transfer list has been added to describe the "fate" of U.S. Navy and Coast Guard ships disposed of since 1970.

In general, the information in this edition is current through late 1980. Standard abbreviations and terms are used for the most part, with all explained in the Glossary in the front of the book and in Appendix A, Ship Classifications. The principal exception is the current status of ships. The official Naval Vessel Register, for example, uses RECU to indicate ships that are "Inactive, in commission, in reserve, undergoing conversion," while the Navy Program Information Center uses INSAC for inactive ships. In *Ships and Aircraft* a more simplified active (AA, PA) and reserve (AR, PR, MR) scheme is used to indicate ship status, with active ships—in commission and in service—being shown in bold face. Ships in the Maritime Administration's National Defense Reserve Fleet (NDRF) that remain under Navy ownership are listed as MR. In addition, a number of amphibious and auxiliary ships are laid up in the NDRF under Maritime Administration ownership.

The author is in debt to many individuals for their guidance and their contributions to this effort, most especially Dr. Giorgio Arra, the world's leading ship photographer, whose views of the U.S. Fleet inundate these pages. Special thanks are also due to Fred Rainbow of the Naval Institute *Proceedings* and his colleagues on that outstanding publication for initiating my column "The U.S. Navy," which is based on this book, to Frank Uhlig, Jr., senior editor of the Naval Institute, and Dr. Norman Friedman of the Hudson Institute for their guidance.

Others who have contributed to this effort include Lieutenant Pete Clayton of the staff of Commander Naval Air Force, Pacific Fleet; Dr. Robert Scheina, Lieutenant Daniel Wood, and Miss Rosemary Whitehurst of the U.S. Coast Guard; Captain Robert B. Sims, Deputy Chief of Navy Information (CHINFO); Robert Carlisle, Lieutenant Commander Jolene K. Keefer, Miss Lynn Sundberg, Journalist Evelyn Jutte, and Miss Judy Van Benthuysen of CHINFO; Mr. Richard C. Bassett and Mrs. Susan Weidner of the Naval Ship Systems Command; Captain James H. Barrett, Lieutenant Commander Michael Wein, Lieutenant William Clyde, and Hoyle A. Taylor of the Naval Military Personnel Command; Vice Admiral Wesley McDonald, Deputy Chief of Naval Operations (Air Warfare), and Captains Gordon Murray, Jr., and Richard E. Allsopp of his staff; Vice Admiral James H. Doyle, former Deputy CNO (Surface Warfare); Rear Admiral Henry C. Mustin, Commander Cruiser-Destroyer Group 2; Mrs. Jane T. Wootton of the Naval Ship Research and Development Center; Lieutenant John Alexander of the Public Affairs Office, Atlantic Fleet; Lou Granger and his predecessor Larry Manning of the Military Sealift Command; Captain James C. Hay, former commanding officer, Naval Submarine Base New London; Captain Stuart D. Landersman, executive director, Pacific Fleet Tactical Training; Lieutenant Commander Mary S. Cooperman, public affairs officer, Chief of Naval Air Training; Commander Donald F. Dvornik, public affairs officer, Pacific Fleet; W. M. Frierson, Jr., Naval Air Station, Patuxent River; Captain Dale K. Patterson, former PAO, Pacific Fleet; Commander T. W. Turman, former PAO, Seventh Fleet; and Lieutenant Commander J. S. Renk, former PAO, Naval Surface Force, Atlantic Fleet.

Also, Robert Lawson, aviation photographer and editor of *The Hook;* Paul Martineau of Ingalls Shipbuilding Division, Litton Industries; E. M. Barnes, McDonnell Douglas, Tulsa; Jack T. Gilbride, president, Todd Shipyards; William S. Lind of the staff of Senator Gary Hart; Bruce R. Blakeley, Lockheed Electronics; Robert M. Hill, Tacoma Boatbuilding; Stephen Letzler, Sperry Rand; Peter Dakan, Boeing Marine Systems; Hal Gettings, Martin Marietta Aerospace; James Saulsbury, Hughes Aircraft; Robert W. Towse, McDonnell Douglas Astronautics; Tommy H. Thomason of Bell Helicopter Textron; Donald J. Norton and Nicholas F. Pensiero of RCA; and W. F. Searle, tug expert *par excellence.*

Several professional colleagues have also given of their time and energy to help this project: Mrs. Patty M. Maddocks, director of Library and Photographic Services of the Naval Institute; William Georgen, Dr. Scott Truver of the Santa Fe Corporation; John Patrick of Vought Corporation; Kohji Ishiwata, editor of *Ships of the World;* Dr. Jürgen Rohwer, historian and editor of *Marine-Rundschau;* and J. Labayle Couhat, editor of *Les Flottes De Combat.*

Mrs. Carol Swartz and Miss Beverly Baum of the Naval Institute are responsible for the editing and design of this edition.

Finally, two wives have tolerated their husbands' exhaustive devotion to the study of the ships and aircraft of the U.S. Fleet; special thanks are due to them for allowing this book to be done: Beverly Polmar and Carla Arra.

Norman Polmar
Alexandria, Virginia

1 State of the Fleet

During the 1980s the United States Fleet will probably decline in size, from the current 460-odd active, Navy-manned ships to possibly as few as 350 ships. At the same time, the Navy will have difficulty in manning even these ships with the quality of personnel needed to operate them effectively and continuously.

This situation could be changed either by a large-scale war involving the United States or by the combined action of the Congress and the Executive Branch. The latter action seems unlikely in the foreseeable future.

The situation is somewhat ironic, because during the 1980s the importance of the seas to American political, economic, and military interests will probably continue to increase. At the same time, Soviet naval forces can be expected to expand in capability and operations, as will the naval forces of some Third World nations with interests inimical to those of the United States.

The U.S. Fleet is being adversely affected by factors both external and internal to the Navy. The external factors include (1) the overall military personnel situation, (2) the high inflation rate, and (3) several years of indifference by the Executive Branch. At the same time, internal conditions have reduced the Navy's ability to solve its own problems: (1) a lack of cohesive and long-term planning, (2) continued internal revisions of shipbuilding plans, (3) frequent changes in organization (and hence placing of responsibility), and (4) the separate paths taken by the "platform unions"—air, surface, and submarine-nuclear.

The results of these conditions are major problems in manning and insufficient ships and aircraft to maintain the current Fleet strength. The effects of future reductions will be somewhat mitigated by more auxiliary ships being operated by civilian crews under the Military Sealift Command, and both amphibious and auxiliary ships being operated by the Naval Reserve Force. While both of these groups have demonstrated a high degree of professionalism in operating the ships they now have, this trend must be recognized as providing less unit effectiveness during crises and actual combat.

With respect to aircraft, the Navy and Marine Corps are not receiving enough of them to even replace operational losses. Attrition due to age and operational losses has resulted in reductions in the number of squadrons and aircraft per squadron. And, for both external and internal reasons, new aircraft development has not kept pace with requirements.

Indeed, the overall approach to the future development of the Fleet has been both slow and conservative. With the end of the Viet-

nam War, large numbers of older ships were retired, some because they were simply worn out (most of those of World War II construction), some because their effectiveness was minimal (such as the minesweeping force), and others because of high maintenance and operating costs. These ships were "traded in" in anticipation of the funds saved being applied to new ships, weapons, and sensors.

A whole phalanx of new programs was put forth to provide a modern fleet for the 1980s and beyond: small aircraft carriers (i.e., Sea Control Ships and VSTOL* Support Ships); advanced hull forms such as hydrofoils, surface effects ships, and SWATH† ships; small frigates that could be produced in larger numbers than could major warships; antiship cruise missiles; the 8-inch lightweight gun; VSTOL aircraft; advanced destroyer-based helicopters (LAMPS‡); and other innovations. Relatively few of these have joined the Fleet. There will be no surface effects ship nor SWATH warship program; the 8-inch gun is dead; only six hydrofoil missile craft of 30 planned will be completed; the small-carrier program died, although it is now being proposed again; the advanced VSTOL program died, but the tenacious Marine Corps will probably acquire an improved version of the decade-old Harrier VSTOL light attack aircraft.

Only the small, "low-mix" frigate program and the cruise missiles seem to have reached the full programs envisioned for them a decade ago. Over 50 of the frigates are being built (the original program provided for some 75). Perhaps more significant, the Harpoon, 60-mile antiship missile is being extensively deployed today in surface ships, attack submarines, and patrol aircraft; the Tomahawk cruise missile is in advanced development, in both Antiship Missile (T-ASM) and Land-Attack Missile (T-LAM) configurations. Those weapons can help compensate for reductions in U.S. naval forces and increasing threats.

However, on a day-to-day basis, it is still numbers of ships and aircraft that are important and only secondly their specific weapons and systems. This is not to say that modern ships, especially nuclear-propelled ships, are not more effective and more capable than their predecessors; rather a large fleet is required to support America's world-wide interests in the 1980s and beyond. For example, when the American hostages were captured in Tehran in November 1979, a carrier battle group was immediately deployed to

---

* Vertical/Short Take-Off and Landing aircraft.
† Small Waterplane Area Twin-Hull
‡ Light Airborne Multi-Purpose System.

the Arabian Sea area; this deployment has continued, with the RH-53D helicopters used for the aborted rescue mission in May 1980 coming from the deck of the carrier NIMITZ (CVN 68), which had raced into the Gulf of Oman for a night launch of the helicopters. (The NIMITZ remained under way for 144 consecutive days during that Mediterranean-Indian Ocean deployment, believed to have been the longest consecutive at-sea period in history for an aircraft carrier.) At almost the same time, the political turmoil in South Korea led the President to dispatch another battle group, led by the aircraft carrier CORAL SEA (CV 43), to Korean waters.

Other crises and tension in the Caribbean area, the Middle East, Africa, and Southeast Asia have also been met with the deployment of naval forces. Indeed, "send an aircraft carrier" has become an almost commonplace response to political and military crises. As Oliver Cromwell reportedly said "a gunboat is the best ambassador," so is a warship the best on-the-scene representation of American military capability and interest in most situations other than strategic confrontation between the United States and Soviet Union. Warships can be active or benign, within sight of the beach or out of sight over the horizon, sustained in the area for long periods, and totally under U.S. control. No other U.S. military forces can provide this mobility and flexibility.

It is difficult to ascertain how many ships and of what kind the U.S. Navy should have. Some qualified participants in the recent debates over future naval forces have argued for an advanced technology fleet; others for a conservative approach, generally for more of what we now have; and others for a variety of positions between the two extremes. Separate but related is the argument over numbers of ships. Prior to the Vietnam War, in 1960 the Navy had over 800 active, Navy-manned ships; in the early 1970s the number 600 was put forward as the minimum number the Navy required to carry out its assigned missions; there are now only some 460 ships.

Discussions of numbers have limited value because of the different types of ships (i.e., the "force mix"); still, such matters are useful to indicate trends and relative capabilities. In this respect, the numbers of ships authorized for the Navy during the past five years (Fiscal Years 1977–1981) have averaged only 15 ships per year; assuming a nominal 30-year service life, this program would support a 450-ship fleet. However, the very large number of ships that will reach their thirtieth year during the decade of the 1990s (e.g., over 50 missile-armed cruisers and destroyers, some 40 amphibious ships) will require larger building programs than even 15 per year to maintain 450 active ships.

Also significant is the force mix of recent construction programs. For example, the FY 1973–1984 shipbuilding programs should provide a total of 56 frigates of the OLIVER HAZARD PERRY (FFG 7) class. These are primarily Antisubmarine Warfare (ASW) ships, with limited antiair and antiship capabilities. Added to the previously built ASW frigates, by 1990 there will be some 120 of these "low-mix" ships in service. Although today's frigates are far more capable than their predecessors, because of the increasing threat presented by modern Soviet naval forces, the frigate remains the Navy's low-mix warship on a relative basis.

Between 1960—the pre-Vietnam period—and 1990 the number of frigates will have increased from 41 to about 120; at the same time the overall fleet will have declined from 812 active ships to an estimated 450. Thus, the portion of the fleet that is low-mix will have increased more than five times:

	1960	1970	1980	1990 (estimated)
Cruisers-Destroyers	240 (30%)	186 (24%)	100 (22%)	110 (24%)[a]
Frigates	41 (5%)	47 (6%)	65 (14%)	120 (27%)
Total Active Fleet	812	769	462	450 *maximum*

[a] Includes 15 CG 47 Aegis ships.

Indeed, in 1981 the only "high-mix" surface combatants under construction are four missile-armed variants of the SPRUANCE design (KIDD class) and the first few Aegis missile cruisers of the TICONDEROGA class (CG 47, formerly DDG 47). The former were acquired by the default of the Iranian government after the fall of the Shah in 1979. (At the same time the Soviet Navy has four classes of missile-armed cruisers and destroyers under construction, the largest being the KIROV class of some 23,000 tons with nuclear propulsion.)

Still another factor is the planned procurement of noncombat ships. Beginning with FY 1979 the Carter Administration has planned to procure 12 sonar surveillance ships (T-AGOS) and 14 forward deployment ships (T-AKX) for Marine weapons and equipment. Of the 97 ships planned for FY 1981–1985, 23 ships would be in these categories, effectively reducing the fleet replacement program to an average of 15 ships per year.

Of course, the 97 ships are the *planned* procurement (see table), with the later years of the five-year program having more ships than the earlier years. The peak years of such plans are rarely reached because each annual revision advances the peak numbers to later years. (The tables show actual FY 1981 authorizations.)

The acquisition of four missile destroyers planned for Iran has helped the situation, as they are in addition to the 15-per-year construction average. There may also be an addition from the mothballed fleet, as several congressmen have urged reactivating one or more of the four IOWA (BB 61)-class battleships, and the aircraft carrier ORISKANY (CV 34). These warships were all constructed during World War II (although the ORISKANY was not completed until 1950). The battleships would be impressive in the political presence role, but on a practical basis their manning requirements—some 1,500 each in their existing configuration—appear to be prohibitive, considering the Navy's current personnel problems. More reasonable would be the carrier, which would require more people, but could provide much more striking capability. Still, one must consider the reactivation and high operating costs, coupled with anticipated service life, compared to the return for investing those dollars in new construction.

The situation with respect to naval aircraft is similar. The Navy and Marine Corps require over 300 new aircraft per year to maintain the current naval air arm of some 5,550 aircraft. This number is derived from aircraft reaching the end of their effective service life (23 to 35 years) plus a peacetime attrition that averages about 120 aircraft. Procurement rates are lower. For example, in FY 1980 the Executive Branch requested 103 aircraft—less than the number that would be lost through attrition. The Congress added 24 aircraft for a total buy of 127. For FY 1981 the Carter Administration asked for 104 aircraft, promising to request 179 in FY 1982 with further increases in future years, reaching 342 aircraft in FY 1985.

The tactical aviation picture is fraught with other problems and uncertainties beyond the numbers problem. The Navy's fighter force is supposed to shift several squadrons from the F-4 Phantom to the F/A-18 Hornet, and 24 attack squadrons from the A-7 Corsair to the F/A-18 during the 1980s. However, the F/A-18 is experiencing significant problems, while Marine desires to buy the AV-8B Harrier VSTOL aircraft instead of the F/A-18 for eight attack squadrons could further increase the already higher-than-expected costs of the F/A-18 program.

If the F/A-18 is delayed, or even canceled, the Navy could accelerate or expand the F-14 production, but the attack-aircraft situation requires further consideration. Similarly, the Navy faces a shortfall in electronic jamming aircraft (EA-6B), tanker aircraft (KA-6D), and electronic surveillance aircraft (EA-3B). The Marines will also face a problem soon, as the CH-46 Sea Knight, the principal assault helicopter, will have to be replaced by the late 1980s. Alternatives include a modification of the CH-46 to prolong its service life (which is not a solution, but a postponement of the problem), procurement of another helicopter (most likely the Army's UH-60A Black Hawk), or shifting to a more-capable VSTOL aircraft—possibly one based on the XV-15 tilt-rotor technology demonstrator.

In these and other areas of aircraft and ship procurement the Navy faces serious problems in the 1980s. Overshadowing all decisions will be the personnel problem. As discussed in Chapter 3, the Navy is experiencing difficulties in a number of manpower areas. Probably the most significant is in manning nuclear-propelled surface ships and submarines. This program will become worse as more nuclear aircraft carriers and submarines are completed during the 1980s, replacing conventionally propelled ships. Long-time practices in the nuclear propulsion field have created manning problems that cannot be solved with existing policies and practices.

The personnel situation has reached the point where ship sailings have been delayed because of critical shortages in certain enlisted specialities. The Navy's leaders feel that the remedy to this problem is twofold: first, a meaningful sea-pay policy to help compensate for the 70-hour work weeks and six- to eight-month ship deployments; second, restoring military pay in general to a level reasonably comparable to that of the civilian sector. For example, a Navy electronics technician stationed in the San Francisco area can earn substantially more in 35 hours of off-duty, "moonlighting" work than he can earn in his 45 to 50 hours of similar Navy work. Of course, the electronics technician cannot earn extra money if he is at sea.

Recent congressional legislation has helped the situation, this despite President Carter, the first Naval Academy graduate to ever serve in the White House, having initially opposed significant pay increases for military personnel. Mr. Carter felt that pay should not be the incentive for Navymen to remain in the service.

Two other positive points have been some relatively minor, but highly significant, organizational changes in OPNAV, the Office of the Chief of Naval Operations. These are the establishment of the position of Director of Naval Warfare (OP-95) under Vice Admiral Kinnard R. McKee, and a new Long Range Planning Office (OP-

FIVE-YEAR SHIPBUILDING PLAN

Class	Type	FY 1980 Actual	FY 1981 Actual	FY 1982	FY 1983	FY 1984	FY 1985	FY 1981 Cost[a]
SSBN 726	Strategic Submarine	1	1	1	1	1	1	$1,129.4
SSN 688	Attack Submarine	2	2	1	1	1	1	$ 597.3
FA-SSN	Advanced Submarine				1	1	4	—
CVN 68	Aircraft Carrier	1						$2,102.0[b]
CG 47	Aegis Missile Cruiser	1	2	3	3	4	4	$ 813.6
DDGX	Advanced Destroyer						1	—
FFG 7	ASW Frigate	6	6	4	3	4		$ 277.3
FFX	ASW Corvette				1		4	—
LSD 41	Dock Landing Ship		1		1		1	$ 340.3
MCM	Mine Countermeasures Ship			1		4	4	—
T-AGOS	Surveillance Ship	1	5	4				$ 36.8
T-AO	Oiler			2	2			—
T-AKX	Maritime Prepositioning Ship			3	3	3	3	$ 103.5
ARS	Salvage Ship		1	2	1			$ 93.0
Total		12	18	19	17	21	23	

[a] Unit costs in millions.
[b] Fiscal Year 1980 cost.

OOX), which is directly under the Chief of Naval Operations, headed by Rear Admiral Charles R. Larson. At the same time, obvious progress is being made by the Navy in the vital operational area of Command, Control, and Communications (C^3), mainly through the efforts of the Naval Ocean Systems Laboratory at San Diego. There are other efforts as well, such as some seniors within the Navy belatedly supporting efforts to construct smaller, rather than larger, undersea craft for the next generation of both attack submarines and strategic missile submarines, and interest by some in smaller aircraft carriers *in addition* to the construction of additional large aircraft carriers of the NIMITZ class.

Solutions to the problems that face the U.S. Fleet in the 1980s and beyond will not be easy nor will they be inexpensive. The election of Ronald Reagan in late 1980 brought the hope that the U.S. armed forces would be rebuilt and modernized. However, the state of the economy, the desire for a tax cut, the magnitude of the needs of the four services, the limited U.S. production capabilities for certain items, and the need to first solve manpower problems, make it unlikely that there will be significant increases in the numbers of ships and aircraft in the Fleet during the coming decade. The problems now present will persist, especially if we seek to continue the same programs and operational concepts of the past. Rather, changes must be made in the types of ships and aircraft that we buy as well as in operating concepts because of the increasing importance of the sea to the future political, economic, and military well-being of the United States.

FIVE-YEAR AIRCRAFT PROCUREMENT PLAN

Aircraft		FY 1980 Actual	FY 1981 Actual	FY 1982	FY 1983	FY 1984	FY 1985	FY 1981 Cost[a]
F-14A	Tomcat	30	30	24	12	6		$23.5
F/A-18	Hornet	25	60	96	147	174	191	$27.9
A-6E	Intruder	6	12					$24.2[b]
EA-6B	Prowler	6	6	3				$39.7
KX	(Tanker)				6	18	32	—
E-2C	Hawkeye	6	6	6	6	6	6	$35.3
EC-130Q	Hercules (TACAMO)	3	1	2	2	2	3	$45.1
P-3C	Orion	12	12	12	12	12	12	$22.7
SH-60B	Seahawk (LAMPS III)			18	58	60	68	$20.4[c]
SH-2F	(LAMPS I)			18	18	10	12	$11.4[c]
AH-1T	SeaCobra					22	22	—
CH-53E	Super Stallion	15	14					$12.4
UC-12B		22						$ 1.2[b]
VCX	(COD)				8	8	8	—
C-9B	Skytrain II		2					$14.8[b]
T-34C	Mentor		45					
TH-57C	Jet Ranger		7					
Total		127	195	179	269	318	354	

[a] Unit costs in millions.
[b] Fiscal Year 1980 cost.
[c] Fiscal Year 1982 cost.

NAVAL FORCE LEVELS (January 1981)

	United States	Soviet Union
Active Fleet		
Strategic Missile Submarines	36	62
Old Strategic Missile Submarines	—	25[a]
Submarines[b]	83	275
Aircraft Carriers	12[c]	3
Cruisers	27	~40[d]
Destroyers	81	~65
Frigates	74	~160[e]
Command Ships	3	—
Amphibious Warfare Ships	58	~85
Patrol Combatants	3	~120
Mine Warfare Ships	3	~160
Auxiliary Ships	~80	~760
Naval Reserve Force (NRF)		
Destroyers	16	—[f]
Amphibious Warfare Ships	6	—[f]
Mine Warfare Ships	22	—[f]
Auxiliary Ships	8	—[f]
Naval Fleet Auxiliary Force (NFAF)		
Auxiliary Ships	25	—[f]
Naval Aircraft (including Marine Corps)		
Tactical	1,900	700
Antisubmarine	650	400
Transport-Training-Utility	2,300	280

[a] Hotel SSBN and Golf SSB classes.
[b] Includes research, training, and special-purpose submarines.
[c] Plus SARATOGA (CV 60) in three-year modernization.
[d] Includes two MOSKVA-class CHG helicopter carrier-missile ships.
[e] Includes approximately 28 Krivak-class frigates.
[f] Data not available.
[g] Civilian-manned (MSC) replenishment and support ships.

2 Fleet Organization

The U.S. Navy's operational forces—ships, submarines, aircraft, Marine units, construction battalions (Seabees), and certain other units—are simultaneously under two organizational structures: administrative and tactical.

The administrative organization of the Navy is responsible for the training and readiness of naval forces. This organization is based on "type" categories, with similar forces grouped together to facilitate training, overhaul, repair, logistics, and other aspects of readiness. Within the Navy, the administrative organization begins with the Secretary of the Navy and continues through the Chief of Naval Operations and the Commandant of the Marine Corps, to the commanders-in-chief of the Atlantic and Pacific Fleets.

Within each fleet there are air, surface, and submarine "type" commanders responsible for their respective forces. In addition, commanding generals of the respective Fleet Marine Forces also function as type commanders. The type commanders have cognizance over the air wings and squadrons, and ship and submarine groups, squadrons, and divisions, as well as the individual aircraft, surface ships, and submarines, and their crews and equipment.

While the type commands are similar in both fleets, the components of those type commands differ considerably. Further, in the surface forces the organizations are not always homogeneous; for example, a destroyer squadron will often include frigates and both missile-armed and all-gun destroyers; some squadrons have both active ships and Naval Reserve Force ships. In the Atlantic Fleet the higher-numbered destroyer squadrons do not have ships assigned; the lower-numbered squadron commanders to whom ships are assigned are responsible for the ships' training, maintenance, and logistics. When the ships go to sea, the higher-numbered squadron commanders are their tactical commanders and assume task force or task group designations. In the Pacific Fleet the destroyer squadron commanders have both functions, i.e., readiness and deployment as operational commanders.

During 1980, both the Atlantic and Pacific Fleets established a single surface squadron for their NRF destroyers. Surface Squadron 1 was established in the Pacific on 1 March 1980 and Surface Squadron 2 in the Atlantic on 15 October 1980.

In the following tables of the administrative organization of the U.S. Fleet, the ships assigned to type commanders are indicated. Such assignments change regularly, as new ships are commissioned, older ships stricken or transferred, or ships are reassigned for overhauls or modernization.

Finally, in addition to the administrative chain of command above, the following fleet-type activities report directly to the Chief of Naval Operations for certain purposes: Commander-in-Chief U.S. Naval Forces Europe, Commander Military Sealift Command, Commander Operational Test and Evaluation Force, Commander Mine Warfare Command, and Commander Naval Air Reserve Force.

The principal operational or tactical forces of the Navy are the Second Fleet in the Atlantic, the Third Fleet in the eastern Pacific, the Sixth Fleet in the Mediterranean, and the Seventh Fleet in the western Pacific-Indian Ocean regions. Operational control of these fleets begins with the National Command Authority (President and Secretary of Defense) through the specified and unified commanders. These commanders have responsibility for the conduct of military operations. A specified command generally has forces assigned only from a single service, as the Strategic Air Command; a unified command has components from two or more services, with the principal unified commands with naval forces being assigned to the Commander-in-Chief Pacific (Pacific Command), Commander-in-Chief Atlantic (Atlantic Command), and Commander-in-Chief U.S. Forces Europe (European Command). The naval forces in the Pacific Command are under the Naval Component Commander, who is the Commander-in-Chief Pacific Fleet. The Atlantic Command's naval forces (Atlantic Fleet) are under Commander-in-Chief Atlantic Fleet, with both positions being held by the same officer; and the European Command's naval forces are under the Commander-in-Chief U.S. Naval Forces Europe.

Thus, the Atlantic and Pacific *fleet* commanders function in both the administrative and tactical chains of command. The fleets' tactical organizations are based on task forces with the TF designation based on the relevant numbered fleet designation. When appropriate, subgroupings are designated as task groups and task units. Thus, TF-62 in the Sixth Fleet could have TG-62.1 assigned, and that, in turn, could have TU-62.1.1.

In general, all major units in the administrative chain of command have operational (TF) designations for use in emergency or contingency situations. For example, in the Pacific Fleet the aviation type command is designated TF-17, the surface type command TF-15, and the submarine type command TF-14 and TF-54. Many other TF designations of the Atlantic and Pacific Fleets exist only on paper. However, they are useful in providing the procedures and communications links necessary for a variety of contingencies.

TABLE 1
UNITED STATES FLEET DEPLOYMENTS[a]

Pacific Fleet		Atlantic Fleet	U.S. Naval Forces Europe	
Seventh Fleet (Western Pacific)	**Third Fleet** (Eastern Pacific)	**Second Fleet** (Atlantic)	**Sixth Fleet** (Mediterranean)	**Middle East Force** (Persian Gulf)
6 attack submarines	28 attack submarines	40 attack submarines	4 attack submarines	2 surface combatants
1 transport submarine	4 aircraft carriers	5 aircraft carriers	2 aircraft carriers	1 flagship (AGF)
2 aircraft carriers	60 surface combatants	60 surface combatants	14 surface combatants	
18 surface combatants[b]	24 amphibious ships	1 flagship (LCC)	5 amphibious ships	
1 flagship (LCC)	38 auxiliary ships	26 amphibious ships	12 auxiliary ships	
8 amphibious ships		40 auxiliary ships		
15 auxiliary ships	Aviation units:	3 minesweepers	Aviation units:	
	4 CVW		2 CVW	
Aviation units:[c]	8 VP	Aviation units:	1½ VP	
	1 VQ[d]		1 VQ	
2 CVW		4 CVW		
4 VP	Marine units:	10½ VP	Marine units:	
1 VQ		1 VQ[d]		
	1 Brigade		1 Battalion	
Marine units:	1 Division	Marine units:	(reinforced)	
	1 Air Wing			
1 Division		1 Division		
1 Air Wing		1 Air Wing		

[a] Nominal assignment of active ships and squadrons; strategic missile submarines are not indicated.
[b] Surface combatants are cruisers, destroyers, and frigates.
[c] See Chapter 21 for aviation abbreviations.
[d] VQ squadrons assigned to the Second and Third Fleets are strategic communications units; the others are electronic surveillance squadrons.

TABLE 2
COMMANDER-IN-CHIEF U.S. NAVAL FORCES EUROPE (★★★)

Sixth Fleet[a] (★★★)
  TF-60 Battle Force (★★)
    TG-60.1 Battle Group 1 (★★)
    TG-60.2 Battle Group 2 (★★)
    TG-60.5 Screen Group
    TG-60.7 Flagship
  TF-61 Amphibious Force
  TF-62 Landing Force
  TF-63 Service Force[b]
  TF-64 FBM Submarine Force[c] (★★)
  TF-66 Area ASW Force
  TF-67 Maritime Surveillance and Reconnaissance Force (★★)
    TG-67.1 Maritime Patrol Air Group Sigonella (Sicily)
    TG-67.2 Maritime Patrol Air Group Rota (Spain)
    TG-67.3 Maritime Patrol Air Group Suda Bay (Crete)
    TG-67.4 Air Reconnaissance Group[d]
  TF-68 Special Operations Force
  TF-69 Attack Submarine Force[c]
    TG-69.7 Submarine Refit and Training Group
  TF-109 Middle East Force (★★)

[a] Also Commander Naval Striking and Support Forces Southern Europe (NATO).
[b] Commander Service Squadron 6.
[c] Commander Submarine Group 8.
[d] Fleet Air Reconnaissance Squadron 2 (VQ-2).

There is an obvious overlap and some confusion over which chain of command has responsibility for a particular function or activity. But the existing organizational concepts do provide a very high degree of flexibility, which is a key characteristic of naval forces. (Indeed, some aspects of the confusion can be seen in comparing the Department of the Navy manual *Organization of the U.S.* *Navy, NWP 2* with the organization documents of the Atlantic and Pacific Fleets; there are significant differences. The following tables are based primarily on the fleet documents.)

In the following tables stars are used to indicate the grades of commanders: ★★★★ for admiral, ★★★ for vice admiral or lieutenant general (Marine Corps), ★★ for rear admiral or major general, and ★ for brigadier general. The U.S. Navy does not use the rank of commodore in peacetime. However, the title of commodore is usually accorded to any officer through the rank of captain who commands a grouping of ships of any size or type.

In general, similar Navy organizations have similar commanders: type commanders are vice admirals, except that Commander Submarine Force in the Pacific Fleet is a rear admiral, group commanders are rear admirals, and squadron commanders are captains. Divisions of ships are now used only for minesweepers. In naval aviation (see Chapter 21), air wings based ashore are generally commanded by rear admirals, carrier air wings by captains, squadrons based ashore by commanders or captains, and carrier squadrons by commanders.

Even-numbered ship groups and squadrons are normally assigned to the Atlantic Fleet and odd-numbered groups and squadrons to the Pacific Fleet.

Table 1 provides the nominal assignment of ships and aircraft squadrons to the numbered fleets. Most ships in the forward-deployed Sixth and Seventh Fleets operate in the forward areas for about six months, and then rotate back to the Second and Third Fleets, respectively. While in the latter fleets the ships undergo overhaul and maintenance, training, participate in exercises, and have some operational assignments. The Second Fleet provides

TABLE 3
COMMANDER-IN-CHIEF ATLANTIC FLEET[a] (★★★★)
Administrative

Naval Air Force[b] (★★★)	Norfolk, Va.	1 AVT	Amphibious Squadron 4	Little Creek, Va.	2 LPD
Carrier Group 2 (★★)	Naples, Italy	—			1 LPH
Carrier Group 4 (★★)	Norfolk, Va.	2 CV			1 LSD
Carrier Group 6 (★★)	Mayport, Fla.	2 CV			3 LST
Carrier Group 8 (★★)	Norfolk, Va.	2 CVN	Amphibious Squadron 6	Norfolk, Va.	2 LPD
		1 CV			1 LPH
					2 LSD
Naval Surface Force (★★★)					2 LST
Flagships LA SALLE (Commander Middle East Force)		AGF 3	Amphibious Squadron 8	Norfolk, Va.	1 LKA
PUGET SOUND (Commander Sixth Fleet)		AD 38			1 LHA
(Saudi training)		2 PG			1 LPD
		1 AFDM			1 LPH
		1 AFDL			1 LSD
Cruiser Destroyer Group 2 (★★)	Charleston, S.C.	2 CG			2 LST
		1 AD	Mine Squadron 12 (NRF)	Charleston, S.C.	3 MSO
Destroyer Squadron 4	Charleston, S.C.	6 DDG	Mine Division 121 (NRF)		5 MSO (NRF)
		10 DD	Mine Division 123 (NRF)		4 MSO (NRF)
		1 FFG	Mine Division 125		7 MSB
		8 FF			1 LCU
Destroyer Squadron 20	Charleston, S.C.	—	Mine Division 126 (NRF)		4 MSO (NRF)
Destroyer Squadron 36	Charleston, S.C.	—	Submarine Force[c] (★★★)	Norfolk, Va.	
Cruiser Destroyer Group 8 (★★)	Norfolk, Va.	5 CGN	Submarine Development Squadron 12	Groton, Conn.[d]	6 SSN
		4 CG	Submarine Group 2 (★★)	Groton, Conn.	3 SSBN[e]
		1 PHM			1 SSN
Destroyer Squadron 2	Norfolk, Va.	10 DDG	Submarine Group 6 (★★)	Charleston, S.C.	7 SSBN
		2 DD			1 AG
		1 FFG	Submarine Group 8 (★★)	Naples, Italy	1 AS
		2 FF	Submarine Squadron 2	Groton, Conn.	9 SSN
Destroyer Squadron 10	Norfolk, Va.	8 DD			1 ASR
		7 FF			NR-1
Destroyer Squadron 22	Norfolk, Va.	—	Submarine Support Facility	Groton, Conn.	2 ARD
Destroyer Squadron 26	Norfolk, Va.	—	New London		1 ARDM
Destroyer Squadron 32	Norfolk, Va.	—	Submarine Squadron 4	Charleston, S.C.	7 SSN
Cruiser Destroyer Group 12 (★★)	Mayport, Fla.	1 CG			1 AS
		1 AD			1 ASR
Destroyer Squadron 8 (est. 20 Oct 1980)	Newport, R.I.	3 FFG	Submarine Squadron 6	Norfolk, Va.	11 SSN
Destroyer Squadron 12	Mayport, Fla.	4 DDG			1 AS
		4 DD			1 ASR
		4 FFG	Submarine Squadron 8	Norfolk, Va.	4 SSN
		8 FF			1 AS
Destroyer Squadron 14	Mayport, Fla.	—			1 ASR
Destroyer Squadron 24	Mayport, Fla.	—	Submarine Squadron 16	Kings Bay, Ga.	5 SSBN
Surface Squadron 2 (NRF)	Newport, R.I.	11 DD (NRF)			1 AS
		4 FF			1 ARDM
Service Group 2 (★★)	Norfolk, Va.	2 AD	Submarine Squadron 18	Charleston, S.C.	4 SSBN
		1 AR			1 AS
Service Squadron 2	Earle, N.J.	5 AE			1 ARDM
		2 AOE			
Service Squadron 4	Norfolk, Va.	3 AFS	Fleet Marine Force (★★★)	Norfolk, Va.	
		2 AO	II Marine Amphibious Force[g] (★★)	Camp Lejeune, N.C.	
		3 AOR	Second Marine Division (★★)	Camp Lejeune, N.C.	
Service Squadron 6	Naples, Italy	—	Second Marine Aircraft Wing[h] (★★)	Cherry Point, N.C.	
Service Squadron 8	Little Creek, Va.	1 AD	Second Force Service Support Group (★)	Camp Lejeune, N.C.	
		3 ARS			
		1 ARS (NRF)			
		2 ATF (NRF)			
		1 ATS			
Amphibious Group 2 (★★)	Norfolk, Va.	1 LHA			
		1 LKA (NRF)			
Flagship MOUNT WHITNEY (Commander Second Fleet)		LCC 20			
Amphibious Squadron 2	Norfolk, Va.	2 LPD			
		1 LPH			
		2 LSD			
		3 LST			

---

[a] Also Commander-in-Chief Atlantic (unified command of all U.S. air, land, sea forces); Supreme Allied Commaner Atlantic (NATO); CinC Western Atlantic Area (NATO).
[b] See Chapter 21 for subordinate aviation units.
[c] Also Submarine Operations Advisor/Poseidon Operations Advisor to CinCLant and SACLant; Commander Submarines Western Atlantic (NATO); Commander Submarine Activities Atlantic.
[d] Groton, Conn., is actually U.S. Naval Submarine Base, New London. SubRon-10 is based at the State Pier in the city of New London.
[e] These submarines are being overhauled at the Portsmouth Naval Shipyard.
[f] The SSBNs are home-ported in the United States.
[g] Also Commanding General Second Marine Division.
[h] Logistics and material support through Naval Air Force, Atlantic

Operational

Commander-in-Chief Atlantic Fleet (★★★★)		TF-134	Naval Forces Caribbean
TF-40	Naval Surface Force (★★★)	TF-136	Naval Base Guantanamo
TF-41	Naval Air Force (★★★)	TF-137	Eastern Atlantic
TF-42	Submarine Force (★★★)	TF-138	South Atlantic Force (★★)
TF-43	Training Command (★★)	TF-142	Operational Test and Evaluation Force (★★)
TF-45	Fleet Marine Force (★★★)	Second Fleet (★★★)	
TF-80	Naval Control and Protection of Shipping Force	TF-20	Battle Force
TF-81	Sea Control and Surveillance Force	TG-20.1	Battle Group 1
TF-82	Amphibious Force	TG-20.9	Flagship
TF-83	Landing Force (★★★) (II Marine Amphibious Force)	TF-21	Sea Control and Surveillance Force
TF-84	ASW Task Force	TF-22	Amphibious Force
TF-85	Mobile Logistics Support Force	TF-23	Landing Force
TF-86	Patrol Air Force (★★) (PatWingsLant)	TF-24	ASW Force
TF-87	Transit Force	TF-25	Mobile Logistics Support Force
TF-88	Training Force	TF-26	Caribbean Contingency Force
TF-89	Mine Warfare Force	TF-27	Ready Action Force

TABLE 4
COMMANDER-IN-CHIEF PACIFIC FLEET[a] (★★★★)
Administrative

Unit	Location	Ships
Naval Air Force[b] (★★★)		
Carrier Group 1 (★★)	San Diego, Calif.	2 CV
Carrier Group 3 (★★)	San Diego, Calif.	2 CV
Carrier Group 5 (★★)	Cubi Point, Philippines	1 CV[c]
Carrier Group 7 (★★)	Alameda, Calif.	1 CVN
Naval Surface Force (★★★)		
Cruiser Destroyer Group 1 (★★)	San Diego, Calif.	3 CGN
		1 AD
Destroyer Squadron 5	San Diego, Calif.	4 FF
Destroyer Squadron 13	San Diego, Calif.	2 DDG
		1 DD
		3 FF
Destroyer Squadron 23	San Diego, Calif.	1 DDG
		1 DD
		1 FFG
		2 FF
Cruiser-Destroyer Group 3 (★★)	San Diego, Calif.	5 CG
		1 AD
		1 AR
Destroyer Squadron 7	San Diego, Calif.	3 DDG
		1 FF
Destroyer Squadron 17	San Diego, Calif.	1 DD
		1 FFG
		3 FF
Cruiser-Destroyer Group 5 (★★)	San Diego, Calif.	4 CG
		1 AD
		1 AR
Destroyer Squadron 9	San Diego, Calif.	8 DD
		4 FFG
		1 AVM
Destroyer Squadron 21	San Diego, Calif.	1 DDG
		5 DD
		2 FF
Destroyer Squadron 31	San Diego, Calif.	3 DDG
		1 DD
		1 FFG
		2 FF

Unit	Location	Ships
Surface Squadron 1 (NRF)	Long Beach, Calif.	6 DD (NRF)
		2 LKA (NRF)
		1 LST (NRF)
		3 ATF (NRF)
Service Group 1	Oakland, Calif.	3 AFS
		1 AO
		2 AOE
		4 AOR
		1 AR
Service Squadron 3	Vallejo, Calif.	8 AE
Mine Squadron 5 (NRF)	Long Beach, Calif.	
Mine Division 51 (NRF)	Long Beach, Calif.	2 MSO (NRF)
Mine Division 52 (NRF)	San Francisco, Calif.	2 MSO (NRF)
Mine Division 53 (NRF)	Seattle, Wash.	3 MSO (NRF)
Mine Division 54 (NRF)	San Diego, Calif.	2 MSO (NRF)
Naval Surface Group Western Pacific (★★)	Subic Bay, Philippines	
Flagship—LCC 19, BLUE RIDGE (Commander Seventh Fleet)		1 CG
		1 AFS
Destroyer Squadron 15	Yokosuka, Japan	1 DDG
		4 FF
Naval Surface Group Mid-Pacific (★★)	Pearl Harbor, Hawaii	1 CG
		1 AD
		2 AO
Destroyer Squadron 25	Pearl Harbor, Hawaii	3 DDG
		2 FF
Destroyer Squadron 33	Pearl Harbor, Hawaii	5 FF
Destroyer Squadron 35	Pearl Harbor, Hawaii	2 DDG
		2 DD
		3 FF
Service Squadron 5	Pearl Harbor, Hawaii	3 ARS
		2 ATS
Amphibious Group 1 (★★)	White Beach, Okinawa	—
Amphibious Group Eastern Pacific (★★)	San Diego, Calif.	1 LHA
Amphibious Squadron 1	San Diego, Calif.	1 LPH
		2 LPD

Amphibious Squadron 3	San Diego, Calif.	3 LST
		1 LPH
		1 LKA
		2 LPD
		2 LSD
		1 LST
Amphibious Squadron 5	San Diego, Calif.	1 LHA
		1 LPH
		2 LPD
		3 LSD
		3 LST
Amphibious Squadron 7	San Diego, Calif.	1 LHA
		1 LKA
		1 LPD
		2 LSD
		2 LST
Submarine Force (★★)	Pearl Harbor, Hawaii	
Submarine Squadron 1	Pearl Harbor, Hawaii	7 SSN
		1 SS
Submarine Squadron 15	Apra Harbor, Guam	5 SSNd
		1 AS
Submarine Development Group 1	San Diego, Calif.	2 SSN
		1 AGSS
		1 AGDS
		2 ASR
		2 DSRV
		3 DSV
Submarine Squadron 3	San Diego, Calif.	8 SSN
		1 AS

Submarine Squadron 7	Pearl Harbor, Hawaii	8 SSN
Submarine Group 5 (★★)	San Diego, Calif.	7 SSN
		2 SS
		1 SSAG
		1 AS
		1 ARD
Submarine Group 7	Yokosuka, Japan	2 SSe
Fleet Marine Force (★★★)	Camp Smith, Hawaii	
I Marine Amphibious Forcef (★★)	Camp Pendleton, Calif.	
First Marine Division (★★)	Camp Pendleton, Calif.	
Third Marine Aircraft Wingg (★★)	El Toro, Calif.	
III Marine Amphibious Forceh (★★)	Okinawa	
Third Marine Division (★★)	Okinawa	
First Marine Aircraft Wingi (★★)	Okinawa	
First Marine Brigadej (★)	Kaneohe Bay, Hawaii	
First Force Service Support Group (★)	Camp Pendleton, Calif.	
Third Force Service Support Group (★)	Okinawa	

a Also Naval Component Commander, U.S. Pacific Command.
b See Chapter 21 for subordinate aviation units.
c The MIDWAY (CV 41) is home-ported at Yokosuka, Japan.
d All SSBNs are based at Pearl Harbor.
e The GRAYBACK (SS 574) is home-ported at Subic Bay, Philippines, and the DARTER (SS 576) at Sasebo, Japan.
f Also Commanding General First Marine Division.
g Logistic and material support through Naval Air Force, Pacific Fleet.
h Also Commanding General Third Marine Division.
i Logistic and material support through Naval Air Force, Pacific Fleet.
j Composed of units from the Third Marine Division, First Marine Aircraft Wing, and Third Force Service Support Group.

Operational

Commander-in-Chief Pacific Fleet (★★★★)
TF-10   Temporary Operations Force
TF-11   Training Force
TF-13   Logistics Support Force
TF-14   Submarine Force
TF-15   Surface Force
TF-17   Naval Air Force
TF-19   Fleet Marine Force
TF-50   Battle Force
TF-51   Command and Coordination Force
TF-52   Patrol and Reconnaissance Force
Tf-53   Logistic Support Force
TF-54   Submarine Force
TF-55   Surface Combatant Force
TF-56   Amphibious Force
TF-57   Carrier Strike Force
TF-59   Landing Force
TG-168.1   Pacific Forward Area Support Team
TF-199   Naval Support Force Antarctica
Third Fleet (★★★)
TF-30   Battle Force
TF-31   Combat Support Forcea (★★★)
TF-32   Patrol and Reconnaissance Force (★★)
TF-33   Logistics Support Force

TF-34   Submarine Forceb (★★)
TF-35   Surface Combatant Force
TF-36   Amphibious Force (★★)
TF-37   Carrier Strike Force
TF-38   Canadian Maritime Forces Pacific
TF-39   Landing Marine Force
Seventh Fleet (★★★)
TF-70   Battle Force (★★)
TF-71   Command and Coordination Forcec (★★★)
TF-72   Patrol and Reconnaissance Force
TF-73   Logistic Support Forced (★★)
TF-74   Submarine Force
TF-75   Surface Combatant Forcee (★★)
TF-76   Amphibious Forcef (★★)
TF-77   Carrier Strike Forceg (★★)
TF-79   Landing Forceh (★★)

a Commander Third Fleet.
b Commander Submarine Force, Pacific Fleet.
c Commander Seventh Fleet.
d Commander Naval Surface Group Western Pacific.
e Commander Cruiser-Destroyer Group 1.
f Commander Amphibious Group 1.
g Commander Carrier Group 5.
h Commanding General, III Marine Amphibious Force.

ships and aircraft for NATO exercises in the Atlantic area. Both the Sixth and Seventh Fleets provide ships for the Indian Ocean deployments that began in November 1979; before that the periodic carrier and surface groups that operated in the Indian Ocean came from the Seventh Fleet while the Sixth Fleet provided the two destroyers or frigates that, with the flagship LA SALLE (AGF 3), formed the U.S. Middle East Force.

MILITARY SEALIFT COMMAND

In addition to the above fleet organization, the Navy operates the Military Sealift Command (MSC) to provide ocean transportation and to support special projects of all of the armed services and other government agencies. The Commander MSC, a rear admiral, is responsible as a "fleet commander" to the Chief of Naval Operations and to the Office of the Secretary of Defense for ocean transportation.

All MSC ships are civilian-manned with Civil Service crews, or are operated by commercial contractors. About 160 Navy personnel serve in MSC ships to provide security for nuclear weapons or operate communications equipment.

MSC ships have the prefix USNS (U.S. Naval Ship) instead of USS, have T-hull designations, and can be identified by blue-and-gold funnel markings.

MSC-operated ships that provide fleet support are considered as active Navy ships and are classified as the Naval Fleet Auxiliary Force. The NFAF ships are civilian-manned ammunition ships (T-AE), store ships (T-AF), fleet oilers (T-AO), cable ships (T-ARC), fleet tugs (T-ATF), and three cargo ships (T-AK) that support forward-deployed SSBN tenders. Other MSC ships provide point-to-point transporta-

tion of Navy and Defense Department cargoes (T-AK, T-AKR, T-AOG, T-AOT), and support various Navy, Defense, and NASA research, surveying, and surveillance projects (T-AG, T-AGM, T-AGOR, T-AGS).

The MSC ships currently in service include point-to-point cargo ships (T-AK, T-AKR, T-AOT), underway replenishment ships (T-AF, T-AO, T-AE), Polaris/Poseidon tender resupply ships (T-AK), cable repairing ships (T-ARC), and special project and research ships (T-AG, T-AGM, T-AGOR, T-AGS).

In addition, MSC charters privately owned U.S. merchant ships to carry defense cargo. Almost 95 percent of all U.S. military material sent overseas is moved in this manner.

NAVAL RESERVE FORCE

The Naval Reserve operates a large number of surface ships and small craft as well as several aircraft wings and squadrons that comprise the Naval Reserve Force (NRF). In addition, there are several reserve construction battalions ("Seabees"), and administrative and other specialized reserve units. The Chief of Naval Reserve is a vice admiral. Ships assigned to the Naval Reserve are operationally controlled by the surface force commanders of the Atlantic and Pacific Fleets.

There are 42 ships operated by the NRF in 1981 with composite active and reserve crews: 6 destroyers, 4 amphibious cargo ships, 2 tank landing ships, 22 ocean minesweepers, 2 ammunition ships, 1 salvage ship, and 5 fleet tugs. The Navy planned to reduce the NRF destroyers to 6 ships during 1981. (See Chapter 9.)

Additionally, the Naval Reserve operates some 560 aircraft (see Chapter 21).

3 Personnel

The U.S. Navy in late 1980 had 528,200 officers and enlisted men and women on active duty, plus 185,200 officers and enlisted men and women in the Marine Corps.

Navy personnel were assigned to the following activities:*

Strategic. Strategic missile submarines and related support, and related command, control, and communications: 20,800.

Tactical/Mobility. Warships (except SSBNs), other Navy-manned ships, other direct support: 180,100; tactical air forces: 61,700; miscellaneous: 3,300; total: 245,100.

Auxiliary Activities. Intelligence, centrally managed communications, research and development, and miscellaneous: 23,000.

Support Activities. Bases, medical, training, central logistics, management headquarters, and miscellaneous: 135,700.

Individuals. Personnel in transit, 25,600; patients, prisoners, and holdees, 4,900; Naval Academy midshipmen, 4,400; other students and personnel in training, 68,500; total, 103,400.

The Navy's personnel strength has leveled off from its rapid decline in the immediate post-Vietnam period (having reached a Vietnam peak in 1969 with 777,100 Navy personnel on active duty). While the overall number of Navy personnel on active duty remained level over the past few years, the number of women on active duty continued to increase. Beginning in 1979, women have been assigned on a permanent basis to noncombat ships and on a temporary basis to other surface ships that are not expected to be in combat as well as to flying duty and ground assignments in aircraft squadrons. Approximately 160 women officers and 4,900 enlisted women are expected to be serving in ships by the mid-1980s.

Despite the increasing assignment of women to duty ashore and afloat, the Navy continues to have major personnel problems in both the enlisted and officer categories. From a quantitative viewpoint, the Navy has sufficient enlisted men and women on active duty, but there is a shortage of some 2,000 mid-grade petty officers, primarily first and second class. Especially critical are shortages in the electronics, propulsion, and nuclear areas of specialization. These shortfalls of technical and supervisory skills impair the Navy's capability for sustained operations and have an adverse impact on day-to-day readiness. This petty officer problem also affects the Navy's schools and on-the-job training, further exacerbating the enlisted personnel problems.

The immediate cause of the petty officer shortage is a decrease in the retention of sailors after their first enlistment. Enlisted retention rates for FY 1979† decreased in every category from the previous year's retention rates. The first-term reenlistment rate was 37.5 percent; the second term was 45.3 percent; and the third term (generally personnel with 13 to 20 years of service) was 91.4 percent. The career force (third term to 30 years of service) had a retention rate of 62.2 percent in FY 1979. But even more significant than declines in overall retention rates are the critical shortages noted above in the electronics, propulsion, and nuclear categories.

Enlisted recruiting increased slightly in FY 1979 (to 94.6 percent of goals compared to 94.0 in FY 1978); nevertheless, this compares to essentially 96 to 100 percent of recruiting goals achieved from FY 1974 (the first full fiscal year without a draft) until FY 1977. From a qualitative viewpoint, however, the Navy's recruiting efforts have been much less successful, as the service has failed to attract the numbers of high school graduates deemed necessary to operate the modern Fleet.

Officer personnel problems have been similar. There are major shortages of unrestricted line officers in the specialties of aircraft pilot and nuclear-training. Again, the problems are in retention and recruiting. Ideally the Navy would like to retain about 60 percent of its officers; actual retention over the past few years has been only 30 to 40 percent, going even lower in some areas.

This situation has two consequences. First, a reasonable rotation of assignments between sea and shore duty becomes impossible. For example, over 80 percent of all nuclear-submarine officers below the grade of captain are at sea. These officers can expect to be at sea for as many as 14 of their first 20 years of service. Second, many positions will go unfilled, causing a larger workload on those officers remaining in the Navy. This situation, in turn, will probably lead to more officers leaving the Navy as soon as their required tenure is completed.

In officer recruiting the Navy achieved only 86 percent of its goal in FY 1979 (a slight improvement from 76 percent in FY 1978). The major officer recruiting problem was for nuclear-power officers. This effort was 206 officers short in FY 1979, attaining only 46 percent of the recruiting quota. Other serious shortfalls (under 50 percent of goal being met) occurred in engineering specialities (Civil

---

* All numbers are rounded.

† The FY 1979 data are the latest available through late 1980.

The super-dreadnought NEW JERSEY (BB 62) on sea trials prior to being commissioned for the fourth time in December 1982. Note the SPS–49 search radar and SLQ–32 electronic systems atop the forward tower; Phalanx Gatling guns atop bridge and amidships; and underway replenishment gear amidships. A second battleship, the IOWA (BB 61) was to rejoin the fleet in December 1984. Some 1,600 officers and enlisted men will sail in each ship. (1982, U.S. Navy, PH1 Harold Gerwein)

Engineer Corps and Aviation Maintenance Duty Officers). Although the number of officers in these categories was small, only 30 percent of the quota was attained.

Officer-recruiting shortages are predicted in the early 1980s for surface warfare specialists and supply officers because of substantial increases in their respective recruiting quotas.

While the Navy faces major problems in both the officer and enlisted categories, the relative sophistication of Navy ships and aircraft continues to increase, making still more demands on the quality of personnel required to operate the modern Fleet.

In addition to active-duty personnel, the Navy has a selected reserve of 87,000 men and women in pay status, while the Marine Corps has 33,700 men and women in reserve pay status.

Planning provided for a late-1981 strength of 533,800 Navy, 185,200 Marines, 395,400 Naval Reserve, and 103,800 Marine Corps Reserve personnel.

ACTIVE DUTY PERSONNEL[a]

	Navy	Marine Corps
Officer	63,900	17,900
Enlisted	459,900	167,300
Midshipmen	4,400	—
Total	528,200	185,200

[a] Numbers are rounded.

4 Glossary

Also see Appendix A, Ship Classifications.

AA	Antiaircraft
AA	Atlantic (Fleet) Active
AAW	Antiair Warfare
Academic	Navy-owned ship operated by academic or research institution
AMCM	Airborne Mine Countermeasures
AR	Atlantic Reserve (Fleet)
ASMD	Antiship Missile Defense
ASROC	Antisubmarine Rocket
ASW	Antisubmarine Warfare
Beam	extreme width of hull
Boilers	psi indicates pounds-per-square-inch pressure
BPDMS	Basic Point Defense Missile System
Catapults	flush, flight-deck catapults in aircraft carriers
CGR	Coast Guard Reserve
CIWS	Close-In Weapon System
COD	Carrier On-board Delivery
DASH	Drone Antisubmarine Helicopter
Displacement	*Light* (ship) is displacement of the ship and all machinery without crew, provisions, fuel, munitions, all other consumables, and aircraft *Standard* is displacement of the ship fully manned and equipped, ready for sea, including all provisions, munitions, and aircraft, but without fuels *Full load* is displacement of the ship complete and ready for service in all respects, including all fuels
DP	Dual-Purpose (for use against air and surface targets)
Draft	maximum draft of ship at full load, including fixed projections below the keel, if any (e.g., sonar domes)
ECM	Electronic Countermeasures
Elevators	aircraft-capable elevators in aircraft carriers
EW	Electronic Warfare
Extreme width	maximum width at or about the flight deck, including fixed projections, if any (e.g., gun "tubs")
FBM	Fleet Ballistic Missile
FCS	Fire Control System
Flag	special accommodations for fleet or task force commander and his staff; lesser division or squadron commanders and their staffs are included in the ship's manning data
FY	Fiscal Year; from 1 October of the calendar year until 30 September of the following year (since 1976; previously from 1 July until 30 June); S in front of an FY number indicates a supplemental authorization
GL	Great Lakes
Guns	mount or turret arrangement is indicated in parentheses (e.g., 2 × 3 indicates two triple turrets)
IO	Indian Ocean
IOC	Initial Operational Capability
IW	Inland Waters
LAMPS	Light Airborne Multi-Purpose System
lbst	pounds static thrust
Length	wl indicates length on waterline (this is the length between perpendiculars in naval practice); oa indicates length overall
Manning	the number of personnel assigned to the ship; the term *complement* is no longer used by the U.S. Navy; O = officers, enlisted = enlisted personnel
MarAd	Maritime Administration
MCLWG	Major Caliber Lightweight Gun
MCM	Mine Countermeasures
Missiles	number of launchers and tubes or rails are indicated; e.g., 2 twin launchers indicates two launchers with twin launching rails; the number of missiles carried in the launcher or magazine is indicated in parentheses for reloadable launchers
Mk	Mark
Mod	Modification
MR	Maritime (Administration) Reserve (i.e., National Defense Reserve Fleet)
MSC	Military Sealift Command (formerly Military Sea Transportation Service)
n. mile	nautical mile
NRF	Naval Reserve Force (A indicates Atlantic, P indicates Pacific)

NTDS	Naval Tactical Data System
OSP	Offshore Procurement (ship built overseas with U.S. funding)
PA	Pacific (Fleet) Active
PR	Pacific Reserve (Fleet)
Propulsion	designed shaft horsepower (shp) is indicated
Radars	radars associated with fire control systems are listed under Fire control
Reactors	first letter of reactor designation indicates platform (A = Aircraft carrier, C = Cruiser, D = frigate (DL), now cruiser, S = Submarine); numeral indicates sequence of reactor design by specific manufacturer; and second letter is manufacturer (C = Combustion Engineering, G = General Electric, W = Westinghouse)
SAM	Surface-to-Air Missile
SCB	Ships Characteristics Board's sequential numbering of all Navy ship designs reaching advanced planning; numbered in a single series from 1947 (SCB-1 was the NORFOLK CLK 1/DL 1) through 1964 (SCB-252 was the FLAGSTAFF PGH 1); from 1964 on numbered in blocks: 001-009 cruisers, 100 carriers, 200 destroyers/frigates, 300 submarines, 400 amphibious, 500 mine warfare, 600 patrol, 700 auxiliary, 800 service craft, 900 special purpose; e.g., SCB-400.65 was the AGC/LCC of the FY 1965 design.
SLBM	Submarine-Launched Ballistic Missile
SLCM	Sea-Launched Cruise Missile (formerly Submarine-Launched Cruise Missile)
Speed	maximum speed unless otherwise indicated
SSM	Surface-to-Surface Missile
STOL	Short Take-Off and Landing
SUBROC	Submarine Rocket
SURTASS	Surveillance Towed Array Sensor System
TACAN	Tactical Aircraft Navigation (shipboard homing beacon)
TACTAS	Tactical Towed Array Sonar
T-ASM	Tomahawk Antiship Missile
3-D	three-dimensional radar
T-LAM	Tomahawk Land-Attack Missile
TRA	Training
Troops	designed accommodations; O = officers, enlisted = enlisted personnel
USNS	United States Naval Ship; civilian-manned ship operated by the Military Sealift Command
USS	United States Ship
UNREP	Underway Replenishment
VERTREP	Vertical Replenishment
VSTOL	Vertical/Short Take-Off and Landing

VSTOL attack aircraft: Marine AV–8A Harriers maneuver after landing at Quantico, Va. Under their wings are four-inch Zuni rocket pods and Mk 77 napalm bombs; 30-mm Aden gun pods are attached to the fuselage. These Harriers are from Marine Attack Squadron (VMA) 231. (U.S. Marine Corps, R. D. Ward)

5 Submarines

The principal types of submarines in service with the world's navies are strategic missile submarines and attack submarines. The former are armed with Submarine-Launched Ballistic Missiles (SLBM), while the latter are armed with torpedoes and, increasingly, guided (cruise) missiles. In addition, three specialized research and troop-carrying submarines are operated by the U.S. Navy.

This chapter lists strategic missile submarines first, followed by the attack and specialized submarines; the listings within the two sections are arranged by class and then hull-number sequence.

STRATEGIC MISSILE SUBMARINES

The number of U.S. strategic missile submarines (SSBN) is declining in the early 1980s, as the oldest Polaris-armed submarines are being retired at a faster rate than the Trident submarines are being completed. As of January 1981 there were some 35 SSBNs in active service carrying 560 missiles. This is a decline from the force of 41 submarines with 656 SLBMs that the U.S. Navy had in commission from 1967 through 1979 (less those submarines being overhauled or modernized).

The Trident program, approved for development in 1972 eventually to replace the Polaris-Poseidon force, is significantly behind schedule. The Trident C-4 missile, with a range of 4,000 nautical miles, first went to sea in late 1979 aboard rearmed Polaris-Poseidon submarines. The lead Trident SSBN would not be completed until a year and a half later. The last Polaris SSBN was scheduled to complete its last deterrent patrol in September 1981.

As the Trident SSBNs are completed, the older submarines, first the Polaris and then the Poseidon, will be retired or possibly reassigned to other roles. With ten Polaris SSBNs being retired from the strategic role in 1979–1981 and only one or two Trident submarines being completed by the end of 1981, the SSBN force will continue to decline. However, because the Trident submarines each have 24 missiles vice 16 in the earlier SSBNs, the decline in missile numbers will not be as severe as the decline in submarine numbers. On a qualitative basis, the SLBM situation also improves because of the backfitting of 12 Poseidon submarines with the Trident C-4 missile (192 weapons) and the greater range and advanced multiple warhead of that weapon compared to the Polaris A-3 and Poseidon C-3 (see Chapter 23).

However, there is a potential long-term SSBN force-level concern. At current Trident submarine building rates, by 1995 there would be only 15 Trident submarines (360 SLBMs) plus, possibly,

some of the 12 rearmed older submarines (192 SLBMs), with the latter having at most another five years of service remaining. Of particular concern will be the small number of submarines at sea, which could simplify Soviet antisubmarine efforts. In an effort to avoid this situation, the Navy and Department of Defense are again examining lower-cost SLBM submarine designs. The current effort is noted below. In the past, proposals have been put forward for smaller, 16-tube SSBNs, with some analysts proposing a modification of the STURGEON or LOS ANGELES SSN design to a strategic missile configuration in the same manner that the SKIPJACK-class SSN was enlarged into the initial U.S. SSBNs.

Names: Beginning in 1958 the 41 Polaris-Poseidon submarines were named for "distinguished Americans who were known for their devotion to freedom." Three submarines, however, were named for non-Americans, the CASIMIR PULASKI, KAMEHAMEHA, and VON STEUBEN.

The use of state names was introduced in 1976 for the Trident SSBNs. That source had been used previously for battleships and, in the recent past, for guided missile cruisers.

Type	Class/Ship	Active	Bldg.[a]	Reserve	Comm.	Missiles
SSBN 726	OHIO	—	9	—	1981–	24 Trident C-4
SSBN 640	BENJAMIN FRANKLIN	12	—	—	1965–1967	16 Trident C-4 / 16 Poseidon C-3
SSBN 616	LAFAYETTE	19	—	—	1963–1964	16 Poseidon C-3
SSBN 608	ETHAN ALLEN	5	—	—	1961–1963	16 Polaris A-3
SSBN 598	GEORGE WASHINGTON	—	—	5	1959–1961	removed

[a] Includes ships authorized through FY 1981.

ATTACK SUBMARINES

The U.S. attack submarine force (SS/SSN) is increasing and will peak above the 90-submarine force-level goal during the mid-1980s. As of January 1981 there were approximately 75 nuclear-propelled attack submarines plus five diesel-electric attack submarines in commission. One of the latter was configured as a troop transport, but retained an SS designation. In addition, three research submarines were in service, the venerable SEAWOLF (still designated SSN), GUDGEON (SSAG), and DOLPHIN (AGSS).

Attack submarine force levels will begin to decline in the later 1980s as the current SSN construction rate of just over one LOS

The Los Angeles (SSN 688) at dawn in Hong Kong harbor. The Los Angeles is the lead submarine of the largest and fastest U.S. attack submarine design. Those characteristics have been costly and have led to the effort to design a smaller and possibly (but not necessarily) less capable attack submarine class to succeed the Los Angeles. (1979, Giorgio Arra)

Angeles per year will not replace the earlier SSNs being retired after 25 years of service.

During 1978–1979, at the insistence of Congress, the Navy conducted a "Submarine Alternatives Study" that proposed a smaller, possibly less-capable SSN design. (However, it has been pointed out by some analysts that current technology may permit the design of a smaller and *more* capable SSN.) The Navy's submarine leadership has opposed such proposals, instead advocating larger and faster (and more costly) SSNs. The Department of Defense has decided to pursue the smaller SSN concept, currently designated as the Fleet Attack submarine (FA-SSN).

There is also limited interest in the construction of non-nuclear attack submarines (SSX), a move strongly opposed by the submarine community leadership. Foreign designs—especially the German HDW 2000 submarine—as well as new American designs have been proposed for the SSX. Such submarines, even in limited numbers, would appear to be useful for the training and target roles that today require SSNs with much higher construction and operating costs. The few surviving U.S. diesel-electric attack submarines will be discarded by the mid-1980s.

When this edition went to press, there was also consideration being given to methods of employing some of the Polaris SSBNs in a tactical role, either in their current configuration or with missile sections removed. Both "straight" SSN and tactical or theater land-attack cruise missile (SSGN) configurations were being considered for these submarines.

Electronics/Radar: All combat submarines have surface search radar for navigational purposes (designated in the BPS series; see Chapter 24). Electronic Warfare (EW) equipment is also provided. Only those systems specifically identified with submarines are listed in the following descriptions.

Names: The first U.S. Navy submarine, the Holland (SS 1), completed in 1900, was named for her Irish-born inventor. Subsequent U.S. submarines were named for fish and other marine life until letter-number names (e.g., A-3) were assigned to all existing submarines on 17 November 1911. Marine-life names were reintroduced in the early 1930s for "fleet" boats, with some units named retroactively.

The source for attack submarine names was changed in 1973 to members of Congress who had supported the nuclear submarine program; in 1974 the names of American cities were introduced (a source that previously provided names for cruisers and, more recently, for amphibious cargo ships and large replenishment ships).

Submersibles: The Navy's Deep Submergence Vehicles (DSV)—including the nuclear-propelled NR-1—are described in Chapter 19 of this edition.

Type	Class/Ship	Active	Bldg.[a]	Reserve	Comm.	Notes
SSN 688	Los Angeles	10	27	—	1976–	
SSN 685	Lipscomb	1	—	—	1974	Deep diving
SSN 671	Narwhal	1	—	—	1969	SUBROC/Mk 48
SSN 637	Sturgeon	37	—	—	1967–1975	Advanced sonar
SSN 594	Permit	13	—	—	1962–1968	
SSN 597	Tullibee	1	—	—	1960	no longer first line
SSN 587	Halibut	—	—	1	1960	ex-guided missile
SSN 586	Triton	—	—	1	1959	ex-radar picket
SSN 585	Skipjack	5	—	—	1959–1961	high speed; first line
SSN 580	Barbel	3	—	—	1959	last U.S. non-nuclear
SSN 578	Skate	4	—	—	1957–1959	no longer first line
SSG 577	Growler	—	—	1	1958	guided missile
SS 576	Darter	1	—	—	1956	
SSN 575	Seawolf	1	—	—	1957	research
SS 574	Grayback	1	—	—	1958	transport
SSN 571	Nautilus	—	—	1	1954	relic
AGSS 569	Albacore	—	—	1	1953	research
SSAG 567	Gudgeon	1	—	—	1952	research
AGSS 555	Dolphin	1	—	—	1968	research

[a] Includes submarines authorized through FY 1981.

ADVANCED STRATEGIC MISSILE SUBMARINES

Funds have been programmed by the Department of Defense for concept and design studies leading to a follow-on, less expensive Trident SSBN. Under current plans, the ship could be a variation of the Trident submarine with a smaller reactor, or a smaller submarine with the same number of SLBM tubes. Through 1980 the Navy had used available funds to determine if the Trident SSBNs could be built more cheaply, the so-called reengineered Trident. None of the funds were used to "look seriously" at new SSBN designs according to the Deputy Chief of Naval Operations (Submarine Warfare).

The Navy considers FY 1985 as the earliest possible authorization date for an advanced SSBN.

(9) NUCLEAR-PROPELLED STRATEGIC MISSILE SUBMARINES: "OHIO" CLASS

Number	Name	FY/SCB	Builder	Laid down	Launched	Commission	Status
SSBN 726	OHIO	74/304	General Dynamics (Electric Boat)	10 Apr 1976	7 Apr 1979	mid-1981 (?)	Bldg.
SSBN 727	MICHIGAN	75/304	General Dynamics (Electric Boat)	4 Apr 1977	26 Apr 1980	1981	Bldg.
SSBN 728		75/304	General Dynamics (Electric Boat)	9 June 1977		1982	Bldg.
SSBN 729	GEORGIA	76/304	General Dynamics (Electric Boat)	7 Apr 1979		1983	Bldg.
SSBN 730		77/304	General Dynamics (Electric Boat)			1983	Bldg.
SSBN 731		78/304	General Dynamics (Electric Boat)			1984	Bldg.
SSBN 732		78/304	General Dynamics (Electric Boat)			1985	Bldg.
SSBN 733		80/304	General Dynamics (Electric Boat)			1985	Auth.
SSBN 734		81/304	General Dynamics (Electric Boat)			1986	Auth.

Displacement:	16,600 tons standard	Speed:	
	18,700 tons submerged		20+ knots submerged
Length:	560 feet (170.7 m) oa	Manning:	153 (13 O + 140 enlisted)
Beam:	42 feet (12.8 m)	Missiles:	24 tubes for Trident C-4 SLBM
Draft:	36½ feet (11.1 m)	Torpedo tubes:	4 21-inch (533-mm) amidships Mk 68
Propulsion:	steam turbines (General Electric); 1 shaft	Sonars:	BQQ-6 bow-mounted
Reactors:	1 pressurized-water S8G	Fire control:	1 Mk 98 missile FCS
			1 Mk 118 torpedo FCS

The first Trident submarine, the USS OHIO (SSBN 726), at sea before transiting to her home port of Bangor, Washington. She sailed on her first deterrent patrol late in 1982. (1981, U.S. Navy, PH2 William Garlinghouse)

Activity at Electric Boat: The attack submarine PHOENIX (SSN 702) had just been launched (left) when this photo was taken at the EB yard in Groton, Connecticut. In the center is the Trident submarine MICHIGAN and, at right, the OHIO. The bow of the third Trident SSBN, the FLORIDA, is at upper left. The PHOENIX is only 20 feet shorter than the first U.S. SSBNs, but 200 feet shorter than the Trident submarines. (1979, General Dynamics/Electric Boat)

The OHIO-class submarines are the largest undersea craft known to have been constructed by any nation. They are more than twice the displacement of the previous LAFAYETTE class.

The Trident program is considerably behind the schedule established in May 1972 when the weapon system was approved for development. The lead submarine was funded in FY 1974 with a schedule drawn up for constructing an initial ten-ship class at an annual rate of 1–3–3–3. The first Trident was ordered on 25 July 1974 with a planned delivery of 30 April 1979. However, the shipyard agreed to attempt to make delivery in December 1977 because of the high priority of the program. Subsequent delays caused by the Navy and problems at the shipyard have resulted in late deliveries of all submarines and the first nine submarines being authorized on a 1–2–1–1–2–0–1–1 schedule.

The Defense Department has approved a construction rate of one SSBN per year to the mid-1980s and then three submarines every two years.

These submarines are scheduled to begin their initial operational deployment nine months after commissioning. The first Trident squadron will be based at Bremerton, Wash., and deploy to the Pacific.

Design: These submarines have a relatively conservative design with an improved LAFAYETTE-class arrangement incorporating the bow sonar dome and amidships torpedo tubes of later attack submarines. These are the only 24-tube strategic missile submarines built by any nation (all others having 20 tubes or less).

Reactors: The S8G reactor was designed to produce 60,000 shp, the most powerful U.S. naval reactor except for the A4W reactors in the aircraft carriers of the NIMITZ (CVN 68) class. A land-based S8G reactor prototype has been constructed.

Sonar: The BQQ-6 sonar is similar to the BQQ-5 in attack submarines less the active sonar elements. A towed sonar array is provided in the BQQ-6 system.

Torpedoes: The SSBNs carry Mk 48 torpedoes.

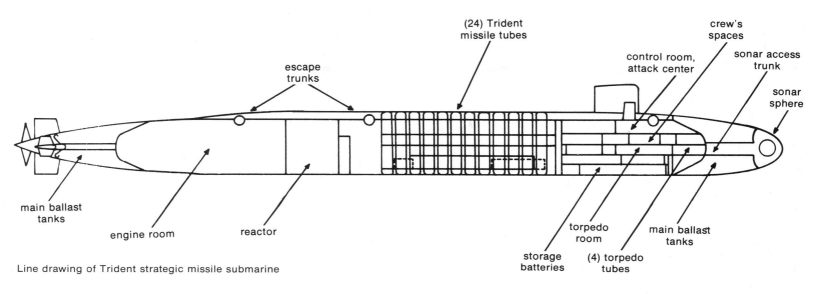

Line drawing of Trident strategic missile submarine

The Oʜɪᴏ at sea during trials. (1981, U.S. Navy, PH2 William Garlinghouse)

31 NUCLEAR-PROPELLED STRATEGIC MISSILE SUBMARINES: "LAFAYETTE" AND "BENJAMIN FRANKLIN" CLASSES

Number	Name	FY/SCB	Builder	Laid down	Launched	Commissioned	Status
SSBN 616	LAFAYETTE	61/216	General Dynamics (Electric Boat)	17 Jan 1961	8 May 1962	23 Apr 1963	**AA**
SSBN 617	ALEXANDER HAMILTON	61/216	General Dynamics (Electric Boat)	26 June 1961	18 Aug 1962	27 June 1963	**AA**
SSBN 619	ANDREW JACKSON	61/216	Mare Island Naval Shipyard	26 Apr 1961	15 Sep 1962	3 July 1963	**AA**
SSBN 620	JOHN ADAMS	61/216	Portsmouth Naval Shipyard	19 May 1961	12 Jan 1963	12 May 1964	**AA**
SSBN 622	JAMES MONROE	S61/216	Newport News	31 July 1961	4 Aug 1962	7 Dec 1963	**AA**
SSBN 623	NATHAN HALE	S61/216	General Dynamics (Electric Boat)	2 Oct 1961	12 Jan 1963	23 Nov 1963	**AA**
SSBN 624	WOODROW WILSON	S61/216	Mare Island Naval Shipyard	13 Sep 1961	22 Feb 1963	27 Dec 1963	**AA**
SSBN 625	HENRY CLAY	S61/216	Newport News	22 Oct 1961	30 Nov 1962	20 Feb 1964	**AA**
SSBN 626	DANIEL WEBSTER	S61/216	General Dynamics (Electric Boat)	28 Dec 1961	27 Apr 1963	9 Apr 1964	**AA**
SSBN 627	JAMES MADISON	62/216	Newport News	5 Mar 1962	15 Mar 1963	28 July 1964	**AA**
SSBN 628	TECUMSEH	62/216	General Dynamics (Electric Boat)	1 June 1962	22 June 1963	29 May 1964	**AA**
SSBN 629	DANIEL BOONE	62/216	Mare Island Naval Shipyard	6 Feb 1962	22 June 1963	23 Apr 1964	**AA**
SSBN 630	JOHN C. CALHOUN	62/216	Newport News	4 June 1962	22 June 1963	15 Sep 1964	**AA**
SSBN 631	ULYSSES S. GRANT	62/216	General Dynamics (Electric Boat)	18 Aug 1962	2 Nov 1963	17 July 1964	**AA**
SSBN 632	VON STEUBEN	62/216	Newport News	4 Sep 1962	18 Oct 1963	30 Sep 1964	**AA**
SSBN 633	CASIMIR PULASKI	62/216	General Dynamics (Electric Boat)	12 Jan 1963	1 Feb 1964	14 Aug 1964	**AA**
SSBN 634	STONEWALL JACKSON	62/216	Mare Island Naval Shipyard	4 July 1962	30 Nov 1963	26 Aug 1964	**AA**
SSBN 635	SAM RAYBURN	62/216	Newport News	3 Dec 1962	20 Dec 1963	2 Dec 1964	**AA**
SSBN 636	NATHANAEL GREENE	62/216	Portsmouth Naval Shipyard	21 May 1962	12 May 1964	19 Dec 1964	**AA**
SSBN 640	BENJAMIN FRANKLIN	63/216	General Dynamics (Electric Boat)	25 May 1963	5 Dec 1964	22 Oct 1965	**AA**
SSBN 641	SIMON BOLIVAR	63/216	Newport News	17 Apr 1963	22 Aug 1964	29 Oct 1965	**AA**
SSBN 642	KAMEHAMEHA	63/216	Mare Island Naval Shipyard	2 May 1963	16 Jan 1965	10 Dec 1965	**AA**
SSBN 643	GEORGE BANCROFT	63/216	General Dynamics (Electric Boat)	24 Aug 1963	20 Mar 1965	22 Jan 1966	**AA**
SSBN 644	LEWIS AND CLARK	63/216	Newport News	29 July 1963	21 Nov 1964	22 Dec 1965	**AA**
SSBN 645	JAMES K. POLK	63/216	General Dynamics (Electric Boat)	23 Nov 1963	22 May 1965	16 Apr 1966	**AA**
SSBN 654	GEORGE C. MARSHALL	64/216	Newport News	2 Mar 1964	21 May 1965	29 Apr 1966	**AA**
SSBN 655	HENRY L. STIMSON	64/216	General Dynamics (Electric Boat)	4 Apr 1964	13 Nov 1965	20 Aug 1966	**AA**
SSBN 656	GEORGE WASHINGTON CARVER	64/216	Newport News	24 Aug 1964	14 Aug 1965	15 June 1966	**AA**
SSBN 657	FRANCIS SCOTT KEY	64/216	General Dynamics (Electric Boat)	5 Dec 1964	23 Apr 1966	3 Dec 1966	**AA**
SSBN 658	MARIANO G. VALLEJO	64/216	Mare Island Naval Shipyard	7 July 1964	23 Oct 1965	16 Dec 1966	**AA**
SSBN 659	WILL ROGERS	64/216	General Dynamics (Electric Boat)	20 Mar 1965	21 July 1966	1 Apr 1967	**AA**

Displacement:	6,650 tons light
	7,250 tons standard
	8,250 tons submerged
Length:	425 feet (129.5 m) oa
Beam:	33 feet (10.1 m)
Draft:	31½ feet (9.6 m)
Propulsion:	steam turbines; 15,000 shp; 1 shaft
Reactors:	1 pressurized-water S5W
Speed:	~20 knots surface
	~25 knots submerged
Manning:	141 (12 O + 129 enlisted)
Missiles:	16 tubes for Poseidon C-3 SLBM or Trident C-4 SLBM
Torpedo tubes:	4 21-inch (533-mm) bow Mk 65
Sonars:	BQR-7
	BQR-15 towed array
	BQR-19
	BQS-4
Fire control:	1 Mk 88 missile FCS
	1 Mk 113 torpedo FCS

The DANIEL WEBSTER maneuvering at the New London Submarine Base (actually in Groton, Conn.) with the assistance of two YTBs. The WEBSTER is the only U.S. SSBN with bow-mounted diving planes. All four British SSBNs have bow-mounted planes, while the modern Soviet and French SSBNs follow the U.S. design. (1975, U.S. Navy, JO2 Gwyneth J. Schultz)

These submarines were built to carry the Polaris SLBM, with all subsequently being modernized to carry the improved Poseidon SLBM and the last 12 submarines now being upgraded to fire the Trident missile. All are operational in the Atlantic-Mediterranean areas.

Class: The last 12 submarines of this design are officially the BEN-
JAMIN FRANKLIN class (see Design notes). Four additional units of
this class were proposed in the fiscal 1965 shipbuilding program to
complete the then-planned 45-submarine Polaris force. The ships
were not built.

Design: These submarines are enlarged versions of the previous
ETHAN ALLEN class. The last 12 submarines have quieter machinery
than their predecessors and other minor differences. The DANIEL
WEBSTER has bow-mounted diving planes instead of sail-mounted
planes.

Missiles: The first eight submarines initially deployed with the
Polaris A-2 missile and the 23 later units with the Polaris A-3 missile.
All were converted during 1970–1978 to launch the Poseidon missile. Subsequently, the last 12 submarines were selected for modification to launch the Trident C-4 missile. The first Trident SSBN was
the FRANCIS SCOTT KEY, modified in 1978–1979 and starting the first
Trident patrol on 20 October 1979. All 12 backfits were to be completed by 1983.

The Mk 88 Mod 2 FCS is fitted in the submarines armed with the
Trident.

The CASIMIR PULASKI under way on the surface on the Navy's Atlantic Undersea Test and Evaluation Center (AUTEC) range near Andros Island, Ba-
hamas. While on strategic deployments SSBNs do not normally operate on
the surface. The hydrodynamic "cigar" design of modern submarines
makes them faster submerged than on the surface for the same horsepower. (1979, U.S. Navy)

The strategic missile submarine SIMON BOLIVAR at sea off Norfolk, Va. The submarine's hull number has been painted out, the standard practice for SSBNs
and SSNs on patrol. The SSBNs normally deploy for up to 60 days, although selected port visits are used to break up the monotony. "Blue" and "Gold"
crews alternate on the patrols, with the off-duty crew undergoing training and leave. (1976, Giorgio Arra)

This rare view of two SSBNs shows the THOMAS A. EDISON, in rear, passing the FRANCIS SCOTT KEY in the Panama Canal. The latter submarine is 15 feet
longer, but has been refitted with the Poseidon C-3 missile in place of the Polaris A-3 weapons of the EDISON. (1973, U.S. Navy)

5 NUCLEAR-PROPELLED STRATEGIC MISSILE SUBMARINES: "ETHAN ALLEN" CLASS

Number	Name	FY/SCB	Builder	Laid down	Launched	Commissioned	Status
SSBN 608	ETHAN ALLEN	59/180	General Dynamics (Electric Boat)	14 Sep 1959	22 Nov 1960	8 Aug 1961	**PA**
SSBN 609	SAM HOUSTON	59/180	Newport News	28 Dec 1959	2 Feb 1961	6 Mar 1962	**PA**
SSBN 610	THOMAS A. EDISON	59/180	General Dynamics (Electric Boat)	15 Mar 1960	15 June 1961	10 Mar 1962	**PA**
SSBN 611	JOHN MARSHALL	59/180	Newport News	4 Apr 1960	15 July 1961	21 May 1962	**PA**
SSBN 618	THOMAS JEFFERSON	61/180	Newport News	3 Feb 1961	24 Feb 1962	4 Jan 1963	**PA**

Displacement:	6,955 tons standard
	7,900 tons submerged
Length:	410½ feet (125.1 m) oa
Beam:	33 feet (10.1 m)
Draft:	30 feet (9.1 m)
Propulsion:	steam turbines; 15,000 shp; 1 shaft
Reactors:	1 pressurized-water S5W
Speed:	~20 knots surface
	~25 knots submerged
Manning:	141 (12 O + 129 enlisted)
Missiles:	16 tubes for Polaris A-3 SLBM
Torpedo tubes:	4 21-inch (533-mm) bow Mk 65
Sonars:	BQS-4
	BQR-15 towed array
	BQR-19
Fire control:	1 Mk 84 missile FCS
	1 Mk 112 torpedo FCS

The ETHAN ALLEN was the first U.S. ballistic missile submarine design, with the previous GEORGE WASHINGTON class having been modified from an SSN design. All five of these submarines have been withdrawn from the strategic missile role. Their future use was uncertain when this edition went to press.

Class: Note that the THOMAS JEFFERSON's hull number is out of sequence.

Missiles: These submarines were initially armed with the Polaris A-2 missile. All five were later modified to launch the Polaris A-3 missile. This class and the previous GEORGE WASHINGTON-class SSBNs could not be fitted to carry the larger-diameter Poseidon missile without extensive hull modification.

The SAM HOUSTON at high speed on the surface off Apra Harbor, Guam, site of the Pacific Fleet's Polaris submarine refit site. All surviving Polaris submarines were scheduled to be decommissioned in 1980–1981, with some possibly being converted to SSN with the removal of the 16-tube missile section (as being done by the Soviets to their older Yankee-class SSBNs). (1979, U.S. Navy, PH2 Edward J. O'Brien)

THOMAS JEFFERSON (1976, U.S. Navy, PH1 A. E. Legare)

5 NUCLEAR-PROPELLED STRATEGIC MISSILE SUBMARINES: "GEORGE WASHINGTON" CLASS

Number	Name	FY/SCB	Builder	Laid down	Launched	Commissioned	Status
SSBN 598	George Washington	S58/180A	General Dynamics (Electric Boat)	1 Nov 1957	9 June 1959	30 Dec 1959	PR
SSBN 599	Patrick Henry	S58/180A	General Dynamics (Electric Boat)	27 May 1958	22 Sep 1959	9 Apr 1960	PR
SSBN 600	Theodore Roosevelt	S58/180A	Mare Island Naval Shipyard	30 May 1958	3 Oct 1959	13 Feb 1961	PR
SSBN 601	Robert E. Lee	59/180A	Newport News	25 Aug 1958	18 Dec 1959	16 Sep 1960	PR
SSBN 602	Abraham Lincoln	59/180A	Portsmouth Naval Shipyard	1 Nov 1958	14 May 1960	11 Mar 1961	PR

Displacement:	6,000 tons standard
	6,700 tons submerged
Length:	381²/₃ feet (116.3 m) oa
Beam:	33 feet (10.1 m)
Draft:	29 feet (8.8 m)
Propulsion:	steam turbines; 15,000 shp; 1 shaft
Reactors:	1 pressurized-water S5W
Speed:	~20 knots surface
	~25 knots submerged
Manning:	139 (12 O + 127 enlisted)
Missiles:	removed
Torpedo tubes:	6 21-inch (533-mm) bow Mk 65
Sonars:	BQS-4
	BQR-19
Fire control:	1 Mk 84 missile FCS
	1 Mk 112 torpedo FCS

The George Washington-class submarines were the first warships in the West to be armed with ballistic missiles. They were predated by the Soviet diesel-electric Zulu-V and Golf SSB classes, and the nuclear-propelled Hotel SSBN class. The George Washington-class SSBNs were armed with more and longer-range missiles than the Soviet submarines.

All are now inactive. The Theodore Roosevelt and Robert E. Lee completed their last Polaris patrols in 1979 and the three other SSBNs in 1980. Their future is uncertain. They may be fitted with vertical-launch Tomahawk cruise missiles or with a new mid-section for launching cruise missiles. Alternatively, the mid-section may be removed (as the Soviet Navy has done in converting several similar Yankee-class SSBNs to the SSN configuration).

Class: These submarines were "converted" during construction from Skipjack-class attack submarines. The FY 1958 supplemental shipbuilding program, signed by President Eisenhower on 11 February 1958, provided for the immediate construction of three SSBNs. In anticipation of this action, the Navy had shortly before directed that two attack submarines be redesigned as missile submarines; they were the Scorpion (SSN 589) and the then-unnamed SSN 590. These were completed as the George Washington and Patrick Henry, respectively.

Design: The redesign of the Skipjack class provided for the addition of almost 130 feet in length to accommodate two rows of eight missile tubes, auxiliary machinery, and missile fire control and inertial navigation systems.

Missiles: As built, these submarines were armed with the Polaris A-1 missile, with the George Washington beginning the first Polaris patrol on 15 November 1960. All five submarines were refitted with the Polaris A-3 missile.

Patrick Henry (1978, U.S. Navy, PHAN Norman Desrochers)

10+27 NUCLEAR-PROPELLED ATTACK SUBMARINES: "LOS ANGELES" CLASS

Number	Name	FY/SCB	Builder	Laid down	Launched	Commissioned	Status
SSN 688	LOS ANGELES	70/303	Newport News	8 Jan 1972	6 Apr 1974	13 Nov 1976	**PA**
SSN 689	BATON ROUGE	70/303	Newport News	18 Nov 1972	26 Apr 1975	25 June 1977	**AA**
SSN 690	PHILADELPHIA	70/303	General Dynamics (Electric Boat)	12 Aug 1972	19 Oct 1974	25 June 1977	**AA**
SSN 691	MEMPHIS	71/303	Newport News	23 June 1973	3 Apr 1976	17 Dec 1977	**AA**
SSN 692	OMAHA	71/303	General Dynamics	27 Jan 1973	21 Feb 1976	11 Mar 1978	**PA**
SSN 693	CINCINNATI	71/303	Newport News	6 Apr 1974	19 Feb 1977	10 June 1978	**AA**
SSN 694	GROTON	71/303	General Dynamics (Electric Boat)	3 Aug 1973	9 Oct 1976	8 July 1978	**AA**
SSN 695	BIRMINGHAM	72/303	Newport News	26 Apr 1975	29 Oct 1977	16 Dec 1978	**AA**
SSN 696	NEW YORK CITY	72/303	General Dynamics (Electric Boat)	15 Dec 1973	18 June 1977	3 Mar 1978	**PA**
SSN 697	INDIANAPOLIS	72/303	General Dynamics (Electric Boat)	19 Oct 1974	30 July 1977	5 Jan 1980	**PA**
SSN 698	BREMERTON	72/303	General Dynamics (Electric Boat)	6 May 1976	22 July 1978	Dec 1981	Bldg.
SSN 699	JACKSONVILLE	72/303	General Dynamics (Electric Boat)	21 Feb 1976	18 Nov 1978	1981	Bldg.
SSN 700	DALLAS	73/303	General Dynamics (Electric Boat)	9 Oct 1976	28 Apr 1979	1981	Bldg.
SSN 701	LA JOLLA	73/303	General Dynamics (Electric Boat)	16 Oct 1976	11 Aug 1979	1981	Bldg.
SSN 702	PHOENIX	73/303	General Dynamics (Electric Boat)	30 July 1977	8 Dec 1979	1981	Bldg.
SSN 703	BOSTON	73/303	General Dynamics (Electric Boat)	11 Aug 1978	19 Apr 1980	1981	Bldg.
SSN 704	BALTIMORE	73/303	General Dynamics (Electric Boat)	21 May 1979	13 Dec 1980	1982	Bldg.
SSN 705	CHICAGO	73/303	General Dynamics (Electric Boat)	4 Sep 1979		1982	Bldg.
SSN 706	. . . .	74/303	General Dynamics (Electric Boat)	27 Dec 1979		1982	Bldg.
SSN 707	. . . .	74/303	General Dynamics (Electric Boat)	8 May 1980		1982	Bldg.
SSN 708	. . . .	74/303	General Dynamics (Electric Boat)			1983	Bldg.
SSN 709	. . . .	74/303	General Dynamics (Electric Boat)			1984	Bldg.
SSN 710	. . . .	74/303	General Dynamics (Electric Boat)			1984	Bldg.
SSN 711	SAN FRANCISCO	75/303	Newport News	26 May 1977	27 Oct 1979	1981	Bldg.
SSN 712	ATLANTA	75/303	Newport News	17 Aug 1978	16 Aug 1980	1981	Bldg.
SSN 713	HOUSTON	75/303	Newport News	29 Jan 1979		1982	Bldg.
SSN 714	. . . .	76/303	Newport News	1 Aug 1979		1983	Bldg.
SSN 715	. . . .	76/303	Newport News	25 Jan 1980		1983	Bldg.
SSN 716	. . . .	77/303	Newport News			1983	Bldg.
SSN 717	. . . .	77/303	Newport News			1984	Bldg.
SSN 718	. . . .	77/303	Newport News			1985	Bldg.
SSN 719	. . . .	78/303	General Dynamics (Electric Boat)			1984	Bldg.
SSN 720	. . . .	79/303	General Dynamics (Electric Boat)			1985	Bldg.
SSN 721	. . . .	80/303				1986	Auth.
SSN 722	. . . .	80/303				1986	Auth.
SSN 723	. . . .	81/303				1987	Auth.
SSN 724	. . . .	81/303				1987	Auth.

Displacement: 6,000 tons standard
6,900 tons submerged
Length: 360 feet (109.7 m) oa
Beam: 33 feet (10.1 m)
Draft: 32$\frac{1}{3}$ feet (9.85 m)
Propulsion: steam turbines; ~30,000 shp; 1 shaft
Reactors: 1 pressurized-water S6G
Speed:
30+ knots submerged
Manning: 127 (12 O + 115 enlisted)
Missiles: Harpoon SSM in eight submarines
Torpedo tubes: 4 21-inch (533-mm) amidships Mk 67
ASW weapons: SUBROC
Mk 48 torpedoes
Radars: BPS-15 surface search
Sonars: BQQ-5 bow-mounted
BQR-26 in some submarines
BQS-13
BQS-15
towed array
Fire control: 1 Mk 113 torpedo FCS in SSN 688–699; Mk 117 in later submarines

These are large, high-speed attack submarines developed to counter the fast Soviet submarines of the Charlie and Victor classes that were first completed in 1967–1968. These submarines are believed to be about five knots faster than the previous STURGEON-class SSNs. They are, of course, significantly slower than the speeds reported for the Soviet Alfa and Papa classes of nuclear-propelled submarines.

Class: Thirty-seven units of the LOS ANGELES class have been authorized through the FY 1981 program. As of 1980, four additional submarines were planned through the FY 1984 budget. These would make this the largest class of nuclear-propelled ships built by any nation (followed by 37 STURGEON-class SSNs and 34 Soviet Yankee-class SSN/SSBNs).

Design: These submarines displace approximately half again as much as the previous STURGEON class, with the additional size being required primarily for the larger propulsion plant. The LOS ANGELES submarines also have improved sonar and fire control systems, although those of the previous SSN classes are being updated.

Missiles: The Harpoon torpedo-tube-launched missile is being fitted in these submarines. When available, the Tomahawk cruise missile can also be carried by this class.

Reactors: The S6G reactor is estimated to have an initial fuel core operating life of 10 to 13 years.

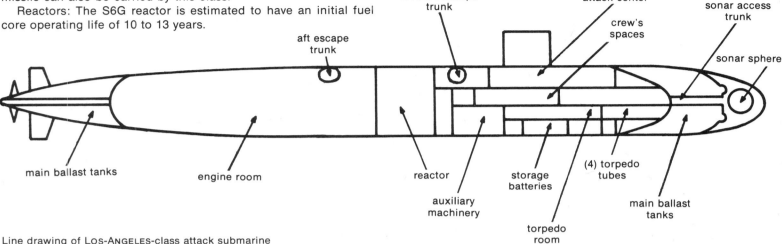

Line drawing of LOS-ANGELES-class attack submarine

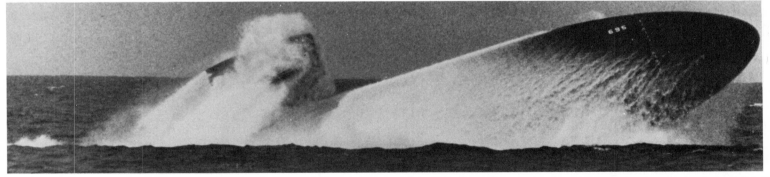

The BIRMINGHAM demonstrates an emergency surfacing evolution during sea trials. Note the water pouring from her sail structure and sail-mounted diving planes, and her relatively pointed bow. The LOS ANGELES-class submarines are the world's largest attack submarines, exceeding the size of even those Soviet nuclear-propelled submarines that have cruise missile tubes in addition to torpedo tubes. (1978, U.S. Navy)

ADVANCED NUCLEAR-PROPELLED ATTACK SUBMARINES

The high costs of the LOS ANGELES-class attack submarines and the need for increased construction rates in the late 1980s to replace older attack submarines being phased out has led the Department of Defense to accept the recommendations of the Navy's "Submarine Alternatives Study" and plan a smaller SSN. Currently designated the Fleet Attack submarine (FA-SSN, and referred to as "Fat Albert"), the craft will be smaller than the LOS ANGELES and possibly slightly slower. Other characteristics are expected to be similar.

The lead FA-SSN has been scheduled for the FY 1983 shipbuild-

ing program, with a second submarine in FY 1984, and four additional units in FY 1985.

The following are comparisons of the leading advanced submarine designs and the LOS ANGELES.

Type	Reactor	Displacement (tons)	Torpedo tubes	Costs*
SSN 688	S6G	6,900	4	1.00
Advanced SSN-688	S6G	7,200+	6	1.01
Reengineered SSN 688	S6G	~7,000	4	.96
FA-SSN	S5W	~5,000	6	.74

* Normalized cost average for ten follow-on ships.

The OMAHA at sea in the Pacific. Raised out of her sail structure are her radio antenna mast, narrow attack periscope, and larger night-reconnaissance periscope. Also housed in the sail structure are the submarine's radar, ECM mast, identification beacon, snorkel induction mast, and other radio antennas. (1979, Giorgio Arra)

LOS ANGELES (1979, Giorgio Arra)

The LOS ANGELES moored to an LST in Hong Kong harbor. Note the safety rail installed atop the sail structure, floodlights at the ends of the diving planes, and working party on deck. (1979, Giorgio Arra)

1 NUCLEAR-PROPELLED ATTACK SUBMARINE: "GLENARD P. LIPSCOMB" TYPE

Number	Name	FY/SCB	Builder	Laid down	Launched	Commissioned	Status
SSN 685	GLENARD P. LIPSCOMB	68/302	General Dynamics (Electric Boat)	5 June 1971	4 Aug 1973	21 Dec 1974	**AA**

Displacement:	5,800 tons standard
	6,480 tons submerged
Length:	365 feet (111.3 m) oa
Beam:	31¾ feet (9.7 m)
Draft:	
Propulsion:	turboelectric drive (General Electric); 1 shaft
Reactors:	1 pressurized-water S5Wa
Speed:	~18 knots surface
	~25 knots submerged
Manning:	120 (12 O + 108 enlisted)
Missiles:	(see notes)
Torpedo tubes:	4 21-inch (533 mm) amidships Mk 63
ASW weapons:	SUBROC
	Mk 48 torpedoes
Radars:	BPS-15
Sonars:	BQQ-2 bow-mounted
	BQS-13
	towed array
Fire control:	1 Mk 113 torpedo FCS

The LIPSCOMB was constructed to evaluate a Turbine-Electric Drive (TED) propulsion plant. Speed was sacrificed to reduce machinery noises. The TULLIBEE, constructed over a decade earlier, was in part a similar effort to replace reduction gear with electric drive. No additional submarines of this type were built because of the decision to have the faster LOS ANGELES class as the standard SSN design. The LIPSCOMB is considerably larger than the contemporary STURGEON-class submarines.

Fire control: The Mk 117 torpedo fire control system will be installed during a future overhaul.

Missiles: Torpedo-tube launched Harpoon and eventually Tomahawk cruise missiles will be carried in the LIPSCOMB.

Sonars: The BQQ-2 sonar system will be upgraded to the BQQ-5 configuration during a future overhaul. An additional sonar was fitted to the forward end of the LIPSCOMB's upper sail structure in June 1977.

The GLENARD P. LIPSCOMB—often referred to as the "Lipscomb fish" in the Fleet—returns to New London after a five-month deployment. Note the YTB on the portside, small sonar dome on the bow, bits and cleats (that retract when at sea), and bulge at the top of the sail for a special sonar installed in 1977. (1979, U.S. Navy; Jean Russell)

GLENARD P. LIPSCOMB making 17.5 knots on trials (1974, General Dynamics/Electric Boat)

1 NUCLEAR-PROPELLED ATTACK SUBMARINE: "NARWHAL" TYPE

Number	Name	FY/SCB	Builder	Laid down	Launched	Commissioned	Status
SSN 671	NARWHAL	64/245	General Dynamics (Electric Boat)	17 Jan 1966	9 Sep 1966	12 July 1969	**AA**

Displacement:	4,450 tons standard
	5,350 tons submerged
Length:	314 feet (95.7 m) oa
Beam:	38 feet (11.6 m)
Draft:	26 feet (7.9 m)
Propulsion:	steam turbines (General Electric); ~17,000 shp; 1 shaft
Reactors:	1 pressurized-water S5G
Speed:	~25 knots surface
	~30 knots submerged
Manning:	120 (12 O + 108 enlisted)
Missiles:	(see notes)
Torpedo tubes:	4 21-inch (533-mm) amidships Mk 63
ASW weapons:	ASROC
	Mk 48 torpedoes
Radars:	BPS-15
Sonars:	BQQ-2 bow-mounted
	BQS-13
	towed array
Fire control:	1 Mk 113 torpedo FCS

The NARWHAL was constructed to evaluate the natural-circulation S5G reactor plant in an attack submarine. Weapons, sensors, and other features of the NARWHAL are similar to the STURGEON class.

Fire control: The Mk 117 torpedo fire control system will be installed during a future overhaul.

Missiles: The NARWHAL will be fitted to fire the Harpoon and eventually the Tomahawk cruise missiles.

Reactors: The S5G reactor plant uses natural convection rather than pumps for heat transfer/coolant transfer at slow speeds, thus reducing self-generated machinery noises. A land-based prototype of the S5G plant was built at Arco, Idaho.

Sonar: The BQQ-2 sonar system will be upgraded to the BQQ-5 configuration during a future overhaul.

NARWHAL (1969, General Dynamics/Electric Boat)

37 NUCLEAR-PROPELLED ATTACK SUBMARINES: "STURGEON" CLASS

Number	Name	FY/SCB	Builder	Laid down	Launched	Commissioned	Status
SSN 637	STURGEON	62/188A	General Dynamics (Electric Boat)	10 Aug 1963	26 Feb 1966	3 Mar 1967	**AA**
SSN 638	WHALE	62/188A	General Dynamics (Quincy)	27 May 1964	14 Oct 1966	12 Oct 1968	**AA**
SSN 639	TAUTOG	62/188A	Ingalls SB Corp	27 Jan 1964	15 Apr 1967	17 Aug 1968	**PA**
SSN 646	GRAYLING	63/188A	Portsmouth Naval Shipyard	12 May 1964	22 June 1967	11 Oct 1969	**AA**
SSN 647	POGY	63/188A	Ingalls SB Corp	4 May 1964	3 June 1967	15 May 1971	**PA**
SSN 648	ASPRO	63/188A	Ingalls SB Corp	23 Nov 1964	29 Nov 1967	20 Feb 1969	**PA**
SSN 649	SUNFISH	63/188A	General Dynamics (Quincy)	15 Jan 1965	14 Oct 1966	15 Mar 1969	**AA**
SSN 650	PARGO	63/188A	General Dynamics (Electric Boat)	3 June 1964	17 Sep 1966	5 Jan 1968	**AA**
SSN 651	QUEENFISH	63/188A	Newport News	11 May 1965	25 Feb 1966	6 Dec 1966	**PA**
SSN 652	PUFFER	63/188A	Ingalls SB Corp	8 Feb 1965	30 Mar 1968	9 Aug 1969	**PA**
SSN 653	RAY	63/188A	Newport News	1 Apr 1965	21 June 1966	12 Apr 1967	**AA**
SSN 660	SAND LANCE	64/188A	Portsmouth Naval Shipyard	15 Jan 1965	11 Nov 1969	25 Sep 1971	**AA**
SSN 661	LAPON	64/188A	Newport News	26 July 1965	16 Dec 1966	14 Dec 1967	**AA**
SSN 662	GURNARD	64/188A	Mare Island Naval Shipyard	22 Dec 1964	20 May 1967	6 Dec 1968	**PA**
SSN 663	HAMMERHEAD	64/188A	Newport News	29 Nov 1965	14 Apr 1967	28 June 1968	**AA**
SSN 664	SEA DEVIL	64/188A	Newport News	12 Apr 1966	5 Oct 1967	30 Jan 1969	**AA**
SSN 665	GUITARRO	65/300	Mare Island Naval Shipyard	9 Dec 1965	27 July 1968	9 Sep 1972	**PA**
SSN 666	HAWKBILL	65/300	Mare Island Naval Shipyard	12 Dec 1966	12 Apr 1969	4 Feb 1971	**PA**
SSN 667	BERGALL	65/300	General Dynamics (Electric Boat)	16 Apr 1966	17 Feb 1968	13 June 1969	**AA**
SSN 668	SPADEFISH	65/300	Newport News	21 Dec 1966	15 May 1968	14 Aug 1969	**AA**
SSN 669	SEAHORSE	65/300	General Dynamics (Electric Boat)	13 Aug 1966	15 June 1968	19 Sep 1969	**AA**
SSN 670	FINBACK	65/300	Newport News	26 June 1966	7 Dec 1968	4 Feb 1970	**AA**
SSN 672	PINTADO	66/300	Mare Island Naval Shipyard	27 Oct 1967	16 Aug 1969	29 Apr 1971	**PA**
SSN 673	FLYING FISH	66/300	General Dynamics (Electric Boat)	30 June 1967	17 May 1969	29 Apr 1970	**AA**
SSN 674	TREPANG	66/300	General Dynamics (Electric Boat)	28 Oct 1967	27 Sep 1969	14 Aug 1970	**AA**
SSN 675	BLUEFISH	66/300	General Dynamics (Electric Boat)	13 Mar 1968	10 Jan 1970	8 Jan 1971	**AA**
SSN 676	BILLFISH	66/300	General Dynamics (Electric Boat)	20 Sep 1968	1 May 1970	12 Mar 1971	**AA**
SSN 677	DRUM	66/300	Mare Island Naval Shipyard	20 Aug 1968	23 May 1970	15 Apr 1972	**PA**
SSN 678	ARCHERFISH	67/300	General Dynamics (Electric Boat)	19 June 1969	16 Jan 1971	17 Dec 1971	**AA**
SSN 679	SILVERSIDES	67/300	General Dynamics (Electric Boat)	13 Oct 1969	4 June 1971	5 May 1972	**AA**
SSN 680	WILLIAM H. BATES	67/300	Ingalls (Litton)	4 Aug 1969	11 Dec 1971	5 May 1973	**PA**
SSN 681	BATFISH	67/300	General Dynamics (Electric Boat)	9 Feb 1970	9 Oct 1971	1 Sep 1972	**AA**
SSN 682	TUNNY	67/300	Ingalls (Litton)	22 May 1970	10 June 1972	26 Jan 1974	**PA**
SSN 683	PARCHE	68/300	Ingalls (Litton)	10 Dec 1970	13 Jan 1973	17 Aug 1974	**PA**
SSN 684	CAVALLA	68/300	General Dynamics	4 June 1970	19 Feb 1972	9 Feb 1973	**PA**
SSN 686	L. MENDEL RIVERS	69/300	Newport News	26 June 1971	2 June 1973	1 Feb 1975	**AA**
SSN 687	RICHARD B. RUSSELL	69/300	Newport News	19 Oct 1971	12 Jan 1974	16 Aug 1975	**AA**

Displacement:	3,640 tons standard
	4,650 tons submerged
Length:	292 1/6 feet (89.0 m) oa
Beam:	31 2/3 feet (9.65 m)
Draft:	29 1/2 feet (8.9 m)
Propulsion:	steam turbines; 15,000 shp; 1 shaft
Reactors:	1 pressurized-water S5W
Speed:	~20 knots surface
	~30 knots submerged
Manning:	121-134 (12-13 O + 109-121 enlisted)
Missiles:	Harpoon SSM in 17 submarines
Torpedo tubes:	4 21-inch (533-mm) amidships Mk 63
ASW weapons:	SUBROC
	Mk 48 torpedoes
Radars:	BPS-15
Sonars:	BQQ-2 or BQQ-5 bow-mounted
	BQS-8/12 in SSN 637–639, 646–653, 660–664; BQS-13 in later units
	BQR-26 in SSN 666
	towed array
Fire control:	1 Mk 113 or Mk 117 torpedo FCS

ASPRO alongside CHOWANOC (ATF 100—now stricken) (1977, Giorgio Arra)

This is the largest class of nuclear-propelled ships built by any nation, although the planned LOS ANGELES class would exceed the 37 submarines in this class. These submarines are improved versions of the previous PERMIT class.

Builders: The POGY was begun by the New York Shipbuilding Corp., Camden, N.J. The contract for her construction was terminated on 5 June 1967, and the unfinished submarine was towed to the Ingalls yard for completion.

Fire control: The original Mk 113 torpedo fire control system originally fitted in this class is being replaced by the Mk 117 during overhauls.

Missiles: The Harpoon cruise missile is being provided to this class, as will the Tomahawk when that weapon is deployed.

Sonar: The BQQ-2 sonar system in these submarines is being upgraded to the BQQ-5 during overhauls. The HAWKBILL is fitted with a protruding BQR-26 sonar in the forward part of her sail structure.

The HAWKBILL and some other submarines have an acoustic device designated GNAT fitted just forward of the upper rudder fin.

The HAWKBILL—a modern SSN—with her masts and scopes raised. Her BPS-15 radar is just visible below the flag; raised are her No. 1 attack scope (Type 2F) with the IFF/UHF antenna mast next to it; the No. 2 attack scope (Type 2) with the loop radio antenna mast barely raised; and the BRA-21 radio antenna mast. Not raised are the submarine's ECM mast, snorkel induction mast, and BRD-6 antenna mast. (1979, Giorgio Arra)

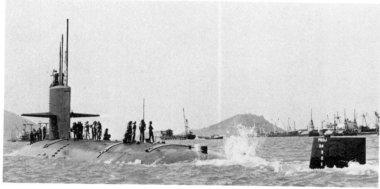

HAWKBILL (1979, Giorgio Arra)

The HAWKBILL off Hong Kong during a respite from a Western Pacific patrol. The submarine has a BQR-26 simultaneous multi-beam lens sonar fitted to the front end of her sail; the bulge forward of her rudder is a GNAT acoustic device. Several small sonar domes protrude from her deck, with the small bow dome being for her WLR-9 (see Chapter 24 for information on sonars). (1979, Giorgio Arra)

13 NUCLEAR-PROPELLED ATTACK SUBMARINES: "PERMIT" CLASS

Number	Name	FY/SCB	Builder	Laid down	Launched	Commissioned	Status
SSN 594	PERMIT	58/188	Mare Island Naval Shipyard	16 July 1959	1 July 1961	29 May 1962	**PA**
SSN 595	PLUNGER	58/188	Mare Island Naval Shipyard	2 Mar 1960	9 Dec 1961	21 Nov 1962	**PA**
SSN 596	BARB	58/188	Ingalls SB Corp	9 Nov 1959	12 Feb 1962	24 Aug 1963	**PA**
SSN 603	POLLACK	59/188	New York SB Corp	14 Mar 1960	17 Mar 1962	26 May 1964	**PA**
SSN 604	HADDO	59/188	New York SB Corp	9 Sep 1960	18 Aug 1962	16 Dec 1964	**PA**
SSN 605	JACK	59/188	Portsmouth Naval Shipyard	16 Sep 1960	24 Apr 1963	31 Mar 1967	**AA**
SSN 606	TINOSA	59/188	Portsmouth Naval Shipyard	24 Nov 1959	9 Dec 1961	17 Oct 1964	**AA**
SSN 607	DACE	59/188	Ingalls SB Corp	6 June 1960	18 Aug 1962	4 Apr 1964	**AA**
SSN 612	GUARDFISH	60/188	New York SB Corp	28 Feb 1961	15 May 1965	20 Dec 1966	**PA**
SSN 613	FLASHER	60/188	General Dynamics (Electric Boat)	14 Apr 1961	22 June 1963	22 July 1966	**PA**
SSN 614	GREENLING	60/188	General Dynamics (Electric Boat)	15 Aug 1961	4 Apr 1964	3 Nov 1967	**AA**
SSN 615	GATO	60/188	General Dynamics (Electric Boat)	15 Dec 1961	14 May 1964	25 Jan 1968	**AA**
SSN 621	HADDOCK	61/188	Ingalls SB Corp	24 Apr 1961	21 May 1966	22 Dec 1967	**PA**

Displacement: 3,750 tons standard (except SSN 605, 613–615, 3,800 tons)
4,300 tons submerged (except SSN 605, 4,500 tons; SSN 613–615, 4,600 tons)
Length: 278$\frac{1}{2}$ feet (84.9 m) oa (except SSN 605, 296$\frac{3}{4}$ feet (89.5 m); SSN 613–615, 292$\frac{1}{6}$ feet (89.1 m))
Beam: 31$\frac{3}{4}$ feet (9.6 m)
Draft: 29 feet (8.8 m)
Propulsion: steam turbines (General Electric in SSN 603–605, 612; De Laval in SSN 606, 613–615; Westinghouse in others)
Reactors: 1 pressurized-water S5W

Speed: ~20 knots surface
~30 knots submerged
Manning: 122-134 (12-13 O + 110-121 enlisted)
Missiles: Harpoon SSM in 2 submarines
Torpedo tubes: 4 21-inch (533-mm) amidships Mk 63
ASW weapons: SUBROC
Mk 48 torpedoes
Radars: BPS-11
Sonars: BQQ-2 or BQQ-5 bow-mounted
towed array
Fire control: 1 Mk 113 torpedo FCS except Mk 117 in SSN 594, 621

FLASHER (1978, Giorgio Arra)

These submarines established the standard for later U.S. Navy nuclear-propelled submarines, having a deep-diving capability, advanced sonars mounted in the optimum bow position, amidships torpedo tubes, SUBROC antisubmarine rocket, and a high degree of machinery quieting.

Builders: The GREENLING and GATO were launched by the Electric Boat yard at Groton, Conn., and then towed to the General Dynamics yard at Quincy, Mass., for completion. The later submarines of this class were delayed for inspection and modification after the loss of the THRESHER.

Class: The lead ship of this class, the THRESHER (SSN 593) was lost at sea on 10 April 1963 with all 129 men on board. Subsequently, the surviving submarines are generally referred to as the PERMIT class. The SSN 594–596 and SSN 607 were originally ordered as guided missile submarines (SSGN with same hull number) to carry the Regulus cruise missile. They were reordered as attack submarines after the Regulus program was canceled in December 1958.

Design: The later submarines of this class were modified during construction to incorporate additional safety features after the loss of the THRESHER. The JACK has a modified propulsion system with a large-diameter, sleeve-like outer propeller shaft housing a smaller-diameter inner shaft. This provides counter-rotating propellers on essentially a single shaft arrangement. The scheme was used to increase efficiency and reduce turbulence. There was no increase in speed, and it has not been repeated in other submarines.

Fire control: The original Mk 113 torpedo fire control system is being replaced during overhauls with the Mk 117.

Missiles: The torpedo-tube-launched Harpoon and later the Tomahawk cruise missiles can be fitted to these submarines.

Names: The names of three submarines were changed during construction: SSN 595 ex-POLLACK, SSN 596 ex-POLLACK, ex-PLUNGER, and SSN 603 ex-BARB.

Sonars: The original BQQ-2 sonar fitted in these submarines is being upgraded during overhauls to the BQQ-5 configuration.

POLLACK (1977, Giorgio Arra)

BARB (1977, Giorgio Arra)

1 NUCLEAR-PROPELLED ATTACK SUBMARINE: "TULLIBEE" TYPE

Number	Name	FY/SCB	Builder	Laid down	Launched	Commissioned	Status
SSN 597	TULLIBEE	58/178	General Dynamics (Electric Boat)	26 May 1958	27 Apr 1960	9 Nov 1960	**AA**

Displacement:	2,317 tons standard
	2,640 tons submerged
Length:	273 feet (83.2 m) oa
Beam:	23 1/3 feet (7.1 m)
Draft:	21 feet (6.4 m)
Propulsion:	turbo-electric with steam turbines (Westinghouse); 2,500 shp; 1 shaft
Reactors:	1 pressurized-water S2C
Speed:	~15 knots surface
	15+ knots submerged
Manning:	102 (11 O + 91 enlisted)
Torpedo tubes:	4 21-inch (533-mm) amidships Mk 64
ASW weapons:	Mk 48 torpedoes
Sonars:	BQQ-2 bow-mounted
	BQG-4 PUFFS
Fire control:	1 Mk 112 torpedo FCS

The TULLIBEE was designed as a small, hunter-killer submarine intended to operate off enemy ports and in narrow waterways, as were the smaller diesel-electric submarines of the SSK 1 class built earlier. The construction of additional submarines of this design was halted in favor of the larger and more-versatile PERMIT class. During the planning process the TULLIBEE was sometimes referred to as an SSKN, but that designation was never officially applied. The TULLIBEE is no longer considered a first-line submarine.

Design: This was the first U.S. submarine to have bow-mounted sonar with the torpedo tubes fitted amidships, and angled out to port and starboard. This sonar arrangement, followed in later SSNs and in the OHIO-class SSBNs, places the acoustic detection equipment in the best position with respect to ship movement and machinery noises.

Engineering: The nuclear power plant is smaller and less powerful than that of other U.S. submarines, with turbo-electric drive used in place of steam turbines and reduction gear to reduce self-generated submarine noises.

Reactor: A prototype reactor of this type (designated S1C) was built at Windsor, Conn.

TULLIBEE (1968, U.S. Navy)

1 NUCLEAR-PROPELLED RESEARCH SUBMARINE: "HALIBUT" TYPE

Number	Name	FY/SCB	Builder	Laid down	Launched	Commissioned	Status
SSN 587	HALIBUT	56/137A	Mare Island Naval Shipyard	11 Apr 1957	9 Jan 1959	4 Jan 1960	PR

Displacement: 3,850 tons standard
               5,000 tons submerged
Length: 350 feet (106.6 m) oa
Beam: 29½ feet (8.9 m)
Draft: 21½ feet (6.5 m)
Propulsion: steam turbines (Westinghouse); 2 shafts
Reactors: 1 pressurized-water S3W
Speed: 15.5 knots surface
               15+ knots submerged
Manning: 120 (12 O + 108 enlisted)
Missiles: removed
Torpedo tubes: 6 21-inch (533-mm) (4 bow Mk 61 + 2 stern Mk 62)
ASW weapons: torpedoes
Sonars: BQS-4
Fire control: 1 Mk 101 torpedo FCS

Engineering: The reactor plant is similar to the SKATE-class SSNs with lower speed because of her hull shape and larger size. The HALIBUT originally was ordered as a diesel-electric submarine, but on 27 February 1956 the Navy announced that she would be provided with nuclear propulsion.

The HALIBUT was designed and constructed as a guided missile submarine (SSGN) to launch the Regulus strategic attack missile; after that weapon was removed from service, the HALIBUT was reclassified as an attack submarine (SSN) on 25 July 1965. She subsequently served as a research submarine until decommissioned on 30 June 1976. In the latter role the HALIBUT's forward missile hangar was modified for research equipment, a ducted bow thruster was provided for precise control and maneuvering, and facilities were installed aft for carrying submersibles.

She is laid up in reserve in Bremerton, Wash.

Class: No additional submarines of this class were planned. An improved Regulus-armed SSGN class was planned, but those submarines were reordered as PERMIT-class submarines.

Design: The HALIBUT has a large hangar faired into her forward hull (capable of storing two Regulus II or five Regulus I missiles). In her SSGN configuration a trainable launcher was fitted between the hangar and sail structure.

HALIBUT (1970, U.S. Navy)

The HALIBUT in San Francisco Bay. A deep submergence vehicle is on the submarine's fantail, "mated" to the HALIBUT's aftermost hatch to permit crewmen to pass between the two while they are submerged. In the objective area the HALIBUT could launch and recover the vehicle while remaining at depth. After several years of research work the HALIBUT was laid up in reserve in 1976. The "hump" on her forward deck is her hangar hatch. (1970, U.S. Navy)

1 NUCLEAR-PROPELLED ATTACK SUBMARINE: "TRITON" TYPE

Number	Name	FY/SCB	Builder	Laid down	Launched	Commissioned	Status
SSN 586	TRITON	56/132	General Dynamics (Electric Boat)	29 May 1956	19 Aug 1958	10 Nov 1959	AR

Displacement:	5,940 tons standard
	6,670 tons submerged
Length:	447½ feet (136.3 m) oa
Beam:	37 feet (11.3 m)
Draft:	24 feet (7.3 m)
Propulsion:	steam turbines (General Electric); ~34,000 shp; 2 shafts
Reactors:	2 pressurized-water S4G
Speed:	27 knots surface
	20+ knots submerged
Manning:	172 as SSRN (16 O + 156 enlisted); 159 as SSN (13 O + 146 enlisted)
Torpedo tubes:	6 21-inch (533-mm) (4 bow + 2 stern) Mk 60
ASW weapons:	torpedoes
Radars:	SPS-26 (see notes)
Sonars:	BQS-4
Fire control:	1 Mk 101 torpedo FCS

The TRITON was designed and constructed as a radar picket submarine (SSRN) to provide early warning of aircraft attacks against a carrier task force. With the end of the radar picket program, the TRITON was reclassified as an SSN on 1 March 1961 and employed in general submarine operations until decommissioned on 3 May 1969 and placed in reserve. The TRITON was the longest U.S. submarine to be constructed until the OHIO-class SSBNs were built almost two decades later.

Design: The TRITON was designed for high-speed surface operations. A large, retractable search radar antenna was fitted in the sail structure; in addition, a large Combat Information Center (CIC) was provided, as well as extensive communication equipment.

Engineering: This is the U.S. Navy's only two-reactor submarine, with a total shp not approached until the LOS ANGELES-class SSNs were built. The two-reactor plant was, in part, a prototype for multi-reactor surface ship propulsion plants.

Radar: The TRITON carried a modified SPS-26 radar, an electronically scanned, three-dimensional search radar that was the forerunner to the SPS-39 radar (see Chapter 24). The only other ship to carry the SPS-26 was the frigate NORFOLK (DL 1), that set being installed in 1957. The TRITON's large radar antenna fully retracted into the sail structure (retracted at 90° to port; see photograph).

Reactor: A single-reactor prototype of the TRITON plant was built as the S3G at West Milton, N.Y.

The giant TRITON rigged for surface running with a removable railing installed forward. She has scopes and masts raised from her large sail structure; her air search radar is retracted, with the opening visible in this view. Although highly innovative, the TRITON was soon overshadowed by the Polaris missile submarines. Proposals to employ the TRITON as an under-ice tug and rescue ship or national command ship were never developed, and she was laid up in reserve in 1969. (1963, U.S. Navy)

5 NUCLEAR-PROPELLED ATTACK SUBMARINES: "SKIPJACK" CLASS

Number	Name	FY/SCB	Builder	Laid down	Launched	Commissioned	Status
SSN 585	SKIPJACK	56/154	General Dynamics (Electric Boat)	29 May 1956	26 May 1958	15 Apr 1959	**AA**
SSN 588	SCAMP	57/154	Mare Island Naval Shipyard	22 Jan 1959	8 Oct 1960	5 June 1961	**AA**
SSN 590	SCULPIN	57/154	Ingalls SB Corp	3 Feb 1958	31 Mar 1960	1 June 1961	**AA**
SSN 591	SHARK	57/154	Newport News	24 Feb 1958	16 Mar 1960	9 Feb 1961	**AA**
SSN 592	SNOOK	57/154	Ingalls SB Corp	7 Apr 1958	31 Oct 1960	24 Oct 1961	**PA**

Displacement:	3,075 tons standard
	3,500 tons submerged
Length:	251¾ feet (76.7 m) oa
Beam:	31½ feet (9.6 m)
Draft:	28 feet (8.5 m)
Propulsion:	steam turbines (Westinghouse in SSN 585; General Electric in others); 15,000 shp; 1 shaft
Reactors:	1 pressurized-water S5W
Speed:	~20 knots surface
	30+ knots submerged
Manning:	114 (11 O + 103 enlisted)
Torpedo tubes:	6 21-inch (533-mm) bow Mk 59
ASW weapons:	Mk 48 torpedoes
Sonars:	BQS-4 (modified)
Fire control:	1 Mk 101 torpedo FCS

The SKIPJACK-class submarines were the first to combine nuclear propulsion with the high-speed, "tear-drop" hull of the experimental submarine ALBACORE. They were the fastest submarines in U.S. service until the LOS ANGELES class. The SKIPJACKS remain first-line submarines, although they lack the large sonars and SUBROC capability of later SSNs.

Class: The SCORPION (SSN 589) was lost with all 99 men on board in May 1968 while some 400 miles southwest of the Azores.

Design: This class formed the basis for the U.S. fleet ballistic missile submarines (SSBN) constructed during the late 1950s and 1960s. See GEORGE WASHINGTON class for details.

SCAMP (1976, Giorgio Arra)

The SCAMP, second ship of the highly successful SKIPJACK class, at anchor in Hong Kong. She has subsequently shifted to the Atlantic Fleet. These were the first high-speed SSNs; later U.S. submarines can dive deeper, are quieter, and have improved sonars, but have fewer torpedo tubes and, until the LOS ANGELES class, were slower. The SKIPJACKS were the last of several postwar submarine classes to have names beginning with the same letter, a common earlier practice. (1976, Giorgio Arra)

4 NUCLEAR-PROPELLED ATTACK SUBMARINES: "SKATE" CLASS

Number	Name	FY/SCB	Builder	Laid down	Launched	Commissioned	Status
SSN 578	SKATE	55/121	General Dynamics (Electric Boat)	21 July 1955	16 May 1957	23 Dec 1957	**PA**
SSN 579	SWORDFISH	55/121	Portsmouth Naval Shipyard	25 Jan 1956	27 Aug 1957	15 Sep 1958	**PA**
SSN 583	SARGO	56/121	Mare Island Naval Shipyard	21 Feb 1956	10 Oct 1957	1 Oct 1958	**PA**
SSN 584	SEADRAGON	56/121	Portsmouth Naval Shipyard	20 June 1956	16 Aug 1958	5 Dec 1959	**PA**

Displacement:	2,570 tons standard
	2,861 tons submerged
Length:	267^7/$_{12}$ feet (81.5 m) oa
Beam:	25 feet (7.6 m)
Draft:	21 feet (6.4 m)
Propulsion:	steam turbines (Westinghouse); ~7,500 shp; 2 shafts
Reactors:	1 pressurized-water S3W in SSN 578 and SSB 583; S4W in SSN 579 and SSN 584
Speed:	15.5 knots surface
	20+ knots submerged
Manning:	111 (11 O + 100 enlisted)
Torpedo tubes:	8 21-inch (533-mm) (6 bow Mk 56 + 2 stern Mk 57)
ASW weapons:	Mk 48 torpedoes
Sonars:	BQS-4
Fire control:	1 Mk 101 torpedo FCS

SARGO (1977, Giorgio Arra)

This class was the first U.S. effort to develop a production-model nuclear-propelled submarine. They are no longer considered first-line submarines and will soon reach the end of their effective service life.

Engineering: The nuclear plant of the SKATE class is similar in arrangement to that of the NAUTILUS, but smaller and simplified. The differences between the S3W and S4W are primarily in plant arrangement.

SARGO   (1977, Giorgio Arra)

1 NUCLEAR-PROPELLED RESEARCH SUBMARINE: "SEAWOLF" TYPE

Number	Name	FY/SCB	Builder	Laid down	Launched	Commissioned	Status
SSN 575	SEAWOLF	53/64A	General Dynamics (Electric Boat)	15 Sep 1953	21 July 1955	30 Mar 1957	**AA**

Displacement:	3,720 tons standard
	4,280 tons submerged
Length:	337½ feet (102.9 m) oa
Beam:	27¾ feet (8.4 m)
Draft:	22 feet (6.7 m)
Propulsion:	steam turbines (General Electric); ~15,000 shp; 2 shafts
Reactors:	1 pressurized-water S2Wa
Speed:	19 knots surface
	20+ knots submerged
Manning:	132 (11 O + 122 enlisted)
Torpedo tubes:	6 21-inch (533-mm) bow Mk 51
Sonars:	BQS-4
Fire control:	1 Mk 101 torpedo FCS

The SEAWOLF was the world's second nuclear-propelled submarine. She was designed to evaluate a competitive nuclear plant to that in the NAUTILUS. She is no longer considered a first-line submarine and has been engaged in research activity since 1969. She can carry submersibles.

Engineering: As built, the SEAWOLF was fitted with the liquid-metal (sodium) S2G reactor plant. After two years of limited operations, the SEAWOLF plant was shut down in December 1958 and a modified NAUTILUS-type plant was installed. The submarine was recommissioned on 30 September 1960.

Reactors: The land-based prototype for the SEAWOLF plant, the S1G, was built at West Milton, N.Y.

SEAWOLF (1974, William Whalen, Jr.)

1 NUCLEAR-PROPELLED ATTACK SUBMARINE: "NAUTILUS" TYPE

Number	Name	FY/SCB	Builder	Laid down	Launched	Commissioned	Status
SSN 571	NAUTILUS	52/64	General Dynamics (Electric Boat)	14 June 1952	21 Jan 1954	30 Sep 1954	Relic

Displacement:	3,530 tons standard
	4,040 tons submerged
Length:	319⁵/₁₂ feet (97.4 m) oa
Beam:	27½ feet (8.4 m)
Draft:	22 feet (6.7 m)
Propulsion:	steam turbines (Westinghouse); 15,000 shp; 2 shafts
Reactors:	1 pressurized-water S2W
Speed:	18 knots surface
	20+ knots submerged
Manning:	120 (10 O + 110 enlisted)
Torpedo tubes:	6 21-inch (533-mm) bow Mk 50
ASW weapons:	torpedoes
Sonars:	BQS-4
Fire control:	1 Mk 101 torpedo FCS

The NAUTILUS was the world's first nuclear-propelled submarine (preceding the first Soviet nuclear-propelled surface ship, the icebreaker LENIN, and the November-class submarines by about five years). The NAUTILUS got under way on nuclear power for the first time on 17 January 1955.

Always based on the East Coast, she shifted her home port to the Mare Island Naval Shipyard at Vallejo, Calif., in May 1979 in preparation for decommissioning. She was formally decommissioned on 3 March 1980 and will become a national memorial (similar to the sail frigate CONSTITUTION at the Boston Naval Shipyard). See Addenda.

Design: The NAUTILUS and the five succeeding nuclear attack submarines have conventional submarine hull forms based on the German Type XXI design of World War II. Although designed to evaluate nuclear propulsion in a ship platform, the NAUTILUS was a fully armed and combat-capable submarine, unlike the unarmed research submarines ALBACORE and DOLPHIN.

Reactor: The land-based prototype of the NAUTILUS plant was the S1W reactor at Arco, Idaho.

NAUTILUS (1975, General Dynamics/Electric Boat)

NAUTILUS (1975, General Dynamics/Electric Boat)

3 ATTACK SUBMARINES: "BARBEL" CLASS

Number	Name	FY/SCB	Builder	Laid down	Launched	Commissioned	Status
SS 580	BARBEL	56/150	Portsmouth Naval Shipyard	18 May 1956	19 July 1958	17 Jan 1959	**PA**
SS 581	BLUEBACK	56/150	Ingalls SB Corp	15 Apr 1957	16 May 1959	15 Oct 1959	**PA**
SS 582	BONEFISH	56/150	New York SB Corp	3 June 1957	22 Nov 1958	9 July 1959	**PA**

Displacement:	2,145 tons standard
	2,895 tons submerged
Length:	219½ feet (66.9 m) oa
Beam:	29 feet (8.8 m)
Draft:	28 feet (8.5 m)
Propulsion:	3 diesels (FM); 4,800 shp
	2 electric motors (GM); 3,150 shp; 1 shaft
Speed:	15 knots surface
	25 knots submerged
Manning:	79 (8 O + 71 enlisted)
Torpedo tubes:	6 21-inch (533-mm) bow Mk 58
ASW weapons:	Mk 48 torpedoes
Sonars:	BQS-4
Fire control:	1 Mk 101 torpedo FCS

These were the last diesel-electric combat submarines to be constructed for the U.S. Navy. They are expected to remain in service until the mid-1980s.

Design: The BARBEL class has the "tear-drop" or modified spindle-hull design best suited for high-speed underwater operation. The design was tested in the research submarine ALBACORE. As built, these submarines had bow-mounted diving planes; these were later refitted to the sail structure.

BLUEBACK (1979, Giorgio Arra)

BARBEL (Giorgio Arra)

BONEFISH (1978, Giorgio Arra)

BLUEBACK (1979, Giorgio Arra)

1 GUIDED MISSILE SUBMARINE: "GROWLER" TYPE

Number	Name	FY/SCB	Builder	Laid down	Launched	Commissioned	Status
SSG 577	GROWLER	55/161	Portsmouth Naval Shipyard	15 Feb 1955	5 Apr 1957	30 Aug 1958	PR

Displacement: 2,540 tons standard
3,515 tons submerged
Length: 317^{7}/$_{12}$ feet (96.8 m) oa
Beam: 27^{1}/$_{6}$ feet (8.3 m)
Draft: 19 feet (5.8 m)
Propulsion: 3 diesels (FM); 4,600 shp
2 electric motors (Elliott); 5,600 shp; 2 shafts
Speed: 20 knots surface
~12 knots submerged
Manning: 88 (10 O + 78 enlisted)
Missiles: (see notes)
Torpedo tubes: 6 21-inch (533-mm) (4 bow Mk 52 + 2 stern Mk 53)
ASW weapons: torpedoes
Sonars: BQS-4
Fire control: 1 Mk 106 torpedo FCS

The GROWLER was one of two conventionally propelled submarines built to carry the Regulus missile; her near-sister submarine GRAYBACK has been converted to a transport submarine. The GROWLER operated in the strategic-missile attack role from her completion until she was decommissioned on 25 May 1964 and placed in reserve. Plans to convert the GROWLER to a transport were halted because of rising ship-conversion costs. She is laid up at Bremerton, Wash.

Design: These were originally ordered as attack submarines of the DARTER class. The GRAYBACK and GROWLER were reordered in 1956 as missile submarines; their hulls were extended approximately 50 feet, and two cylindrical hangars (each 70 feet long and 11 feet high) were superimposed on their bows. They were also fitted with a launching rail located between the hangars and the sail structure, and with the necessary navigation and fire control equipment.

Missiles: As SSGs, the GRAYBACK and GROWLER were designed to carry two Regulus II strategic attack guided or "cruise" missiles; however, development of that missile was halted, and from 1959 to 1964 these submarines each made nine "deterrent" patrols in the Western Pacific carrying four Regulus I missiles.

The GROWLER, laid up in reserve, is the only guided missile submarine in the Naval Register. She was to have undergone conversion to a transport submarine, as did her near-sister GRAYBACK. However, the project was dropped during the Vietnam War for higher-priority ship programs. The Harpoon and Tomahawk missiles can be fired from standard SSN torpedo tubes. (U.S. Navy)

1 ATTACK SUBMARINE: "DARTER" TYPE

Number	Name	FY/SCB	Builder	Laid down	Launched	Commissioned	Status
SS 576	DARTER	54/116	General Dynamics (Electric Boat)	10 Nov 1954	28 May 1956	20 Oct 1956	**PA**

Displacement: 1,720 tons surface
2,388 tons submerged
Length: 268$^{7}/_{12}$ feet (81.9 m) oa
Beam: 27$^{1}/_{6}$ feet (8.3 m)
Draft: 19 feet (5.8 m)
Propulsion: 3 diesels (FM), 4,500 shp
2 electric motors (Elliott); 4,500 shp; 2 shafts
Speed: 19.5 knots surface
14 knots submerged
Manning: 88 (8 O + 80 enlisted)
Torpedo tubes: 8 21-inch (533-mm) (6 bow Mk 54 + 2 stern Mk 55)
Torpedoes: Mk 48
Sonars: BQS-4
BQG-4 PUFFS
Fire control: 1 Mk 106 torpedo FCS

The DARTER was built to an improved TANG-class design. This design was superceded by the improved BARBEL class before additional units were constructed. The DARTER was scheduled to be stricken in 1978, but has been retained in service. In 1979 she was home-ported in Sasebo, Japan.

Class: The GRAYBACK and GROWLER were to have been of this class; both were instead completed as guided missile submarines.

DARTER (1980, Giorgio Arra)

The DARTER at high speed on the surface in the Far East. Previously scheduled to be stricken in FY 1978, she will now see service at least into the early 1980s. Note her distinctive BQG-4 PUFFS sonar domes; radar mounted on mast, and windows of sheltered navigating bridge atop sail. (1980, Giorgio Arra)

1 ATTACK SUBMARINE: "GRAYBACK" TYPE

Number	Name	FY/SCB	Builder	Laid down	Launched	SSG Comm.	LPSS Comm.	Status
SS 574	GRAYBACK	53/161	Mare Island Naval Shipyard	1 July 1954	2 July 1957	7 Mar 1958	9 May 1969	**PA**

Displacement:	2,670 tons standard
	3,650 tons submerged
Length:	334 feet (101.8 m) oa
Beam:	30 feet (9.1 m)
Draft:	19 feet (5.8 m)
Propulsion:	3 diesels (FM); 4,500 shp
	2 electric motors (Elliott); 5,600 shp; 2 shafts
Speed:	20 knots surface
	~12 knots submerged
Manning:	96 (10 O + 86 enlisted)
Troops:	67 (7 O + 60 enlisted)
Torpedo tubes:	8 21-inch (533-mm) (6 bow Mk 52 + 2 stern Mk 53)
Torpedoes:	Mk 14
	Mk 37
Sonars:	BQS-4
	BQG-4 PUFFS
Fire control:	1 Mk 106 torpedo FCS

The GRAYBACK and GROWLER (see previous page) were built as guided missile submarines to carry the Regulus strategic cruise missile. The GRAYBACK operated in the SSG role from her completion until she was decommissioned on 25 May 1964. She was subsequently converted to a transport submarine. She retains her submarine transport configuration while currently operating in that role as well as an attack submarine. Based at Subic Bay in the Philippines, the GRAYBACK does not carry Mk 48 torpedoes because of the lack of support facilities for that weapon at her home port.

Classification: The GRAYBACK was commissioned as a guided missile submarine (SSG). During her subsequent conversion to a transport she was listed as APSS but was formally changed to an LPSS on 30 August 1968. She was reclassified as an attack submarine (SS) on 30 June 1975 for administrative purposes. There were no physical changes to the ship.

Conversion: The GRAYBACK was converted to a transport submarine at the San Francisco Bay Naval Shipyard (Mare Island) from November 1967 to May 1969. She was lengthened (from 322⅓ feet) and fitted to berth and mess commando or UDT (Underwater Demolition Team) personnel. The forward missile hangars were modified to "lock out" swimmers and six Swimmer Delivery Vehicles (SDV). Her sail structure was heightened and a PUFFS sonar system was installed during the conversion. The conversion was No. 350.65 under the new SCB scheme.

Marines on GRAYBACK (1975, U.S. Marine Corps)

GRAYBACK with starboard hangar door open (1978, Giorgio Arra)

1 RESEARCH SUBMARINE: "TANG" CLASS

Number	Name	FY/SCB	Builder	Laid down	Launched	Commissioned	Status
SSAG 567	GUDGEON	49/2A	Portsmouth Naval Shipyard	20 May 1950	11 June 1952	21 Nov 1952	**PA**

Displacement:	2,100 tons standard
	2,700 tons submerged
Length:	287 feet (87.5 m) oa
Beam:	27¹/₆ feet (8.3 m)
Draft:	19 feet (5.8 m)
Propulsion:	3 diesels (FM); 4,500 shp
	2 electric motors (Westinghouse); 5,600 shp; 2 shafts
Speed:	16 knots surface
	16 knots submerged
Manning:	88 (8 O + 80 enlisted) as SS
Torpedo tubes:	8 21-inch (533-mm) (6 bow Mk 43 + 2 stern Mk 44)
ASW weapons:	torpedoes
Sonars:	BQS-4
	BQG-4 PUFFS
Fire control:	1 Mk 10 torpedo FCS

The GUDGEON is the last of six TANG-class submarines (SS 563–568), the first undersea craft constructed by the U.S. Navy after World War II. The GUDGEON is employed in acoustic and other research. See Appendix C for disposals of the five other submarines of this class, three of which were to have been transferred to Iran.

Classification: The GUDGEON was changed from her original SS designation to AGSS on 1 April 1979, when she replaced the TANG (AGSS 563) in the research role. On 5 November 1979 the GUDGEON was changed to SSAG to reflect her retaining a combat capability in contrast to the other AGSS then in service, the DOLPHIN, which has no torpedo tubes or other weapons.

Design: The TANG class had the hull form, large batteries, streamlined superstructure, snorkel breathing device, and other features of the German Type XXI advanced submarines. These features were also incorporated into 52 World War II submarines modernized under the GUPPY program (for Greater Underwater Propulsive Power).

Engineering: As built, the TANG-class submarines were 296¹/₆ feet long and fitted with radial "pancake" diesel engines. These engines were subsequently replaced when the submarines were lengthened. The DARTER is a modified TANG-class submarine.

GUDGEON (1967, U.S. Navy)

1 RESEARCH SUBMARINE: "ALBACORE" TYPE

Number	Name	FY/SCB	Builder	Laid down	Launched	Commissioned	Status
AGSS 569	ALBACORE	50/56	Portsmouth Naval Shipyard	15 Mar 1952	1 Aug 1953	5 Dec 1953	AR

Displacement:	1,500 tons standard
	1,850 tons submerged
Length:	210½ feet (64.2 m) oa
Beam:	27⅓ feet (8.3 m)
Draft:	18½ feet (5.6 m)
Propulsion:	2 diesels (GM); 1,500 shp
	1 electric motor (Westinghouse); 15,000 shp; 1 shaft
Speed:	25 knots surfaced
	33 knots submerged
Manning:	52 (5 O + 47 enlisted)
Torpedo tubes:	none

ALBACORE (U.S. Navy)

1 RESEARCH SUBMARINE: "DOLPHIN" TYPE

Number	Name	FY/SCB	Builder	Laid down	Launched	Commissioned	Status
AGSS 555	DOLPHIN	61/207	Portsmouth Naval Shipyard	9 Nov 1962	8 June 1968	17 Aug 1968	**PA**

Displacement:	800 tons standard
	930 tons submerged
Length:	152 feet (46.3 m) oa
Beam:	19⁵/₁₂ feet (5.9 m)
Draft:	18 feet (5.5 m)
Propulsion:	2 diesels (Detroit)
	1 electric motor (Elliott); 1,650 shp; 1 shaft
Speed:	
	12+ knots submerged
Manning:	29 (3 O + 26 enlisted); 4 to 7 scientists
Torpedo tubes:	removed
Sonars:	(see notes)

The DOLPHIN is an experimental deep-diving submarine. Reportedly, she has operated at greater depths than any other operating submarines.

Design: The DOLPHIN has a constant-diameter pressure hull with an outside diameter of approximately 15 feet and hemisphere heads at both ends. An improved rudder design and other features permit maneuverability without the use of conventional submarine diving planes; there are built-in safety systems that automatically surface the submarine in an emergency, and there are few pressure-hull penetrations (e.g., only one access hatch). An experimental torpedo tube that was originally mounted was removed in 1970.

Engineering: Submerged endurance is approximately 24 hours; her endurance at sea is about 14 days.

Sonar: Various experimental sonars have been fitted in the DOLPHIN. Her original bow sonar, which had four arrays that could be extended at 90° angles to the submarine's bow-stern axis, has been removed.

A BQS-15 sonar was installed in 1971.

DOLPHIN with BQS-15 sonar in bow (U.S. Navy)

POST–WORLD WAR II SUBMARINE PROGRAMS

United States submarine construction during the World War II reached hull number SS 550 (with hulls SS 526–550 being canceled). SS 551–562 were not used in the immediate postwar programs; subsequently, five of these numbers were assigned, two of them to U.S.-financed, foreign-built submarines (Offshore Procurement).

The last wartime submarine on the Naval Register was the transport submarine SEALION (LPSS 315), decommissioned and laid up in 1970, and stricken on 15 March 1977. The last active submarine of World War II construction was the TIGRONE (AGSS 419), decommissioned on 30 June 1975 and stricken on 27 June 1975 (i.e., three days before formally being decommissioned!).

All postwar U.S. submarines have been numbered in the same series except for three small hunter-killer submarines (SSK) and three training submarines (SST), which were in separate series.

The U.S. Navy's lone midget submarine, the X-1, completed in 1955, was stricken on 16 February 1973.

SS 551	BASS (ex-K 2/SSK 2)	stricken 1 Apr 1965
SS 552	BONITA (ex-K 3/SSK 3)	stricken 1 Apr 1965
SS 553	(KINN)	Norway OSP 1964
SS 554	(SPRINGEREN)	Denmark OSP 1964
SS 555	DOLPHIN	
SS 556–562	Not used	
SS 563–568	TANG class	
AGSS 569	ALBACORE	
AGSS 570	completed as SST 1	
SSN 571	NAUTILUS	
SSR 572–573	SAILFISH class	
SSG 574	GRAYBACK	to LPSS 574/SS 574
SSN 575	SEAWOLF	
SS 576	DARTER	
SSG 577	GROWLER	
SSN 578–579	SKATE class	
SS 580–582	BARBEL class	
SSN 583–584	SKATE class	
SSN 585	SKIPJACK	
SSRN 586	TRITON	to SSN 586
SSGN 587	HALIBUT	to SSN 587
SSN 588–592	SKIPJACK class	
SSN 593	THRESHER	sunk 1963
SSN 594–596	PERMIT class (ex-THRESHER class)	
SSN 597	TULLIBEE	

SSBN 598–602	GEORGE WASHINGTON class
SSN 603–607	PERMIT class
SSBN 608–611	ETHAN ALLEN class
SSN 612–615	PERMIT class
SSBN 616–617	LAFAYETTE class
SSBN 618	ETHAN ALLEN class
SSBN 619–620	LAFAYETTE class
SSN 621	PERMIT class
SSBN 622–636	LAFAYETTE class
SSN 637–639	STURGEON class
SSBN 640–645	LAFAYETTE class
SSN 646–653	STURGEON class
SSBN 654–659	LAFAYETTE class
SSN 660–670	STURGEON class
SSN 671	NARWHAL
SSN 672–684	STURGEON class
SSN 685	GLENARD P. LIPSCOMB
SSN 686–687	STURGEON class
SSN 688–725	LOS ANGELES class
SSBN 726–735	OHIO class

HUNTER-KILLER SUBMARINES

SSK 1	BARRACUDA (ex-K 1)	Comm. 1951	to SST 3
SSK 2	BASS (ex-K 2)	Comm. 1951	to SS 551
SSK 3	BONITA (ex-K 3)	Comm. 1952	to SS 552

These were small (1,000-ton, 196-foot) hunter-killer submarines, intended to lie in wait to attack Soviet submarines off foreign ports and in narrow waterways. Several hundred were to have been produced in time of war. Originally assigned K-number "names," they were given fish names in 1955. The BASS and BONITA were reclassified as SS in 1959 for use in the training role; the BARRACUDA was changed to SST in 1959 for training.

TRAINING SUBMARINES

SST 1	MACKEREL (ex-T 1)	Comm. 1953	stricken 31 Jan 1973
SST 2	MARLIN (ex-T 2)	Comm. 1953	stricken 31 Jan 1973
SST 3	BARRACUDA (ex-K 1/SSK 1)		stricken 1 Oct 1973

The SST 1–2 were small (310-ton, 133-foot) training submarines. The MACKEREL was ordered as AGSS 570. Originally assigned T-number "names," they were given fish names in 1956.

6 Aircraft Carriers

The U.S. Navy had 13 aircraft carriers (CV/CVN) available as of January 1981. In addition, an older carrier is employed as a pilot training ship (AVT). Of the 13 first-line flattops, one carrier is undergoing a longer-term modernization termed SLEP (Service Life Extension Program). Thus, there are 12 "deployable" carriers, permitting four ships to be maintained in forward areas on a continuous basis (Mediterranean, Far East, and Indian Ocean) with the eight other ships in overhaul, training, and transit. This 1-in-3 deployment cycle is caused primarily by personnel considerations.

Two additional nuclear-propelled carriers of the NIMITZ class are under construction. These ships will replace two MIDWAY-class ships of World War II construction that will be unserviceable by the late 1980s. Thus, with the two ships under construction, the maximum probable carrier force level of the late 1980s will be five nuclear ships plus eight conventional, oil-burning ships (with one of the latter undergoing SLEP modernization). This projection assumes that the SLEP effort will be continued and can be kept within a 2½-year time period. Under these conditions, the current force-level goal of 12 carriers can be maintained until about the year 2000, with the SLEP process adding an expected 10 to 15 years of service life to each ship.

Since the early 1970s, the Navy's leadership has proposed a number of smaller aircraft carrier designs as potential supplements to the CV/CVN force. The design concepts were the Sea Control Ship (SCS) and VSTOL Support Ship (VSS). In addition, a "mid-size" carrier of approximately 55,000 tons (CVV) was proposed by the Executive Branch in the late 1970s as an alternative to constructing additional CV/CVNs. However, in response to the Carter Administration's proposal of a CVV in FY 1979, the Congress appropriated funds for an additional (fourth) NIMITZ-class nuclear carrier. Mr. Carter vetoed the FY 1979 ship but was forced to accept such a ship in the FY 1980 budget (the CVN 71).

At the insistence of Congress, the Navy is considering the construction of additional aviation ships—generally referred to as "light aircraft carriers." When this edition went to press the most-favored design concept was the so-called SSS (STOL Support Ship), a ship intended to operate conventional and VSTOL aircraft, albeit with certain weight/payload restrictions on the former.

The current five-year defense plan does not provide for any new construction of aviation ships. However, congressional and Navy interest in additional aircraft carriers of some type make the funding of a light carrier probable in the near future, with the possibility of another large ship (CVN) also being proposed in the mid-1980s.

Classification: Into the 1970s two principal types of aircraft carriers were in service: attack aircraft carriers (CVA/CVAN) and ASW aircraft carriers (CVS), whose classifications dated from 1952-1953. The last ASW carrier was decommissioned in 1974. With the phase-out of the CVS-type ships, their squadrons of fixed-wing ASW aircraft and helicopters were integrated into the CVA/CVAN air wings. Those ships with the ASW aircraft were then redesignated as multi-mission carriers (CV). However, on 30 June 1975 all other active carriers were changed to CV/CVN regardless of whether ASW aircraft were assigned. All aircraft carriers have ASW aircraft assigned except the MIDWAY and CORAL SEA.

Electronics: All U.S. aircraft carriers have, or are being fitted with, the SLQ-17 Deceptive Electronic Countermeasures (DECM) and WLR-8 radar receiver sets. When installed together these are known as the SLQ-29 EW system.

Names: The Navy's first aircraft carrier, the LANGLEY (CV 1), was named for an aviation pioneer who proposed a flying machine for naval use in 1898. Subsequently, aircraft carriers were named for older warships (RANGER, INTREPID) and battles (MIDWAY, SARATOGA). The FRANKLIN D. ROOSEVELT was named for the 32nd president, who died in office, setting the precedent for naming aircraft carriers for public officials. The CARL VINSON is the first U.S. Navy ship to be named for a living American since about 1800. (The ship honors a member of the House of Representatives from 1914 to 1965, who was a major supporter of American naval power.)

Radar: All carriers have, or will receive, the SPS-48 three-dimensional search radar and SPS-49 long-range search radar. Most ships will receive the SPS-65 threat-detection radar for defense against cruise missiles.

Type	Class/Ship	Active	Building[a]	Reserve	Comm.	Aircraft
CVN 68	NIMITZ	2	2	—	1975–	~90
CVN 65	ENTERPRISE	1	—	—	1961	~90
CV 63	KITTY HAWK	4	—	—	1961–1968	~85
CV 59	FORRESTAL	3[b]	—	—	1955–1959	~85
CV 41	MIDWAY	2	—	—	1945–1947	~75
CV/CVA/CVS	HANCOCK	—	—	4	1943–1950	~45–80
AVT 16	LEXINGTON	1	—	—	1943	—

[a] Includes CVN 71 authorized in FY 1980.
[b] Excludes SARATOGA undergoing three-year SLEP modernization.

Coming home: The NIMITZ returns to Norfolk, Va., in May 1980, completing an unprecedented 144 days at sea for an aircraft carrier. Highlight of her Atlantic-Mediterranean-Indian Ocean deployment was launching RH-53D Sea Stallion helicopters on the ill-fated effort to rescue American hostages in Tehran. Subsequently, her sister ship EISENHOWER spent 154 days at sea during that carrier's 251-day Indian Ocean deployment that ended in December 1980. (1980, U.S. Navy, LCDR Gordon I. Peterson)

STOL SUPPORT SHIP

Displacement:	~40,000-50,000 tons full load
Length:	~800-900 feet oa
Beam:	
Draft:	
Propulsion:	gas turbines (General Electric); 2 shafts
Speed:	27-30 knots
Manning:	~3,000 (ship and air wing)
Aircraft:	~25 fully supported
	~55 surge capability
Catapults:	none
Elevators:	2
Missiles:	none
Guns:	3 20-mm Phalanx CIWS Mk 16

At left are nominal characteristics for the light aircraft carrier that was expected to be proposed for the FY 1983 or FY 1984 shipbuilding program. The STOL (Short Take-Off and Landing) Support Ship would operate both conventional carrier aircraft, primarily the F/A-18 Hornet, as well as helicopters and VSTOL aircraft.

The Congress has expressed considerable interest in a light carrier design to supplement the limited number of large carriers in the Navy. Two other, less-likely candidates have been proposed for this role, a 29,000-ton VSTOL carrier (VSTOL Support Ship, designated VSS) and an enlarged and reconfigured SPRUANCE (DD 963)-class destroyer of some 18,000 tons (designated DDV).

Loading up: The RANGER takes aboard Carrier Air Wing 2 (CVW-2) at NAS North Island, San Diego, prior to deploying to the Western Pacific. Her fighter squadrons—VF-21 and VF-154—with their F-4 Phantoms are already on board. Her other squadrons line up to be taken aboard. The aircraft closest to the camera is an EA-6B Prowler electronic warfare/jamming aircraft from VAQ-137. (1979, Robert L. Lawson)

2 + 2 NUCLEAR-PROPELLED AIRCRAFT CARRIERS: "NIMITZ" CLASS

Number	Name	FY/SCB	Builder	Laid down	Launched	Commissioned	Status
CVN 68	NIMITZ	67/102	Newport News	22 June 1968	13 May 1972	3 May 1975	**AA**
CVN 69	DWIGHT D. EISENHOWER	70/102	Newport News	14 Aug 1970	11 Oct 1975	18 Oct 1977	**AA**
CVN 70	CARL VINSON	74/102	Newport News	11 Oct 1975	15 Mar 1980	1982	Bldg.
CVN 71	. . . .	80/102	Newport News			late 1987	Bldg.

Displacement:	81,600 tons standard
	91,400 tons full load
	93,400 tons combat load
Length:	1,040 feet (317 m) wl
	1,092 feet (332.8 m) oa
Beam:	134 feet (40.8 m)
Extreme width:	250⅚ feet (76.4 m)
Draft:	37 feet (11.3 m)
Propulsion:	steam turbines; 260,000 + shp; 4 shafts
Reactors:	2 pressurized-water A4W
Speed:	30+ knots
Manning:	3,073 (147 O + 2,926 enlisted) in CVN 68
	3,151 (147 O + 3,004 enlisted) in CVN 69
Air wing:	~2,625 (300 O + 2,325 enlisted)
Aircraft:	~90
Catapults:	4 steam C13-1
Elevators:	4 deck edge (85 × 52 feet; 130,000-pound capacity)
Missiles:	3 8-tube Sea Sparrow BPDMS launchers Mk 25 in CVN 68–69
	3 8-tube NATO Sea Sparrow launchers Mk 29 in CVN 70
Guns:	(see notes)
Radars:	SPS-10 surface search
	SPS-43A air search in CVN 68–70
	SPS-48 3-D search
Fire control:	3 Mk 115 missile FCS in CVN 68–69
	3 Mk 91 missile FCS in CVN 70

These are the world's largest warships. Three ships originally were proposed in the mid-1960s as replacements for the MIDWAY-class carriers. The NIMITZ-class ships have been delayed by shipyard strikes and labor shortages at the Newport News shipyard. The NIMITZ was seven years from keel laying to commissioning compared to less than four years for the earlier, eight-reactor ENTERPRISE.

A contract for the CVN 71 was awarded to the Newport News shipyard on 1 October 1980.

Classification: The NIMITZ and EISENHOWER were ordered as attack aircraft carriers (CVAN); they were changed to multi-mission aircraft carriers (CVN) on 30 June 1975. The VINSON was ordered as a CVN.

Design: The general arrangement of these ships is similar to the previous KITTY HAWK class with respect to flight deck, elevators, and island structure. Full load displacement is the maximum load for entering port; combat load is the maximum amount of aviation fuel and ordnance that can be loaded at sea. The hangar deck in these ships is 684 feet long, 108 feet wide, and 26½ feet high.

Guns: The NIMITZ and EISENHOWER will be fitted with three 20-mm Phalanx CIWS and the VINSON with four CIWS when that weapon becomes available.

Radar: The first three ships have an SPS-43A search radar mounted on a lattice mast abaft the island. This will be replaced with an SPS-49. The multi-function, phased-array SPY-1A radar has been proposed for the CVN 71 in place of the SPS-48 and SPS-49, as well as some aircraft control radars.

Reactors: These carriers have only two reactors compared to eight in the first nuclear carrier, the ENTERPRISE. The initial fuel cores in these ships are estimated to have a service life of at least 13 years (800,000 to one million miles).

DWIGHT D. EISENHOWER during sea trials, almost nude of aircraft. Note the ship's sleek hull lines, the portside sponson supporting the angled flight deck. (1977, Newport News)

NIMITZ (1979, Giorgio Arra)

The NIMITZ operating in the Mediterranean, with an RA-5C Vigilante and three A-6 Intruders being readied for launch from her forward catapults, and F-4 Phantoms being readied at her two waist "cats." The "Viggies" have been discarded, and the NIMITZ's fighter squadrons, VF-41 and VF-84, now fly the F-14 Tomcat. Note the saucer-topped E-2 Hawkeyes parked on the elevator abaft the island; a neat line of A-7 Corsairs on the deck, and more F-4 Phantoms huddled aft. (1976, U.S. Navy, JO2 R. Leonard)

The EISENHOWER and CALIFORNIA (CGN 36) maneuver close aboard during exercises. In the late 1980s, when the fourth NIMITZ-class carrier is completed, the Navy will have five CVNs in service with nine nuclear escorts. Although nuclear escorts greatly enhance the effectiveness of nuclear carriers, their high cost and manning problems in the nuclear area make the future construction of nuclear escorts unlikely. (1978, U.S. Navy, PH1 William C. Wickham)

The NIMITZ replenishing at sea from the ammunition ship MOUNT BAKER (AE 34) during training operations off Guantanamo Bay, Cuba. Two of the NIMITZ's three starboard deck-edge elevators are lowered to the hangar deck, with munitions coming into the ship across the forward elevator and into the hangar for striking below. (1975, U.S. Navy)

1 NUCLEAR-PROPELLED AIRCRAFT CARRIER: "ENTERPRISE" TYPE

Number	Name	FY/SCB	Builder	Laid down	Launched	Commissioned	Status
CVN 65	ENTERPRISE	58/160	Newport News	4 Feb 1958	24 Sep 1960	25 Nov 1961	**PA**

Displacement: 75,700 tons standard
 89,600 tons full load
Length: 1,040 feet (317.0 m) wl
 1,123 feet (342.3 m) oa
Beam: 133 feet (40.5 m)
Extreme width: 248⅓ feet (75.7 m)
Draft: 35¾ feet (10.9 m)
Propulsion: steam turbines (Westinghouse); ~280,000 shp; 4 shafts
Reactors: 8 pressurized-water A2W
Speed: 30+ knots
Manning: 3,157 (152 O + 3,005 enlisted)
Air wing: 2,628 (305 O + 2,323 enlisted)
Aircraft: ~90
Catapults: 4 steam C13
Elevators: 4 deck edge (85 × 52 feet; 130,000-pound capacity)
Missiles: 3 8-tube NATO Sea Sparrow launchers Mk 29
Guns: 3 20-mm Phalanx CIWS Mk 15 (3 × 1)
Radars: SPS-10 surface search
 SPS-48 3-D
 SPS-49 air search
 SPS-65 threat warning
Fire control: 3 Mk 91 missile FCS

The island structure of the ENTERPRISE after her "facelift" and removal of her SPS–32/33 "billboard" radars. The Gatling gun in the foreground is mounted on the port side of the flight deck, one of three Gatling guns on the ship. She also has three Mk 68 single 20–mm gun mounts and two MK 29 Sea Sparrow missile launchers. (1982, U.S. Navy, PHAN Kathy Moss)

The ENTERPRISE was the world's second nuclear-propelled surface warship (preceded by the cruiser LONG BEACH). She entered the Puget Sound Naval Shipyard in January 1979 for a major overhaul that was to last into mid-1981.

Class: The Congress provided $35 million in the FY 1960 budget for long-lead time nuclear components for a second aircraft carrier of this type. However, the Eisenhower Administration deferred the project. The next nuclear carrier, the NIMITZ, was not ordered until 9½ years after the ENTERPRISE with two oil-burning carriers being constructed in the interim period.

Classification: Originally an attack aircraft carrier (CVAN), the ENTERPRISE was changed to a multi-mission carrier (CVN) on 30 June 1975.

Design: The ENTERPRISE was built to a modified KITTY HAWK design, but in her original configuration she had a distinctive island because of the arrangement of "billboard" radar antennas. Her hangar deck is 860 feet long, 107 feet wide, and 25 feet high.

Guns: Phalanx CIWS installed during 1980–1981 yard period.

Missiles: As built, the ENTERPRISE had neither missiles nor guns. Late in 1967 she was fitted with two Sea Sparrow Mk 25 launchers. During her 1979–1981 overhaul three Mk 29 NATO Sea Sparrow launchers were installed.

Radar: The ENTERPRISE and the LONG BEACH (CGN 9) were the only ships fitted with the SPS-32 and SPS-33 fixed-array radars. They were replaced with conventional, rotating SPS-48 and SPS-49 radars during the carrier's 1979–1981 overhaul.

Reactors: The two-reactor A1W prototype of the ENTERPRISE's propulsion plant was constructed at Arco, Idaho.

The ENTERPRISE at Subic Bay in the Philippines. Her distinctive island structure with "billboard" antennas for the SPS-32/33 radars were being changed radically during the ship's 1979–1981 overhaul. The radars were too difficult to maintain. She now has a smaller island structure, topped by SPS-48 and SPS-49 as well as lesser electronic antennas. (1978, Giorgio Arra)

The ENTERPRISE operating off southern California with Carrier Air Wing 14 (NK) on board. Air wings periodically shift carriers, with 12 wings being available for 13 flattops, since the latter periodically undergo lengthy overhauls and modernizations. CVW-14 subsequently operated from the CORAL SEA, with two Marine F-4 Phantom squadrons replacing the two F-14 squadrons normally assigned to the wing (see Chapter 21). (1976, U.S. Navy, PH3 Howard Burgess)

The ENTERPRISE during her reconstruction at Puget Sound. Note her new, conventional island structure taking shape, topped by a large pole mast. (1980, U.S. Navy, D. Yacko)

4 AIRCRAFT CARRIERS: "KITTY HAWK" CLASS

Number	Name	FY/SCB	Builder	Laid down	Launched	Commissioned	Status
CV 63	KITTY HAWK	56/127	New York SB Corp	27 Dec 1956	21 May 1960	29 Apr 1961	**PA**
CV 64	CONSTELLATION	57/127A	New York Naval Shipyard	14 Sep 1957	8 Oct 1960	27 Oct 1961	**PA**
CV 66	AMERICA	61/127B	Newport News	9 Jan 1961	1 Feb 1964	23 Jan 1965	**AA**
CV 67	JOHN F. KENNEDY	63/127C	Newport News	22 Oct 1964	27 May 1967	7 Sep 1968	**AA**

Displacement: 60,100 tons standard CV 63–64
60,300 tons standard CV 66
61,000 tons standard CV 67
80,800 tons full load CV 63–64, 66
82,000 tons full load CV 67
Length: 990 feet (301.8 m) wl
1,062½ feet (323.9 m) oa CV 63
1,072½ feet (326.9 m) oa CV 64
1,047½ feet (319.3 m) oa CV 66–67
Beam: 129½ feet (39.5 m) CV 63–64
130 feet (39.6 m) CV 66–67
Extreme width: 250 feet (76.2 m) CV 63–64
266 feet (81.2 m) CV 66 (see notes)
267½ feet (81.5 m) CV 67 (see notes)
Draft: 36 feet (11.0 m)
Propulsion: steam turbines (Westinghouse); 280,000 shp; 4 shafts
Boilers: 8 1,200-psi (Foster Wheeler)
Speed: 30+ knots
Manning: ~2,879 (143 O + 2,736 enlisted) in CV 63
2,879 (142 O + 2,737 enlisted) in CV 64
2,990 (143 O + 2,847 enlisted) in CV 66
2,924 (139 O + 2,785 enlisted) in CV 67
Air Wing: ~2,500 (290 O + 2,200 enlisted)

Aircraft: ~85
Catapults: 4 steam C13 in CV 63–64
3 steam C13 + 1 steam C13-1 in CV 66–67
Elevators: 4 deck edge (85 × 52 feet; 130,000-pound capacity)
Missiles: 2 8-tube NATO Sea Sparrow launchers Mk 29 in CV 63; 3 in CV 66–67
2 twin launchers for Terrier SAM Mk 10 Mod 3/4 in CV 64
Guns: 3 20-mm Phalanx CIWS Mk 15 (3 × 1) in CV 66

Radars:	CV 63	CV 64	CV 66	CV 67
	SPS-10B	SPS-10	SPS-10F	SPS-10F
	SPS-37A	SPS-48	SPS-48C	SPS-48C
	SPS-48C	SPS-49	SPS-49	SPS-49
				SPS-65

Sonars: SQS-23 bow-mounted in CV 66

Fire control:	CV 63	CV 64	CV 66	CV 67
	2 Mk 91	4 Mk 76	3 Mk 91	3 Mk 91
		4 SPG-55A		

These ships are improved FORRESTAL-class carriers with an improved elevator and flight deck arrangement. Construction of the KENNEDY was delayed because of debates over whether the ship should have conventional or nuclear propulsion.

JOHN F. KENNEDY fueling from the KALAMAZOO (AOR 6) in the Atlantic (1978, U.S. Navy)

Class: The KENNEDY is officially considered a separate, one-ship class. These ships are often grouped with the FORRESTAL class in force-level discussions.

Classification: All four ships were originally attack aircraft carriers (CVA); two ships were changed to multi-mission aircraft carriers (CV) when modified to operate ASW aircraft, the KITTY HAWK on 29 April 1973 and the KENNEDY on 1 December 1974; the CONSTELLATION and AMERICA were changed to CV on 30 June 1975, prior to being modified.

Design: These ships are larger than the FORRESTAL class and have an improved flight deck arrangement. The later class has two elevators forward of the island structure (instead of one in the FORRESTALS), and the port-side elevator on the stern quarter rather than at the forward end of the angled flight deck. The extreme (flight deck) width listed above includes a removable deck extension at the forward end of the angled deck that extends the

AMERICA's overall width by 16½ feet and the KENNEDY's width by 22½ feet.

The hangar deck in the first three ships is 740 feet long, 101 feet wide, and 25 feet high; in the KENNEDY the hangar deck is 688 feet long, 106 feet wide, and 25 feet high. The KENNEDY has her stack angled out to starboard.

Guns: Each ship is scheduled to have three 20-mm Phalanx CIWS installed when that weapon becomes available.

Missiles: The first three ships were built with Terrier missile launchers (Mk 10 Mod 3 on starboard quarter and Mk 10 Mod 4 on port quarter). The KENNEDY originally had three Sea Sparrow Mk 25 launchers. All four ships will eventually have three NATO Sea Sparrow Mk 29 launchers and three Mk 91 missile fire control systems.

Sonar: The AMERICA and KENNEDY have bow sonar domes, but only the AMERICA has actually had sonar installed. She is the only U.S. carrier so fitted at this time.

KITTY HAWK at anchor in Hong Kong with Carrier Air Wing 15 (1978, Giorgio Arra)

KITTY HAWK (1979, Giorgio Arra)

KITTY HAWK (1978, Giorgio Arra)

CONSTELLATION (1980, Giorgio Arra)

4 AIRCRAFT CARRIERS: "FORRESTAL" CLASS

Number	Name	FY/SCB	Builder	Laid down	Launched	Commissioned	Status
CV 59	FORRESTAL	52/80	Newport News	14 July 1952	11 Dec 1954	1 Oct 1955	**AA**
CV 60	SARATOGA	53/80	New York Naval Shipyard	16 Dec 1952	8 Oct 1955	14 Apr 1956	Yard
CV 61	RANGER	54/80	Newport News	2 Aug 1954	29 Sep 1956	10 Aug 1957	**PA**
CV 62	INDEPENDENCE	55/80	New York Naval Shipyard	1 July 1955	6 June 1958	10 Jan 1959	**AA**

Displacement: 59,650 tons standard CV 59
60,000 tons standard CV 60–62
78,000 tons full load
Length: 990 feet (316.7 m) wl
1,039 feet (316.7 m) CV 59–61
1,046½ feet (319.0 m) CV 62
Beam: 129½ feet (38.5 m)
Extreme width: 238 feet (72.5 m) CV 59–61
238½ feet (72.7 m) CV 62
Draft: 37 feet (11.3 m)
Propulsion: steam turbines (Westinghouse); 260,000 shp in CV 59, 280,000 shp in CV 60–62; 4 shafts
Boilers: 8 600-psi (Babcock & Wilcox) CV 59
8 1,200-psi (Babcock & Wilcox) CV 60–62
Speed: 33 knots CV 59
34 knots CV 60–62
Manning: 2,875 (139 O + 2,736 enlisted) in CV 59
2,911 (140 O + 2,771 enlisted) in CV 60
2,848 (141 O + 2,707 enlisted) in CV 61
2,889 (142 O + 2,747 enlisted) in CV 62
Air wing: ~2,500 (290 O + 2,200 enlisted)
Aircraft: ~85
Catapults: 2 steam C7 + 2 steam C11-1 in CV 59–60
4 steam C7 in CV 61–62
Elevators: 4 deck edge (63 × 52 feet; 80,000-pound capacity)
Missiles: 2 8-tube Sea Sparrow BPDMS launchers Mk 25 in CV 59–60
2 8-tube NATO Sea Sparrow launchers Mk 29 in CV 61–62
Guns: (see notes)

Radars:

CV 59	CV 60	CV 61	CV 61
SPS-10	SPS-10	SPS-10	SPS-10
SPS-43A	SPS-30	SPS-43A	SPS-43A
SPS-48	SPS-43A	SPS-48C	SPS-48
SPS-58	SPS-58		SPS-58

Fire control: 2 Mk 115 missile FCS in CV 59–60
2 Mk 91 missile FCS in CV 61–62

These were the first U.S. aircraft carriers constructed after World War II. The only other nation to build fixed-wing aircraft carriers in the three decades after World War II was France, with the smaller CLEMENCEAU and FOCH, completed in 1961 and 1963, respectively. Subsequently, the Soviet Union has built the KIEV class and Great Britain the INVINCIBLE class, both for VSTOL aircraft, with the Soviets having a larger, approximately 60,000-ton aircraft carrier under construction. This newest Soviet ship may have nuclear propulsion.

The SARATOGA is undergoing a major modernization (SLEP) that began in October 1980 at the Philadelphia Naval Shipyard and was expected to last almost three years. The update is expected to add 10 to 15 years to the ship's nominal 30-year service life. The FORRESTAL and then the other ships of the class are scheduled to follow the "Sara" in SLEP.

Classification: The FORRESTAL and SARATOGA were ordered as large aircraft carriers (CVB); they were reclassified as attack aircraft carriers (CVA) on 1 October 1952. Two ships were changed to multimission aircraft carriers (CV) when modified to operate ASW aircraft, the SARATOGA on 30 June 1972 and INDEPENDENCE on 28 February 1973. The FORRESTAL and RANGER were changed to CV on 30 June 1975, prior to modification.

Design: These ships incorporated many design features of the aborted carrier UNITED STATES (CVA 58). They were originally designed as axial (straight) deck ships; the FORRESTAL was modified during construction to incorporate the British-developed angled flight deck. As built, the FORRESTAL had a large second mast to carry electronic antennas; it was subsequently replaced by a smaller pole mast. Details of the ships differ considerably.

The FORRESTAL with Carrier Air Wing 17 (AA) during a Mediterranean deployment. The FORRESTAL is the oldest of the Navy's large-deck, modern aircraft carriers; the flattop is scheduled to undergo an extensive SLEP (Service Life Extension Program) modernization from early 1983 to mid-1985, following the SARATOGA SLEP, which was scheduled from October 1980 to early 1983. (1978, PH2 Jim Urick)

The hangar decks of these ships are 740 feet long, 101 feet wide, and 25 feet high.

Guns: All four ships were completed with eight 5-inch/54 cal DP Mk 42 single guns, mounted in pairs on sponsons. The forward sponsons were removed early in service because of damage in heavy seas (except that after deletion of guns, the RANGER retains forward sponsons—the only ship to be assigned to the Pacific and thus not have to operate in the rougher seas of the North Atlantic). The after guns were removed as Sea Sparrow launchers became available for these ships.

Each ship is scheduled to have three 20-mm Phalanx CIWS installed.

Missiles: All four ships will eventually have three NATO Sea Sparrow Mk 29 launchers and three Mk 91 missile fire control systems.

Radar: The SARATOGA will receive SPS-48 and SPS-49 radars during her SLEP modernization. She was the last postwar-built ship to have the SPS-30 height-finding radar; SPS-30 retained by war-built MIDWAY until late 1980.

FORRESTAL fueling from British fleet tanker OLNA in the Mediterranean (1978, U.S. Navy, PH2 Jim Urick)

RANGER with Carrier Air Wing 2 (NE) (1979, Giorgio Arra)

The RANGER at anchor with Carrier Air Wing 2 (NE) on board. Note the F-4 Phantom and A-7E Corsair on her bow. She is the only FORRESTAL-class carrier retaining forward sponsons. An almost-square SPS-48C 3-D radar tops her island structure, and an SPS-43A radar is mounted to starboard. Carrier islands are also studded with antennas for electronic warfare and aircraft control systems. (1979, Giorgio Arra)

2 AIRCRAFT CARRIERS: "MIDWAY" CLASS

Number	Name	Builder	Laid down	Launched	Commissioned	Status
CV 41	MIDWAY	Newport News	27 Oct 1943	20 Mar 1945	10 Sep 1945	**PA**
CV 43	CORAL SEA	Newport News	10 July 1944	2 Apr 1946	1 Oct 1947	**PA**

Displacement:	51,000 tons standard CV 41
	52,500 tons standard CV 43
	64,000 tons full load
Length:	900 feet (274.3 m) wl
	979 feet (298.4 m) oa
Beam:	121 feet (36.9 m)
Extreme width:	258½ feet (78.8 m) CV 41 (see notes)
	236 feet (71.9 m) CV 43
Draft:	36 feet (11.0 m)
Propulsion:	steam turbines (Westinghouse); 212,000 shp; 4 shafts
Boilers:	12 600-psi (Babcock & Wilcox)
Speed:	32 knots
Manning:	2,616 (125 O + 2,491 enlisted) in CV 41
	2,523 (123 O + 2,400 enlisted) in CV 43
Air wing:	~1,945 (220 O + 1,725 enlisted)
Aircraft:	~75
Catapults:	2 steam C13 in CV 41
	3 steam C11-1 in CV 43
Elevators:	3 deck edge (63 × 52 feet; 130,000-pound capacity) in CV 41
	3 deck edge (56 × 44 feet; 74,000-pound capacity) in CV 43
Missiles:	2 8-tube Sea Sparrow BPDMS launcher Mk 25 in CV 41
Guns:	3 20-mm Phalanx CIWS Mk 15 (3 × 1) in CV 41
Radars:	CV 41 CV 43
	SPS-10 SPS-10
	SPS-37A SPS-30
	SPS-48A SPS-43A
Fire control:	2 Mk 115 missile FCS in CV 41

These ships were the largest warships built by the United States during World War II and the first designed with a beam too great to pass through the Panama Canal locks (110 feet). The CORAL SEA was not placed in a reduced commission status as planned in the late 1970s, but has remained in full commission. She is scheduled to re-place the LEXINGTON as a training carrier (AVT) in 1984, and in turn the MIDWAY is scheduled to replace the CORAL SEA in the AVT role in 1988.

The MIDWAY is based at Yokosuka, Japan.

Aircraft: These carriers do not operate F-14 Tomcat fighters or S-3A Viking ASW aircraft; the F-4 Phantom is flown from these ships in the VF role.

Class: Three ships of this class were built, with the FRANKLIN D. ROOSEVELT (CV 42) stricken in 1977. Three additional ships were planned: the CVB 44 was canceled on 1 November 1943 and CVBs, 56–57 were canceled on 28 March 1945. None had been laid down.

Classification: The MIDWAY-class ships were completed as large aircraft carriers (CVB); they were reclassified as attack aircraft carriers (CVA) on 1 October 1952, and changed to multi-mission aircraft carriers (CV) on 30 June 1975.

Design: These ships were designed to provide greater aircraft capacity and improved protection over the previous ESSEX-class aircraft carriers. The MIDWAYS were the first U.S. carriers with armored flight decks. Their original standard displacement was 45,-000 tons and full load was approximately 60,000 tons. As built, each ship had two catapults and three elevators (two centerline and one deck edge).

Hangar decks are 692 feet long, 85 feet wide, and 17½ feet high. The MIDWAY has a 13-foot-wide removable extension on the port edge of her flight deck.

Guns: As built, the MIDWAY mounted 18 and the CORAL SEA 14 single 5-inch/54 cal DP Mk 39 guns, arranged on both sides at the main deck level, just below the flight deck. Secondary gun arma-

The MIDWAY at anchor in Hong Kong. She is based at Yokosuka, Japan, the only overseas-based U.S. carrier. In the early 1970s the Navy had planned to forward-base a carrier at Piraeus, Greece, but that proposal ran afoul of political problems. Note that the MIDWAY has a lattice mast atop her island while the CORAL SEA has a large pylon mast; the FRANKLIN D. ROOSEVELT (CV 42) had an arrangement similar to the CORAL SEA. (1979, Giorgio Arra)

ment consisted of 84 40-mm AA guns and 28 20-mm AA guns at completion. The 40-mm and 20-mm were replaced by twin 3-inch/50 AA gun mounts. The guns were subsequently reduced until, by the late 1970s, each ship had only three 5-inch guns. The MIDWAY's 1980–1981 overhaul provided the ship with three 20-mm Phalanx CIWS, the first U.S. ship to have the rapid-fire weapon installed for service. (Two destroyer-type ships were fitted with the Phalanx during at-sea evaluation of the weapon.)

Missiles: The MIDWAY had two Sea Sparrow BPDMS launchers installed in 1979.

Modernization: Both of these ships have been extensively modernized, receiving enclosed ("hurricane") bows, angled flight decks, strengthened decks, and their elevators were rearranged and strengthened.

The major modernizations of these ships were:

CV 41	SCB-110	Puget Sound Naval Shipyard from 1 Sep 1955 to 30 Sep 1957
	SCB-101*	San Francisco Naval Shipyard from 15 Feb 1966 to 31 Jan 1970
CV 43	SCB-110A	Puget Sound Naval Shipyard from 16 Apr 1957 to 25 Jan 1960

Radars: These ships are receiving SPS-48 and SPS-49 radars.

*New SCB series (101.66).

The Navy's oldest operational carrier, the MIDWAY, at sea in the Indian Ocean during the Iranian crisis with Carrier Air Wing 5 (NF) embarked. Note her electronics mast abaft the enlarged island structure, the A-6E Intruder on the lowered elevator forward of the island, and fuel hoses rigged just abaft the elevator indicating the proximity of an oiler or of an escort that needs fuel. (1979, U.S. Navy)

The CORAL SEA under way in the Indian Ocean with Carrier Air Wing 14 (NK). She has a banner displayed on her island welcoming the "Connie"—the CONSTELLATION. Although newer than the MIDWAY, the CORAL SEA has not been as extensively modernized and was, when this photo was taken, unarmed with respect to guns or missile launchers. (1980, U.S. Navy)

5 AIRCRAFT CARRIERS: "HANCOCK" CLASS

No.	Name	Builder	Laid down	Launched	Commissioned	Status
CVS 11	INTREPID	Newport News	1 Dec 1941	26 Apr 1943	16 Aug 1943	AR
AVT 16	LEXINGTON	Bethlehem Steel (Quincy)	15 July 1941	26 Sep 1942	17 Feb 1943	**TRA-A**
CVA 31	BON HOMME RICHARD	New York Navy Yard	1 Feb 1943	29 Apr 1944	26 Nov 1944	PR
CV 34	ORISKANY	New York Navy Yard	1 May 1944	13 Oct 1945	25 Sep 1950	PR
CVS 38	SHANGRI-LA	Norfolk Navy Yard	15 Jan 1943	24 Feb 1944	15 Sep 1944	AR

Displacement: ~33,000 tons standard except
33,250 tons standard CV 34
42,000 tons full load except
44,700 tons full load CVA 31
39,000 tons full load AVT 16

Length: 820 feet (249.9 m) wl
894½ feet (272.6 m) oa except
890 feet (271.3 m) oa CV 34

Beam: 103 feet (30.8 m) except
106½ feet (32.5 m) CV 34

Extreme width: 185 feet (56.4 m) (see notes)

Draft: 31 feet (9.4 m)

Propulsion: steam turbines (Westinghouse); 150,000 shp; 4 shafts

Boilers: 8 600-psi (Babcock & Wilcox)

Speed: 30+ knots

Manning: ~2,090 (110 O + 1,980 enlisted) in CV/CVA
~1,615 (115 O + 1,500 enlisted) in CVS
1,375 in AVT 16

Air wing: ~1,200 in CV/CVA
~800 in CVS
none in AVT 16

Aircraft: ~70–80 in CV/CVA
~45 in CVS

Catapults: 2 steam C11-1

Elevators: 3 { centerline 70 × 44 feet; 46,000-pound capacity
port deck edge 56 × 44 feet; 46,000-pound capacity
starboard deck edge 56 × 44 feet; 56,500-pound capacity

Guns: 4 5-inch (127-mm) 38 cal DP Mk 24 (4 × 1) except 2 guns in CV 34;
removed from AVT 16

Radars: SPS-10 surface search
SPS-12 air search in AVT 16
SPS-30 height-finding except AVT 16
SPS-37 or SPS-43A air search

Fire control: 1 Mk 37 gun FCS except 2 in CV 34; none in AVT 16
2 or 3 Mk 56 gun FCS except none in CV 34, AVT 16

These ships are the survivors of the 24 ESSEX-class aircraft carriers completed during and after World War II. All have been extensively modernized and are considered as part of the HANCOCK (CV 19) class. The LEXINGTON is operational as a pilot training ship, and the four others are laid up in reserve. The LEXINGTON, based at Pensacola, Fla., cannot maintain or otherwise support aircraft. She was to have been decommissioned in FY 1979 (and replaced by the CORAL SEA); however, the "Lex" will be retained into the early 1980s. The "Lex" recorded her 390,000th arrested landing in May 1979; this is significantly more than any other carrier in history.

The BON HOMME RICHARD was decommissioned on 2 July 1971 (laid up at Bremerton, Wash.), SHANGRI-LA on 30 July 1971 (Philadelphia, Pa.), INTREPID on 15 March 1974 (Philadelphia), and ORISKANY on 30 September 1976 (Bremerton).

Class: Twenty-four ESSEX-class ships were completed (CV 9–21, 31–34, 36–40, 45, and 47); two started ships were canceled at the end of World War II (CV 35, 46), while six not-yet-started ships were canceled on 27 March 1945 (CV 50–55).

Classification: All ships were designated CV when built; all were reclassified as attack aircraft carriers (CVA) on 1 October 1952.

Three ships were changed to ASW aircraft carriers (CVS); the INTREPID on 31 March 1962, the LEXINGTON on 1 October 1962, and the SHANGRI-LA on 30 June 1969. The LEXINGTON was again changed to a training carrier (CVT) on 1 January 1969 and to auxiliary aircraft landing training ship (AVT) on 1 July 1978. The ORISKANY was changed to a multi-mission aircraft carrier (CV) on 30 June 1975.

Design: Original standard displacement was 27,100 tons and full-load displacement 33,000 tons. Construction of the ORISKANY

ORISKANY (1970, U.S. Navy)

was suspended in 1946; resumed in 1947, she was completed to a modified design. Hangar decks are 644 feet long, 70 feet wide, and 17½ feet high.

Guns: As built, these ships had 12 5-inch 38 cal DP guns plus 68 to 72 40-mm AA guns and 52 20-mm AA guns, except ORISKANY, which was completed with eight 5-inch guns and 28 3-inch 50 cal AA guns. Most ships had their lighter weapons replaced by twin 3-inch mounts during the 1950s. Subsequently, gun armament was reduced to the minimal number of weapons shown above. The LEXINGTON is unarmed.

Modernization: All of these ships have been extensively modernized, receiving enclosed ("hurricane") bows, strengthened and angled flight decks, improved elevators, etc.

Their modernization periods were:

CV 11	SCB-27C	Newport News SB & DD Co 1951–1954
	SCB-125	New York Naval Shipyard 1956–1957
CV 16	SCB-27C	Puget Sound Naval Shipyard 1952–1955
CV 31	SCB-27C	San Francisco Naval Shipyard 1952–1955
CV 34	SCB-125A	San Francisco Naval Shipyard 1957–1959
CV 38	SCB-27C	Puget Sound Naval Shipyard 1951–1955

Radar: The radars listed above are those installed at time of decommissioning.

Sonar: FRAM-modernized CVS-type ships had been fitted with SQS-23 bow-mounted sonar, including INTREPID.

The BON HOMME RICHARD during an UNREP evolution with the large oiler-ammunition ship SACRAMENTO (AOE 1) and the destroyer THOMASON (DD 760). The 44 aircraft on her flight deck represent just over half of her air wing. The deck-edge elevator abaft the "Bonnie Dick's" island is folded upward to facilitate replenishment. Just abaft the island are a pair of A-3 Skywarriors; other aircraft are E-1B Tracers, F-8 Crusaders, and A-4 Skyhawks. (1969, U.S. Navy)

The Oriskany was the last Essex-class aircraft carrier to be completed and the last to operate as a combat carrier. Shown here in the Pacific during the Vietnam War, she has an E-1B Tracer on her starboard catapult, with F-8 Crusaders and A-7 Corsairs parked aft. Proposals were put forward in 1980 to re-activate her, although providing a crew and aircraft would be problems. (The ship is too small to operate F-4 Phantom or F-14 Tomcat fighters.) (1970, U.S. Navy)

2 ASW AIRCRAFT CARRIERS: MODERNIZED "ESSEX" CLASS

Number	Name	Builder	Laid down	Launched	Commissioned	Status
CVS 12	HORNET	Newport News	3 Aug 1942	29 Aug 1943	29 Nov 1943	PR
CVS 20	BENNINGTON	New York Navy Yard	15 Dec 1942	26 Feb 1944	6 Aug 1944	PR

Displacement:	~33,000 tons standard
	40,000 tons full load
Length:	820 feet (249.9 m) wl
	890 feet (271.3 m) oa
Beam:	103 feet (30.8 m)
Extreme width:	~195 feet (59.5 m)
Draft:	31 feet (9.4 m)
Propulsion:	steam turbines (Westinghouse); 150,000 shp; 4 shafts
Boilers:	8 600-psi (Babcock & Wilcox)
Speed:	30+ knots
Manning:	~1,615 (115 0 + 1,500 enlisted)
Air wing:	~800
Aircraft:	~45 as CVS
Catapults:	2 hydraulic H–8 in CVS 12
Elevators:	3 (2 deck edge + 1 centerline)
Guns:	4 5-inch (127-mm) 38–cal DP Mk 24 (4 × 1)
Radars:	SPS-10 surface search
	SPS-30 height finding
	SPS-43A air search
Sonars:	SQS-23 bow-mounted

Fire control:	1 Mk 37 gun FCS	1 Mk 25 radar
	3 Mk 56 gun FCS	2 Mk 35 radar

These two ships retain many of their original Essex characteristics, not having the degree of modernization of the Hancock-class carriers. The Bennington was decommissioned on 15 January 1970 and the Hornet on 26 June 1970. See Hancock class (page 63) for additional details.

Aircraft: In the CVS role at the time of being laid up, these ships each carried two squadrons of S-2 Tracker fixed-wing ASW aircraft and one squadron of SH-3 Sea King helicopters plus various detachments.

Classification: Built with CV classification; changed to CVA in October 1952; the Hornet changed to CVS on 27 June 1958 and the Bennington on 30 June 1959.

Modernization: These ships have been extensively modernized and have enclosed (hurricane) bows, angled flight decks, strengthened decks, etc.; their elevators have been rearranged and strengthened.

Sonar: Both ships have SQS-23 sonar.

The last active ESSEX/HANCOCK-class carrier is the LEXINGTON, employed for training carrier pilots. She has no aircraft maintenance or rearming capabilities. Based at Pensacola, Fla., she was to have been replaced in the AVT role by the CORAL SEA, but will now remain in service as a training ship at least into the early 1980s. (U.S. Navy, PH2 Burns Palmer)

POST–WORLD WAR II AIRCRAFT CARRIER PROGRAMS

U.S. World War II aircraft carrier construction programs reached hull number CVB 57 (a canceled MIDWAY-class ship). The "heavy" aircraft carrier UNITED STATES (CVA 58) was ordered on 10 August 1948 from Newport News, laid down on 18 April 1949, and canceled on 23 April 1949. She was to have displaced 65,000 tons standard, 80,000 tons full load; her length was 1,090 feet overall with flush deck (i.e., no angled deck and a retracting control station); she was designed with conventional steam-turbine propulsion.

7 Battleships

The U.S. Navy maintains four Iowa-class battleships in reserve. These are the only battleships remaining afloat with any navy. All four ships were in combat in World War II and in the Korean War, with the NEW JERSEY having also been reactivated in 1968–1969 for the Vietnam War.

Periodically during the 1960s and 1970s there have been proposals to reactivate some or all of the ships for various roles. Suggested configurations have included: basically the same as built with their nine 16-inch guns or gunfire support and "political presence"; commando ships; guided missile ships for task force air defense; strategic missile monitor carrying Polaris missiles; and fleet command ship. In 1980, primarily as a result of the Afghanistan and Iran crises, consideration was given to reactivating the ships. Some of the proposals at that time called for removal of the ships' after 16-inch triple gun turret to provide space for a large battery of land-attack cruise missiles or facilities for VSTOL aircraft and possibly a limited troop-carrying capability.

All proposals to reactivate these ships suffer from their large manpower requirements.

Names: U.S. battleships have almost exclusively been named for States of the Union. That name source has subsequently been assigned to Trident missile submarines and cruisers.

Radar and Fire Control: The equipment listed below is that installed prior to the last decommissioning.

4 BATTLESHIPS: "IOWA" CLASS

Number	Name	Builder	Laid down	Launched	Commissioned	Status
BB 61	IOWA	New York Navy Yard	27 June 1940	27 Aug 1942	22 Feb 1943	AR
BB 62	NEW JERSEY	Philadelphia Navy Yard	16 Sep 1940	7 Dec 1942	23 May 1943	PR
BB 63	MISSOURI	New York Navy Yard	6 Jan 1941	29 Jan 1944	11 June 1944	PR
BB 64	WISCONSIN	Philadelphia Navy Yard	25 Jan 1941	7 Dec 1943	16 Apr 1944	AR

Displacement:	48,425 tons standard
	57,500 tons full load
Length:	860 feet (262.1 m) wl
	887$\frac{1}{4}$ feet (270.4 m) oa except BB 62 887$\frac{7}{12}$ feet
Beam:	108$\frac{1}{6}$ feet (33 m)
Draft:	38 feet (11.6 m)
Propulsion:	steam turbines (General Electric in BB 61, 63; Westinghouse in BB 62, 64); 212,000 shp; 4 shafts
Boilers:	8 600-psi (Babcock & Wilcox)
Speed:	33 knots
Manning:	2,753–2,911 as designed; 1,626 (70 O + 1,556 enlisted) in BB 62 during 1968 deployment to Vietnam
Guns:	9 16-inch (406 mm) 50 cal Mk Mod 0 (3 × 3)
	20 5-inch (127-mm) 38 cal DP Mk 28 Mod 0/10 (10 × 2)
	several 40-mm AA Mk 2 (? × 4), except removed from BB 62
Radars:	SG-6 surface search, except removed from BB 62
	SPS-6 air search
	SPS-8A height-finding, except removed from BB 62
	SPS-10F surface search in BB 62
	SPS-53 surface search in BB 62
Fire control:	4 Mk 37 gun FCS
	2 Mk 38 gun directors
	1 Mk 40 gun director
	1 Mk 51 gun director
	6 Mk 56 gun FCS, except removed from BB 62
	2 Mk 63 gun FCS, except removed from BB 62

The four IOWAs were the last U.S. battleships to be constructed. (Two foreign ships were completed later, the British VANGUARD in 1946, and French JEAN BART in 1952.) In size and firepower the IOWAs were exceeded only by the Japanese battleships YAMATO and MUSASHI (~70,000 tons full load, with nine 18.1-inch guns).

After World War II three ships were mothballed in 1948–1949, while the MISSOURI was retained in reduced commission as a training ship. All four ships returned to full service in 1950–1951 for the Korean War; all were decommissioned between 1953 and 1958. The NEW JERSEY was commissioned for the third time on 6 April 1968 for the Vietnam War; she was subsequently decommissioned on 17 December 1969.

The MISSOURI and NEW JERSEY are laid up at Bremerton, Wash., and the IOWA and WISCONSIN at Philadelphia, Pa.

Aircraft: These ships were built with two rotating stern catapults and an aircraft crane for handling floatplanes. Three were normally embarked for scouting and gunfire spotting. The catapults were beached during the Korean War, and the ships subsequently embarked utility helicopters. During the Vietnam War the NEW JERSEY also flew QH-50C "snoopy dash" drones for gunfire spotting.

Armor: Armor was provided to protect vital areas of the ships from the enemy's 16-inch guns. The Class A steel armor belt tapers vertically from 12.1 inches to 1.62 inches; to protect the propeller shafts, there is a lower armot belt, which is 13.5 inches, abaft the No. 3 main battery turret. Turret faces are 17 inches, turret tops are 7.25 inches, turret backs are 12 inches, barbettes have a maximum armor of 11.6 inches, second deck armor is 6 inches, and the three-level conning tower sides are 17.3 inches with roof armor of 7.25 inches.

Class: Six ships of this class were ordered; the ILLINOIS (BB 65) was canceled on 12 August 1945 when 22 percent complete; construction of the KENTUCKY (BB 66) was halted after the war, and she was canceled on 22 January 1950 when 73.1 percent complete.

Electronics: When recommissioned in 1968, the NEW JERSEY was fitted with additional electronic warfare equipment (note modified conning tower).

Guns: As built, these ships mounted 80 40-mm AA guns and 49 to 60 20-mm AA guns. The 20-mm weapons were removed after World War II and the number of 40-mm guns successively reduced; all were removed from the NEW JERSEY by 1968 with only a few remaining in the other ships.

Operational: During her 1968–1969 reactivation the NEW JERSEY made one deployment to the Western Pacific. She was on the "gun line" off South Vietnam for 120 days during which she fired 5,688 rounds of 16-inch ammunition and 14,891 rounds of 5-inch ammunition. (The NEW JERSEY fired a total of 6,200 main-battery rounds in her 1968–1969 commission; she fired 771 rounds from 1943 to 1948, and 6,671 during her participation in the Korean War and midshipman cruises from 1950 to 1957.)

The NEW JERSEY during her sea trials prior to recommissioning in December 1982. (1982, U.S. Navy, PH1 Harold Gerwien)

The NEW JERSEY in the Delaware River, going to sea after reactivation in 1968. She retained the circular "tubs" for 40-mm gun mounts, but those and her lighter 20-mm weapons all had been removed. Plans to replace the quad "forties" with twin 3-inch/50 caliber mounts were never carried out. She has an aircraft crane aft; helicopter deck markings were not yet painted in this photo. (1968, U.S. Navy)

The NEW JERSEY fires a round from her No. 2 turret of 16–inch guns during weapons tests. She carries the largest guns afloat and will be joined by at least one sister ship in the near future. (1982, U.S. Navy, PHC Terry C. Mitchell)

8 Cruisers

The distinction between the cruiser and destroyer ship types has become irrelevant in the U.S. Navy, as both categories of warships have come to be considered "task force escorts" or "battle group escorts." As of January 1981 the Navy had 27 cruisers (CG/CGN) and 81 destroyers (DD/DDG) in active service. In addition, 16 old destroyers (DD) were being retained in the Naval Reserve Force, manned by composite active-reserve crews.

The Navy's force-level objective for active cruisers and destroyers is 111 ships based on the following ship assignments:

6 Carrier Battle Groups	{	18 CG (Aegis)
		30 CG/CGN/DDG
		24 DD
3 Surface Action Groups	{	3 CG (Aegis)
		9 DDG
Amphibious Force Escorts	{	12 DDG
		5 FF/FFG
Convoy Escorts	{	7 DD
		63 FF/FFG
Underway Replenishment Group Escorts	{	8 DDG
		24 FF/FFG

Total	27 Cruisers
	84 Destroyers
	(92 Frigates)

Except for the nuclear-propelled LONG BEACH, all U.S. Navy cruisers now in commission are large, destroyer-type ships (formerly DDG/DLG/DLGN types) that have been reclassified from 1975 onward. These former "destroyers" are large and heavily armed ships, but lack the flag accommodations and armor of earlier cruiser designs. Also, except for the Aegis-equipped TICONDEROGA class, these ships lack the Command, Control, and Communications (C³) facilities generally required for major-force flagships, and except for the nuclear ships, they lack the endurance previously associated with cruisers.

The only "cruisers" now under construction are the TICONDEROGA-class ships. These are highly capable, multi-purpose ships, with four having been authorized through FY 1981. Continued construction of these ships is planned at the rate of three to four ships per year toward a force goal of the 18 that are currently approved by the Department of Defense (i.e., three Aegis ships for each two-carrier battle group). No other "cruiser" construction is now planned, although an enlarged TICONDEROGA (carrying more Tomahawk cruise missiles) has been unofficially proposed. Some of the proposed configurations of the DDGX (see Chapter 9) are similar to the TICONDEROGA class.

Electronics: All missile cruisers have, or are being fitted with, the SLQ-32(V)3 electronic warfare system, replacing several earlier EW sets.

Names: U.S. cruisers traditionally have been named for American cities. In 1971 the name source for ships then classified as frigates (DLGN) was changed to states, with the CALIFORNIA being named for the home state of the incumbent President Richard M. Nixon. In 1975 those ships were reclassified as cruisers, thus six cruisers carry state names. In 1980 the Navy announced that the Aegis "cruisers" (formerly classified as destroyers) would have battle names, with the lead ship being named TICONDEROGA. Previously battle names had been assigned to aircraft carriers, with the preceding TICONDEROGA having been the CV 14.

Radars: The radars listed for decommissioned ships are those installed at the time the ships were decommissioned.

(In the following table, AAW indicates Terrier/Standard surface-to-air missile systems; ASW indicates ASROC and SQS-23/26/53 sonar; Helicopter indicates that ships have a hangar facility; and Guns are the largest caliber installed.)

Type	Class/Ship	Active	Buildingᵃ	Reserve	Commission	AAW	ASW	Helicopter	Guns
CG 47	TICONDEROGA	—	4	—	1983–	✔	✔	✔	5-inch
CGN 38	VIRGINIA	4	—	—	1976–1980	✔	✔	✔	5-inch
CGN 36	CALIFORNIA	2	—	—	1974–1975	✔	✔	—	5-inch
CGN 35	TRUXTUN	1	—	—	1967	✔	✔	✔	5-inch
CG 26	BELKNAP	9	—	—	1964–1967	✔	✔	✔	5-inch
CGN 25	BAINBRIDGE	1	—	—	1962	✔	✔	—	removed
CG 16	LEAHY	9	—	—	1962–1964	✔	✔	—	removed
CG 10	ALBANY	—	—	2	1945–1946	✔	✔	—	5-inch
CGN 9	LONG BEACH	1	—	—	1961	✔	✔	—	5-inch
CG 5	OKLAHOMA CITY	—	—	1	1944	✔	—	—	6-inch
CA 134	DES MOINES	—	—	2	1948–1949	—	—	—	8-inch

ᵃ Includes ships authorized through FY 1981.

The Navy's first three nuclear escorts, the BAINBRIDGE, TRUXTUN, and LONG BEACH of Cruiser-Destroyer Group 1 at Subic Bay with the tender SAMUEL GOMPERS (AD 37). Note the different hull lines of the warships, with the TRUXTUN and BAINBRIDGE having sleeker, destroyer hulls indicating their DLGN "frigate" origins. Both have stem anchors to facilitate mooring with their bow-mounted sonar. (1978, U.S. Navy)

(4) AEGIS GUIDED MISSILE CRUISERS: "TICONDEROGA" CLASS

Number	Name	FY/SCB	Builder	Laid down	Launch	Commission	Status
CG 47	TICONDEROGA	78/226	Litton/Ingalls (Pascagoula)	21 Jan 1980	1981	1983	Bldg.
CG 48	. . . .	80/226	Litton/Ingalls (Pascagoula)	1981		1984	Bldg.
CG 49	. . . .	81/226				1985	Auth.
CG 50	. . . .	81/226				1985	Auth.

Displacement:	9,100 tons full load
Length:	529 feet (161.2 m) wl
	563$^{1}/_{3}$ feet (171.7 m) oa
Beam:	55 feet (17.6 m)
Draft:	31 feet (9.4 m)
Propulsion:	gas turbines (General Electric); 80,000 shp; 2 shafts
Speed:	30+ knots
Range:	~600 n.miles at 20 knots
Manning:	360 (33 O + 327 enlisted); expected to be reduced in ships with Vertical Launch System
Helicopters:	2 SH-60B LAMPS
Missiles:	2 twin Mk 26 Mod 1 launchers for Standard-MR SAM (88)
	2 Ex 41 vertical launchers for Harpoon/Standard/Tomahawk in later ships (61 + 61)
	2 quad launchers for Harpoon SSM Mk 141 in CG 47–48
Guns:	2 5-inch (127-mm) 54 cal DP Mk 45 (2 × 1)
	2 20-mm Phalanx CIWS Mk 15 (2 × 1)
ASW weapons:	ASROC fired from forward Mk 26 launcher in CG 47–48
	ASROC fired from Ex 41 launchers in CG 49 and later ships
	6 12.75-inch (324-mm) torpedo tubes Mk 32 (2 × 3)
Radars:	SPS-49 air search
	SPS-55 surface search
	(4) SPY-1A phased-array multi-function
Sonars:	SQS-53A bow-mounted
	SQR-19 TACTAS
Fire control:	1 Mk 7 Aegis weapon system
	1 Mk 86 gun FCS
	4 Mk 99 missile directors
	1 Mk 116 ASW FCS
	1 SPQ-9A radar

These cruisers are intended to provide AAW defense for carrier battle groups. The use of Vertical Launch Systems in the later ships will also provide a potent offensive capability with a "load out" of Harpoon or Tomahawk cruise missiles at the expense of some AAW missiles or ASW rockets.

Several previous Aegis ship designs and classes were being considered for deployment prior to this class. In 1968–1969 there were proposals to arm the then-DLGN 38 class and a new class of nuclear ships (DGN), a total of some 30 units, with Aegis; subsequently, in 1972–1974 a conventionally propelled destroyer class (DG) was planned; in late 1974 a large, 14,000-ton strike cruiser (CSGN) was put forward as an Aegis ship; in early 1975 conversion of the cruiser LONG BEACH was planned; and in the late 1970s a redesigned, 12,000-ton VIRGINIA-class cruiser with Aegis was proposed.

Classification: These ships were changed from guided missile destroyers (DDG) to cruisers on 1 January 1980 to reflect their capabilities and cost, according to official Navy statements.

Design: The DDG/CG 47 design is a modification of the SPRUANCE (DD 963) design with an enlarged superstructure to accommodate the SPY-1A radars. Internal changes include installation of the other components of the Aegis system, armor plating for magazine and critical electronics spaces, increases in the ship's service generators from three 2,000 kw to three 2,500 kw, additional accommodations, and additional fuel tanks.

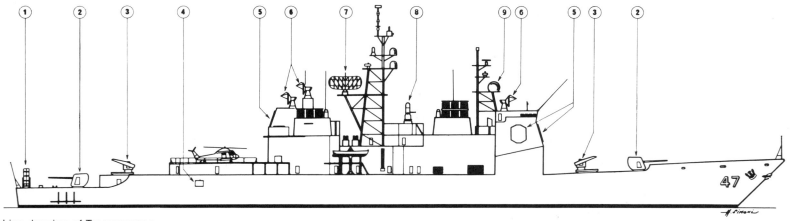

Line drawing of TICONDEROGA

1. Harpoon launchers (port and starboard) 2. 5-inch DP MK 45 gun 3. Mk 26 missile launcher 4. Mk 32 ASW torpedo tubes (P&S) 5. SPY-1A radar (port and aft) 6. Mk 99 missile directors (2 forward and 2 aft) 7. SPS-49 radar 8. Phalanx CIWS (P&S) 9. SPQ-9A radar

During construction the TICONDEROGA's design was changed to provide higher machinery exhaust stacks and a bow bulwark.

Electronics: These ships are fitted with SLQ-32(V)3 electronic countermeasures.

Missiles: The later TICONDEROGAS are scheduled to have two Ex 41 Vertical Launch Systems in place of Mk 26 launchers. This change will provide more rapid and flexible missile firings, plus a larger magazine capacity.

The Aegis guided missile cruiser TICONDEROGA at sea. The forward and starboard "faces" of her SPY–1A radar are visible on the forward superstructure; the port and after antennas are on the after structure. Gatling guns are fitted amidships, and she carries two quad banks of Harpoon missiles on her fantail. (1982, Ingalls Shipbuilding)

4 NUCLEAR-PROPELLED GUIDED MISSILE CRUISERS: "VIRGINIA" CLASS

Number	Name	FY/SCB	Builder	Laid down	Launched	Commissioned	Status
CGN 38	VIRGINIA	70/246	Newport News	19 Aug 1972	14 Dec 1974	11 Sep 1976	**AA**
CGN 39	TEXAS	71/246	Newport News	18 Aug 1973	9 Aug 1975	10 Sep 1977	**AA**
CGN 40	MISSISSIPPI	72/246	Newport News	22 Feb 1975	31 July 1976	5 Aug 1978	**AA**
CGN 41	ARKANSAS	75/246	Newport News	17 Jan 1977	21 Oct 1978	18 Oct 1980	**AA**

Displacement:	11,000 tons full load
Length:	585 feet (178.3 m) oa
Beam:	63 feet (19.2 m)
Draft:	29$\frac{1}{2}$ feet (9.0 m)
Propulsion:	steam turbines; ~60,000 shp; 2 shafts
Reactors:	2 pressurized-water D2G
Speed:	30+ knots
Manning:	519 (30 O + 489 enlisted)
Helicopters:	1 LAMPS (see notes)
Missiles:	2 twin Mk 26 Mod 0/1 launchers for Tartar/Standard-MR SAM (68)
Guns:	2 5-inch (127-mm) 54 cal DP Mk 45 (2 × 1)
ASW weapons:	ASROC fired from forward Mk 26 launcher
	6 12.75-inch (324-mm) torpedo tubes Mk 32 (2 × 3)

Radars:	SPS-40B air search
	SPS-48C 3-D search
	SPS-55 surface search
Sonars:	SQS-53A bow-mounted
Fire control:	1 Mk 13 weapons direction system
	1 Mk 86 gun FCS
	1 Mk 74 missile FCS
	1 Mk 116 ASW FCS
	2 SPG-51D radar
	1 SPG-60 radar
	1 SPQ-9A radar

Line drawing of VIRGINIA

1. helicopter hangar   2. Mk 26 missile launcher   3. 5-inch DP Mk 45 gun   4. Mk 32 ASW torpedo tubes (port and starboard)   5. SPG-51D radar   6. SPS-40B radar   7. SPS-48C radar   8. SPS-55 radar   9. SPQ-9A radar   10. SPG-60 radar

MISSISSIPPI under way in Hampton Roads, Va. (1978, Newport News)

These are large escort ships for nuclear-propelled aircraft carriers. All were delayed considerably because of shipyard labor problems and contractual disagreements between the yard and the government.

Class: Early planning called for at least 11 ships of this class to provide, along with five earlier CGNs, four nuclear-propelled escorts for each of four nuclear carriers (then CVAN 65, 68–70). A fifth ship of the VIRGINIA class was proposed in the FY 1976 budget but was not approved by Congress pending development of the strike cruiser (CSGN) program. After the strike cruiser effort was halted, an improved VIRGINIA-class ship of approximately 12,000 tons and fitted with the Aegis AAW system was proposed for construction in FY 1980. However, all further consideration of nuclear-propelled Aegis ships has been dropped in favor of constructing the TICONDEROGA-class ships.

Classification: CGNs 38–40 were originally classified as frigates (DLGN 38–40); they were changed to cruisers on 30 June 1975. The ARKANSAS was ordered as CGN 41.

Design: These ships are of an improved design, superior to the previous CALIFORNIA class with their Mk 26 missile launchers and provision for a helicopter hangar and elevator in their stern. These were the first U.S. ships built since World War II to have the latter feature.

Guns: Two Phalanx CIWS are planned for installation in each of these ships.

Helicopters: Helicopters are not normally embarked in these ships. The hangar is connected to the main deck by a stern elevator covered by a folding hatch. The hangar is 42-feet long and 14-feet wide. Eventual assignment of SH-2F LAMPS helicopters is planned.

Missiles: These ships will be fitted with Tomahawk and Harpoon cruise missiles at a later date.

TEXAS (1977, U.S. Navy, PH2 Thomas J. Baroody)

The MISSISSIPPI on trials with her after 5-inch mount and Mk 26 launcher trained to port. Note her lowered radio antennas and helicopter safety nets. Her superstructure has a bare look pending installation of SLQ-32(V)3 and other electronic equipment. (1978, Newport News)

MISSISSIPPI under way in Chesapeake Bay (1978, Newport News)

2 NUCLEAR-PROPELLED GUIDED MISSILE CRUISERS: "CALIFORNIA" CLASS

Number	Name	FY/SCB	Builder	Laid down	Launched	Commissioned	Status
CGN 36	CALIFORNIA	67/241	Newport News	23 Jan 1970	22 Sep 1971	16 Feb 1974	**AA**
CGN 37	SOUTH CAROLINA	68/241	Newport News	1 Dec 1970	1 July 1972	25 Jan 1975	**AA**

Displacement:	10,150 tons full load	Radars:	SPS-40B air search
Length:	596 feet (181.7 m) oa		SPS-48C 3-D search
Beam:	61 feet (18.6 m)		SPS-55 surface search
Draft:	31½ feet (9.6 m)	Sonars:	SQS-26CX bow-mounted
Propulsion:	2 steam turbines; ~60,000 shp; 2 shafts	Fire control:	1 Mk 11 weapon direction system
Reactors:	2 pressurized-water D2G		2 Mk 74 missile FCS
Speed:	30+ knots		1 Mk 86 gun FCS
Manning:	533 (31 O + 502 enlisted)		1 Mk 114 ASW FCS
Helicopters:	none		4 SPG-51D radar
Missiles:	2 single Mk 13 Mod 3 launchers for Tartar/Standard-MR SAM (80)		1 SPG-60 radar
Guns:	2 5-inch (127-mm) 54 cal DP Mk 45 (2 × 1)		1 SPQ-9A radar
ASW weapons:	1 8-tube ASROC launcher Mk 16		
	4 12.75-inch (324-mm) torpedo tubes Mk 32 (4 × 1 fixed)		

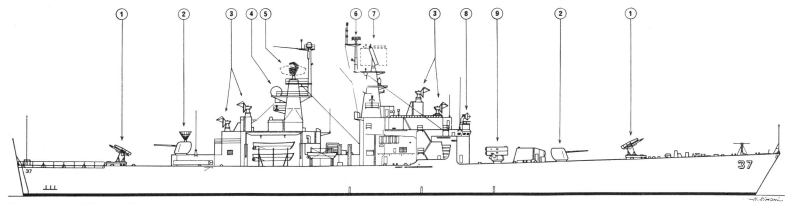

Line drawing of SOUTH CAROLINA

1. Mk 13 missile launcher　2. 5-inch DP Mk 45 gun　3. SPG-51D radar　4. SPQ-9A radar　5. SPS-40B radar　6. SPS-55 radar　7. SPS-48C radar　8. SPG-60 radar　9. ASROC launcher

The CALIFORNIA at Portsmouth, England, in full dress. She has single-arm Mk 13 missile launchers, an ASROC reload structure and box launcher forward, and her after 5-inch mount on the 01 level to distinguish her from the improved VIRGINIA class. The later ships are more capable in the Antiair Warfare (AAW) role and have helicopter support facilities, although they have not yet embarked LAMPS. (1977, Giorgio Arra)

This was the first class of nuclear-propelled surface warships intended for series production. They are employed as escorts for nuclear carriers. The construction of additional units was deferred in favor of the more-capable VIRGINIA class.

Class: A third ship of this design was authorized in FY 1968 but was not built because of rising costs and the development of the VIRGINIA class.

Classification: Both ships originally were classified as guided missile frigates (DLGN); they were changed to cruisers on 30 June 1975.

Design: These ships have a large helicopter landing area aft, but no hangar or maintenance facilities. They have a separate ASROC "box" launcher because of the Mk 13 launchers that cannot accommodate the antisubmarine rockets.

Their SCB number is part of the new SCB series (241.65).

Guns: These ships are scheduled to be fitted with two Phalanx CIWS.

Missiles: Harpoon and Tomahawk cruise missiles are scheduled for installation in these ships.

SOUTH CAROLINA (1976, U.S. Navy, JO2 R. Leonard)

SOUTH CAROLINA (1976, U.S. Navy, JO2 R. Leonard)

1 NUCLEAR-PROPELLED GUIDED MISSILE CRUISER: "TRUXTUN" TYPE

Number	Name	FY/SCB	Builder	Laid down	Launched	Commissioned	Status
CGN 35	TRUXTUN	62/222	New York SB Corp	17 June 1963	19 Dec 1964	27 May 1967	**PA**

Displacement:	8,200 tons standard
	9,200 tons full load
Length:	564 feet (117.9 m) oa
Beam:	58 feet (17.7 m)
Draft:	31 feet (9.4 m)
Propulsion:	steam turbines; ~60,000 shp; 2 shafts
Reactors:	2 pressurized-water D2G
Speed:	30+ knots
Range:	150,000 n. miles at full speed
Manning:	538 (32 O + 506 enlisted)
Helicopters:	1 SH-2 LAMPS
Missiles:	1 twin Mk 10 Mod 8 launcher for Terrier/Standard-ER SAM (60)
	2 quad launchers for Harpoon SSM Mk 141
Guns:	1 5-inch (127-mm) 54 cal DP Mk 42 (1 × 1)
ASW weapons:	ASROC fired from missile launcher
	4 12.75-inch (324-mm) torpedo tubes Mk 32 (4 × 1 fixed)
Radars:	SPS-10 surface search
	SPS-40 air search
	SPS-48 3-D search
Sonars:	SQS-26 bow-mounted
Fire control:	1 Mk 11 weapon direction system
	1 Mk 68 gun FCS
	2 Mk 76 missile FCS
	1 Mk 114 ASW FCS
	1 SPG-53F radar
	2 SPG-55B radar

The TRUXTUN was the U.S. Navy's fourth nuclear-propelled surface warship. The ship was requested by the Navy as one of seven oil-burning frigates in the FY 1962 program; however, the Congress directed that one unit be nuclear-propelled.

Classification: Originally classified as a guided missile frigate (DLGN); changed to cruiser (CGN) on 30 June 1975.

Design: The TRUXTUN was built to a modified BELKNAP-class design, with the gun and missile-launcher arrangement reversed; distinctive lattice masts replace "macks" of the oil-burning ships.

Guns: As built, the TRUXTUN also had two 3-inch/50 cal AA gun mounts amidships. They have been replaced by the Harpoon missile tubes. The ship is scheduled to receive two Phalanx CIWS.

Helicopters: The TRUXTUN's hangar is 40 1/3-feet long and 16 3/4-feet wide.

Torpedoes: As built, the ship had two Mk 25 torpedo tubes mounted in the stern counter.

The one-of-a-kind TRUXTUN at Pearl Harbor. The large Mk 10 missile launcher is aft, as indicated by the two large, SPG-55B fire control radars. In this view the TRUXTUN has quad Harpoon launchers amidships, in the "tubs" that previously carried twin 3-inch AA guns. The TRUXTUN has the same weapons and sensors as the oil-burning BELKNAP class, but with the 5-inch gun and Mk 10 launcher arrangement reversed. (1980, Giorgio Arra)

TRUXTUN with 3-inch guns (1978, Giorgio Arra)

TRUXTUN (1977, Giorgio Arra)

9 GUIDED MISSILE CRUISERS: "BELKNAP" CLASS

Number	Name	FY/SCB	Builder	Laid down	Launched	Commissioned	Status
CG 26	BELKNAP	61/212	Bath Iron Works	5 Feb 1962	20 July 1963	7 Nov 1964	**AA**
CG 27	JOSEPHUS DANIELS	61/212	Bath Iron Works	23 Apr 1962	2 Dec 1963	8 May 1965	**AA**
CG 28	WAINWRIGHT	61/212	Bath Iron Works	2 July 1962	25 Apr 1964	8 Jan 1966	**AA**
CG 29	JOUETT	62/212	Puget Sound Naval Shipyard	25 Sep 1962	30 June 1964	3 Dec 1966	**PA**
CG 30	HORNE	62/212	San Francisco Naval Shipyard	12 Dec 1962	30 Oct 1964	15 Apr 1967	**PA**
CG 31	STERETT	62/212	Puget Sound Naval Shipyard	25 Sep 1962	30 June 1964	8 Apr 1967	**PA**
CG 32	WILLIAM H. STANDLEY	62/212	Bath Iron Works	29 July 1963	19 Dec 1964	9 July 1966	**PA**
CG 33	FOX	62/212	Todd Shipyard (San Pedro)	15 Jan 1963	21 Nov 1964	28 May 1966	**PA**
CG 34	BIDDLE	62/212	Bath Iron Works	9 Dec 1963	2 July 1965	21 Jan 1967	**AA**

Displacement:	6,570 tons standard
	7,930 tons full load
Length:	547 feet (166.7 m) oa
Beam:	54¾ feet (16.7 m)
Draft:	28¾ feet (8.7 m)
Propulsion:	steam turbines (GE in CG 26–28, 32, 34; De Laval in CG 29–31, 33); 85,000 shp; 2 shafts
Boilers:	4 1,200-psi (Babcock & Wilcox in CG 26–28, 32, 34; Combustion Engineering in CG 29–31, 33)
Speed:	33 knots
Range:	7,100 n. miles at 20 knots
Manning:	446–452 (23–25 O + 410–427 enlisted)
Helicopters:	1 SH-2 LAMPS
Missiles:	1 twin Mk 10 Mod 7 launcher for Terrier/Standard-ER SAM (60)
	2 quad launchers for Harpoon SSM Mk 141
Guns:	1 5-inch (127-mm) 54 cal DP Mk 42 (1 × 1)
	1 20-mm Phalanx CIWS (Mk 15) in CG 34 (installed in 1980)
ASW weapons:	ASROC fired from missile launcher
	6 12.75-inch (324-mm) torpedo tubes Mk 32 (2 × 3)
Radars:	SPS-10F surface search
	SPS-40 air search in CG 29, 31–34; being replaced by SPS-49
	SPS-43 air search in CG 27–28, 30; being replaced by SPS-49
	SPS-48 3-D search
	SPS-49 air search in CG 26
Sonars:	SQS-26BX bow-mounted except SQS-53A in CG 26
Fire control:	1 Mk 7 weapon direction system in CG 27
	1 Mk 11 weapon direction system in CG 28–34
	1 Mk 14 weapon direction system in CG 26
	1 Mk 68 gun FCS
	1 Mk 114 ASW FCS except Mk 116 in CG 26
	1 SPG-53A radar in CG 26, 29, 32, 34
	1 SPG-53F radar in CG 27–28, 30–31, 33
	1 SPG-55B radar

These are "single-end" guided missile cruisers built to screen aircraft carriers. The nuclear-propelled TRUXTUN is similar.

The BELKNAP was severely damaged in a collision with the carrier JOHN F. KENNEDY (CV 67) in the Ionian Sea on the night of 22 November 1975. The cruiser was rebuilt at the Philadelphia Naval Shipyard, arriving at the yard on 30 January 1976 and returning to sea in April 1980. (Recommissioned on 10 May 1980.)

Classification: These ships were originally classified as guided missile frigates (DLG 26–34); they were changed to CG on 30 June 1975.

Guns: Two 3-inch/50 cal AA single guns originally mounted amidships have been removed with quad Harpoon missile tubes fitted in their place. Two Phalanx CIWS are to be installed in these ships.

Helicopters: The helicopter hangar in these ships varies in size; most are approximately 43 feet long and 14 feet wide; the JOUETT and STANDLEY have hangars approximately 55 feet long.

Missiles: The WAINWRIGHT was the first ship to be fitted with the SM-2 version of the Standard missile, conducting evaluation of that missile in 1977.

Torpedoes: As built, these ships had two Mk 25 torpedo tubes in their after superstructure, angled out one to starboard and one to port. They have been removed.

BELKNAP (1980, U.S. Navy, Walt Fields)

The BELKNAP going to sea after her rehabilitation at the Philadelphia Naval Shipyard from 1976–1980. The cruiser retains her basic DLG/CG configuration, with updated systems. Quad Harpoon launchers will be fitted on the platforms abaft the LAMPS hangar. (Single Harpoon tubes were installed at the time of her recommissioning.) In the accompanying photo note the stern openings for SLQ-25 Nixie torpedo countermeasures and the SLQ-32(V)3 EW suite on the port bridge wing. (1980, U.S. Navy)

The STERETT at Hong Kong. Visible are the quad Harpoon missile launchers and, forward of the Harpoons, chaff rockets to decoy hostile antiship missiles. Although these ships lack the second missile launcher of the previous DLG/CG classes, the LAMPS capability and 5-inch DP gun make them more versatile ships. (1979, Giorgio Arra)

1 NUCLEAR-PROPELLED GUIDED MISSILE CRUISER: "BAINBRIDGE" TYPE

Number	Name	FY/SCB	Builder	Laid down	Launched	Commissioned	Status
CGN 25	BAINBRIDGE	56/189	Bethlehem Steel Co (Quincy)	15 May 1959	15 Apr 1961	6 Oct 1962	**PA**

Displacement:	7,700 tons standard
	8,580 tons full load
Length:	550 feet (167.6 m) wl
	565 feet (172.5 m) oa
Beam:	58 feet (17.7 m)
Draft:	29 feet (7.9 m)
Propulsion:	steam turbines; 60,000 shp; 2 shafts
Reactors:	2 pressurized-water D2G
Speed:	30+ knots
Manning:	499 (30 O + 469 enlisted)
Helicopters:	None
Missiles:	2 twin Mk 10 Mod 5/6 launchers for Terrier/Standard-ER SAM (80)
	2 quad launchers for Harpoon SSM Mk 141
Guns:	2 20-mm AA Mk 67 (2 × 1)
ASW weapons:	1 8-tube ASROC launcher Mk 16
	6 12.75-inch (324-mm) torpedo tubes Mk 32 (2 × 3)
Radars:	SPS-10D surface search
	SPS-37 air search
	SPS-39 3-D search
Sonars:	SQS-23 bow-mounted
Fire control:	1 Mk 11 weapon direction system
	4 Mk 76 missile FCS
	1 Mk 111 ASW FCS
	4 SPG-55B radar

The BAINBRIDGE was the U.S. Navy's third nuclear-propelled surface warship. She differs from the later TRUXTUN in being a "double-ended" missile ship and in not having a helicopter-support capability.

Classification: Originally classified as a guided missile frigate (DLGN 25); changed to cruiser on 30 June 1975.

Guns: The two 3-inch/50 cal AA twin mounts previously fitted amidships have been removed. Two single-barrel 20-mm guns can be mounted on pedestals alongside the after missile directors. Two Phalanx CIWS are to be installed in the BAINBRIDGE.

BAINBRIDGE (1980, U.S. Navy, PH3 Roland Otero)

The BAINBRIDGE steaming at high speed off the coast of southern California. Her late-1970s modernization enlarged the superstructure to accommodate additional electronic equipment. The Harpoon launchers are abaft the after SPG-55B radars; the Mk 32 torpedo tubes are barely visible forward of the motor launchers. When installed, the 20-mm guns are fitted near the Harpoons. (1979, U.S. Navy, PH2 P. J. Salesi)

9 GUIDED MISSILE CRUISERS: "LEAHY" CLASS

Number	Name	FY/SCB	Builder	Laid down	Launched	Commissioned	Status
CG 16	LEAHY	58/172	Bath Iron Works	3 Dec 1959	1 July 1961	4 Aug 1962	**PA**
CG 17	HARRY E. YARNELL	58/172	Bath Iron Works	31 May 1960	9 Dec 1961	2 Feb 1963	**AA**
CG 18	WORDEN	58/172	Bath Iron Works	19 Sep 1960	2 June 1962	3 Aug 1963	**PA**
CG 19	DALE	59/172	New York Shipbuilding	6 Sep 1960	28 July 1962	23 Nov 1963	**AA**
CG 20	RICHMOND K. TURNER	59/172	New York Shipbuilding	9 Jan 1961	6 Apr 1963	13 June 1964	**AA**
CG 21	GRIDLEY	59/172	Puget Sound Bridge & DD Co	15 July 1960	31 July 1961	25 May 1963	**PA**
CG 22	ENGLAND	59/172	Todd Shipyards (San Pedro)	4 Oct 1960	6 Mar 1962	7 Dec 1963	**PA**
CG 23	HALSEY	59/172	San Francisco Naval Shipyard	26 Aug 1960	15 Jan 1962	20 July 1963	**PA**
CG 24	REEVES	59/172	Puget Sound Naval Shipyard	1 July 1960	12 May 1962	15 May 1964	**PA**

Displacement:	5,670 tons standard
	7,800 tons full load
Length:	533 feet (162.5 m) oa
Beam:	55 feet (16.8 m)
Draft:	25 feet (7.62 m)
Propulsion:	steam turbines (GE in CG 16–18, De Laval in CG 19–22, Allis-Chalmers in CG 23–24); 85,000 shp; 2 shafts
Boilers:	4 1,200-psi (Babcock & Wilcox in CG 16–18, Foster Wheeler in CG 19–24)
Speed:	32 knots
Range:	8,000 n. miles at 20 knots
Manning:	399–407 (23–24 O + 376–383 enlisted)
Helicopters:	none
Missiles:	2 twin Mk 10 Mod 5/6 launchers for Terrier/Standard-ER SAM (80)
Guns:	4 3-inch (76-mm) 50 cal AA Mk 33 (2 × 2) in CG 16, 18–19, 22 (see notes)
ASW weapons:	1 8-tube ASROC launcher Mk 16
	6 12.75-inch (324-mm) torpedo tubes Mk 32 (2 × 3)
Radars:	SPS-10 surface search
	SPS-43 air search; being replaced by SPS-49
	SPS-48 3-D search
Sonars:	SQS-23 bow-mounted
Fire control:	1 Mk 11 weapon direction system
	4 Mk 76 missile FCS
	1 Mk 114 ASW FCS
	4 SPG-55B radar

These are "double-ended" missile cruisers, the smallest U.S. Navy ships classified as cruisers. The WORDEN is home-ported in Yokosuka, Japan.

Classification: Originally these ships were classified as guided missile frigates (DLG 16–24); they were changed to cruisers on 30 June 1975.

Design: These ships introduced the "mack" superstructure (combination masts and exhausts stacks) in U.S. warships.

Guns: As built, all ships of this class had two 3-inch gun mounts amidships. They are being removed, with Harpoon missile launchers installed in their place. The two Mk 63 gun FCS associated with the 3-inch guns have been removed from all ships.

These ships are scheduled to receive the Phalanx CIWS.

Sonars: The SQQ-23 PAIR sonar will be fitted in these ships.

ENGLAND (1978, Giorgio Arra)

LEAHY (1980, Giorgio Arra)

LEAHY (1980, Giorgio Arra)

2 GUIDED MISSILE CRUISERS: "ALBANY" CLASS

Number	Name	Builder	Laid down	Launched	CA Comm.	CG Comm.	Status
CG 10	ALBANY (ex-CA 123)	Bethlehem Steel Co (Quincy)	6 Mar 1944	30 June 1945	15 June 1946	3 Nov 1962	AR
CG 11	CHICAGO (ex-CA 136)	Philadelphia Navy Yard	28 July 1943	20 Aug 1944	1 Jan 1945	2 May 1964	PR

Displacement:	13,700 tons standard
	17,500 tons full load
Length:	664 feet (202.4 m) wl
	673 feet (205.3 m) oa
Beam:	70 feet (21.6 m)
Draft:	27 feet (8.2 m)
Propulsion:	steam turbines (GE); 120,000 shp; 4 shafts
Boilers:	4 600-psi (Babcock & Wilcox)
Speed:	32.5 knots
Manning:	835 (51 O + 784 enlisted)
Helicopters:	utility helicopter in CG 11
Missiles:	2 twin Mk 12 Mod 1 launchers for Talos SAM (92)
	2 twin Mk 11 Mod 1/2 launchers for Tartar SAM (80)
Guns:	2 5-inch (127-mm) 38 cal DP Mk 24 (2 × 1)
ASW weapons:	1 8-tube ASROC launcher Mk 16
	6 12.75-inch (324-mm) torpedo tubes Mk 32 (2 × 3)
Radars:	SPS-10C surface search
	SPS-30 height-finding in CG 11
	SPS-43A air search
	SPS-48 3-D search
Sonars:	SQS-23 keel-mounted
Fire control:	1 Mk 6 weapon direction system
	2 Mk 56 gun FCS
	4 Mk 74 missile FCS
	2 Mk 77 missile FCS
	1 Mk 111 ASW FCS
	4 SPG-49B radar
	4 SPG-51C radar
	4 SPW-2B radar
	2 Mk 35 radar

ALBANY during NATO Operation Display in the Mediterranean. She served as flagship of the U.S. Sixth Fleet until 1980 when relieved by the destroyer tender PUGET SOUND (AD 38). Both SPS-30 radars have been removed while the CHICAGO retained one aft when decommissioned in 1980. (1976, U.S. Navy, PHAN M. S. Adams)

These ships were fully converted to "double-ended" missile cruisers from conventional heavy (8-inch gun) cruisers. The ALBANY was originally of the OREGON CITY (CA 122) class and the CHICAGO of the BALTIMORE (CA 68) class. The ALBANY was decommissioned on 1 February 1980 and the CHICAGO on 1 March 1980; they were the last war-built cruisers in active service with the U.S. Navy.

Aircraft: The CHICAGO retained her cruiser stern aircraft hangar after her conversion to a missile ship. The hangar was 41 1/2-feet long and 16-feet wide, connected to the main deck by an elevator 39 2/3-feet long and 14 1/2-feet wide.

Class: The COLUMBUS (CG 12, ex-CA 74), the third conversion of this class, was laid up in reserve in 1975 and stricken on 9 August 1976.

Conversion: During their missile conversion these ships were stripped down to their main deck, with all their guns and existing superstructure removed. The new superstructure is largely aluminum, with a large "mack" structure combining masts and exhaust stacks. Conversion was SCB-173.

Guns: After their conversion to missile ships, these ships were not fitted with guns; they subsequently were fitted with single, open-mount 5-inch guns to provide minimal defense against low-flying subsonic aircraft and small-boat attacks.

Missiles: The original missile cruiser conversion provided for these ships to carry the Regulus II strategic cruise missile. After cancellation of that program in 1958, plans were developed to arm these ships with eight Polaris SLBMs; however, those weapons were not installed.

CHICAGO (1979, Giorgio Arra)

CHICAGO (1979, Giorgio Arra)

1 NUCLEAR-PROPELLED GUIDED MISSILE CRUISER: "LONG BEACH" TYPE

Number	Name	FY/SCB	Builder	Laid down	Launched	Commissioned	Status
CGN 9 (ex-CLGN 160)	LONG BEACH	57/169	Bethlehem Steel Co (Quincy)	2 Dec 1957	14 July 1959	9 Sep 1961	**PA**

Displacement:	14,200 tons standard
	17,350 tons full load
Length:	721¼ feet (219.8 m) oa
Beam:	73¼ feet (22.3 m)
Draft:	29 feet (8.8 m)
Propulsion:	steam turbines (GE); ~80,000 shp; 2 shafts
Reactors:	2 pressurized-water C1W
Speed:	30+ knots
Range:	90,000 n. miles at 30 knots
	360,000 n. miles at 20 knots
Manning:	983 (61 O + 922 enlisted)
Helicopters:	none
Missiles:	2 twin Mk 10 Mod 1/2 launchers for Terrier/Standard-ER SAM (120)
	2 quad launchers for Harpoon SSM Mk 141
Guns:	2 5-inch (127-mm) 38 cal DP Mk 30 (2 × 1)
ASW weapons:	1 8-tube ASROC launcher Mk 16
	6 12.75-inch (324-mm) torpedo tubes Mk 32 (2 × 2)

Radars:	SPS-12 air search
	(4) SPS-32 fixed-array air search
	(4) SPS-33 fixed-array 3-D search
	SPS-65 threat warning
Sonars:	SQS-23 bow-mounted
Fire control:	1 Mk 6 weapon direction system
	2 Mk 56 gun FCS
	4 Mk 76 missile FCS
	1 Mk 111 ASW FCS
	4 SPG-55A radar
	2 Mk 35 radar

The LONG BEACH was the first U.S. cruiser to be constructed since World War II, the first nuclear-propelled surface warship, and the first warship to be built with guided missiles as the main battery.

Classification: The LONG BEACH was ordered as a guided missile light cruiser (CLGN 160) on 15 October 1956, reclassified as a

An artist's impression of the LONG BEACH after her modernization in the early 1980s. The distinctive SPS-32/33 "billboard" radars are removed and conventional SPS-48 and SPS-49 installed, the latter on a lattice mast aft. Harpoon launchers are fitted amidships (just forward of the lattice mast) and Tomahawk launchers aft. Note that both Phalanx guns are fitted on the after superstructure. (U.S. Navy drawing by T. Jones)

guided missile cruiser (CGN 160) on 6 December 1956, and renumbered CGN 9 on 1 July 1957.

Design: The LONG BEACH was initially proposed as a large destroyer or "frigate" of some 7,800 tons (standard displacement): subsequently her design was enlarged to accommodate additional missile systems to take maximum advantage of the benefits of nuclear propulsion.

Engineering: The C1W reactors in the LONG BEACH are essentially the same as the A2Ws in the aircraft carrier ENTERPRISE (CVN 65). After having steamed more than 167,700 miles on her initial reactor cores, the LONG BEACH was refueled during an overhaul from August 1965 to February 1966.

Guns: As built, the LONG BEACH had no guns; subsequently she was fitted with two 5-inch guns to provide minimal defense against attacks by subsonic aircraft or small craft.

The ship is scheduled to receive two Phalanx CIWS.

Missiles: The LONG BEACH was built with a twin Talos Mk 12 launcher aft. It was removed in 1979 along with the associated Mk 77 missile FCS, SPG-49B and SPW-2B radars. Harpoon SSM tubes were installed aft of the superstructure on the main deck.

Mk 26 Standard missile launchers were to have been installed in place of the Mk 10 launchers during the planned Aegis conversion. (See Radars, below.)

The original LONG BEACH design provided for the ship to carry the Regulus II strategic cruise missile and, after cancellation of that program in 1958, the Polaris SLBM. Neither weapon was installed.

Radars: The FY 1978 budget provided $371 million to begin Aegis conversion. The Aegis AAW system would have included the fixed-array SPY-1A radars in place of the current SPS-32/33 radars (plus two Mk 26 missile launchers). However, the conversion was canceled because of concern that the new cruiser construction program would be reduced.

Instead, during her 1980 modernization the LONG BEACH received SPS-48C and SPS-49 radars in place of her SPS-32/33 radars. (The square island structure is retained with 1¾-inch armor being fitted from the 05 to 08 levels.)

Sonars: The ship is being fitted with SQQ-23 PAIR sonar.

LONG BEACH (1980, Giorgio Arra)

The LONG BEACH off San Diego, Calif., with her Mk 12 Talos launcher and associated radars and fire control removed. Note the cut-down after structure; barely visible are eight Harpoon launchers just behind the after structure. Plans to provide the LONG BEACH with Aegis were shot down by nuclear-propulsion advocates who feared the conversion would lead to a cutback in nuclear cruiser construction. The two 5-inch DP mounts are located in the amidships clutter. (1979, Giorgio Arra)

1 GUIDED MISSILE CRUISER: CONVERTED "CLEVELAND" CLASS

Number	Name	Builder	Laid down	Launched	CL Comm.	CLG Comm.	Status
CG 5 (ex-CL 91)	OKLAHOMA CITY	Cramp Shipbuilding (Philadelphia)	8 Mar 1942	20 Feb 1944	22 Dec 1944	7 Sep 1960	PR

Displacement:	10,670 tons standard
	14,600 tons full load
Length:	600 feet (182.9 m) wl
	610$^{1}/_{12}$ feet (185.9 m) oa
Beam:	66$^{1}/_{3}$ feet (20.2 m)
Draft:	25 feet (7.6 m)
Propulsion:	steam turbines (GE); 100,000 shp; 4 shafts
Boilers:	4 600-psi (Babcock & Wilcox)
Speed:	31 knots
Manning:	~860 (~60 O + ~800 enlisted)
Flag:	216 (50 O + 166 enlisted)
Helicopters:	utility helicopter embarked (no hangar)
Missiles:	1 twin Mk 7 Mod 0 launcher for Talso SAM (46)
Guns:	3 6-inch (152-mm) 47 cal Mk 16 (1 × 3)
	2 5-inch (127-mm) 38 cal DP Mk 32 (1 × 2)
ASW weapons:	none
Radars:	SPS-10C surface search
	SPS-30 height-finding
	SPS-43A air search
Sonars:	none

Fire control:	1 Mk 2 weapon direction system	2 SPG-49A radar
	1 Mk 34 gun director	2 SPW-2A radar
	1 Mk 37 gun FCS	1 Mk 13 radar
	1 Mk 77 missile FCS	1 Mk 25 radar

The OKLAHOMA CITY is the only survivor of six CLEVELAND (CL 55)-class cruisers converted to "single-ended" missile ships. Three were converted to Talos missiles (CLG 3-5) and three to Terrier missiles (CLG 6-8), with two of each type being additionally fitted as fleet flagships. The OKLAHOMA CITY served as flagship of the Seventh Fleet in the Far East (based at Yokosuka, Japan) until 1979 when relieved by the BLUE RIDGE (LCC 19). She was decommissioned on 15 December 1979.

Classification: The ship was built as the CL 91, reclassified as CLG 5 upon conversion to missile configuration, and subsequently changed to CG 5 on 30 June 1975.

Conversion: The ship is a partial conversion; unlike the ALBANY class, she retained much of the original superstructure and twin-funnel arrangement; the after 6-inch gun turrets were replaced by a missile launcher; the forward superstructure was enlarged for flag accommodations, and only one forward 6-inch gun turret with one 5-inch gun mount was retained.

The original armament was: 12 6-inch guns, 12 5-inch guns, 28 40-mm guns, plus 20-mm AA guns. Original pole masts were replaced by elaborate lattice masts and platforms for radar, TACAN, and EW antennas. The Talos conversion was SCB-140.

OKLAHOMA CITY (1978, Giorgio Arra)

The last of six CLEVELAND-class light cruisers converted to gun-missile configuration, the OKLAHOMA CITY was Seventh Fleet flagship until laid up in 1979. Two BALTIMORE-class heavy cruisers were similarly converted in the 1950s. The "Okay City" and three others were fitted as fleet flagships, with enlarged bridges, additional accommodations and communications spaces, and special electronic equipment. Note the helicopter on her fantail. (1979, Giorgio Arra)

2 HEAVY CRUISERS: "DES MOINES" CLASS

Number	Name	Builder	Laid down	Launched	Commissioned	Status
CA 134	DES MOINES	Bethlehem Steel Co (Quincy)	28 May 1945	27 Sep 1946	16 Nov 1948	AR
CA 139	SALEM	Bethlehem Steel Co (Quincy)	4 June 1945	25 Mar 1947	14 May 1949	AR

Displacement:	17,000 tons standard
	21,500 tons full load
Length:	700 feet (213.4 m) wl
	716½ feet (218.4 m) oa
Beam:	76⅓ feet (23.3 m)
Draft:	26 feet (7.9 m)
Propulsion:	steam turbines (GE); 120,000 shp; 4 shafts
Boilers:	4 600-psi (Babcock & Wilcox)
Speed:	33 knots
Manning:	1,800 (~115 O + 1,685 enlisted)
Helicopters:	utility helicopter embarked (no hangar)
Guns:	9 8-inch (203-mm) 55 cal Mk 16 (3 × 3)
	12 5-inch (127-mm) 38 cal DP Mk 32 (6 × 2)
	16 3-inch (76-mm) 50 cal AA Mk 32 (8 × 2)
ASW weapons:	none
Radars:	SG-6 air search
	SPS-8A height-finding
	SPS-12 air search in CA 139
Sonars:	none

Fire control:	
4 Mk 37 gun FCS	2 Mk 13 radar
2 Mk 54 gun director	4 Mk 25 radar
4 Mk 56 gun FCS	2 Mk 34 radar in CA 139
2 Mk 63 gun FCS	4 Mk 35 radar
2 SPG-50 radar in CA 134	

The DES MOINES class represents the final heavy cruiser (8-inch gun) design to be constructed by any navy. They are the largest nonmissile cruisers afloat. They were completed too late for service in World War II, but were employed extensively as fleet flagships during their active careers. The SALEM was decommissioned on 30 January 1959 and the DES MOINES on 14 July 1961.

Aircraft: The DES MOINES was completed with two stern catapults and embarked four floatplanes. The catapults were subsequently removed, and all ships of the class operated utility helicopters.

Class: Twelve ships of this class were planned, the CA 134, 139–143, and 148–153. Only three ships were completed, the two above units and the NEWPORT NEWS (CA 148), stricken in 1978. The NEWPORT NEWS was the world's last active heavy cruiser. Nine ships were canceled in 1945–1946, prior to completion.

Design: The class was designed specifically to carry the 8-inch gun Mk 16; they thus needed a larger hull than previous heavy cruisers. The design is an improved version of the previous OREGON CITY (CA 122) class which, in turn, was a modification of the BALTIMORE (CA 68) class.

Guns: The principal innovation of this class was the rapid-firing 8-inch gun Mk 16, which used metal cartridge cases in place of the bagged powder charges used in all other 8-inch-gun cruisers.

As built, these ships had a secondary battery of 12 5-inch DP guns, as many as 24 3-inch AA guns, and 12 20-mm AA guns. The 20-mm weapons were quickly removed and the 3-inch guns reduced, with the SALEM and DES MOINES being mothballed with only 16 3-inch guns installed.

The DES MOINES steams through the Mediterranean during her 1958–1961 tour as Sixth Fleet flagship. She has HUP "hupmobile" helicopters and the admiral's vehicles and boats parked aft. The SALEM and DES MOINES are the only heavy cruisers still afloat; their Mk 54 gun directors are on tall, distinctive towers fore and aft; they were among the relatively few single-funnel cruisers to be built. (1960, U.S. Navy)

POST–WORLD WAR II CRUISER PROGRAMS

U.S. World War II cruiser programs reached hull number CL 159 (with hulls CL 154–159 being canceled in 1945). All heavy (CA), light (CL), and antiaircraft (CLAA) cruisers were numbered in the same series. Only one ship was added to this cruiser list in the postwar period: the nuclear-propelled LONG BEACH, ordered as CLGN 160, changed to CGN 160, and completed as CGN 9.

HUNTER-KILLER CRUISERS

CLK 1	NORFOLK	completed as DL 1
CLK 2	NEW HAVEN	deferred 1949; canceled 1951

After World War II the U.S. Navy established the classification of hunter-killer cruiser (CLK) for a planned series of small cruisers designed for ASW operations against high-speed submarines. Only one ship, the NORFOLK, was completed; classified as a frigate (DL), she was employed mainly in ASW test and evaluation (e.g., as ASROC test ship).

GUIDED MISSILE CRUISERS

CAG 1	BOSTON (ex-CA 69) reverted to CA; stricken 1973
CAG 2	CANBERRA (ex-CA 70) reverted to CA, stricken in July 1978
CLG 3–8	Converted CLEVELAND class (CL)
CGN 9	LONG BEACH (ex-CLGN/CGN 160)
CG 10	ALBANY (ex-CA 123)
CG 11	CHICAGO (ex-CA 135)
CG 12	COLUMBUS (ex-CA 74)
CG 13	BALTIMORE class; conversion canceled
CG 14	BALTIMORE class; conversion canceled
CG 15	Not used
CG 16–24	LEAHY class (ex-DLG 16–24)
CGN 25	BAINBRIDGE (ex-DLGN 25)
CG 26–34	BELKNAP (ex-DLG 26–34)
CGN 35	TRUXTUN (ex-DLGN 35)
CGN 36–37	CALIFORNIA class (ex-DLGN 36–37)
CGN 38–40	VIRGINIA class (ex-DLGN 38–40)
CGN 41	VIRGINIA class
CG 42–46	Not used
CG 47	TICONDEROGA class (ex-DDG 47)

The guided missile cruiser classifications were established in 1952 to reflect specialized weapons and AAW roles of these ships. In 1975, 25 guided missile frigates (DLG/DLGN) were changed to cruisers, and in 1980 the Aegis-equipped destroyers were reclassified as cruisers.

FRIGATE PROGRAMS

The frigate classifications (DL/DLG/DLGN) were established after 1951 for large destroyers that were designed to operate with fast carrier forces. In general, emphasis has been on AAW systems, although some ships also had the most capable ASW systems available (i.e., large sonar, helicopter, ASROC). The hunter-killer cruiser NORFOLK was completed as the DL 1, while four MITSCHER-class ships ordered as destroyers were completed as DL 2–5.

This frigate classification was abolished on 30 June 1975, and frigate (FF/FFG) was established to indicate smaller ocean escort ships (formerly DE/DEG).

DL 1	NORFOLK (ex-CLK 1)	commissioned 1953; stricken 1973
DL 2	MITSCHER (ex-DD 927)	converted to DDG 35; stricken 1978
DL 3	JOHN S. MCCAIN (ex-DD 928)	converted to DDG 36; stricken 1978
DL 4	WILLIS A. LEE (ex-DD 929)	commissioned 1954; stricken 1972
DL 5	WILKINSON (ex-DD 930)	commissioned 1954; stricken 1974
DLG 6–15	COONTZ class	to DDG 37–46
DLG 16–24	LEAHY class	to CG 16–24
DLGN 25	BAINBRIDGE	to CGN 25
DLG 26–34	BELKNAP class	to CG 26–34
DLGN 35	TRUXTUN	to CGN 35
DLGN 36–37	CALIFORNIA class	to CGN 36–37
DLGN 38–40	VIRGINIA class	to CGN 38–40

STERETT (1977, Giorgio Arra)

9 Destroyers

The Navy's cruiser and destroyer force-level goals are described at the beginning of Chapter 8 of this edition. The Navy had 37 missile-armed destroyers (DDG) and 43 all-gun destroyers (DD) in active service at the beginning of 1981. Another 16 older destroyers manned by composite reserve and active crews were in the Naval Reserve Force (see below).

Four missile-armed ships of the KIDD class were under construction as was the 31st ship of the SPRUANCE class. In addition, a new class of destroyers, now designated DDGX, is proposed for construction, with the lead ship scheduled for the FY 1985 shipbuilding program. Forty-nine ships are planned as replacements for CG/DDG-type ships that will be retired in the late 1980s and 1990s.

The DDGXs will be primarily AAW ships armed with Vertical Launch Systems (VLS) for firing combinations of antiaircraft, antiship, and land-attack missiles, as well as possibly an ASROC-type weapon. Current Navy planning is for a ship of about 7,000 tons full load, i.e., smaller than the SPRUANCE and TICONDEROGA classes. However, the need for advanced radars for the future AAW role may require the ship to have the Aegis/SPY-1 electronics, resulting in a larger ship.

The proposed air-capable destroyer program has been canceled because of lack of Navy interest and support. The program was strongly supported by several members of Congress. The basic concept provided for constructing additional SPRUANCE-class destroyers with increased aviation facilities for operating additional helicopters or VSTOL aircraft. Two ships were authorized by Congress in FY 1979 and one ship was funded. However, the Navy preferred to order another SPRUANCE-class ship.

Electronics: The CHARLES F. ADAMS and SPRUANCE classes are being fitted with the SLQ-32(V)2 electronic warfare system.

Names: Destroyers are named for officers and enlisted personnel of the Navy and Marine Corps, secretaries of the Navy, members of Congress, and inventors who have influenced naval affairs.

Naval Reserve Force: In January 1981 there were 16 destroyers assigned to the Naval Reserve Force, 15 modernized (FRAM) Gearing-class destroyers of World War II construction and the postwar-built EDSON, which serves as both an NRF ship and a training ship at Newport, R.I.

The Navy had planned to scrap or transfer all but five of these ships during 1980–1981 because of their poor material condition and high operating costs. However, congressional opposition to any further reduction of the NRF force has delayed their disposal. Still, it appears likely that all of the ships will be decommissioned and stricken in 1981. The 16 ships are listed in this chapter, with only the five scheduled for retention.

(In the following table, AAW indicates Terrier/Standard-ER or Tartar/Standard-MR surface-to-air missile systems; ASW indicates ASROC and SQS-23/26/53 sonar; Helicopter indicates helicopter support facilities; and Guns indicates the largest caliber fitted in the ships.)

Type	Class/Ship	Active	Building[a]	NRF	Commission	AAW	ASW	Helicopter	Guns
DDG 993	KIDD	—	4	—	1980–1981	✔	✔	✔	5-inch
DDG 37	COONTZ	10	—	—	1960–1961	✔	✔	—	5-inch
DDG 31	Conv. SHERMAN	4	—	—	1956–1959	✔	✔	—	5-inch
DDG 2	ADAMS	23	—	—	1960–1964	✔	✔	—	5-inch
DD 963	SPRUANCE	30	1	—	1975–1980	—	✔	✔	5-inch
DD 931	Mod. SHERMAN	8	—	—	1956–1959	✔	✔	—	5-inch
DD 931	SHERMAN	5	—	1	1955–1959	—	—	—	5-inch
DD 710	GEARING	—	—	15	1945–1946	—	✔	—	5-inch

[a] Includes ships authorized through FY 1981.

Harbinger of future destroyer firepower? A Tomahawk cruise missile is launched from the SPRUANCE-class destroyer MERRILL during the first test firing of the missile from a surface ship. Destroyer-type ships, since World War II employed primarily in the AAW/ASW defensive role, have gained new capabilities during the past few years with the Harpoon antiship missile. The Tomahawk, in the antiship (T-ASM) and land-attack (T-LAM) configurations, offers the opportunity for even more potent surface combatants. (1980, U.S. Navy)

ADVANCED GUIDED MISSILE DESTROYERS (DDGX)

The DDGX program is being developed to provide replacement ships for the large number of U.S. cruisers and destroyers that will be retired by the year 2000, primarily the CG 16, CG 26, DDG 2, and DDG 37 classes. A total of 49 ships is planned in the DDGX program, based on the following schedule:

lead DDGX in FY 1985
2 DDGX in FY 1987
5 DDGX in FY 1988 and succeeding years

However, the Congress has expressed concern over this schedule and has urged an earlier start date. A FY 1983 authorization for the lead ship has been proposed by several members of Congress as well as some shipbuilders.

These ships will emphasize AAW and strike capabilities at the expense of ASW and gunfire support capabilities.

The data presented here are preliminary, with a rather long (five-year) design and development period planned by the Navy prior to awarding the contract for the lead DDGX in January 1985. Delivery of the lead ship would occur about 1990.

Builders: The Navy intends that two shipyards will construct the DDGX class, with the second yard constructing one FY 1987 ship and two or three of the FY 1988 ships and sharing subsequent programs with the lead shipyard.

Displacement:	~7,000 tons full load
Length:	~500 feet (152.4 m) oa
Beam:	
Draft:	
Propulsion:	gas turbines; 2 shafts
Speed:	~30 knots
Manning	~325 (~25 O + ~300 enlisted)
Helicopters:	no facilities
Missiles:	2 vertical launchers for Harpoon/Standard/Tomahawk (61 + 29)

Guns:	1 76-mm 62 cal AA Mk 75 (1 × 1)
	2 20-mm Phalanx CIWS Mk 15 (2 × 1)
ASW weapons:	ASROC fired from vertical launchers
	6 12.75-inch (324-mm) torpedo tubes Mk 32 (2 × 3)
Radars:	(4) MFAR (Multi-Function Array Radar)
	SPS-55 threat warning
Sonars:	SQS-53 (modified) bow-mounted
Fire control:	2 Mk 99 missile directors

Cost: The principal design constraint on these ships is a $500 million cost in FY 1980 monies for follow-on ships. This compares to an $800 million cost for a TICONDEROGA (CG 47)-class ship.

Design: The above characteristics reflect the so-called 3-A option of a series of designs that evolved from the Navy's DDX study of 1979. That study sought lower-cost alternatives to the TICONDEROGA-class ships to provide the large numbers of AAW-oriented surface combatants the Navy requires.

Electronics: These ships will have a more austere electronics suite than the TICONDEROGA class's Aegis system. However, a leading candidate for the MFAR is an improved (and smaller) variant of the RCA SPY-1 radar. Operationally, the DDGX would operate with a CG 47-class ship with the latter performing certain detection, tracking, and guidance functions for both ships through data links.

The DDGX will have the SLQ-32(V)2 electronic warfare system.

Guns: All U.S. destroyers since the FARRAGUT (DD 348) of 1934 have been armed with 5-inch guns. The 76-mm gun of the DDGX design is considered optional; however, space and weight will be reserved, if possible, for installation of a 5-inch Mk 45 lightweight gun.

Helicopters: These ships will not have a helicopter flight deck or hangar under the 3-A option. However, data links will be provided to enable the ships to operate with SH-60B LAMPS helicopters. Also, facilities will be provided to permit refueling of helicopters while they hover over the ship.

This is an artist's impression of the mid–1982 version of the DDG 51 (formerly DDGX). The final design was not complete when this second printing of the 12th edition went to press. As shown here, the ship has a 61–tube vertical launch system forward, probably a 29–tube launcher and 5–inch gun aft, and two Gatling guns. Four "faces" of an SPY–1D radar are on the single superstructure.

These ships are AAW variants of the SPRUANCE-class destroyers. As conceived in the late 1960s, the so-called DX/DXG program was to produce ASW and AAW variants of the same basic destroyer design. The ASW variant evolved into the SPRUANCE class; however, the U.S. Navy did not order any of the AAW ships. The Iranian government announced plans to order two AAW ships based on the SPRUANCE design on 15 December 1973, with an announcement for four additional ships on 27 August 1974. Only four ships were formally ordered on 23 March 1978 under the U.S. Foreign Military Sales program.

The CALLAGHAN under construction at the Litton/Ingalls West Bank yard in Pascagoula, Miss. The masts of the SCOTT are seen at right. The similarity of the KIDD and SPRUANCE classes of destroyers and the TICONDEROGA (CG 47)-class cruisers will simplify logistics, training, and maintenance for all of these ships. Proposals to develop still another SPRUANCE variant as the DDGX have been put forward by Litton/Ingalls as well as some members of Congress and naval analysts. (1980, Litton/Ingalls)

The KIDD is the first of four modified SPRUANCE-class missile destroyers ordered by the late Shah of Iran but taken over by the U.S. Navy after the Iranian Revolution. The planned SPRUANCE DGX series of missile ships were not built except for these four variations. (1981, Ingalls Shipbuilding)

(4) GUIDED MISSILE DESTROYERS: "KIDD" CLASS (FORMER IRANIAN SHIPS)

Number	Name	FY/SCB	Builder	Laid down	Launched	Commissioned	Status
DDG 993	KIDD	79S	Litton/Ingalls (Pascagoula)	26 June 1978	13 Oct 1979	1981	Bldg.
DDG 994	CALLAGHAN	79S	Litton/Ingalls (Pascagoula)	23 Oct 1978	19 Jan 1980	1981	Bldg.
DDG 995	SCOTT	79S	Litton/Ingalls (Pascagoula)	12 Feb 1979	29 Mar 1980	1981	Bldg.
DDG 996	CHANDLER	79S	Litton/Ingalls (Pascagoula)	12 May 1979	28 June 1980	1981	Bldg.

Displacement:	8,140 tons full load	ASW weapons:	ASROC fired from forward Mk 26 launcher
Length:	529 feet (161.2 m) wl		6 12.75-inch (324-mm) torpedo tubes Mk 32 (2 × 3)
	563$^{1}/_{3}$ feet (171.1 m) oa	Radars:	SPS-48 3-D search
Beam:	55 feet (16.8 m)		SPS-55 surface search
Draft:	29.9 feet (9.1 m)	Sonars:	SQS-53 bow-mounted
Propulsion:	gas turbines (General Electric); 80,000 shp; 2 shafts	Fire control:	2 Mk 74 missile FCS
Speed:	30+ knots		1 Mk 86 gun FCS
Manning:	338 (20 O + 318 enlisted)		1 Mk 116 ASW FCS
Helicopters:	2 SH-60B Seahawk		2 SPG-51 radar
Missiles:	2 twin Mk 26 Mod 0/1 launchers for Standard-MR SAM (68)		1 SPG-60 radar
	2 quad Mk 141 tubes for Harpoon SSM		1 SPQ-9A radar
Guns:	2 5-inch (127-mm) 54 cal DP Mk 45 (2 × 1)		

The SCOTT at high speed. The hull and machinery of the SPRUANCE, TICONDEROGA, and KIDD classes are identical; some had sought to have the same hull and power plant similarly used in the DDGX/DDG 51 program. (1981, Ingalls Shipbuilding)

After the fall of the Shah's government in Iran in early 1979 the U.S. Navy sought to acquire the four ships then under construction. The FY 1979 supplemental budget provided $1,353 million for the purchase of the ships, and they were formally acquired on 25 July 1979.

These ships differ from the contemporary CG 47 Aegis cruisers primarily in not having the Aegis/SPY-1A system.

Classification: These ships were originally ordered as F-DD 993–996, indicating that they were basically SPRUANCE-class ships intended for foreign use. They were changed to DDG with the same nonmissile hull numbers on 8 August 1979.

Design: The Iranian government required that these ships be provided with increased air-conditioning capacity and dust separators for their engine air intakes. See SPRUANCE class for additional notes.

Guns: The Mk 26 Mod 0 missile launcher installed forward has a smaller (24-missile) magazine than the after Mk 26 Mod 1 launcher to provide space for possible installation of the 8-inch Mk 71 gun. These ships are scheduled to receive two Phalanx CIWS.

10 GUIDED MISSILE DESTROYERS: "COONTZ" CLASS

Number	Name	FY/SCB	Builder	Laid down	Launched	Commissioned	Status
DDG 37 (ex-DLG 6)	FARRAGUT	56/142	Bethlehem Steel Co (Quincy)	3 June 1957	18 July 1958	10 Dec 1960	**AA**
DDG 38 (ex-DLG 7)	LUCE	56/142	Bethlehem Steel Co (Quincy)	1 Oct 1957	11 Dec 1958	20 May 1961	**AA**
DDG 39 (ex-DLG 8)	MACDONOUGH	56/142	Bethlehem Steel Co (Quincy)	15 Apr 1958	9 July 1959	4 Nov 1961	**AA**
DDG 40 (ex-DLG 9)	COONTZ	56/142	Puget Sound Naval Shipyard	1 Mar 1957	6 Dec 1958	15 July 1960	**AA**
DDG 41 (ex-DLG 10)	KING	56/142	Puget Sound Naval Shipyard	1 Mar 1957	6 Dec 1958	17 Nov 1960	**AA**
DDG 42 (ex-DLG 11)	MAHAN	56/142	San Francisco Naval Shipyard	31 July 1957	7 Oct 1959	25 Aug 1960	**AA**
DDG 43 (ex-DLG 12)	DAHLGREN	57/142	Philadelphia Naval Shipyard	1 Mar 1958	16 Mar 1960	8 Apr 1961	**AA**
DDG 44 (ex-DLG 13)	WM V. PRATT	57/142	Philadelphia Naval Shipyard	1 Mar 1958	16 Mar 1960	4 Nov 1961	**AA**
DDG 45 (ex-DLG 14)	DEWEY	57/142	Bath Iron Works	10 Aug 1957	30 Nov 1958	7 Dec 1959	**AA**
DDG 46 (ex-DLG 15)	PREBLE	57/142	Bath Iron Works	16 Dec 1957	23 May 1959	9 May 1960	**PA**

Displacement:	4,700 tons standard
	5,800 tons full load
Length:	512½ feet (156.2 m) oa
Beam:	52½ feet (15.9 m)
Draft:	25 feet (7.6 m)
Propulsion:	steam turbines (De Laval in DDG 37–39, 45–46; Allis-Chalmers in DDG 40–44); 85,000 shp; 2 shafts
Boilers:	4 1,200-psi (Foster Wheeler in DDG 37–39; Babcock & Wilcox in DDG 40–46)
Speed:	33 knots
Range:	4,000+ n. miles at 20 knots
Manning:	398–399 (24 O + 374–375 enlisted)
Helicopters:	none
Missiles:	1 twin Mk 10 Mod 0 launcher for Terrier/Standard-ER SAM (40)
	2 quad Mk 141 tubes for Harpoon SSM in DDG 37, 40
Guns:	1 5-inch (127-mm) 54 cal DP Mk 42 (1 × 1)
ASW weapons:	1 8-tube ASROC launcher Mk 16
	6 12.75-inch (324-mm) torpedo tubes Mk 32 (2 × 3)
Radars:	SPS-10B search radar
	SPS-29 or SPS-37 air search; being replaced by SPS-49
	SPS-48 3-D search
Sonars:	SQS-23 keel-mounted
Fire control:	1 Mk 11 weapon direction system except Mk 14 in DDG 42
	1 Mk 68 gun FCS
	2 Mk 74 missile FCS
	1 Mk 111 ASW FCS
	1 SPG-53A radar
	2 SPG-55B radar

These ships originally were classified as "frigates" (DLG); although they are now considered destroyers, they have the Terrier/Standard-ER missile system and Naval Tactical Data System (NTDS) of U.S. cruiser classes.

Classification: The first three ships of this class were ordered on 27 January 1956 as all-gun frigates (DL 6–8); they were changed to guided missile frigates (DLG 6–8) on 14 November 1956. These ships were classified as DLG 6–15 from the time of their commissioning until 30 June 1975 when they were changed to guided missile destroyers.

Guns: As built, each ship had two 3-inch/50 cal Mk 33 twin gun mounts aft of the second funnel; these have been removed from all ships. The KING was fitted with the Phalanx CIWS from August 1973 until March 1974 for at-sea evaluation; installed on fantail. These ships are not scheduled to receive the Phalanx CIWS.

Missiles: The MAHAN was the first ship of the class to be fitted with the improved Standard-ER SM-2 missile (1979); the cruiser

WAINWRIGHT was the first ship fitted with the SM-2, in 1978. The Mk 14 weapon direction system and improved Mk 76 Mod 9 missile FCS are installed with the SM-2 refit.

These ships are being armed with the Harpoon antiship missile.

Modernization: All ships underwent AAW modernization between 1968 and 1977 (SCB-243). Radars and fire control systems were updated, NTDS installed (updated in KING and MAHAN) and 3-inch guns removed.

Names: The LUCE was to have been named DEWEY; changed in 1957.

Sonars: These ships will be refitted with the SQQ-23 PAIR sonar.

The COONTZ at Norfolk displays the NATO flag while assigned to the Standing Naval Force Atlantic (STANAVFORLANT). Destroyer-type ships of several NATO navies rotate through the command, established in 1967, for experience in multi-national operations. The COONTZ has her quad Harpoon launchers abaft the after superstructure; at right is the Canadian frigate OTTAWA with her hangar door open. (1979, Giorgio Arra)

The LUCE under way off the southern coast of Cuba. These ships—formerly designated as frigates (DLG)—can be easily distinguished from the smaller DDGs by their ASROC launcher forward and absence of 5-inch gun aft. Although these ships can launch Terrier/Standard-ER missiles, their lack of a helicopter capability limits their versatility. (1978, U.S. Navy)

FARRAGUT (1978, U.S. Navy, PHAN T. K. Grandfield and PH2 B. F. Parker)

4 GUIDED MISSILE DESTROYERS: CONVERTED "SHERMAN" CLASS

Number	Name	FY/SCB	Builder	Laid down	Launched	DL Comm.	DDG Comm.	Status
DDG 31 (ex-DD 936)	DECATUR	54/85	Bethlehem Steel Co (Quincy)	13 Sep 1954	15 Dec 1955	7 Dec 1956	29 Apr 1967	**PA**
DDG 32 (ex-DD 932)	JOHN PAUL JONES	53/85	Bath Iron Works	18 Jan 1954	7 May 1955	5 Apr 1956	23 Sep 1967	**PA**
DDG 33 (ex-DD 949)	PARSONS	56/85A	Ingalls SB Corp	17 June 1957	19 Aug 1958	29 Oct 1959	3 Nov 1967	**PA**
DDG 34 (ex-DD 947)	SOMERS	56/85A	Bath Iron Works	4 Mar 1957	30 May 1958	3 Apr 1959	10 Feb 1968	**PA**

Displacement:	4,150 tons full load	Missiles:	1 single Mk 13 Mod 1 launcher for Tartar/Standard-MR SAM (40)
Length:	407 feet (124.0 m) wl	Guns:	1 5-inch (127-mm) 54 cal DP Mk 42 (1 × 1)
	DDG 31–32 418$^5/_{12}$ feet (127.5 m) oa	ASW weapons:	1 8-tube ASROC launcher Mk 16
	DDG 33–34 418 feet (127.4 m) oa		6 12.75-inch (324-mm) torpedo tubes Mk 32 (2 × 3)
Beam:	DDG 31–32 45$^1/_6$ feet (13.8 m)	Radars:	SPS-10B surface search
	DDG 33–34 45 feet (13.7 m)		SPS-29E air search, except SPS-40 in DDG 34
Draft:	20 feet (6.1 m)		SPS-48 3-D search
Propulsion:	steam turbines (General Electric, except Westinghouse in DDG 32); 70,000 shp; 2 shafts	Sonars:	SQS-23
		Fire control:	1 Mk 4 weapon direction system
Boilers:	4 1,200-psi (Foster Wheeler in DDG 31, 33; Babcock & Wilcox in DDG 32, 34)		1 Mk 68 gun FCS
			1 Mk 74 missile FCS
Speed:	32.5 knots		1 Mk 114 ASW FCS
Range:	3,800+ n. miles at 20 knots		1 SPG-51C radar
Manning:	333–344 (20 O + 313–324 enlisted)		1 SPG-53B radar
Helicopters:	none		

The destroyer PARSONS under way. She has satellite communication antennas on a short mast behind the 5-inch gun and aft attached to the deckhouse (left of the SPG-51C radar). The dome on the second mast is TACAN (Tactical Aircraft Navigation). Note the massive lattice masts to support antennas in the DDG role. (1979, Giorgio Arra)

These ships were converted from FORREST SHERMAN-class destroyers. They have a limited ASW capability and retain only one 5-inch gun; along with the larger COONTZ-class ships, they are the U.S. Navy's only one-gun destroyers, with one 5-inch gun. The PARSONS is based in Yokosuka.

Class: Fourteen other SHERMAN-class destroyers remain in service with the DD designation.

Classification: The DECATUR (ex-DD 936) was changed to DDG 31 on 15 September 1966; the three other ships were changed to DDG on 15 March 1967.

Conversion: Converted to Tartar missile configuration beginning in 1965–1966. The original tripod masts were replaced with lattice masts to support additional radars; ASROC and deckhouse were added aft of second funnel; two after 5-inch gun mounts were removed, and a single-arm missile launcher was installed. The original DDG conversion plan (SCB-240) provided for a Drone Antisubmarine Helicopter (DASH) facility; however, this was deleted in favor of ASROC.

Missiles: These ships have been fitted with the Mk 13 lightweight launcher, which is capable of a high rate of fire (eight rounds per minute). They are limited in firepower by having only one director compared to two directors per launcher in other U.S. missile destroyers.

PARSONS (1979, Giorgio Arra)

SOMERS (1979, Giorgio Arra)

23 GUIDED MISSILE DESTROYERS: "CHARLES F. ADAMS" CLASS

Number	Name	FY/SCB	Builder	Laid down	Launched	Commissioned	Status
DDG 2	CHARLES F. ADAMS	57/155	Bath Iron Works	16 June 1958	8 Sep 1959	10 Sep 1960	**AA**
DDG 3	JOHN KING	57/155	Bath Iron Works	25 Aug 1958	30 Jan 1960	4 Feb 1961	**AA**
DDG 4	LAWRENCE	57/155	New York SB Corp	27 Oct 1958	27 Feb 1960	6 Jan 1962	**AA**
DDG 5	CLAUDE V. RICKETTS	57/155	New York SB Corp	18 May 1959	4 June 1960	5 May 1962	**AA**
DDG 6	BARNEY	57/155	New York SB Corp	18 May 1959	10 Dec 1960	11 Aug 1962	**AA**
DDG 7	HENRY B. WILSON	57/155	Defoe SB Co	28 Feb 1958	23 Apr 1959	17 Dec 1960	**PA**
DDG 8	LYNDE MCCORMICK	57/155	Defoe SB Co	4 Apr 1958	9 Sep 1960	3 June 1961	**PA**
DDG 9	TOWERS	57/155	Todd Shipyards (Seattle)	1 Apr 1958	23 Apr 1959	6 June 1961	**PA**
DDG 10	SAMPSON	58/155	Bath Iron Works	2 Mar 1959	9 Sep 1960	24 June 1961	**AA**
DDG 11	SELLERS	58/155	Bath Iron Works	3 Aug 1959	9 Sep 1960	28 Oct 1961	**AA**
DDG 12	ROBISON	58/155	Defoe SB Co	23 Apr 1959	27 Apr 1960	9 Dec 1961	**PA**
DDG 13	HOEL	58/155	Defoe SB Co	1 June 1960	4 Aug 1960	16 June 1962	**PA**
DDG 14	BUCHANAN	58/155	Todd Shipyards (Seattle)	23 Apr 1959	11 May 1960	7 Feb 1962	**PA**
DDG 15	BERKELEY	59/155	New York SB Corp	1 June 1960	29 July 1961	15 Dec 1962	**PA**
DDG 16	JOSEPH STRAUSS	59/155	New York SB Corp	27 Dec 1960	9 Dec 1961	20 Apr 1963	**PA**
DDG 17	CONYNGHAM	59/155	New York SB Corp	1 May 1961	19 May 1962	13 July 1963	**AA**
DDG 18	SEMMES	59/155	Avondale Marine Ways	18 Aug 1960	20 May 1961	10 Dec 1962	**AA**
DDG 19	TATTNALL	59/155	Avondale Marine Ways	14 Nov 1960	26 Aug 1961	13 Apr 1963	**AA**
DDG 20	GOLDSBOROUGH	60/155	Puget Sound Bridge & Dry Dock Co	3 Jan 1961	15 Dec 1961	9 Nov 1963	**PA**
DDG 21	COCHRANE	60/155	Puget Sound Bridge & Dry Dock Co	31 July 1961	18 July 1962	21 Mar 1964	**PA**
DDG 22	BENJAMIN STODDERT	60/155	Puget Sound Bridge & Dry Dock Co	11 June 1962	8 Jan 1963	12 Sep 1964	**PA**
DDG 23	RICHARD E. BYRD	61/155	Todd Shipyards (Seattle)	12 Apr 1961	6 Feb 1962	7 Mar 1964	**AA**
DDG 24	WADDELL	61/155	Todd Shipyards (Seattle)	6 Feb 1962	26 Feb 1963	28 Aug 1964	**PA**

Displacement:	3,370 tons standard
	4,500 tons full load
Length:	420 feet (128 m) wl
	437 feet (133.2 m) oa
Beam:	47 feet (14.3 m)
Draft:	22 feet (6.7 m)
Propulsion:	steam turbines (General Electric in DDG 2–3, 7–8, 10–13, 15–22; Westinghouse in DDG 4–6, 9, 14, 23–24); 70,000 shp; 2 shafts
Boilers:	4 1,200-psi (Babcock & Wilcox in DDG 2–3, 7–8, 10–13, 20–22; Foster Wheeler in DDG 4–6, 9, 14; Combustion Engineering in DDG 15–19)
Speed:	31.5 knots
Range:	4,500 n. miles at 20 knots
Manning:	333–350 (20 O + 313–330 enlisted)
Helicopters:	none
Missiles:	1 twin Mk 11 Mod 0 launcher for Tartan/Standard-MR SAM (42) in DDG 2–14
	1 twin Mk 13 Mod 0 launcher for Tartar(Standard-MR SAM (40) in DDG 15–24 (see notes)
Guns:	2 5-inch (127-mm) 54 cal DP Mk 42 (2 × 1)
ASW weapons:	1 8-tube ASROC launcher Mk 16
	6 12.75-inch (324-mm) torpedo tubes Mk 32 (2 × 3)
Radars:	SPS-10C/D surface search
	SPS-29 or SPS-37 air search in DDG 2–14
	SPS-40 air search in DDG 15–24
	SPS-39 3-D search
Sonars:	SPS-23 keel-mounted except bow-mounted in DDG 20–24
Fire control:	1 Mk 4 weapon direction system
	1 Mk 68 gun FCS
	2 Mk 74 missile FCS
	1 Mk 111 ASW FCS in DDG 2–15
	1 Mk 114 ASW FCS in DDG 16–24
	2 SPG-51C radar
	1 SPG-53A/E/F radar

This is the largest class of missile-armed surface warships to be constructed for the U.S. Navy, comprising just over one-third of the AAW-capable screening ships available for carrier forces. They are considered highly capable for their size.

Class: Three additional ships of this class were built for Australia

HENRY B. WILSON (1979, Giorgio Arra)

(assigned U.S. hull numbers DDG 25–27) and three for West Germany (DDG 28–30).

Classification: The first eight ships of this class were authorized as all-gun/ASW destroyers (DD 952–959), then changed to guided missile ships and reclassified DDG 952–959 on 16 August 1956; they were changed to DDG 2–9 on 26 June 1957.

Design: The ADAMS design is based on an improved FORREST SHERMAN arrangement, with a Tartar missile launching system in place of the SHERMAN's aftermost 5-inch gun. The last five ships have their sonar in the improved, bow position.

Missiles: These ships can fire the Harpoon antiship missile from their Mk 11 or Mk 13 launcher.

Modernization: The Navy had planned to modernize all 23 ships of this class, extending their useful service life for 15 years beyond the nominal 30 years. The modernizations were to be funded in FY 1980–1983. However, increasing costs and congressional interest in constructing new destroyer-type ships rather than upgrading older units has led to a cutback in the modernization program for the last ten ships. Existing systems will be overhauled and upgraded with the following major equipment changes:

Radars
SPS-65 in place of SPS-10
SPS-40C/D in place of SPS-29 or SPS-37
SPS-52B in place of SPS-39
Sonars
SQQ-23 PAIR in place of SQS-23 (in all ships)
Fire control
Mk 13 weapon direction system in place of Mk 4
Mk 86 gun FCS in place of Mk 68
Mk 74 Mod 8 missile FCS (upgrade)
SPG-60 radar (addition)
SPQ-9A radar (addition)
Command and Control
SYS-1 integrated automatic detection and tracking system (addition)
NTDS improvements
Electronic Warfare
SLQ-32(V)2 (addition)

The modernizations will require at least 18 months per ship.

Names: DDG 5 was originally named BIDDLE; renamed CLAUDE V. RICKETTS on 28 July 1964 (with DLG/CG 34 subsequently named BIDDLE).

CHARLES F. ADAMS (1978, U.S. Navy)

HENRY B. WILSON (1977, Giorgio Arra)

The BENJAMIN STODDERT steams through the mirror-smooth Pacific. A later ADAMS-class ship, the STODDERT has SPS-40 radar on the tripod mast and a single-arm Mk 13 launcher aft. The SPS-39A 3-D radar is on a platform attached to the second funnel, alleviating the weight of a second mast. Unlike the SHERMAN DDG conversions, the ADAMS-class ships have a second 5-inch gun. (1979, U.S. Navy, PH2 D. R. James)

The BUCHANAN at high speed. She has gear on her fantail, which is too small for helicopter landings. The twin-arm Mk 11 Tartar/Standard-MR launcher has an ''E'' and chevron indicating excellence in missilery for two years. The two SPG-51C radars provide the ability to guide two missiles simultaneously, compared to the single missile guidance capability of the SHERMAN DDGs.

30 + 1 DESTROYERS: "SPRUANCE" CLASS

Number	Name	FY/SCB	Builder	Laid down	Launched	Commissioned	Status
DD 963	SPRUANCE	70/224	Litton/Ingalls (Pascagoula)	17 Nov 1972	10 Nov 1973	20 Sep 1975	**AA**
DD 964	PAUL F. FOSTER	70/224	Litton/Ingalls (Pascagoula)	6 Feb 1973	23 Feb 1974	21 Feb 1976	**PA**
DD 965	KINKAID	70/224	Litton/Ingalls (Pascagoula)	19 Apr 1973	25 May 1974	10 July 1976	**PA**
DD 966	HEWITT	71/224	Litton/Ingalls (Pascagoula)	23 July 1973	24 Aug 1974	25 Sep 1976	**PA**
DD 967	ELLIOT	71/224	Litton/Ingalls (Pascagoula)	15 Oct 1973	19 Dec 1974	22 Jan 1977	**PA**
DD 968	ARTHUR W. RADFORD	71/224	Litton/Ingalls (Pascagoula)	14 Jan 1974	1 Mar 1975	9 Apr 1977	**AA**
DD 969	PETERSON	71/224	Litton/Ingalls (Pascagoula)	29 Apr 1974	21 June 1975	9 July 1977	**AA**
DD 970	CARON	71/224	Litton/Ingalls (Pascagoula)	1 July 1974	24 June 1975	1 Oct 1977	**AA**
DD 971	DAVID R. RAY	71/224	Litton/Ingalls (Pascagoula)	23 Sep 1974	23 Aug 1975	19 Nov 1977	**PA**
DD 972	OLDENDORF	72/224	Litton/Ingalls (Pascagoula)	27 Dec 1974	21 Oct 1975	4 Mar 1978	**PA**
DD 973	JOHN YOUNG	72/224	Litton/Ingalls (Pascagoula)	17 Feb 1975	7 Feb 1976	20 May 1978	**PA**
DD 974	COMTE DE GRASSE	72/224	Litton/Ingalls (Pascagoula)	4 Apr 1975	26 Mar 1976	5 Aug 1978	**PA**
DD 975	O'BRIEN	72/224	Litton/Ingalls (Pascagoula)	9 May 1975	8 July 1976	3 Dec 1977	**PA**
DD 976	MERRILL	72/224	Litton/Ingalls (Pascagoula)	16 June 1975	1 Sep 1976	11 Mar 1978	**PA**
DD 977	BRISCOE	72/224	Litton/Ingalls (Pascagoula)	21 July 1975	8 Jan 1977	3 June 1978	**AA**
DD 978	STUMP	72/224	Litton/Ingalls (Pascagoula)	22 Aug 1975	30 Apr 1977	19 Aug 1978	**AA**
DD 979	CONOLLY	74/224	Litton/Ingalls (Pascagoula)	29 Sep 1975	25 June 1977	14 Oct 1978	**AA**
DD 980	MOOSBRUGGER	74/224	Litton/Ingalls (Pascagoula)	3 Nov 1975	20 Aug 1977	16 Dec 1978	**AA**
DD 981	JOHN HANCOCK	74/224	Litton/Ingalls (Pascagoula)	16 Jan 1976	29 Oct 1977	10 Mar 1979	**AA**
DD 982	NICHOLSON	74/224	Litton/Ingalls (Pascagoula)	20 Feb 1976	28 Jan 1978	12 May 1979	**AA**
DD 983	JOHN RODGERS	74/224	Litton/Ingalls (Pascagoula)	12 Aug 1976	25 Feb 1978	14 July 1979	**AA**
DD 984	LEFTWICH	74/224	Litton/Ingalls (Pascagoula)	12 Nov 1976	8 Apr 1978	25 Aug 1979	**PA**
DD 985	CUSHING	74/224	Litton/Ingalls (Pascagoula)	2 Feb 1977	17 June 1978	20 Oct 1979	**PA**
DD 986	HARRY W. HILL	75/224	Litton/Ingalls (Pascagoula)	1 Apr 1977	10 Aug 1978	17 Nov 1979	**PA**
DD 987	O'BANNON	75/224	Litton/Ingalls (Pascagoula)	24 June 1977	25 Sep 1978	15 Dec 1979	**AA**
DD 988	THORN	75/224	Litton/Ingalls (Pascagoula)	29 Aug 1977	14 Nov 1978	16 Feb 1980	**AA**
DD 989	DEYO	75/224	Litton/Ingalls (Pascagoula)	14 Oct 1977	20 Jan 1979	22 Mar 1980	**AA**
DD 990	INGERSOLL	75/224	Litton/Ingalls (Pascagoula)	16 Dec 1977	10 Mar 1979	12 Apr 1980	**PA**
DD 991	FIFE	75/224	Litton/Ingalls (Pascagoula)	6 Mar 1978	1 May 1979	31 May 1980	**PA**
DD 992	FLETCHER	75/224	Litton/Ingalls (Pascagoula)	24 Apr 1978	16 June 1979	12 July 1980	**PA**
DD 997	HAYLER	78/224	Litton/Ingalls (Pascagoula)	1980	1982	1983	Bldg.

Displacement:	7,800 tons full load
Length:	529 feet (161.2 m) wl
	563⅓ feet (171.1 m) oa
Beam:	55 feet (17.6 m)
Draft:	29 feet (8.8 m)
Propulsion:	gas turbines (General Electric); 80,000 shp; 2 shafts
Speed:	30+ knots
Range:	6,000 + n.miles at 20 knots
Manning:	288-302 (18-19 O + 270-283 enlisted)
Helicopters:	1 SH-3 Sea King or 2 SH-60B LAMPS
Missiles:	1 8-tube NATO Sea Sparrow launcher Mk 29
	2 quad tubes for Harpoon SSM Mk 141
Guns:	2 5-inch (127-mm) 54 cal DP Mk 45 (2 × 1)
ASW weapons:	1 8-tube ASROC launcher Mk 16
	6 12.75-inch (324-mm) torpedo tubes Mk 32 (2 × 3)
Radars:	SPS-40B air search
	SPS-55 surface search
Sonars:	SQS-53 bow-mounted
Fire control:	1 Mk 86 gun FCS
	1 Mk 91 missile FCS
	1 Mk 116 ASW FCS
	1 SPG-60 radar
	1 SPQ-9A radar

The SPRUANCE-class destroyers were developed as replacements for the large number of World War II-built general purpose destroyers of the ALLEN M. SUMNER (DD 692) and GEARING (DD 710) classes that reached the end of their service lives in the mid-1970s. These are specialized ASW ships, built with only point-defense missiles. However, they are now scheduled for the installation of Vertical Launch Systems.

The four KIDD-class missile destroyers and TICONDEROGA (CG 47)-class missile cruisers have the same hull, propulsion, and auxiliary systems. The SPRUANCE class represents the largest number of surface combatants built to the same design by any Western navy except for the frigates of the KNOX (FF 1052) and OLIVER HAZARD PERRY (FFG 7) classes.

Builders: The entire SPRUANCE class was contracted with a single shipyard to facilitate design and mass production. A contract for the development and production of 30 ships was awarded on 23 June 1970 to a new yard established by the Ingalls Shipbuilding Division of Litton Industries at Pascagoula, Mississippi. Labor and technical problems delayed the construction of these ships.

Class: In addition to these 31 ships, four were ordered with the Mk 26/Standard AAW missile system for the Iranian Navy, but were completed as the KIDD class, accounting for hull numbers DD 993–996.

One additional ship of this class was ordered on 29 September 1979 (DD 997). This ship was one of two authorized (one funded) by Congress with the proviso that, in the wording of the Senate Committee on Armed Services, "The committee does not intend for these funds to be used for acquisition of two standard 963 class destroyers; rather, it is the committee's intention that these ships be the first element in a new technology approach to the problems of designing surface escorts. The standard 963 class design should be modified to substantially increase the number of helicopter aircraft carried." This feature could permit the eventual modification of the ships to operate VSTOL aircraft as well. However, the Navy chose to build the ship as a standard SPRUANCE, and no additional ships were funded by Congress.

Design: The SPRUANCE design provides for the subsequent installation of additional weapon systems, specifically the Mk 26 missile launcher (and subsequently the Ex 41 VLS) forward with removal of the ASROC launcher and aft with removal of the Sea Sparrow launcher. In addition, the forward 5-inch gun could be replaced by the now-canceled Mk 71 8-inch Major Caliber Lightweight Gun.

Engineering: These are the first U.S. Navy surface combatants to have gas-turbine propulsion. Previously, gas turbines were installed in several Navy patrol combatants and in HAMILTON-class (WHEC 715) and some RELIANCE-class (WMEC 615) cutters.

The SPRUANCE-class ships have four LM2500 gas turbines, which are modified TF39 aircraft turbofan engines. One engine can propel the ships at about 19 knots, two engines at about 27 knots, and three and four engines can provide speeds in excess of 30 knots.

Guns: These ships are each scheduled to receive two Phalanx CIWS.

Helicopters: The hanger sizes in these ships vary; they are 49 to 54 feet long and 21 to 23½ feet wide.

Missiles: The MERRILL was fitted with an armored launcher for four Tomahawk antiship cruise missiles in 1980. All of these ships are scheduled to receive two vertical launchers for ASW and antiship cruise missiles; each launcher will hold 61 weapons, which will make these among the most heavily armed surface combatants afloat.

Sonars: Original plans provided for these ships to have the SQS-35 Independent Variable Depth Sonar (IVDS) in addition to their bow-mounted SQS-53. The IVDS was deleted because of the effectiveness of the SQS-53. The decision has subsequently been made to fit these ships with the SQR-19 TACTAS when that sonar becomes available.

The JOHN HANCOCK's stern displays the signature of the ship's namesake instead of the normal block letters. The openings at right are for the ship's SLQ-25 Nixie torpedo countermeasures system. (1979, courtesy USS JOHN HANCOCK)

ELLIOTT (1978, U.S. Navy, PHC William E. Kendall)

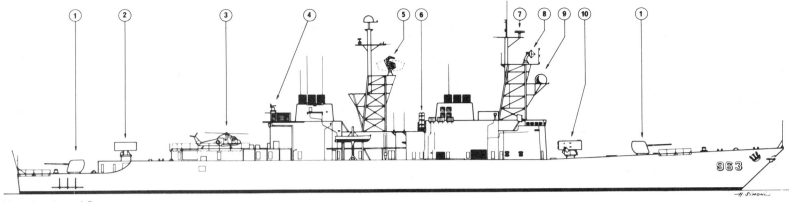

Line drawing of SPRUANCE

1. 5-inch DP Mk 45 gun.   2. NATO Sea Sparrow launcher   3. SH-2F LAMPS helicopter on flight deck   4. Mk 91 missile FCS   5. SPS-40B radar   6. Harpoon missiles   7. SPS-55 radar   8. SPG-60 radar   9. SPQ-9A radar   10. ASROC launcher

HEWITT with SH-2F LAMPS on flight deck (1979, Giorgio Arra)

BRISCOE (1979, Giorgio Arra)

Mass production: The FLETCHER and FIFE at the Litton/Ingalls yard the day before their dual christening ceremonies. The yard completed 30 of these destroyers in a five-year period. The same ship-assembly facility is building one additional SPRUANCE plus the KIDD and TICONDEROGA classes. (1979, Litton/Ingalls)

14 DESTROYERS: "FORREST SHERMAN" CLASS

Number	Name	FY/SCB	Builder	Laid down	Launched	Commissioned	Status
DD 931	FORREST SHERMAN	53/85	Bath Iron Works	27 Oct 1953	5 Feb 1955	9 Nov 1955	**AA**
*DD 933	BARRY	53/85	Bath Iron Works	15 Mar 1954	1 Oct 1955	31 Aug 1956	**AA**
*DD 937	DAVIS	54/85	Bethlehem Steel (Quincy)	1 Feb 1955	28 Mar 1956	28 Feb 1957	**AA**
*DD 938	JONAS INGRAM	54/85	Bethlehem Steel (Quincy)	15 June 1955	8 July 1956	19 July 1957	**AA**
*DD 940	MANLEY	55/85	Bath Iron Works	10 Feb 1955	12 Apr 1956	1 Feb 1957	**AA**
*DD 941	DU PONT	55/85	Bath Iron Works	11 May 1955	8 Sep 1956	1 July 1957	**AA**
DD 942	BIGELOW	55/85	Bath Iron Works	6 July 1955	2 Feb 1957	8 Nov 1957	**AA**
*DD 943	BLANDY	55/85	Bethlehem Steel (Quincy)	29 Dec 1955	19 Dec 1956	26 Nov 1957	**AA**
DD 944	MULLINNIX	55/85	Bethlehem Steel (Quincy)	5 Apr 1956	18 Mar 1957	7 Mar 1958	**AA**
DD 945	HULL	56/85A	Bath Iron Works	12 Sep 1956	10 Aug 1957	3 July 1958	**PA**
DD 946	EDSON	56/85A	Bath Iron Works	3 Dec 1956	1 Jan 1958	7 Nov 1958	**NRF-A**
*DD 948	MORTON	56/85A	Ingalls Shipbuilding Corp	4 Mar 1957	23 May 1958	26 May 1959	**PA**
*DD 950	RICHARD S. EDWARDS	56/85A	Puget Sound Bridge & D D Co	20 Dec 1956	24 Sep 1957	5 Feb 1959	**PA**
DD 951	TURNER JOY	56/85A	Puget Sound Bridge & D D Co	30 Sep 1957	5 May 1958	3 Aug 1959	**PA**

* ASW-modified ships

Displacement:	~2,800 tons standard
	~4,050 tons full load
Length:	407 feet (124 m) wl
	DD 931–944 418 feet (127.4 m) oa, except DD 933, 425 feet (125.9 m)
	DD 945–951 418$^5/_{12}$ feet (127.5 m) oa
Beam:	DD 931–944 45 feet (13.7 m)
	DD 945–951 45$^1/_{12}$ feet (13.8 m)
Draft:	22 feet (6.7 m)
Propulsion:	steam turbines (General Electric, except Westinghouse in DD 931, 933); 70,000 shp; 2 shafts
Boilers:	4 1,200-psi (Foster Wheeler, except Babcock & Wilcox in DD 937–938, 943–944, 948)
Speed:	32.5 knots
Range:	4,000+ n. miles at 20 knots
Manning:	319–332 (19 O + 300–313 enlisted) except 309 (17 O + 292 enlisted) in ASW-modified ships(*)
	208 (13 O + 195 enlisted) active Navy in DD 946

Helicopters:	none
Guns:	3 5-inch (127-mm) 54 cal DP Mk 42 (3 × 1) except 2 guns in ASW-modified ships(*)
ASW weapons:	1 8-tube ASROC launcher Mk 16 in ASW-modified ships (*)
	6 12.75-inch (324-mm) torpedo tubes Mk 32 (2 × 3)
Radars:	SPS-10 surface search
	SPS-37 air search in DD 933, 937, 940, 942, 946, 948, 950–951
	SPS-40 air search in DD 931, 938, 941, 943–945
Sonars:	SQS-23 keel-mounted except bow-mounted in DD 933
	SQS-35 IVDS in ASW-modified ships(*)
Fire control:	1 Mk 5 target designation system
	1 Mk 56 gun FCS
	1 Mk 68 gun FCS
	1 Mk 105 ASW FCS except Mk 114 in ASW-modified ships(*)
	1 SPG-53/53A radar
	1 Mk 35 radar

MORTON—ASW modified. (1979, Giorgio Arra)

The HULL was the only destroyer ever to be armed with an 8-inch gun. The Mk 71 MCLWG was removed in April 1979, shortly after the photo was taken as the ship lay at anchor in Hong Kong. The ship reverted to a three-gun configuration. The Mk 32 torpedo tubes (covered with canvas) are amidships; the MORTON's are forward of the bridge. (1978, Giorgio Arra)

The TURNER JOY off Pearl Harbor. She has satellite communication antennas forward of the Mk 68 GFCS (above bridge) and aft of the Mk 56 GFCS (on after structure). Arrangement of the Mk 68 and Mk 56 directors vary. The SHERMANs are the only modern U.S. surface warships with more guns aft than forward. (1980, Giorgio Arra)

The 18 FORREST SHERMAN-class ships were the first U.S. destroyers designed and constructed after World War II, following the large DL 2–5 (DD 927–930). Four have been converted to guided missile ships and are listed separately (DDG 31–34); eight others have undergone an ASW modification (indicated by asterisks), with six ships retaining essentially their original configuration.

The EDSON was assigned to the Naval Reserve Force on 1 April 1977; she also provides training for students at the Surface Warfare Officers School in Newport, Rhode Island. The assignment of other SHERMANS to the NRF is no longer anticipated.

Design: These were the first major U.S. combatants with more firepower aft than forward. The DECATUR and later ships have higher bows; the HULL and later ships have slightly different bow designs. These were the first U.S. destroyers not to have antiship torpedo tubes (built with four fixed 21-inch "long" ASW torpedo tubes Mk 25 plus depth-charge racks and hedgehogs).

Guns: As built, the SHERMANS each had three 5-inch Mk 42 guns and four 3-inch Mk 33 guns, the latter in twin mounts forward and aft. The 3-inch guns were removed during the 1960s and 1970s. In addition, the No. 3 5-inch gun was removed from the eight modernized ships.

The BIGELOW carried the Phalanx CIWS in the late 1970s for at-sea evaluation (fitted forward of her No. 3 gun mount).

The HULL was test ship for the Mk 71 8-inch MCLWG. The gun, installed from 1975 until early 1979, replaced the ship's forward 5-inch mount.

Modernization: Eight SHERMANS were modernized to improve their ASW capabilities; the number of guns was reduced, and ASROC was installed in conjunction with general updating; the BARRY was fitted with bow-mounted SQS-23; all were provided with variable-depth sonar. The BARRY modernization was SCB-251; the other seven were SCB-221. Plans to modernize six additional ships were dropped because of increasing costs.

RICHARD S. EDWARDS—ASW modification (1977, Giorgio Arra)

BARRY—ASW modification (1978, U.S. Navy)

MORTON—ASW modified (1979, Giorgio Arra)

15 DESTROYERS: "GEARING" AND "CARPENTER" CLASSES

Number	Name	Builder	Laid down	Launched	Commissioned	Status
DD 743	SOUTHERLAND	Bath Iron Works	27 May 1944	5 Oct 1944	22 Dec 1944	**NRF-P**
DD 763	WILLIAM C. LAWE	Bethlehem Steel (San Francisco)	12 Mar 1944	21 May 1945	18 Dec 1946	**NRF-A**
DD 784	MCKEAN	Todd-Pacific Shipyards (Seattle)	15 Sep 1944	31 Mar 1945	9 June 1945	**NRF-P**
DD 817	CORRY	Consolidated Steel Corp	5 Apr 1945	28 July 1945	26 Feb 1946	**NRF-A**
DD 821	JOHNSTON	Consolidated Steel Corp	26 Mar 1945	19 Oct 1945	23 Aug 1946	**NRF-A**
DD 825	CARPENTER	Consolidated Steel Corp	30 July 1945	30 Dec 1945	15 Dec 1949	**NRF-P**
DD 827	ROBERT A. OWENS	Bath Iron Works	29 Oct 1945	15 July 1946	5 Nov 1949	**NRF-A**
DD 862	VOGELGESANG	Bethlehem Steel (Staten Island)	3 Aug 1944	15 Jan 1945	28 Apr 1945	**NRF-A**
DD 863	STEINAKER	Bethlehem Steel (Staten Island)	1 Sep 1944	13 Feb 1945	26 May 1945	**NRF-A**
DD 864	HAROLD J. ELLISON	Bethlehem Steel (Staten Island)	3 Oct 1944	14 Mar 1945	23 June 1945	**NRF-A**
DD 866	CONE	Bethlehem Steel (Staten Island)	30 Nov 1944	10 May 1945	18 Aug 1945	**NRF-A**
DD 876	ROGERS	Consolidated Steel Corp	3 June 1944	20 Nov 1944	26 Mar 1945	**NRF-P**
DD 880	DYESS	Consolidated Steel Corp	17 Aug 1944	26 Jan 1945	21 May 1945	**NRF-A**
DD 883	NEWMAN K. PERRY	Consolidated Steel Corp	10 Oct 1944	17 Mar 1945	26 July 1945	**NRF-A**
DD 886	ORLECK	Consolidated Steel Corp	28 Nov 1944	12 May 1945	15 Sep 1945	**NRF-P**

Displacement:	2,425 tons standard	Helicopters:	none
	3,410-3,520 tons full load	Guns:	4 5-inch (127-mm) 38 cal DP Mk 38 (2 × 2) except 2 guns in DD 827
Length:	383 feet (116.6 m) wl	ASW weapons:	1 8-tube ASROC launcher Mk 16
	390$^1/_2$ feet (119.0 m) oa		6 12.75-inch (324-mm) torpedo tubes Mk 32 (2 × 6)
Beam:	40$^5/_6$ feet (12.4 m)	Radars:	SPS-10 surface search
Draft:	19 feet (5.8 m)		SPS-29 or SPS-37 or SPS-40 air search
Propulsion:	steam turbines; 60,000 shp; 2 shafts	Sonars:	SQS-23 keel-mounted
Boilers:	4,600-psi	Fire control:	1 Mk 5 target designation system except Mk 1 in DD 827
Speed:	32 knots		1 Mk 37 gun FCS except Mk 56 in DD 827
Range:	4,000+ n.miles at 20 knots		1 Mk 114 ASW FCS except Mk 111 in DD 785
Manning:	307 as NRF ships (12 O + 176 enlisted active; 7 O + 112 enlisted reserve)		1 Mk 25 radar except Mk 35 in DD 827

These are the only U.S. warships constructed during World War II that remain in service except for the aircraft carriers MIDWAY (CV 41) and CORAL SEA (CV 43). All fifteen ships are assigned to the Naval Reserve Force and are manned by composite active and reserve crews. The Navy planned to strike all but four of these ships by 1981 (DD 763, 784, 864, 866); however, congressional mandate has kept them in NRF service at least into 1981.

Builders: After launching, the CARPENTER and ROBERT A. OWENS were towed to the Newport News SB & DD Company for completion as specialized ASW ships.

Class: The GEARING class was the final U.S. destroyer design to be constructed during World War II. The class consisted of hulls DD 710–721, 742–743, 763–769, 782–791, and 905–926; 98 ships were completed through 1952, the last being the TIMMERMAN (DD 828/AG 152) built with experimental lightweight propulsion machinery. Forty-nine ships were canceled in 1945, and four unfinished ships were scrapped in the 1950s.

Ships of this class and several earlier U.S. destroyer classes continue to serve in a number of foreign navies.

Design: The GEARING-class ships were identical to the previous ALLEN M. SUMNER (DD 692) class, except for the addition of 14 feet to their length to provide additional fuel capacity.

Guns: As built, the GEARINGS had six 5-inch guns, 12 40-mm AA guns, and 11 20-mm AA guns (plus 10 21-inch torpedo tubes and depth charges). After World War II the after bank of tubes was replaced by an additional quad 40-mm gun mount; those ships modified as radar pickets lost the other five-tube bank in favor of a tripod radar mast. Subsequently, all 20mm-guns were removed and 40-mm weapons replaced by up to six 3-inch guns. During FRAM modernization in the 1960s, gun armament was reduced to four 5-inch guns, and ASROC and Mk 32 tubes were installed. The ships have a "balanced" gun arrangement (A and Y positions).

The ROBERT A. OWENS was completed with four 3-inch 50-cal AA guns in enclosed mounts (plus two Weapon Able ASW weapons), rearmed with four 3-inch 70-cal rapid-fire guns in 1957. A single 5-inch gun twin mount was fitted forward during FRAM modernization.

Modernization: All of the surviving ships of this class were modernized in the 1960s under the FRAM I program. Machinery and electrical systems were updated, new electronic equipment installed, gun armament reduced, ASROC and Mk 32 tubes installed, and facilities provided for the DASH (Drone Antisubmarine Helicopter), although that program was canceled before being provided to all modified destroyers.

POST–WORLD WAR II DESTROYER PROGRAMS

U.S. World War II destroyer programs reached hull number DD 926 (with hulls DD 891–926 being canceled in 1945). Many ships built during the war were subsequently reclassified as escort destroyers (DDE), hunter-killer destroyers (DDK), radar picket destroyers (DDR), and experimental destroyers (EDD), keeping the same hull numbers; all survivors reverted to the "straight" DD classification.

As noted below, several war prizes and foreign-built ships (offshore procurement) had DD-series hull numbers, as did one British destroyer acquired for transfer to Pakistan with U.S. funds.

Six missile-armed ships of the SPRUANCE class ordered by Iran were assigned DD hull numbers by the U.S. Navy. Four ships actually begun went to the U.S. Navy with DDG designations but with their original hull numbers; the two other numbers were canceled, with one being subsequently assigned to the thirty-first SPRUANCE-class ship.

DD 927–930	MITSCHER class	completed as DL 2–5
DD 931–933	FORREST SHERMAN class	
DD 934	ex-Japanese HANAZUKI	
DD 935	ex-German T-35	
DD 936–938	FORREST SHERMAN class	
DD 939	ex-German Z-39	
DD 940–951	FORREST SHERMAN class	
DD 952–959	CHARLES F. ADAMS class	completed as DDG 2–9
DD 960	(AKIZUKI)	Japan OSP 1960
DD 961	(TERUZUKI)	Japan OSP 1960
DD 962	(ex-British CHARITY)	to Pakistan 1958 (SHAH JAHAN)
DD 963–992	SPRUANCE class	
DD 993	(ex-Iranian KOUROSH)	completed as DDG 993
DD 994	(ex-Iranian DARYUSH)	completed as DDG 994
DD 995	(ex-Iranian ARDESHIR)	completed as DDG 995
DD 996	(ex-Iranian NADER)	completed as DDG 996
DD 997	(Iranian SHAPOUR)	canceled 1976; reassigned as U.S. DD 997; SPRUANCE class
DD 998	(Iranian ANOUSHIRVAN)	canceled 1976

GUIDED MISSILE DESTROYERS

DDG 1	GYATT (ex-DD 712)	Comm. 1956; stricken (as DD 712)
DDG 2–24	CHARLES F. ADAMS class	
DDG 25	(Australian PERTH)	Comm. 1965
DDG 26	(Australian HOBART)	Comm. 1965
DDG 27	(Australian BRISBANE)	Comm. 1967
DDG 28	(German LÜTJENS)	Comm. 1969
DDG 29	(German MÖLDERS)	Comm. 1969
DDG 30	(German ROMMEL)	Comm. 1970
DDG 31–34	Conv. FORREST SHERMAN class (ex-DD 936, 932, 949, 947)	
DDG 35	MITSCHER (ex-DL 2)	Comm. 1968; stricken 1978
DDG 36	JOHN S. McCAIN (ex-DL 3)	Comm. 1969; stricken 1978
DDG 37–46	COONTZ class (ex-DLG 6–15)	
DDG 47	TICONDEROGA	completed as CG 47

The guided missile destroyer (DDG) classification was established in 1956. The first DDG was the GEARING-class destroyer GYATT (DD 712), fitted with a twin Terrier SAM launcher aft, replacing the after 5-inch twin gun mount. The GYATT became DDG 712 on 3 December 1956 and DDG 1 on 23 April 1957. Subsequent DDGs had the smaller Tartar (later Standard-MR) missile, until the COONTZ-class frigates were reclassified as destroyers in 1975. Note that the missile-armed ships of the SPRUANCE class being built for Iran had U.S. hull numbers in the DD series because they were modifications of the U.S. nonmissile design, and are not a new class. Six ADAMS-class DDGs for Germany and Australia were built in the United States.

The NEWMAN K. PERRY at Hong Kong. This FRAM configuration is the ship's third; built as a six-gun, ten-torpedo tube DD, converted to a radar picket ship (DDR) in 1950, and subsequently rebuilt under the FRAM program and redesignated DD. Note the large tripod mast forward and EW "stack" aft. (1973, Giorgio Arra)

NEWMAN K. PERRY (1973, Giorgio Arra)

10 Frigates

The Navy had some 70 frigates (FF/FFG) in commission in January 1981, with an additional 40 ships of the OLIVER HAZARD PERRY class under construction. The planned FY 1982–1985 shipbuilding program would add another 11 ships of this type to the Fleet. Thus, by the early 1990s the Navy should have some 120 frigates in commission.

The current Navy force-level objective for frigates is 92 ships based on the following requirements:

Amphibious Force Escorts	5 FF/FFG
Convoy Escorts	63 FF/FFG
Underway Replenishment Group Escorts	24 FF/FFG

These are the minimum requirements in this category of warships. It is anticipated that in a future conflict involving NATO, frigate-type ships would be the major contribution of allied navies to complement the U.S. Fleet.

The Navy is now examining the requirement and alternatives for a new type of "low-mix" escort ships that would be less capable and less costly than the PERRY-class ships, but still capable of the ocean escort role. The ship would be manned primarily by reservists and assigned to the Naval Reserve Force. For planning purposes this ship is being designated as a "corvette" (FFX).

No characteristics for the FFX had been determined when this edition went to press. The lead ship is tentatively scheduled for funding in the FY 1983 shipbuilding program. However, some congressional opposition to the proposal is expected.

The long-planned Surface Effect Ship design that was intended for the next generation of frigates has been canceled. A contract for a detailed design and to initiate construction of the ship was issued to Rohr Marine Inc. on 9 December 1976. This was to have been a 3,000-ton, 80-plus knot prototype. Existing weapon and sensor systems were to have been adopted to the ship.

The Carter Administration had opposed funding for the ship and was overruled by Congress in FY 1978 and 1979; no funding for the ship was provided in the FY 1980 budget.

Classification: This type of warship was classified as destroyer escort (DE) from its inception in the U.S. Navy in 1941 until the early 1950s when DE was changed to "ocean escort." Subsequently, guided missile ships were designated DEG and the escort research ship GLOVER became an AGDE. On 30 June 1975 all escort ships were changed to "frigate" (FF/FFG/AGFF).

Electronics: The PERRY-class ships will receive the SLQ-32(V)2 EW system and other frigates the SLQ-32(V)1.

Names: Frigates are named for deceased Navy, Marine Corps, and Coast Guard personnel.

(In the following table AAW indicates ships armed with Tartar/Standard-MR surface-to-air missile systems; ASW indicates SQS-26/56 sonar; Helicopter indicates helicopter hangar and other support facilities; and Guns lists the largest caliber gun fitted in the ships.)

Type	Class/Ship	Active	Building[a]	Reserve	Commission	AAW	ASW	Helicopter	Guns
FFG 7	OLIVER HAZARD PERRY	7	39	—	1977–	✔	✔	✔	3-inch
FFG 1	BROOKE	6	—	—	1966–1968	✔	✔	✔	5-inch
FF 1098	GLOVER	1	—	—	1965	—	✔	✔	5-inch
FF 1052	KNOX	46	—	—	1969–1974	—	✔	✔	5-inch
FF 1040	GARCIA	10	—	—	1964–1968	—	✔	✔	5-inch
FF 1037	BRONSTEIN	2	—	—	1963	—	✔	—	3-inch

[a] Includes ships authorized through FY 1981.

The frigates WADSWORTH (left) and GEORGE PHILIP at high speed. Frigates—intended for ASW escort—probably will comprise more than one-fourth of the active U.S. Fleet in the 1990s. This is a higher fraction of "low-mix" warships in the active fleet than at any time since escort/frigate-type ships were introduced in the U.S. Fleet early in World War II. (1980, Todd Shipyards)

Five PERRY-class frigates being constructed at the Todd Seattle yard: at left the ANTRIM (FFG 20), HMAS ADELAIDE (02), and BOONE (FFG 28), with two later ships at right. (1980, Todd Shipyards)

7 + 39 GUIDED MISSILE FRIGATES: "OLIVER HAZARD PERRY" CLASS

Number	Name	FY/SCB	Builder	Laid down	Launched	Commissioned	Status
FFG 7	OLIVER HAZARD PERRY	73/261	Bath Iron Works	12 June 1976	25 Sep 1978	17 Dec 1977	**AA**
FFG 8	MCINERNEY	75/261	Bath Iron Works	16 Jan 1978	4 Nov 1978	15 Dec 1979	**AA**
FFG 9	WADSWORTH	75/261	Todd Shipyards (San Pedro)	13 July 1977	29 July 1978	2 Apr 1980	**PA**
FFG 10	DUNCAN	75/261	Todd Shipyards (Seattle)	29 Apr 1977	1 Mar 1978	24 May 1980	**PA**
FFG 11	CLARK	76/261	Bath Iron Works	17 July 1978	24 Mar 1979	17 May 1980	**AA**
FFG 12	GEORGE PHILIP	76/261	Todd Shipyards (San Pedro)	14 Dec 1977	16 Dec 1978	12 Nov 1980	**PA**
FFG 13	SAMUEL ELIOT MORISON	76/261	Bath Iron Works	4 Dec 1978	14 July 1979	11 Oct 1980	**AA**
FFG 14	SIDES	76/261	Todd Shipyards (San Pedro)	7 Aug 1978	19 May 1979	1981	Bldg.
FFG 15	ESTOCIN	76/261	Bath Iron Works	2 Apr 1979	3 Nov 1979	1981	Bldg.
FFG 16	CLIFTON SPRAGUE	76/261	Bath Iron Works	30 July 1979	16 Feb 1980	1981	Bldg.
FFG 19	JOHN A. MOORE	77/261	Todd Shipyards (San Pedro)	19 Dec 1978	20 Oct 1979	1981	Bldg.
FFG 20	ANTRIM	77/261	Todd Shipyards (Seattle)	21 June 1978	27 Mar 1979	1981	Bldg.
FFG 21	FLATLEY	77/261	Bath Iron Works	13 Nov 1979	15 May 1980	1981	Bldg.
FFG 22	FAHRION	77/261	Todd Shipyards (Seattle)	1 Dec 1978	24 Aug 1979	1981	Bldg.
FFG 23	LEWIS B. PULLER	77/261	Todd Shipyards (San Pedro)	23 May 1979	15 Mar 1980	1981	Bldg.
FFG 24	JACK WILLIAMS	77/261	Bath Iron Works	25 Feb 1980	30 Aug 1980	1981	Bldg.
FFG 25	COPELAND	77/261	Todd Shipyards (San Pedro)	24 Oct 1979	26 July 1980	1982	Bldg.
FFG 26	GALLERY	77/261	Bath Iron Works	17 May 1980	20 Dec 1980	1982	Bldg.
FFG 27	MAHLON S. TISDALE	78/261	Todd Shipyards (San Pedro)	19 Mar 1980	7 Feb 1981	1982	Bldg.
FFG 28	BOONE	78/261	Todd Shipyards (Seattle)	27 Mar 1979	16 Jan 1980	1982	Bldg.
FFG 29	. . . .	78/261	Bath Iron Works			1982	Bldg.
FFG 30	REID	78/261	Todd Shipyards (San Pedro)			1982	Bldg.
FFG 31	STARK	78/261	Todd Shipyards (Seattle)	24 Aug 1979	30 May 1980	1982	Bldg.
FFG 32	. . . .	78/261	Bath Iron Works			1982	Bldg.
FFG 33	. . . .	78/261	Todd Shipyards (San Pedro)			1983	Bldg.
FFG 34	. . . .	78/261	Bath Iron Works			1983	Bldg.
FFG 36	. . . .	79/261	Bath Iron Works			1983	Bldg.
FFG 37	CROMMELIN	79/261	Todd Shipyards (Seattle)	30 May 1980		1983	Bldg.
FFG 38	. . . .	79/261	Todd Shipyards (San Pedro)			1983	Bldg.
FFG 39	. . . .	79/261	Bath Iron Works			1983	Bldg.
FFG 40	. . . .	79/261	Todd Shipyards (Seattle)			1983	Bldg.
FFG 41	. . . .	79/261	Todd Shipyards (San Pedro)			1983	Bldg.
FFG 42	. . . .	79/261	Bath Iron Works			1983	Bldg.
FFG 43	. . . .	79/261	Todd Shipyards (San Pedro)			1984	Bldg.
6 FFG		80/261				1984–1985	Auth.
6 FFG		81/261				1985–1986	Auth.

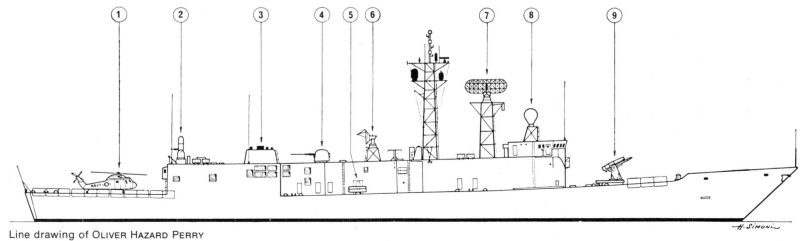

Line drawing of OLIVER HAZARD PERRY

1. LAMPS helicopter   2. Phalanx CIWS   3. stack.   4. 76-mm AA Mk 75 gun   5. Mk 32 ASW torpedo tubes   6. STIR radar   7. SPS-49 radar   8. Mk 92 FCS   9. Mk 13 missile launcher

Displacement:	3,710 tons full load
Length:	445 feet (135.6 m) oa
Beam:	45 feet (13.7 m)
Draft:	24½ feet (7.5 m)
Propulsion:	gas turbines (General Electric); 40,000 shp; 1 shaft
Speed:	28 knots (sustained)
Range:	4,500 n.miles at 20 knots
Manning:	179 (12 O + 167 enlisted)
Helicopters:	2 SH-60B LAMPS (when available)
Missiles:	1 single Mk 13 Mod 4 launcher for Standard-MR SAM and Harpoon SSM (40)
Guns:	1 76-mm 62 cal AA Mk 75 (1 × 1)
ASW weapons:	6 12.75-inch (324-mm) torpedo tubes Mk 32 (2 × 3)
Radars:	SPS-49 air search
	SPS-55 surface search
Sonars:	SQS-56 keel-mounted
Fire control:	1 Mk 13 weapon direction system
	1 Mk 92 weapon FCS
	1 SPG-60 radar

The PERRY-class frigates are intended to provide open ocean defense of merchant convoys, undersea replenishment groups, and amphibious forces. They have less on-board ASW capability than the previous KNOX-class ships (no ASROC and smaller sonar), but they can operate two ASW helicopters and have more AAW capability with the Standard-MR/Harpoon launching system. The PERRY's gun, fire control, and sonar systems were evaluated at sea in the frigate TALBOT.

Class: Three additional ships of this class have been built by Todd Shipyards (Seattle) for the Royal Australian Navy: ADELAIDE (F-FFG 17), CANBERRA (F-FFG 18), and SYDNEY (F-FFG 35). The F-FFG 44 is under construction for the RAN. Original U.S. Navy planning provided for approximately 75 ships of this class. Current programs provide for 54 ships to be authorized through the FY 1984 shipbuilding program when the class is completed.

Classification: When conceived, these ships were classified as "patrol frigates" (PF), a term previously applied to a series of smaller, World War II-era ships (PF 1–102) and postwar coastal escorts that were constructed specifically for foreign transfer (PF 103–108). The PERRY was designated hull PF 109 until changed to "frigate" FFG 7 on 30 June 1975.

Design: These ships were designed specifically for modular assembly and mass production. All major components were tested at sea or in land facilities before completion of the lead ship. Space and weight are reserved for fin stabilizers. Early designs provided a single hangar aft with twin funnels ("split" by the hangar). The design was revised to provide side-by-side hangars to accommodate two SH-60B helicopters. A single anchor is fitted.

Engineering: These ships have two LM2500 gas turbine engines (also installed in CG 47/DDG 997/DD 963/PHM 1 classes). They can attain 25 knots on one engine. On trials the PERRY reached 31 knots.

Two auxiliary propulsion pods are fitted under the hull, aft of the sonar dome; these are 325-shp auxiliary engines that can propel the ship up to six knots in the event of a casualty to the main propulsion plant.

Guns: A single Phalanx CIWS will be fitted to each of these ships.

Helicopters: A haul-down and deck handling system will be provided in these ships.

Sonars: An SQR-19 towed array will be fitted in these ships.

OLIVER HAZARD PERRY (1978, U.S. Navy, PHC J. E. Higgins)

The DUNCAN on acceptance trials. The Phalanx CIWS and SH-60B LAMPS helicopters will not be available for these ships until the early 1980s, with the McINERNEY scheduled to conduct helicopter compatibility tests. A Canadian-developed Recovery Assist, Securing, and Traversing (RAST) will be fitted to help land and, once on deck, move the large SH-60B Seahawk. (1980, Camera Craft/Todd Shipyards)

RAMSEY (1979, Giorgio Arra)

6 GUIDED MISSILE FRIGATES: "BROOKE" CLASS

Number	Name	FY/SCB	Builder	Laid down	Launched	Commissioned	Status
FFG 1	BROOKE	62/199B	Lockheed SB & Constn Co (Seattle)	10 Dec 1962	19 July 1963	12 Mar 1966	**PA**
FFG 2	RAMSEY	62/199B	Lockheed SB & Constn Co (Seattle)	4 Feb 1963	15 Oct 1963	3 June 1967	**PA**
FFG 3	SCHOFIELD	62/199B	Lockheed SB & Constn Co (Seattle)	15 Apr 1963	7 Dec 1963	11 May 1968	**PA**
FFG 4	TALBOT	63/199B	Bath Iron Works	4 May 1964	6 Jan 1966	22 Apr 1967	**AA**
FFG 5	RICHARD L. PAGE	63/199B	Bath Iron Works	4 Jan 1965	4 Apr 1966	5 Aug 1967	**AA**
FFG 6	JULIUS A. FURER	63/199B	Bath Iron Works	12 July 1965	22 July 1966	11 Nov 1967	**AA**

Displacement:	2,640 tons standard
	3,245 tons full load
Length:	390 feet (118.9 m) wl
	414½ feet (126.3 m) oa
Beam:	44$\frac{1}{6}$ feet (13.5 m)
Draft:	24 feet (7.3 m)
Propulsion:	steam turbine (Westinghouse); 35,000 shp; 1 shaft
Boilers:	2 1,200-psi (Foster Wheeler)
Speed:	27 knots
Range:	4,000 n. miles at 20 knots
Manning:	253–256 (16 O + 237–240 enlisted)
Helicopters:	1 SH-2 LAMPS
Missiles:	1 single Mk 22 Mod 0 launcher for Tartar/Standard-MR SAM (16)
Guns:	1 5-inch (127-mm) 38 cal DP Mk 30 (1 × 1)
ASW weapons:	1 8-tube ASROC launcher Mk 16
	6 12.75-inch (324-mm) torpedo tubes Mk 32 (2 × 3)
Radars:	SPS-10F surface search
	SPS-52D 3-D search
Sonars:	SQS-26AX bow-mounted
Fire control:	1 Mk 4 weapon direction system
	1 Mk 56 gun FCS
	1 Mk 74 missile FCS
	1 Mk 114 ASW FCS
	1 SPG-51C radar
	1 Mk 35 radar

This class is essentially the same as the GARCIA class but with a SAM launcher in place of the second 5-inch gun.

Class: Ten additional ships planned for the FY 1964 shipbuilding program and three later units were not built because of the significantly higher costs for the missile and fire control systems, compared to all-gun ships.

Classification: As built, these ships were classified as guided missile escort ships (DEG); they were changed to FFG on 30 June 1975.

Design: The original hangar has been expanded and fitted with a flexible extension. Hangar size varies from approximately 39½ to 52 feet in length and 14½ to 16⅚ feet wide.

Helicopters: These ships were to have operated the Drone Antisubmarine Helicopter (DASH). They were subsequently modified to operate the LAMP I helicopter.

Torpedoes: Two Mk 25 torpedo tubes were installed in the stern of these ships as built but were subsequently removed.

BROOKE (1979, Giorgio Arra)

SCHOFIELD (1978, Giorgio Arra)

1 FRIGATE: "GLOVER" TYPE

Number	Name	FY/SCB	Builder	Laid down	Launched	Commissioned	Status
FF 1098 (ex-AGFF 1)	GLOVER	61/198	Bath Iron Works	29 July 1963	17 Apr 1965	13 Nov 1965	**AA**

Displacement:	2,643 tons
	3,426 tons full load
Length:	414½ feet (126.3 m) oa
Beam:	44⅙ feet (13.5 m)
Draft:	14½ feet (4.3 m)
Propulsion:	steam turbines (Westinghouse); 35,000 shp; 1 shaft
Boilers:	2 1,200-psi (Foster Wheeler)
Speed:	27 knots
Range:	4,000 n. miles at 20 knots
Manning:	316 (17 O + 309 enlisted)
Helicopters:	none
Guns:	1 5-inch (127-mm) 38 cal DP Mk 30 (1 × 1)
ASW weapons:	1 8-tube ASROC launcher Mk 16
	6 12.75-inch (324-mm) torpedo tubes Mk 32 (2 × 3)
Radars:	SPS-10 surface search
	SPS-40 air search
Sonars:	SQS-26AXR bow-mounted
Fire control:	1 Mk 1 target designation system 1 Mk 114 ASW FCS
	1 Mk 56 gun FCS 1 Mk 35 radar

The GLOVER was built as an experimental frigate with a modified hull to facilitate research. The ship originally was authorized in the FY 1960 program but postponed until FY 1961. The ship was used primarily for research into the late 1970s; subsequently the GLOVER has served in an operational frigate role.

Classification: The GLOVER was authorized as a miscellaneous auxiliary (AG 163); completed as an escort research ship (AGDE 1) and changed to frigate research ship (AGFF 1) on 30 June 1975. The ship was redesignated as a frigate (FF 1098) on 1 October 1979, taking on a hull number previously assigned to a canceled ship of the KNOX class.

Design: The design of the GLOVER is similar to the BROOKE and GARCIA classes, but with a modified hull. The ship has a raised platform aft 2 feet 8 inches above the main deck. There is no Tartar launcher or second 5-inch gun amidships.

Helicopter: The ship was built to accommodate two DASH helicopters; the hangar has not been modified for LAMPS operation.

Torpedoes: As built, the ship had two Mk 24 torpedo tubes; these have been removed.

GLOVER—now FF 1098 (1975, Giorgio Arra)

OUELLET with raised forecastle to improve seakeeping (1980, Giorgio Arra)

46 FRIGATES: "KNOX" CLASS

Number	Name	FY/SCB	Builder	Laid down	Launched	Commissioned	Status
FF 1052	KNOX	64/199C	Todd Shipyards (Seattle)	5 Oct 1965	19 Nov 1966	12 Apr 1969	**PA**
FF 1053	ROARK	64/199C	Todd Shipyards (Seattle)	2 Feb 1966	24 Apr 1967	22 Nov 1969	**PA**
FF 1054	GRAY	64/199C	Todd Shipyards (Seattle)	19 Nov 1966	3 Nov 1967	4 Apr 1970	**PA**
FF 1055	HEPBURN	64/199C	Todd Shipyards (San Pedro)	1 June 1966	25 Mar 1967	3 July 1969	**PA**
FF 1056	CONNOLE	64/199C	Avondale Shipyards	23 Mar 1967	20 July 1968	30 Aug 1969	**AA**
FF 1057	RATHBURNE	64/199C	Lockheed SB & Constn Co	8 Jan 1968	2 May 1969	16 May 1970	**PA**
FF 1058	MEYERKORD	64/199C	Todd Shipyards (San Pedro)	1 Sep 1966	15 July 1967	28 Nov 1969	**PA**
FF 1059	W. S. SIMS	64/199C	Avondale Shipyards	10 Apr 1967	4 Jan 1969	3 Jan 1970	**AA**
FF 1060	LANG	64/199C	Todd Shipyards (San Pedro)	25 Mar 1967	17 Feb 1968	28 Mar 1970	**PA**
FF 1061	PATTERSON	64/199C	Avondale Shipyards	12 Oct 1967	3 May 1969	14 Mar 1970	**AA**
FF 1062	WHIPPLE	65/200	Todd Shipyards (Seattle)	24 Apr 1967	12 Apr 1968	22 Aug 1970	**PA**
FF 1063	REASONER	65/200	Lockheed SB & Constn Co	6 Jan 1969	1 Aug 1970	31 July 1971	**PA**
FF 1064	LOCKWOOD	65/200	Todd Shipyards (Seattle)	3 Nov 1967	5 Sep 1964	5 Dec 1970	**PA**
FF 1065	STEIN	65/200	Lockheed SB & Constn Co	1 June 1970	19 Dec 1970	8 Jan 1972	**PA**
FF 1066	MARVIN SHIELDS	65/200	Todd Shipyards (Seattle)	12 Apr 1968	23 Oct 1969	10 Apr 1971	**PA**
FF 1067	FRANCIS HAMMOND	65/200	Todd Shipyards (San Pedro)	15 July 1967	11 May 1968	25 July 1970	**PA**
FF 1068	VREELAND	65/200	Avondale Shipyards	20 Mar 1968	14 June 1969	13 June 1970	**AA**
FF 1069	BAGLEY	65/200	Lockheed SB & Constn Co	22 Sep 1970	24 Apr 1971	9 May 1972	**PA**
FF 1070	DOWNES	65/200	Todd Shipyards (Seattle)	5 Sep 1968	13 Dec 1969	28 Aug 1971	**PA**
FF 1071	BADGER	65/200	Todd Shipyards (Seattle)	17 Feb 1968	7 Dec 1968	1 Dec 1970	**PA**
FF 1072	BLAKELY	65/200	Avondale Shipyards	3 June 1968	23 Aug 1969	18 July 1970	**AA**
FF 1073	ROBERT E. PEARY	65/200	Lockheed SB & Constn Co	20 Dec 1970	23 June 1971	23 Sep 1972	**PA**
FF 1074	HAROLD E. HOLT	65/200	Todd Shipyards (San Pedro)	11 May 1968	3 May 1969	26 Mar 1971	**PA**
FF 1075	TRIPPE	65/200	Avondale Shipyards	29 July 1968	1 Nov 1969	19 Sep 1970	**AA**
FF 1076	FANNING	65/200	Todd Shipyards (San Pedro)	7 Dec 1968	24 Jan 1970	23 July 1971	**PA**
FF 1077	OUELLET	65/200	Avondale Shipyards	15 Jan 1969	17 Jan 1970	12 Dec 1970	**PA**
FF 1078	JOSEPH HEWES	66/200	Avondale Shipyards	15 May 1969	7 Mar 1970	27 Feb 1971	**AA**
FF 1079	BOWEN	66/200	Avondale Shipyards	11 July 1969	2 May 1970	22 May 1971	**AA**
FF 1080	PAUL	66/200	Avondale Shipyards	12 Sep 1969	20 June 1970	14 Aug 1971	**AA**
FF 1081	AYLWIN	66/200	Avondale Shipyards	13 Nov 1969	29 Aug 1970	18 Sep 1971	**AA**
FF 1082	ELMER MONTGOMERY	66/200	Avondale Shipyards	23 Jan 1970	21 Nov 1970	30 Oct 1971	**PA**
FF 1083	COOK	66/200	Avondale Shipyards	20 Mar 1970	23 Jan 1971	18 Dec 1971	**AA**
FF 1084	McCANDLESS	66/200	Avondale Shipyards	4 June 1970	20 Mar 1971	18 Mar 1972	**AA**
FF 1085	DONALD B. BEARY	66/200	Avondale Shipyards	24 July 1970	22 May 1971	22 July 1972	**AA**
FF 1086	BREWTON	66/200	Avondale Shipyards	2 Oct 1970	24 July 1971	8 July 1972	**PA**
FF 1087	KIRK	66/200	Avondale Shipyards	4 Dec 1970	25 Sep 1971	9 Sep 1972	**PA**
FF 1088	BARBEY	67/200	Avondale Shipyards	5 Feb 1971	4 Dec 1971	11 Nov 1972	**PA**
FF 1089	JESSE L. BROWN	67/200	Avondale Shipyards	8 Apr 1971	18 Mar 1972	17 Feb 1973	**AA**
FF 1090	AINSWORTH	67/200	Avondale Shipyards	11 June 1971	15 Apr 1972	31 Mar 1973	**AA**
FF 1091	MILLER	67/200	Avondale Shipyards	6 Aug 1971	3 June 1972	30 June 1973	**AA**
FF 1092	THOMAS C. HART	67/200	Avondale Shipyards	8 Oct 1971	12 Aug 1972	28 July 1973	**AA**
FF 1093	CAPODANNO	67/200	Avondale Shipyards	12 Oct 1971	21 Oct 1972	17 Nov 1973	**AA**
FF 1094	PHARRIS	67/200	Avondale Shipyards	11 Feb 1972	16 Dec 1972	26 Jan 1974	**AA**
FF 1095	TRUETT	67/200	Avondale Shipyards	27 Apr 1972	3 Feb 1973	1 June 1974	**AA**
FF 1096	VALDEZ	67/200	Avondale Shipyards	30 June 1972	24 Mar 1973	27 July 1974	**AA**
FF 1097	MOINESTER	67/200	Avondale Shipyards	25 Aug 1972	12 May 1973	2 Nov 1974	**AA**

Displacement:	3,011 tons standard	**Guns:**	1 5-inch (127-mm) 54 cal DP Mk 42 (1 × 1)
	4,100 tons full load	**ASW weapons:**	1 8-tube ASROC launcher Mk 16
Length:	415 feet (126.5 m) wl		4 12.75-inch (324-mm) torpedo tubes Mk 32 (4 × 1 fixed)
	438 feet (133.5 m) oa	**Radars:**	SPS-10 surface search
Beam:	46¾ feet (14.25 m)		SPS-40 air search
Draft:	24¾ feet (7.6 m)		SPS-58 threat warning in some ships
Propulsion:	steam turbines (Westinghouse); 35,000 shp; 1 shaft	**Sonars:**	SQS-26CX bow-mounted
Boilers:	2 1,200-psi (Combustion Engineering)		SQS-35 IVDS in FF 1052, 1056, 1063–1071, 1073–1076, 1078–1097
Speed:	27+ knots (sustained)		SQR-18 towed array being fitted in all ships
Range:	4,500 n.miles at 20 knots	**Fire control:**	1 Mk 1 target designation system
Manning:	257-266 (16 O + 241-250 enlisted)		1 Mk 68 gun FCS
Helicopters:	1 SH-2 LAMPS		1 Mk 114 ASW FCS
Missiles:	1 8-tube Sea Sparrow launcher Mk 25 BPDMS except NATO Sea Sparrow launcher Mk 29 in FF 1070		1 Mk 115 missile FCS except Mk 91 in FF 1070
	Harpoon can be fired from ASROC launcher		1 SPG-53A/D/F radar

This is the largest class of surface combatants constructed in the West since World War II, although a larger number of PERRY-class frigates are planned. (The only Soviet class of surface combatants with more units was the SKORYY class of destroyers, with an estimated 72 ships completed from 1949 to 1955.)

The KIRK is home-ported in Yokosuka, Japan.

Class: Ten additional ships were authorized in the FY 1968 budget (DE 1098–1107); the construction of six ships (DE 1102–1107) was deferred in 1968 in favor of more-capable destroyer type ships (i.e., the SPRUANCE program); three ships were deferred later that year (DE 1099–1101) to help pay for cost overruns of nuclear-propelled submarines; and one ship (DE 1098) was deferred in 1969. Note that the hull number 1098 has been assigned to the earlier GLOVER (formerly AGFF/AGDE 1).

Classification: These ships were built as ocean escorts (DE); changed to frigates on 30 June 1975.

Design: This design is significantly larger than the BROOKE and GARCIA classes because of the use of non-pressure-fired boilers. The superstructure is topped by a distinctive cylindrical "mack" which combines masts and stacks. A port-side anchor is fitted at the bow, and a larger anchor retracts into the after end of the bow sonar dome.

The original hangar has been enlarged in most ships to accommodate the SH-2F LAMPS helicopter. Hangars vary in size from 41½ to 47⅙ feet in length and 14½ to 18¼ feet in width.

Helicopters: These ships were designed to operate DASH. Subsequently most ships have been refitted to operate the SH-2F LAMPS.

Missiles: The DOWNES was evaluation ship for the NATO Sea Sparrow missile. The ships are being modified to fire Harpoon SSMs from the ASROC launcher.

Torpedoes: The Mk 32 tubes are fixed in the after superstructure.

PHARRIS with VDS lowered (1978, U.S. Navy, PHAN C. E. Fritz)

The DOWNES was the test ship for the NATO Sea Sparrow launcher. Mk 91 FCS directors are on a lattice mast atop the bridge and atop the helicopter hangar; the SPS-40 antenna has been moved to a second lattice mast atop the hangar, with its place on the "mack" taken by a Mk 23 Target Acquisition System (TAS) antenna. (1972, U.S. Navy)

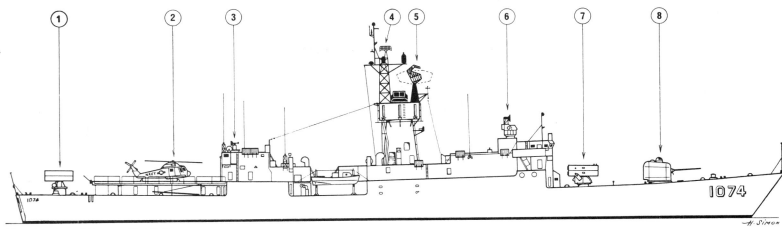

Line drawing of HAROLD E. HOLT

1. Sea Sparrow BPDMS   2. SH-2 LAMPS helicopter   3. Mk 115 Sea Sparrow director   4. SPS-10 radar   5. SPS-40 radar   6. Mk 68 FCS   7. ASROC launcher   8. 5-inch DP Mk 42 gun

HAROLD E. HOLT with HAWKBILL (SSN 666) (1979, Giorgio Arra)

Lockwood with SH-2F LAMPS from HSL-37 (1979, Giorgio Arra)

10 FRIGATES: "GARCIA" CLASS

Number	Name	FY/SCB	Builder	Laid down	Launched	Commissioned	Status
FF 1040	GARCIA	61/199A	Bethlehem Steel (San Francisco)	16 Oct 1962	31 Oct 1963	21 Dec 1964	**AA**
FF 1041	BRADLEY	61/199A	Bethlehem Steel (San Francisco)	17 Jan 1963	26 Mar 1964	15 May 1965	**PA**
FF 1043	EDWARD McDONNELL	62/199A	Avondale Shipyards	1 Apr 1963	15 Feb 1964	15 Feb 1965	**AA**
FF 1044	BRUMBY	62/199A	Avondale Shipyards	1 Aug 1963	6 June 1964	5 Aug 1965	**AA**
FF 1045	DAVIDSON	62/199A	Avondale Shipyards	20 Sep 1963	2 Oct 1964	7 Dec 1965	**PA**
FF 1047	VOGE	63/199A	Defoe Shipbuilding	21 Nov 1963	4 Feb 1965	25 Nov 1966	**AA**
FF 1048	SAMPLE	63/199A	Lockheed SB & Constn Co	19 July 1963	28 Apr 1964	23 Mar 1968	**PA**
FF 1049	KOELSCH	63/199A	Defoe Shipbuilding	19 Feb 1964	8 June 1965	10 June 1967	**AA**
FF 1050	ALBERT DAVID	63/199A	Lockheed SB & Constn Co	29 Apr 1964	19 Dec 1964	19 Oct 1968	**PA**
FF 1051	O'CALLAHAN	63/199A	Defoe Shipbuilding	19 Feb 1964	20 Oct 1965	13 July 1968	**PA**

Displacement:	2,620 tons standard
	3,400 tons full load
Length:	390 feet (118.9 m) wl
	414½ feet (126.3 m) oa
Beam:	44⅙ feet (13.5 m)
Draft:	24 feet (7.3 m)
Propulsion:	steam turbine (Westinghouse); 35,000 shp; 1 shaft
Boilers:	2 1,200-psi (Foster Wheeler)
Speed:	27 knots
Range:	4,000 n. miles at 20 knots
Manning:	258–270 (17 O + 241–253 enlisted)
Helicopters:	1 SH-2F LAMPS except none in FF 1048, 1050
Guns:	2 5-inch (127-mm) 38 cal SP Mk 30 (2 × 1)
ASW weapons:	1 8-tube ASROC launcher Mk 16
	6 12.75-inch (324-mm) torpedo tubes Mk 32 (2 × 3)
Radars:	SPS-10 surface search
	SPS-40 air search
Sonars:	SQS-26AXR bow-mounted in FF 1040–1045
	SQS-26BX bow-mounted in FF 1046–1051
	SQR-15 TASS in FF 1048, 1050
Fire control:	1 Mk 1 target designation system
	1 Mk 56 gun FCS
	1 Mk 114 ASW FCS
	1 Mk 35 radar

These ships are similar to the contemporary BROOKE-class frigates, but with a second 5-inch gun in place of the latter's Tartar missile launcher.

Aircraft: DASH facilities were originally provided in these ships; modified to operate SH-2 LAMPS in the 1970s.

Classification: As built, these ships were classified as ocean escorts (DE); changed to frigates (FF) on 30 June 1975.

Missiles: The BRADLEY evaluated the Sea Sparrow BPDMS in 1967–1968, with the launcher being fitted between the funnel and the after 5-inch gun mount.

Torpedoes: Several ships were built with two Mk 25 tubes for ASW torpedoes in their stern; these have been removed from the earlier ships and were not fitted in the later ships.

DAVIDSON (1980, Giorgio Arra)

DAVIDSON (1979, Giorgio Arra)

2 FRIGATES: "BRONSTEIN" CLASS

Number	Name	FY/SCB	Builder	Laid down	Launched	Commissioned	Status
FF 1037	BRONSTEIN	60/199	Avondale Shipyards	16 May 1961	31 Mar 1962	15 June 1963	**PA**
FF 1038	McCLOY	60/199	Avondale Shipyards	15 Sep 1961	9 June 1962	21 Oct 1963	**AA**

Displacement:	2,360 tons standard
	2,650 tons full load
Length:	350 feet (106.7 m) wl
	371½ feet (113.2 m) oa
Beam:	40½ feet (12.3 m)
Draft:	23 feet (7 m)
Propulsion:	steam turbine (De Laval); 20,000 shp; 1 shaft
Boilers:	2 600-psi (Foster Wheeler)
Speed:	24 knots
Range:	2,300 n. miles at 20 knots
Manning:	208 (13 O + 195 enlisted) in FF 1037
	209 (13 O + 196 enlisted) in FF 1038
Guns:	2 3-inch (76-mm) 50 cal AA Mk 33 (1 × 2)
ASW weapons:	1 8-tube ASROC launcher Mk 16
	6 12.75-inch (324-mm) torpedo tubes Mk 32 (2 × 3)
Radars:	SPS-10 surface search
	SPS-40 air search
Sonars:	SQS-26 bow-mounted
	SQR-15 TASS
Fire control:	1 Mk 1 target designation system
	1 Mk 56 gun FCS
	1 Mk 114 ASW FCS
	1 Mk 35 radar

These were the lead ships for a new generation of ASW ocean escorts, introducing the large SQS-26 bow-mounted sonar and ASROC. However, they lack the 5-inch guns, helicopter facilities, and sea-keeping characteristics of the later BROOKE, GARCIA, and KNOX classes.

Classification: Both ships were built as ocean escorts (DE); changed to frigates on 30 June 1975.

Design: The BRONSTEIN design provided for a DASH helicopter facility. These ships cannot operate larger, manned helicopters.

Guns: As built, a third 3-inch gun (single) was mounted aft; subsequently removed. The next 63 frigates built by the U.S. Navy had 5-inch guns. The PERRY class introduced the 76-mm gun in 1978.

Sonars: A Towed Array Surveillance System (TASS) was fitted to both ships in the mid-1970s. The BRONSTEIN currently has an SQR-15 TASS.

McCLOY (1976, U.S. Navy, PH2 D.L. Thompson)

McCLOY (1975, U.S. Navy, Ed Dowling)

POST–WORLD WAR II ESCORT/FRIGATE PROGRAMS

U.S. World War II destroyer escort programs reached hull number DE 1005 (with DE 801–1005 being canceled). After the war several ships were converted to radar picket escorts (DER), a few for the tactical fleet role, but most for strategic early warning. A few also were modified to a control escort (DEC) configuration to support amphibious landings. With the start of postwar construction, these ships were reclassified as ocean escorts (DE), partly so that they would not be confused with escort destroyers (DDE). U.S. hull numbers were assigned to 17 ships built in Europe with American funds (Offshore Procurement or OSP). Thirteen U.S. ships were completed between 1954 and 1957, built to the similar DEALEY and COURTNEY designs, and four ships to the CLAUD JONES design.

DE 1006	DEALEY	Comm. 1954; to Uruguay 1972
DE 1007	(French LE NORMAND)	OSP 1956
DE 1008	(French LE LORRAIN)	OSP 1956
DE 1009	(French LE PICARD)	OSP 1956
DE 1010	(French LE GASCON)	OSP 1957
DE 1011	(French LE CHAMPENOIS)	OSP 1957
DE 1012	(French LE SAVOYARD)	OSP 1957
DE 1013	(French LE BOURGUIGNON)	OSP 1957
DE 1014	CROMWELL	Comm. 1954; stricken 1972
DE 1015	HAMMERBERG	Comm. 1955; stricken 1973
DE 1016	(French LE CORSE)	OSP 1952
DE 1017	(French LE BRESTOIS)	OSP 1952
DE 1018	(French LE BOULONNAIS)	OSP 1953
DE 1019	(French LE BORDELAIS)	OSP 1953
DE 1020	(Italian CIGNO)	OSP 1957
DE 1021	COURTNEY	Comm. 1956; stricken 1973
DE 1022	LESTER	Comm. 1957; stricken 1973
DE 1023	EVANS	Comm. 1957; stricken 1973
DE 1024	BRIDGET	Comm. 1957; stricken 1973
DE 1025	BAUER	Comm. 1957; stricken 1973
DE 1026	HOOPER	Comm. 1958; stricken 1973
DE 1027	JOHN WILLIS	Comm. 1957; stricken 1972
DE 1028	VAN VOORHIS	Comm. 1957; stricken 1972
DE 1029	HARTLEY	Comm. 1957; to Colombia 1972
DE 1030	JOSEPH K. TAUSSIG	Comm. 1957; stricken 1972
DE 1031	(Italian CASTORE)	OSP 1957
DE 1032	(Portuguese PERO ESCOBAR)	OSP 1957
DE 1033	CLAUD JONES	Comm. 1959; to Indonesia 1974
DE 1034	JOHN R. PERRY	Comm. 1959; to Indonesia 1973
DE 1035	CHARLES BERRY	Comm. 1959; to Indonesia 1974
DE 1036	McMORRISS	Comm. 1960; to Indonesia 1974
DE 1037–1038	BRONSTEIN class	
DE 1039	(Portuguese ALMIRANTE PEREIRA DA SILVA)	OSP 1966
DE 1040–1041	GARCIA class	
DE 1042	(Portuguese ALMIRANTE GAGO COUTINHO)	OSP 1967
DE 1043–1045	GARCIA class	
DE 1046	(Portuguese ALMIRANTE MAGALHAES CORREA)	OSP 1967
DE 1047–1051	GARCIA class	
DE 1052–1107[a]	KNOX class	

[a] FF 1098 subsequently reassigned to GLOVER (formerly AGFF/AGDE 1).

11 Command Ships

The U.S. Navy has three specialized flagships in service: The LA SALLE, which serves as flagship for Commander, U.S. Middle East Force; the BLUE RIDGE, flagship for the Commander, Seventh Fleet; and the MOUNT WHITNEY, flagship for Commander Second Fleet.

The LA SALLE and MOUNT WHITNEY are home-ported at Norfolk, with the former ship operating in the Persian Gulf and Indian Ocean area. The BLUE RIDGE is home-ported in Yokosuka, Japan. The LA SALLE is officially classified as an auxiliary ship and the BLUE RIDGE and MOUNT WHITNEY as amphibious ships. In late 1980, the amphibious dock CORONADO (LPD 11) was modified to serve as a flagship to relieve the LASALLE while she returned to the United States for overhaul. The CORONADO, described in Chapter 12, was given the temporary designation AGF 11 for the assignment.

1 MISCELLANEOUS FLAGSHIP: CONVERTED "RALEIGH" CLASS

Number	Name	FY/SCB	Builder	Laid down	Launched	Commissioned	Status
AGF 3 (ex-LPD 3)	LA SALLE	61/187A	New York Naval Shipyard	2 Apr 1962	3 Aug 1963	22 Feb 1964	Yard

Displacement:	8,040 tons light
	13,900 tons full load
Length:	500 feet (152.0 m) wl
	521¾ feet (158.4 m) oa
Beam:	84 feet (25.6 m)
Draft:	21 feet (6.4 m)
Propulsion:	steam turbines (De Laval); 24,000 shp; 2 shafts
Boilers:	2 600-psi (Babcock & Wilcox)
Speed:	21.6 knots (20 knots sustained)
Manning:	421 (21 O + 400 enlisted)
Flag:	59 (12 O + 47 enlisted)
Helicopters:	utility helicopter
Guns:	8 3-inch (76-mm) 50 cal AA Mk 33 (4 × 2)
Radars:	SPS-10 surface search
	SPS-40 air search
Fire control:	(local control only)

The LA SALLE was converted from an amphibious transport dock specifically to serve as flagship for the U.S. Middle East Force. She has retained her docking well and other amphibious ship features. The LASALLE entered the Philadelphia Naval Shipyard in January 1981 for a major overhaul that was to last until early 1982. During the overhaul the CORONADO was assigned as flagship for Commander, Middle East Force.

Class: The LA SALLE was one of three RALEIGH (LPD 1)-class amphibious transport docks.

Classification: Built as LPD 3 and served with that designation until 1 July 1972 when changed to AGF 3.

Conversion: During 1972 the LA SALLE was fitted with command and communications facilities, accommodations for an admiral and his staff, a helicopter hangar, and additional air-conditioning. The amidships hangar is 48⅓-feet long and 18-feet wide. The ship is painted white to help reflect heat.

Guns: The LA SALLE is scheduled to have one twin 3-inch gun mount removed and two Phalanx CIWS installed.

LA SALLE (1972, U.S. Navy)

One of two white warships, the LA SALLE steams through the Indian Ocean with three of her Mk 33 Mod 13 twin 3-inch gun mounts trained on the camera. The LA SALLE retains most of her LPD assault capability but has a helicopter hangar and covered assembly area on her flight deck. Note the lattice mast for a satellite antenna abaft her portside stack. In 1980–81, the CORONADO (LPD 11) stood in for the LA SALLE as Middle East flagship and was similarly painted white. (1977, U.S. Navy)

BLUE RIDGE (1979, Giorgio Arra)

2 AMPHIBIOUS COMMAND SHIPS: "BLUE RIDGE" CLASS

Number	Name	FY/SCB	Builder	Laid down	Launched	Commissioned	Status
LCC 19	BLUE RIDGE	65/400	Philadelphia Naval Shipyard	27 Feb 1967	4 Jan 1969	14 Nov 1970	**PA**
LCC 20	MOUNT WHITNEY	66/400	Newport News	8 Jan 1969	8 Jan 1970	16 Jan 1971	**AA**

Displacement:	19,290 tons full load	Fire control:	1 Mk 1 target designation system
Length:	620 feet (188.5 m) oa		2 Mk 56 gun FCS
Beam:	82 feet (25.3 m)		2 Mk 115 missile FCS
Extreme width:	108 feet (33 m)		2 Mk 35 radar
Draft:	27 feet (8.2 m)		

Displacement: 19,290 tons full load
Length: 620 feet (188.5 m) oa
Beam: 82 feet (25.3 m)
Extreme width: 108 feet (33 m)
Draft: 27 feet (8.2 m)
Propulsion: steam turbine (General Electric); 22,000 shp; 1 shaft
Boilers: 2 600-psi (Foster Wheeler)
Speed: 20 knots (sustained)
Manning: 799 (41 O + 758 enlisted) in LCC 19
516 (41 O + 475 enlisted) in LCC 20
Flag: ~250 (50 O + 200 enlisted) in LCC 19
~420 (160 O + 260 enlisted) in LCC 20
Helicopters: utility helicopters
Missiles: 2 8-tube Sea Sparrow BPDMS launchers Mk 25
Guns: 4 3-inch (76-mm) 50 cal AA Mk 33 (2 × 2)
Radar: SPS-10 surface search
SPS-40 air search
SPS-48 3-D search

Fire control: 1 Mk 1 target designation system
2 Mk 56 gun FCS
2 Mk 115 missile FCS
2 Mk 35 radar

These are large amphibious command ships, the first and only ships to be constructed by any nation specifically for that role. Both ships are now employed as fleet flagships, replacing cruisers in that role. The BLUE RIDGE is home-ported in Yokosuka, Japan, having relieved the cruiser OKLAHOMA CITY (CG 5) there in October 1979.

Class: A third ship of this design (AGC 21) was planned; she was to have been designed from the outset for both amphibious force and fleet command functions.

MOUNT WHITNEY (1978, U.S. Navy, LCDR Joe Mancias, Jr.)

BLUE RIDGE (1979, Giorgio Arra)

BLUE RIDGE (1977, Giorgio Arra)

Classification: These ships were originally classified as amphibious force flagships (AGC); they were changed to amphibious command ships (LCC) on 1 January 1969.

Design: The command ship facilities originally provided in this class were for a Navy amphibious task force command and a Marine assault-force commander and their staffs. Designed flag/staff accommodations were for 200 officers and 500 enlisted men.

They have large open decks to provide for antenna placement. There is a helicopter landing area aft, but no hangar. (A small vehicle hangar and elevator is provided.) The hull and propulsion machinery are similar to the Iwo JIMA (LPH 2)-class helicopter carriers.

Flag: In addition to Commander Second Fleet (39 + 82), the MOUNT WHITNEY in early 1981 carried the Commander Amphibious Group 2 (45 + 75) and Commander Fourth Marine Amphibious Brigade (with a full staff strength of approximately 75 + 100).

Guns: The original armament was two 3-inch AA gun mounts as now installed. Early designs provided for two additional 3-inch twin mounts on the forecastle; they were not installed.

Missiles: The Sea Sparrow BPDMS launchers were fitted in 1974.

MISCELLANEOUS FLAGSHIPS

From the late 1940s until 1972 the Navy employed small seaplane tenders (AVP) as flagships for U.S. forces in the Persian Gulf area. Subsequently, one of those ships, the VALCOUR (AVP 55), was reclassified as a miscellaneous flagship (AGF 1) on 15 December 1965 specifically for that role and home-ported in Bahrain. She was replaced in that role by the LA SALLE in 1972. In order to permit the LA SALLE to retain the "3" of the original designation.

COMMAND SHIPS

The Navy built one ship and converted another specifically for use as major command ships, while a third such ship was planned.

The heavy cruiser NORTHAMPTON (CA 125), canceled in 1945 while under construction, was subsequently reordered in 1948 as a tactical light command ship (CLC 1) and completed in that configuration in 1953. After operating as a fleet flagship, she was reconfigured to serve as a National Emergency Command Post Afloat (NECPA) in 1961 and reclassified as CC 1. She was decommissioned in 1970 and laid up in reserve until stricken in 1977.

The light carriers WRIGHT (originally CVL 49) and SAIPAN (CVL 48) were similarly designated for conversion to the NECPA role. The WRIGHT, also designated AVT 6 while in reserve, was converted in 1962–1963 and became CC 2; she operated in the NECPA role until 1970 when she was laid up in reserve. She was stricken in 1977.

The SAIPAN, also AVT 6 while in reserve after World War II, began conversion to the CC 3 in 1964, but was instead completed as a major communications relay ship in 1966 (renamed ARLINGTON and classified AGMR 2).

In the NECPA role these ships were to provide afloat facilities for the President in the event of a national emergency or war.

12 Amphibious Warfare Ships

The U.S. Navy had 58 amphibious ships in active commission as of January 1981. With six additional amphibious ships assigned to the Naval Reserve Force and manned by composite active-reserve crews, this force has a nominal lift capacity of slightly more than one reinforced Marine division and air wing (approximately 30,000 troops; designated a Marine Assault Force or MAF). The term *nominal* is used because only some 85 percent of the ships normally are operational, with the remainder being in overhaul or undergoing modernization. Of the operational ships, at any given time one squadron is forward-deployed in the Mediterranean and two in the Western Pacific-Indian Ocean region, while others are in transit to or from forward deployments. Thus, the ability to concentrate a major amphibious lift capability is limited. (One of these ships, the CORONADO, was temporarily employed as a special flagship during 1981.)

In addition to the 64 amphibious ships listed in this chapter, two amphibious command ships are listed separately because of their current employment as fleet flagships, as is the flagship LA SALLE (Chapter 11) and the transport submarine GRAYBACK (Chapter 5).

The amphibious force will lose eight dock landing ships during the 1980s as the THOMASTON-class ships reach their thirtieth year of service. The planned LSD 41 class that was to replace those ships is expected to have only six units built during the 1980s, a net loss of two ships. More significant, a score of additional amphibious ships will reach the end of their predicted service lives in the 1990s, requiring a replacement rate of more than two ships per year to begin in the late 1980s. At this writing there is no official program for their replacement. However, preliminary studies have suggested one or two ship types that could serve as a "universal" amphibious ship, much the same as the LHA design was a partial replacement for the LKA, LPA, LPH, and LSD types. The single ship concept—unofficially designated LHX—would have a flight-deck configuration, with a possible variant additionally having a docking well specifically for carrying air cushion landing craft (LCAC).

In addition to amphibious warfare ships, which are designed to carry and unload amphibious forces on hostile beaches, the U.S. Navy is now developing a force of forward-deployment ships. This concept, which was developed in the early 1960s, calls for cargo-type ships to be kept in overseas areas with weapons and munitions that can be "married" with troops that are flown into the area during a crisis. See Chapter 17 for additional information.

Electronics: The LHA and LPH classes are being fitted with the SLQ-32(V)3 electronic warfare suite; the LKA, LPD, LSD, and LST classes are receiving the SLQ-32(V)1.

Names: Amphibious assault ships are named for major battles or landings in which U.S. Marines participated; amphibious cargo ships for counties; amphibious transport docks for cities that honor explorers and pioneers; dock landing ships for historic sites and cities; and tank landing ships for counties and parishes.

Type	Class/Ship	Active	Bldg.[a]	NRF	Reserve[b]	Commission
LCC 19[b]	BLUE RIDGE	2	—	—	—	1970–1971
LHA 1	TARAWA	5	—	—	—	1976–1980
LPH 2	IWO JIMA	7	—	—	—	1961–1970
LKA 113	CHARLESTON	1	—	4	—	1968–1970
LKA 112	MARINER	—	—	—	1	1956
LPD 4	AUSTIN	12	—	—	—	1965–1971
LPD 2	RALEIGH	2	—	—	—	1962–1963
LSD 41	. . . .	—	1	—	—	
LSD 36	ANCHORAGE	5	—	—	—	1969–1972
LSD 28	THOMASTON	8	—	—	—	1954–1957
LST 1179	NEWPORT	18	—	2	—	1969–1972
LST 1156	TERREBONNE PARISH	—	—	—	6	1953
LST 1	. . . .	—	—	—	2	1943–1944
SS 574[c]	GRAYBACK	1	—	—	—	1958

[a] Includes ships authorized through FY 1981.
[b] Includes ships laid up in National Defense Reserve Fleet.
[c] Ships listed in other chapters.

Sign of the future? The JEFF-B Amphibious Assault Landing Craft (AALC) sails into the dry well of the dock landing ship SPIEGEL GROVE during trials off Panama City, Fla. The U.S. Marine Corps plans to procure some 50 to 80 air cushion landing craft during the 1980s. At this writing the Soviet Navy already had some 40 such craft in service. Despite the development of large helicopter ships, LSDs and LPDs remain important to amphibious operations because of their ability to carry a variety of vehicles, landing craft, and equipment, plus, in the case of the LPDs, large numbers of troops. (1979, U.S. Navy)

5 AMPHIBIOUS ASSAULT SHIPS: "TARAWA" CLASS

Number	Name	FY/SCB	Builder	Laid down	Launched	Commissioned	Status
LHA 1	Tarawa	69/410	Litton/Ingalls (Pascagoula)	15 Nov 1971	1 Dec 1973	29 May 1976	**PA**
LHA 2	Saipan	70/410	Litton/Ingalls (Pascagoula)	21 July 1972	18 July 1974	15 Oct 1977	**AA**
LHA 3	Belleau Wood	70/410	Litton/Ingalls (Pascagoula)	5 Mar 1973	11 Apr 1977	23 Sep 1978	**PA**
LHA 4	Nassau	71/410	Litton/Ingalls (Pascagoula)	13 Aug 1973	28 Jan 1978	28 July 1979	**AA**
LHA 5	Peleliu	71/410	Litton/Ingalls (Pascagoula)	12 Nov 1976	6 Jan 1979	3 May 1980	**PA**

Displacement: 39,300 tons full load
Length: 778 feet (237.1 m) wl
820 feet (249.9 m) oa
Beam: 106²/₃ feet (32.5 m)
Extreme width: 126 feet (38.4 m)
Draft: 26 feet (7.9 m)
Propulsion: steam turbines (Westinghouse); 70,000 shp; 2 shafts
Boilers: 2 600-psi (Combustion Engineering)
Speed: 24 knots (22 knots sustained)
Manning: ~894 (~54 O + ~840 enlisted)
Troops: 2,000+
Helicopters: ~30
Catapults: none

Elevators: 2 { 1 deck edge (50 × 34 feet; 40,000-pound capacity)
1 stern (59¾ × 34¾ feet; 80,000-pound capacity)
Missiles: 2 8-tube Sea Sparrow launchers BPDMS Mk 25
Guns: 3 5-inch (127-mm) 54 cal DP Mk 45 (3 × 1)
6 20-mm AA Mk 67 (6 × 1)
Radars: SPS-10F air search
SPS-40B air search
SPS-52B 3-D search
Fire control: 1 Mk 86 gun FCS
2 Mk 115 missile FCS
1 SPG-60 radar
1 SPQ-9A radar

The Saipan with Army and Air Force helicopters spotted on her flight deck steams off the coast of Nicaragua during a rescue operation after a natural disaster struck the Central American state. Search, rescue, and relief operations are a regular function of Navy ships. Note the large, blockhouse island structure, with the vehicle ramp opening visible just under the Sea Sparrow launcher forward of the island. (1979, U.S. Navy, PH1 Thomas E. Kosbiel)

These are the largest amphibious ships ever built. They were intended to combine the capabilities of several types of amphibious ship in one hull. In addition to helicopters, these ships periodically have operated AV-8 Harrier VSTOL aircraft and OV-10 Bronco STOL aircraft.

Class: Nine ships of this class were originally planned. The Navy announced on 20 January 1971 that LHA 6–9 would not be constructed.

Design: Special features of this class include an 18-foot section of the mast that is hinged to permit passage under bridges; a 5,000-square-foot training and acclimatization room to permit troops to exercise in a controlled environment; 30,000 square feet of vehicle storage decks connected by ramps to the flight deck and docking well; five cargo elevators that move equipment between the holds and flight deck; and extensive command and communications facilities are provided for an amphibious force commander.

The hangar deck is 820-feet long and 78-feet wide with a 20-foot overhead.

The stern docking well is 268-feet long and 78-feet wide and can accommodate 4 LCU-1610 landing craft or 2 LCUs and 3 LCM-8s or 17 LCM-6s. (In addition, 40 LVTs can be carried on the vehicle decks.)

Engineering: A 900-hp through-tunnel thruster is fitted in the forward part of the hull to assist in maneuvering while launching landing craft. The boilers are the largest ever manufactured in the United States.

Guns: These are the only U.S. amphibious ships that are armed with 5-inch guns. The 20-mm Mk 67 guns are manually operated weapons for defense against small craft and swimmers. Each ship is scheduled to receive two Phalanx CIWS when that weapon becomes available.

Helicopters: These ships were designed to simultaneously operate 12 CH-46 Sea Knight or 9 CH-53 Sea Stallion helicopters from the flight deck. The hangar deck can accommodate 30 Sea Knights or 19 Sea Stallions or various combinations of aircraft. A normal LHA "air wing" consists of 18 Sea Knights, 4 Sea Stallions, and 4 AH-1 SeaCobra helicopters.

Medical: Extensive medical facilities are provided with permanent intensive care space for 300 patients.

Names: The PELELIU was originally named DA NANG; the ship was renamed on 15 February 1978 after the fall of the Republic of (South) Vietnam to communist forces.

TARAWA (1979, Giorgio Arra)

NASSAU (1979, Litton/Ingalls)

TARAWA with three LCMs visible in docking well (1979, Giorgio Arra)

TARAWA (1979, Giorgio Arra)

7 AMPHIBIOUS ASSAULT SHIPS: "IWO JIMA" CLASS

Number	Name	FY/SCB	Builder	Laid down	Launched	Commissioned	Status
LPH 2	Iwo Jima	58/157	Puget Sound Naval Shipyard	2 Apr 1959	17 Sep 1960	26 Aug 1961	**AA**
LPH 3	Okinawa	59/157	Philadelphia Naval Shipyard	1 Apr 1960	14 Aug 1961	14 Apr 1962	**PA**
LPH 7	Guadalcanal	60/157	Philadelphia Naval Shipyard	1 Sep 1961	16 Mar 1963	20 July 1963	**AA**
LPH 9	Guam	62/157	Philadelphia Naval Shipyard	15 Nov 1962	22 Aug 1964	16 Jan 1965	**AA**
LPH 10	Tripoli	63/157	Ingalls SB Corp	15 June 1964	31 July 1965	6 Aug 1966	**PA**
LPH 11	New Orleans	65/157	Philadelphia Naval Shipyard	1 Mar 1966	3 Feb 1968	16 Nov 1968	**PA**
LPH 12	Inchon	66/157	Ingalls SB Corp	8 Apr 1968	24 May 1969	20 June 1970	**AA**

Displacement:	17,000 tons light
	18,300 tons full load
Length:	592 feet (180 m) oa
Beam:	84 feet (25.6 m)
Extreme width:	112 feet (34.1 m)
Draft:	26 feet (7.9 m)
Propulsion:	steam turbine (Westinghouse); 22,000 shp; 1 shaft
Boilers:	2 600-psi (Combustion Engineering or Babcock & Wilcox)
Speed:	20 knots (sustained)
Manning:	~652 (~44 O + ~608 enlisted)
Troops:	2,000+
Helicopters:	~25
Catapults:	none
Elevators:	2 deck edge (50 × 34 feet; 50,000-pound capacity in LPH 2–3, 11–12) (50 × 34 feet; 44,000-pound capacity in LPH 7, 9–10)
Missiles:	2 8-tube Sea Sparrow launchers BPDMS Mk 25
Guns:	4 3-inch (76-mm) 50 cal AA Mk 33 (2 × 2)
Radars:	SPS-10 surface search
	SPS-40 air search
Fire control:	2 Mk 115 missile FCS

These ships were the first of any navy designed specifically to operate helicopters. Unlike the Royal Navy's commando ships and the later Tarawa class, the ships do not carry landing craft and are thus limited in the size of vehicles that they can carry (except for LCVP davits in the Inchon).

The Guam of this class operated from 1972 to 1974 as an interim sea-control ship to evaluate the concept of flying VSTOL aircraft and ASW helicopters from a ship of this size in the convoy defense role; she subsequently reverted to an amphibious-assault role. These ships have also operated minesweeping helicopters.

Design: These ships represent an improved World War II-type escort carrier design with accommodations for a Marine battalion. The Inchon has davits aft for two LCVPs. No catapults or arresting gear are fitted.

Guns: As built, these ships had four 3-inch twin gun mounts. Between 1970 and 1974 all ships had two mounts replaced by the Sea Sparrow launchers (one on the flight deck forward of the island structure, and one on the port quarter).

All gun FCS have been removed and only local control is now available.

The ships are each scheduled to receive two Phalanx CIWS.

Helicopters: The ships can simultaneously launch and recover up to seven CH-46 Sea Knight or four CH-53 Sea Stallion helicopters from their flight decks. The hangar deck can accommodate 19 Sea Knights or 11 Sea Stallions or various mixes of helicopters.

Medical: These ships have extensive medical facilities.

AMPHIBIOUS ASSAULT SHIP PROGRAMS

The LPH classification was established in 1955. The World War II-era escort carrier Block Island was to have been LPH 1, but her conversion was canceled. Three Essex-class carriers were subsequently modified to LPHs, as was the escort carrier Thetis Bay. The smaller ship had been designated a helicopter assault carrier (CVHA 1) upon her conversion in 1955–1956. She was changed to LPH to avoid confusion and budget competition with CV-type aircraft carriers.

LPH 1	Block Island (ex-CVE 106)	conversion canceled
LPH 2–3	Iwo Jima class	
LPH 4	Boxer (ex-CVA/CVS 21)	to LPH 1959; stricken 1969
LPH 5	Princeton (ex-CVA/CVS 37)	to LPH 1959; stricken 1970
LPH 6	Thetis Bay (ex-CVE 90)	to CVHA 1/LPH 1956; stricken 1966
LPH 7	Iwo Jima class	
LPH 8	Valley Forge (ex-CVA/CVS 45)	to LPH 1961; stricken 1970
LPH 9–12	Iwo Jima class	

GUADALCANAL (1979, Giorgio Arra)

The TRIPOLI at anchor in Hong Kong harbor with Marine CH-46 Sea Knights and CH-53 Sea Stallions on her deck, plus a single UH-1 Huey parked on the forward end of her flight deck. The LPHs have been used primarily for vertical assault operations, but also for mine countermeasures in Vietnam and Suez with CH-53/RH-53 AMCM helicopters. (1980, Giorgio Arra)

TRIPOLI (1980, Giorgio Arra)

GUADALCANAL (1978, U.S. Navy, LCDR Joe Mancias, Jr.)

TRIPOLI with SCHOFIELD (FFG 3) in background (1980, Giorgio Arra)

5 AMPHIBIOUS CARGO SHIPS: "CHARLESTON" CLASS

Number	Name	FY/SCB	Builder	Laid down	Launched	Commissioned	Status
LKA 113	CHARLESTON	65/403	Newport News	5 Dec 1966	2 Dec 1967	14 Dec 1968	**NRF-A**
LKA 114	DURHAM	65/403	Newport News	10 July 1967	29 Mar 1968	24 May 1969	**NRF-P**
LKA 115	MOBILE	65/403	Newport News	15 Jan 1968	19 Oct 1968	20 Sep 1969	**NRF-P**
LKA 116	ST. LOUIS	65/403	Newport News	3 Apr 1968	4 Jan 1969	22 Nov 1969	**PA**
LKA 117	EL PASO	66/403	Newport News	22 Oct 1968	17 May 1969	17 Jan 1970	**NRF-A**

Displacement:	20,700 tons full load
Length:	575½ feet (175.4 m) oa
Beam:	82 feet (25 m)
Draft:	25½ feet (7.7 m)
Propulsion:	steam turbine (Westinghouse); 22,000 shp; 1 shaft
Boilers:	2 600-psi (Combustion Engineering)
Speed:	20+ knots (sustained)
Manning:	325 (24 O + 301 enlisted) in active ships
Troops:	225
Guns:	6 3-inch (76-mm) 50 cal AA Mk 33 (3 × 2)
Radars:	SPS-10 surface search
Fire control:	(local control only)

These ships carry heavy equipment and supplies for amphibious assaults. They are the first ships to be designed and constructed specifically for this role; all previous ships of the LKA/AKA type were converted or built to merchant designs.

The DURHAM was transferred to the Naval Reserve Force on 1 October 1979, the CHARLESTON on 21 November 1979, the MOBILE on 1 September 1980, and the EL PASO late in 1980.

Classification: As ordered, these ships were classified as attack cargo ships (AKA); the CHARLESTON was changed to an amphibious cargo ship (LKA) on 14 December 1968; the others were changed to LKA on 1 January 1969.

Design: These ships have a helicopter landing area aft, but no hangar or maintenance facilities. The ships can carry nine LCMs as deck cargo. There are two 78-ton capacity cranes, two 40-ton capacity booms, and eight 15-ton capacity booms.

Guns: As built, four 3-inch twin mounts were provided. One mount has been removed from each ship as well as the Mk 56 gun FCS.

DURHAM (1979, Giorgio Arra)

1 AMPHIBIOUS CARGO SHIP: "MARINER" CLASS

Number	Name	Builder	Laid down	Launched	Commissioned	Status
LKA 112	TULARE	Bethlehem Steel (San Francisco)	16 Feb 1953	22 Dec 1953	12 Jan 1956	MR

Displacement:	12,000 tons light
	16,800 tons full load
Length:	564 feet (171.9 m) oa
Beam:	76 feet (23.2 m)
Draft:	26 feet (7.9 m)
Propulsion:	steam turbine (De Laval); 22,000 shp; 1 shaft
Boilers:	2 (Combustion Engineering)
Manning:	325 (24 O + 301 enlisted active; 21 O + 208 enlisted reserve)
Troops:	320
Guns:	6 3-inch (76-mm) 50 cal AA Mk 33 (3 × 2)
Radars:	SPS-10 surface search
	SPS-12 air search
Fire control:	(local control only)

The TULARE was a "Mariner"-class merchant ship acquired by the Navy on 12 January 1956 for conversion to an amphibious cargo ship. After active service for almost two decades she was transferred to the Naval Reserve Force on 1 July 1975. She was decommissioned on 15 February 1980 and laid up in the National Defense Reserve Fleet (i.e., Maritime Reserve).

Class: Thirty-five "Mariner"-class cargo ships were built during the early 1950s. Five ships were acquired by the Navy: two for conversion to attack transports (APA/LPA) and two to support fleet ballistic missile development programs (AG), plus the TULARE. At one point a sixth Navy acquisition was planned, also to support the Polaris FBM program.

Classification: The TULARE originally was classified as an attack cargo ship (AKA); she was changed to amphibious cargo ship (LKA) on 1 January 1969.

Design: A helicopter platform is fitted aft, but no hangar or maintenance facilities were provided. The ship has 60-ton capacity booms and can deck load 9 LCM-6s and 11 LCVPs. The Maritime Administration type was C4-S-1A and the Navy conversion SCB-77.

Guns: Initially as an AKA the TULARE was armed with 12 3-inch guns in twin mounts. The number of guns was reduced in the 1970s and her Mk 63 gun FCS were removed.

Names: As ordered, all "Mariner"-class ships were assigned nicknames for states of the Union, with all but one also having the name suffix "Mariner." The TULARE was named EVERGREEN MARINER in commercial service.

TULARE (1969, U.S. Navy)

12 AMPHIBIOUS TRANSPORT DOCKS: "AUSTIN" CLASS

Number	Name	FY/SCB	Builder	Laid down	Launched	Commissioned	Status
LPD 4	AUSTIN	62/187B	New York Naval Shipyard	4 Feb 1963	27 June 1964	6 Feb 1965	**AA**
LPD 5	OGDEN	62/187B	New York Naval Shipyard	4 Feb 1963	27 June 1964	19 June 1965	**PA**
LPD 6	DULUTH	62/187B	New York Naval Shipyard	18 Dec 1963	14 Aug 1965	18 Dec 1965	**PA**
LPD 7	CLEVELAND	63/187B	Ingalls SB Corp	30 Nov 1964	7 May 1966	21 Apr 1967	**PA**
LPD 8	DUBUQUE	63/187B	Ingalls SB Corp	25 Jan 1965	6 Aug 1966	1 Sep 1967	**PA**
LPD 9	DENVER	63/187B	Lockheed SB & Constn Co	7 Feb 1964	23 Jan 1965	26 Oct 1968	**PA**
LPD 10	JUNEAU	63/187B	Lockheed SB & Constn Co	23 Jan 1965	12 Feb 1966	12 July 1969	**PA**
AGF 11	CORONADO	64/187C	Lockheed SB & Constn Co	3 May 1965	30 July 1966	23 May 1970	**IO**
LPD 12	SHREVEPORT	64/187C	Lockheed SB & Constn Co	27 Dec 1965	25 Oct 1966	12 Dec 1970	**AA**
LPD 13	NASHVILLE	64/187C	Lockheed SB & Constn Co	14 Mar 1966	7 Oct 1967	14 Feb 1970	**AA**
LPD 14	TRENTON	65/402	Lockheed SB & Constn Co	8 Aug 1966	3 Aug 1968	6 Mar 1971	**AA**
LPD 15	PONCE	65/402	Lockheed SB & Constn Co	31 Oct 1966	30 May 1970	10 July 1971	**AA**

Displacement:	10,000 tons light
	16,900 tons full load
Length:	570 feet (173.3 m) oa
Beam:	84 feet (25.6 m)
Draft:	23 feet (7.0 m)
Propulsion:	steam turbines (De Laval); 24,000 shp; 2 shafts
Boilers:	2 600-psi (Babcock & Wilcox)
Speed:	20 knots (sustained)
Manning:	410–447 (24–25 O + 386–422 enlisted)
Troops:	930 in LPD 4–6
	840 in LPD 7–13
Flag:	90 in LPD 7–13
Helicopters:	up to 6 CH-46 Sea Knight (see notes)
Guns:	4 3-inch (76-mm) 50 cal AA Mk 33 (2 × 2)
Radars:	SPS-10 surface search
	SPS-40 air search
Fire control:	(local control only)

These ships are enlarged versions of the previous RALEIGH-class LPDs. They are intended to carry Marines into the forward area and unload them by landing craft and vehicles carried on board, and by helicopters provided mainly from amphibious assault ships (LHA/LPH). The general configuration of these ships is similar to dock landing ships, but with a relatively smaller docking well and additional space for troop berthing and vehicle parks. The CORONADO was temporarily redesignated AGF 11 (LPD 11) on 1 October 1980 to replace the LA SALLE as flagship of Commander, Middle East Force, while the latter ship was in overhaul.

Builders: The DULUTH was completed at the Philadelphia Naval Shipyard after the closing of the New York Naval Shipyard; she was assigned to the former yard on 24 November 1965.

Class: An additional ship (LPD 16) was provided in the FY 1966 shipbuilding program, but construction of the ship was deferred in favor of the LHA program and officially canceled in February 1969.

Design: The LPD 7–13 are configured as amphibious squadron flagships and have an additional bridge level. The docking well in these ships is 168-feet long and 50-feet wide; see RALEIGH-class listing for well capacity. These ships have a fixed flight deck above the docking well with two landing spots. All except the AUSTIN are fitted with a hangar varying from 58 to 64 feet in length and 18 1/2 to 24 feet in width; the hangars have an extension that can expand to provide a length of approximately 80 feet.

Guns: As built, these ships had eight 3-inch guns in twin mounts. The number was reduced in the late 1970s and the associated Mk 56 and Mk 63 gun FCS were removed. All ships are scheduled to receive two Phalanx CIWS.

Helicopters: These ships have deployed with up to six CH-46 Sea Knights embarked.

Two LCMs enter the docking well of the CLEVELAND while the ship's crane lifts aboard an LCVP. Note the two-spot helicopter deck; partially opened hangar door with movie screen attached in preparation for the nightly show. (U.S. Navy)

JUNEAU (1979, Giorgio Arra)

CORONADO (1980, U.S. Navy)

2 AMPHIBOUS TRANSPORT DOCKS: "RALEIGH" CLASS

Number	Name	FY/SCB	Builder	Laid down	Launched	Commissioned	Status
LPD 1	RALEIGH	59/187	New York Naval Shipyard	23 June 1960	17 Mar 1962	8 Sep 1962	**AA**
LPD 2	VANCOUVER	60/187	New York Naval Shipyard	19 Nov 1960	15 Sep 1962	11 May 1963	**PA**

Displacement:	8,040 tons light
	13,900 tons full load
Length:	521¾ feet (158.4 m) oa
Beam:	84 feet (25.6 m)
Draft:	21 feet (6.4 m)
Propulsion:	steam turbines (De Laval); 24,000 shp; 2 shafts
Boilers:	2 600-psi (Babcock & Wilcox)
Speed:	20 knots (sustained)
Manning:	413 (24 O + 389 enlisted) in LPD 1
	410 (23 O + 387 enlisted) in LPD 2
Troops:	930
Helicopters:	none
Guns:	6 3-inch (76-mm) 50 cal AA Mk 33 (3 × 2)
Radars:	SPS-10 surface search
	SPS-40 air search
Fire control:	(local control only)

The LPD is a development of the dock landing ship (LSD) concept with increased troop and vehicle capacity and a relatively smaller docking well.

Class: The third ship of this class, the LA SALLE (LPD 3), has been reclassified as a miscellaneous flagship (AGF 3); see Chapter 11.

Design: There is a fixed helicopter deck fitted over the docking well in these ships. The well is 168 feet long and 50 feet wide and can accommodate one LCU and three LCM-6s or four LCM-8s or 20 LVTs. In addition, two LCM-6s or four LCPLs are normally carried on the helicopter deck. No helicopter hangar or maintenance facilities are provided.

Guns: All guns originally installed have been retained; however, the Mk 56 and Mk 51 gun FCS have been removed from both ships. The Phalanx CIWS are to be fitted in these ships.

VANCOUVER (1976, John Mortimer)

VANCOUVER—no hangar (1976, Giorgio Arra)

(1) DOCK LANDING SHIP: LSD 41 CLASS

Number	Name	FY/SCB	Builder	Status
LSD 41	. . . .	81	Lockheed SB & Constn Co	Bldg.

Displacement:	11,140 tons light
	15,745 tons full load
Length:	609 feet (185.6 m)
Beam:	84 feet (25.6 m)
Draft:	19½ feet (5.9 m)
Propulsion:	diesels; 40,000 shp; 2 shafts
Speed:	20+ knots (sustained)
Manning:	413 (22 O + 391 enlisted)
Troops:	340

Helicopters:	none
Guns:	2 20-mm Phalanx CIWS Mk 15 (2 × 1)
Radars:	SPS-55 surface search

The LSD 41 class was originally proposed to replace the eight THOMASTON-class ships. However, the Carter Administration deferred construction of the ships until FY 1980 when Congress voted $41 million as long-lead funding for the class, forcing their construction. Subsequently, the Administration announced a plan to construct six ships in alternate years beginning with FY 1981.

Design: These are improved ANCHORAGE-class ships with their docking well 440-feet long and 50-feet wide to enable them to carry four air cushion landing craft (LCAC).

5 DOCK LANDING SHIPS: "ANCHORAGE" CLASS

Number	Name	FY/SCB	Builder	Laid down	Launched	Commissioned	Status
LSD 36	ANCHORAGE	65/404	Ingalls SB Corp	13 Mar 1967	5 May 1968	15 Mar 1969	**PA**
LSD 37	PORTLAND	66/404	General Dynamics (Quincy)	21 Sep 1967	20 Dec 1969	3 Oct 1970	**AA**
LSD 38	PENSACOLA	66/404	General Dynamics (Quincy)	12 Mar 1969	11 July 1970	27 Mar 1971	**AA**
LSD 39	MOUNT VERNON	66/404	General Dynamics (Quincy)	29 Jan 1970	17 Apr 1971	13 May 1972	**PA**
LSD 40	FORT FISHER	67/404	General Dynamics (Quincy)	15 July 1970	22 Apr 1972	9 Dec 1972	**PA**

Displacement:	8,600 tons light
	13,700 tons full load
Length:	553⅓ feet (168.6 m) oa
Beam:	84 feet (25.6 m)
Draft:	18½ feet (5.6 m)
Propulsion:	steam turbines (De Laval); 24,000 shp; 2 shafts
Boilers:	2 600-psi (Foster Wheeler, except Combustion Engineering in LSD 36)
Speed:	20 knots (sustained)
Manning:	341–346 (18 O + 323–328 enlisted)
Troops:	375
Helicopters:	none
Guns:	6 3-inch (76-mm) 50 cal AA Mk 33 (3 × 2)
Radars:	SPS-10 surface search
	SPS-40 air search
Fire control:	(local control only)

MOUNT VERNON (1979, Giorgio Arra)

These LSDs were part of the large amphibious ship program of the early 1960s and were to supplement the LPDs (and later LHAs) by carrying additional landing craft to the assault area.

Design: The docking well is 430-feet long and 50-feet wide; it can accommodate 3 LCUs or 9 LCM-8s or approximately 50 LVTs. A re- movable helicopter deck is fitted over the docking well. No helicop- ter hangar or maintenance facilities are provided.

Guns: As built, these ships had eight 3-inch guns in twin mounts; one amidships mount and all fire control systems were removed in the late 1970s. Two CIWS will be fitted in each of these ships.

The FORT FISHER, one of five LSDs constructed during the rejuvenation of the amphibious force in the 1960s. These ships carry cargo and landing craft. The ANCHORAGE-class LSDs are similar in design to the previous THOMASTON class. LSDs are named for historic sites, with the first three ships of this class also honoring cities. (1979, Giorgio Arra)

8 DOCK LANDING SHIPS: "THOMASTON" CLASS

Number	Name	FY/SCB	Builder	Laid down	Launched	Commissioned	Status
LSD 28	THOMASTON	52/75	Ingalls SB Corp	3 Mar 1953	9 Feb 1954	17 Sep 1954	**PA**
LSD 29	PLYMOUTH ROCK	52/75	Ingalls SB Corp	5 May 1953	7 May 1954	29 Nov 1954	**AA**
LSD 30	FORT SNELLING	52/75	Ingalls SB Corp	17 Aug 1953	16 July 1954	24 Jan 1955	**AA**
LSD 31	POINT DEFIANCE	52/75	Ingalls SB Corp	23 Nov 1953	28 Sep 1954	31 Mar 1955	**PA**
LSD 32	SPIEGEL GROVE	54/75	Ingalls SB Corp	7 Sep 1954	10 Nov 1955	8 June 1956	**AA**
LSD 33	ALAMO	54/75	Ingalls SB Corp	11 Oct 1954	20 Jan 1956	24 Aug 1956	**PA**
LSD 34	HERMITAGE	55/75	Ingalls SB Corp	11 Apr 1955	12 June 1956	14 Dec 1956	**AA**
LSD 35	MONTICELLO	55/75	Ingalls SB Corp	6 June 1955	10 Aug 1956	29 Mar 1957	**PA**

Displacement:	6,880 tons light
	11,270 tons full load, except LSD 32–34 12,150 tons
Length:	510 feet (155.5 m) oa
Beam:	84 feet (25.6 m)
Draft:	19 feet (5.8 m)
Propulsion:	steam turbines (General Electric); 24,000 shp; 2 shafts
Boilers:	2 600-psi (Babcock & Wilcox)
Speed:	22.5 knots
Manning:	331–341 (18 O + 313–323 enlisted)
Troops:	340
Helicopters:	none
Guns:	6 3-inch (76-mm) 50 cal AA Mk 33 (3 × 2)
Radars:	SPS-6 air search
	SPS-10 surface search
Fire control:	(local control only)

These ships were built as a result of the renewed interest in am- phibious operations during the Korean War. They are the only am- phibious ships of that era that remain in active Navy service; they are scheduled to be stricken or transferred to other nations during the mid- to late-1980s.

Design: The docking well in these ships is 391-feet long and 48- feet wide, and can transport 3 LCUs or 9 LCM-8s or about 50 LVTs. A removable helicopter deck is fitted above the well deck, but there is no hangar and helicopters cannot be maintained on board.

Guns: These ships were built with an armament of 16 3-inch guns in twin mounts plus 12 20-mm AA guns. Their armament was reduced to 12 3-inch guns during the 1960s and to the above arma- ment during the late 1970s. Their fire control systems were also re- moved, leaving local gun control only.

THOMASTON (1980, Giorgio Arra)

THOMASTON (1980, Giorgio Arra)

A Marine Corps M48 medium tank rolls aboard the Australian landing craft BALIKPAPA from the USS POINT DEFIANCE during preparations for an exercise assault during Operation Kangaroo II. (1976, U.S. Navy, PH3 D. A. Fort)

20 TANK LANDING SHIPS: "NEWPORT" CLASS

Number	Name	FY/SCB	Builder	Laid down	Launched	Commissioned	Status
LST 1179	NEWPORT	65/405	Philadelphia Naval Shipyard	1 Nov 1966	3 Feb 1968	7 June 1969	**AA**
LST 1180	MANITOWOC	66/405	Philadelphia Naval Shipyard	1 Feb 1967	4 June 1969	24 Jan 1970	**AA**
LST 1181	SUMTER	66/405	Philadelphia Naval Shipyard	14 Nov 1967	13 Dec 1969	20 June 1970	**AA**
LST 1182	FRESNO	66/405	National Steel & SB Co	16 Dec 1967	20 Sep 1968	22 Nov 1969	**PA**
LST 1183	PEORIA	66/405	National Steel & SB Co	22 Feb 1968	23 Nov 1968	21 Feb 1970	**PA**
LST 1184	FREDERICK	66/405	National Steel & SB Co	13 Apr 1968	8 Mar 1969	11 Apr 1970	**PA**
LST 1185	SCHENECTADY	66/405	National Steel & SB Co	2 Aug 1968	24 May 1969	13 June 1970	**PA**
LST 1186	CAYUGA	66/405	National Steel & SB Co	28 Sep 1968	12 July 1969	8 Aug 1970	**PA**
LST 1187	TUSCALOOSA	66/405	National Steel & SB Co	23 Nov 1968	6 Sep 1969	24 Oct 1970	**PA**
LST 1188	SAGINAW	67/405	National Steel & SB Co	24 May 1969	7 Feb 1970	23 Jan 1971	**AA**
LST 1189	SAN BERNARDINO	67/405	National Steel & SB Co	12 July 1969	28 Mar 1970	27 Mar 1971	**PA**
LST 1190	BOULDER	67/405	National Steel & SB Co	6 Sep 1969	22 May 1970	4 June 1971	**NRF-A**
LST 1191	RACINE	67/405	National Steel & SB Co	13 Dec 1969	15 Aug 1970	9 July 1971	**NRF-P**
LST 1192	SPARTANBURG COUNTY	67/405	National Steel & SB Co	7 Feb 1970	11 Nov 1970	1 Sep 1971	**AA**
LST 1193	FAIRFAX COUNTY	67/405	National Steel & SB Co	28 Mar 1970	19 Dec 1970	16 Oct 1971	**AA**
LST 1194	LA MOURE COUNTY	67/405	National Steel & SB Co	22 May 1970	13 Feb 1971	18 Dec 1971	**AA**
LST 1195	BARBOUR COUNTY	67/405	National Steel & SB Co	15 Aug 1970	15 May 1971	12 Feb 1972	**PA**
LST 1196	HARLAN COUNTY	67/405	National Steel & SB Co	7 Nov 1970	24 July 1971	8 Apr 1972	**AA**
LST 1197	BARNSTABLE COUNTY	67/405	National Steel & SB Co	19 Dec 1970	2 Oct 1971	27 May 1972	**AA**
LST 1198	BRISTOL COUNTY	67/405	National Steel & SB Co	13 Feb 1971	4 Dec 1971	5 Aug 1972	**PA**

Displacement:	8,342 tons full load
Length:	522⅓ feet (159.2 m) hull oa; 562 feet (171.3 m) over derrick arms
Beam:	69½ feet (21.2 m)
Draft:	17½ feet (5.3 m)
Propulsion:	diesels (Alco); 16,500 bhp; 2 shafts
Speed:	20 knots (sustained)
Manning:	~218 (13 O + ~205 enlisted)
Troops:	385
Guns:	4 3-inch (76-mm) 50 cal AA Mk 32 (2 × 2)
Radars:	SPS-10 surface search
Fire control:	(local control only)

These ships represent the "ultimate" design in landing ships that can be "beached." They depart from the traditional LST bow-door design by using a pointed bow; this allows them to sustain a speed of 20 knots.

The BOULDER and RACINE were assigned to the Naval Reserve Force during 1980.

Design: This design has bow and stern ramps for unloading tanks and other vehicles. The bow ramp is 112 feet long and is handled over the bow by twin fixed derrick arms. Vehicles can be driven

The CAYUGA off Apra Harbor, Guam, displays the modern LST's unusual design, with uneven funnels, amidships davits for four small craft, and twin 3-inch gun mounts lost in the superstructure clutter. LSTs are assigned county or parish names; until the NEWPORT, all had county or parish suffixes to their names. (1979, U.S. Navy, PH2 Newell D. Schultz)

to the lower deck via a ramp, or through a passage in the super-structure which leads to the helicopter deck aft. The stern ramp permits unloading of amphibious vehicles into water, or "mating" to landing craft or a pier. The cargo capacity of these ships is 500 tons of vehicles on 19,000 square feet of parking area (not including the helicopter deck). The draft listed above is maximum aft; the full-load draft forward is $11^{1}/_2$ feet.

A helicopter landing area is provided but the ships have no hangar.

Engineering: They are fitted with six diesel engines. A through-hull bow thruster is provided to maintain the ship's position while unloading amphibious vehicles.

Guns: The twin 3-inch gun mounts, installed atop the super-structure, will be replaced by two 20-mm CIWS when the latter become available.

Names: The first 13 ships do not have "county" or "parish" name suffixes as had all previous named LSTs.

The Newport with bow ramp being lowered; note open bulwarks and derrick arms for lifting landing ramp; an LCVP is being lowered from davits on the port side. (1978, U.S. Navy, PHAN T. P. McAuliffe)

Tuscaloosa (1979, U.S. Navy, PHC Robert R. Howard, Jr.)

Spartanburg County (1978, U.S. Navy)

A Marine LVTP-7 leaves the stern of the Fairfax County during training in restricted waters off Detroit, Mich. The stern ramp is slightly offset to port with a retracting anchor on the starboard side of the stern. (1979, U.S. Navy)

6 TANK LANDING SHIPS: "TERREBONNE PARISH" CLASS

Number		FY/SCB	Builder	Laid down	Launched	Commissioned	Status
LST 1158	TIOGA COUNTY	53/9	Bath Iron Works		11 Apr 1953	20 June 1953	MR
LST 1160	TRAVERSE COUNTY	53/9	Bath Iron Works		3 Oct 1953	19 Dec 1953	MR
LST 1162	WAHKIAKUM COUNTY	53/9	Ingalls Shipbuilding Corp		23 Jan 1953	13 Aug 1953	MR
LST 1163	WALDO COUNTY	53/9	Ingalls Shipbuilding Corp		17 Mar 1953	17 Sep 1953	MR
LST 1164	WALWORTH COUNTY	53/9	Ingalls Shipbuilding Corp		18 May 1953	26 Oct 1953	MR
LST 1165	WASHOE COUNTY	53/9	Ingalls Shipbuilding Corp		14 July 1953	30 Nov 1953	MR

Displacement:	2,590 tons light
	5,800 tons full load
Length:	384 feet (117.0 m) oa
Beam:	55 feet (16.8 m)
Draft:	17 feet (5.2 m)
Propulsion:	diesels (General Motors); 6,000 shp; 2 shafts
Speed:	15 knots
Manning:	116
Troops:	~400
Guns:	6 3-inch (76-mm) 30 cal AA Mk 33 (3 × 2)

Radars:	SPS-10 surface search
Fire control:	2 Mk 63 gun FCS
	2 SPG-34 radar

These LSTs are the survivors of a class of 15 built during the Korean War. They were the first post–World War II LST design. All were decommissioned 1969–1971 and transferred to the National Defense Reserve Fleet.

Class: This class originally included hull numbers LST 1156–1170.

TRAVERSE COUNTY (1970, U.S. Navy)

2 TANK LANDING SHIPS: LST 1 AND LST 542 CLASSES

Number	Name	Builder	Laid down	Launched	Commissioned	Status
LST 399	(unnamed)	Boston Navy Yard	28 Sep 1942	23 Nov 1942	4 Jan 1943	MR
LST 715	DE KALB COUNTY	Jeffersonville Boiler and Mach. Co, Ind.	7 June 1944	20 July 1944	15 Aug 1944	MR

Displacement:	1,653 tons standard
	2,366 tons beaching
	4,080 tons full load
Length:	328 feet (100.0 m) oa
Beam:	50 feet (15.25 m)
Draft:	14 feet (4.3 m)
Propulsion:	diesels (General Motors); 1,700 shp; 2 shafts
Speed:	11.6 knots
Manning:	120
Troops:	~150
Guns:	several 40-mm AA (? × 1, ? × 2)

Radars:	SPS-10 surface search
Fire control:	2 Mk 51 directors

Of the 1,052 LSTs built during the World War II for the U.S. Navy, these are the only two ships remaining under U.S. government ownership. Both are laid up in the National Defense Reserve Fleet.

Design: There were minor differences between the LST 1 and LST 542 classes: deck ramps, connecting the main deck and tank deck forward were substituted for elevators of the earlier ships;

De Kalb County (U.S. Navy)

space was provided on the main deck for transporting LCTs; and a raised conning position was added over the original pilot house to facilitate conning the ship with an LCT on the main deck. Maritime Administration design S3-M2-K2.

Guns: The original armament for these ships was two 40-mm AA twin mounts, four 40-mm AA single mounts, and 12 20-mm AA single mounts.

Names: LST 715 named 1 July 1955.

FIRE SUPPORT SHIP PROGRAMS

In World War II numerous production landing ships were modified during construction or converted to the fire-support role for amphibious landings (LCIG, LCIM, LCIR, LSMR) and the LCSL was constructed specifically for that role. The CARRONADE was an improved LSMR with a single 5-inch gun and rapid-fire rocket launchers (designation changed from IFS to LFR 1 on 1 January 1969, along with surviving LSMRs).

IFS 1	CARRONADE	Comm. 1955; stricken 1973 (LFR 1)

POST–WORLD WAR II TANK LANDING SHIP PROGRAMS

Through June 1945 a total of 1,052 LSTs were completed for the U.S. Navy (numbered LST 1–1152, with 100 ships canceled). All were of the same basic design, with the latter 611 ships (LST 542 onward) having minor improvements over the earlier series. Three larger, improved LSTs with steam-turbine propulsion were ordered during the war with two being completed in 1947. (All other U.S. LSTs have had diesel propulsion.) All postwar-built LSTs have been stricken except for the 20-ship NEWPORT class. (See Appendix C; LST 1155 was canceled in 1946 and LST 1172 was canceled in 1955.)

LST 1153	TALBOT COUNTY	Comm. 1947; stricken 1973
LST 1154	TALLAHATCHEE COUNTY	Comm. 1949; conv. to AVB 2
LST 1155	canceled 1946	
LST 1156–1170	TERREBONNE PARISH class	
LST 1171–1178	SUFFOLK COUNTY class	
LST 1179–1198	NEWPORT class	

13 Landing Craft

The U.S. Navy has several hundred landing craft. The principal types as well as the two prototype air cushion vehicle landing craft are described here, as are the plans for production air cushion craft. The amphibious tractors operated by the Marine Corps are listed separately (see Chapter 14).

Several other types of landing craft and vehicles are operated by the Navy in small numbers.

LANDING CRAFT AIR CUSHION

The Navy plans to procure some 50 to 80 Landing Craft Air Cushion (LCAC) during the 1980s. These craft will be based on the JEFF-A and JEFF-B prototypes.

They will be capable of carrying one M60 medium tank (48 tons) or six towed howitzers and trucks, with a range of 200 n.miles at 50 knots and the ability to negotiate eight-foot plunging surf. The LCAC will be carried by the following classes of amphibious ships: LHA 1 (one LCAC), LPD 1 and 4 (two LCAC), LSD 41 (four LCAC), LSD 36 (four LCAC), and LSD 28 (three LCAC).

1 AMPHIBIOUS ASSAULT LANDING CRAFT: "JEFF-A"

Number	Name	Status
(AALC)	JEFF-A	**Test**

Weight:	85.8 tons empty
	186.4 tons gross
Length:	97 feet (29.6 m) hullborne
	99 1/6 feet (29.3 m) on air cushion
Beam:	44 feet (13.4 m) hullborne
	48 feet (14.6 m) on air cushion
Propulsion:	4 gas turbines (Avco Lycoming); 11,200 shp; 4 aircraft-type propellers in shrouds
Lift:	2 gas turbines (Avco Lycoming); 5,600 shp; 8 horizontal fans
Speed:	~50 knots
Manning:	6 (enlisted)
Guns:	none

The JEFF-A is one of two competitive prototypes of Amphibious Assault Landing Craft (AALC) constructed for Navy-Marine Corps evaluation. The JEFF-A design was developed by the Aerojet-Gen-

JEFF-B (foreground) and JEFF-A during trials off Panama City, Fla. (1980, U.S. Navy)

eral Corporation, built by Todd Shipyards, Seattle (Washington), and delivered in 1977.

Design: The all-aluminum craft has bow and stern ramps, 1,850 square feet of open cargo area, and can carry 120,000 pounds of cargo or vehicles. No SCB number is assigned.

1 AMPHIBIOUS ASSAULT LANDING CRAFT: "JEFF-B"

Number	Name	Status
(AALC)	JEFF-B	**Test**

Weight:	162.5 tons gross
Length:	80 feet (24.4 m) hullborne
	86¾ feet (26.4 m) on air cushion
Beam:	43 feet (13.1 m) hullborne
	47 feet (14.3 m) on air cushion
Propulsion:	6 gas turbines (Avco Lycoming); 16,800 shp; 2 aircraft-type propellers in shrouds
Lift:	4 horizontal fans (interconnected to propulsion engines)
Speed:	~50 knots
Manning:	6 (enlisted)
Guns:	none

The JEFF-B is a competitive prototype with the JEFF-A landing craft. This craft was developed and built by Bell Aerosystems at the National Aeronautics and Space Administration's former facility in Michoud, Louisiana, and delivered in 1977.

Design: The craft has bow and stern ramps, 1,738 square feet of open cargo area, and a cargo capacity of about 120,000 pounds. The JEFF-B is all-aluminum construction. Unlike the JEFF-A, this craft does not have separate lift engines. No SCB number is assigned to this craft.

JEFF-B (1979, U.S. Navy)

Marine M60 main battle tank rolls from JEFF-B (1979, U.S. Navy)

JEFF-A (foreground), JEFF-B, and UH-1 Huey (1980, U.S. Navy)

54 UTILITY LANDING CRAFT: "LCU 1610" CLASS

Number	Number	Number	Number
LCU 1613	LCU 1632	LCU 1655	LCU 1669
LCU 1614	LCU 1633	LCU 1656	LCU 1670
LCU 1616	LCU 1634	LCU 1657	LCU 1671
LCU 1617	LCU 1641	LCU 1658	LCU 1672
LCU 1618	LCU 1644	LCU 1659	LCU 1673
LCU 1619	LCU 1645	LCU 1660	LCU 1674
LCU 1621	LCU 1646	LCU 1661	LCU 1675
LCU 1623	LCU 1647	LCU 1662	LCU 1676
LCU 1624	LCU 1648	LCU 1663	LCU 1677
LCU 1627	LCU 1649	LCU 1664	LCU 1678
LCU 1628	LCU 1650	LCU 1665	LCU 1679
LCU 1629	LCU 1651	LCU 1666	LCU 1680
LCU 1630	LCU 1653	LCU 1667	
LCU 1631	LCU 1654	LCU 1668	

Displacement:	170 tons light
	390 tons full load
Length:	134¾ feet (41 m) oa
Beam:	29¾ feet (9 m)
Draft:	6 feet (1.8 m)
Propulsion:	geared diesels (Detroit); 2,000 shp; 2 shafts (see Engineering notes)
Speed:	11 knots
Range:	1,200 n. miles at 11 knots (loaded)
Manning:	6 (enlisted)
Troops:	8
Guns:	2 20-mm AA or 2 .50-cal MG (2 × 1)

These are improved LCUs with 15 units (LCU 1610–1624) completed in 1960, and the remainder from 1967 to 1976. Several small shipyards constructed these craft.

The LCU 1618 is configured to support test operations of the Naval Ocean Systems Center at San Diego, and the LCU 1641 operates with Mine Division 125 at Charleston.

Class: This class originally consisted of hull numbers LCU 1610–1624 and 1627–1680. Several units have been transferred to other navies, stricken, or reclassified as ferry boats (YFB) or harbor utility craft (YFU). The latter are listed with Service Craft (Chapter 18).

Design: These LCUs have a "drive-through" configuration with bow and stern ramps, and a small, starboard-side island structure housing controls and accommodations. They are of welded-steel construction. The mast folds down for entering well decks in amphibious ships. Cargo capacity is three M48 or M103 tanks or up to about 150 tons. The LCU 1610–1624 were SCB-149 and the LCU 1627 and later units were SCB-149B (later series SCB-406).

Engineering: The LCU 1621 has vertical shafts fitted with a vertical axis, cycloidal six-bladed propellers. All other units have Kort-nozzle propellers.

Guns: Weapons are not normally fitted in these craft.

LCU 1632 (1979, Giorgio Arra)

LCU 1653 with mast lowered (1975, Giorgio Arra)

LCU 1632 (1979, Giorgio Arra)

LCU 1641 (U.S. Navy)

1 UTILITY LANDING CRAFT: "LCU 1637"

Number
LCU 1637

Displacement:	135 tons light
	357 tons full load
Length:	134¾ feet (14 m) oa
Beam:	29¾ feet (9 m)
Draft:	6 feet (1.8 m)
Propulsion:	geared diesels (Detroit); 2,000 shp; 2 shafts
Speed:	12 knots
Manning:	6 (enlisted)
Troops:	8
Guns:	2 20-mm AA (2 × 1)

The LCU 1637 was a prototype craft of all-aluminum construction which is otherwise identical to the LCU 1610 class. The LCU 1637 is slightly faster than a steel LCU. The mast folds down, as in other LCUs, for transport in amphibious docking wells. No additional units of this type have been constructed.

25 UTILITY LANDING CRAFT: "LCU 1466" CLASS

Number	Number	Number	Number
LCU 1466	LCU 1477	LCU 1489	LCU 1539
LCU 1467	LCU 1482	LCU 1490	LCU 1547
LCU 1468	LCU 1484	LCU 1492	LCU 1548
LCU 1469	LCU 1485	LCU 1525	LCU 1559
LCU 1470	LCU 1486	LCU 1535	
LCU 1472	LCU 1487	LCU 1536	
LCU 1473	LCU 1488	LCU 1537	

Displacement:	180 tons light
	360 tons full load
Length:	119 feet (39 m) oa
Beam:	34 feet (10.4 m)
Draft:	6 feet (1.8 m)
Propulsion:	geared diesels (Gray Marine); 675 shp; 3 shafts
Speed:	8 knots
Manning:	6 (enlisted)
Troops:	8
Guns:	2 20-mm AA (2 × 1)

These LCUs are similar to their World War II-era predecessors. The units delivered to the U.S. Navy were completed between 1954 and 1957. The LCU 1473, which had been laid up in reserve, was reactivated in 1973 and assigned to the Naval Reserve Force (Reserve Assault Craft Unit 2).

Class: This class covered hull numbers LCU 1466–1609, with 14 units constructed in Japan under offshore procurement for foreign service (LCU 1594–1601 completed for Taiwan and LCU 1602–1607 completed for Japan, all in 1955); others were built for U.S. Army service.

Several U.S. units have been transferred to other navies, and others have been scrapped. Some became harbor utility craft (YFU); one of these, the LCU 1488 (ex-YFU 94) reverted to LCU status on 1 February 1972.

LCU 1469 with mast lowered, unloading mobile crane (U.S. Navy)

LCU 1488 (U.S. Navy)

LCU 1491 carrying three Marine medium tanks (U.S. Navy)

Classification: The LCU 1466–1503 were ordered as utility landing ships (LSU 1466–1503) on 31 October 1951; they were reclassified as LCUs on 15 April 1952.

Design: These craft have a bow ramp and stern superstructure. They are welded-steel construction. Design was SCB-25.

22 UTILITY LANDING CRAFT: "LCU 501" CLASS

Number	Number	Number	Number
LCU 539	LCU 666	LCU 871	LCU 1387
LCU 588	LCU 667	LCU 893	LCU 1430
LCU 599	LCU 674	LCU 1045	LCU 1451
LCU 608	LCU 742	LCU 1124	LCU 1462
LCU 654	LCU 768	LCU 1241	
LCU 660	LCU 803	LCU 1348	

Displacement:	143–160 tons light
	309–320 tons full load
Length:	119$^{1}/_{12}$ feet (39 m) oa
Beam:	32$^{2}/_{3}$ feet (10 m)
Draft:	3¾ feet (1.1 m)
Propulsion:	diesels (Gray Marine); 675 shp; 3 shafts
Speed:	10 knots
Manning:	} 12–13 (enlisted)
Troops:	
Guns:	2 20-mm AA (2 × 1)

These craft were completed in 1943–1944.

Class: This class originally consisted of hull numbers 501–1465. Numerous units were transferred to other navies, scrapped, or lost; several employed as harbor utility craft (YFU) or salvage lifting craft (YLLC), with the LCU 666 (ex-YFU 9) reverting to LCU status on 1 January 1962.

Classification: These craft were built as tank landing craft (LCT(6) 501–1465). The surviving units were reclassified as utility landing ships (LSU) in 1949 and were changed again to LCUs on 15 April 1952.

The subsequent LCT(7) 1501–1830 were completed with the designation LSM for medium landing ship, with hull numbers beginning with LSM 1.

Design: These craft have a bow ramp and superstructure aft. They were built in three sections for transport as deck cargo and welded together at forward bases. Cargo capacity is almost 200 tons.

MECHANIZED LANDING CRAFT: LCM-8 MOD 2 DESIGN

Displacement:	36.5 tons light
	106.75 tons full load
Length:	74$^{1}/_{12}$ feet (22.7 m) oa
Beam:	21$^{1}/_{12}$ feet (6.4 m)
Draft:	4$^{1}/_{2}$ feet (1.4 m)
Propulsion:	diesels (Detroit); 1,300 shp; 2 shafts
Speed	12 knots
Manning:	5 (enlisted)
Guns:	none

LCM(8) landing craft carrying Marine medium tanks are unloaded from the dock landing ship FORT FISHER (LSD 40) during multi-national exercises off Queensland, Australia. These landing craft are carried to the assault area by LSD, LPD, LHA, and LKA-type ships. (1974, U.S. Navy)

The LCM-8 Mod 2 is an aluminum version of the steel LCM-8 and was developed for use with the CHARLESTON (LKA 113)-class amphibious cargo ships.

Design: These craft are constructed of welded aluminum. Their cargo capacity is one M60 tank or 65 tons.

Engineering: Some units have been refitted with Kort nozzles.

MECHANIZED LANDING CRAFT: LCM-8 Mod 1 DESIGN

Displacement:	62.65 tons light
	130.25 tons full load
Length:	73$^{7}/_{12}$ feet (22.4 m) oa
Beam:	21$^{1}/_{12}$ feet (6.4 m)
Draft:	5$^{1}/_{6}$ feet (1.6 m)
Propulsion:	diesels (Detroit); 1,300 shp; 2 shafts
Speed:	9 knots
Manning:	5 (enlisted)
Guns:	none

LCM(8) with Marine medium tank and troops (1970, U.S. Navy)

Design: These are welded-steel landing craft with a cargo capacity of one M60 tank or 65 tons.

Engineering: Some units have been refitted with Kort nozzles.

MECHANIZED LANDING CRAFT: LCM-6 Mod 2 DESIGN

Displacement:	26.7 tons light
	62.35 tons full load
Length:	56 feet (17 m) oa
Beam:	14$\frac{1}{3}$ feet (4.4 m)
Draft:	3$\frac{5}{6}$ feet (1.2 m)
Propulsion:	diesels (Gray Marine); 450 shp; 2 shafts
Speed:	10 knots
Manning:	5 (enlisted)
Guns:	none

Many of these craft have been converted to riverine combat craft.

Design: These craft are constructed of welded steel. Their cargo capacity is 34 tons or 80 troops.

LANDING CRAFT VEHICLE AND PERSONNEL (LCVP)

Displacement:	13.5 tons full load
Length:	35$\frac{3}{4}$ feet (11.7 m) oa
Beam:	10$\frac{1}{2}$ feet (3.4 m)
Draft:	3$\frac{1}{2}$ feet (1.1 m)
Propulsion:	diesel; 325 shp; 1 shaft
Speed:	9 knots
Manning:	2–3 (enlisted)
Guns:	none

Design: These craft are built of wood or fiberglass-reinforced plastic. They can carry light vehicles or four tons of cargo.

LCM(6)s in TORTUGA (LSD 26) (U.S. Navy)

LCVP from MOUNT WHITNEY (LCC 20) (1973, Giorgio Arra)

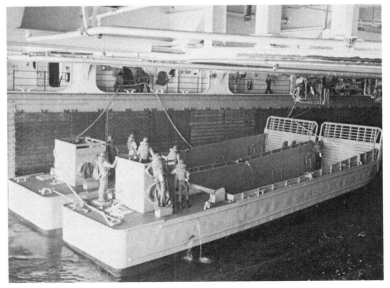

LCM(6)s in TARAWA (LHA 1) (1976, U.S. Navy, PH3 D. A. Fort)

LCVP from BLUE RIDGE (LCC 19) (U.S. Navy)

14 Landing Vehicles

Tracked landing vehicles are used by the Marine Corps for assault landings and, as feasible, for subsequent operations ashore. The Marines currently operate some 985 amphibious tractors or "amtracs" of the LVT-7 series—the LVTP-7 troop carrier, LVTC-7 command and control vehicle, and LVTR-7 recovery vehicle. Although these vehicles can be used on land, they lack the heavier armor common to most Armored Personnel Carriers (APC).

The Marine Corps has three amphibious tractor battalions: the 3rd Amphibious Tractor Battalion at Camp Pendleton, Calif., to support the 1st Marine Division; the 2nd Amphibious Tractor Battalion at Camp Lejeune, N.C., to support the 2nd Marine Division; and the 1st Tracked Vehicle Battalion on Okinawa, to support the 3rd Marine Division. The 2nd and 3rd battalions are each assigned 187 LVTP-7s, 15 LVTC-7s, and 6 LVTR-7s, with the capability of simultaneously lifting the assault echelons of a regimental landing team. The 1st Tracked Vehicle Battalion is assigned 96 LVTP-7s, 8 LVTCs, and 3 LVTRs. (The last also has 34 M60 tanks and 3 tank-recovery vehicles; other Marine tanks are in separate tank battalions.)

The service life of the present LVT-7 family of vehicles is expected to end in the mid-1980s. The Marines have embarked on a program to extend the life of the existing vehicles by modernizing, pending introduction of a follow-on vehicle in the 1990s. The following are the major improvements to the LVT-7A1: improved power train, automatic fire detection and suppression systems, night-vision driving devices, position locating and reporting system, secure voice radio system, smoke generators, improved ventilation systems, and maintenance diagnostics system.

The Marines initially had planned to replace the LVT-7A1 with a higher-speed Landing Vehicle Assault (LVA). The LVA was to have had a water speed of 25 to 40 mph and carry 18 troops. The LVA program was canceled in January 1979, because the vehicle was judged to be too large, too difficult to maintain, and too expensive to procure. Because of delays in the LVT(X) program, the FY 1982 budget requests 73 new LVTP-7A1 vehicles at a cost of $68.7 million.

ADVANCED TRACKED LANDING VEHICLE

The Marine Corps is planning a follow-on tracked landing vehicle as an alternative to the canceled LVA to replace the LVT-7 series. Currently designated LVT(X), the new vehicle would be used for combat ashore as well as ship-to-shore movement. A troop capacity of 18 to 19 is used for planning purposes.

The water speed of the LVT(X) is envisioned to be at least eight mph, with the rotary diesel engine, developed in conjunction with the LVA, planned for this vehicle. Armament for the LVT(X) has not been selected, but the 25-mm rapid-fire cannon is a candidate weapon.

In service the LVT(X) will probably be designated LVT-8; command and control (LVTC) and recovery (LVTR) variants are also being developed.

In order to equip the three assault amphibian battalions and to meet reserve and pipeline requirements, approximately 1,285 LVT(X)s are planned.

TRACKED LANDING VEHICLES, PERSONNEL: LVTP-7 SERIES

Weight:	38,450 pounds empty
	50,350 pounds loaded
Length:	26 feet (7.9 m) oa
Width:	10¾ feet (3.27 m)
Height:	10¼ feet (3.1 m)
Draft:	5-2/3 feet (1.72 m)
Propulsion:	turbo-supercharged diesel (Detroit); 400 hp; tracked running gear on land
	2 waterjets in water (3,025 lbst each)
Speed:	40 mph maximum, 20–30 mph cruise on land
	8.4 mph maximum, 8 mph cruise in water
Range:	300 miles at 25 mph on land
	~55 miles at 8 mph in water
Crew:	3
Troops:	25
Guns:	1 .50-cal. MG M85 (1 × 1)

The LVTP-7 is a full-tracked, amphibious vehicle, providing an over-the-beach capability for landing troops and material through heavy surf. It is the world's only vehicle capable of operating in rough seas and plunging surf (up to ten feet high).

Armament: The LVTP-7 was designed to mount a 20-mm cannon coaxially with a 7.62-mm machine gun; however, due to development problems the cannon was deleted. The .50-cal. MG is in a 360° powered turret and has 1,000 rounds of ammunition.

Class: The prototypes for the LVTP-7 design were 15 LVTPX-12 vehicles delivered to the Marines in 1967–1968. These were followed by a production run of 965 LVTP-7s delivered from 1970 to 1974 plus the specialized LVTC and LVTR vehicles described below. In addition, one LVTE-7, a prototype assault engineer/mine clearance vehicle, was delivered in 1970 but no more were produced.

Design: The LVTP-7 was designed to replace the LVTP-5 series amtracs and offered increased land and water speeds, more range, with less vehicle weight. In lieu of troops, the LVTP-7 can carry 10,000 pounds of cargo. The LVTP-7 has a stern door and ramp for rapidly unloading troops or cargo; it can turn 360° within its own length on land or in water.

Modernization: A SLEP modernization program beginning in 1981 is updating 985 vehicles of the LVT-7 series (including personnel, command and recovery vehicles) to permit their use until the LVT(X) is available. Modified LVT-7s will be designated LVT-7A1s. The original Detroit diesel 8V53T engine is being replaced by a Cummins VT 400 (providing the same horsepower).

LVTP-7 with ramp lowered (U.S. Marine Corps)

LVTP-7 (U.S. Marine Corps)

LVTP-7 landing vehicles spew forth from the amphibious transport dock CORONADO (LPD 11) during exercises off North Carolina. (U.S. Navy, Milt Putnam)

LVTP-7s come ashore during Operation Brave Soldier in Hawaii. Their markings indicate they are from Company D, 3rd Amphibious Tractor Battalion. In combat the vehicle gunners and commanders would be "buttoned up" inside the vehicles. (U.S. Marine Corps)

TRACKED LANDING VEHICLES, COMMAND: LVTC-7 SERIES

Weight: 40,187 pounds empty
                 44,111 pounds loaded
Crew: 12 (3 vehicle crew, 5 radiomen, 4 unit commander and staff)
Troops: none
Guns: 1 7.62-mm MG M60D (1 × 1)

Except as indicated above, the LVTC-7 characteristics are similar to those of the LVTP-7 series. Eighty-five of these vehicles were procured for use as command vehicles during amphibious operations. They are fitted with radios, crypto equipment, and telephones. Seventy-seven vehicles are being modernized (redesignated LVTC-7A1).

TRACKED LANDING VEHICLES, RECOVERY: LVTR-7 SERIES

Weight: 47,304 pounds empty
                 49,853 pounds loaded
Crew: 5 (3 vehicle crew, 2 tracked vehicle mechanics)
Troops: none
Guns: 1 7.62-mm MG M60D (1 × 1)

Except as indicated above, the LVTR-7 characteristics are similar to those of the LVTP-7 series. Sixty of these vehicles were procured for recovery of damaged amtracs during amphibious operations. They are fitted with a 6,000-pound-capacity, telescoping boom-type crane and 30,000-pound line-pull winch, plus maintenance equipment. Fifty-four vehicles are being modernized (redesignated LVTR-7A1).

LVTC-7 with ramp door open (U.S. Marine Corps)

LVTR-7 (U.S. Marine Corps)

LVTP-7 (U.S. Marine Corps)

LTVP-7s waddle ashore at Queensland, Australia, during Operation Kangaroo II. (1976, U.S. Navy, PH1 John R. Sheppard)

15 Patrol Ships and Craft

The U.S. Navy has minimal interest in patrol or "light" forces, instead stressing larger, long-range naval forces. In the early 1970s the Navy did plan a 30-ship class of hydrofoil missile craft, primarily for use in the Baltic and Mediterranean areas. However, reduced funding for ship construction, technical problems, and higher priority programs led to the cancellation of all but the first six units. Subsequently, the Department of Defense attempted to halt the construction of five of those units, but congressional action forced their completion.

The Navy also operates the surviving two of 17 motor gunboats built during the 1960s in response to the need to patrol the Caribbean against Cuban-based activities. These craft are retained to train Saudi naval personnel.

The surviving Navy coastal and riverine craft are operated by the active Navy and the Naval Reserve Force.

A number of patrol ships and craft are under construction for foreign navies. These efforts, coupled with the earlier Coastal Patrol and Interdiction Craft (CPIC) developed in the 1970s (the prototype was transferred to South Korea) and private shipbuilding activities, have provided a considerable knowledge of light forces in the U.S. Navy despite the lack of formal interest. During 1980–1982 the Tacoma Boatbuilding Company was delivering four missile craft to Saudi Arabia (F-PCG 1–4), and Peterson Builders was delivering nine missile patrol gunboats (F-PGG 1–9) to Saudi Arabia. Smaller PB-type craft are also being built for foreign users.

Classification: The smaller, unnamed patrol boats and craft are individually designated by their hull length, hull type, calendar year of construction, and consecutive hull of that type built during the year. Thus, 65PB776 indicates the sixth 65-foot PB-type craft built in 1977. The first two letters are generally used in the designation except RP is used for PBRs and NS for PCFs.

1 + 5 PATROL COMBATANTS—MISSILE (HYDROFOIL): "PEGASUS" CLASS

Number	Name	FY/SCB	Builder	Laid down	Launched	Commissioned	Status
PHM 1	PEGASUS	73/602	Boeing Co, Seattle	10 May 1973	9 Nov 1974	9 July 1977	**AA**
PHM 2	HERCULES	76/602	Boeing Co, Seattle	13 Sep 1980	1982	1982	Bldg.
PHM 3	TAURUS	75/602	Boeing Co, Seattle	30 Jan 1979	1981	1981	Bldg.
PHM 4	AQUILA	75/602	Boeing Co, Seattle	10 July 1979	1981	1981	Bldg.
PHM 5	ARIES	75/602	Boeing Co, Seattle	7 Jan 1980	1981	1982	Bldg.
PHM 6	GEMINI	75/602	Boeing Co, Seattle	13 May 1980	1982	1982	Bldg.

Displacement: 231 tons full load
Length: 147$\frac{1}{6}$ feet (45.0 m) oa foils retracted
131$\frac{1}{2}$ feet (40.0 m) oa foils extended
Beam: 28$\frac{1}{6}$ feet (8.6 m)
Draft: 6$\frac{1}{6}$ feet (1.9 m) foils retracted
23$\frac{1}{6}$ feet (7.1 m) foils extended
Propulsion: 2 diesels (Mercedes-Benz); 1,600 shp; 2 waterjets hullborne
1 gas turbine (General Electric); 18,000 shp; 2 waterjets on foils
Speed: 12 knots hullborne
40+ knots on foils
Manning: 22 (4 O + 18 enlisted)
Missiles: 2 quad launchers for Harpoon SSM Mk 140
Guns: 1 76-mm 62 cal AA Mk 75 (1 × 1)
Radars: (see Fire Control)
Fire control: 1 Mk 94 weapons FCS in PHM 1
1 Mk 92 weapons FCS in PHM 2–6

The PEGASUS is the lead ship of 30 hydrofoil missile combatants originally planned for the FY 1973–1977 shipbuilding programs. Two ships were authorized with FY 1973 research and development funds. Construction of the second ship (PHM 2) was suspended in 1976 when she was about 20 percent complete, to provide funds for completion of the PEGASUS. Four additional ships were funded in FY 1974.

The original 30-PHM program was reduced to the six funded ships in February 1976, partially because of cost increases. Subsequently, Secretary of Defense Harold Brown on 6 April 1977 announced his decision to cancel the entire PHM program except for the lead ship. He cited the program's high costs and limited operational effectiveness. However, the Congress refused to rescind the authorization and funding of the PHM 2-6, and in August 1977 the Department of Defense approved construction of the five additional ships. However, because of structural problems encountered in construction, the HERCULES, originally laid down on 30 May 1974, was "restarted" and will be the last completed.

Classification: When originally established, the designation PHM meant Patrol Hydrofoil—Missile. On 30 June 1975, however, the

PEGASUS being "paced" by an A-4 Skyhawk (U.S. Navy)

The TARUS, second ship of the PEGASUS class to be delivered, streaks on her foils near Renton, Washington. The PHMs are being based at Key West, Florida. There are no plans to deploy them to the Mediterranean, one of the principal operating areas put forward when the PHM concept was developed. (1981, Boeing Marine)

name of this type was changed to Patrol Combatant—Missile (Hydrofoil), with its designation remaining PHM.

Design: The PHM design evolved from a NATO requirement. The Italian and West German governments participated in the development of the design, with the latter navy planning to build up to 12 ships of this design in German shipyards. But after the U.S. program cutback, none will be built.

Engineering: Fitted with two separate diesel engines and one LM2500 gas turbine. A through-bow thruster is provided for low-speed maneuvering. Endurance is 32 hours at 38.28 knots (1,225 n. miles).

Fire control: Mk 94 is the U.S. designation for the Netherlands Hollandse Signaalapparaten WM-28 fire control system. The PHM 2-6 are to be fitted with the Mk 92 Mod 1, a modified WM-28 manufactured by the Sperry Company (also used in the PERRY-class (FFG 7) frigates).

Guns: No secondary gun battery is provided in the U.S. ships; the PHM design provides for two 20-mm Mk 20 single gun mounts to be fitted abaft the mast.

Missiles: The original PHM design provided four single Harpoon SSM tubes; the design was revised to permit carrying two quad launchers on the fantail.

Names: The PHM 1 originally was named the DELPHINUS. She was renamed the PEGASUS on 26 April 1974.

PEGASUS with foils raised (1979, Giorgio Arra)

PEGASUS with foils raised (1979, Giorgio Arra)

PEGASUS (1979, U.S. Navy)

2 PATROL COMBATANTS: "ASHEVILLE" CLASS

Number	Name	FY/SCB	Builder	Laid down	Launched	Commissioned	Status
PG 92	TACOMA	66/600	Tacoma Boatbuilding	24 July 1967	13 April 1968	14 July 1969	**AA**
PG 93	WELCH	66/600	Peterson Builders	8 Aug 1967	25 July 1968	8 Sep 1969	**AA**

Displacement:	225 tons standard
	245 tons full load
Length:	164½ feet (50.1 m) oa
Beam:	23¹¹/₁₂ feet (7.3 m)
Draft:	9½ feet (2.9 m)
Propulsion:	2 diesels (Cummins), 1,750 bhp; 1 gas turbine (General Electric), 14,000 shp; 2 shafts (controllable-pitch propellers)
Speed:	16 knots on diesels; 40+ knots on gas turbine
Manning:	28 (4 O + 24 enlisted)
Guns:	1 3-inch (76-mm) 50 cal AA Mk 34 (1 × 1)
	1 40-mm AA Mk 3 (1 × 1)
	4 .50-cal MG (2 × 2)
Radars:	Raytheon Pathfinder surface search
Fire control:	1 Mk 63 gun FCS
	1 SPG-50 radar

Seventeen ASHEVILLE-class patrol gunboats were completed 1966–1971 for coastal patrol and blockade missions. They were developed in response to the Cuban situation of the early 1960s; subsequently they were used extensively in the Vietnam War, and in the 1970s four of them operated in the Mediterranean carrying Standard-ARM SSMs.

The two surviving units are used at Norfolk, Virginia, to train Saudi Arabian naval personnel.

Class: This class originally consisted of PGM/PG 84–90 and 92–101. (The hull numbers PGM 33–83, 91, and 102–121 were assigned to gunboats built from 1955 onward for transfer to foreign navies; the PGG 1–9 are under construction for Saudi Arabia, to be delivered in 1980–1982.)

The CHEHALIS (PG 94) and GRAND RAPIDS (PG 98) have been stripped of armament and are employed as research craft (see Chapter 18).

Classification: As built, these ships were classified as motor gunboats (PGM). They were reclassified as patrol gunboats (PG) on 1 April 1967. The designation of the fourteen surviving units was eventually changed to patrol combatants (PG) on 30 June 1975.

Design: These ships have aluminum hulls and aluminum-fiberglass superstructures.

Engineering: CODOG (Combination Diesel or Gas-turbine) propulsion is provided, with two diesels for cruising and a single, LM1500 gas turbine for high-speed operations. The ships can transfer from diesel to gas turbine (or back) without loss of power; they also can accelerate from a full stop to 40 knots in one minute.

Missiles: The BENICIA (PG 96) was fitted with a single "box" launcher for the Standard-ARM SSM in 1971. Following successful test firings, two launchers were installed in four units (PG 86–87, 98, and 100).

TACOMA (1975, Giorgio Arra)

WELCH (1975, Stefan Terzibaschitsch)

1 COASTAL PATROL AND INTERDICTION CRAFT

Displacement:	~75 tons full load
Length:	100 feet (30.5 m) oa
Beam:	18½ feet (5.6 m)
Draft:	~6 feet (1.8 m)
Propulsion:	gas turbines (Avco Lycoming); 6,750 shp; 3 shafts; auxiliary propulsion, diesels (Volvo); 500 shp; 2 outboard drive units
Speed:	40+ knots
Manning:	~11 (1 O + 10 enlisted); varies with armament provided
Missiles:	(see notes)
Guns:	(see notes)

CPIC on U.S. sea trials (1974, U.S. Navy)

The CPIC was developed by the U.S. Navy as a successor to PT/PTF-type small combatants in U.S. service and for foreign sales. The prototype CPIC was built by Tacoma Boatbuilding, launched in 1974, and after extensive trials was transferred to South Korea on 1 August 1975. Four additional craft of this type were reportedly built in Korea.

The prototype CPIC was designated PKM 123 and named GIREOGI in Korean service; she was returned to the United States in 1980 for a research project.

Design: The CPIC is designed for maximum mission and weapons flexibility, with provisions for up to 20,000 pounds of weapons. There is provision for a major weapon installation forward and aft of the bridge structure and also for pintel mountings for machine guns along the sides. Guns, rockets, missiles, torpedoes, or mines can be fitted. (See Gun notes)

The craft has accommodations for 11. Fin stabilizers are fitted.

2 PATROL BOATS: PB Mk I DESIGN

Displacement:	26.9 tons light
	36.3 tons full load
Length:	65 feet (19.8 m) oa
Beam:	16 feet (4.9 m)
Draft:	4⅚ feet (1.5 m)
Propulsion:	diesels (Detroit); 1,635 shp; 3 shafts
Speed:	26 knots
Manning:	
Guns:	6 20-mm or .50-cal MG (1 × 2, 4 × 1)

PB Mk I (U.S. Navy)

These are prototype patrol boats developed as replacements for the "Swift" PCFs. Both were built by Sewart Seacraft of Berwick, La. They were completed in 1972 and delivered to the Navy in 1973 for evaluation. Subsequently they were transferred to the Naval Reserve Force.

2 INSHORE PATROL CRAFT: PCF Mk I DESIGN

Displacement:	22.5 tons full load
Length:	50¹⁄₁₂ feet (15.3 m) oa
Beam:	13 feet (4 m)
Draft:	3½ feet (1.1 m)
Propulsion:	diesels (General Motors); 960 shp; 2 shafts
Speed:	28 knots
Manning:	6 (1 O + 5 enlisted)
Guns:	2 .50-cal MG (1 × 2)
	1 81-mm mortar Mk 2/1 .50-cal MG M2 (1 × 1/1)

PCF Mk I (1969, U.S. Navy)

Engineering: Two independent propulsion systems are fitted: three TF-25 gas turbines with high-speed propellers for high-speed operations and two TAMD-70 diesels with outboard drive for lower-speed cruising. The primary machinery cooling systems have external, hull-mounted heat exchangers without seawater intakes, permitting the craft to operate in shallow and debris-filled water. The gas turbines are of modular design to facilitate maintenance and replacement.

Guns: During U.S. Navy trials in 1974–1975 the CPIC was fitted with a single Mk 74 twin 30-mm gun mount forward. The gun has a 600-round-per-minute rate of fire per barrel with 2,000 rounds of ammunition provided in the mount. A second mount could be fitted aft of the bridge.

17 PATROL BOATS: PB Mk III DESIGN

Displacement:	31.5 tons light
	41.25 tons full load
Length:	$64^{11}/_{12}$ feet (19.8 m) oa
Beam:	$18^{1}/_{12}$ feet (5.5 m)
Draft:	$5^{5}/_{6}$ feet (1.8 m)
Propulsion:	diesels (General Motors); 1,800 shp; 3 shafts
Speed:	26 knots
Range:	450 n.miles at full power; 2,000 n.miles at slow speed
Manning:	5 (1 O + 4 enlisted minimum)
Missiles:	(see notes)
Guns:	(see notes)

The PB Mk III was developed as a multi-mission inshore warfare craft for U.S. and foreign naval service. These craft are operated by the active Navy and the Naval Reserve Force.

Builders: The PB Mk IIIs were built by the Marinette Marine Corporation and Peterson Builders, Inc.

Classification: The Naval Sea Systems Command designates these craft as PB Mk 3; however, they are designated as Mk III in the Fleet.

PB Mk III (1978, U.S. Navy)

Three PB Mk III patrol boats from Coastal Riverine Squadron 2 cruise on Chesapeake Bay. (1978, U.S. Navy)

PB Mk III (Peterson Builders)

PBR Mk II (1968, U.S. Navy)

Design: The Mk III is a modified commercial craft used to support offshore drilling platforms in the Gulf of Mexico. The craft are of all-aluminum construction with their pilot house offset to starboard to provide maximum deck space for weapons and equipment. The craft has a low radar cross section and quiet engines for clandestine operations.

Guns: These craft are designed to mount up to four .50-cal machine guns on pintle mountings; there are also hard points on the deck for mounting larger guns and missiles. They can also be rigged to carry mines, torpedoes, or minesweeping gear.

Missiles: The PB Mk III is being used to evaluate the Norwegian-developed Penguin SSM, with four stowage/launcher containers being fitted on the after portion of the deck.

These are all-metal inshore patrol craft, generally referred to as "Swift" boats. All are assigned to the Naval Reserve Force.

Class: Approximately 125 units have been built since 1965. Most were used by the U.S. Navy in Vietnam, with 104 being transferred to the South Vietnamese government in 1968–1970. Others have been built for South Korea, the Philippines, and Thailand.

Classification: PCF originally stood for fast patrol craft; changed to inshore patrol craft on 14 August 1968.

Design: This design is adapted from a commercial crew boat employed in support of offshore oil platforms in the Gulf of Mexico.

27 RIVER PATROL BOATS: PBR Mk II DESIGN

Displacement:	7.5 tons light
	8.9 tons full load
Length:	32 feet (9.8 m) oa
Beam:	$11^2/_3$ feet (3.5 m)
Draft:	$2^7/_{12}$ feet (0.8 m)
Propulsion:	geared diesels (General Motors); 420 shp; waterjets
Speed:	25+ knots
Manning:	4-5 (enlisted)
Guns:	3 .50-cal MG (1 × 2, 1 × 1)
	1 40-mm grenade launcher Mk 19 (1 × 1)
	1 60-mm mortar Mk 4 in some units

These craft were developed for riverine combat in the Vietnam War. They have fiberglass-reinforced plastic hulls and ceramic

armor. The surviving U.S. units are operated by the Naval Reserve Force.

Class: More than 500 PBRs were built in 1967–1973, with most transferred to South Vietnam.

2 ASSAULT SUPPORT PATROL BOATS: ASPB Mk I DESIGN

Displacement:	33.25 tons light
	39.35 tons full load
Length:	$50^1/_6$ feet (15.3 m) oa
Beam:	$17^5/_{12}$ feet (5.3 m)
Draft:	$3^3/_4$ feet (1.1 m)
Propulsion:	diesels (General Motors; 850 shp; 2 shafts
Speed:	14 knots (sustained)
Manning:	5-6 (enlisted)
Guns:	1 or 2 20-mm (1–2 × 2)
	2 .50-cal MG in boats with 1 20-mm gun (1 × 2)
	2 .30-cal MG (2 × 1)
	2 40-mm grenade launchers (2 × 1)

These riverine "battleships" were developed to provide fire support for other craft, counter shallow-water mines, and interdict enemy river traffic. They have welded-steel hulls and aluminum superstructures.

Both units are operated by the Naval Reserve Force.

Guns: In some units the forward "turret" had two machine guns in lieu of the single 20-mm gun. Some units also had an 81-mm mortar/.50-cal MG mount aft.

ASPB with 81-mm mortar aft (U.S. Navy)

18 ARMORED TROOP CARRIERS: "MINI" ATC DESIGN

Displacement:	11 tons light
	14.75 tons full load
Length:	36 feet (11.0 m) oa
Beam:	12¾ feet (3.9 m)
Draft:	3½ feet (1.1 m)
Propulsion:	diesels (General Motors); 560 shp; waterjets
Speed:	28 knots
Manning:	2 (enlisted)
Troops:	15
Guns:	(see notes)

These craft were developed from lessons of the Vietnam War and are intended for clandestine operations. They are difficult to detect by radar and have quiet engines. They have aluminum hulls and ceramic armor. At high speeds they have a one-foot draft.

All are operated by the Naval Reserve Force.

Guns: Up to seven pintle-mounted weapons can be fitted in these craft (machine guns, grenade launchers, mortars).

1 COMMAND AND CONTROL BOAT: CCB Mk I DESIGN

Displacement:	67 tons light
	83.5 tons full load
Length:	60 feet (18.3 m) oa
Beam:	17½ feet (5.3 m)
Draft:	3⅓ feet (1.0 m)
Propulsion:	diesels (Gray Marine); 450 shp; 2 shafts
Speed:	8.5 knots (6 knots sustained)
Manning:	11
Guns:	1 40-mm/1 20-mm (1 × 1/1)
	several 20-mm (? × 1)
	several .30-cal MG (? × 1)

The CCB was developed as a command post for riverine operations. A command "module" is fitted between the after "superstructure" and forward gun "turret." The craft was converted from an LCM; it is similar to the now-discarded riverine monitors (MON) which had an 81-mm mortar in place of the command module. Several command radios are fitted.

"MINI" ATC (U.S. Navy)

3 FAST PATROL BOATS: "OSPREY" CLASS

Number	FY	In service
PTF 23	67	13 Mar 1968
PTF 24	67	13 Mar 1968
PTF 26	67	8 Apr 1968

Builders:	Stewart Seacraft, Berwick, La.
Displacement:	80 tons light
	105 tons full load
Length:	94¾ feet (28.8 m) oa
Beam:	23⅙ feet (7.0 m)
Draft:	7 feet (2.1 m)
Propulsion:	diesels (Napier-Deltic); 6,200 shp; 2 shafts
Speed:	~40 knots
Manning:	19 (1 O + 18 enlisted)
Guns:	1 40-mm AA Mk 3 (1 × 1)
	2 20-mm AA Mk 67 (2 × 1)
	1 81-mm mortar Mk 2/1 .50-cal MG M2 (1 × 1/1)
Radars:	commercial surface search

Only these four units remain of 24 fast patrol boats acquired during the Vietnam War plus two additional units redesignated PTF after originally being built in the late 1940s to evaluate new PT-boat designs. After Vietnam these boats were operated by the Naval Reserve Force until laid up in the late 1970s. They have aluminum hulls and improved habitability compared to their predecessors of the Norwegian-designed "Nasty" class. "Osprey" is the commercial name. All are laid up.

These boats can be configured as torpedo boats, minelayers, or submarine chasers.

Class: Four boats of this design were constructed, PTF 23-26. The PTF 25 was experimentally fitted with gas turbine engines in 1978; stricken in 1980. The remaining boats are classified as service craft.

CCB (U.S. Navy)

PTF 23 at Little Creek, Va. (1975, Giorgio Arra)

16 Mine Warfare Ships and Craft

The U.S. Navy maintains a small and largely outdated mine countermeasures capability. Three ocean minesweepers (MSO) are in active service, primarily to support mine research and development activities. Another 22 MSOs are operated by the Naval Reserve Force.

Type	Class/Ship	Active	Bldg.	NRF	Comm.
MSO	ACME	—	—	2	1957–1958
MSO	AGILE/AGGRESSIVE	3	—	20	1953–1956
MSB	(unnamed)	7	—.	—	

The principal Navy mine countermeasures capability consists of RH-53D Sea Stallion helicopters. Originally 30 were produced for the U.S. Navy (plus six for the Iranian Navy). Seven of the U.S. helicopters were destroyed during the ill-fated attempt to rescue the American hostages in Tehran in April 1980, and the use of several for research and development has left few available for service use. An improved MH-53E mine countermeasures helicopter is being procured, but in limited numbers and with the additional role of at-sea replenishment (Vertical On-board Delivery, or VOD).

A new class of mine countermeasures ships (designated MCM) is planned. When the MCM program was initiated in the 1970s, the goal was a deep-ocean capability to counter advanced Soviet mines, with 19 ships being proposed. The basic MCM design provided for a 1,640-ton, 265-foot ship (see 11th Edition of *The Ships and Aircraft of the U.S. Fleet,* Chapter 2). Subsequently, the MCM concept has been revised to provide an improved MSO-type ship.

All coastal minesweepers (MSC) have been discarded and the sur-

ADVANCED MINE COUNTERMEASURES SHIPS

Displacement:	~1,100 tons full load	Speed:	13.5 knots
Length:	~200 feet (61.0 m) oa	Range:	2,500 n. miles at
Beam:	~37 feet (11.3)		10 knots
Draft:		Manning:	80
Propulsion:	diesels; 2,400 shp; 2 shafts	Sonars:	(see notes)

viving minesweeping launches (MSL) have been stripped of their specialized equipment and are employed as utility launches. Two former inshore minesweepers (MSI) are employed as research craft (listed in Chapter 18).

Names: Ocean minesweepers have "action word" names.

The Department of Defense has approved a Navy plan for the construction of nine of these MCMs in the FY 1982–1985 shipbuilding programs. A total of 20 to 30 ships of this type are projected for construction during the 1980s to replace the obsolete MSO force.

Design: The MCM design is based on the improved MSO design that had been planned for construction in the late 1960s (MSO 523 class). The MCMs will have mine-hunting sonars (see below) and carry remote-controlled Mine Neutralization Vehicles (MNV) and other advanced mine countermeasures equipment.

Sonars: These ships will have the SQQ-30 minehunting sonar, an improved version of the SQQ-14 that is lowered from the hull of the ship. In addition, some of the devices being developed for airborne MCM use may be employed aboard these ships, especially the ALQ-141 electronic sweep device. The MCMs will also have the SSN-2 precision navigation system for plotting and relocating minefields.

2 OCEAN MINESWEEPERS: "ACME" CLASS

Number	Name	FY/SCB	Builder	Laid down	Launched	Commissioned	Status
MSO 509	ADROIT	54/45A	Frank L. Sample, Jr., Boothbay Harbor, Maine	18 Nov 1954	20 Aug 1955	4 Mar 1957	**NRF-A**
MSO 511	AFFRAY	54/45A	Frank L. Sample, Jr., Boothbay Harbor, Maine	24 Aug 1955	18 Dec 1956	8 Dec 1958	**NRF-A**

Displacement:	720 tons light	Radars:	SPS-53L in MSO 509; SPS-53E in MSO 511
	780 tons full load	Sonars:	SQQ-14 mine detection
Length:	173 feet (52.7 m) oa		
Beam:	36 feet (11.0 m)		
Draft:	14 feet (4.3 m)		
Propulsion:	diesels (Packard); 2,800 shp; 2 shafts		
Speed:	14 knots		
Range:	3,300 n. miles at 10 knots		
Manning:	86 (3 O + 36 enlisted active; 3 O + 44 enlisted reserve)		
Guns:	1 20-mm AA Mk 24 (1 × 1)		

These ships are improved versions of the AGILE and AGGRESSIVE classes. They are fitted as mine division flagships. The notes for the earlier MSO classes apply to this class.

Class: Four ships of this class were built for the U.S. Navy (MSO 508–511).

The AFFRAY was one of four "sweeps" built to an improved AGILE/AGGRESSIVE design. The forward 40-mm gun has since been removed to provide space for the SQQ-14 sonar. Note the reels for cable stowage abaft the funnel and the floats or "pigs" on the fantail for streaming mine gear. (1969, U.S. Navy)

The FIDELITY at sea. She is one of three MSOs manned by active Navy crews and employed primarily in MCM research and development. Note the large sonar hosting gear on her forecastle. As in other modernized MSOs, the superstructure has been built up aft of the bridge. (1978, U.S. Navy)

23 OCEAN MINESWEEPERS: "AGILE" AND "AGGRESSIVE" CLASSES

Number	Name	FY/SCB	Builder	Laid down	Launched	Commissioned	Status
MSO 427	CONSTANT	51/45A	Fulton Shipyard Co, Antioch, Calif.	16 Aug 1951	14 Feb 1953	8 Sep 1954	**NRF-P**
MSO 428	DASH	51/45A	Astoria Marine Constn Co, Astoria, Oregon	2 July 1951	20 Sep 1952	14 Aug 1953	**NRF-A**
MSO 429	DETECTOR	51/45A	Astoria Marine Constn Co, Astoria, Oregon	1 Oct 1951	5 Dec 1952	26 Jan 1954	**NRF-A**
MSO 430	DIRECT	51/45A	C. Hiltebrant DD Co, Kingston, NY	2 Feb 1952	27 May 1953	9 July 1954	**NRF-A**
MSO 431	DOMINANT	51/45A	C. Hiltebrant DD Co, Kingston, NY	23 Apr 1952	5 Nov 1953	8 Nov 1954	**NRF-A**
MSO 433	ENGAGE	51/45A	Colberg Boat Works, Stockton, Calif.	7 Nov 1951	18 June 1953	16 Apr 1955	**NRF-P**
MSO 437	ENHANCE	51/45A	Martinolich SB Co., San Diego, Calif.	12 July 1952	11 Oct 1952	10 Sep 1955	**NRF-P**
MSO 438	ESTEEM	51/45A	Martinolich SB Co, San Diego, Calif.	1 Sep 1952	20 Dec 1952	24 Feb 1955	**NRF-P**
MSO 439	EXCEL	51/45A	Higgins Inc, New Orleans, La.	9 Feb 1953	25 Sep 1953	31 Mar 1954	**NRF-A**
MSO 440	EXPLOIT	51/45A	Higgins Inc, New Orleans, La.	28 Dec 1951	10 Apr 1953	22 June 1954	**NRF-A**
MSO 441	EXULTANT	51/45A	Higgins Inc, New Orleans, La.	22 May 1952	6 June 1953	22 Sep 1954	**NRF-A**
MSO 442	FEARLESS	51/45A	Higgins Inc, New Orleans, La.	23 July 1952	17 July 1953	19 Jan 1955	**AA**
MSO 443	FIDELITY	51/45A	Higgins Inc, New Orleans, La.	15 Dec 1952	21 Aug 1953	16 July 1954	**NRF-A**
MSO 446	FORTIFY	51/45A	Seattle SB & DD Co, Seattle, Wash.	30 Nov 1951	14 Feb 1953	14 Nov 1953	**AA**
MSO 448	ILLUSIVE	51/45A	Martinolich SB Co, San Diego, Calif.	23 Oct 1951	12 July 1952	15 July 1954	**NRF-A**
MSO 449	IMPERVIOUS	51/45A	Martinolich SB Co, San Diego, Calif.	18 Nov 1951	29 Aug 1952	10 Mar 1954	**NRF-P**
MSO 455	IMPLICIT	52/45A	Wilmington Boat Works Inc, Calif.	29 Oct 1951	1 Aug 1953	11 May 1954	**NRF-A**
MSO 456	INFLICT	52/45A	Wilmington Boat Works Inc, Calif.	29 Oct 1951	6 Oct 1953	11 Aug 1954	**NRF-P**
MSO 464	PLUCK	52/45A	Wilmington Boat Works Inc, Calif.	31 Mar 1952	6 Feb 1954	20 July 1955	**NRF-P**
MSO 488	CONQUEST	53/45A	J. M. Martinac SB Corp, Tacoma, Wash.	26 Mar 1953	20 May 1954	14 Sep 1955	**NRF-P**
MSO 489	GALLANT	53/45A	J. M. Martinac SB Corp, Tacoma, Wash.	21 May 1953	4 June 1954	16 Nov 1955	**AA**
MSO 490	LEADER	53/45A	J. M. Martinac SB Corp, Tacoma, Wash.	22 Sep 1953	15 Sep 1954	20 Apr 1956	**NRF-P**
MSO 492	PLEDGE	53/45A	J. M. Martinac SB Corp, Tacoma, Wash.	24 June 1954	20 July 1955		

Displacement:	665 tons light
	750 tons full load
Length:	172 feet (52.4 m) oa
Beam:	35 feet (10.7 m)
Draft:	14 feet (4.3 m)
Propulsion:	diesels (Packard except General Motors in MSO 428–431, Waukesha in MSO 433, 437–438, 441–443, 446, 448–449, 456, 488, 490); 2,280 shp except 1,520 shp in ships with GM diesels; 2 shafts (controllable-pitch propellers)
Speed:	15.5 knots except 15 knots in ships with GM diesels
Range:	3,300 n. miles at 10 knots
Manning:	72 (8 O + 64 enlisted) in active ships
	40 (4 O + 36 enlisted active) in NRF ships
	71 (6 O + 65 enlisted) in MSO 443, 448, 490
Guns:	1 40-mm AA M3 (1 × 1) or
	1 20-mm AA Mk 68 (1 × 1)
Radars:	SPS-5C or SPS-53E/L surface search
Sonars:	UQS-1 or SQQ-14 mine detection

The large ocean minesweeper construction program of the 1950s was initiated in response to the extensive use of Soviet-provided mines in the Korean War (1950–1953). Large numbers of these ships were built for the U.S. Navy and several NATO navies (see Class notes). Of the surviving ships, 3 are in active Navy service and 20 are NRF ships.

Builders: Most of the MSOs were constructed at small boatyards.

Class: Fifty-eight ships of these classes were built for the U.S. Navy plus seven ships of the similar ACME and ABILITY classes, which are listed separately. Another 3 MSOs of these classes were built specifically for other NATO navies (plus the canceled MSO 497). The total MSO program covered hull numbers 421–522. Sixteen additional MSOs funded in FY 1966–1968 were not built.

Classification: All MSOs originally were classified as minesweepers (AM); they were changed to MSOs on 7 February 1955.

Design: These ships are of lightweight wooden construction with laminated timbers; the fittings and machinery are of bronze and stainless steel. Magnetic items have been reduced to a minimum.

They were fitted for sweeping contact, magnetic, and acoustic mines.

Guns: As built, these ships had one 40-mm gun and two .50-cal MG. Most have been rearmed with provisions for a 20-mm mount forward, originally a twin-barrel Mk 24 and subsequently a single-barrel MK 68 gun. The smaller 20-mm mount was required in modernized ships to permit installation of the larger, retractable SQQ-14 sonar in the forward hull.

Modernization: In FY 1968 a program was begun to modernize the existing MSOs (SCB-502). New engines, communications, and sonar (SQQ-14) were to be installed, habitability improved, and advanced sweep gear provided. However, increasing costs and conversion delays caused the program to be halted after only 13 ships had been fully modernized (MSO 433, 437–438, 441–443, 445–446, 448–449, 456, 488, and 490). Subsequently, some features, especially the improved sonar, were fitted to several additional ships.

Sonars: These ships originally had UQS-1 mine-detecting sonar; most have been refitted with SQQ-14, which has additional mine classification capabilities.

EXCEL (1979, MacIver Studio/Todd Shipyards)

PLEDGE under way off Point Loma, San Diego; note built-up superstructure. A rubber boat is on the port quarter. (1979, U.S. Navy, PHC William E. Kendall)

GALLANT (1979, U.S. Navy)

MSB 15—Vietnam configuration (1967, U.S. Navy)

Coastal Minesweepers

All U.S. Navy coastal minesweepers of the similar FALCON (MSC 190–199) and REDWING (MSC 200–209) classes have been discarded. Most of these 145-foot craft were operated by the NRF during their last years of U.S. service. See Appendix C.

7 MINESWEEPING BOATS

Number	Number	Number
MSB 15	MSB 28	MSB 51
MSB 16	MSB 29	
MSB 25	MSB 41	

Displacement:	30 tons light 42 tons full load except MSB 29 80 tons
Length:	57¼ feet (17.4 m) oa except MSB 29 82 feet (25.0 m)
Beam:	15⅚ feet (4.8 m) except MSB 29 19 feet (5.8 m)
Draft:	4⅓ feet (1.3 m) except MSB 29 5½ feet (1.7 m)
Propulsion:	diesel (Packard); 600 shp; 2 shafts
Speed:	12 knots
Manning:	6–7 (enlisted)
Guns:	several MG can be fitted

MSB crewmen handling sweep gear (U.S. Navy)

These are wooden-hulled minesweeping boats that were designed to be carried to amphibious assault areas aboard ship. However, they are too large to be easily handled by crane and instead have been employed to sweep harbors and rivers. They were extensively used in the Vietnam War.

The seven surviving MSBs are assigned to Mine Division 125 at Charleston, S.C.

Class: The above class originally included MSB 5-54, less the MSB 24 that was not built and the MSB 29 that was built to an enlarged design in an effort to improve seakeeping qualities. All were completed 1952–1956. The MSB 1-4 were former Army minesweepers built in 1946.

MSB 29 (U.S. Navy)

Riverine Minesweeping Craft

A variety of minesweeping craft were developed during the Vietnam War for clearing rivers of mines and booby traps. These were the patrol minesweepers (MSR), river minesweepers (MSM), and drone minesweepers (MSD). All have been discarded.

17 Auxiliary Ships

Auxiliary ships are noncombatant ships that provide support for the "fighting fleet." This category is made up of a variety of types and classes, most of which are highly specialized. All of these ships are government-owned (some acquired through long-term government financing); however, many of the Underway Replenishment (UNREP) ships, tugs, logistic ships, and research ships are operated by the Navy's Military Sealift Command (MSC) with civilian crews—either Civil Service or merchant seamen under commercial operating contracts. Several research ships are operated by scientific and educational institutions. In addition, beginning in 1977 several UNREP and tug-type ships have been assigned to the Naval Reserve Force (NRF) with composite active-reserve crews.

Those ships operated by MSC have the prefix USNS for United States Naval Ship, and their hull designations are prefixed with the letter "T."

Several ships officially classified as auxiliaries are listed elsewhere in this volume and are not included in the following table. Those ships are the miscellaneous command ships (AGF), auxiliary submarines (AGSS), and training aircraft carrier (AVT).

Guns: All MSC civilian-manned ships are unarmed. Navy-manned ships have minimal 20-mm or 3-inch gun armament. UNREP ships that operate with carrier battle groups will receive Phalanx CIWS and/or NATO Sea Sparrow.

The following groupings have been developed by the author, based on types of functions; they are not official groupings.

UNDERWAY REPLENISHMENT SHIPS

AE, AF, AFS, AO, AOE, and AOR ships provide provisions, munitions, and fuels to forward-deployed naval forces. These ships can transfer material to warships while under way, steaming on parallel courses a few hundred feet apart. Helicopters can transfer all material except fuels to ships alongside or miles apart.

Electronics: The AOE- and AOR-type ships are being fitted with SLQ-32(V)3, and the AE- and AFS-type ships with SLQ-32(V)1 electronic warfare systems. Other auxiliary ships are not being provided with advanced EW systems.

Names: Ammunition ships traditionally have been named for explosives (NITRO for nitroglycerine) or for volcanoes (the SURIBACHI); store ships for stars or constellations (VEGA); and oilers for rivers with Indian names (NEOSHO). The new types of underway replenishment ships that began entering service in the 1960s, the combat

store ships, fast combat-support ships, and replenishment oilers, are named for American cities. That name source previously had been used for U.S. Navy cruisers and since 1971 has been used for attack submarines, demonstrating the considerable confusion in U.S. ship nomenclature.

SUPPORT SHIPS

AD, AGDS, APB, AR, ARC, ARL, and AS ships provide maintenance, repairs, and other support to the Fleet. The destroyer and submarine tenders provide a wide range of services to their "broods," both at U.S. ports and overseas. The submarine tenders supply electrical power for "hotel" services to nuclear submarines whose reactor plants are closed down; the SSBN tenders also have Trident or Poseidon missile reloads. The cable ships lay and maintain seafloor acoustic sensors. The only seaplane tender (AV) remaining in Navy service is the NORTON SOUND, which has long been employed as a guided missile and gunnery test ship (designated AVM 1).

Names: Destroyer tenders generally are named for geographic areas (DIXIE), except for the SAMUEL GOMPERS, which honors an American labor leader. The lone deep-submergence support ship, the POINT LOMA, is named for an area of San Diego that serves as base for the Navy's deep-submergence activities. Repair ships are named for mythological characters (VULCAN), and submarine tenders for mythological characters (ORION) or pioneers in submarine development or submarine heroes (L. Y. SPEAR and HOWARD W. GILMORE, respectively).

TUG-TYPE SHIPS

ARS, ASR, ATA, ATF, and ATS ships provide towing, salvage, target, submarine rescue, and other services to the Fleet. The salvage ships, submarine rescue ships, and ATS tugs are fitted for heavy salvage work. The ASRs are the Navy's principal deep-ocean diver support ships, and have the McCann submarine rescue chamber and, in the newer ships, Deep Submergence Rescue Vehicles (DSRV) to save crewmen trapped in submarines disabled on the ocean floor at depths above their hull-collapse depth.

Names: Salvage ships are named for terms related to salvage activity (CLAMP); submarine rescue ships have bird names (PIGEON), a scheme begun when the first ASRs were converted from World War I "Bird"-class minesweepers; and Navy tugs traditionally have had Indian names (SHAKORI, SAMOSET, and KOKA). The large EDENTON-class tugs have been named for American towns with English namesakes—a reasonable scheme for these ships, which were constructed in England.

SEALIFT SHIPS
AK, AKR, AOT, and AOG ships carry cargo from point to point and do not undertake underway replenishment or amphibious operations. Modified "Victory" cargo ships are employed exclusively in supplying Trident/Poseidon submarine tenders forward deployed at Holy Loch, Scotland, and at U.S. ports. All other sealift ships carry cargo for all Department of Defense agencies. (These ships all are civilian-manned under MSC control, with Poseidon resupply ships having small Navy detachments for missile warhead security and communications.)

Names: Most MSC-operated cargo ships are named for U.S. Army heroes of World War II (PVT. LEONARD C. BROSTROM), while the ADMIRAL WILLIAM M. CALLAGHAN honors the first commander of the Military Sea Transportation Service (the previous name of MSC from 1949 to 1970); tankers have Indian river names (POTOMAC), and the new "Sealift" class has geographic area names (SEALIFT PACIFIC). Ships named for persons are generally referred to by last names only.

PRE-POSITIONING SHIPS
The Soviet invasion of Afghanistan and the revolutionary Iranian government's seizure of American hostages in late 1979 called attention to the lack of U.S. conventional military capability in the Indian Ocean area. Accordingly, the following year the Department

The landing ship SUMTER (LST 1181) is refueled in the North Atlantic by the fleet oiler TRUCKEE (AO 147) during the NATO Exercise Northern Wedding. Auxiliary ships provide the Fleet with mobility and staying power. Even nuclear surface ships are dependent upon oilers, ammunition ships, and store ships for "consumables." In this photo the SUMTER is carrying four pontoons along her sides for use as unloading causeways; her deck is crowded with Marine vehicles and equipment. The TRUCKEE, Navy-manned when this photo was taken, has a large structure forward of her after superstructure and a large helicopter deck. The ship has since been assigned a civilian crew under the Navy's Military Sealift Command. (1978, U.S. Navy)

of Defense established a pre-positioning force of merchant-type ships to carry Marine equipment, weapons, and provisions to support a 12,000-man Marine Amphibious Brigade (MAB) for 15 days of operations. The troops themselves would be flown out to the area and "married" with the equipment in a friendly port area.

The near-term pre-positioning force of seven ships was established off the island of Diego Garcia in July 1980. The force consists of three roll-on/roll-off vehicle ships, the METEOR (T-AKR 9), MERCURY (T-AKR 10), and JUPITER (T-AKR 11); and two commercial C-4 break-bulk cargo ships and two commercial medium-sized tankers.

During the mid-1980s these ships were to be supplemented by commercial SL-7 high-speed (33-knot) container ships, acquired by the government and modified for the pre-positioning role. Those ships are no longer considered suitable for commercial operation.

Subsequently, a class of 14 built-for-the-purpose pre-positioning ships were to be constructed for this role (tentatively designated T-AKX). In early 1980 this plan was modified for eight new ships (Maritime Administration C8-M-MA134) and four conversions of commercial roll-on/roll-off ships. See page 203 of this edition.

To supplement the pre-positioning ships, the Congress has provided funding for the Navy to look into the use of a surface effects ship for the long-range logistics role. A baseline design for such a ship is 5,000–7,000 tons with a speed of 70 knots or more, capable of carrying perhaps one-third or one-half of a division's equipment, vehicles, and munitions.

EXPERIMENTAL, RESEARCH, SURVEYING SHIPS

AG, AGM, AGMR, AGOR, AGOS, AGS, AVM, and certain IX ships perform a variety of services in support of Navy programs and national ocean and space activities. Most of these ships are manned by civilians under MSC control or are operated by institutions. Details of their employment and operation are found under the individual ship listings.

Names: Name sources for these ships vary; most ocean research and surveying ships are named for oceanographers and other ocean-science pioneers (LYNCH and HAYES, respectively; the latter honors the "father of sonar" in the U.S. Navy).

Type		Active					Building[a]	Reserve[b]
		Total	Navy	MSC	NRF	Academic		
AD	Destroyer Tenders	8	8				3	2
AE	Ammunition Ships	10	7	1	2			
AF	Store Ships	1	1					
AFS	Combat Store Ships	8	7	1				
AG	Miscellaneous Auxiliaries	1	1					1
AGDS	Deep-Submergence Support Ships	1	1					
AGM	Missile Range Instrumentation Ships	7	7					
AGOR	Oceanographic Research Ships	13		5		8		1
AGOS	Ocean Surveillance Ships						8	
AGS	Surveying Ships	8		8				1
AH	Hospital Ships							1
AK	Cargo Ships	7		7			1	7
AKR	Vehicle Cargo Ships	5		5				
AO	Oilers	16	6	10			3	2
AOE	Fast Combat Support Ships	4	4					
AOG	Gasoline Tankers	5		5				
AOR	Replenishment Oilers	7	7					
AOT	Transport Oilers	18	18					7[d]
AP	Transports							17[e]
AR	Repair Ships	4	4					
ARC	Cable Repairing Ships	3		3			1	
ARL	Landing Craft Repair Ships							1
ARS	Salvage Ships	7	6		1		1	1
AS	Submarine Tenders	12	12				1	3
ASR	Submarine Rescue Ships	6	6					
ATA	Auxiliary Ocean Tugs							5
ATF	Fleet Ocean Tugs	12		7	5		2	10
ATS	Salvage and Rescue Ships	3	3					
AVM	Guided Missile Ships	1	1					
IX	Unclassified Miscellaneous Ships	9	9					1[c]

[a] Includes ships authorized through FY 1981.
[b] Includes ships in National Defense Reserve Fleet.
[c] Relic CONSTITUTION.
[d] Includes one ship on loan to Department of Energy.
[e] Includes three ships on loan to state maritime schools.

1 + 3 DESTROYER TENDERS: "YELLOWSTONE" CLASS

Number	Name	FY/SCB	Launched	Commissioned	Status
AD 41	YELLOWSTONE	75/700	27 Jan 1979	28 June 1980	**AA**
AD 42	ACADIA	76/700	28 July 1979	1981	Bldg.
AD 43	CAPE COD	77/700	2 Aug 1980	1982	Bldg.
AD 44	. . . .	79/700	1982	1983	Bldg.

Builders: National Steel & Shipbuilding, San Diego, Calif.
Displacement: 22,800 tons full load
Length: 643 feet (196.0 m) oa
Beam: 85 feet (25.9 m)
Draft: 22½ feet (6.9 m)
Propulsion: steam turbine; 20,000 shp; 1 shaft
Boilers: 2
Speed: 20 knots (18 knots sustained)

Manning: 1,051 (36 O + 1,015 enlisted)
Helicopters: none assigned
Guns: 2 40-mm Mk 19 (2 × 1)
            2 20-mm Mk 67 (2 × 1)

These are improved GOMPERS-class tenders, intended to provide a wide range of support to surface combatants, including ships with gas turbine and nuclear propulsion.

Class: The AD 45 planned for the FY 1980 shipbuilding program was not funded. No additional destroyer tenders are planned in the FY 1981–1986 period.

Design: These ships are generally similar to the two previous AD classes. They have two 30-ton-capacity cranes and two 6½-ton-capacity cranes. See GOMPERS class for additional details.

YELLOWSTONE on trials (1979, National Steel)

2 DESTROYER TENDERS: "SAMUEL GOMPERS" CLASS

Number	Name	FY/SCB	Launched	Commissioned	Status
AD 37	SAMUEL GOMPERS	64/244	14 May 1966	1 July 1967	**PA**
AD 38	PUGET SOUND	65/700	16 Sep 1966	27 Apr 1968	**AA**

Builders:	Puget Sound Naval Shipyard, Bremerton, Wash.
Displacement:	22,260 tons full load
Length:	643 feet (196.0 m) oa
Beam:	85 feet (25.9 m)
Draft:	22½ feet (6.9 m)
Propulsion:	steam turbine (De Laval); 20,000 shp; 1 shaft
Boilers:	2 (Combustion Engineering)
Speed:	20 knots (18 knots sustained)
Manning:	1,206 (37 O + 1,169 enlisted) in AD 37
	1,314 (40 O + 1,274 enlisted) in AD 38
Helicopters:	none assigned
Guns:	4 20-mm Mk 67 (4 × 1)

These were Navy's first post–World War II destroyer tenders, designed specifically to support surface combatants with guided missiles and gas turbine or nuclear propulsion.

Class: The AD 39 was authorized in the FY 1969 shipbuilding program but was canceled prior to start of construction because of cost overruns in other new ship programs; the AD 40 was authorized in FY 1963 but was not built.

Design: These ships are similar in design to the L. Y. SPEAR (AS 36)-class submarine tenders. A landing platform and hangar were provided for the DASH helicopter. In the GOMPERS the hangar has been converted to a boat repair shop.

Guns: As built, the AD 37 and 38 had a single 5-inch 38 cal DP gun forward with a Mk 56 gun FCS; this armament was removed, and plans to install NATO Sea Sparrow missiles were dropped.

SAMUEL GOMPERS (1977, Giorgio Arra)

The SAMUEL GOMPERS is the lead ship of the Navy's postwar destroyer tender program. These ADs are similar in design to the L. Y. SPEAR-class submarine tenders. The 5-inch 38 cal DP gun originally mounted forward of the bridge has been removed. Note servicing boats under cranes. These ships have a large stern anchor as well as two bow anchors. (1978, Giorgio Arra)

2 DESTROYER TENDERS: "KLONDIKE" AND "SHENANDOAH" CLASSES

Number	Name	Launched	Commissioned	Status
AD 24	EVERGLADES	28 Jan 1945	25 May 1951	MR
AD 36	BRYCE CANYON	7 Mar 1946	15 Sep 1950	PR

Builders:	AD 24 Los Angeles Shipbuilding & DD Co, Calif.
	AD 36 Charleston Navy Yard, S.C.
Displacement:	8,165 tons standard
	16,635–16,900 tons full load
Length:	492 feet (150.0 m) oa
Beam:	69½ feet (21.2 m)
Draft:	27¹⁄₆ feet (8.3 m)
Propulsion:	steam turbine (General Electric in AD 24, Westinghouse in AD 36);
	8,500 shp; 1 shaft
Boilers:	2 (Babcock & Wilcox in AD 24, Foster Wheeler in AD 36)
Speed:	18 knots
Manning:	
Helicopters:	no facilities
Guns:	2 3-inch (76-mm) 50 cal AA Mk 26 (2 × 1) in AD 24
Fire control:	1 Mk 51 gun director in AD 24
	1 Mk 52 gun FCS in AD 24
	1 Mk 26 radar in AD 24

These ships were built to a merchant design specifically for the tender role. Completion of these two ships was delayed after World War II.

Class: Ten destroyer tenders were built to this configuration: the KLONDIKE class (AD 22–25) and the SHENANDOAH class (AD 26–29, 31, 36). Three additional ships were canceled (AD 30, 33, 35). The AD 16 and 20–21 were similar to these ships. The KLONDIKE (AD 22) and GRAND CANYON (AD 28) were reclassified as repair ships (changed to AR with same hull numbers) in 1960 and 1971, respectively.

Classification: The BRYCE CANYON originally was ordered as a seaplane tender (AV 20).

Design: Maritime Administration C3 design, modified for the AD role.

Guns: The original armament for the KLONDIKE class was 1 5-inch gun, 4 3-inch guns, and 4 40-mm guns; for the SHENANDOAH class, 2 5-inch guns and 8 40-mm guns. The BRYCE CANYON was armed with a single 5-inch gun forward until shortly before being decommissioned in 1979.

Modernization: These ships have been extensively modernized to permit them to support modern destroyers and frigates; the helicopter platform and hangar were provided to support the Drone Antisubmarine Helicopter (DASH) program and cannot land manned helicopters.

BRYCE CANYON—with 5-inch gun forward (1978, U.S. Navy)

BRYCE CANYON (1979, Giorgio Arra)

5 DESTROYER TENDERS: "DIXIE" CLASS

Number	Name	Launched	Commissioned	Status
AD 14	DIXIE	27 May 1939	25 Apr 1940	**PA**
AD 15	PRAIRIE	9 Dec 1939	5 Aug 1940	**PA**
AD 17	PIEDMONT	7 Dec 1942	5 Jan 1944	**AA**
AD 18	SIERRA	23 Feb 1943	20 Mar 1944	**AA**
AD 19	YOSEMITE	16 May 1943	25 May 1944	**AA**

Builders:	AD 14–15 New York Shipbuilding Corp, Camden, N.J.
	AD 17–19 Tampa Shipbuilding Co, Fla.
Displacement:	9,450 tons standard
	17,176 tons full load
Length:	530½ feet (161.7 m) oa
Beam:	73⅓ feet (22.3 m)
Draft:	25½ feet (7.8 m)
Propulsion:	steam turbines (Parsons in AD 14–15, Allis Chalmers in AD 17–19);
	11,000 shp; 2 shafts
Boilers:	4 (Babcock & Wilcox)
Speed:	19.6 knots
Manning:	929 (31 O + 898 enlisted) in AD 14–15
	855 (31 O + 824 enlisted) in AD 17–19
Helicopters:	no facilities
Guns:	4 20-mm Mk 68 (4 × 1)

These are the oldest ships in U.S. Navy commission except for the sail frigate CONSTITUTION, which is retained as a relic. They have been modernized to service ships with ASROC, improved electronics, etc.

Class: Five ships were built to this design (AD 14–15, 17–19); the later NEW ENGLAND (AD 32, ex-AS 28), canceled in 1945, was to have been similar.

Guns: As completed, these ships had four 5-inch DP guns and eight 40-mm AA guns; these were reduced up to the mid-1970s when minimal 20-mm armament was provided.

Modernization: Modernization programs provided helicopter hangar and flight deck to support DASH helicopters. Manned helicopters cannot operate from these ships.

PIEDMONT (1976, Giorgio Arra)

The PRAIRIE under way; tenders are usually found at anchor or moored, with a "nest" of destroyers or submarines alongside. The DIXIE of this class is the oldest U.S. Navy ship in commission except for the relic CONSTITUTION. During 1979 the DIXIE deployed to the Indian Ocean, setting up shop at Diego Garcia to support naval forces operating in that area after the seizure of the American embassy in Tehran by Iranian terrorists. During 4½ months at Diego Garcia the DIXIE performed work on 31 ships. (1979, Giorgio Arra)

8 AMMUNITION SHIPS: "KILAUEA" CLASS

Number	Name	FY/SCB	Launched	Commissioned	Status
AE 26	KILAUEA	65/703	9 Aug 1967	10 Aug 1968	**MSC-P**
AE 27	BUTTE	65/703	9 Aug 1967	29 Nov 1968	**AA**
AE 28	SANTA BARBARA	66/703	23 Jan 1968	11 July 1970	**AA**
AE 29	MOUNT HOOD	66/703	17 July 1968	1 May 1971	**PA**
AE 32	FLINT	67/703	9 Nov 1970	20 Nov 1971	**PA**
AE 33	SHASTA	67/703	3 Apr 1971	26 Feb 1972	**PA**
AE 34	MOUNT BAKER	68/703	23 Oct 1971	22 July 1972	**AA**
AE 35	KISKA	68/703	11 Mar 1972	16 Dec 1972	**PA**

Builders:	AE 26–27 General Dynamics Corp, Quincy, Mass.
	AE 28–29 Bethlehem Steel Corp, Sparrows Point, Md.
	AE 30–35 Ingalls Shipbuilding Corp, Pascagoula, Miss.
Displacement:	20,500 tons full load
Length:	564 feet (171.9 m) oa
Beam:	81 feet (24.7 m)
Draft:	25¾ feet (7.8 m)
Propulsion:	steam turbine (General Electric); 22,000 shp; 1 shaft
Boilers:	3 (Foster Wheeler)
Speed:	22 knots (20 knots sustained)
Manning:	347–353 (~15 O + 332–338 enlisted)
Helicopters:	2 UH-46 Sea Knight
Guns:	4 3-inch (76-mm) 50 cal AA Mk 33 (2 × 2)

These are high-capability underway replenishment ships, fitted for the rapid transfer of missiles and other munitions.

Design: The KILAUEA design provides for the ship's main cargo spaces forward of the superstructure, with a helicopter landing area aft. A hangar approximately 50 feet long and 15½ to 17½ feet wide is built into the superstructure. Cargo capacity is approximately 6,500 tons.

Guns: As built, these ships had eight 3-inch guns in twin mounts (with two Mk 56 gun FCS). Their armament was reduced during the lated 1970s. Two Phalanx CIWS are scheduled for installation in each ship.

KILAUEA (1980, Giorgio Arra)

The KILAUEA displays the unique design of this advanced class of "ammo ships." Two UH-46 Sea Knights can be embarked for vertical replenishment of warships, alleviating the need for the ships to close and steam together for rearming. (1980, Giorgio Arra)

5 AMMUNITION SHIPS: "SURIBACHI" CLASS

Number	Name	FY/SCB	Launched	Commissioned	Status
AE 21	SURIBACHI	54/114A	2 Nov 1955	17 Nov 1956	**AA**
AE 22	MAUNA KEA	54/114A	3 May 1956	30 Mar 1957	**NRF-P**
AE 23	NITRO	56/114A	25 June 1958	1 May 1959	**AA**
AE 24	PYRO	56/114A	5 Nov 1958	24 July 1959	**NRF-P**
AE 25	HALEAKALA	57/114A	17 Feb 1959	3 Nov 1959	**PA**

Builders:	Bethlehem Steel Corp, Sparrows Point, Md.
Displacement:	10,000 tons standard
	17,500 tons full load
Length:	512 feet (156.1 m) oa
Beam:	72 feet (21.9 m)
Draft:	29 feet (8.8 m)
Propulsion:	steam turbine (Bethlehem); 16,000 shp; 1 shaft
Boilers:	2 (Combustion Engineering)
Speed:	20.6 knots
Manning:	322–327 (14–15 O + 308–312 enlisted)
Helicopters:	none assigned
Guns:	4 3-inch (76-mm) 50 cal AA Mk 33 (2 × 2)

These ships were designed specifically for munitions underway replenishment. The MAUNA KEA was transferred to the Naval Reserve Force on 1 October 1979 and the PYRO on 1 September 1980.

Design: Cargo capacity is 7,500 tons.

Guns: As built, eight 3-inch guns were installed in twin mounts (see Modernization notes). The arrangement of the forward guns varies; some ships have 3-inch mounts in tandem and others side by side. The Mk 56 and Mk 63 gun FCS have been removed.

Modernization: All five ships were extensively modernized during the 1960s (SCB-232); they were fitted to carry and transfer guided missiles; the after 3-inch gun mounts were removed, and a helicopter deck was installed. No hangar was provided.

PYRO (1978, Giorgio Arra)

HALEAKALA (1979, Giorgio Arra)

1 STORE SHIP: "RIGEL" CLASS

Number	Name	FY/SCB	Launched	Commissioned	Status
T-AF 58	RIGEL	53/97	15 Mar 1955	2 Sep 1955	**MSC-A**

Builders:	Ingalls Shipbuilding Corp, Pascagoula, Miss.
Displacement:	7,950 tons light
	15,540 tons full load
Length:	502 feet (153.0 m) oa
Beam:	72 feet (22.0 m)
Draft:	29 feet (8.8 m)
Propulsion:	steam turbine (General Electric); 16,000 shp; 1 shaft
Boilers:	2 (Combustion Engineering)
Speed:	20 knots
Manning:	115 (civilian)
Helicopters:	no facilities
Guns:	removed

The RIGEL was one of two built-for-the-purpose refrigerated store ships. She was assigned to the Military Sealift Command on 23 June 1975.

Design: Modified Maritime Administration R3-S-A4 design. Cargo capacity is 4,650 tons.

Guns: The RIGEL was completed with eight 3-inch AA Mk 33 guns in twin mounts. The two after mounts were removed for installation of a helicopter platform. The forward guns were removed when the ship was assigned to MSC, as were the Mk 56 and Mk 63 gun FCS.

1 COMBAT STORES SHIP: Ex-ROYAL NAVY TYPE

Number	Name	Launched	RFA Comm.	Status
T-AFS 8	SIRIUS	7 Apr 1966	22 Dec 1966	**MSC-A**

Builders:	Swan Hunter & Wighman Richardson, Wallsend-on-Tyne, England
Displacement:	9,010 tons light
	16,792 tons full load
Length:	524 feet (159.7 m) oa
Beam:	72 feet (21.9 m)
Draft:	22 feet (6.7 m)
Propulsion:	diesel (Wallsend-Sulzer); 11,520 shp; 1 shaft
Speed:	18 knots
Manning:	116 (civilian) + 17 Navy
Helicopters:	none assigned
Guns:	none

The SIRIUS was built as the Royal Navy stores support ship LYNESS (civilian manned by the Royal Fleet Auxiliary). In response to the U.S. Navy's massive logistic problems in maintaining two carrier battle groups in the Indian Ocean, she was acquired on 1 November 1980 by the Military Sealift Command under time charter with a nongovernment civilian crew. Subsequently her status was changed to bare boat charter and she was turned over to MSC in ceremonies at Norfolk, Va., on 17 January 1981. At that time the ship was renamed SIRIUS and designated T-AFS 8. (U.S. Navy purchase of the ship was to occur about the same time.)

Class: Originally a class of three ships, the others being the RFA TARBATNESS (now laid up) and RFA STROMNESS (active with the Royal Navy in the Pacific).

Helicopters: Large landing area but no hangar facilities.

RIGEL (1977, Giorgio Arra)

7 COMBAT STORE SHIPS: "MARS" CLASS

Number	Name	FY/SCB	Launched	Commissioned	Status
AFS 1	MARS	61/208	15 June 1963	21 Dec 1963	**PA**
AFS 2	SYLVANIA	62/208	15 Aug 1963	11 July 1964	**AA**
AFS 3	NIAGARA FALLS	64/208	26 Mar 1966	29 Apr 1967	**PA**
AFS 4	WHITE PLAINS	65/705	23 July 1966	23 Nov 1968	**PA**
AFS 5	CONCORD	65/705	17 Dec 1966	27 Nov 1968	**AA**
AFS 6	SAN DIEGO	66/705	13 Apr 1968	24 May 1969	**AA**
AFS 7	SAN JOSE	67/705	13 Dec 1969	23 Oct 1970	**PA**

Builders:	National Steel & Shipbuilding Co, San Diego, Calif.
Displacement:	16,500 tons full load
Length:	581 feet (177.1 m) oa
Beam:	79 feet (24.1 m)
Draft:	24 feet (7.3 m)
Propulsion:	steam turbine (De Laval in AFS 1–2, 4–5, 7); 22,000 shp; 1 shaft
Boilers:	3 (Babcock & Wilcox)
Speed:	20 knots
Manning:	431–442 (24–25 O + 407–417 enlisted)
Helicopters:	2 UH-46 Sea Knight
Guns:	4 3-inch (76-mm) AA Mk 33 (2 × 2)

These are large, built-for-the-purpose underway replenishment ships combining the capabilities of store ships (AF), stores-issue ships (AKS), and aviation store ships (AVS). They do not carry bulk petroleum products as do the AOE-AOR replenishment ships.

The WHITE PLAINS is home-ported in Yokosuka, Japan.

Class: Three additional ships that were planned for the FY 1977 –1978 shipbuilding programs were not requested when the annual budgets were submitted to Congress. No additional ships of the AF/AFS type are planned for construction during the 1980s.

Design: These ships have advanced cargo transfer equipment; they are fitted with five cargo holds (one refrigerated), and have a 7,000-ton cargo capacity. A helicopter hangar 46¾ to 51 feet in length and 16- to 23-feet wide is provided at the after end of the superstructure, with a landing area aft.

Engineering: Two boilers are normally used for full-power steaming, with the third shut down for maintenance.

Guns: These ships were completed with four 3-inch twin gun mounts and the Mk 56 gun FCS. Two mounts and the FCS were removed during the late 1970s.

CONCORD—open 3-inch mounts forward (1979, U.S. Navy)

The SYLVANIA under way at slow speed; note the ship's amidships superstructure and hangar structure aft. Two enclosed 3-inch twin gun mounts have been retained forward; the twin 3-inch open mounts abaft the funnel have been removed. These ships are also configured to support two UH-46 Sea Knights for vertical replenishment. (1979, Giorgio Arra)

1 HYDROGRAPHIC RESEARCH SHIP: "VICTORY" CLASS

Number	Name	Launched	In service	Status
T-AG 164	KINGSPORT	29 May 1944	1 Mar 1950	**MSC-A**

Builders:	California Shipbuilding Corp, Los Angeles
Displacement:	7,190 tons light
	10,680 tons full load
Length:	455 feet (138.7 m) oa
Beam:	62 feet (18.9 m)
Draft:	22 feet (6.7 m)
Propulsion:	steam turbine; 8,500 shp; 1 shaft
Boilers:	2
Speed:	15.2 knots
Manning:	54 (civilian) + 15 technical personnel
Helicopters:	no facilities
Guns:	none

The KINGSPORT was built as a cargo ship and was employed in carrying military cargoes until acquired by the Navy on 1 March 1950 and assigned to MSTS (retaining her original name KINGSPORT VICTORY). She continued in the cargo role as the T-AK 239 until 1961, when she was converted to support the Project Advent defense satellite communications program; in that role she was renamed the KINGSPORT and changed to T-AG 164. The support of Project Advent and other space programs was completed in 1966, and the KINGSPORT was reassigned to hydrographic research activities in support of undersea surveillance programs. Operated by MSC in support of the Naval Electronic Systems Command, she is civilian-manned.

Classification: She was changed from T-AK 239 to T-AG 164 (and renamed) on 14 November 1961.

Conversion: Conversion to a satellite communications ship included provision of extensive communications and satellite tracking equipment, including a 30-foot parabolic communications antenna housed in a 53-foot diameter plastic radome aft of the superstructure. (This was later removed.) The ship was painted white for operations in the tropics. The conversion was SCB-225.

Design: Maritime Administration VC2-S-AP3 design.

KINGSPORT (U.S. Navy)

1 NAVIGATION RESEARCH SHIP: "MARINER" CLASS

Number	Name	Launched	Commissioned	Status
AG 153	COMPASS ISLAND	24 Oct 1953	3 Dec 1956	MR

Builders:	New York Shipbuilding Corp, Camden, N.J.
Displacement:	16,076 tons full load
Length:	563 feet (171.6 m) oa
Beam:	76 feet (23.2 m)
Draft:	29 feet (8.8 m)
Propulsion:	steam turbine (General Electric); 22,000 shp; 1 shaft
Boilers:	2
Speed:	20 knots
Manning:	265 (17 O + 248 enlisted)
Helicopters:	none assigned
Guns:	none

The COMPASS ISLAND was completed as a commercial merchant ship in October 1953. She was subsequently laid up in reserve until acquired by the Navy on 29 March 1956 for conversion to a test ship for inertial navigation systems to be used in Polaris submarines. She was Navy-manned and continued to be used in the development of navigation equipment until decommissioned on 1 May 1980 and laid up in the National Defense Reserve Fleet. Replaced in the research role by the VANGUARD (T-AGM 19).

Classification: Originally classified YAG 56, she was changed to AG 153 on 19 June 1956; she was listed as EAG 153 until 1 April 1968, when she was "reclassified" as AG 153.

Conversion: She is fitted with Ships Inertial Navigation System (SINS), with star trackers mounted in a 67-ton stabilized tower or observatory forward of the bridge. Active-fin roll stabilizers are installed, and she has been fitted with a large sonar dome.

Design: Maritime Administration C4-S-1A design.

Names: Merchant name was the GARDEN MARINER.

COMPASS ISLAND (U.S. Navy)

1 AUXILIARY DEEP SUBMERGENCE SUPPORT SHIP: "POINT LOMA" TYPE

Number	Name	Launched	T-AKD in service	AGDS Comm.	Status
AGDS 2	POINT LOMA	25 May 1957	29 May 1958	3 July 1976	**PA**

Builders:	Maryland Shipbuilding & Dry Dock Co, Baltimore
Displacement:	9,415 tons standard
	14,094 tons full load
Length:	492 feet (150.0 m) oa
Beam:	90 feet (27.4 m)
Draft:	26 feet (7.9 m)
Propulsion:	steam turbines; 6,000 shp; 2 shafts
Boilers:	2
Speed:	15 knots
Manning:	240 (10 O + 230 enlisted) + 8 technicians
Helicopters:	no facilities
Guns:	none

The POINT LOMA was built as a "wet well" dock cargo ship (originally the POINT BARROW, T-AKD 1) to carry vehicles, supplies, and landing craft to U.S. radar warning installations in the Arctic. She was assigned to MSTS upon completion and operated in that role until 1965 (during that period she also transported the fixed-array radar antennas for the carrier ENTERPRISE and cruiser LONG BEACH); she was modified in 1965 and then used until 1970 to carry Saturn rockets and other space program equipment from California to Cape Kennedy. She also made some trips to Vietnam carrying landing craft.

The ship was laid up in 1971–1972, then returned to general cargo work under Military Sealift Command; she was converted in 1974–1976 to carry and support the research submersible TRIESTE.

The POINT LOMA is operated by Submarine Development Group 1 at Point Loma (San Diego), California.

Classification: The classification AGDS was established on 3 January 1974. The previous TRIESTE II support ship, the modified floating dry dock WHITE SANDS (ARD 20), was briefly assigned the hull number AGDS 1.

Conversion: The ship was specifically converted in 1974–1976 for use with the TRIESTE II; she can carry, launch, recover, and service the submersible. Tankage is provided for approximately 100,000 gallons of aviation gasoline that is used for flotation by the TRIESTE II, and the lead shot that is used by the submersible for ballast.

Design: Maritime Administration S2-ST-23A design. The ship is ice-strengthened and winterized for Arctic operation.

POINT LOMA (1979, Giorgio Arra)

1 MISSILE RANGE INSTRUMENTATION SHIP: "MARINER" CLASS

Number	Name	Launched	Commissioned	Status
T-AGM 23 (ex-AG 154)	OBSERVATION ISLAND	15 Aug 1953	5 Dec 1958	**MSC-A**

Builders:	New York Shipbuilding Corp, Camden, N.J.
Displacement:	
Length:	563 feet (171.6 m) oa
Beam:	76 feet (23.2 m)
Draft:	29 feet (8.8 m)
Propulsion:	steam turbine (General Electric); 22,000 shp; 1 shaft
Boilers:	2
Speed:	20 knots
Manning:	
Helicopters:	no facilities
Guns:	none

The ship was completed for commercial service in February 1954, and after operating briefly she was laid up in the National Defense Reserve Fleet in November 1954. She was transferred to the Navy on 10 September 1956 for conversion to a missile test ship for the Polaris SLBM, being commissioned in 1958. She was subsequently modified to launch the Poseidon missile.

After completion of the Poseidon development program, the ship was laid up in the National Defense Fleet, being decommissioned on 25 September 1972. The OBSERVATION ISLAND was retained on the Naval Register, and on 18 August 1977 she was selected for conversion to a missile range instrumentation ship. As an AGM she has been fitted with the Cobra Judy phased-array radar aft, and two radar spheres atop her superstructure. She is operated by the Military Sealift Command with a civilian crew for the Air Force Eastern Test Range.

Class: Plans to acquire a third "Mariner" (i.e., AG 155) to support the Polaris program were canceled.

Classification: Originally classified YAG 57 for Navy service. Changed to AG 154 on 19 June 1956; listed as EAG 154 until 1 April 1968 when the ship was "reclassified" as AG 154 to avoid confusion. The ship was again changed to T-AGM 23 on 1 May 1979.

Conversion: Converted to AGM configuration at the Maryland Shipbuilding & Drydock Co, Baltimore, Md., from 1977–1981.

Design: Maritime Administration C4-S-1A design. As an AG she was fitted with two SLBM launch tubes.

Names: Her merchant name was EMPIRE STATE MARINER.

OBSERVATION ISLAND after conversion to T-AGM 23 (Raytheon)

OBSERVATION ISLAND as AG 154 (U.S. Navy)

2 MISSILE RANGE INSTRUMENTATION SHIPS: "VICTORY" CLASS

Number	Name	Launched	APA Comm.	T-AGM in service	Status
T-AGM 8	WHEELING	22 May 1945	—	28 May 1964	**MSC-P**
T-AGM 22	RANGE SENTINEL	10 July 1944	20 Sep 1944	14 Oct 1971	**MSC-A**

Builders:	T-AGM 8 Oregon Shipbuilding Corp, Portland T-AGM 22 Permanente Metals Corp, Richmond, Calif.
Displacement:	10,680 tons full load T-AGM 8 11,860 tons full load T-AGM 22
Length:	455 feet (138.7 m) oa
Beam:	62 feet (18.9 m)
Draft:	
Propulsion:	steam turbine (Westinghouse); 8,500 shp; 1 shaft
Boilers:	2
Speed:	17.7 knots
Manning:	58 (civilian) + 48 technicians in T-AGM 8 68 (civilian) + 27 technicians in T-AGM 22
Helicopters:	none assigned to T-AGM 8; no facilities in T-AGM 22
Guns:	none

These ships are a former merchant ship and Navy attack transport (APA 205), respectively, converted to missile range instrumentation ships. The WHEELING is the survivor of several "Victory"-class ships that were converted to the AGM role during the intensive U.S. space and strategic weapon programs of the 1960s (AGM 1, 3–8).

The RANGE SENTINEL served as an APA during World War II; she was subsequently laid up and stricken on 1 October 1958. She was reacquired from the Maritime Administration on 22 October 1969 for conversion to an AGM, and reclassified as AGM 22 on 26 April 1971.

Both ships are civilian-manned.

Design: Maritime Administration VC2-S-AP3 and VC2-S-AP5 designs, respectively. Their configurations differ considerably. The WHEELING has a helicopter hangar and flight deck aft.

Names: The RANGE SENTINEL was formerly the SHERBURNE (APA 205).

RANGE SENTINEL (1973, U.S. Navy)

WHEELING (U.S. Navy)

1 NAVIGATION RESEARCH SHIP AND 1 MISSILE RANGE INSTRUMENTATION SHIP—CONVERTED OILERS

Number	Name	Launched	AO Comm.	T-AGM in service	Status
T-AGM 19 (ex-AO 122)	VANGUARD	25 Nov 1943	21 Oct 1947	28 Feb 1966	**MSC-A**
T-AGM 20 (ex-AO 114)	REDSTONE	28 Feb 1944	22 Oct 1947	30 June 1966	**MSC-A**

Builders:　　　　Marine Ship Corp, Sausalito, Calif.
Displacement:　 21,626 tons full load
Length:　　　　 595 feet (181.4 m) oa
Beam:　　　　　 75 feet (22.9 m)
Draft:　　　　　 25 feet (7.6 m)
Propulsion:　　 turbo-electric drive (General Electric); 10,000 shp; 1 shaft
Boilers:　　　　 2 (Babcock & Wilcox)
Speed:　　　　　16 knots
Manning:　　　　76 (civilian) + 120 technicians in T-AGM 20
Helicopters:　　no facilities
Guns:　　　　　 none

These ships are former "Mission"-class tankers that were extensively converted for the missile range instrumentation role. Both ships initially served as Navy oilers and were then transferred to MSTS when that service was created on 1 October 1949. The VANGUARD was stricken as AO 122 on 4 September 1957 and then reacquired by the Navy on 28 September 1964 for conversion to AGM 19; the REDSTONE was stricken as AO 114 on 13 March 1958 and reacquired on 19 September 1964 to become AGM 20.

The VANGUARD was assigned to the Navy's Strategic Systems Project Office on 1 October 1978 for conversion to a navigation research ship to replace the COMPASS ISLAND (AG 153). She was to have been reclassified AG 194 in her new role but instead serves as

T-AGM 19. The VANGUARD's conversion was completed in mid-1980. Both ships are civilian-manned by MSC, with the REDSTONE supporting NASA activities.

Class: A third ship of this type, the MERCURY (T-AGM 21) has been stricken. (See Appendix C.)

Conversion: Both ships were extensively converted to the AGM configuration at the General Dynamics yard at Quincy, Mass.; a 72-foot midships section was installed, increasing the ships' length and beam. They were fitted with missile/space tracking systems, extensive communications equipment was installed, and accommodations were provided for a large technical staff. Their configurations as AGMs differed.

The VANGUARD was converted to a navigation research ship at the Todd Shipyards Corporation's Brooklyn facility in 1979–1980.

Design: Original Maritime Administration design as oilers was T2-SE-A2.

Names: The VANGUARD was built as the MISSION SAN FERNANDO; renamed MUSCLE SHOALS on 8 April 1965, and then VANGUARD on 1 September 1965. The REDSTONE was built as the MISSION DE PALA; changed to JOHNSTOWN on 8 April 1965, and to REDSTONE on 1 September 1965.

REDSTONE (1970, U.S. Air Force)

VANGUARD (U.S. Navy)

2 MISSILE RANGE INSTRUMENTATION SHIPS: CONVERTED TRANSPORTS

Number	Name	Launched	AP Comm.	T-AGM in service	Status
T-AGM 9	GENERAL H. H. ARNOLD	23 May 1944	17 Aug 1944	1 July 1964	**MSC-P**
T-AGM 10	GENERAL HOYT S. VANDENBERG	10 October 1943	1 Apr 1944	13 July 1964	**MSC-A**

Builders:	Kaiser Co, Richmond, Calif.
Displacement:	16,600 tons full load
Length:	522⁵/₆ feet (159.4 m) oa
Beam:	71½ feet (21.8 m)
Draft:	26¹/₃ feet (8 m)
Propulsion:	steam turbine (Westinghouse); 9,000 shp; 1 shaft
Boilers:	2 (Babcock & Wilcox)
Speed:	16.5 knots
Manning:	90 (civilian) + 113 technicians
Helicopters:	no facilities
Guns:	none

These ships were converted from "General"-class transports (T-AP 139 and T-AP 145, respectively) into missile range ships to support Air Force ICBM tests. Upon conversion both ships were placed in Air Force service in 1963 with civilian contract crews. They were subsequently designated T-AGMs and assigned to MSTS in 1964.

Both ships are civilian-manned.

Design: Maritime Administration C4-S-A1 design. As transports, these ships each carried approximately 3,300 troops.

Names: T-AGM 9 originally was named the GENERAL R. E. CALLAN and the T-AGM 10 was the GENERAL HARRY TAYLOR.

GENERAL H. H. ARNOLD (U.S. Navy)

GENERAL H. H. ARNOLD (1977, Giorgio Arra)

GENERAL HOYT S. VANDENBERG (U.S. Navy)

GENERAL HOYT S. VANDENBERG at Port Canaveral (1980, U.S. Navy, CDR Gordon Peterson)

2 OCEANOGRAPHIC RESEARCH SHIPS: "GYRE" CLASS

Number	Name	FY/SCB	Launched	Delivered	Status
(AGOR 21)	GYRE	71/734	25 May 1973	14 Nov 1973	**Academic**
(AGOR 22)	MOANA WAVE	71/734	18 June 1973	16 Jan 1974	**Academic**

Builders:	Halter Marine Service, New Orleans
Displacement:	950 tons full load
Length:	176 feet (53.6 m) oa
Beam:	36 feet (11.0 m)
Draft:	14½ feet (4.4 m)
Propulsion:	turbo-charged diesels (Caterpillar); 1,700 shp; 2 shafts
Speed:	13 knots
Manning:	10 (civilian) + 11 scientists
Helicopters:	no facilities
Guns:	none

These are small, "utility" research ships designed specifically for use by research institutions. They are operated for the Oceanographer of the Navy by Texas A&M University and the University of Hawaii, respectively. The MOANA WAVE has been employed for at-sea testing of the T-AGOS towed sonar array.

Design: These ships are based on a commercial design. The open deck aft provides space for special-purpose vans and research equipment.

Engineering: A small, 50-hp retractable propeller pod is fitted for low-speed maneuvering or station-keeping during research operations, thus permitting main engines to be shut down to reduce noise and vibration.

GYRE (Halter Marine Service)

MOANA WAVE (1979, Giorgio Arra)

1 OCEANOGRAPHIC RESEARCH SHIP: "HAYES" TYPE

Number	Name	FY/SCB	Launched	In service	Status
T-AGOR 16	HAYES	67/726	2 July 1970	21 July 1971	**MSC-A**

Builders:	Todd Shipyards, Seattle
Displacement:	3,080 tons full load
Length:	246$^5/_{12}$ feet (75.1 m) oa
Beam:	75 feet (22.9 m)
Draft:	18½ feet (5.6 m)
Propulsion:	geared diesels (General Motors); 5,400 shp; 2 shafts
Speed:	15 knots (sustained)
Manning:	44 (civilian) + 30 scientists
Helicopters:	no facilities
Guns:	none

The HAYES is the Navy's largest built-for-the-purpose oceanographic research ship. The catamaran design provides a stable work platform with a large, open deck area; also, a center-line well makes it possible to lower research equipment into sheltered water between the two hulls. However, some seakeeping problems were encountered in this design, and it has not been repeated.

The HAYES is operated by MSC for the Office of Naval Research under the technical control of the Oceanographer of the Navy, with a civilian crew.

Design: The HAYES has two hulls, each with a 24-foot beam, spaced 27 feet apart for an overall ship beam of 75 feet. Berthing and messing spaces are located in the forward superstructure "block," while the laboratories are located aft.

Engineering: An auxiliary, 165-ship diesel engine is provided in each hull to permit a "creeping" speed of 2 to 4 knots.

HAYES (1975, U.S. Navy, CAPT A. J. Cotterell)

2 OCEANOGRAPHIC RESEARCH SHIPS: "MELVILLE" CLASS

Number	Name	FY/SCB	Launched	Commissioned	Status
(AGOR 14)	MELVILLE	66/710	10 July 1968	27 Aug 1969	**Academic**
(AGOR 15)	KNORR	66/710	21 Aug 1968	14 Jan 1970	**Academic**

Builders:	Defoe Shipbuilding Co, Bay City, Mich.
Displacement:	1,915 tons standard
	2,080 tons full load
Length:	244$^5/_6$ feet (74.6 m) oa
Beam:	46$^1/_3$ feet (14.1 m)
Draft:	15 feet (4.6 m)
Propulsion:	diesel (Enterprise); 2,500 shp; 2 cycloidal propellers
Speed:	12.5 knots (sustained)
Manning:	25 (civilian) + 25 scientists
Helicopters:	no facilities
Guns:	none

These ships are the U.S. Navy's first oceangoing ships with cycloidal propellers (see Engineering notes). These ships have essentially the same capabilities as the previous CONRAD class.

The MELVILLE is operated by the Scripps Institution of Oceanography and the KNORR by the Woods Hole Oceanographic Institution, both for the Office of Naval Research under the technical control of the Oceanographer of the Navy. They are civilian-manned.

Class: AGOR 19–20 were in the FY 1968 program, but their construction was canceled.

Design: These ships are radically different in design from the CONRAD class, although both classes share a common SCB number. There is a bow observation dome.

Engineering: These ships have a single diesel engine, driving two cycloidal (vertical) propellers; the forward propeller is just abaft the bow observation dome and the after propeller is forward of the

HAYES (U.S. Navy)

rudder. Cycloidal propulsion—controlled by a "joystick"—allows the ships to be propelled in any direction and to turn up to 360° in their own length. This type of propulsion also allows precise station-keeping and slow speeds, without the use of auxiliary propulsion units. The ships have experienced some transmission system difficulties.

MELVILLE (U.S. Navy)

Cycloidal propellers on MELVILLE (Courtesy Stewart Nelson)

KNORR (U.S. Navy)

7 OCEANOGRAPHIC RESEARCH SHIPS: "CONRAD" CLASS

Number	Name	FY/SCB	Launched	Delivered	Status
(AGOR 3)	ROBERT D. CONRAD	60/185	26 May 1962	29 Nov 1962	**Academic**
(AGOR 4)	JAMES M. GILLISS	60/185	19 May 1962	5 Nov 1962	**Academic**
T-AGOR 7	LYNCH	62/185	17 Mar 1964	22 Oct 1965	**MSC-A**
(AGOR 9)	THOMAS G. THOMPSON	63/185	18 July 1964	4 Sep 1965	**Academic**
(AGOR 10)	THOMAS WASHINGTON	63/185	1 Aug 1964	17 Sep 1965	**Academic**
T-AGOR 12	DE STEIGUER	65/710	21 Mar 1966	28 Feb 1969	**MSC-P**
T-AGOR 13	BARTLETT	65/710	24 May 1966	15 Apr 1969	**MSC-A**

Builders:	AGOR 3	Gibbs Corp, Jacksonville, Fla.
	AGOR 4	Christy Corp, Sturgeon Bay, Wisc.
	AGOR 7	Marietta Manufacturing Co, Point Pleasant, West Va.
	AGOR 9–10	Marinette Marine Corp, Marinette, Wisc.
	AGOR 12–13	Northwest Marine Iron Works, Portland, Ore.
Displacement:		(varies) ~1,200 tons standard
		~1,380 tons full load
Length:		208⅚ feet (63.7 m) oa
Beam:		37⁵⁄₁₂ feet (11.4 m)
Draft:		~15⅓ feet (4.7 m)
Propulsion:		diesel-electric (Caterpillar Tractor diesels); 10,000 shp; 1 shaft
Speed:		13.5 knots
Manning:		26–27 (civilian) + 15 scientists
Helicopters:		no facilities
Guns:		none

These were the U.S. Navy's first built-for-the-purpose oceanographic research ships. Three ships are operated by MSC; the CONRAD is operated by the Lamont Geological Observatory of Columbia University, the GILLISS by the University of Miami (Florida), the THOMPSON by the University of Washington (state), and the WASHINGTON by the Scripps Institution of Oceanography; all are under the technical control of the Oceanographer of the Navy, and all have civilian crews.

Class: Two ships have been transferred to other nations: the CHARLES H. DAVIS (AGOR 5) to New Zealand in 1970, and the SANDS (AGOR 6) to Brazil in 1974.

Design: These ships vary in detail, each with different bridge, amidships side structure, mast, and laboratory arrangements. The last two ships have SCB numbers in the new scheme (i.e., SCB-185 and -710 are the same design).

Engineering: The large stacks contain a small diesel exhaust funnel and provide space for the small 620-shp gas-turbine engine used to provide "quiet" power during experiments in which the noise generated by the main propulsion diesel would be unacceptable. The gas turbine can be linked to the propeller shaft for speeds of up to 6.5 knots. There is also a bow propeller pod which allows precise maneuvering and can propel the ship at speeds up to 4.5 knots.

LYNCH (1973, Giorgio Arra)

THOMAS WASHINGTON (U.S. Navy)

2 OCEANOGRAPHIC RESEARCH SHIPS: CONVERTED CARGO SHIPS

Number	Name	Launched	AK in service	AGOR in service	Status
T-AGOR 8	ELTANIN	16 Jan 1957		1962	MR
T-AGOR 11	MIZAR	7 Oct 1957	7 Mar 1958	1965	**MSC-P**

Builders:	Avondale Marine Ways, New Orleans, La.
Displacement:	2,036 tons light
	4,942 tons full load
Length:	262¹/₆ feet (79.9 m) oa
Beam:	51½ feet (15.7 m)
Draft:	22¾ feet (7.0 m)
Propulsion:	diesel-electric (Alco diesels; Westinghouse electric motors); 3,200 shp; 2 shafts
Speed:	12 knots
Manning:	T-AGOR 11 46 (civilian) + 15 scientists
Helicopters:	no facilities
Guns:	none

The MIZAR was converted from an ice-strengthened cargo ship (T-AK 272) to a deep-ocean research ship. She is operated by MSC for the Naval Research Laboratory and is under the technical control of the Oceanographer of the Navy. The ELTANIN (ex-T-AK 270) was transferred to Argentina in 1972; she was returned to the United States and laid up in the National Defense Reserve Fleet.

Class: Three cargo ships were built to this design (T-AK 270–272). The MIZAR and ELTANIN were converted to oceanographic research ships.

Classification: The ELTANIN changed from AK 270 to AGOR 8 on 23 August 1962; the MIZAR changed from AK 272 to AGOR 11 on 15 April 1964.

Conversion: The MIZAR was converted to an AGOR in 1964–1965, being fitted with a center well for lowering towed sensors and instruments. She was also fitted with laboratories and photographic facilities. She has an elaborate computer-controlled hydrophone system that makes precise sea-floor navigation possible, and assists in locating underwater objects. The center well is 23-feet long and 10-feet wide.

After partial conversion in 1964, the MIZAR participated in the search for the sunken submarine THRESHER (SSN 593). She completed conversion to an AGOR after the completion of that operation. The MIZAR subsequently helped to locate the sunken USS SCORPION (SSN 589) and the Soviet Golf-class diesel submarine that was lost in the Pacific in 1968.

The ELTANIN was converted to an oceanographic research ship in 1961, being fitted with scientific equipment for Antarctic research in support of the National Science Foundation.

Design: Originally Maritime Administration C1-ME2-13a design.

ELTANIN (U.S. Navy)

The MIZAR (above) and her sister ship ELTANIN have distinctive enclosed crow's nests on their forward mast and icebreaking bows, reflecting their original role of Arctic supply ships. The MIZAR has an amidships structure covering her center well used for lowering research and search equipment. The ELTANIN has an amidships mast and built-up structure forward. (1973, Wright & Logan)

(8) OCEAN SURVEILLANCE SHIPS

Number	Name	FY/SCB	Launch	Commission	Status
T-AGOS 1	. . . .	79			Bldg.
T-AGOS 2	. . . .	79			Bldg.
T-AGOS 3	. . . .	80			Bldg.
T-AGOS 4	. . . .	81			Auth.
T-AGOS 5	. . . .	81			Auth.
T-AGOS 6	. . . .	81			Auth.
T-AGOS 7	. . . .	81			Auth.
T-AGOS 8	. . . .	81			Auth.

Builders:	Tacoma Boatbuilding Co., Wash.
Displacement:	~1,900 tons full load
Length:	~217 feet (65.1 m) oa
Beam:	~42 feet (12.8 m)
Draft:	~14 feet (4.3 m)
Propulsion:	diesel-electric; 2 shafts
Speed:	11 knots (transit; 3 knots towing)
Manning:	~20 (civilian) + 5–6 technicians
Helicopters:	no facilities
Guns:	none

The T-AGOS ships are being constructed to supplement the Navy's SOSUS (Sound Surveillance System)—a series of fixed, acoustic detection devices moored to the ocean floor. The ships will tow the SURTASS (Surveillance Towed Array Sensor System), a passive hydrophone array intended to provide long-range detection of hostile submarines. The SURTASS array, which is several hundred feet long, will be towed at the end of a 6,000-foot cable. This array is considerably longer than the tactical arrays towed by anti-submarine ships. The T-AGOS will have no ASW capability, but will transmit data to shore stations or, under certain circumstances, to warships.

Four additional T-AGOS were planned for the FY 1982 budget to provide a 12-ship force. Tacoma Boatbuilding received a contract in September 1980 with multi-year provisions to construct the entire class.

Design: The T-AGOS design is a modification of an offshore oil-drilling rig support ship.

Electronics: Data from the hydrophone array will be generated at a very high rate. They will be "pre-processed" on board the T-AGOS and sent at a much lower data rate (reduced by a factor of ten) via satellite link to shore stations. The data rate from ship to shore is about 32,000 bits (32 kilobits) per second.

Operations: The Navy originally planned for 12 T-AGOS that would each undertake 90-day patrols towing SURTASS plus about eight days in transit. Subsequent analysis and civilian manning considerations have led to a revised patrol schedule of 60 to 74 days plus transit, thus reducing the area coverage over that planned when the 12-ship force was developed.

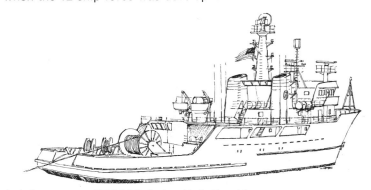

Artist's concept of T-AGOS design (J. C. Roach)

1 SURVEYING SHIP: "H. H. HESS" TYPE

Number	Name	Launched	In service	Status
T-AGS 38	H. H. HESS	30 May 1964	16 Jan 1978	**MSC-P**

Builders:	National Steel and Shipbuilding Co, San Diego, Calif.
Displacement:	3,127 tons light
	17,874 tons full load
Length:	564 feet (171.9 m) oa
Beam:	76 feet (23.2 m)
Draft:	32¾ feet (10.0 m)
Propulsion:	steam turbine (General Electric); 19,250 shp; 1 shaft
Boilers:	2 (Foster Wheeler)
Speed:	20 knots
Manning:	69 (civilian) + 14 scientists + 27 Navy technicians
Helicopters:	none assigned
Guns:	none

This ship is the former merchant ship CANADA MAIL acquired by the Navy in 1975 for conversion to an AGS to replace the MICHELSON (T-AGS 23). She is operated by MSC for the Oceanographer of the Navy, with a civilian crew.

Classification: Classified as an AGS and renamed on 1 November 1976.

Conversion: Converted to an AGS in 1975–1977.

H. H. HESS (1977, Giorgio Arra)

H. H. Hess (U.S. Navy)

4 SURVEYING SHIPS: "SILAS BENT" CLASS

Number	Name	FY/SCB	Launched	Delivered	Status
T-AGS 26	Silas Bent	63/226	16 May 1964	23 July 1965	**MSC-P**
T-AGS 27	Kane	64/226	20 Nov 1965	19 May 1967	**MSC-A**
T-AGS 33	Wilkes	67/725	31 July 1969	28 June 1971	**MSC-A**
T-AGS 34	Wyman	67/728	30 Oct 1969	3 Nov 1971	**MSC-A**

Builders:	AGS 26	American Shipbuilding Co, Lorain, Ohio
	AGS 27	Christy Corp, Sturgeon Bay, Wisc.
	AGS 33–34	Defoe Shipbuilding Co, Bay City, Mich.
Displacement:	1,935 tons standard	
	AGS 26–27 2,558 tons full load, AGS 33 2,540 tons, AGS 34 2,420 tons	
Length:	285⅓ feet (87.0 m) oa	
Beam:	48 feet (14.6 m)	
Draft:	15 feet (4.6 m)	
Propulsion:	diesel-electric (Westinghouse diesels); 3,600 shp; 1 shaft	
Speed:	14 knots	
Manning:	50 (civilian) + 26 scientists, except	
	41 (civilian) + 20 scientists in T-AGS 34	
Helicopters:	no facilities	
Guns:	none	

These ships were designed specifically for surveying operations. They differ in detail. All four ships are operated by MSC for the Oceanographer of the Navy with civilian crews.

Design: Two ships have old-system SCB numbers, and two have new-system numbers.

Engineering: These ships have bow propulsion units for precise maneuvering and station-keeping.

Kane (1979, Giorgio Arra)

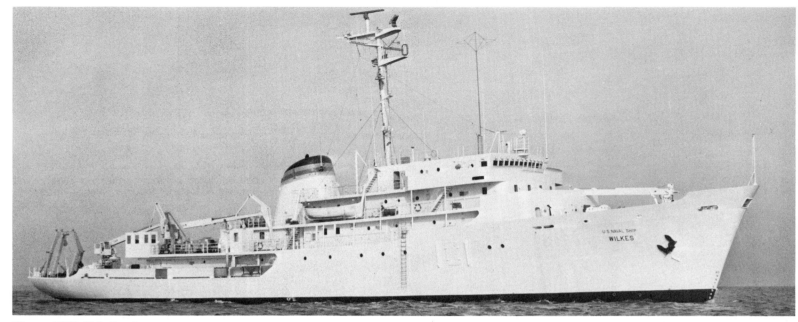

WILKES (1971, U.S. Navy)

2 SURVEYING SHIPS: "CHAUVENET" CLASS

Number	Name	FY/SCB	Launched	Delivered	Status
T-AGS 29	CHAUVENET	65/723	13 May 1968	13 Nov 1970	**MSC-P**
T-AGS 32	HARKNESS	66/723	12 June 1968	29 Jan 1971	MR

Builders:	Upper Clyde Shipbuilders, Glasgow, Scotland
Displacement:	4,200 tons full load
Length:	393 1/6 feet (119.8 m) oa
Beam:	54 feet (16.5 m)
Draft:	16 feet (4.9 m)
Propulsion:	diesel (Westinghouse); 3,600 shp; 1 shaft
Speed:	15 knots
Manning:	69 (civilian) + 12 scientists + 74 Navy technicians
Helicopters:	1 or 2 utility helicopters
Guns:	none

The CHAUVENET and the HARKNESS were the largest surveying or research ships built specifically for this role for the U.S. Navy.

The CHAUVENET is operated by MSC for the Oceanographer of the Navy. The Navy technicians include a 19-man helicopter detachment. The HARKNESS was decommissioned in April 1979 and transferred to the National Defense Reserve Fleet.

Builders: This was the first class of ships to be built since World War II in Britain for U.S. naval service. Also see EDENTON (ATS 1)-class salvage and rescue ships.

Design: This is the only AGOR/AGS class with a full helicopter support capability, including a hangar 45½-feet long and 12-feet wide.

The CHAUVENET (above) and HARKNESS are the largest ships to be constructed for the U.S. Navy specifically for the research role. Note the davits for surveying boats and the twin helicopter hangars aft. (U.S. Navy)

CHAUVENET (1980, U.S. Navy, PH3 Richard Ludwig)

2 SURVEYING SHIPS: "VICTORY" CLASS

Number	Name	Launched	In service	Status
T-AGS 21	BOWDITCH	30 June 1945	8 Oct 1958	**MSC-A**
T-AGS 22	DUTTON	8 May 1945	1 Nov 1958	**MSC-P**

Builders:	Oregon Shipbuilding Co, Portland
Displacement:	13,050 tons full load
Length:	455$\frac{1}{6}$ feet (138.7 m) oa
Beam:	62$\frac{1}{6}$ feet (19.0 m)
Draft:	25 feet (7.6 m)
Propulsion:	steam turbine (GE in T-AGS 21, Westinghouse in T-AGS 22); 8,500 shp; 1 shaft
Boilers:	2
Speed:	15 knots
Manning:	67 (civilian) + 12 scientists + ~25 Navy technicians
Helicopters:	no facilities
Guns:	none

These are converted "Victory"-class merchant ships, which were acquired by the Navy in 1957 for sea-floor charting and magnetic surveys to support the fleet ballistic missile program. They are operated by MSC for the Oceanographer of the Navy, with civilian crews.

Class: A third ship of this configuration, the MICHELSON (T-AGS 23), was stricken on 15 April 1975.

Conversion: Both ships were converted in 1957–1958; the conversion was SCB-179.

Design: These ships are Maritime Administration VC2-S-AP3 design.

Names: Their merchant names were the SOUTH BEND VICTORY and TUSKEGEE VICTORY, respectively.

DUTTON (1976, U.S. Navy)

1 HOSPITAL SHIP: "HAVEN" CLASS

Number	Name	Launched	Commissioned	Status
AH 17	SANCTUARY	15 Aug 1944	20 June 1945	MR

Builders:	Sun SB & DD Co, Chester, Pa.
Displacement:	11,141 tons standard
	15,400 tons full load
Length:	529 feet (161.2 m) oa
Beam:	71½ feet (21.8 m)
Draft:	24 feet (7.3 m)
Propulsion:	steam turbine (General Electric); 9,000 shp; 1 shaft
Boilers:	2 (Babcock & Wilcox)
Speed:	18.3 knots
Manning:	530 (70 O + 460 enlisted)
Helicopters:	none assigned

The SANCTUARY was converted while under construction to serve as a naval hospital ship. She was decommissioned from 1946 until stricken from the Navy list on 1 September 1961 and transferred to the Maritime Administration. The ship was reacquired by the Navy on 1 March 1966 and, after modernization, served extensively in the Vietnam area. She was converted in 1971–1973 to serve as a dependent support ship in conjunction with plans to base an aircraft carrier at Piraeus, Greece. She was assigned the first mixed male–female crew in the history of the U.S. Navy (excluding female medical personnel). The ship was again decommissioned on 28 March 1974 and laid up in reserve.

During 1980, the subject was raised in the Department of Defense of reactivating this ship to support the pre-positioning ships in the Indian Ocean with major medical facilities. No action had been taken when this edition went to press.

Class: Six ships of this class were completed as hospital ships, AH 12–17.

Conversion: As a dependent support ship the SANCTUARY was fitted with special facilities for obstetrics, gynecology, maternity, and nursery services, and was fitted with a 74-bed hospital that could be expanded to 300 beds in 72 hours; she also had a commissary.

Design: Maritime Administration C4-S-B2 design.

Names: Her merchant name was to have been the MARINE OWL.

SANCTUARY (1973, U.S. Navy)

SANCTUARY (1974, U.S. Navy)

(1) PRE-POSITIONING SHIP

Number	Name	FY/SCB	Launch	Commission	Status
T-AKX	......	81		mid-1983	Auth.

Builders:	
Displacement:	48,800 tons full load
Length:	831½ feet (253.4 m) oa
Beam:	105½ feet (32.2 m)
Draft:	30 feet (9.1 m)
Propulsion:	medium-speed diesels; 27,000 shp; 2 shafts
Speed:	20.4 knots
Manning:	(civilian)
Helicopters:	landing area
Guns:	none

During 1980 the Department of Defense developed a requirement for 14 maritime pre-positioning ships to be forward deployed—carrying vehicles, supplies, and munitions for approximately 16,500 Marines (a Marine Amphibious Brigade). However, the requirement was subsequently changed in 1980 to eight of these ships (to be authorized FY 1981–1986) and four roll-on/roll-off ships of the commercial MAINE class (Maritime C8-S-95A). The latter will be conversions.

The new ships will be built under Maritime Administration contracts. They will be civilian manned by MSC.

Class: The Department of Defense planned a similar class of Forward Deployed Logistic (FDL) ships in the early 1960s, but that program was not funded by Congress. However, some older cargo ships (T-AK) and LSTs were used in that role in the 1960s, being forward deployed in the Far East.

Design: These ships will have a carrying capacity of 28,000 deadweight tons, with 225,000 square feet of vehicle parking area. The vehicles will be loaded and unloaded via a stern ramp. There will be five cargo holds and cranes for handling heavy cargo. Maritime Administration type C8-M-MA134J.

Engineering: Endurance at 20 knots will be 13,000 nautical miles.

2 FORWARD DEPLOYMENT SHIPS: "MORMAC" CLASS

Number	Name	Launched	In service	Status
T-AK 284	NORTHERN LIGHT	29 June 1961	22 Apr 1980	MSC-IO
T-AK 285	SOUTHERN CROSS	23 Jan 1962	1 May 1980	MSC-IO

Builders:	Sun Shipbuilding and DD Co, Chester, Pa.
Displacement:	T-AK 284 9,361 tons gross; 12,537 tons deadweight
	T-AK 285 9,259 tons gross; 12,519 tons deadweight
Length:	T-AK 284 488 feet (148.7 m) oa
	T-AK 285 483 feet (147.2 m) oa
Beam:	68 feet (20.7 m)
Draft:	31 feet (9.4 m)
Propulsion:	steam turbines; 11,000 shp; 1 shaft
Boilers:	2
Speed:	18 knots
Manning:	T-AK 284 50 (civilian)
	T-AK 285 39 (civilian)
Helicopters:	no facilities
Guns:	none

NORTHERN LIGHT (1980, U.S. Navy)

These were commercial cargo ships built for Moore-McCormack Lines and subsequently laid up in Maritime Administration reserve. They were acquired in 1980 for use as prepositioning ships in the Indian Ocean. They carry Marine equipment and supplies.

Design: Maritime Administration type C3-S-33a. Eight ships were built to this design for commercial use, with the COVE (now T-AK 284) having a modified bow that makes her slightly larger than the other ships in the class.

Names: Merchant names were MORMAC COVE and MORMAC TRADE, respectively.

NORTHERN LIGHT prior to modification to naval role (as SS MORMAC COVE).

1 CARGO SHIP: Ex-ATTACK CARGO SHIP

Number	Name	Launched	Commissioned	Status
T-AK 283	WYANDOT	28 June 1944	30 Sep 1944	MR

Builders:	Moore Dry Dock Co, Oakland, Calif.
Displacement:	7,430 tons light
	14,000 tons full load
Length:	459¹/₆ feet (140.0 m) oa
Beam:	63 feet (19.2 m)
Draft:	24 feet (7.3 m)
Propulsion:	steam turbine (General Electric); 6,000 shp; 1 shaft
Boilers:	2 (Combustion Engineering)
Speed:	16.5 knots
Manning:	
Helicopters:	no facilities
Guns:	removed

WYANDOT (U.S. Navy)

The WYANDOT was completed as an attack cargo ship (AKA 92) of the ANDROMEDA (AKA 15) class. She was stricken from the Naval Register after the Korean War, but reacquired in 1961 and assigned to MSTS in 1963 as a cargo ship (T-AKA 92). She is now laid up in the National Defense Reserve Fleet.

Classification: Changed from AKA 92 to AK 283 on 1 January 1969.

Design: Maritime Administration C2-S-B1 design.

Guns: Original armament as an AKA consisted of one 5-inch 38 cal DP gun, eight 40-mm AA guns, plus 20-mm AA guns.

3 FLEET BALLISTIC MISSILE CARGO SHIPS: "VICTORY" CLASS

Number	Name	Launched	In service	Status
T-AK 280	FURMAN	6 May 1945	18 Sep 1963	**MSC-P**
T-AK 281	VICTORIA	28 April 1944	11 Oct 1965	**MSC-A**
T-AK 282	MARSHFIELD	15 May 1944	28 May 1970	**MSC-A**

Builders: Oregon Shipbuilding Corp, Portland, except T-AK 281 Permanente Metals Corp, Richmond, Calif.
Displacement: 6,700 tons light
11,150 tons full load
Length: 455¼ feet (138.8 m) oa
Beam: 62 feet (18.9 m)
Draft: 24 feet (7.3 m)
Propulsion: steam turbine; 8,500 shp; 1 shaft
Boilers: 2
Speed: 17 knots
Manning: 66–69 (civilian) + Navy security detachment
Helicopters: no facilities
Guns: none

These are former merchant ships taken over by the Navy specifically for conversion into supply ships to support SSBN tenders. All three ships are operated by MSC with civilian crews; Navy security personnel are assigned to safeguard the missiles and their nuclear warheads.

Class: Three earlier FBM supply ships have been stricken (T-AK 259–260 and T-AK 279). See Appendix C.

Conversion: As SSBN tender supply ships all three were refitted to carry black oil (for tenders), diesel fuel, bottled gases, dry and frozen provisions, packaged petroleum products, spare parts, and torpedoes. The No. 3 hold was configured to carry 16 missiles. Also fitted for carrying radioactive waste. (Cargo tanks can hold 355,000 gallons of diesel oil, 430,000 gallons of fuel oil in addition to ships' bunkers.) Conversion was SCB-234.

Design: Maritime Administration VC2-S-AP3 design.

Names: Merchant names were FURMAN VICTORY, ETHIOPIA VICTORY, and MARSHFIELD VICTORY, respectively.

1 FLEET BALLISTIC MISSILE CARGO SHIP

Number	Name	Launched	In service	Status
T-AK	. . . .			Conv.

Builders:
Displacement: 15,200 tons full load
Length: 483¼ feet (147.3 m) oa
Beam: 68 feet (20.7 m)
Draft: 27⅙ feet (8.3 m)
Propulsion: steam turbine; 12,000 shp; 1 shaft
Boilers: 2
Manning: 75 (civilian) + Navy security detachment
Helicopters: no facilities
Guns: none

The conversion of a commercial cargo ship to the FBM tender supply role was authorized in the FY 1981 budget.

MARSHFIELD (1970, U.S. Navy)

2 HEAVY-LIFT CARGO SHIPS: "BROSTROM" CLASS

Number	Name	Launched	In service	Status
T-AK 255	Pvt. Leonard C. Brostrom	10 May 1943	30 Aug 1950	**MSC-P**
T-AK 267	Marine Fiddler	15 May 1945	10 Dec 1952	MR

Builders: Sun Shipbuilding and DD Co, Chester, Pa.
Displacement: 22,056 tons full load
Length: 520 feet (158.5 m) oa
Beam: 71½ feet (21.8 m)
Draft: 33 feet (10.1 m)
Propulsion: steam turbine (GE); 9,000 shp; 1 shaft
Boilers: 2 (Babcock & Wilcox)
Speed: 15.8 knots
Manning: 52 (civilian)
Helicopters: no facilities
Guns: none

Both ships were built for merchant service. The Brostrom operated until laid up 1946–1948, when assigned to Army for ser-

vice. Assigned to National Defense Reserve Fleet in 1950. Reactivated and transferred to the Navy later in 1950; converted to a heavy-lift ship in 1953–1954. She has been MSTS/MSC operated with a civilian crew since 1950.

The Marine Fiddler was laid up after merchant service 1946–1952; reactivated in 1952 for commercial service but acquired by the Navy for MSTS operation that same year and converted to a heavy-lift ship in 1954. She remained in service until laid up in 1973 in the National Defense Reserve Fleet.

Design: Originally Maritime Administration C4-S-B1 design. These ships are fitted with 150-ton-capacity booms, the largest of any U.S. ships, for lifting locomotives, mooring buoys, and other large objects.

Names: The Brostrom was originally named Marine Eagle. She was renamed in 1948 and her Army name was retained when transferred to the Navy. The Marine Fiddler has kept her merchant name.

Pvt. Leonard C. Brostrom (U.S. Navy)

5 CARGO SHIPS: "VICTORY" CLASS

Number	Name	Launched	In service	Status
T-AK 237	Greenville Victory	28 May 1944	1 Mar 1950	MR
T-AK 240	Pvt. John R. Towle	19 Jan 1945	1 Mar 1950	**MSC-A**
T-AK 242	Sgt. Andrew Miller	4 Apr 1945	1 Mar 1950	MR
T-AK 254	Sgt. Truman Kimbro	30 Nov 1944	5 Aug 1950	MR
T-AK 274	Lieut. James E. Robinson	20 Jan 1944	1 Mar 1950	MR

Builders: Oregon Shipbuilding Corp, Portland
Displacement: 6,700 tons light
12,450 tons full load
Length: 455½ feet (138.9 m) oa
Beam: 62 feet (18.9 m)
Draft: 28½ feet (8.9 m)
Propulsion: steam turbine (General Electric); 8,500 shp; 1 shaft
Boilers: 2
Speed: 17 knots except T-AK 254 15 knots
Manning: ~50 (civilian)
Helicopters: no facilities
Guns: none

These ships and the previously listed FBM cargo ships are the last of a large number of "Victory" merchant ships acquired by the Navy after World War II. All but one have been laid up in the National Defense Reserve Fleet.

The Robinson was originally acquired for use as an aircraft transport and designated T-AKV 3; the ship was subsequently redesignated T-AK 274 and employed in general cargo work. In 1963 she was modified for special project work and changed to T-AG 170, but reverted to T-AK 274 on 1 July 1964.

Design: Maritime Administration VC2-S-AP3 except T-AK 254 is VC2-S-AP2 type.

Names: The Greenville Victory retains her original merchant name; the others carry Army names assigned prior to transfer to the Navy in 1950. Their original merchant names were: AK 240 Appleton Victory, AK 242 Radcliffe Victory, AK 254 Hastings Victory, AK 274 Czechoslovakia Victory.

Pvt. John R. Towle (U.S. Navy)

1 CARGO SHIP: "ELTANIN" CLASS

Number	Name	Launched	In service	Status
T-AK 271	Mirfak	5 Aug 1957	30 Dec 1957	MR

Builders:	Avondale Marine Ways, New Orleans, La.
Displacement:	2,036 tons light
	4,942 tons full load
Length:	262$^{1}/_{6}$ feet (79.9 m) oa
Beam:	51½ feet (15.7 m)
Draft:	
Propulsion:	diesel-electric (Alco diesels; Westinghouse electric motors); 3,200 shp; 2 shafts
Speed:	13 knots
Manning:	
Helicopters:	no facilities
Guns:	none

The Mirfak was one of three small cargo ships built specifically for Arctic resupply. She was operated by MSTS (subsequently MSC) with a civilian crew until laid up in the National Defense Reserve Fleet.

Class: Sister ships Eltanin (AK 270) and Mizar (AK 272) were converted to oceanographic research ships, AGOR 8 and AGOR 11, respectively.

Design: Maritime Administration C1-ME2-13a design with strengthened hull and icebreaking bow, enclosed crows nests and control spaces, and other features for Arctic operation.

Mirfak (U.S. Navy)

1 VEHICLE CARGO SHIP: "CALLAGHAN" TYPE

Number	Name	Launched	In service	Status
—	ADM. WM. M. CALLAGHAN	17 Oct 1967	19 Dec 1967	**MSC-A**

Builders:	Sun Shipbuilding and DD Co., Chester, Pa.
Displacement:	24,500 tons full load
Length:	694 feet (211.5 m) oa
Beam:	92 feet (28.0 m)
Draft:	29 feet (8.8 m)
Propulsion:	2 gas turbines (General Electric); 50,000 shp; 2 shafts
Speed:	26 knots
Manning:	33 (civilian)
Helicopters:	no facilities
Guns:	none

The CALLAGHAN is technically a chartered ship rather than a Navy-owned ship of the MSC "nucleus" fleet. However, the ship was designed and constructed specifically for Navy charter and as such is fully committed to MSC. The ship is manned by a civilian crew and has no Navy hull number.

Design: The ship has internal parking decks and ramps for carrying some 750 vehicles on 167,537 square feet of deck. They can be loaded or unloaded via four side ramps and a stern ramp. The ship can offload and reload a full cargo of vehicles in 27 hours.

Engineering: The CALLAGHAN was the first all-gas-turbine ship constructed for the U.S. Navy. The engines are LM2500s, of the type used in subsequent warship classes.

ADMIRAL WM. M. CALLAGHAN (U.S. Navy)

ADMIRAL WM. M. CALLAGHAN (U.S. Navy)

2 VEHICLE CARGO SHIPS: "MAINE" CLASS

Number	Name	Launched	In service	Status
T-AKR 10	Mercury	21 Dec 1976	3 June 1980	**MSC-IO**
T-AKR 11	Jupiter	1 Nov 1975	7 May 1980	**MSC-IO**

Builders:	Bath Iron Works, Me.
Displacement:	13,156 tons gross; 19,172 tons deadweight
Length:	685 feet (208.8 m) oa
Beam:	102 feet (31.1 m)
Draft:	32 feet (9.1 m)
Propulsion:	steam turbines; 37,000 shp; 1 shaft
Boilers:	2
Speed:	23 knots
Manning:	42 (civilian)
Helicopters:	no facilities
Guns:	none

These ships were built for commercial use by the States Steamship Company. They were transferred to MSC in 1980 for use as forward prepositioning ships in the Indian Ocean. They carry Marine vehicles, supplies, and ammunition.

Design: Maritime Administration type C7-S-95a. These ships are designed to carry vehicles, unloading them through side ports and over a slewing stern ramp.

Names: Merchant names were ILLINOIS and TYLSON LYKES, respectively; renamed by MSC on 14 May 1980 (before one ship was formally transferred to MSC).

The MERCURY loading Marine amphibious tractors prior to deployment to the Indian Ocean in mid-1980. Note the slewed stern loading ramp; camouflaged LVTP-7. (1980, U.S. Navy)

JUPITER (1980, U.S. Navy)

MERCURY (1980, U.S. Navy, PH3 George Bruder)

1 VEHICLE CARGO SHIP: "METEOR" TYPE

Number	Name	FY/SCB	Launched	In service	Status
T-AKR 9	METEOR	63/236	18 Apr 1965	19 May 1967	**MSC-IO**

Builders:	Lockheed Shipbuilding & Construction Co, Seattle, Wash.
Displacement:	11,130 tons standard
	16,940 tons standard
	21,700 tons full load
Length:	540 feet (164.6 m) oa
Beam:	83 feet (25.3 m)
Draft:	29 feet (8.8 m)
Propulsion:	steam turbines; 19,400 shp; 2 shafts
Boilers:	2
Speed:	20 knots
Manning:	47 (civilian)
Helicopters:	no facilities
Guns:	none

The METEOR, originally named SEA LIFT, was built specifically as a roll-on/roll-off (ro/ro) ship for Navy service. She is operated by MSC with a civilian crew. In mid-1980 she deployed to the Indian Ocean loaded with Marine Corps equipment, munitions, and supplies as part of an afloat maritime pre-positioning force. (The other ships assigned to the force at the time were merchant ships under Navy charter.)

Classification: Authorized as T-AK 278 but changed to T-LSV 9 while under construction; changed again to vehicle cargo ship T-AKR 9 on 14 August 1969.

Design: The METEOR is one of the few ships to have both an SCB (236) and Maritime Administration design (C4-ST-67a) designation.

Names: Changed from SEA LIFT to METEOR on 12 September 1975 to avoid confusion with "Sealift"-class tankers.

1 VEHICLE CARGO SHIP: "COMET" TYPE

Number	Name	Launched	In service	Status
T-AKR 7	COMET	31 July 1957	27 Jan 1958	**MSC-A**

Builders:	Sun Shipbuilding and DD Co, Chester, Pa.
Displacement:	7,605 tons light
	18,150 tons full load
Length:	499 feet (152.1 m) oa
Beam:	78 feet (23.8 m)
Draft:	28¾ feet (8.8 m)
Propulsion:	steam turbines (General Electric); 13,200 shp; 2 shafts
Boilers:	2 (Babcock & Wilcox)
Speed:	18 knots
Manning:	56 (civilian)
Helicopters:	no facilities
Guns:	none

The COMET was built specifically for the Navy. She is operated by MSC with a civilian crew.

Classification: The COMET originally was classified T-AK 269. She was changed to vehicle cargo ship T-LSV 7 on 1 June 1963, and again to T-AKR 7 on 1 January 1969.

Design: Maritime Administration C3-ST-14a design. She can accommodate several hundred vehicles in her two after holds, with the two forward holds intended for general cargo.

METEOR (Lockheed)

COMET (U.S. Navy)

2 + 3 OILERS: "CIMARRON" CLASS

Number	Name	FY/SCB	Launched	Commissioned	Status
AO 177	CIMARRON	76/739	28 Apr 1979	1980	**PA**
AO 178	MONONGAHELA	76/739	4 Aug 1979	1980	**AA**
AO 179	MERRIMACK	77/739	17 May 1980	1981	Bldg.
AO 180	. . . .	78/739	1981	1982	Bldg.
T-AO 186	. . . .	78/739	1981	1982	Bldg.

Builders:	Avondale Shipyards, New Orleans, La.
Displacement:	27,500 tons full load
Length:	591½ feet (178.8 m) oa
Beam:	88 feet (26.8 m)
Draft:	33½ feet (10.2 m)
Propulsion:	steam turbine; 24,000 shp; 1 shaft
Boilers:	2
Speed:	20 knots (sustained)
Manning:	181 (11 O + 170 enlisted) in early ships; 92 (civilian) + 21 Navy personnel in later ships
Helicopters:	no facilities
Guns:	2 20-mm Phalanx CIWS Mk 15 (2 × 1) in Navy-manned ships

These fleet oilers are designed to provide two complete fuelings for a conventional aircraft carrier and six to eight accompanying escort ships. The U.S. Navy has a requirement for 21 fleet oilers (AO/T-AO); with the five CIMARRON-class ships there will be 11 modern fleet oilers available in the mid-1980s, with that number then declining unless there is additional new construction. At this writing four additional ships are planned in the FY 1983–1984 shipbuilding programs. Earlier plans for additional ships of this class in the FY 1979–1982 programs were dropped because of overall reductions in Navy ship construction.

Although designed for Navy manning, personnel problems have led to later ships being civilian-manned under MSC control.

Classification: Note that AO-series hull numbers 182–185 are assigned to the "Falcon"-class transport tankers (T-AOT), hence the sequence break in this class of ships. The POTOMAC is T-AOT 181.

Design: These ships carry 120,000 barrels of petroleum products. They have an elliptical underwater bow for improved seakeeping. A vertical replenishment (VERTREP) platform is provided, but no helicopter landing or support facilities are in the ships.

Guns: An armament of two Phalanx CIWS can be installed in these ships.

Manning: Original Navy manning was to be approximately 135; it was increased to provide maintenance self-sufficiency for prolonged deployments. MSC civilian manning is planned for the later ships of this class.

The MONONGAHELA under way. Note similarity in general arrangement to the SEALIFT (T–AOT 168)-class transport oilers. The replenishment gear on her deck identifies the MONONGAHELA as an UNREP ship vice point-to-point transport oiler or "tanker." (1981, Avondale Shipyards)

6 OILERS: "NEOSHO" CLASS

Number	Name	FY/SCB	Launched	Commissioned	Status
T-AO 143	NEOSHO	52/82	10 Nov 1953	24 Sep 1954	**MSC-A**
T-AO 144	MISSISSINEWA	52/82	12 June 1954	18 Jan 1955	**MSC-A**
T-AO 145	HASSAYAMPA	52/82	12 Sep 1954	19 Apr 1955	**MSC-P**
T-AO 146	KAWISHIWI	52/82	11 Dec 1954	6 July 1955	**MSC-P**
T-AO 147	TRUCKEE	52/82	10 Mar 1955	23 Nov 1955	**MSC-A**
AO 148	PONCHATOULA	52/82	9 July 1955	12 Jan 1956	**PA**

Builders:	AO 143 Bethlehem Steel Co, Quincy, Mass.
	AO 144–148 New York Shipbuilding Corp, Camden, N.J.
Displacement:	11,600 tons light
	38,000–40,000 tons full load
Length:	655 feet (199.6 m) oa
Beam:	86 feet (26.2 m)
Draft:	35 feet (10.7 m)
Propulsion:	steam turbines (General Electric); 28,000 shp; 2 shafts
Boilers:	2 (Babcock & Wilcox)
Speed:	20 knots
Manning:	~105 (civilian) except 301 (14 O + 287 enlisted) in AO 148
Helicopters:	none assigned (no facilities in T-AO 145–146, AO 148)
Guns:	4 3-inch (76-mm) 50 cal AA Mk 33 (2 × 2) in AO 148; removed from other ships

PONCHATOULA (1979, Giorgio Arra)

KAWISHIWI prior to transfer to MSC (note gun mount forward) (1979, Giorgio Arra)

These ships are the largest "straight" oilers constructed by the U.S. Navy for underway replenishment. The MISSISSINEWA was transferred to MSC for operation with a civilian crew on 2 February 1976; the NEOSHO on 26 May 1978; HASSAYAMPA on 17 November 1978; the TRUCKEE on 30 January 1980; and the KAWISHIWI on 1 October 1979. All continue in the UNREP role.

Design: Cargo capacity is approximately 180,000 barrels of petroleum products. Three ships had a helicopter platform installed aft.

Guns: As built, these ships each had two 5-inch 38 cal DP guns in single mounts plus 12 3-inch 50 cal AA guns in twin mounts. The former were removed in 1969 and the latter subsequently reduced until most had only two mounts when transferred to MSC and disarmed.

The PONCHATOULA was the only ship of the NEOSHO class remaining in active Navy service when this volume went to press. Note her minimal 3-inch gun armament—one twin mount forward on the starboard side and one aft on the port side; she bears a red engineering "E" on her funnel. (1979, Giorgio Arra)

5 OILERS: "MISPILLION" CLASS

Number	Name	Launched	Commissioned	Status
T-AO 105	MISPILLION	10 Aug 1945	29 Dec 1945	**MSC-P**
T-AO 106	NAVASOTA	30 Aug 1945	27 Feb 1946	**MSC-P**
T-AO 107	PASSUMPSIC	31 Oct 1945	1 Apr 1946	**MSC-P**
T-AO 108	PAWCATUCK	19 Feb 1945	10 May 1946	**MSC-A**
T-AO 109	WACCAMAW	30 Mar 1946	25 June 1946	**MSC-A**

Builders:	Sun Shipbuilding and DD Co, Chester, Pa.
Displacement:	11,000 tons light
	34,750 tons full load
Length:	646 feet (196.9 m) oa
Beam:	75 feet (22.9 m)
Draft:	35½ feet (10.8 m)
Propulsion:	steam turbines (Westinghouse); 13,500 shp; 2 shafts
Boilers:	4 (Babcock & Wilcox)
Speed:	16 knots
Manning:	110 (civilian)
Helicopters:	none assigned
Guns:	removed

These ships were built during World War II as Navy oilers. They were converted under the "jumbo" process in the mid-1960s to increase their cargo capacity, thus forming a new five-ship class. (Three Navy-manned "jumboized" oilers are similar; see next listing.) These five ships were assigned to MSC in 1974–1975; they are civilian-manned and serve in the UNREP role.

Design: These ships originally were Maritime Administration T3-S2-A3 type. They were converted ("jumboized") in the mid-1960s with the addition of a 93-foot midsection, thus increasing cargo capacity to approximately 150,000 barrels. A helicopter area is provided *forward*, but it is used primarily for vertical replenishment and not for landings. No hangar is provided.

Guns: As built, these ships had a designed armament of 1 5-inch DP gun, 4 3-inch AA guns, and 8 40-mm AA guns. These were successively reduced until only four 3-inch single mounts were left when they were transferred to MSC.

MISPILLION (1976, Giorgio Arra)

PASSUMPSIC refueling CHICAGO (CG 11) (1978, U.S. Navy, PH1 Arthur E. Legare)

3 OILERS: "ASHTABULA" CLASS

Number	Name	Launched	Commissioned	Status
AO 51	ASHTABULA	22 May 1943	7 Aug 1943	**PA**
AO 98	CALOOSAHATCHEE	2 June 1945	10 Oct 1945	**AA**
AO 99	CANISTEO	6 July 1945	3 Dec 1945	**AA**

Builders:	Bethlehem Steel Co, Sparrows Point, Md.
Displacement:	34,750 tons full load
Length:	644 feet (196.3 m) oa
Beam:	75 feet (22.9 m)
Draft:	31½ feet (9.6 m)
Propulsion:	steam turbines (Bethlehem); 13,500 shp; 2 shafts
Boilers:	4 (Foster Wheeler)
Speed:	18 knots
Manning:	343–350 (20 O + 323–330 enlisted except 284 enlisted in AO 98)
Helicopters:	no facilities
Guns:	2 3-inch (76-mm) 50 cal AA Mk 26 (2 × 1)

These oilers were built for Navy use. They were "jumboized" to increase their cargo capacity. All three are Navy-manned.

Design: Originally Maritime Administration T3-S2-A1 type, they were converted in the mid-1960s under the "jumbo" program (SCB-224). They were lengthened 91 feet to increase their cargo capacity to approximately 143,000 barrels, along with a limited capacity for munitions and stores. A small VERTREP platform is fitted forward.

Guns: See the MISPILLION class for notes on original armament.

ASHTABULA (1978, U.S. Navy, PH3 T. J. Pfrang)

CANISTEO (1979, Giorgio Arra)

ASHTABULA (1979, Giorgio Arra)

2 OILERS: "CIMARRON" CLASS

Number	Name	Launched	Commissioned	Status
T-AO 57	MARIAS	21 Dec 1943	12 Feb 1944	MR
T-AO 62	TALUGA	10 July 1944	25 Aug 1944	MR

Builders:	Bethlehem Steel Co, Sparrows Point, Md.
Displacement:	25,525 tons full load
Length:	553 feet (168.6 m) oa
Beam:	75 feet (22.9 m)
Draft:	31½ feet (9.6 m)
Propulsion:	steam turbines (Bethlehem); 13,500 shp; 2 shafts
Boilers:	4 (Foster Wheeler)
Speed:	18 knots
Manning:	105 (civilian)
Helicopters:	no facilities
Guns:	removed

TALUGA (1978, U.S. Navy)

These are the survivors of a large number of twin-screw fleet oilers constructed during World War II. Ships of this design that have been enlarged under the "jumbo" program are listed separately. The TALUGA was transferred from active naval service to MSC on 4 May 1972 and the MARIAS on 2 October 1973; both ships were laid up on 30 September 1980.

Design: Maritime Administration T3-S2-A1 design. Cargo capacity was originally 145,000 barrels of petroleum products, but was reduced to 115,000 barrels with installation of improved communications equipment and increased accommodations (when Navy manned). A VERTREP platform is provided forward.

Guns: See MISPILLION class for notes on original armament.

TALUGA (1977, Giorgio Arra)

4 FAST COMBAT SUPPORT SHIPS: "SACRAMENTO" CLASS

Number	Name	FY/SCB	Launched	Commissioned	Status
AOE 1	SACRAMENTO	61/196	14 Sep 1963	14 Mar 1964	**PA**
AOE 2	CAMDEN	63/196	29 May 1965	1 Apr 1967	**PA**
AOE 3	SEATTLE	65/196	2 Mar 1968	5 Apr 1969	**AA**
AOE 4	DETROIT	66/196	21 June 1969	28 Mar 1970	**AA**

Builders:	AOE 1, 3–4 Puget Sound Naval Shipyard, Wash.
	AOE 2 New York Shipbuilding Corp, Camden, N.J.
Displacement:	19,200 tons light
	53,600 tons full load
Length:	793 feet (241.7 m) oa
Beam:	107 feet (32.6 m)
Draft:	39⅓ feet (12.0 m)
Propulsion:	steam turbines (General Electric); 100,000 shp; 2 shafts
Boilers:	4 (Combustion Engineering)
Speed:	26 knots
Manning:	563–574 (23–24 O + 536–551 enlisted)
Helicopters:	2 UH-46 Sea Knight
Missiles:	1 8-tube NATO Sea Sparrow launcher Mk 29
Guns:	4 3-inch (76-mm) 50 cal AA Mk 33 (2 × 2)
Fire control:	1 Mk 91 missile FCS

These are the world's largest underway replenishment ships, designed to provide a carrier battle group with fuels, munitions, dry and frozen provisions, and other supplies. A fifth ship of this design was planned for the FY 1968 and then the FY 1980 shipbuilding programs, but the ship was not built. The smaller and less expensive AOR design was developed as an alternative to additional ships of this class. The Soviet BEREZINA-class ships of some 40,000-tons displacement, which first went to sea in 1978, are similar in design and concept.

The Navy has a requirement for 12 "multi-product" UNREP ships of the AOE and AOR types to support 12 carrier battle groups. Eleven such ships are available; there are no near-term plans to construct additional AOE/AOR-type ships.

Design: These ships can carry 177,000 barrels of fuels, 2,150 tons of munitions, 250 tons of dry stores, and 250 tons of refrigerated stores. The ships are provided with highly automated cargo-handling equipment. A large helicopter deck is fitted aft with a three-bay hangar for VERTREP helicopters. Each bay is 47- to 52-feet long and 17- to 19-feet wide.

Engineering: The first two ships have machinery produced for the canceled battleship KENTUCKY (BB 66).

Guns: As built, these ships each had eight 3-inch guns in twin mounts and Mk 56 gun FCS. They were reduced in the mid-1970s and NATO Sea Sparrow was installed. The remaining 3-inch guns are scheduled to be replaced by two Phalanx CIWS when that weapon is available.

SACRAMENTO (1978, Giorgio Arra)

CAMDEN (1979, Giorgio Arra)

2 GASOLINE TANKERS: "ALATNA" CLASS

Number	Name	FY/SCB	Launched	In service	Status
T-AOG 81	ALATNA	55/—	6 Sep 1956	June 1957	**MSC**
T-AOG 82	CHATTAHOOCHEE	55/—	4 Dec 1956	Aug 1957	**MSC**

Builders:	Bethlehem Steel, Staten Island, N.Y.
Displacement:	5,720 tons full load
Length:	302 feet (92.0 m) oa
Beam:	61 feet (18.6 m)
Draft:	19 feet (5.8 m)
Propulsion:	diesel-electric (Alco diesels); 4,000 shp; 2 shafts
Speed:	13 knots
Manning:	40 (civilian)
Helicopters:	none assigned
Guns:	none

CHATTAHOOCHEE in Antarctic (U.S. Navy)

These ships were designed and built specifically for operation by the Military Sealift Command in support of U.S. Arctic military installations. Both ships were operated by MSTS (later MSC) until taken out of service (inactivated on 8 August 1972) and laid up in the National Defense Reserve Fleet. Both ships were reacquired by the Navy on 31 July 1979 while still laid up; they will be extensively modernized and in 1981 replace three older AOGs in MSC service.

Design: The ships have ice-strengthened bows and are otherwise fitted for Arctic operation (similar to the T-AK 270 class). Cargo capacity is 30,000 barrels of petroleum products plus some 2,700 tons of dry cargo. A helicopter platform was fitted aft in original configuration. Maritime Administration T1-MET-24a design.

ALATNA ballasted down aft (U.S. Navy)

3 GASOLINE TANKERS: "TONTI" CLASS

Number	Name	Launched	In service	Status
T-AOG 77	Rincon	5 Jan 1945	1 July 1950	**MSC-P**
T-AOG 78	Nodaway	15 May 1945	7 Sep 1950	**MSC-P**
T-AOG 79	Petaluma	9 Aug 1945	7 Sep 1950	**MSC-P**

Builders:	Todd Shipyards, Houston, Texas
Displacement:	2,060 tons light
	6,000 tons full load
Length:	325$^{1}/_{6}$ feet (99.1 m) oa
Beam:	48$^{1}/_{6}$ feet (14.7 m)
Draft:	19 feet (5.8 m)
Propulsion:	diesel (Nordberg); 1,400 shp; 1 shaft
Speed:	10 knots
Manning:	36 (civilian)
Helicopters:	no facilities
Guns:	none

These are the only survivors in U.S. Navy service of a once numerous type of small gasoline tankers. Five ships of this particular design were built as merchant tankers; all were acquired by the Navy in 1950 and assigned to MSTS, the forerunner of the Military Sealift Command. These ships are operated by MSC in the point-to-point carrying of petroleum products and are not fitted for underway replenishment.

The Navy plans to replace these three ships about 1981–1982 with the previously described Alatna and Chattahoochee.

Class: T-AOG 76–80 were originally in this class. The AOG 64–75 were similar (BT1 design).

Design: Maritime Administration T1-M-BT2 design. Cargo capacity is 30,000 barrels.

Names: Merchant names were Tarland, Belridge, and Raccoon Bend (ex-Tavispan), respectively.

Rincon (U.S. Navy)

Kalamazoo (1978, PH1 Osborne, U.S. Navy)

7 REPLENISHMENT OILERS: "WICHITA" CLASS

Number	Name	FY/SCB	Launched	Commissioned	Status
AOR 1	WICHITA	65/707	18 Mar 1968	7 June 1969	**PA**
AOR 2	MILWAUKEE	65/707	17 Jan 1969	1 Nov 1969	**AA**
AOR 3	KANSAS CITY	66/707	28 June 1969	6 June 1970	**PA**
AOR 4	SAVANNAH	66/707	25 Apr 1970	5 Dec 1970	**AA**
AOR 5	WABASH	67/707	6 Feb 1971	20 Nov 1971	**PA**
AOR 6	KALAMAZOO	67/707	11 Nov 1972	11 Aug 1973	**AA**
AOR 7	ROANOKE	72/707	7 Dec 1974	15 Dec 1975	**PA**

Builders:	AOR 1–6 General Dynamics Corp, Quincy, Mass.
	AOR 7 National Steel and SB Co, San Diego
Displacement:	38,100 tons full load
Length:	659 feet (206.9 m) oa
Beam:	96 feet (29.3 m)
Draft:	33⅓ feet (10.2 m)
Propulsion:	steam turbines; 32,000 shp; 2 shafts
Boilers:	3 (Foster Wheeler)
Speed:	20 knots
Manning:	418–431 (19 O + 399–412 enlisted)
Helicopters:	2 UH-46 Sea Knights in AOR 2–3, 5, 7
Missiles:	1 8-tube NATO Sea Sparrow launcher Mk 29 in AOR 3, 7
Guns:	4 3-inch (76-mm) 50 cal AA Mk 33 (2 × 2) in AOR 1, 4, 6
	2 20-mm Mk 67 (2 × 1) in AOR 7
	4 20-mm Mk 68 (4 × 1) in AOR 2

These ships carry petroleum and munitions, and have a limited capacity for dry and frozen provisions. As built, AOR 1–6 had large helicopter decks but no hangar; all are being modified to provide two hangars abaft the funnel.

Classification: The German war prize CONECUH, formerly a U-boat tender, was employed as a replenishment fleet tanker (AOR 110) in the 1950s. The WACCAMAW was to be similarly modified (AOR 109), but she remained a "straight" fleet oiler. The classification AOR was established as replenishment oiler in 1964.

Design: These ships can carry 160,000 barrels of liquid cargo, 600 tons of munitions, 200 tons of dry stores, and 100 tons of refrigerated stores. They have highly automated cargo-handling equipment.

Engineering: Ships of this class can steam at 18 knots on two boilers while one is being maintained.

Guns: AOR 1–6 were built with two 3-inch twin gun mounts aft and the Mk 56 gun FCS. The 3-inch guns have been removed with the installation of helicopter hangars. A minimal 20-mm gun armament has been installed in some ships without 3-inch guns. All AORs are scheduled to receive two Phalanx CIWS.

Helicopters: AOR 7 was built with twin helicopter hangars. All other ships of the class are being similarly refitted; the hangars are 61½- to 63-feet long and 19- to 21-feet wide.

Missiles: NATO Sea Sparrow is being installed in all ships of this class.

Stern of KANSAS CITY showing both hangar doors open. She has a NATO Sea Sparrow launcher above the hangar and two Mk 91 FCS on lattice masts (the port-side mast is hidden by the funnel). All seven ships will be modified to support helicopters. (1979, Giorgio Arra)

WABASH with UH-46 Sea Knight from HC-11 (1979, Giorgio Arra)

4 TRANSPORT OILERS: "FALCON" CLASS

Number	Name	Launched	In service	Status
T-AOT 182	COLUMBIA	12 Sep 1970	15 Jan 1976	**MSC**
T-AOT 183	NECHES	30 Jan 1971	11 Feb 1976	**MSC**
T-AOT 184	HUDSON	8 Jan 1972	23 Apr 1976	**MSC**
T-AOT 185	SUSQUEHANNA	2 Oct 1971	11 May 1976	**MSC**

Builders:	Ingalls Shipbuilding Corp, Pascagoula, Miss.
Displacement:	8,601 tons light
	45,877 tons full load
Length:	672 feet (204.8 m) oa
Beam:	89 feet (27.1 m)
Draft:	36 feet (11.0 m)
Propulsion:	diesel (Pielstick); 15,000 shp; 1 shaft
Speed:	16.5 knots
Manning:	23 (civilian)
Helicopters:	no facilities
Guns:	none

These ships were delivered as merchant tankers in 1971 (two ships) and 1972 (two ships); they were chartered by MSC until acquired by the Navy in 1976. They are operated by a commercial firm under contract to MSC.

Classification: These ships were designated AO after acquisition by the Navy; changed to AOT on 30 September 1978. On that date 18 tankers operated by MSC were changed to AOT as were seven ships laid up in the National Defense Reserve Fleet (AO 50, 67, 73, 75–76, 78, 134).

Design: Cargo capacity is 310,000 barrels.

Names: The merchant names for these ships were, respectively, FALCON LADY, FALCON DUTCHESS, FALCON PRINCESS, and FALCON COUNTESS. They were renamed for rivers when acquired by the Navy in 1976. In naval service they are referred to as the "Falcon" class.

TALUGA (top) and COLUMBIA (U.S. Navy)

SUSQUEHANNA (1979, Georgio Arra)

1 TRANSPORT OILER: "POTOMAC" TYPE

Number	Name	Launched	In service	Status
T-AOT 181	POTOMAC	8 Oct 1956	12 Jan 1976	**MSC**

Builders:	Sun Shipbuilding and DD Co, Chester, Pa.
Displacement:	7,333 tons light
	34,800 tons full load
Length:	620 feet (189.0 m) oa
Beam:	83½ feet (25.5 m)
Draft:	34 feet (10.4 m)
Propulsion:	steam turbine; 20,460 shp; 1 shaft
Boilers:	2
Speed:	18 knots
Manning:	
Helicopter:	no facilities
Guns:	none

The POTOMAC was constructed from the stern of an earlier naval tanker, with mid-body and bow sections built to mate with that stern section. The "new" tanker, named the SHENANDOAH, was operated under commercial charter to MSC for several years until she was formally acquired in 1976. The ship's current MSC name is the same as the original naval tanker (T-AO 150) from which the stern section was salvaged. (The earlier POTOMAC was partially destroyed by fire on 26 September 1961, but the stern section and machinery were relatively intact. The POTOMAC's original design was T5-S-12a.)

The POTOMAC is contractor-operated for MSC with a civilian crew.

Design: Cargo capacity is 200,000 barrels.

9 TRANSPORT OILERS: "SEALIFT" CLASS

Number	Name	Launched	In service	Status
T-AOT 168	SEALIFT PACIFIC	13 Oct 1973	14 Aug 1974	**MSC**
T-AOT 169	SEALIFT ARABIAN SEA	26 Jan 1974	6 Feb 1975	**MSC**
T-AOT 170	SEALIFT CHINA SEA	20 Apr 1974	19 May 1975	**MSC**
T-AOT 171	SEALIFT INDIAN OCEAN	27 July 1974	29 Aug 1975	**MSC**
T-AOT 172	SEALIFT ATLANTIC	26 Jan 1974	26 Aug 1974	**MSC**
T-AOT 173	SEALIFT MEDITERRANEAN	9 Mar 1974	6 Nov 1974	**MSC**
T-AOT 174	SEALIFT CARIBBEAN	8 June 1974	10 Feb 1975	**MSC**
T-AOT 175	SEALIFT ARCTIC	31 Aug 1974	22 May 1975	**MSC**
T-AOT 176	SEALIFT ANTARCTIC	26 Oct 1974	1 Aug 1975	**MSC**

Builders:	T-AOT 168–171 Todd Shipyards, San Pedro, Calif.
	T-AOT 172–176 Bath Iron Works, Me.
Displacement:	32,000 tons full load
Length:	587 feet (178.9 m) oa
Beam:	84 feet (25.6 m)
Draft:	34⅓ feet (10.5 m)
Propulsion:	turbo-charged diesels (Pielstick); 14,000 shp; 1 shaft
Speed:	16 knots
Manning:	30 (civilian) + 2 Maritime Academy cadets
Helicopters:	no facilities
Guns:	none

These ships were built specifically for MSC to replace World War II-era tankers of the T2 series. The ships are contractor-operated for MSC with civilian crews.

Design: These ships have a cargo capacity of 220,000 barrels.

Engineering: A bow thruster is provided to assist in docking the ships.

SEALIFT ANTARCTIC (1975, U.S. Navy)

SEALIFT PACIFIC (U.S. Navy)

1 TRANSPORT OILER: "AMERICAN EXPLORER" TYPE

Number	Name	Launched	In service	Status
T-AOT 165	AMERICAN EXPLORER	11 Apr 1958	27 Oct 1959	**MSC**

Builders:	Ingalls Shipbuilding Corp, Pascagoula, Miss.
Displacement:	31,300 tons full load
Length:	615 feet (187.5 m) oa
Beam:	80 feet (24.4 m)
Draft:	32 feet (9.8 m)
Propulsion:	steam turbine (De Laval); 22,000 shp; 1 shaft
Boilers:	2 (Babcock & Wilcox)
Speed:	20 knots
Manning:	
Helicopters:	no facilities
Guns:	none

The AMERICAN EXPLORER was built for merchant use, but upon completion she was acquired by the Navy. She is similar to the MAUMEE-class ships. The AMERICAN EXPLORER is contractor-operated for MSC with a civilian crew.

Design: Maritime Administration T5-S-RM2a design. Cargo capacity is 190,300 barrels of petroleum.

AMERICAN EXPLORER (U.S. Navy)

3 TRANSPORT OILERS: "MAUMEE" CLASS

Number	Name	Launched	In service	Status
T-AOT 149	MAUMEE	16 Feb 1956	12 Dec 1956	**MSC**
T-AOT 151	SHOSHONE	17 Jan 1957	15 Apr 1957	**MSC**
T-AOT 152	YUKON	16 Mar 1956	17 May 1957	**MSC**

Builders:	T-AOT 149, 152 Ingalls Shipbuilding Corp, Pascagoula, Miss.
	T-AOT 151 Sun Shipbuilding & DD Co, Chester, Pa.
Displacement:	32,953 tons full load
Length:	620 feet (189.0 m) oa
Beam:	83½ feet (25.5 m)
Draft:	32 feet (9.6 m)
Propulsion:	steam turbine (Westinghouse); 20,460 shp; 1 shaft
Boilers:	2 (Combustion Engineering)
Speed:	18 knots
Manning:	
Helicopters:	no facilities
Guns:	none

These ships were built for naval service. All are contractor-operated for MSC with civilian crews.

Class: The POTOMAC (T-AO 150) of this class was partially destroyed by fire in 1961; she was rebuilt in 1963–1964 and is listed separately as the T-AO 181. Hull numbers AO 166–167 were reserved for planned "Mission"-class (T2-SE-A2) tanker "jumbo" conversions (to have been SCB-713); the T-AO 153–164 were T2-SE-A1 tankers acquired during the 1956 Suez crisis and stricken 1957–1958.

Design: Maritime Administration T5-S-12a type. Cargo capacity is 203,200 barrels. The MAUMEE was modified in 1969–1970, being fitted with a strengthened prow and other features enabling her to transport petroleum to U.S. Arctic research sites.

SHOSHONE (1979, Giorgio Arra)

1 TRANSPORT OILER: "MISSION" CLASS

Number	Name	Launched	Commissioned	Status
T-AOT 134	MISSION SANTA YNEZ	19 Dec 1943	(see notes)	MR

Builders:	Marine Ship Corp, Sausalito, Calif.
Displacement:	5,730 tons light
	22,380 tons full load
Length:	523½ feet (159.6 m) oa
Beam:	68 feet (20.7 m)
Draft:	30⅚ feet (9.4 m)
Propulsion:	turbo-electric; 10,000 shp; 1 shaft
Boilers:	2
Speed:	16 knots
Manning:	
Helicopters:	no facilities
Guns:	none

The MISSION SANTA YNEZ is the lone survivor retained in reserve of a series of merchant tankers delivered late in World War II and acquired by the Navy after the war. This ship was delivered as a merchant tanker on 13 March 1944 and acquired by the Navy for use as a tanker on 22 October 1947. Except for propulsion, the "Mission" class tankers were similar to the SUAMICO-class ships. (See page 224.)

Design: Maritimes Administration T2-SE-A2 design. Cargo capacity approximately 134,000 barrels of petroleum products.

Guns: Unarmed when acquired by the Navy; no guns installed.

Names: Merchant name retained in naval service.

MISSION SANTA YNEZ (U.S. Navy)

6 TRANSPORT OILERS: "SUAMICO" CLASS

Number	Name	Launched	Commissioned	Status
T-AOT 50	TALLULAH	25 June 1942	5 Sep 1942	MR
T-AOT 67	CACHE	7 Sep 1942	3 Nov 1942	MR
T-AOT 73	MILLICOMA	21 Jan 1943	5 Mar 1943	MR
T-AOT 75	SAUGATUCK	7 Dec 1942	19 Feb 1943	MR
T-AOT 76	SCHUYLKILL	16 Feb 1943	9 Apr 1943	MR
T-AOT 78	CHEPACHET	10 Mar 1943	27 Apr 1943	Loan

Builders:	Sun Shipbuilding and DD Co, Chester, Pa.
Displacement:	5,730 tons light
	22,380 tons full load
Length:	523½ feet (159.6 m) oa
Beam:	68 feet (20.7 m)
Draft:	30⅚ feet (9.4 m)
Propulsion:	turbo-electric (GE turbine, except Westinghouse in T-AOT 67 and 75); 6,000 shp; 1 shaft
Boilers:	2 (Babcock & Wilcox)
Speed:	15 knots
Manning:	
Helicopters:	no facilities
Guns:	removed

All of these ships were begun as merchant tankers but acquired by the Navy in 1942–1943 and completed as fleet oilers (AO). After World War II they were employed in the tanker role by MSTS (later MSC). All have been decommissioned, with some stricken from the Naval Register, and laid up in the National Defense Reserve Fleet, except the CHEPACHET, which is on loan from NDRF to the Department of Energy.

Classification: Changed from AO to AOT on 30 September 1978 (while laid up in reserve).

Design: Maritime Administration T2-SE-A1 design. Cargo capacity is approximately 134,000 barrels.

Guns: As built, this class was armed with one 5-inch 38 cal DP gun, four 3-inch 50 cal AA guns, and eight 40-mm AA guns. All disarmed after World War II when employed in tanker role.

Names: Original merchant names were: T-AOT 50 TALLULAH; T-AOT 67 STILLWATER; T-AOT 73 CONESTOGA, KING'S MOUNTAIN; T-AOT 75 NEWTON; T-AOT 76 LOUISBURG.

SCHUYLKILL (U.S. Navy)

3 TRANSPORTS: "BARRETT" CLASS

Number	Name	Launched	In service	Status
T-AP 196	BARRETT	27 June 1950	15 Dec 1951	Loan
T-AP 197	GEIGER	9 Oct 1950	13 Sep 1952	Loan
T-AP 198	UPSHUR	19 Jan 1951	20 Dec 1952	Loan

Builders:	New York Shipbuilding Corp, Camden, N.J.
Displacement:	17,600 tons standard
	19,600 tons full load
Length:	533 feet (162.7 m) oa
Beam:	73 feet (22.25 m)
Draft:	27 feet (8.2 m)
Propulsion:	steam turbines; 13,750 shp; 1 shaft
Boilers:	2
Speed:	19 knots
Manning:	
Troops:	1,500 + 400 cabin passengers
Helicopters:	no facilities
Guns:	none

These ships were begun as passenger liners for the American President Lines; taken over by the Navy during construction and completed as troop transports. Placed in service 1951–1952 with MSTS and operated by civilian crews.

All three ships are assigned to the National Defense Reserve Fleet but operated by state maritime academies, the GEIGER by the Massachusetts Maritime Academy (as the Training Ship BAY STATE), the BARRETT by the University of New York Maritime College (as the TS EMPIRE STATE), and the UPSHUR by the Maine Maritime Academy (TS STATE OF MAINE).

Design: Maritime Administration P2-S1-DN1 design. All troop, cabin, mess, and recreation spaces are fully air-conditioned. Some 1,000 additional troops can be carried by converting recreation areas into high-density berthing spaces. Cabin spaces are for officers and dependents.

Names: Merchant names were to have been AP 196 PRESIDENT JACKSON, AP 197 PRESIDENT ADAMS, and AP 198 PRESIDENT HAYES.

Propulsion: The BARRETT attained 21.5 knots on trials.

UPSHUR (U.S. Navy)

GEIGER (U.S. Navy)

7 TRANSPORTS: "ADMIRAL" CLASS

Number	Name	Launched	Commissioned	Status
T-AP 120	GEN. DANIEL I. SULTAN	28 Nov 1943	23 Aug 1944	MR
T-AP 122	GEN. ALEXANDER M. PATCH	22 Apr 1944	21 Nov 1944	MR
T-AP 123	GEN. SIMON B. BUCKNER	14 June 1944	24 Jan 1945	MR
T-AP 124	GEN. EDWIN D. PATRICK	27 July 1944	31 Jan 1945	MR
T-AP 125	GEN. NELSON M. WALKER	26 Nov 1944	24 Apr 1945	MR
T-AP 126	GEN. MAURICE ROSE	25 Feb 1945	10 July 1945	MR
T-AP 127	GEN. WILLIAM O. DARBY	4 June 1945	27 Sep 1945	MR

Builders:	Bethlehem Steel Co, Alameda, Calif.
Displacement:	9,676 tons standard
	20,120 tons full load
Length:	608^{11}/$_{12}$ feet (185.6 m) oa
Beam:	75½ feet (23.0 m)
Draft:	29 feet (8.8 m)
Propulsion:	turbo-electric (General Electric turbines); 18,000 shp; 2 shafts
Boilers:	4 (Combustion Engineering)
Speed:	19 knots
Manning:	500–650 (full wartime)
Troops:	4,650–5,000
Helicopters:	no facilities
Guns:	removed

These ships were acquired by the Navy while under construction and placed in commission as troop transports. They were transferred to the Army in 1946 for use as transports and renamed for deceased generals. They were reacquired by the Navy in 1950 but retained their Army names. All are laid up in the National Defense Reserve Fleet, reserved for operation by MSC in time of national emergency or war.

Design: Maritime Administration P2-SE2-R1 design. This class is similar in general design to the slightly larger "General" class. These ships, however, have kingposts forward and aft while the "General" class has single pole masts forward and aft.

Guns: As built, an armament of four 5-inch 38 cal DP guns and eight 40-mm AA guns was fitted, plus 20-mm guns in some ships.

Names: Original "Admiral" class names were: AP 120 ADM. W. S. BENSON, AP 122 ADM. R. E. COONTZ, AP 123 ADM. E. W. EBERLE, AP 124 ADM. C. F. HUGHES, AP 125 ADM. H. T. MAYO, AP 126 ADM. HUGH RODMAN, and AP 127 ADM. W. S. SIMS. Some of these names are now carried by warships.

(GEN. MAURICE ROSE (U.S. Navy))

GEN. MAURICE ROSE (U.S. Navy)

7 TRANSPORTS: "GENERAL" CLASS

Number	Name	Launched	Commissioned	Status
T-AP 110	GEN. JOHN POPE	21 Mar 1943	5 Aug 1943	MR
T-AP 111	GEN. A. E. ANDERSON	2 May 1943	5 Oct 1943	MR
T-AP 112	GEN. W. A. MANN	18 July 1943	13 Oct 1943	MR
T-AP 114	GEN. WILLIAM MITCHELL	31 Oct 1943	19 Jan 1944	MR
T-AP 117	GEN. W. H. GORDON	7 May 1944	29 June 1944	MR
T-AP 119	GEN. WILLIAM WEIGEL	3 Sep 1944	6 Jan 1945	MR
T-AP 176	GEN. J. C. BRECKINRIDGE	18 Mar 1945	30 June 1945	MR

Builders:	Federal Shipbuilding & DD Co, Kearny, N.J.
Displacement:	11,828 tons standard
	20,175 tons full load
Length:	622$^{7}/_{12}$ feet (189.8 m) oa
Beam:	75½ feet (23.0 m)
Draft:	25½ feet (7.8 m)
Propulsion:	steam turbines (De Laval); 17,000 shp; 2 shafts
Boilers:	4 (Foster Wheeler)
Speed:	20.6 knots
Manning:	450–530 (full wartime)
Troops:	~5,300
Helicopters:	no facilities
Guns:	removed

These large troop transports are laid up in the National Defense Reserve Fleet, reserved for MSC operation in time of national emergency or war. All were acquired by the Navy while under construction, with some placed in partial commission for transfer to another shipyard for outfitting as a troop transport. (Full commission dates after conversion are given above.)

All saw Navy service in World War II. The GORDON was turned over to the Army for use as a transport from 1946 to 1951 and the WEIGEL from 1946 to 1950; both reacquired by the Navy and used with the other ships during the Korean War. Some were laid up in reserve (actually transferred to Maritime Administration) for brief periods after World War II and again in the 1950s. The POPE was laid up for the last time in 1970, the ANDERSON in 1958, the MANN and MITCHELL in 1966, the GORDON in 1961, the WEIGEL in 1967, and the BRECKINRIDGE in 1966.

Design: These ships are Maritime Administration P2-S2-R2 design.

Guns: As built, an armament of four 5-inch 38 cal DP guns and eight 40-mm AA guns was fitted, plus 20-mm guns in some ships.

Names: AP 119 was originally named GEN. C. H. BARTH; changed during construction.

(GEN. W. H. GORDON (U.S. Navy)

GEN. JOHN POPE (U.S. Navy)

4 REPAIR SHIPS: "VULCAN" CLASS

Number	Name	Launched	Commissioned	Status
AR 5	VULCAN	14 Dec 1940	16 June 1941	**AA**
AR 6	AJAX	22 Aug 1942	30 Oct 1943	**PA**
AR 7	HECTOR	11 Nov 1942	7 Feb 1944	**PA**
AR 8	JASON	3 Apr 1943	19 June 1944	**PA**

Builders:	AR 5 New York Shipbuilding Corp, Camden, N.J.
	AR 6–8 Los Angeles Shipbuilding and DD Corp
Displacement:	9,140 tons standard
	16,200 tons full load
Length:	529½ feet (161.4 m) oa except AR 8 530 feet
Beam:	73⅓ feet (22.3 m)
Draft:	23⅓ feet (7.1 m)
Propulsion:	steam turbines (Allis Chalmers, except New York Shipbuilding in AR 5); 11,000 shp; 2 shafts
Boilers:	4 (Babcock & Wilcox)
Speed:	19.2 knots
Manning:	734–870 (29 O + 705–841 enlisted)
Helicopters:	no facilities
Guns:	4 20-mm Mk 67 (4 × 1)

These are large, highly capable repair ships, although they lack the ability to support more sophisticated weapons and electronic systems. Plans to construct a new class of repair ships in the 1980s to replace the VULCANS have been dropped.

Classification: The JASON was completed as a heavy hull repair ship (ARH 1); she was reclassified as AR 8 on 9 September 1957.

Guns: As built, these ships each had four 5-inch DP guns and eight 40-mm AA guns. The 5-inch guns were retained into the 1970s when they were beached in favor of minimal 20-mm weapons.

JASON (1979, Giorgio Arra)

JASON (1979, Giorgio Arra)

(1) CABLE REPAIRING SHIP

Number	Name	FY/SCB	Launch	In service	Status
T-ARC 7	. . . .	79/—	1981	1983	Bldg.

Builders:	National Steel & SB Co, San Diego, Calif.
Displacement:	8,370 tons light
	14,157 tons full load
Length:	502½ feet (153.2 m) oa
Beam:	73 feet (22.25 m)
Draft:	24 feet (7.3 m)
Propulsion:	diesel-electric; 10,200 shp; 2 shafts
Speed:	15 knots
Manning:	88 (civilian) + 38 technicians (including six Navy communications personnel)
Helicopters:	no facilities
Guns:	none

This ship is being constructed to maintain the Navy's capability for laying and repairing underwater cables and related hardware, including sea-floor acoustic detection systems. In addition, the ships undertake acoustic, hydrographic, oceanographic, and ocean engineering surveys. (Commercial ships are also chartered for this type of work, although few are available that meet Navy requirements.)

Two ships of this class were planned, one to replace the now-stricken THOR (ARC 4) and the AEOLUS (ARC 3). Only one has been authorized, and no additional ships are planned at this time.

The ship will be civilian-manned by MSC.

Design: Two bow and two stern thrusters will be installed to facilitate station keeping while handling cable.

NEPTUNE (1975, Giorgio Arra)

2 CABLE REPAIRING SHIPS: "NEPTUNE" CLASS

Number	Name	Launched	Commissioned	Status
T-ARC 2	NEPTUNE		1 June 1953	**MSC-A**
T-ARC 6	ALBERT J. MEYER		(13 May 1963)	**MSC-P**

Builders:	T-ARC 2 Pusey and Jones Corp, Wilmington, Del.
Displacement:	7,400 tons full load
Length:	370 feet (112.8 m) oa
Beam:	47 feet (14.3 m)
Draft:	18 feet (5.5 m)
Propulsion:	reciprocating engines (Skinner); 4,800 ihp; 2 shafts
Boilers:	2 (Combustion Engineering)
Speed:	14 knots
Manning:	71 (civilian) + 25 technicians + 6 Navy communications detachment
Helicopters:	no facilities (see notes)
Guns:	none

These are large cable repair and laying ships employed in the support of sea-floor surveillance (SOSUS) and communications systems. The NEPTUNE was completed in February 1946 as a commercial cable ship. She was acquired by the Navy from the Maritime Administration in 1953 and Navy-manned until transferred to MSC in 1973.

The ALBERT J. MEYER was used by the Army Signal Corps until transferred to the Navy in 1963 on loan (changed to permanent transfer in 1966); the ship was placed in service (instead of in commission) with MSTS/MSC in 1963. Both ships are civilian-manned.

Design: These ships are Maritime Administration S3-S2-BP1 design. They have electric cable-handling machinery (in place of the original steam equipment) and SSN-2 precise sea-floor navigation equipment. The NEPTUNE has a helicopter platform aft, but it is useful only for VERTREP.

Engineering: These are the last ships in U.S. naval service with reciprocating engines; they use the measurement for *indicated* horsepower vice shaft horsepower.

Modernization: These ships are scheduled for major modernizations to permit their use into the 1990s.

Names: The NEPTUNE was named WILLIAM H. G. BULLARD in merchant service.

ALBERT J. MEYER (1977, Giorgio Arra)

1 CABLE REPAIRING SHIP: "AEOLUS" CLASS

Number	Name	Launched	AKA Comm.	ARC Comm.	Status
T-ARC 3	AEOLUS	29 May 1945	18 June 1945	14 May 1955	**MSC-P**

Builders:	Walsh-Kaiser Co, Providence, R.I.
Displacement:	7,040 tons full load
Length:	438 feet (133.5 m) oa
Beam:	58 feet (17.7 m)
Draft:	19¼ feet (5.9 m)
Propulsion:	turbo-electric (Westinghouse turbines); 6,000 shp; 2 shafts
Boilers:	2 (Wickes)
Speed:	16.9 knots
Manning:	
Helicopters:	no facilities (see notes)
Guns:	removed

The AEOLUS was completed as an attack cargo ship (AKA); laid up in reserve from 1946 until converted to a cable ship in 1955. She was provided with bow sheaves, cable stowage tanks, cable repair facilities, and a helicopter platform. SSN-2 precise bottom navigation system is fitted.

The ship was Navy-manned from 1955 until 1973 when transferred to MSC for operation with a civilian crew.

Class: A sister ship, the THOR (T-ARC 4, formerly AKA 49), was stricken in 1975.

Design: Originally Maritime Administration design S4-SE2-BE1. The AEOLUS has a helicopter platform aft, but it can no longer be used for that purpose and instead provides a working area and VERTREP platform.

Guns: All armament was removed during ARC conversion.

Names: Named TURANDOT as AKA 47.

AEOLUS (1970, U.S. Navy)

1 LANDING CRAFT REPAIR SHIP: CONVERTED LST

Number	Name	Launched	Commissioned	Status
ARL 24 (ex-LST 963)	SPHINX	18 Nov 1944	12 Dec 1944	PR

Builders:	Bethlehem Steel Co, Hingham, Mass.
Displacement:	1,625 tons light
	4,100 tons full load
Length:	328 feet (100.0 m) oa
Beam:	50 feet (15.2 m)
Draft:	11 feet (3.4 m)
Propulsion:	diesels (General Motors); 1,800 shp; 2 shafts
Manning:	~250 (20 O + 130 enlisted)
Helicopters:	no facilities
Guns:	8 40-mm AA Mk 2 (2 × 4)

The SPHINX is the last of several score LSTs converted to various types of repair and support ships remaining on the Naval Register.

She has been in reserve from 1947–1950 (reactivated for the Korean War), 1956–1967 (reactivated for the Vietnam War), and from 1971 onward.

Class: Thirty-nine ships were converted to the ARL configuration (ARL 1–24, 26–33, 35–41, with ARL 25 and ARL 34 canceled). Several survive in foreign navies.

Guns: The original ARL armament consisted of one 3-inch 50 cal AA gun and eight 20-mm AA guns in addition to the two 40-mm quad mounts.

Conversion: The ARL conversion provided repair and support capabilities for landing craft and small boats. The ships were fitted with machine shops, a carpenter's shop, brass foundry, welding facilities, increased distilling capacity, and additional electric power generators. Two 10-ton-capacity booms are fitted forward, and a 50-ton-capacity sheerleg is mounted on the portside of the deckhouse. A tripod mast has been fitted in the SPHINX in place of her original pole mast.

The SPHINX under way off San Diego. She is the only one of several score of LSTs converted to various repair and support roles that remains on the Naval Register. Note the covered quad "forties" at her bow and stern; built up shop and storage spaces amidships; and tripod mast aft. Many sister ships of various configurations serve in foreign navies. (1968, U.S. Navy)

(1) SALVAGE SHIP: NEW CONSTRUCTION

Number	Name	FY/SCB	Status
ARS 50	. . . .	81	Auth.

Builders:
Displacement:	2,900 tons full load
Length:	255 feet (77.7 m) oa
Beam:	50 feet (15.2 m)
Draft:	15 feet (4.6 m)
Propulsion:	geared diesels; 4,200 shp; 2 shafts
Speed:	14 knots
Manning:	87 (6 O + 81 enlisted)
Helicopters:	no facilities
Guns:	not determined

The Navy plans to construct four or five salvage ships of this design to replace the existing ARS-type ships, with the first new ship authorized in FY 1981. These ships, plus the three large, ATS-type ships, will permit the continuous forward deployment of one ship in the Mediterranean and one ship in the Western Pacific, plus limited operations in other areas.

(The Navy has a national responsibility for salvaging of all U.S. ships, both government-owned and private, under Public Law 80-513.)

8 SALVAGE SHIPS: "ESCAPE" AND "BOLSTER" CLASSES

Number	Name	Launched	Commissioned	Status
ARS 6	ESCAPE	22 Nov 1942	20 Nov 1943	AR
ARS 8	PRESERVER	1 Apr 1943	11 Jan 1944	**NRF-A**
ARS 38	BOLSTER	23 Dec 1944	1 May 1945	**PA**
ARS 39	CONSERVER	27 Jan 1945	9 June 1945	**PA**
ARS 40	HOIST	31 Mar 1945	21 July 1945	**AA**
ARS 41	OPPORTUNE	31 Mar 1945	5 Oct 1945	**AA**
ARS 42	RECLAIMER	25 June 1945	20 Dec 1945	**PA**
ARS 43	RECOVERY	4 Aug 1945	15 May 1946	**AA**

Builders:	Basalt Rock Co, Napa, Calif.
Displacement:	1,530 tons standard
	1,900 tons full load
Length:	213½ feet (65.1 m) oa
Beam:	39 feet (11.9 m) except ARS 38–43, 43 feet
Draft:	13 feet (4.0 m)
Propulsion:	diesel-electric (Cooper Bessemer diesels); 3,000 shp; 2 shafts
Speed:	14.8 knots except ARS 38, 43 knots
Manning:	90 (6 O + 84 enlisted)
Helicopters:	no facilities
Guns:	2 20-mm Mk 67 (2 × 1) in ARS 39, 41
	2 20-mm Mk 68 (2 × 1) in ARS 6, 8, 38, 40, 42–43

These ships are fitted for salvage and towing. They have compressed-air diving equipment; the early ships have 8-ton- and 10-ton-capacity booms while the later ships have 10-ton and 20-ton booms.

The Escape was decommissioned on 1 September 1978; the Preserver was transferred to the Naval Reserve Force on 1 November 1979 and is manned by a composite active-reserve crew.

Class: These classes originally included 22 ships (ARS 5–9, 19–28, 38–43 plus the canceled ARS 44–49). Two ships were converted to oceanographic research ships (AGOR 17 ex-ARS 20 and AGOR 18 ex-ARS 27); two others serve with the Coast Guard (WMEC 167, ex-ARS 9, and WMEC 168, ex-ARS 26).

Guns: The original armament of these classes was two or four 20-mm guns in twin mounts. After World War II most of the ships carried a single 40-mm gun atop the superstructure.

Bolster (1980, Giorgio Arra)

Reclaimer (1976, Giorgio Arra)

2 + 1 SUBMARINE TENDERS: "EMORY S. LAND" CLASS

Number	Name	FY/SCB	Launched	Commissioned	Status
AS 39	Emory S. Land	72/737	4 May 1977	7 July 1979	**AA**
AS 40	Frank Cable	73/737	14 Jan 1978	5 Feb 1980	**AA**
AS 41	McKee	77/737	16 Feb 1980	1981	Bldg.

Builders:	Lockheed Shipbuilding and Constn Co, Seattle, Wash.
Displacement:	13,842 tons light
	23,000 tons full load
Length:	645²/₃ feet (196.8 m) oa
Beam:	85 feet (25.9 m)
Draft:	25 feet (7.6 m)
Propulsion:	steam turbines (De Laval); 20,000 shp; 1 shaft
Boilers:	2 (Combustion Engineering)
Speed:	18 knots (sustained)
Manning:	1,099 (43 O + 1,056 enlisted)
Flag:	69 (25 O + 44 enlisted)
Helicopters:	none assigned
Guns:	2 40-mm Mk 19 (2 × 1)
	4 20-mm Mk 67 (4 × 1)

These are improved versions of the L. Y. Spear-class submarine tenders, with the AS 39–41 fitted specifically for supporting the Los Angeles (SSN 688)-class attack submarines. Up to four submarines can be supported alongside simultaneously. The McKee is scheduled to be assigned to the Pacific Fleet.

Design: Submarine tenders have maintenance shops for various submarine systems and equipment, weapon and provision stowage, and other facilities to support attack submarines. A helicopter landing platform is fitted, but no hangar is provided.

Emory S. Land (1979, Jim Davis Photography)

FRANK CABLE (U.S. Navy)

2 SUBMARINE TENDERS: "L. Y. SPEAR" CLASS

Number	Name	FY/SCB	Launched	Commissioned	Status
AS 36	L. Y. SPEAR	65/702	7 Sep 1967	28 Feb 1970	**AA**
AS 37	DIXON	66/702	20 June 1970	7 Aug 1971	**PA**

Builders:	General Dynamics Corp, Quincy, Mass.
Displacement:	12,770 tons light
	22,628 tons full load
Length:	645²/₃ feet (196.8 m) oa
Beam:	85 feet (25.9 m)
Draft:	24²/₃ feet (7.5 m)
Propulsion:	steam turbines (General Electric); 20,000 shp; 1 shaft
Boilers:	2 (Foster Wheeler)

Speed:	18 knots (sustained)
Manning:	1,112 (43 O + 1,069 enlisted) in AS 36
	1,161 (43 O + 1,118 enlisted) in AS 37
Flag:	69 (25 O + 44 enlisted)
Helicopters:	none assigned
Guns:	4 20-mm Mk 67 (4 × 1)

These are the Navy's first submarine tenders designed to support SSNs. See LAND class for general notes.

Class: The AS 39 of this design was provided in the FY 1969 budget, but was not built because of fund shortages in other programs.

Guns: As built, these ships each had two 5-inch 38 cal DP guns. They were removed in favor of minimal 20-mm gun armament.

DIXON (1979, Giorgio Arra)

2 FBM SUBMARINE TENDERS: "SIMON LAKE" CLASS

Number	Name	FY/SCB	Launched	Commissioned	Status
AS 33	SIMON LAKE	63/238	8 Feb 1964	7 Nov 1964	**AA**
AS 34	CANOPUS	64/238	12 Feb 1965	4 Nov 1965	**AA**

Builders:	AS 33 Puget Sound Naval Shipyard, Bremerton, Wash.
	AS 34 Ingalls Shipbuilding Corp, Pascagoula, Miss.
Displacement:	21,500 tons full load
Length:	643¾ feet (196.2 m) oa
Beam:	85 feet (25.9 m)
Draft:	24½ feet (7.5 m)
Propulsion:	steam turbines; 20,000 shp; 1 shaft
Boilers:	2 (Combustion Engineering)
Speed:	18 knots (sustained)
Manning:	1,232 (54 O + 1,178 enlisted) in AS 33
	1,228 (54 O + 1,174 enlisted) in AS 34
Helicopters:	none assigned
Guns:	4 3-inch (76-mm) 50 cal AA Mk 33 (2 × 2)

These tenders are designed to support FBM submarines with up to three SSBNs moored alongside simultaneously. The ships have extensive machine shops, weapons and provisions stowage, spare parts lockers, and replacement missiles. They were originally configured to support Polaris missiles; the SIMON LAKE was modified in 1970–1971 and the CANOPUS in 1969–1970 to handle Poseidon missiles. The SIMON LAKE has subsequently been modified to support the Trident missile.

Class: The AS 35 of this design was authorized in FY 1965, but her construction was deferred and the ship was not built. The ship would have provided one tender for each of five planned SSBN squadrons with a sixth ship in overhaul and transit. However, the Polaris SSBN program was cut from a proposed 45 submarines to 41, and only four squadrons were established.

Design: A helicopter platform is fitted aft, but the ships do not have hangars or support facilities.

2 FBM SUBMARINE TENDERS: "HUNLEY" CLASS

Number	Name	FY/SCB	Launched	Commissioned	Status
AS 31	HUNLEY	60/194	28 Sep 1961	16 June 1962	**PA**
AS 32	HOLLAND	62/194	19 Jan 1963	7 Sep 1963	**AA**

Builders:	AS 31 Newport News Shipbuilding and DD Co, Va.
	AS 32 Ingalls Shipbuilding Corp, Pascagoula, Miss.
Displacement:	10,500 tons standard
	18,300 tons full load
Length:	599 feet (182.6 m) oa
Beam:	83 feet (25.3 m)
Draft:	24 feet (7.3 m)
Propulsion:	diesel-electric (Fairbanks-Morse diesels); 15,000 shp; 1 shaft
Speed:	19 knots
Manning:	1,244 (54 O + 1,190 enlisted) in AS 31
	1,335 (56 O + 1,279 enlisted) in AS 32
Helicopters:	no facilities
Guns:	4 20-mm Mk 67 (2 × 2)

These ships were the first U.S. submarine tenders constructed to support FBM submarines; three SSBNs can be serviced alongside simultaneously. They have extensive maintenance and stowage facilities, including vertical stowage for replacement missiles. As built, they could handle Polaris missiles; the HUNLEY was modified in 1973–1974 and the HOLLAND in 1974–1975 to support Poseidon-armed submarines.

Design: As built, these ships had a 32-ton-capacity hammerhead crane fitted aft. It has been replaced in both ships with amidships cranes, as in the later SIMON LAKE class. As in all postwar sub tenders, there is a helicopter deck, but no hangar; the deck is used for VERTREP and is no longer certified for helicopter landings.

Guns: The original armament in both ships was four 3-inch 50 cal AA guns.

The CANOPUS servicing an SSBN at Holy Loch, Scotland, during the tenth annual Polaris sailing regatta sponsored by the U.S. Navy and the Holy Loch Sailing Club. An Excellent relationship has been developed by the Navy personnel at Holy Loch and the local population. (1970, U.S. Navy)

HOLLAND with two SSBNs (1970, U.S. Navy)

1 FBM SUBMARINE TENDER: "PROTEUS" TYPE

Number	Name	Launched	Commissioned	Status
AS 19	PROTEUS	12 Nov 1942	31 Jan 1944	**PA**

Builders:	Moore Shipbuilding and Dry Dock Co, Oakland, Calif.
Displacement:	10,234 tons standard
	18,500 tons full load
Length:	574½ feet (175.1 m) oa
Beam:	73 feet (22.3 m)
Draft:	25½ feet (7.8 m)
Propulsion:	diesel-electric (General Motors diesels); 11,200 shp; 2 shafts
Speed:	15 knots
Manning:	1,329 (52 O + 1,277 enlisted)
Helicopters:	no facilities
Guns:	4 20-mm Mk 68 (4 × 1)

The PROTEUS originally was a submarine tender of the FULTON class. She was laid up in reserve in 1974; from 1959–1960 she was extensively converted (SCB-190) to support Polaris-armed SSBNs (see Conversion notes). She was recommissioned on 8 July 1960.

Conversion: The PROTEUS was converted at the Charleston Naval Shipyard to the first U.S. Navy FBM submarine tender. A 44-foot amidships section was added to provide space for additional shops and support facilities as well as vertical Polaris-missile stowage. This "insert" was six decks high and weighed about 500 tons. A traveling crane was installed to handle the missiles. Nuclear support capability was added, with the gun battery being reduced to two (forward) 5-inch guns; these guns were removed in the mid-1970s.

PROTEUS—before removal of forward 5-inch gun (U.S. Navy)

6 SUBMARINE TENDERS: "FULTON" CLASS

Number	Name	Launched	Commissioned	Status
AS 11	FULTON	27 Dec 1940	12 Sep 1941	**AA**
AS 12	SPERRY	17 Dec 1941	1 May 1942	**PA**
AS 15	BUSHNELL	14 Sep 1942	10 Apr 1943	AR
AS 16	HOWARD W. GILMORE	16 Sep 1943	24 May 1944	AR
AS 17	NEREUS	12 Feb 1945	27 Oct 1945	PR
AS 18	ORION	14 Oct 1942	30 Sep 1943	**PA**

Builders:	AS 11, 15–17 Mare Island Navy Yard, Vallejo, Calif.
	AS 12, 18 Moore Shipbuilding and DD Co, Oakland, Calif.
Displacement:	9,734 tons standard
	18,000 tons full load
Length:	529½ feet (161.4 m) oa except AS 12, 15, 530½ feet
Beam:	73⅓ feet (22.3 m)
Draft:	25½ feet (7.8 m)
Propulsion:	diesel-electric (General Motors diesels); 11,200 shp except AS 11, 11,500 shp, AS 12, 11,800 shp; 2 shafts
Speed:	15 knots
Manning:	997–1,003 (36–39 O + 958–965 enlisted)
Helicopters:	no facilities
Guns:	2 5-inch (127-mm) 38 cal DP Mk 30 (2 × 1) in AS 15, 17
	4 20-mm Mk 68 (4 × 1) in AS 11–12, 16, 18
Fire control:	1 Mk 37 gun FCS in AS 15, 17
	1 Mk 25 radar in AS 15, 17

These ships are similar in design to the contemporary DIXIE (AD 14)-class destroyer tenders. The FULTONS have been modernized to provide a limited capability to support nuclear attack submarines. Their helicopter decks are suitable only for VERTREP and not for landings. The original 20-ton-capacity cranes have been replaced in the GILMORE.

The BUSHNELL was decommissioned on 30 June 1970, the NEREUS on 27 October 1971, and the HOWARD W. GILMORE on 30 September 1980.

Class: There are seven ships in this class. The PROTEUS, modified to support FBM submarines, is listed separately.

Guns: As built, each ship had four 5-inch guns and eight 40-mm AA guns.

Names: The AS 16 was originally named NEPTUNE; changed in 1943.

HOWARD W. GILMORE (1973, Giorgio Arra)

SPERRY (1979, U.S. Navy, PH2 Jeffrey L. Aswegan)

2 SUBMARINE RESCUE SHIPS: "PIGEON" CLASS

Number	Name	FY/SCB	Launched	Commissioned	Status
ASR 21	PIGEON	67/721	13 Aug 1969	28 Apr 1973	**PA**
ASR 22	ORTOLAN	68/721	10 Sep 1969	14 July 1973	**AA**

Builders:	Alabama Dry Dock and Shipbuilding Co, Mobile, Ala.
Displacement:	4,200 tons full load
Length:	251 feet (76.5 m) oa
Beam:	86 feet (26.2 m)
Draft:	21¼ feet (6.5 m)
Propulsion:	diesels; 6,000 shp; 2 shafts
Speed:	15 knots
Manning:	181 (9 O + 172 enlisted)
Helicopters:	no facilities
Guns:	2 20-mm Mk 68 (2 × 1)

These are the world's first built-for-the-purpose submarine rescue ships. They were constructed specifically to carry Deep Submergence Rescue Vehicles (DSRV) and support deep-ocean diving operations. For the latter role they have the Mk II Deep Diving System (DDS) which can support up to eight divers operating to depths of 1,000 feet in helium-oxygen saturation conditions.

These ships were delayed by problems in design, construction, and fitting out.

Class: The Navy had planned to construct a minimum of three ships of this class to support six DSRVs at three rescue unit home ports. At one point long-range planning called for ten ships as replacements for the older ASR force. However, only two ships were funded. Additional ASRs are not now planned.

Design: These are the Navy's largest catamaran ships, being larger than the research ship HAYES (T-AGOR 16). Each ASR hull is 26 feet wide with a separation of 34 feet between the two. The open well facilitates the raising and lowering of DSRVs and diving chambers. These ships have a precision three-dimensional sonar tracking system for directing DSRV operations, and a helicopter deck is fitted aft but is suited only for VERTREP and not landings. Accommodations are provided for a salvage staff of 14 and a DSRV operator and maintenance team of 24.

Engineering: Through-bow thrusters are fitted in each hull for maneuvering and station-keeping during diving and salvage operations (the ships are not moored while operating DSRVs).

Guns: As built, the PIGEON had two 3-inch AA guns in "tubs" forward on her hulls. After their removal the large mooring buoys ("spuds") were mounted in their place; previously she had two buoys forward of the bridge and two between the hulls aft.

ORTOLAN (1976, Giorgio Arra)

ORTOLAN (1973, U.S. Navy, Albert E. Flournoy)

ORTOLAN (1979, Giorgio Arra)

4 SUBMARINE RESCUE SHIPS: "CHANTICLEER" CLASS

Number	Name	Launched	Commissioned	Status
ASR 9	FLORIKAN	14 June 1942	5 Apr 1943	**PA**
ASR 13	KITTIWAKE	10 July 1945	18 July 1946	**AA**
ASR 14	PETREL	25 Sep 1945	24 Sep 1946	**AA**
ASR 15	SUNBIRD	25 June 1945	28 Jan 1947	**AA**

Builders:	ASR 9 Moore Shipbuilding and Dry Dock Co, Oakland, Calif.
	ASR 13–15 Savannah Machine and Foundry Co, Ga.
Displacement:	1,635 tons standard
Length:	251$\frac{1}{3}$ feet (76.7 m) oa
Beam:	42 feet (12.8 m)
Draft:	14$\frac{5}{6}$ feet (4.5 m)
Propulsion:	diesel-electric (General Motors diesel, except Alco in ASR 9); 3,000 shp; 1 shaft
Speed:	15 knots
Manning:	99 (6 O + 93 enlisted)
Helicopters:	no facilities
Guns:	2 20-mm Mk 68 (2 × 1)

These are large tug-type ships fitted for salvage and helium-oxygen diving operations.

Class: Originally there were eight ships in this class (ASR 7–11, 13–15, plus the canceled ASR 16–18).

Guns: The designed armament of these ships was two 3-inch 50 cal AA guns in single mounts and two 20-mm single guns.

5 AUXILIARY TUGS: "SOTOYOMO" CLASS

Number	Name	Launched	Commissioned	Status
ATA 178	TUNICA	15 June 1944	15 Sep 1944	MR
ATA 181	ACCOKEEK	27 July 1944	7 Oct 1944	MR
ATA 190	SAMOSET	26 Oct 1944	1 Jan 1945	MR
ATA 193	STALLION	24 Nov 1944	26 Feb 1945	MR
ATA 213	KEYWADIN	9 Apr 1945	1 June 1945	MR

Builders:	Levingston Shipbuilding Co, Orange, Texas, except ATA 213 Gulfport Boiler and Welding Works, Port Arthur, Texas
Displacement:	534 tons standard
Length:	143 feet (43.6 m) oa
Beam:	33$\frac{5}{6}$ feet (10.3 m)
Draft:	14 feet (4.3 m)
Propulsion:	diesel-electric (General Motors diesels); 1,500 shp; 1 shaft
Speed:	13 knots
Manning:	45 (5 O + 40 enlisted)
Helicopters:	no facilities
Guns:	1 3-inch (76-mm) 50 cal AA (1 × 1)
	or 4 20-mm AA Mk 24 (2 × 2); all guns removed from some ships

These are the survivors of a class of small oceangoing tugs; they lack the salvage capability of the larger ATFs. All are laid up in the National Defense Reserve Fleet.

Class: Seventy ships of this class were built (ATA 121–125, 146, 170–213, 219–238).

Classification: These ships originally were classified as rescue tugs (ATR); they were renumbered in the same series as the larger fleet tugs on 15 May 1944.

Names: Names of discarded fleet and yard tugs were assigned to these ships in 1948.

Guns: As built, an armament of one 3-inch 50 cal AA gun and two 20-mm AA guns was provided in these tugs.

FLORIKAN (1979, Giorgio Arra)

KITTIWAKE with submarine rescue chamber on fantail (1976, Stefan Terzibaschitsch)

ACCOKEEK (1970, U.S. Navy)

5 + 2 FLEET TUGS: "POWHATAN" CLASS

Number	None	FY/SCB	Launched	In service	Status
T-ATF 166	POWHATAN	75/744	24 June 1978	15 June 1979	**MSC-A**
T-ATF 167	NARRAGANSETT	75/744	12 May 1979	30 Sep 1979	**MSC-P**
T-ATF 168	CATAWBA	75/744	22 Sep 1979	1980	**MSC**
T-ATF 169	NAVAJO	75/744	20 Dec 1979	1980	**MSC**
T-ATF 170	MOHAWK	78/744		1980	**MSC**
T-ATF 171	SIOUX	78/744		1981	Bldg.
T-ATF 172	APACHE	78/744		1981	Bldg.

Builders:	Marinette Marine Corp, Wisc.
Displacement:	2,200 tons full load
Length:	225 feet (68.6 m) oa
Beam:	42 feet (12.8 m)
Draft:	15 feet (4.6 m)
Propulsion:	diesel; 4,500 shp; 2 shafts
Speed:	15 knots
Manning:	16 (civilian) + 4 Navy communications detachment + 20 transients (salvage and diving personnel)
Helicopters:	no facilities
Guns:	none

These tugs are based on a commercial design. They are intended to replace the war-built ATFs. They are MSC operated with civilian crews.

Design: There is a clear afterdeck for diving and salvage equipment. The starboard-side boom has a 10-ton capacity.

Engineering: A 300-hp bow thruster is provided.

POWHATAN (U.S. Navy)

17 FLEET TUGS: "CHEROKEE" CLASS

Number	Name	Launched	Commissioned	Status
ATF 69	CHIPPEWA	25 July 1942	14 Feb 1943	MR
ATF 71	HOPI	7 Sep 1942	31 Mar 1943	MR
T-ATF 76	UTE	24 June 1942	31 Dec 1942	MR
T-ATF 85	LIPAN	17 Sep 1942	29 Apr 1943	MR
ATF 87	MORENO	9 July 1942	30 Nov 1942	MR
ATF 88	NARRAGANSETT	8 Aug 1942	15 Jan 1943	MR
ATF 91	SENECA	2 Feb 1943	30 Apr 1943	MR
ATF 105	MOCTOBI	25 Mar 1944	25 July 1944	**NRF-P**
ATF 110	QUAPAW	15 May 1943	6 May 1944	**NRF-P**
ATF 113	TAKELMA	18 Sep 1943	3 Aug 1944	**NRF-P**
ATF 115	TENINO	10 Jan 1944	18 Nov 1944	MR
ATF 118	WENATCHEE	7 Sep 1944	24 Mar 1945	MR
ATF 148	ACHOMAWI	10 Sep 1944	11 Nov 1944	MR
T-ATF 149	ATAKAPA	11 July 1944	8 Dec 1944	**MSC-A**
T-ATF 158	MOSOPELEA	7 Mar 1945	28 July 1945	**MSC-A**
ATF-159	PAIUTE	4 June 1945	27 Aug 1945	**NRF-A**
ATF 160	PAPAGO	21 June 1945	3 Oct 1945	**NRF-P**

Builders:	ATF 69, 71, 105, 148–149, 158–159, 160 Charleston Shipbuilding and DD Co, S.C.
	ATF 76, 85, 110, 113, 115, 118 United Engineering Co, Alameda, Calif.
	ATF 87–88, 91 Cramp Shipbuilding Co, Philadelphia, Pa.
Displacement:	1,235 tons standard
	1,675 tons full load
Length:	205 feet (62.5 m) oa
Beam:	38½ feet (11.7 m)
Draft:	15½ feet (4.7 m)
Propulsion:	diesel-electric; 3,000 shp; 1 shaft
Speed:	16.5 knots

Manning:	27–28 (civilian) + 6 Navy technicians in MSC ships
Helicopters:	no facilities
Guns:	removed from NRF and MSC ships; 1 3-inch (76-mm) 50 cal AA Mk 22 (1 × 1) in most laid-up ships

These ships are the survivors of a large, highly successful series of ATFs. Ten ships are laid up in the National Defense Reserve Fleet: ATF 69, 87, and 88 since 1961; ATF 115, 118, and 148 since 1962; ATF 71 since 1964; ATF 91 since 1971; and ATF 76 and 85 since 1980. The last two ships were operated by MSC with civilian crews from 1974–1980.

Two ships are currently civilian-manned by MSC, the ATF 149 since 1974 and ATF 158 since 1973. The former is scheduled to be laid up in the fall of 1981.

Five ships are assigned to the Naval Reserve Force and are manned by composite active-reserve crews: The ATF 105, 110, 159, and 160 since 1977, and the ATF 113 since 1979.

The last Navy-manned ship, the SHAKORI (ATF 162), was decommissioned on 29 February 1980 and transferred to Taiwan.

Class: The AT 66–76 and 81–118 were built to the same basic design (see Engineering notes). They are officially known as the CHEROKEE (ATF 66) after the loss of the NAVAJO (AT 64) in 1943 and the SEMINOLE (AT 65) in 1942. Later ships are unofficially referred to as the ABNAKI (ATF 96) class. Several of these ships serve in the U.S. Coast Guard and a number of foreign navies.

Classification: These ships all were ordered with the AT designation. The AT 66 and later ships were changed to ATF on 15 May 1944.

Design: These are steel-hulled ships. They are fitted with a 10- or 20-ton-capacity boom. Most have compressed-air diving equipment.

Engineering: Ships numbered below ATF 96 have four diesels, four generators, and four electric motors driving through a gear to a single propeller shaft; the later ships have only one, very large electric motor. The earlier ships have a short, squat exhaust funnel; the later ships have waterline exhausts for their diesels (as in submarines) and a tall, thin galley funnel (i.e., ''Charlie Noble'').

Guns: The original armament of these tugs was a single 3-inch 50 cal AA gun, two single 40-mm AA guns, and two 20-mm AA guns.

Takelma—small-funnel type (1978, Giorgio Arra)

Ute—large-funnel type (1978, Giorgio Arra)

Lipan—large-funnel type (1977, Giorgio Arra)

Quapaw—small-funnel type (1970, U.S. Navy, PH1 E. L. Goligoski)

3 SALVAGE AND RESCUE SHIPS: "EDENTON" CLASS

Number	Name	FY/SCB	Launched	Commissioned	Status
ATS 1	EDENTON	66/719	15 May 1968	23 Jan 1971	**AA**
ATS 2	BEAUFORT	67/719	20 Dec 1968	22 Jan 1972	**PA**
ATS 3	BRUNSWICK	67/719	14 Oct 1969	10 Dec 1972	**PA**

Builders:	Brooke Marine, Lowestoft, England
Displacement:	3,117 tons full load
Length:	282⅔ feet (86.1 m) oa
Beam:	50 feet (15.2 m)
Draft:	15⅙ feet (4.6 m)
Propulsion:	diesels (Paxman); 6,000 shp; 2 shafts
Speed:	16 knots
Manning:	103 (7 O + 96 enlisted)
Helicopters:	no facilities
Guns:	2 20-mm Mk 67 (2 × 1) in ATS 1
	2 20-mm Mk 68 (2 × 1) in ATS 2–3

These are large ocean tugs with salvage and diving capabilities. They are one of two British-built classes of auxiliary ships constructed in the post–World War II period for the U.S. Navy (see the CHAUVENET class, T-AGS 29). There have been difficulties in maintaining these ships because of their foreign-manufactured components.

Class: The ATS 4 was authorized in FY 1972 and the ATS 5 in FY 1973. Their construction was deferred in 1973 and plans for additional ships of this class were dropped because of the high costs; instead, the commercial-design ATF 166 has been procured.

Classification: The classification ATS was changed from salvage tug to salvage and rescue ship on 16 February 1971.

Design: These ships have large open work spaces forward and aft. They have four mooring buoys, two on each side of the funnel, similar to those carried by submarine rescue ships to facilitate four-point moors. A 10-ton-capacity crane is fitted forward and a 20-ton capacity crane aft. The ships have compressed-air diving equipment.

Engineering: The ships are fitted with through-bow thrusters for precise maneuvering and station-keeping.

BEAUFORT (1974, U.S. Navy)

BRUNSWICK (1979, Giorgio Arra)

1 GUIDED MISSILE SHIP: "NORTON SOUND" TYPE

Number	Name	Launched	Commissioned	Status
AVM 1	NORTON SOUND	28 Nov 1943	8 Jan 1945	**PA**

Builders:.	Los Angeles Shipbuilding and DD Co
Displacement:	9,106 tons standard
	15,170 tons full load
Length:	540¼ feet (164.7 m) wl
	543¼ feet (165.6 m) oa
Beam:	71 feet (21.8 m)
Draft:	21½ feet (6.6 m)
Propulsion:	steam turbines (Allis Chalmers); 12,000 shp; 2 shafts
Boilers:	4 (Babcock & Wilcox)
Speed:	19 knots
Manning:	369 (19 O + 350 enlisted) + 87 civilian technicians
Helicopters:	none assigned
Missiles:	1 twin Mk 26 Mod 0 launcher for Standard SAM
	fitted with vertical launch tubes
Guns:	removed
Radars:	SPS-10 surface search
	SPS-40 air search
	SPS-52 3-D air search
	SPY-1A phased-array (one face)

The NORTON SOUND is a test ship for advanced weapons development. She originally was a seaplane tender of the CURRITUCK (AV 7) class. From 1948 onward she has been employed in the test and evaluation of missiles, guns, and electronic systems (see Guns and Missiles notes). In 1974 she was modified to serve as the test ship for the Aegis system. One "face" of the four-array SPY-1 radar system was fitted on the ship's starboard side above the bridge (with a dummy face to port). The related Aegis computers and fire control systems have been installed and a twin Mk 26 missile launcher installed aft.

Classification: The NORTON SOUND was reclassified from AV 11 to AVM 1 on 8 August 1951.

Design: A 30-ton-capacity crane is fitted. The former seaplane hangar is used for office and stowage space.

Guns: The ship's original armament as AV 11 consisted of 4 5-inch 38 cal DP guns, 20 40-mm AA guns, and 8 20-mm AA guns. All original armament has been removed. In 1968 the 5-inch 54 cal lightweight Mk 45 gun was installed with associated Mk 86 gun FCS for at-sea evaluation; they were subsequently involved.

Missiles: The NORTON SOUND has served as test ship for several missiles and rockets, among them the Loon (American version of the German V-1 "buzz bomb"), Aerobee, Viking, Lark, Regulus I, Terrier, Tartar, Sea Sparrow, and Standard SAM. In 1958 the ship launched multi-stage missiles carrying low-yield nuclear warheads that were detonated some 300 miles above the earth (Project Argus).

In 1973–1974 the ship was fitted with the Mk 26 missile launcher; in 1980 the ship was fitted with vertical launch tubes.

NORTON SOUND (1979, Giorgio Arra)

UNCLASSIFIED MISCELLANEOUS SHIPS

These ships are officially considered to be Service Craft, but are traditionally listed as Auxiliaries.

The hull number IX 505 was assigned to the former medium harbor tug YTM 759; that craft was stricken on 1 December 1977.

The hull number IX 310 is assigned to two test barges linked together and used for research at the Naval Underwater System Center's laboratory at Lake Seneca, N.Y. No name is assigned to this "craft."

The IX 509 is a former underwater explosive test barge. It was instated on the Naval Register on 1 December 1979 (previously listed as floating equipment). The unnamed craft is at the David Taylor Naval Ship Research and Development Center in Maryland.

1 BARRACKS SHIP: FORMER TRANSPORT

Number	Name	Launched	Commissioned	Status
IX 507 (ex-AP 121)	Gen. Hugh J. Gaffey	20 Feb 1944	18 Sep 1944	**PA**

Builders:	Bethlehem Steel Co, Alameda, Calif.
Displacement:	
Length:	608$^{11}/_{12}$ feet (185.6 m) oa
Beam:	75½ feet (23.0 m)
Draft:	26½ feet (8.2 m)
Propulsion:	turbo-electric (General Electric); 18,000 shp; 2 shafts
Boilers:	4 (Combustion Engineering)
Speed:	19 knots
Manning:	
Troops:	~2,500

The Gaffey was originally an "Admiral"-class transport. The ship served in the Navy from 1944–1946; subsequently used by the Army as a troop transport from 1946–1950, when returned to the Navy and assigned to MSTS for operation. She was laid up in the National Defense Reserve Fleet on 14 November 1968.

The Gaffey was modified in 1979–1980 for use as a stationary berthing ship at the Bremerton Naval Shipyard to provide berthing and messing accommodations for the crews of aircraft carriers undergoing overhaul at the yard. The ship arrived at Bremerton early in 1980 and is expected to remain in service there at least until 1985. Modifications for the barracks ship role included upgrading of berths, mess facilities, plumbing, and certain other spaces; installation of lockers, provisions for recreation and class rooms, provision of laundry and hospital facilities; the ship is not capable of steaming.

Class: Additional ships of this class are laid up in the National Defense Reserve Fleet. (See page 226.)

Classification: The Gaffey was changed from T-AP 121 to IX 507 on 1 November 1978.

Names: The ship was originally named Adm. W. L. Capps; changed when transferred to the Army. The Army name was retained when returned to the Navy.

1 RESEARCH SUPPORT SHIP: CONVERTED YFU

Number	Status
IX 506 (ex-YFU 82)	**PA**

Builders:	Pacific Coast Engineering Co, Alameda, Calif.
Displacement:	550 tons full load
Length:	125 feet (40.9 m) oa
Beam:	36 feet (11.8 m)
Draft:	5½ ft (1.7 m)
Propulsion:	diesels; 2 shafts
Speed:	
Manning:	18 (enlisted)

This craft is a former harbor utility craft, converted for use as a research platform by the Naval Ocean Systems Center's facility at Long Beach, Calif. Converted 1978–1980.

Classification: Changed from YFU 82 to IX 506 on 1 April 1978.

IX 506 (1980, U.S. Navy)

IX 506 (1980, U.S. Navy)

3 SELF-PROPELLED BARRACKS SHIPS: MODIFIED LST DESIGN

Number	Name	Launched	Commissioned	Status
IX 502 (ex-APB 39)	MERCER	17 Nov 1944	19 Sep 1945	**PA**
IX 503 (ex-APB 40)	NUECES	6 May 1945	30 Nov 1945	**PA**
IX 504 (ex-APB 37)	ECHOLS	30 July 1945	(1 Jan 1947)	**AA**

Builders:	Boston Navy Yard, Mass.
Displacement:	2,190 tons light
	4,080 tons full load
Length:	328 feet (100 m) oa
Beam:	50 feet (15.2 m)
Draft:	11 feet (3.4 m)
Propulsion:	diesels (General Motors); 1,600 shp; 2 shafts
Speed:	10 knots
Manning:	193 (13 O + 180 enlisted) as APB
Troops:	~900
Guns:	removed

These ships were built to provide accommodations and support for small craft and riverine forces. All three ships were built as barracks ships (APL, later APB) to serve at shipyards for crews of ships being built or under repair. They were then given "unclassified" (IX) designations with their APB hull numbers in 1975–1976.

The ECHOLS was placed in service, instead of being commissioned, in 1947. All of these ships were laid up in reserve after World War II. The MERCER and NUECES were recommissioned in 1968 for service in Vietnam. They were rearmed with two 3-inch guns, eight 40-mm guns (2 × 4), and several MGs. As modified to support riverine forces, they had crews of 12 officers and 186 enlisted men, and could accommodate 900 troops and small-boat crewmen. Both ships were again laid up in 1969–1971 until reactivated in 1975; the ECHOLS was reactivated in 1976.

Class: There were originally 14 ships of this class (APB 35–48).

Classification: IX 502 ex-APB 39, ex-APL 39; IX 503 ex-APB 40, ex-APL 40; and IX 504 ex-APB 37, ex-APL 37; the MERCER and NUECES were changed to IX on 1 November 1975; the ECHOLS on 1 February 1976.

1 TEST RANGE SUPPORT SHIP: "ELK RIVER"

Number	Name	Launched	Commissioned	Status
IX 501 (ex-LSMR 501)	ELK RIVER	21 Apr 1945	27 May 1945	**PA**

Builders:	Brown Shipbuilding Co, Houston, Texas
Displacement:	1,100 tons full load
Length:	230 feet (70.1 m) oa
Beam:	50 feet (15.2 m)
Draft:	$9^5/_6$ feet (3 m)
Propulsion:	diesels; 1,400 shp; 2 shafts
Speed:	6 knots
Manning:	71 (20 O + 51 enlisted)
Guns:	none

The ELK RIVER is a converted rocket landing ship employed as a test and training ship for deep-sea diving and salvage. She is operated by the Naval Ocean Systems Center in San Diego.

Class: The ELK RIVER was one of several medium landing ships (LSM) completed as rocket fire support ships. All other ships of this type have been stricken, the last three having been used in the Vietnam War.

Conversion: The ELK RIVER was converted to a test range support ship in 1967–1968 at Avondale Shipyards, Westwego, La., and the San Francisco Naval Shipyard. The basic 203½-foot LSMR hull was lengthened and eight-foot sponsons were added to both sides to improve the ship's stability and increase working space. A superstructure was added forward and an open center well was provided for lowering and raising equipment. The 65-ton-capacity gantry crane runs on tracks above the opening to handle submersibles and diver-transfer chambers. An active precision maneuvering system is installed for holding position without mooring.

The prototype Mk II Deep Diving System (DDS) has been installed. It can support eight divers operating at depths of 1,000 feet in helium-oxygen saturation conditions. This is the most advanced diving system in use today; the Mk II DDS is also in the PIGEON (ASR 21)-class ships.

ECHOLS in reserve as APB 37 (1976, Giorgio Arra)

ELK RIVER (U.S. Navy)

Elk River (1968, U.S. Navy)

1 TORPEDO TEST SHIP: Ex-CARGO SHIP

Number	Name	Status
IX 308 (ex-AKL 17)	New Bedford	**PA**

Builders:	Wheeler S.B. Corp, Long Island, N.Y.
Displacement:	700 tons
Length:	176½ feet (53.8 m) oa
Beam:	32¾ feet (10.0 m)
Draft:	10 feet (3.1 m)
Propulsion:	diesel; 1,000 shp; 1 shaft
Speed:	13 knots
Manning:	
Guns:	none

The New Bedford is a former Army cargo ship acquired by the Navy on 1 March 1950 for cargo work. She was subsequently converted for torpedo testing and since 1963 operated by the Naval Torpedo Station, Keyport, Wash.

Classification: Originally U.S. Army FS 289; operated by Military Sea Transportation Service as T-AKL 17.

1 INSTRUMENTATION PLATFORM

Number	Name	Status
IX 307 (ex-WLI 299)	Brier	**AA**

Builders:	
Displacement:	178 tons full load
Length:	100 feet (30.1 m) oa
Beam:	24 feet (7.3 m)
Draft:	4½ feet (1.4 m)
Propulsion:	diesel; 300 shp; 2 shafts
Speed:	8.5 knots
Manning:	
Guns:	none

The Brier is a former Coast Guard buoy tender. She was acquired by the Navy on 10 March 1969 to be used as an instrument platform in explosive testing at the Naval Ordnance Center's facility at Solomons Island, Md.

Classification: The Brier was listed as an inland buoy tender (WLI 299) in Coast Guard service; changed to IX 307 on 29 August 1970.

1 TORPEDO TEST SHIP: Ex-CARGO SHIP

Number	Name	Status
IX 306	(unnamed)	**AA**

Builders:	Higgins Industries, New Orleans, La.
Displacement:	906 tons full load
Length:	179 feet (54.6 m) oa
Beam:	33 feet (10.1 m)
Draft:	10 feet (3.1 m)
Propulsion:	diesel; 1 shaft
Speed:	12 knots
Manning:	
Guns:	none

The IX 306 is a former Army cargo ship (FS 221). She was acquired from the Army in January 1969 and converted to a torpedo test ship, being placed in service late in 1969. The ship supports research activities at the Naval Underwater Weapons Research and Engineering Station, Newport, R.I., and operates in the Atlantic Underwater Test and Evaluation Center (AUTEC) range in the Caribbean. The ship is manned by Navy and RCA personnel.

New Bedford (1973, U.S. Navy)

IX 306 (1969, U.S. Navy)

1 RELIC: "CONSTITUTION"

Number	Name	Launched	Commissioned	Status
(IX 21)	CONSTITUTION	21 Oct 1797	1798	Relic

Builders:	Hartt's Shipyard, Boston, Mass.
Displacement:	2,200 tons
Length:	175 feet (53.3 m) gun deck
Beam:	45 feet (13.7 m)
Draft:	20 feet (6.1 m)
Masts:	fore 94 feet (28.7 m)
	main 104 feet (31.7 m)
	mizzen 81 feet (24.7 m)
Speed:	13 knots (under sail)
Manning:	49 (2 O + 47 enlisted) as relic; up to 500 as frigate
Guns:	several smooth-bore cannon

The CONSTITUTION is the oldest U.S. ship in Navy commission. Her original commissioning date is not known; she first put to sea on 22 July 1798. She is moored as a relic at the Boston Naval Shipyard in Boston. (She is afloat, unlike HMS VICTORY, Nelson's flagship at Trafalgar, which is preserved in concrete at Portsmouth, England.)

As a sail frigate, the CONSTITUTION fought in the Quasi-War with France, against the Barbary pirates, and in the War of 1812 against Great Britain. She has been rebuilt several times and restored as much as possible to her original configuration.

No sails are fitted. Twice a year she is taken out into Boston harbor under tow and "turned around," so that her masts do not bend from the effects of sun and wind.

Class: The CONSTITUTION was one of six sail frigates built under an act of Congress of 1794. The CONSTELLATION (36 guns) was built under the same act and broken up at Norfolk, Va., in 1852–1853 with much of her material being used to build another sailing ship of that name. That ship served in the Navy as the IX 20 until transferred in 1954 to a private group in Baltimore, Md., where she is maintained.

Classification: The CONSTITUTION was classified as an "unclassified" ship in 1920 (IX without a hull number). She became IX 21 on 8 December 1941 and carried that classification until 1 September 1975 when it was withdrawn because, according to Navy officials, the designation "tended to demean and degrade the CONSTITUTION through association with a group of insignificant craft of varied missions and configurations."

Names: From 1917 until 1925 the ship was named OLD CONSTITUTION while the name CONSTITUTION was assigned to a battle cruiser (CC5); that ship was never completed.

Guns: When built, the CONSTITUTION was rated as a 44-gun frigate. The actual number of guns installed has varied considerably over her long career.

CONSTITUTION (U.S. Navy)

18 Service Craft

The U.S. Navy operates several hundred service craft, both self-propelled and non-self-propelled, at bases in the United States and overseas. These craft perform a variety of Fleet support services. Only the self-propelled craft are described here, with several "different" craft officially designated as service craft being listed separately: the unclassified miscellaneous ships (IX) are described under Auxiliary Ships (Chapter 17), while Submersibles and Floating Dry Docks are listed in subsequent chapters.

All service craft are Navy-manned with a few having all-female crews.

Classification: The service craft Y designations were initiated when they were considered "yard" craft.

Guns: Service craft are usually unarmed. The seamanship training craft (YP) can be armed with light weapons for use as harbor patrol craft.

The MONOB ONE is shown under way in this photo, taken in the late 1970s. Her deck is crowded with reels for underwater cables and other equipment. Service craft are "in service" rather than being "in commission" (as are some ships, especially those designated IX). Service craft have their full designation (e.g., YAG 61) painted on their hulls; ships have either just their number or, in the case of some auxiliaries, their designation less the letter "A" as TF 113 for ATF 113. (U.S. Navy)

1 MOBILE LISTENING BARGE: CONVERTED WATER BARGE

Number	Name
YAG 61 (ex-IX 309)	MONOB 1

Builders:	Zenith Dredge Co, Duluth, Minn.
Displacement:	1,390 tons full load
Length:	174 feet (53.0 m) oa
Beam:	32 feet (9.75 m)
Draft:	
Propulsion:	diesel; 560 shp; 1 shaft
Speed:	7 knots
Manning:	19 (1 O + 18 enlisted) + technicians

The YAG 61 was originally completed in 1943 as a self-propelled water barge (YW 87). She was converted to a Mobile Noise Barge (MONOB) for acoustic research in 1969 and placed in service conducting research for the Naval Ship Research and Development Center; assigned to Port Canaveral, Fla.

Classification: Reclassified from YW 87 to IX 309 in 1969; changed to YAG 61 on 1 July 1970.

3 COVERED LIGHTERS

Number	Name
YF 862	(unnamed)
YF 866	KODIAK
YF 885	KEYPORT

Builders:	YF 862, 866 Missouri Valley Bridge and Steel Co, Evansville, Ind.
	YF 885 Defoe Shipbuilding Co, Bay City, Mich.
Displacement:	650 tons full load
Length:	132 feet (40.2 m) oa
Beam:	30 feet (9.1 m)
Draft:	
Propulsion:	diesel; 600 shp; 2 shafts
Speed:	10 knots
Manning:	11 (enlisted)

These are small, coastal supply craft with a 250-ton cargo capacity. They were constructed during World War II. The YF 862 and KODIAK are laid up. The KEYPORT is in service at Guam.

YF-type service craft laid up in reserve (1975, A. D. Baker)

YFB 88 (ex-LCU 1636) (U.S. Navy)

2 FERRYBOATS

Number	Number
YFB 83	YFB 87

Builders:		Draft:	
Displacement:	773 tons full load	Propulsion:	diesels; 2 shafts
Length:	180 feet (54.9 m) oa	Speed:	
Beam:	59 feet (18.0 m)	Manning:	

These are small, built-for-the-purpose ferryboats which service naval bases. Both are active.

YFB 87 (1970, U.S. Navy)

4 FERRYBOATS: CONVERTED LCU 1610 CLASS

Number	Number
YFB 88 (ex-LCU 1636)	YFB 90 (ex-LCU 1639)
YFB 89 (ex-LCU 1638)	YFB 91 (ex-LCU 1640)

Builders:	
Displacement:	~390 tons full load
Length:	134¾ feet (41.0 m) oa
Beam:	29¾ feet (9.0 m)
Draft:	6 feet (1.8 m)
Propulsion:	geared diesels (Detroit); 2,000 shp; 2 shafts
Speed:	11 knots
Manning:	6 (enlisted)

These are former LCU 1610-class landing craft modified for use as ferryboats. Their designation was changed from LCU to YFB on 1 September 1969.

1 REFRIGERATED COVERED LIGHTER

Number
YFR 888

Builders:	Defoe Shipbuilding Co, Bay City, Mich.
Displacement:	610 tons full load
Length:	132 feet (40.2 m) oa
Beam:	30 feet (9.1 m)
Draft:	
Propulsion:	diesel; 600 shp; 2 shafts
Speed:	10 knots
Manning:	11 (enlisted)

This craft is of the same design as the Navy's surviving covered lighters (YF), but is provided with refrigerated cargo space. She is now laid up in reserve.

5 COVERED LIGHTERS (RANGE TENDER)

Number	Number	Number
YFRT 287	YFRT 451	YFRT 520
YFRT 418	YFRT 523	

Builders:	YFRT 287	Norfolk Navy Yard, Va.
	YFRT 418, 520, 523	Erie Concrete and Steel Supply Co, Erie, Pa.
	YFRT 451	Basalt Rock Co, Napa, Calif.
Displacement:	650 tons full load	
Length:	132½ feet (40.4 m) oa	
Beam:	30 feet (9.1 m)	
Draft:		
Propulsion:	diesel (Union except Cooper-Bessemer in YFRT 287); 600 shp; 2 shafts	
Speed:	10 knots	
Manning:	11 (enlisted)	

These craft are used for miscellaneous support purposes. They are YF-type craft, all completed during 1941–1945 (with some originally employed in the YF role). Cargo capacity was 250 tons. The YFRT 418 is laid up in reserve; the other units are active.

Classification: The YRFT 287 and 418 originally were classified as YF, with the same hull numbers; the YFRT 523 was the YF 852.

YFRT 520 (1969, U.S. Navy)

6 HARBOR UTILITY CRAFT: CONVERTED LCU 1610 CLASS

Number	Number
YFU 83	YFU 100 (ex-LCU 1610)
YFU 97 (ex-LCU 1611)	YFU 101 (ex-LCU 1612)
YFU 98 (ex-LCU 1615)	YFU 102 (ex-LCU 1462)

Builders:	Defoe Shipbuilding Co., Bay City, Mich.
Displacement:	~390 tons full load
Length:	134¾ feet (41.0 m) oa
Beam:	29¾ feet (9.0 m)
Draft:	6 feet (1.8 m)
Propulsion:	geared diesels (Detroit); 2,000 shp; 2 shafts
Speed:	11 knots
Manning:	6 (enlisted)

Five of these craft are converted landing craft; the YFU was built to the same design specifically for the utility craft role. They carry cargo in coastal and harbor areas. All are active.

YFU 83 (1971, Defoe)

9 HARBOR UTILITY CRAFT: YFU 71 CLASS

Number	Number	Number	Number
YFU 71	YFU 74	YFU 76	YFU 79
YFU 72	YFU 75	YFU 77	YFU 81
YFU 73			

Builders:	Pacific Coast Engineering Co, Alameda, Calif.
Displacement:	
Length:	125 feet (40.9 m) oa
Beam:	36 feet (11.8 m)
Draft:	7½ feet (2.4 m)
Propulsion:	diesels; 2 shafts
Speed:	8 knots
Manning:	

These craft were constructed specifically for use as coastal cargo craft in Vietnam. They were built to a modified commercial design, with 12 units (YFU 71–82) being completed in 1967–1968. Their cargo capacity is 300 tons. The YFU 71–77 and 80–82 were transferred to the U.S. Army in 1970 for use in South Vietnam; they were returned to the Navy in 1973. The YFU 82 was converted to a research craft and is listed as the IX 506. Only the YFU 73 is active.

Guns: During their Vietnam service these craft each had two or more .50-cal MG fitted.

YFU 75 (1968, U.S. Navy)

3 HARBOR UTILITY CRAFT: CONVERTED LCU 1466 CLASS

Number
YFU 50 (ex-LCU 1486)
YFU 91 (ex-LCU 1608)
YFU 94 (ex-LCU 1488)

Builders:	Defoe Shipbuilding Co.
Displacement:	~360 tons full load
Length:	119 feet (39.0 m) oa
Beam:	34 feet (10.4 m)
Draft:	6 feet (1.8 m)
Propulsion:	geared diesels (Gray Marine); 675 shp; 3 shafts
Speed:	8 knots
Manning:	6 (enlisted)

These are converted landing craft used for harbor and coastal cargo carrying. The YFU 91 is operational; the others are laid up.

16 FUEL OIL BARGES

Number	Number	Number	Number
YO 106	YO 200	YO 223	YO 230
YO 129	YO 202	YO 224	YO 241
YO 171	YO 203	YO 225	YO 257
YO 174	YO 220	YO 228	YO 264

Builders:	YO 106, 174	Albina Engine and Machine Works, Portland, Ore.
	YO 129	Pensacola Shipyard and Engine Co, Fla.
	YO 171	R.T.C. Shipbuilding Co, Camden, N.J.
	YO 200–203	Manitowoc Shipbuilding Co, Wisc.
	YO 220–230	Jeffersonville Boat and Machinery Co, Ind.
	YO 241	John H. Mathis Co, Camden, N.J.
	YO 257	Puget Sound Navy Yard, Bremerton, Wash.
	YO 264	Leatham D. Smith Co, Sturgeon Bay, Wisc.

Displacement:	1,400 tons full load
Length:	174 feet (53.0 m) oa
Beam:	32 feet (9.8 m)
Draft:	13¹/₃ feet (4.0 m)
Propulsion:	diesels; 560 shp; 1 shaft
Speed:	10.5 knots
Manning:	11 (enlisted)

These are coastal tankers with a cargo capacity of 6,570 barrels. Eleven of these craft are active with the YO 171, 174, 228, 230, and 241 laid up.

Classification: Three craft were originally classified as gasoline barges: YO 241 ex-YOG 5, YO 257 ex-YOG 72, and YO 264 ex-YOG 105.

YO-type service craft (1970, U.S. Navy)

1 FUEL OIL BARGE

Number
YO 153

Builders:	Ira S. Bushey and Sons, Brooklyn, N.Y.
Displacement:	1,076 tons full load
Length:	156¼ feet (47.6 m) oa
Beam:	30⁷/₁₂ feet (9.3 m)
Draft:	11¾ feet (3.6 m)
Propulsion:	diesels (Fairbanks-Morse); 525 shp; 1 shaft
Speed:	10 knots
Manning:	15 (enlisted)

The YO 153 is the only survivor in U.S. service of a class of coastal and harbor tankers. Her cargo capacity is 6,000 barrels. The craft is laid up in reserve.

1 FUEL OIL BARGE

Number	Name
YO 47	CASING HEAD

Builders:	YO 47 Lake Superior Shipbuilding Co, Superior, Wisc.
Displacement:	1,731 tons full load
Length:	235 feet (71.6 m) oa

Beam:	37 feet (11.3 m)
Draft:	16½ feet (5.0 m)
Propulsion:	diesels (Enterprise); 2 shafts
Speed:	9 knots
Manning:	

This is a coastal gasoline carrier built in 1941. Its cargo capacity is 10,000 barrels. The CASING HEAD is in reserve.

8 GASOLINE BARGES

Number	Number	Number	Number
YOG 58	YOG 78	YOG 87	YOG 93
YOG 68	YOG 79	YOG 88	YOG 196

Builders:	YOG 58, 87–93 R.T.C. Shipbuilding Co, Camden, N.J.
	YOG 68 George Lawley and Sons, Neponset, Mass.
	YOG 78–79 Puget Sound Navy Yard, Bremerton, Wash.
	YOG 196 Manitowoc Shipbuilding Co, Wisc.
Displacement:	
Length:	174 feet (53.0 m) oa
Beam:	32 feet (9.8 m)
Draft:	
Propulsion:	diesel (General Motors except Union in YOG 58); 640 shp except 560 in YOG 58; 1 shaft
Speed:	
Manning:	

These are self-propelled gasoline barges with a cargo capacity of 6,570 barrels. They are virtually identical to the 174-foot fuel oil barges. The YOG 78, 87, 88, and 196 are in service; the others are in reserve. The YOG 196 was formerly designated YO 196.

YOG 78 and YW 119 (1979, Giorgio Arra)

22 SEAMANSHIP TRAINING CRAFT: YP 654 CLASS

Number	Number	Number	Number
YP 654	YP 660	YP 666	YP 672
YP 655	YP 661	YP 667	YP 673
YP 656	YP 662	YP 668	YP 674
YP 657	YP 663	YP 669	YP 675
YP 658	YP 664	YP 670	
YP 659	YP 665	YP 671	

Builders:	YP 654–663 Stephen Brothers, Stockton, Calif.
	YP 664–665 Elizabeth City Shipbuilders, N.C.
	YP 666–675 Peterson Brothers, Sturgeon Bay, Wisc.
Displacement:	69.5 tons full load
Length:	80$\frac{1}{3}$ feet (26.4 m) oa
Beam:	18$\frac{1}{3}$ feet (6.1 m)
Draft:	5$\frac{1}{3}$ feet (1.7 m)
Propulsion:	diesels (General Motors); 660 shp; 2 shafts
Speed:	13.5 knots
Manning:	

These craft are used for seamanship and navigation training at the Naval Academy in Annapolis, Md., and at the Naval Officer Candidate School and Naval Surface Warfare Officers School, both at Newport, R.I. All could be armed with machine guns and employed as harbor patrol craft.

They were built from 1965 onward, with the last three craft being authorized in FY 1977 and delivered to the Navy in 1979. A new, fiberglass hull YP design is being developed for future procurement.

Design: These craft have wood hulls with aluminum deckhouses. The YP 655 has oceanographic research equipment installed for instructional use at the Naval Academy. The design is SCB-139 (later SCB-800 in the new series).

YP 658 (U.S. Navy)

6 SEAPLANE WRECKING DERRICKS: YSD 11 CLASS

Number	Number	Number
YSD 39	YSD 63	YSD 74
YSD 53	YSD 72	YSD 77

Builders:	YSD 39	Norfolk Navy Yard
	YSD 53	Gulfport Boiler and Welding Works, Port Arthur, Texas
	YSD 63	Sonle Steel Co
	YSD 72	Omaha Steel Works
	YSD 74	Pearl Harbor Navy Yard
	YSD 77	Missouri Valley Bridge and Iron Co, Leavenworth, Kansas
Displacement:	270 tons full load	
Length:	104 feet (31.7 m) oa	
Beam:	31$\frac{1}{6}$ feet (9.5 m)	
Draft:		
Propulsion:	diesels; 640 shp; 1 shaft	
Speed:	10 knots	
Manning:	13–15 (enlisted)	

These are small, self-propelled floating cranes completed in 1943–1944. They have 10-ton-capacity cranes. All are active. YSDs are called "Mary Anns."

YP 657 off Naval Academy (U.S. Navy)

YSD 63 (1977, Giorgio Arra)

75 LARGE HARBOR TUGS: YTB 760 CLASS

Number	Name	Number	Name
YTB 760	NATICK	YTB 800	EUFAULA
YTB 761	OTTUMWA	YTB 801	PALATKA
YTB 762	TUSCUMBIA	YTB 802	CHERAW
YTB 763	MUSKEGON	YTB 803	NANTICOKE
YTB 764	MISHAWAKA	YTB 804	AHOSKIE
YTB 765	OKMULGEE	YTB 805	OCALA
YTB 766	WAPAKONETA	YTB 806	TUSKEGEE
YTB 767	APALACHICOLA	YTB 807	MASSAPEQUA
YTB 768	ARCATA	YTB 808	WEMATCHEE
YTB 769	CHESANING	YTB 809	AGAWAN
YTB 770	DAHLONEGA	YTB 810	ANOKA
YTB 771	KEOKUK	YTB 811	HOUMA
YTB 774	NASHUA	YTB 812	ACCOMAC
YTB 775	WAUWATOSA	YTB 813	POUGHKEEPSIE
YTB 776	WEEHAWKEN	YTB 814	WAXAHATCHIE
YTB 777	NOGALES	YTB 815	NEODESHA
YTB 778	APOPKA	YTB 816	CAMPTI
YTB 779	MANHATTAN	YTB 817	HYANNIS
YTB 780	SAUGUS	YTB 818	MECOSTA
YTB 781	NIANTIC	YTB 819	IUKA
YTB 782	MANISTEE	YTB 820	WANAMASSA
YTB 783	REDWING	YTB 821	TONTOGANY
YTB 784	KALISPELL	YTB 822	PAWHUSKA
YTB 785	WINNEMUCCA	YTB 823	CANONCHET
YTB 786	TONKAWA	YTB 824	SANTAQUIN
YTB 787	KITTANNING	YTB 825	WATHENA
YTB 788	WAPATO	YTB 826	WASHTUCNA
YTB 789	TOMAHAWK	YTB 827	CHETEK
YTB 790	MENOMINEE	YTB 828	CATAHECASSA
YTB 791	MARINETTE	YTB 829	METACOM
YTB 792	ANTIGO	YTB 830	PUSHMATAHA
YTB 793	PIQUA	YTB 831	DEKANAWIDA
YTB 794	MANDAN	YTB 832	PETALESHARO
YTB 795	KETCHIKAN	YTB 833	SHABONEE
YTB 796	SACO	YTB 834	NEGWAGON
YTB 797	TAMAQUA	YTB 835	SKENANDOA
YTB 798	OPELIKA	YTB 836	POKAGON
YTB 799	NATCHITOCHES		

Builders:	Marinette Marine Corp, Wisc.
	Southern SB Corp, Slidell, La.
	Mobile Ship Repair Inc., Mobile, Ala.
Displacement:	350–400 tons full load
Length:	109 feet (35.7 m) oa
Beam:	30½ feet (9.3 m)
Draft:	13½ feet (4.1 m)
Propulsion:	diesels; 2,000 shp; 2 shafts
Speed:	12.5 knots
Manning:	11–12 (enlisted)

KALISPELL—mast lowered (1979, Giorgio Arra)

CANONCHET—mast lowered (1979, Giorgio Arra)

6 LARGE HARBOR TUGS: YTB 752 CLASS

Number	Name	Number	Name
YTB 752	EDENSHAW	YTB 757	OSHKOSH
YTB 753	MARIN	YTB 758	PADUCAH
YTB 756	PONTIAC	YTB 759	BOGALUSA

Builders:	YTB 752–753 Christy Corp, Sturgeon Bay, Wisc.
	YTB 756–759 Southern Shipbuilding Corp, Slidell, La.
Displacement:	341 tons full load
Length:	85 feet (25.9 m) oa
Beam:	24 feet (7.3 m)
Draft:	13¼ feet (4.0 m)
Propulsion:	diesel; 1 shaft
Speed:	
Manning:	10–12 (enlisted)

These tugs were completed during 1961–1975. (The similar YTB 837–838 were transferred to Saudi Arabia in 1975.) All of these tugs are in active service.

Design: SCB-147A. These and other Navy harbor tugs are used for towing and maneuvering ships in harbors and coastal waters. Their masts fold down to facilitate working alongside large ships.

The tugs are also equipped for firefighting.

These tugs were completed in 1960–1961. Their design is SCB-147. All are active.

2 MEDIUM HARBOR TUGS: FORMER ARMY TUGS

Number	Name
YTM 748	YUMA
YTM 750	HACKENSACK

Builders:	National Steel and Shipbuilding Co, San Diego, Calif.
Displacement:	470 tons full load
Length:	107 feet (32.6 m) oa
Beam:	26½ feet (8.0 m)
Draft:	14⅚ feet (4.5 m)
Propulsion:	diesel; 1,200 shp; 1 shaft
Speed:	12 knots
Manning:	8 (enlisted)

These are former U.S. Army tugs, the LT 2078 and LT 2089, respectively. The HACKENSACK is in service, the YUMA laid up.

Class: The former Army tug LT 2077 was acquired by the Navy as the YTM 759. She was changed to IX 505 on 1 November 1975 and employed to support research activities, and was stricken on 1 December 1977. No name was assigned during naval service.

2 MEDIUM HARBOR TUGS: "YTM 760" CLASS

Number	Name
YTM 760	MASCOUTAH
YTM 761	MENASHA

Builders:	Jacobson Shipyard, Oyster Bay, N.Y.
Displacement:	~200 tons full load
Length:	85 feet (25.9 m) oa
Beam:	24 feet (7.3 m)
Draft:	11 feet (3.4 m)
Propulsion:	diesels; 2 cycloidal propellers
Speed:	12 knots
Manning:	8 (enlisted)

These tugs were built to an experimental design with cycloidal propellers that provide a high degree of maneuverability and enable them to turn 360° within their length. Both units are active.

Classification: These tugs were built as YTB 772–773, respectively; they were changed to YTM 760–761 in September 1965.

PADUCAH with JOHN F. KENNEDY (CV 67) (U.S. Navy)

6 SMALL HARBOR TUGS: YTL 422 CLASS

Number	Number	Number
YTL 422	YTL 434	YTL 583
YTL 431	YTL 438	YTL 602

Builders:	YTL 422, 431, 434 Everett-Pacific Shipbuilding and DD, Wash.
	YTL 583 Bellingham Iron Works, Wash.
	YTL 438, 602 Robert Jacobs Inc, City Island, N.Y.
Displacement:	80 tons full load
Length:	66⅙ feet (20.2 m) oa
Beam:	17 feet (5.2 m)
Draft:	5 feet (1.5 m)
Propulsion:	diesel; 300 shp; 1 shaft
Speed:	10 knots
Manning:	5 (enlisted)

These are the survivors of several hundred small tugs built during World War II. The YTL 431, 434, and 602 are in service; the others are laid up.

Classification: These craft originally were classified YT with the same hull numbers. YTL originally was harbor tug, "little."

MENASHA (1976, U.S. Navy, Richard A. Banks)

MASCOUTAH (YTM 760), left, and BOGALUSA (YTB 759) (1971, U.S. Navy)

7 MEDIUM HARBOR TUGS: YTM 174 CLASS

Number	Name	Number	Name
YTM 176	JUNALUSKA	YTM 381	CHEPANOC
YTM 252	DEKANISORA	YTM 382	COATOPA
YTM 359	PAWTUCKET	YTM 383	COCHALI
YTM 380	CHANAGI		

Builders:	Gulfport Boiler and Welding Works, Port Arthur, Texas
Displacement:	~200 tons full load
Length:	102 feet (31.1 m) oa
Beam:	25 feet (7.6 m)
Draft:	10 feet (3 m)
Propulsion:	diesel; 1,000 shp; 1 shaft
Speed:	12 knots
Manning:	8 (enlisted)

Two units of this class are active (YTM 252, 380); the others are in reserve.

Classification: These tugs were originally classified YT; changed to large harbor tugs (YTB) in 1944 and reclassified as YTM on 1 February 1962. (Same hull numbers as YT/YTB/YTM.)

50 MEDIUM HARBOR TUGS: YTM 138 AND YTM 518 CLASSES

Number	Name	Number	Name
YTM 149	TOKA	YTM 359	PAWTUCKET
YTM 151	KONOKA	YTM 364	SASSA
YTM 178	DEKAURY	YTM 366	WAUBANSEE
YTM 180	MADOKAWANDO	YTM 390	GANADOGA
YTM 189	NEPANET	YTM 391	ITARA
YTM 265	HIAWATHA	YTM 392	MECOSTA
YTM 268	RED CLOUD	YTM 394	WINAMAC
YTM 395	WINGINA	YTM 527	WAHPETON
YTM 397	YANEGUA	YTM 534	NADLI
YTM 398	NATAHKI	YTM 536	NAHOKE
YTM 399	NUMA	YTM 542	CHEGODOEGA
YTM 400	OTOKOMI	YTM 543	ETAWINA
YTM 403	PITAMAKAN	YTM 544	YATANOCAS
YTM 404	COSHECTON	YTM 545	ACCOHANOC
YTM 405	CUSSETA	YTM 546	TAKOS
YTM 406	KITTATON	YTM 547	YANABA
YTM 413	POROBAGO	YTM 548	MATUNAK
YTM 415	SECOTA	YTM 549	MIGADAN
YTM 417	TACONNET	YTM 701	ACOMA
YTM 496	CHAHAO	YTM 702	ARAWAK
YTM 521	NABIGWON	YTM 704	MORATOC
YTM 522	SAGAWAMICK	YTM 768	APOHOLA
YTM 523	SENASQUA	YTM 770	MIMAC
YTM 524	TUTAHACO	YTM 776	HIAMONEE
YTM 526	WAHAKA	YTM 779	POCASSET

Builders:	Defoe Boiler & Machine Works, Bay City, Mich.; Gibbs Gas Engine Co, Jacksonville, Fla.; Pacific Coast Engineering Co, Oakland, Calif.; Gulfport Boiler & Welding Works, Port Arthur, Texas; Consolidated SB Corp, Morris Heights, N.Y.; Ira S. Bushey & Sons, Brooklyn, N.Y.; Coast Guard Yard, Curtis Bay, Md.; Bethlehem Steel Co, San Pedro, Calif.; Commercial Iron Works, Portland, Ore.
Displacement:	
Length:	100 feet (30.5 m) oa
Beam:	25 feet (7.6 m)
Draft:	9⁷/₁₂ feet (3.0 m)
Propulsion:	diesel; 1,000 shp; 1 shaft
Speed:	14 knots
Manning:	8 (enlisted)

These are harbor tugs employed at most U.S. naval bases. Plans to construct additional YTMs (initially YTM 800–802, authorized in FY 1973) were dropped in favor of additional YTB construction. Mosts units are active, with 18 laid up in reserve. All were built in 1940–1945.

Classification: These craft originally were classified as large harbor tugs (YTB) with the same hull numbers, except YTM 768 ex-YTB 502, YTM 770 ex-YTB 507, YTM 513 ex-YTB 513, and YTM 779 ex-YTB 516.

ETAWINA (1975, Giorgio Arra)

11 WATER BARGES

Number	Number	Number	Number
YW 83	YW 101	YW 119	YW 127
YW 86	YW 108	YW 123	YW 128
YW 98	YW 113	YW 126	

Builders:	YW 83	John H. Mathis Co, Camden, N.J.
	YW 86, 108	Zenith Dredge Co, Duluth, Minn.
	YW 98	George Lawley and Sons, Neponset, Mass.
	YW 101	Mare Island Navy Yard, Vallejo, Calif.
	YW 113	Marine Iron and Shipbuilding Co, Duluth, Minn.
	YW 119	Henry C. Grebe and Co, Chicago
	YW 123, 126–128	Leathem D. Smith Shipbuilding Co, Sturgeon Bay, Wisc.

Displacement:	1,235 tons full load
Length:	174 feet (53.0 m) oa
Beam:	32 feet (9.7 m)
Draft:	15 feet (4.6 m)
Propulsion:	diesel; 560 shp; 1 shaft
Speed:	8 knots
Manning:	

These craft are similar to the YO/YOG types, but are employed to carry fresh water. Cargo capacity is 200,000 gallons. Four craft are in service (YW 113, 119, 123, 128); the others are laid up.

YW 119 (1976, Giorgio Arra)

2 RESEARCH CRAFT: "ASHEVILLE CLASS"

Number	Name	Launched	PGM Commission	Status
(ex-PG 94)	ATHENA I	8 June 1968	8 Nov 1969	**AA**
(ex-PG 98)	ATHENA II	4 Apr 1970	5 Sep 1970	**AA**

Builders:	Tacoma Boatbuilding Co, Wash.
Displacement:	~245 tons full load
Length:	164½ feet (50.1 m) oa
Beam:	23¾ feet (7.3 m)
Draft:	9½ feet (2.9 m)
Propulsion:	2 diesels (Cummins), 1,750 shp; 1 gas turbine (General Electric), 14,000 shp; 2 shafts (controllable-pitch propellers)
Speed:	16 knots on diesels; 40+ knots on gas turbine
Manning:	(civilian contractor)
Guns:	removed

These are former ASHEVILLE-class patrol combatants/gunboats. They were transferred to the Naval Ship Research and Development Center on 21 August 1975 and 3 October 1977, respectively, for use in towing high-speed underwater shapes in research and development programs.

Classification: No hull classifications are assigned in their current role.

Names: Renamed in 1975 and 1977, respectively; formerly the CHEHALIS and GRAND RAPIDS.

ATHENA I (foreground) and ATHENA II (1980, U.S. Navy)

1 DRONE RECOVERY CRAFT: FORMER MOTOR TORPEDO BOAT

Number	Name	Launched	PT in Service	Status
DR-1 (ex-PT 809)	RETRIEVER	7 Aug 1950	1950	**AA**

Builders:	Electric Boat Co, Groton, Conn.
Displacement:	125 tons full load
Length:	98 feet 6 in (30.0 m)
Beam:	26 feet (7.9 m)
Draft:	7 feet (2.1 m)
Propulsion:	4 diesel (General Motors); 4 shafts
Speed:	22–25 knots
Manning:	14 (1 O + 13 enlisted)
Guns:	removed

The DR-1 was originally one of four experimental torpedo boats (PT 809–812) built as prototypes for post–World War II PT boats. After extensive trials and limited service, the PT 809 was laid up in reserve. She was subsequently reactivated and employed to carry Secret Service agents screening the presidential yacht on the Potomac River (based at the Washington Navy Yard). The craft was named GUARDIAN in that role.

In December 1974 the craft was transferred to Fleet Composite Squadron 6 at Little Creek, Va., for operation as a recovery boat for aerial drones and a control boat for surface target drone craft. She was designated DR-1 (for Drone Recovery) and named RETRIEVER on 1 July 1975.

Design: The DR-1 is all-aluminum construction. As a PT she carried four over-the-side torpedo launchers plus 20-mm and 40-mm guns.

RETRIEVER (1980, U.S. Navy, courtesy VC-6)

2 RESEARCH SHIPS: Ex-MINESWEEPERS

Number	Name	FY/SCB	Launched	In service	Status
(MSI 1)	COVE	56/136	8 Feb 1958	22 Nov 1958	**Academic**
(MSI 2)	CAPE	56/136	5 Apr 1958	27 Feb 1959	**Academic**

Builders:	Bethlehem Steel Co, Bellingham, Wash.
Displacement:	120 tons light
	240 tons full load
Length:	105 feet (32.0 m) oa
Beam:	22 feet (6.7 m)
Draft:	10 feet (3.0 m)
Propulsion:	diesel (General Motors); 650 shp; 1 shaft
Speed:	12 knots
Manning:	

These were prototype inshore minesweepers. After several years of service in the MSI role they were assigned to research tasks. Both are now operated by the Johns Hopkins Applied Physics Laboratory.

Additional MSIs have been built specifically for foreign transfer.

CAPE as MSI 2 (1968, U.S. Navy)

1 RANGE SUPPORT SHIP: SWATH DESIGN

Number	Name	Launched	In service	Status
. . . .	KAIMALINO	7 Mar 1973	1973	Conv.

Builders:	Coast Guard Yard, Curtis Bay, Md.
Displacement:	190 tons full load
Length:	88 feet (26.8 m) oa
Beam:	45 feet (13.7 m)
Draft:	
Propulsion:	2 gas turbines (General Electric); 4,200 shp; 2 shafts
Speed:	25 knots
Manning:	

The Stable Semi-submerged Platform (SSP) KAIMALINO is an experimental design craft employed in the range support role at the Naval Ocean Systems Center's underwater test range in Hawaii. After several years of successful trials and service, during 1980–1981 the KAIMALINO was rebuilt to enlarge the underwater hulls and main structure. The above characteristics are as built; in her new configuration the KAIMALINO displaces some 600 tons.

Aircraft: The KAIMALINO has been used extensively to test the feasibility of landing helicopters on an SSP/SWATH-type ship in high sea states at speeds up to 25 knots. Operations with an SH-2F LAMPS were completely successful.

Design: The SSP is a Small Waterplane Area Twin-Hull (SWATH) craft developed to test this hull concept with a craft of about 200 tons. The SWATH has two fully submerged, torpedo-shaped hulls, each 6½-feet in diameter, with vertical struts penetrating the water surface to support the superstructure and flight deck. The flight deck area in the original configuration was 61 by 45 feet.

The SSP/SWATH concept differs from that of a catamaran, which has two conventional ship hulls. The SWATH design provides a comparatively large deck area with a minimum of heave, pitch, and roll. In a sea state 6 the craft acts about the same as a larger, conventional destroyer would in a sea state 4. Tests indicate the SWATH design would be suitable for ships up to about 20,000 tons. Ship motion for such a vessel in seas up to state 10 is considered minimal.

The KAIMALINO has a hull-stabilizing fin connecting the two submerged hulls and two small canard fins forward, one inboard on each hull. There is an opening in the craft's main deck for lowering research and recovery devices. (The opening is covered over for helicopter operations.) The beam listed is the maximum over both torpedo-shaped hulls.

Engineering: Two T64 aircraft-type gas turbine engines provide propulsion power.

KAIMALINO under construction (1973, U.S. Navy)

KAIMALINO with SH-2F (1976, U.S. Navy)

KAIMALINO (U.S. Navy)

1 EXPERIMENTAL SURFACE EFFECT SHIP: BELL AEROSYSTEMS DESIGN

Number	Name	Launched	Commissioned	Status
SES-100 B	(unnamed)	6 Mar 1971	Feb 1972	**Test**

Builders:	Bell Aerosystems, Michoud, La.
Displacement:	100 tons gross
Length:	77¾ feet (23.7 m) oa
Beam:	35 feet (10.7 m)
Draft:	
Propulsion:	3 gas turbines (Pratt & Whitney); 13,500 shp; 2 semisubmerged super-cavitating propellers
Lift:	3 gas turbines (United Aircraft of Canada); 1,500 shp; 8 horizontal fans
Speed:	80+ knots
Manning:	4 + 6 observers

The SES-100B was built as a competitive prototype with the SES-100A to test surface-effect-ship concepts for the Navy in preparation for the large, 2,000–3,000-ton SES (see page 113). The 100-ton SES program was initiated in January 1969 as a joint Navy–Maritime Administration effort; however, MarAd withdrew in 1971, partly because it could not provide the required funding.

The SES-100B was developed by the Bell Aerosystems Division of the Textron Corporation and constructed at Bell Aerosystem's Michoud facility (a part of the National Aeronautics and Space Administration's assembly complex). The launch date above is the date of formal christening.

The craft reached a speed of 91.9 knots during trials in Chesapeake Bay on 25 January 1980. The SES-100B was also used for missile firing tests and vertically launched an SM-1 missile while traveling 60 knots.

Cost: Estimated cost to construct the SES-100B is $14 million.

Design: The craft is constructed of aluminum and has a 10-ton cargo capacity. No SCB number is assigned.

Missiles: During April 1976 the SES-100B was used to test vertical launch techniques for the use of the Standard SM-1 missile in a surface-to-surface role. A successful launch was made at a speed of 60 knots.

Propulsion: The SES has three FT12A-6 propulsion engines and three ST6J-70 lift engines.

SES-100B (U.S. Navy, 1976, Dave Wilson)

1 EXPERIMENTAL SURFACE EFFECT SHIP: AEROJET-GENERAL DESIGN

Number	Name	Launched	Completed	Status
SES-100A	(unnamed)	24 July 1971	May 1972	Stripped

Builders:	Tacoma Boatbuilding Co, Wash.
Displacement:	72.8 tons light
	100 tons gross
Length:	81¹¹/₁₂ feet (24.9 m) oa
Beam:	41¹¹/₁₂ feet (21.7 m)
Draft:	10¹/₃ feet (3.22 m) hullborne
Propulsion:	4 gas turbines (Avco Lycoming); 12,000 shp; 2 waterjets
Lift:	3 horizontal fans (interconnected to propulsion engines)
Speed:	80+ knots (designed)
Manning:	4 + 6 observers

The SES-100A was developed by the Aerojet-General Corporation as a competitive prototype with the SES-100B. The launch date above is the christening date.

The SES-100A was essentially dismantled during 1979–1980 after completion of planned trials.

Cost: Estimated construction cost was $18 million.

Design: The SES-100A is constructed of aluminum. The craft has a 10-ton cargo capacity. Protruding outboard from each sidewall just below the displacement condition waterline are a stabilizer (forward, directly under "SES-100A") and a steering skeg (amidships, abaft the after end of the cabin). No SCB number is assigned.

Propulsion: The craft is fitted with TF-35 engines which are marine versions of the T55-L-11A aircraft engine. The SES-100A reached 76 knots on trials in 1973.

The Navy is testing the commercial Bell-Halter 110 surface effects ship during 1981 at the SES Test Facility at the Patuxent River Naval Air Station. The craft is 110 feet in length, has a beam of 39 feet, and is capable of reaching 40 knots.

SES-100A (U.S. Navy, 1976)

19 Submersibles

Several submersibles are operated by the U.S. Navy to support search, rescue, research, and deep-ocean recovery activities. These craft have also been used to maintain sea-floor test range and surveillance equipment.

Submarine Development Group 1 at San Diego operates the bathyscaph TRIESTE, the rescue submersibles MYSTIC and AVALON, and the research submersibles TURTLE and SEA CLIFF. SubDevGru-1 also operates the submarines SEAWOLF (SSN 575) and PARCHE (SSN 683), the support ship POINT LOMA (AGDS 2), the research submarine DOLPHIN (AGSS 555), and the submarine rescue ships FLORIKAN (ASR 9) and PIGEON (ASR 21).

Submarine Squadron 2 at Groton, Conn., operates the nuclear submersible NR-1 as well as a number of attack submarines. The research submersible ALVIN is operated by the Woods Hole Oceanographic Institution in Mass.

(1) NUCLEAR-PROPELLED RESEARCH SUBMERSIBLE: HTV DESIGN

Displacement:
Length: 153 feet (46.6 m) oa
Beam: 14½ feet (4.4 m)
Draft:
Propulsion: electric motors
Reactors: 1 pressurized water
Speed:
Operating depth: 3,000+ feet (914.4+ m)
Manning:

The so-called Hull Test Vehicle (HTV) was originally proposed as the NR-2 in 1976 by Adm. H. G. Rickover, Deputy Commander for Nuclear Propulsion, Naval Sea Systems Command, to provide a deep-ocean test platform for a nuclear reactor. Subsequently the craft was redesignated HTV to emphasize its use of HY-130 steel. The steel used in PERMIT (SSN 594) and later deep-diving submarines is HY-80; the HY-130, originally proposed but not used for the LOS ANGELES (SSN 688) class.

Adm. Rickover first requested funding for the NR-2 in late 1976, seeking $130 million to build the craft. Neither the Navy nor Congress supported the program at that time. Detailed design of the HTV began in FY 1979. Actual construction has been delayed, with a start now scheduled for 1986. This could permit the use of HY-130 steel in the combat submarines constructed in the mid-1990s (i.e., the class after the mid-1980s FA-SSN).

The NR-1 was built as a test platform for a small submarine nuclear power plant. The craft has a deep-ocean research and recov-

1 NUCLEAR-PROPELLED RESEARCH SUBMERSIBLE: NR-1

Number	Name	Launched	Completed	Status
NR-1	(none)	25 Jan 1969	1969	**AA**

Builders: General Dynamics (Electric Boat), Groton, Conn.
Displacement: 400 tons submerged
Length: 136⁵/₁₂ feet (41.6 m) oa
Beam: 12⁵/₁₂ feet (3.8 m)
Draft: 12 feet (3.7 m)
Propulsion: electric motors; 2 shafts
Reactors: 1 pressurized-water
Speed:
Operating depth: ~3,000 feet (914.4 m)
Crew: 5 (2 O + 3 enlisted) + 2 scientists

ery capability. The craft was funded as a nuclear-propulsion effort and was laid down on 10 June 1967. She is commanded by an officer-in-charge rather than a commanding officer.

Classification: NR-1 indicates Nuclear Research vehicle although the craft is officially listed as a submersible research vehicle (see Appendix A).

Costs: The estimated cost of the NR-1 in 1965 was $30 million, using "state of the art" equipment. Subsequently, specialized equipment had to be developed and a hull larger than the one originally intended was designed, with congressional approval of a cost of $58 million being given in 1967. The estimated cost of the NR-1 when launched in 1969 was $67.5 million plus $19.9 million for oceanographic equipment and sensors, and $11.8 million for research and development, a total cost of $99.2 million. No final cost data have been released by the Navy.

Design: The NR-1 does not have periscopes, but instead has a fixed mast with a top-mounted television camera. The craft is fitted with external lights, a remote-control manipulator, and recovery devices.

Engineering: The NR-1 is propelled by twin propellers driven by electric motors outside of the pressure hull. Four ducted thrusters, two horizontal and two vertical, give the NR-1 a capability for precise maneuvering.

Operations: Published reports credit the NR-1 with having been used to maintain sea-floor equipment and to recover items sunk at great depths. In 1976 the NR-1 helped to recover an F-14 Tomcat fighter armed with a Phoenix missile that rolled off the deck of the carrier JOHN F. KENNEDY (CV 67) and came to rest at a depth of 1,960 feet off the coast of Scotland.

NR-1 (1976, U.S. Navy, Jean Pellegrino)

NR-1 at launching (1969, General Dynamics/Electric Boat)

NR-1 under tow (U.S. Navy)

2 DEEP SUBMERGENCE RESCUE VEHICLES

Number	Name	Launched	Completed	Status
DSRV-1	MYSTIC	24 Jan 1970	6 Aug 1971	**PA**
DSRV-2	AVALON	1 May 1971	28 July 1972	**PA**

Builders:	Lockheed Missiles and Space Co, Sunnyvale, Calif.
Weight:	37 tons
Length:	49²/₃ feet (15 m) oa
Diameter:	8 feet (2.4 m)
Propulsion:	electric motor; 1 propeller-mounted in control shroud (see Engineering notes)
Speed:	4 knots
Operating depth:	5,000 feet (1,524 m)
Crew:	3 + 24 rescued

These submersibles were developed after the loss of the submarine THRESHER (SSN 593) in 1963 to provide a capability for rescuing survivors from submarines disabled on the ocean floor above their hull-collapse depth. Initially 12 rescue vehicles were planned, each capable of carrying 12 survivors. Subsequently, their capacity was increased to 24 survivors and the proposed number of DSRVs was reduced to six. Only two have been built and no additional units are planned. After extensive tests and evaluation, both DSRVs were declared fully operational in late 1977.

Costs: The estimated construction cost of the DSRV-1 was $41 million, and the DSRV-2 cost $23 million. The total development, construction, test, and support for these craft have cost in excess of $220 million.

Design: The DSRV consists of three interconnected personnel spheres, each 7½ feet in diameter, constructed of HY-140 steel, encased in a fiberglass-reinforced plastic shell. The forward sphere contains the vehicle's controls and is manned by the pilot and co-pilot; the center and after spheres can accommodate 24 survivors and a third crewman.

The DSRV is configured to be launched and recovered by a submerged attack submarine or by a PIGEON (ASR 21)-class submarine rescue ship. After launching, the DSRV can descend to the disabled submarine, "mate" with one of the submarine's escape hatches, take on board up to 24 survivors, and return to the "mother" submarine or ASR. The submersible can be air-transported in C-141 aircraft, and ground-transported by a special trailer. It is fitted with a remote-control manipulator.

Electronics: The DSRV is fitted with elaborate search and navigation sonars, closed-circuit television, and optical viewing devices for locating a disabled submarine and mating with the hatches.

Engineering: The DSRVs have a single propeller driven by a 15 hp electric motor for forward propulsion. The propeller is in a rotating control shroud which alleviates the need for rudders and diving planes (which could interfere with a rescue mission). Four ducted thrusters, two vertical and two horizontal, each powered by a 7½ hp electric motor, provide precise maneuvering. The craft has an endurance of five hours at a speed of 4 knots.

Names: Names were assigned in 1977.

Operational: The DSRV rapid-deployment concept was tested in 1978 and again in 1979. In 1978 the MYSTIC was flown from San Diego to Norfolk, Va., and to New London, Conn., in a C-5A transport and deployed aboard U.S. attack submarines; in 1979 the AVALON was flown by C-5A from San Diego to Glasgow, Scotland, for deployment aboard the British SSBN REPULSE.

AVALON aboard HMS REPULSE in the Firth of Clyde (1979, U.S. Navy)

AVALON aboard HMS REPULSE (1979, U.S. Navy)

AVALON being unloaded from C-5A transport at Glasgow, Scotland; the DSRV "mating skirt" is removed for truck/air transport. Note the trainable propeller shroud at the DSRV's stern; the dark, circular opening is one of the ducted thrusters. After being transported to port, a DSRV can be carried to sea aboard a modified SSN/SSBN, or one of the PIGEON (ASR 21)-class submarine rescue ships, or towed to sea by a tug-type ship. (1979, U.S. Navy)

2 RESEARCH SUBMERSIBLES: MODIFIED "ALVIN" CLASS

Number	Name	Launched	Completed	Status
DSV-3	TURTLE	11 Dec 1968	1969	**PA**
DSV-4	SEA CLIFF	11 Dec 1968	1969	Conv.

Builders:	General Dynamics Corp (Electric Boat), Groton, Conn.
Weight:	21 tons
Length:	26 feet (7.9 m) oa
Beam:	8 feet (2.4 m); 12 feet (3.7 m) over propeller pods
Propulsion:	electric motor; 1 propeller (see Engineering notes)
Speed:	2.5 knots
Operating depth:	10,000 feet (3,048 m) for TURTLE; 20,000 feet (6,096 m) for SEA CLIFF
Crew:	2 + 1 scientist

These are small submersibles used for deep-ocean research. They were originally constructed using an HY-100 steel test sphere and an HY-100 replacement sphere originally fabricated for the ALVIN. Their operating depth with the HY-100 spheres was 6,500 feet; subsequently, in 1979 the TURTLE was refitted with a modified sphere providing a 10,000-foot operating depth and the SEA CLIFF was to be fitted with a titanium sphere in 1981–1982 for 20,000-foot operations.

Classification: These craft were designated DSV-3 and DSV-4 on 1 June 1971.

Design: The original HY-100 steel spheres were seven feet in diameter. A light, fiberglass outer hull is fitted to the spheres. The craft have closed-circuit televison, external lights, sonars, cameras, and hydraulic remote-control manipulators.

These craft can be transported by C-5A transports.

Engineering: A single stern propeller is fitted for ahead propulsion and two pod-mounted external electric motors rotate for ma-

neuvering. No thrusters are fitted. Endurance is one hour at 2.5 knots and eight hours at one knot.

Names: During construction these submersibles were named the AUTEC I and II, respectively, because they were initially to be used to support the Navy's Atlantic Undersea Test and Evaluation Center (AUTEC). The names TURTLE and SEA CLIFF were assigned at their joint launching.

SEA CLIFF (U.S. Navy)

SEA CLIFF being loaded in a C-5A transport. (U.S. Navy)

1 RESEARCH SUBMERSIBLE: "ALVIN"

Number	Name	Launched	Completed	Status
DSV-2	ALVIN	5 June 1964	1965	**Academic**

Builders:	General Mills Inc, Minneapolis, Minn.
Weight:	16 tons
Length:	22½ feet (6.9 m) oa
Beam:	8 feet (2.4 m); 12 feet (3.7 m) over propeller pods
Propulsion:	electric motor; 1 propeller (see Engineering notes)
Speed:	2 knots
Operating depth:	13,124 feet (4,000 m)
Crew:	1 + 2 scientists

The ALVIN is operated by the Woods Hole Oceanographic Institution for the Office of Naval Research, which sponsored construction of the craft.

The ALVIN accidentally sank in 5,051 feet of water on 16 October 1968 and her sphere was flooded (there were no casualties). She was raised in August 1969 and refurbished from May 1971 to October 1972, and became operational in November 1972.

Classification: Classified DSV-2 on 1 June 1971.

Design: As built, the ALVIN had a single, 7-foot-diameter pressure sphere made of HY-100 steel, which gave her a 6,000-foot operating depth. She was refitted with a titanium sphere in 1971–1972, which increased her capabilities. She is fitted with a remote-control manipulator.

Engineering: See the TURTLE and SEA CLIFF for propulsion and maneuvering arrangement.

Operational: The ALVIN made her 1,000th dive on 15 January 1980. The dive was part of NOAA studies of the intersection of the Ecuador Rift just north of the equator in the Pacific Ocean.

ALVIN (U.S. Navy)

1 BATHYSCAPH RESEARCH VEHICLE: "TRIESTE"

Number	Name	Launched	Completed	Status
DSV-1	TRIESTE II	(see comments)	1966	**PA**

Builders:	Mare Island Naval Shipyard, Vallejo, Calif.
Displacement:	84 tons surface (empty)
	300 tons submerged
Length:	78 feet (23.8 m) oa
Beam:	15 feet (4.6 m); 18¾ feet (5.7 m) over propeller pods
Propulsion:	electric motors; 3 propeller pods aft
Speed:	2 knots
Operating depth:	20,000 feet (6,096 m)
Crew:	2 + 1 scientist

The TRIESTE is the U.S. Navy's only "bathyscaph" (from the Greek for "deep boat") designed to travel straight up and down in the water rather than maneuver like a submarine.

The original TRIESTE was built by Auguste Piccard in Italy and launched on 1 August 1953. That vehicle was acquired by the Navy in 1958 and, piloted by Lieutenant Don Walsh, USN, and Jacques Piccard, reached a depth of 35,800 feet on 23 January 1960. The craft was rebuilt in 1963–1964 at the Mare Island Naval Shipyard, with a new sphere replacing the deep-dive Krupp chamber and a new float provided. In this configuration the craft was renamed TRIESTE II. The craft was again rebuilt in 1965–1966 and modified in 1967, all at Mare Island. Thus, the current vehicle is the "third generation-plus" bathyscaph.

The TRIESTE II is transported and supported by the POINT LOMA (AGDS 2). The craft has been scheduled to be retired about 1982 when the SEA CLIFF is available for operations to 20,000 feet.

Classication: The TRIESTE originally was classified as an unnumbered "submersible craft." She was assigned the hull number X-2 on 1 September 1969 and was subsequently changed to DSV-1 on 1 June 1971. (The X-1 was an unnamed midget submarine, the only craft of this type built for the U.S. Navy. The X-1 was stricken on 16 February 1973.)

Design: The TRIESTE II has a single, 7-foot-diameter pressure sphere, made of HY-120 steel. Originally rated for 12,000 feet, with the updating of certain subsystems the sphere and vehicle are now capable of 20,000-foot operations. The sphere is mounted at the bottom of a float-like hull which is filled with aviation gasoline to provide buoyancy. External lights, sonars, cameras, and a remote-control manipulator are fitted to the bottom of the float . "Leg"-like structures on each side of the sphere prevent it from sinking into the ocean floor and blocking the viewport (forward).

Engineering: The craft has three 6.5-hp electric motor pods at her stern for propulsion and limited maneuvering, and one 6.5-hp bow thruster for holding position in currents and for precise maneuvering. Her endurance is eight hours at two knots.

Names: The TRIESTE was Piccard's name for the original craft.

TRIESTE II (U.S. Navy)

TRIESTE II (U.S. Navy)

20 Floating Dry Docks

The Navy operates floating dry docks at several bases in the United States and overseas for the repair and maintenance of ships. These are non-self-propelled docks, but all have electrical generators to provide power for their tools and equipment. Normally they operate with a flotilla of non-self-propelled barges that provide specialized services, including messing and berthing for the ships being dry docked.

The floating dry docks are arranged in this chapter in alphabetical order according to their classification. Technically they are con-

sidered service craft. Unless otherwise indicated, all sectional docks are assembled.

Those docks in active Navy service have their locations indicated; several others are operated by commercial firms under lease from the Navy, and the Coast Guard has one dock at its shipyard near Baltimore, Md.

Guns: No floating docks are armed, although many were designed to mount light antiaircraft weapons.

7 LARGE AUXILIARY FLOATING DRY DOCKS

Number	Sections	Name	Completed	Length	Width	Capacity	Construction	Status	Notes
AFDB 1	B-C-D-E-F	ARTISAN	1943	~500 ft (152.4 m)	256 ft (78.0 m)	50,000 tons	steel	Subic Bay, Philippines	5 sections disposed of; ex-ABSD 1
AFDB 2	10		1944	927 ft (282.5 m)	256 ft (78.0 m)	90,000 tons	steel	reserve	ex-ABSD 2
AFDB 3	9		1944	844 ft (257.3 m)	256 ft (78.0 m)	81,000 tons	steel	reserve	ex-ABSD 3
AFDB 4	7		1944	825 ft (251.5 m)	240 ft (73.2 m)	55,000 tons	steel	reserve	ex-ABSD 4
AFDB 5	7		1944	825 ft (251.5 m)	240 ft (73.2 m)	55,000 tons	steel	reserve	ex-ABSD 5
AFDB 7	C-D		1944	~260 ft (79.2 m)	240 ft (73.2 m)	20,000 tons	steel	Norfolk, Va.	ex-ABSD 7
AFDB 7	A-B-E-G	LOS ALAMOS	1944	~420 ft (128.0 m)	240 ft (73.2 m)	40,000 tons	steel	Holy Loch, Scotland	1 section disposed of; ex-ABSD 7

These docks formerly were classified as Advanced Base Sectional Docks (ABSD). They consist of 256- or 240-feet sections, about 80 feet wide with wing walls 83 feet high. The walls house accommodations, machinery, and storage spaces, and fold down for towing. The docks are assembled by the sections being connected

side by side. The overall length of the assembled docks includes a 50-foot outrigger at each end.

Most of these docks originally were classified as Auxiliary Floating Docks (AFD) or Auxiliary Repair Docks—Concrete (ARDC).

WHITE PLAINS (AFS 4) in ARTISAN (AFDB 1) (1975, U.S. Navy, PH1 R. H. Green)

7 SMALL AUXILIARY FLOATING DRY DOCKS

Number	Name	Completed	Length	Width	Capacity	Construction	Status	Notes
AFDL 1	Endeavor	1943	200 ft (61 m)	64 ft (19.5 m)	1,000 tons	steel	Guantanamo Bay, Cuba	ex-AFD 1
AFDL 2		1943	200 ft (61 m)	64 ft (19.5 m)	1,000 tons	steel	lease	ex-AFD 2
AFDL 6	Dynamic	1944	200 ft (61 m)	64 ft (19.5 m)	1,000 tons	steel	Little Creek, Va.	ex-AFD 6
AFDL 7	Ability	1944	288 ft (87.8 m)	64 ft (19.5 m)	1,900 tons	steel	Guam	ex-AFD 7
AFDL 8		1943	200 ft (61 m)	64 ft (19.5 m)	1,000 tons	steel	lease	ex-AFD 8
AFDL 9		1943	200 ft (61 m)	64 ft (19.5 m)	1,000 tons	steel	lease	ex-AFD 9
AFDL 10		1943	200 ft (61 m)	64 ft (19.5 m)	1,000 tons	steel	lease	ex-AFD 10
AFDL 11		1943	200 ft (61 m)	64 ft (19.5 m)	1,000 tons	steel	lease	ex-AFD 11
AFDL 12		1943	200 ft (61 m)	64 ft (19.5 m)	1,000 tons	steel	lease	ex-AFD 12
AFDL 15		1943	200 ft (61 m)	64 ft (19.5 m)	1,000 tons	steel	lease	ex-AFD 15
AFDL 16		1943	200 ft (61 m)	64 ft (19.5 m)	1,000 tons	steel	lease	ex-AFD 16
AFDL 19		1944	200 ft (61 m)	64 ft (19.5 m)	1,000 tons	steel	lease	ex-AFD 19
AFDL 21		1944	200 ft (61 m)	64 ft (19.5 m)	1,000 tons	steel	lease	ex-AFD 21
AFDL 23	Adept	1944	288 ft (87.8 m)	64 ft (19.5 m)	1,900 tons	steel	Subic Bay, Philippines	ex-AFD 23
AFDL 25		1944	200 ft (61 m)	64 ft (19.5 m)	1,000 tons	steel	U.S. Army	ex-AFD 25
AFDL 29		1944	200 ft (61 m)	64 ft (19.5 m)	1,000 tons	steel	lease	ex-AFD 29
AFDL 35		1944	389 ft (118.6 m)	84 ft (25.6 m)	2,800 tons	concrete	reserve	ex-ARDC 2
AFDL 37		1944	389 ft (118.6 m)	84 ft (25.6 m)	2,800 tons	concrete	lease	ex-ARDC 4
AFDL 38		1944	389 ft (118.6 m)	84 ft (25.6 m)	2,800 tons	concrete	lease	ex-ARDC 5
AFDL 40		1944	389 ft (118.6 m)	84 ft (25.6 m)	2,800 tons	concrete	lease	ex-ARDC 7
AFDL 41		1944	389 ft (118.6 m)	84 ft (25.6 m)	2,800 tons	concrete	lease	ex-ARDC 8
AFDL 45		1944	389 ft (118.6 m)	84 ft (25.6 m)	2,800 tons	concrete	lease	ex-ARDC 12
AFDL 47	Reliance	1946	448 ft (140.6 m)	97 ft (30.4 m)	6,500 tons	steel	being reactivated	ex-ARD 33
AFDL 48	Diligence	1956	402 ft (126.2 m)	96 ft (30.1 m)	4,000 tons	concrete	Long Beach, Calif.	

Ability (AFDL 7) in reserve with mothballed yard tug on blocks inside (U.S. Navy)

AFDL 21 under tow (U.S. Navy)

LCU in DYNAMIC (AFDL 6) (1975, Giorgio Arra)

4 MEDIUM AUXILIARY FLOATING DRY DOCKS

Number	Name	Completed	Length	Width	Capacity	Construction	Status	Notes
AFDM 1		1942	544 ft (165.8 m)	116 ft (35.4 m)	15,000 tons	steel	lease	3 sections; ex-YFD 3
AFDM 2		1942	544 ft (165.8 m)	116 ft (35.4 m)	15,000 tons	steel	lease	3 sections; ex-YFD 4
AFDM 3	ENDURANCE	1943	552 ft (168.2 m)	124 ft (37.8 m)	18,000 tons	steel	lease	3 sections; ex-YFD 6
AFDM 5	RESOURCEFUL	1943	552 ft (168.2 m)	124 ft (37.8 m)	18,000 tons	steel		3 sections; ex-YFD 21
AFDM 6	COMPETENT	1944	552 ft (168.2 m)	124 ft (37.8 m)	18,000 tons	steel	Subic Bay, Philippines	3 sections; ex-YFD 62
AFDM 7	SUSTAIN	1945	552 ft (168.2 m)	124 ft (37.8 m)	18,000 tons	steel	Norfolk, Va.	3 sections; ex-YFD 63
AFDM 8	RICHLAND	1944	552 ft (168.2 m)	124 ft (37.8 m)	18,000 tons	steel	Guam, Marianas	3 sections; ex-YFD 64
AFDM 9		1945	552 ft (168.2 m)	124 ft (37.8 m)	18,000 tons	steel	lease	3 sections; ex-YFD 65
AFDM 10		1945	552 ft (168.2 m)	124 ft (37.8 m)	18,000 tons	steel	lease	3 sections; ex-YFD 67

These docks all originally were classified as floating dry docks (YFD), informally known as yard floating dry docks.

SSBN in RICHLAND (AFDM 8) (Robert Fudge)

COMPETENT (AFDM 6) (U.S. Navy)

3 AUXILIARY REPAIR DOCKS

Number	Name	Completed	Length	Width	Capacity	Construction	Status
ARD 5	WATERFORD	1942	485²/₃ ft (148 m)	71 ft (21.6 m)	3,500 tons	steel	New London, Conn.
ARD 7	WEST MILTON	1943	485²/₃ ft (148 m)	71 ft (21.6 m)	3,500 tons	steel	New London, Conn.
ARD 12		1943	491²/₃ ft (149.9 m)	81 ft (24.7 m)	3,500 tons	steel	lease
ARD 30	SAN ONOFRE	1944	491²/₃ ft (149.9 m)	81 ft (24.7 m)	3,600 tons	steel	Pearl Harbor, Hawaii
ARD 32		1944	491²/₃ ft (149.9 m)	81 ft (24.7 m)	3,500 tons	steel	lease

4 MEDIUM AUXILIARY REPAIR DOCKS

Number	Name	Completed	Length	Width	Capacity	Construction	Status	Notes
ARDM 1	OAK RIDGE	1944	536 ft (163.4 m)	81 ft (24.7 m)	3,500 tons	steel	King's Bay, Ga.	ex-ARD 19
ARDM 2	ALAMOGORDO	1944			3,500 tons	steel	Charleston, S.C.	ex-ARD 26
ARDM 3		1944			5,500 tons	steel	Charleston, S.C.	ex-ARD 18
ARDM 4	SHIPPINGPORT	1978	492 ft (150 m)	96 ft (29.3 m)	7,800 tons	steel	New London, Conn.	FY 1975 program

The ARDM 1–3 were extensively modified from Auxiliary Repair Docks (ARD) to support ballistic misssile submarines. The SHIPPINGPORT was built specifically to support SSBNs. Launched on 2 September 1977, at Bethlehem, Sparrows Point, Md.

The OAK RIDGE was moved from Rota, Spain, to King's Bay, Ga., to support Submarine Squadron 16 when that unit shifted in 1979.

SSBN in OAK RIDGE (ARDM 1) (U.S. Navy)

Strategic missile submarine base in action: In the foreground is the floating dry dock OAK RIDGE (ARDM 1) docking an SSBN; in the background are the CANOPUS (AS 34), arriving, and the HOLLAND (AS 32), at Rota, Spain. Note the revolving crane on the HOLLAND compared to the later view on page 235. Submarine Squadron 16, with its support ships, has since shifted to King's Bay, Ga. (1966, U.S. Navy)

PHILADELPHIA (SSN 690) in SHIPPINGPORT (ARDM 4) at New London (U.S. Navy, Jean Russell)

BOW DRY DOCKS

The bow dry dock program (YBD 1–4) was canceled in 1979. These docks were to be 104 feet long and 84 feet wide, and would have permitted the partial docking of surface combatants for maintenance on SQS-23/26/53 bow sonar domes.

The four-dock program was canceled because of reduced maintenance requirements on the sonar domes and the need to fully dock ships for other reasons. (See 11th edition, page 247, for additional details.)

2 YARD FLOATING DRY DOCKS

Number	Completed	Length	Width	Capacity	Construction	Status	Notes
YFD 7	1943	552 ft (168.2 m)	124 ft (37.8 m)	18,000 tons	steel	lease	3 sections
YFD 8	1942	587¼ ft (180 m)	132½ ft (40.4 m)	20,000 tons	wood	lease	6 sections
YFD 23	1943	472 ft (143.9 m)	114 ft (34.7 m)	10,500 tons	wood	lease	6 sections
YFD 54	1943	352 ft (107.3 m)	90 ft (27.4 m)	5,000 tons	wood	lease	1 section
YFD 68	1945	528 ft (160.9 m)	118 ft (36 m)	14,000 tons	steel	lease	3 sections
YFD 69	1945	528 ft (160.9 m)	118 ft (36 m)	14,000 tons	steel	lease	3 sections
YFD 70	1945	528 ft (160.9 m)	118 ft (36 m)	14,000 tons	steel	lease	3 sections
YFD 71	1945	528 ft (160.9 m)	118 ft (36 m)	14,000 tons	steel	San Diego, Calif.	3 sections
YFD 83	1943	200 ft (61 m)	64 ft (19.5 m)	1,000 tons	steel	U.S. Coast Guard; Curtis Bay, Md.	ex-AFDL 31

21 Naval Aviation

U.S. Naval Aviation operates approximately 5,550 aircraft, more than any of the world's air forces except those of the United States, Soviet Union, and China. Included in the generic term "naval aviation" is the air arm of the U.S. Marine Corps, which is the only marine force in the world with a major aviation component. (Britain's Royal Marines, who fly helicopters, are believed to be the only other marine force with an aviation component.)

The following table lists the aircraft as of September 1980 (the end of FY 1980) including Marine and reserve components. "Pipeline" aircraft are those in major rework, overhaul, or en route to or from operational units.

Status	Type	Number
Operating Aircraft	Fighter	714
	Attack	1,060
	Antisubmarine	144
	Patrol	386
	Early Warning	112
	Transport	173
	Tanker	43
	Observation	74
	Training	952
	Drone Control	8
	Utility	53
	Helicopter	1,213
Pipeline		623

A large number of fixed-wing aircraft and helicopters are dedicated to providing basic and advanced flight training to Navy, Marine Corps, and Coast Guard fliers as well as to a few foreign aviators. In addition, first-line aircraft are assigned to Navy and Marine Corps "readiness" or combat training squadrons that ready pilots and air crewmen for combat squadrons. (Although the Navy trains Coast Guard pilots, Coast Guard aircraft are not a part of Naval Aviation.)

The following pages describe the organizational aspects of Naval Aviation. Most units are designated by two systems of abbreviations, pronounceable acronyms and simpler, letter-number combinations. Thus, Training Squadron Eight is known as both TraRon-Eight and as VT-8.

The V prefix for naval aircraft types and units dates back to 1922 when V indicated heavier-than-air and Z meant lighter-than-air blimps or airships. The V and Z were used for ships as well as aircraft and air organizations, hence CV for aircraft carriers, AV for seaplane tenders, AZ for airship tenders, VF for fighter squadrons,

ZP for patrol airships, etc. (The last U.S. Navy airship, a ZPG-2W, was decommissioned in 1962.) Subsequently, H was introduced as the helicopter type letter in 1943 for aircraft (HNS-1) and for squadrons in 1947 (HMX-1; followed in 1948 by HU-1 and HU-2).

The following V and H designations are in current use; for Marine Corps squadrons an M is indicated immediately after the V or H. The T suffix added to Marine squadrons indicates training units.

HC	Helicopter Combat Support
HM	Helicopter Mine Countermeasures
MHA	(Marine) Helicopter Attack
HMH	(Marine) Heavy Helicopter
HML	(Marine) Light Helicopter
HMM	(Marine) Medium Helicopter
HMX	(Marine) Helicopter
HS	Helicopter Antisubmarine
HSL	Light Helicopter Antisubmarine
HT	Helicopter Training
VA	Attack
VAK	Tanker
VAQ	Tactical Electronic Warfare
VAW	Carrier Airborne Early Warning
VC	Fleet Composite
VF	Fighter
VFP	Light Photographic
VMA	(Marine) Attack
VMA (AW)	(Marine) Attack (All Weather)
VMAQ	(Marine) Electronic Warfare
VMFA	(Marine) Fighter-Attack
VMFP	(Marine) Photo Reconnaissance
VMGR	(Marine) Refueller-Transport
VMO	(Marine) Observation
VP	Patrol
VQ	Fleet Air Reconnaissance
VR	Fleet Logistics Support
VRC	Fleet Logistics Support (COD)
VRF	Aircraft Ferry
VS	Air Antisubmarine
VT	Training
VX	Air Test and Evaluation
VXE	Antarctic Development
VXN	Oceanographic Development

Other major naval aviation organizational abbreviations include:

CVW	Carrier Air Wing
CVWR	Reserve Carrier Air Wing
H&MS	(Marine) Headquarters & Maintenance Squadron
MAW	Marine Aircraft Wing
MCAF	Marine Corps Air Facility (Quantico, Va.)
MCAS	Marine Corps Air Station
NAEC	Naval Air Engineering Center (Lakehurst, N.J.)
NAF	Naval Air Facility
NARU	Naval Air Reserve Unit

An F-4J Phantom from Fighter Squadron 161—the"Chargers"—and an A-7E Corsair from Attack Squadron 56—the "Champions"—look over a Soviet An-12 Cub reconnaissance aircraft over the Indian Ocean. The Cub has civilian (Aeroflot #11875) markings, but is flying a reconnaissance mission over U.S. naval forces. The Sidewinder-armed Phantom has standard carrier aircraft markings; the 106 indicates the sixth plane of the first squadron (VF); the "E" is a squadron efficiency award; the "stars and bars" (white star with blue circle and outline and red bars) has been the national insignia since 1947; after fuselage markings include name of carrier, "Navy," the aircraft type (F-4J), and aircraft "bureau" number (from old Bureau of Aeronautics)—158374. On the tail are the air wing code (NF for CVW-5), lightning bolt from the squadron's insignia, and 06 for the sixth plane in the squadron. Color codes also identify units. See page 285 for additional details on naval aircraft markings. (1980, U.S. Navy)

NAS	Naval Air Station
NAVFAC	Naval Facility
PatWing	Patrol Wing

Although carrier air wings were established on 23 December 1963 in place of carrier air groups, the term CAG (for Commander, Air Group) is still widely used in the Fleet to designate the wing commander.

ORGANIZATION

All aviation units belong to an administrative organization, with most units also under tactical organizations. For example, a patrol squadron is administratively under a patrol wing, and while forward deployed it would be under a numbered fleet (task force) commander.

The administrative organization is headed by the Deputy Chief of Naval Operations (Air Warfare) and extends through the Commanders, Naval Air Force Atlantic (NavAirLant) and Pacific (NavAirPac) and their respective wing commanders. The following are the principal administrative wing organizations. Carrier-based squadrons report through their wing (CVW) when assigned to a carrier, and through their "type command" when ashore, e.g., VA-34 to CVW-1 when aboard ship and to Medium Attack Wing 1 when ashore.

Naval Air Force Atlantic Fleet

Air Antisubmarine Wing 1	NAS Cecil Field, Fla.
Airborne Early Warning Wing 12	NAS Norfolk, Va.
Carrier Air Wings 1, 3, 6, 7, 8, 17	
Fighter Wing 1	NAS Oceana, Va.
Fleet Tactical Support Wing 1	NAS Norfolk, Va.

Helicopter Antisubmarine Wing 1 — NAS Jacksonville, Fla.
Helicopter Sea Control Wing 1 — NAS Norfolk, Va.
Light Attack Wing 1 — NAS Cecil Field, Fla.
Medium Attack Wing 1 — NAS Oceana, Va.
Patrol Wing 5 — NAS Brunswick, Maine
Patrol Wing 11 — NAS Jacksonville, Fla.
Patrol Wings Atlantic — NAS Brunswick, Maine
Sea Based Antisubmarine Wings Atlantic — NAS Jacksonville, Fla.
Tactical Wings Atlantic — NAS Oceana, Va.

Naval Air Force Pacific Fleet

Antisubmarine Wing Pacific — NAS North Island (San Diego), Calif.

Carrier Air Wings 2, 5, 9, 11, 14, 15
Fighter/Airborne Early Warning Wing Pacific — NAS Miramar, Calif.
Fleet Air Western Pacific — NAS Atsugi, Japan
Light Attack Wing Pacific — NAS Lemoore, Calif.
Medium Attack Wing/Tactical Electronic Warfare Wing Pacific — NAS Whidbey, Wash.
Patrol Wing 1 — NAVFAC Kamiseya, Japan
Patrol Wing 2 — NAS Barber's Point, Hawaii
Patrol Wings Pacific — NAS Moffett Field, Calif.

AirLant and AirPac wings and squadrons have two-letter identification codes. The system was established on 11 July 1946 and revised on 1 June 1957 to the current fleet "split," with the first letter indicating the fleet assignment: A to M for Atlantic and N to Z for Pacific. The letters I and O are not used to avoid confusion with numerals; AF was dropped because of confusion with the Air Force (used by Carrier Air Group 6, which then took AE code letters, previously used for a brief period by Carrier Air Group 13). Carrier wing and squadron assignments change periodically; the intensive U.S. carrier deployments to the Indian Ocean that began in late 1979 and the SLEP modernizations have exacerbated these changes. The following tables are based on late 1980 carrier assignments.

CARRIER AIR WINGS

CVW	Code	Ship	VF	VA	VAQ	VAW	VS	HS
1	AB	Kennedy	14 32	34 46 72	138	126	32	11
2	NE	Ranger	21 154	25 113 145	137	117	29	2
3	AC	Saratoga	31 103	37 75 105		123	22	7
5	NF	Midway	151 161	56 93 115	136	115		

CVW	Code	Ship	VF	VA	VAQ	VAW	VS	HS
6	AE	Independence	33 102	15 87 176	130	122	28	15
7	AG	Eisenhower	142 143	12 65 66	132	121	31	5
8	AJ	Nimitz	41 84	35 82 86	134	112	24	9
9	NG	Constellation	24 211	146 147 165	132	116	37	8
11	NH	Enterprise	114 213	95 192 195	131	124	33	12
14	NK	Coral Sea	VMFA 323 531	27 97 196		113		
15	NL	Kitty Hawk	51 111	22 52 94	135	114	21	
17	AA	Forrestal	11 74	81 83 85	133	125	30	3

LIGHT ATTACK SQUADRONS

Squadron	Code	Name	Squadron	Code	Name
VA-12	AG	Flying Ubangis	VA-86	AJ	Sidewinders
VA-15	AE	Valions	VA-87	AE	Golden Warriors
VA-22	NL	Fighting Redcocks	VA-93	NF	Ravens
VA-25	NE	Fist of the Fleet	VA-94	NL	Mighty Shrikes
VA-27	NK	Royal Maces	VA-97	NK	Warhawks
VA-37	AC	Bulls	VA-105	AC	Gladiators
VA-45	AD	Blackbirds	VA-113	NE	Stingers
VA-46	AB	Clansmen	VA-122	NJ	Flying Eagles
VA-56	NF	Champions	VA-127	NJ	Royal Blues
VA-66	AG	Waldomen	VA-146	NG	Blue Diamonds
VA-72	AB	Blue Hawks	VA-147	NG	Argonauts
VA-81	AA	Sunliners	VA-174	AD	Hell Razors
VA-82	AJ	Marauders	VA-192	NH	Golden Dragons
VA-83	AA	Rampagers	VA-195	NH	Dam Busters

Each carrier air wing has two squadrons flying A-7E Corsair attack aircraft. The squadrons are designated VA although they are considered light attack units and the Corsair was developed in a VAL design competition. All 24 squadrons are scheduled to convert to the F/A-18 Hornet during the late 1980s and early 1990s.

There are four light attack readiness squadrons; VA-174 provides East Coast A-7 transition and VA-122 the same on the West Coast, while VA-45 on the East Coast and VA-127 on the West Coast provide instrument, navigation, and air combat training, mainly with Skyhawks.

East Coast VA squadrons report to Light Attack Wing 1 while West Coast squadrons are under the command of Light Attack Wing Pacific.

MEDIUM ATTACK SQUADRONS

Squadron	Code	Name	Squadron	Code	Name
VA-34	AB	Blue Blasters	VA-95	NH	Green Lizards
VA-35	AJ	Black Panthers	VA-115	NF	Eagles
VA-42	AD	Green Pawns	VA-128	NJ	Golden Intruders
VA-52	NL	Knightriders	VA-145	NE	Swordsmen
VA-65	AG	Tigers	VA-165	NG	Boomers
VA-75	AC	Sunday Punchers	VA-176	AE	Thunderbolts
VA-85	AA	Black Falcons	VA-196	NK	Main Battery

One medium attack squadron (designated VA, not VAM) is assigned to each carrier air wing. These squadrons all fly ten A-6E Intruder all-weather attack aircraft, with most also being assigned four KA-6D tanker aircraft. The latter are scheduled to be replaced in the late 1980s by a new tanker (KX). The leading candidates are a tanker based on the EA-6B airframe (KA-6H) or new production KS-3 Viking aircraft.

The A-6 readiness squadrons are VA-42 and VA-128. Atlantic squadrons report to Medium Attack Wing 1 at NAS Oceana while Pacific A-6 units are under Medium Attack/Tactical Electronic Warfare Wing Pacific at NAS Whidbey Island, Wash.

TACTICAL ELECTRONIC WARFARE SQUADRONS

Squadron	Code	Name	Squadron	Code	Name
VAQ-33	GD	Fire Birds	VAQ-134	AJ	Garudas
VAQ-129	NJ	Vikings	VAQ-135	NL	Ravens
VAQ-130	AE	Zappers	VAQ-136	NF	Gauntlets
VAQ-131	NH	Lancers	VAQ-137	NE	Rooks
VAQ-132	AG	Scorpions	VAQ-138	AB	Yellowjackets
VAQ-133	AA	Wizards			

There are nine carrier-based VAQ squadrons, three short of the Navy's requirement for one such unit for each carrier air wing. These squadrons each fly four EA-6B Prowler aircraft in the tactical jamming role.

VAQ-129 provides EA-6B readiness training. VAQ-33 provides electronic warfare support to the Atlantic and Pacific Fleets, flying EA-6B Prowlers, an ERA-3B Skywarrior, an NC-121K Warning Star, and EA-4F aircraft. (The C-121 was the militarized version of the Lockheed Super Constellation; the Navy flew a number of EC-121s in the AEW role.) All VAQ-33 aircraft are used to simulate Soviet ECM/EW/radar transmissions. The squadron, based at NAS Key West, Fla., discarded two EF-4J Phantoms in 1980.

VAQ-33 is under Tactical Support Wing 1; all other VAQ squadrons are part of Medium Attack/Tactical Electronic Warfare Wing Pacific at NAS Whidbey Island (code NJ). Some VAQ squadrons are former heavy attack squadrons (VAH), having changed their designation when they shifted from the EKA-3B to EA-6B aircraft in the late 1960s.

Each carrier air wing has an AEW squadron of four E-2B or E-2C Hawkeye aircraft, with the latter variant scheduled for all squad-

AIRBORNE EARLY WARNING SQUADRONS

Squadron	Code	Name	Squadron	Code	Name
RVAW-110	TT	Firebirds	RVAW-120	GE	Hummers
VAW-112	AJ	Golden Hawks	VAW-121	AG	Bluetails
VAW-113	NK	Black Eagles	VAW-122	AE	Steeljaws
VAW-114	NL	Hawgs	VAW-123	AC	Screw Tops
VAW-115	NF	Sentinels	VAW-124	NH	Bear Aces (1980)
VAW-116	NG	Sun Kings	VAW-125	AA	Tiger Tails
VAW-117	NE	Wall Bangers	VAW-126	AB	Seahawks

rons. Readiness training is provided by RVAW-110 for Pacific squadrons and RVAW-120 for Atlantic units. RVAW-110's Detachment 4 flew the Navy's last E-1B Tracers from the FRANKLIN D. ROOSEVELT (CV 42) in 1977.

Carrier AEW Wing 12 at NAS Norfolk controls AEW squadrons in the Atlantic and Fighter/AEW Wing Pacific for that fleet. The current VAW squadron structure dates from 1967, when seven squadrons numbered in sequence were established in each fleet. Note the R in the designation of the AEW readiness squadrons, the only such units with that designation prefix.

FLEET COMPOSITE SQUADRONS

Squadron	Code	Name	Aircraft
VC-1	UA	Unique Antiques	A-4E, TA-4J, SH-3G, VP-3A
VC-3	UF	Iron Men	DC-130A
VC-5	UE	Checkertails	TA-4J, SH-3G
VC-6	JG	Skeeters	none assigned
VC-8	GF	Redtails	EP-2H, TA-4J, SH-3G
VC-10	JH	Crusaders	TA-4J

Composite squadrons provide a variety of utility services for the Fleet including noncombat photography, target tow, radar calibration, and transport. Their aircraft include a variety of types, the principal ones being listed above.

VC-1 flies from Barber's Point, Oahu; VC-3, based at NAS North Island, flies DC-130A Hercules to launch aerial drones; VC-3 at Cubi Point in the Philippines provides services to ships deployed in the Western Pacific; VC-6 at Norfolk flies no aircraft, but operates aerial and surface target drones for the Fleet; and VC-8 at Roosevelt Roads, Puerto Rico, provides services to Atlantic Fleet units training in the Caribbean area, as does VC-10 at Guantanamo Bay, Cuba. VC-10 is the only composite squadron with a combat mission, being responsible for air support in the event of a Cuban attack against the U.S. base.

VC-10 was to be decommissioned during 1981. VC-2 at NAS Oceana (code JE) flying TA-4J Skyhawks, and VC-7 at NAS Miramar (code UH) flying A-4F and TA-4J Skyhawks were decommissioned in 1980.

Pacific VC squadrons have the initial letter U in their codes, recalling their former designations as "utility" squadrons, while Atlantic squadrons have the J from the old utility squadron designation VJ. The Pacific squadrons are assigned to Fighter/AEW Wing

Pacific except for VC-5 at Cubi Point, Philippines, which is under Fleet Air Western Pacific. The Atlantic VC squadrons are under Tactical Support Wing 1. (HU/VU became HC/VC on 1 July 1965.)

FIGHTER SQUADRONS

Squadron	Code	Name	Squadron	Code	Name
*VF-1	NK	Wolfpack	VF-102	AE	Diamondbacks
*VF-2	NK	Bounty Hunters	*VF-103	AC	Sluggers
*VF-11	AA	Red Rippers	*VF-111	NL	Sundowners
*VF-14	AB	Tophatters	*VF-114	NH	Aardvarks
VF-21	NE	Freelancers	VF-124	NJ	Gunfighters
*VF-24	NG	Fighting Red	VFA-125	NJ	
		Checkertails	VF-126	NJ	Fighting Sea Hawks
*VF-31	AC	Tomcatters	*VF-142	AG	Ghostriders
*VF-32	AB	Swordsmen	*VF-143	AG	Puking Dogs
VF-33	AE	Tarsiers	VF-151	NF	Vigilantes
*VF-41	AJ	Black Aces	VF-154	NE	Black Knights
VF-43	AD	Challengers	VF-161	NF	Chargers
*VF-51	NL	Screaming Eagles	VF-171	AD	Aces
VF-74	AA	Bedevilers	*VF-211	NG	Checkmates
*VF-84	AJ	Jolly Rogers	*VF-213	NH	Black Lions
VF-101	AD	Grim Reapers			

* Fly the F-14 Tomcat

The Navy has 24 fighter squadrons assigned to 12 carrier air wings. In 1980 16 of the squadrons flew the F-14 Tomcat, with VF-33 and VF-102 transitioning to the F-14 during 1981. The other squadrons fly the F-4J/S Phantom. CVW-14 "beached" VF-1 and VF-2 when the wing deployed aboard the CORAL SEA (CV 43) in 1979–1980, because the ship could not accommodate F-14s. Two Marine F-4 squadrons took their place. From 1984 onward the six remaining F-4 squadrons are scheduled to convert to the F/A-18 Hornet. Subsequently, assuming full F/A-18 procurement, some F-14 squadrons will probably convert as they lose aircraft through attrition.

In addition to these 24 squadrons, VF-43 provides East Coast Air Combat Maneuvering (ACM), instrument, and spin training with A-4E/F and TA-4J Skyhawk, F-5E Tiger, T-38 Talon, and T-2A Buckeye aircraft; VF-126 fulfills a similar function on the West Coast; VF-101 is the East-Coast F-14 readiness squadron; VF-124 transitions F-14 pilots on the West Coast; and VF-171 is the F-4 readiness squadron, also providing ACM training in A-4E and TA-4J aircraft. The Navy's Fighter Weapons School (Top Gun), operating F-5E/F, A-4E, and T-38 aircraft, was established in September 1969 to develop realistic adversary tactics and training for Navy fliers. It was started by VF-121 and became a separate command on 1 July 1972. VF-121, the West Coast F-4 readiness squadron, was decommissioned on 26 September 1980. It was the first F-4 squadron.

Fighter Attack Squadron 125 was commissioned on 13 November 1980 as the F/A-18 readiness squadron for Navy and Marine pilots.

All East Coast VF activities are controlled by Fighter Wing 1 at NAS Oceana, Va., while West Coast VF activities come under Fighter/AEW Wing Pacific at NAS Miramar (San Diego), Calif.

LIGHT PHOTOGRAPHIC SQUADRONS

Squadron	Code	Name
VFP-63	PP	Eyes of the Fleet

VFP-63 provides the Navy's only carrier-based photographic reconnaissance capability. The squadron provides five three-plane detachments of RF-8G Crusader aircraft to most forward-deployed carriers. The shortage of these aircraft has required the assignment of RF-4B Phantoms from VMFP-3 to the MIDWAY (CV 41). The RF-8G aircraft will be replaced in the CV/CVN air wings from 1981 onward by RF-14 Tomcat fighters carrying a Tactical Air Reconnaissance Pod System (TARPS). The RF-14s will be assigned to fighter squadrons and will retain a Sparrow/Sidewinder missile capability in the recce role. Subsequently, a reconnaissance variant of the F/A-18 Hornet is expected to be developed for service from the mid-1980s onward.

VFP-63, based at NAS Miramar, Calif., is assigned to Fighter/Airborne Early Warning Wing Pacific.

PATROL SQUADRONS

Squadron	Code	Name	Squadron	Code	Name
VP-1	YB	Fleets Finest	VP-24	LR	Batmen
VP-4	YD	Skinny Dragons	VP-26	LK	Tridents
VP-5	LA	Mad Foxes	VP-30	LL	Crow's Nest
VP-6	PC	Blue Sharks	VP-31	RP	The Genies
VP-8	LC	Tigers	VP-40	QE	Fighting Marlins
VP-9	PD	Golden Eagles	VP-44	LM	Golden Pelicans
VP-10	LD	Red Lancers	VP-45	LN	Pelicans
VP-11	LE	Proud Pegasus	VP-46	RC	Gray Knights
VP-16	LF	Eagles	VP-47	RD	Golden Swordsmen
VP-17	ZE	White Lightning	VP-48	SF	Boomerangers
VP-19	PE	Big Red	VP-49	LP	Woodpeckers
VP-22	QA	Blue Goose	VP-50	SG	Blue Dragons
VP-23	LJ	Sea Hawks	VP-56	LQ	Dragons

The Navy's 24 first-line patrol squadrons each fly nine P-3B/C Orion patrol aircraft. The last squadron with the P-3A was VP-44, which completed conversion to the P-3C in November 1978. Sixteen squadrons flew the P-3C in 1980, with the remaining squadrons scheduled to convert to that aircraft by 1987. Operational East Coast squadrons are assigned to Patrol Wing 5 at Brunswick, Maine, and PatWing-11 at Jacksonville, Fla. Their Orion squadrons deploy in the Atlantic and Mediterranean areas. On the West Coast, operational squadrons are assigned to PatWings Pacific at NAS Moffett near San Francisco and PatWing-2 at Barber's Point on Oahu, Hawaii. PatWing-1 at Kamiseya, Japan, directs VP squadrons that rotate to the Western Pacific. VP-30 at Brunswick and VP-31 at Moffett provide Orion readiness training.

FLEET AIR RECONNAISSANCE SQUADRONS

Squadron	Code	Squadron	Code
VQ-1	PR	VQ-3	TC
VQ-2	JQ	VQ-4	HL

VQ-1 and VQ-2 provide electronic surveillance in direct support of fleet operations and carry out special reconnaissance along the borders of foreign territory. VQ-1 at Agana, Guam, and VQ-2 at Rota, Spain, both fly EP-3B/E Orions and EA-3B Skywarriors, the latter aircraft being assigned to forward-deployed carriers. An ES-3 variant of the Viking has been proposed as a successor to the aging Skywarrior.

VQ-3 and VQ-4 fly specially equipped EC-130G/Q Hercules to provide LF/VLF communications relay to strategic missile submarines under a program known as TACAMO (Take Charge and Move Out). VQ-3, at Agana, has about four aircraft assigned and VQ-4, at Patuxent River, Md., has seven and is able to provide one aircraft airborne and a second ready for almost immediate takeoff on a continuous basis. The remainder of the 14 available aircraft are in overhaul. Three additional EC-130Q aircraft were funded in FY 1980 and will be delivered during the latter half of 1982, permitting VQ-3 to maintain one aircraft airborne on a continuous basis. An additional EC-130Q is provided in the FY 1981 budget.

Lockheed and Boeing have proposed various aircraft configured for the TACAMO role for procurement beginning in the mid- to late-1980s.

FLEET LOGISTIC SUPPORT SQUADRONS

Squadron	Code	Name	Squadron	Code	Name
VR-24	JM	World's Biggest Little Airline	VRC-40	CD	
			VRC-50	RG	Cod-Fish Airlines
VRC-30	RW	Truckin' Traders			

These squadrons transport passengers and high-priority cargo in direct support of Fleet operations. They fly the C-1A Trader, C-2A Greyhound, C-9B Skytrain II, CT-39 Sabreliner, and C-130 Hercules aircraft. In addition, VR-24 also flew three RH-53D Sea Stallion helicopters during the late 1970s for Vertical Onboard Delivery (VOD), with those being reassigned to HM squadrons after the aborted Tehran rescue operation in April 1980.

A fifth logistics support squadron, VR-1, which had been commissioned on 9 March 1942, was decommissioned in October 1978.

VR-24 at Sigonella, Sicily, is under Fleet Air Mediterranean; VRC-30 at NAS North Island is under ASW Wing Pacific; VRC-40 at NAS Norfolk is under Tactical Support Wing 1; and VRC-50 at Cubi Point in the Philippines reports to Fleet Air Pacific. All formerly Fleet Tactical Support Squadrons; changed on 1 April 1976.

AIRCRAFT FERRY SQUADRONS

Squadron	Code	Name
VRF-31	(none)	Storkline

VRF-31 provides pilots to transfer Navy and Marine Corps aircraft throughout the world. The squadron is based at NAS Norfolk under Tactical Support Wing 1.

AIR ANTISUBMARINE SQUADRONS

Squadron	Code	Name	Squadron	Code	Name
VS-21	NL	Fighting Red Tails	VS-31	AG	Top Cats
VS-22	AC	Checkmates	VS-32	AB	Yellow Tails
VS-24	AJ	Duty Cats	VS-33	NH	Screwbirds
VS-28	AE	Hukkers	VS-37	NG	Rooster-Tails
VS-29	NE	Vikings	VS-38	NK	Red Griffins
VS-30	AA	Diamond Cutters	VS-41	RA	Shamrocks

The Navy's 11 operational air ASW squadrons each fly ten S-3A Viking aircraft. They are assigned to air wings aboard all carriers except the older MIDWAY (CV 41) and CORAL SEA (CV 43), which do not have ASW coordination centers and are too small to accommodate the additional aircraft squadron.

VS-41 handles all S-3A readiness training. Squadrons on the East Coast come under Air ASW Wing 1 at NAS Cecil Field, and those on the West Coast under ASW Wing Pacific at NAS North Island.

TRAINING SQUADRONS

Squadron	Code	Name	Aircraft	Training
VT-2	E	The Doer Birds	T-28B/C, T-34C	Primary/Intermediate
VT-3	E	Red Knights	T-2C, TA-4J	Primary/Intermediate
VT-4	F	Rubber Ducks	T-2C, TA-4J	Intermediate/Strike
VT-6	E	(none)	T-28B/C, T-34C	Primary/Intermediate
VT-7	A	Eagles	TA-4J	Strike
VT-9	A	Tigers	T-2C	Intermediate
VT-10	F	Cosmic Rats	T-2C, T-39D	Basic/Intermediate NFO
VT-19	A	Fighting Frogs	T-2C	Intermediate
VT-21	B	Red Hawks	TA-4J	Strike
VT-22	B	King Eagles	TA-4J	Strike
VT-23	B	The Professionals	T-2C	Intermediate
VT-24	C	Bobcats	TA-4J	Strike
VT-25	C	Cougars	TA-4J	Strike
VT-26	C	Tigers	T-2C	Intermediate
VT-27	D	Boomers	T-28B	Primary/Intermediate
VT-28	D	Rangers	T-44A	Maritime
VT-31	D	Wise Owls	T-44A	Maritime
VT-86	F	Sabre Hawks	TA-4J, T-39D	Advanced NFO

These 18 squadrons provide training for Navy, Marine Corps, Coast Guard, and foreign pilots and air crewmen under direction of the Naval Air Training Command. The last US-2B and TS-2A Trackers were retired from VT-28 and VT-31 in 1979 with introduction of the T-44A. Single code letters indicate training wings: A for TraWing-1, B for TraWing-2, etc. Note that VT-9 and VT-26 are both "Tigers." VT-27 was not decommissioned in 1979 as previously scheduled.

AIR TEST AND EVALUATION SQUADRONS

Squadron	Code	Name
VX-1	JA	ASW Pioneers
VX-4	XF	Vanguards
VX-5	XE	Vampires

These squadrons test and evaluate weapon systems. VX-1 at NAS Patuxent River, Md., specializes in ASW systems under Sea-Based ASW Wings Atlantic; VX-4 at Point Mugu, Calif., specializes in fighter weapons and tactics under Fighter/AEW Wing Pacific; and VX-5 at China Lake, Calif., supports air-to-surface weapons and tactics development under the administrative control of Light Attack Wing Pacific. The squadrons fly a variety of operational and test aircraft. Note that two specialized development squadrons—VXE-6 and VXN-8—are numbered in the basic VX series.

ANTARCTIC DEVELOPMENT SQUADRONS

Squadron	Code	Name
VXE-6	XD	Puckered Penguins

VXE-6, home-ported at Point Mugu, Calif., operates ski-equipped C-130F Hercules and UH-1 Huey helicopters in support of Navy and national Antarctic research programs. The squadron was commissioned as Air Development Squadron 6 (VX-6) on 17 January 1955; subsequently redesignated to indicate its specialized role. The Navy has operated aircraft in the Antarctic since 1928 when Commander (later Rear Admiral) R. E. Byrd took three aircraft on his expedition to the South Pole.

OCEANOGRAPHIC DEVELOPMENT SQUADRONS

Squadron	Code	Name
VXN-8	JB	World Travelers

VXN-8 at NAS Patuxent River operates two RP-3D Orion aircraft in support of world-wide research projects: Project Magnet is a gravity and geomagnetic study; Project Birdseye is an ice reconnaissance and physical oceanography study; and Project Seascan is an aerial oceanographic effort. A P-3A is assigned to the squadron for training. The squadron is assigned to Tactical Support Wing 1.

RECONNAISSANCE HEAVY ATTACK SQUADRONS

The last RVAH squadron was decommissioned in September 1979, ending the reconnaissance/attack era aboard U.S. aircraft carriers. There were ten RVAH squadrons from 1964 onward, all flying the RA-5C Vigilante in a multi-sensor mode. Eight of those squadrons were previously heavy attack (VAH) units, flying the AJ/A-2 Savage and A3D/A-3 Skywarrior attack planes. The supersonic A3J Vigilante heavy attack aircraft began entering squadron service with VAH-3 in June 1961; however, difficulties with the Vigilante's internal (tunnel) weapons delivery system and the availability of small nuclear weapons that could be carried by other carrier aircraft rapidly led to reconfiguration of all Vigilantes for high-speed reconnaissance (A3J-3P/RA-5C). A secondary nuclear strike capability was retained (up to four Mk 28 or Mk 43 nuclear weapons on wing pylons).

The ten RVAH squadrons were assigned to Reconnaissance Attack Wing 1 (established on 1 February 1951 as Heavy Attack Wing 1). The squadrons deployed as four- and later three-plane units to carriers except for RVAH-3, which served as the Vigilante readiness training squadron from 1958 on. The accompanying table lists the RVAH squadrons and their previous designations. The old heavy attack force consisted of VAH-1 through 11, 13, plus two tanker units, VAH-15 and VAH-16, and VAH-123 for readiness training. The composite squadrons (VC) established from 1948 on initially flew the P2V-3C Neptune and then the AJ Savage to provide the Navy's first nuclear strike capability.

The last RA-5C squadron was RVAH-7, which made its final deployment in the RANGER (CV 61), returning to San Diego on 15 September 1979. RVAH-7 was decommissioned on 30 September 1979 at its home base of NAS Key West, Fla., and Reconnaissance Heavy Attack Wing 1 was decommissioned on 7 January 1980.

HELICOPTER COMBAT SUPPORT SQUADRONS

Squadron	Code	Name	Squadron	Code	Name
HC-1	UP	Pacific Fleet Angels	HC-11	VR	Gunbearers
HC-3	SA	Packrats	HC-16	BF	
HC-6	HW	Chargers			

These squadrons provide helicopters for Search and Rescue (SAR) and VERTREP/VOD operations in direct support of the Fleet. In addition, HC-1 provides SAR helicopters for carrier deployments. The VERTREP requirement calls for 26 detachments of two helicopters each. HC-16, formerly HCT-16, provides readiness training for Sea Knight crewmen.

The principal aircraft flown by these squadrons are variants of

VP-3 to VAH-1 on 1 Nov 1955	to RVAH-1 on 1 Sep 1964	decomm. 29 Jan 1979	Tigers
VP-34 to VAH-3 on 15 June 1956	to RVAH-3 on 1 July 1964	decomm. 17 Aug 1979	Sea Dragons
VC-5 to VAH-5 on 3 Feb 1956	to RVAH-5 on May 1964	decomm. 30 Sep 1977	Savage Sons
VC-6 to VAH-6 on 1 July 1956	to RVAH-6 on 23 Sep 1965	decomm. 20 Oct 1978	Fleurs
VC-7 to VAH-7 on 1 July 1955	to RVAH-7 on 1 Dec 1964	decomm. 28 Sep 1979	Peacemakers of the Fleet
VC-9 to VAH-9 on Nov 1955	to RVAH-9 on 3 June 1964	decomm. 30 Sep 1977	Hoot Owls
VC-8 to VAH-11 on 1 Nov 1955	to RVAH-11 on July 1966	decomm. 1 June 1975	Checkertails
RVAH-12 comm. 1 July 1965		decomm. 2 July 1979	Speartips
VAH-13 comm. 3 Jan 1961	to RVAH-13 on 1 Nov 1964	decomm. 30 June 1976	Bats
RVAH-14 comm. 1 Feb 1968		decomm. 1 May 1974	

the H-46, plus lesser numbers of the UH-1N Huey and SH-3G Sea King.

All helicopter utility squadrons (HU) were changed to HC on 1 July 1965. The genesis of these squadrons was VX-3, the Navy's first helicopter squadron, established in 1947. The following year it was split into HU-1 and HU-2, on the East and West Coasts, respectively.

HELICOPTER MINE COUNTERMEASURES SQUADRONS

Squadron	Code	Name
HM-12	DH	Seadragons
HM-14	BJ	Vanguard
HM-16	GC	Seahawks

The Navy established its first helicopter minesweeping squadron —HM-12—on 1 April 1971 after 19 years of experiments with helicopters in this field. Initially flying CH-53A Sea Stallions and the RH-53D helicopters, HM-12 operated off North Vietnam in 1972 and at the northern end of the Suez Canal in 1973. In the former operation the Navy squadron was assisted by Marine CH-53 helicopters. HM-12 was designated as the airborne mine countermeasures readiness training squadron in 1978, with HM-14, commissioned 12 May 1978, and HM-16, commissioned 27 October 1978, used for operational deployments. When established, HM-14 and HM-16 each had eight RH-53D helicopters with HM-12 retaining five; seven additional helicopters were used for test and evaluation at the time.

Subsequently, three RH-53Ds were reassigned to VR-24 for VERTREP/VOD operations. Seven of the helicopters were destroyed during the ill-fated rescue effort in Iran in May of 1980. This led to reassignment of the VR-24 helicopters to give HM-12 four helicopters and seven each to HM-14 and HM-16. (Total RH-53D production was 30 helicopters for the U.S. Navy and six delivered to the Iranian Navy.) During the early 1980s the Navy will begin operating the improved MH-53E in both the VERTREP and airborne MCM roles.

These squadrons report to Helicopter Sea Control Wing 1 at Norfolk.

HELICOPTER ANTISUBMARINE SQUADRONS

Squadron	Code	Name	Squadron	Code	Name
HS-1	AR	Seahorses	HS-8	NG	Eight Ballers
HS-2	NE	Golden Falcons	HS-9	AJ	Sea Griffins
HS-3	AA	Tridents	HS-10	RA	Task Masters
HS-4		Black Knights	HS-11	AB	Dragon Slayers
HS-5	AG	Night Dippers	HS-12	NH	Wyverns
HS-6	NG	Indians	HS-15	AE	Red Lions
HS-7	AC	Shamrocks			

There are 11 helicopter ASW squadrons that operate with carrier air wings, each flying six SH-3D/G/H Sea King helicopters. These squadrons were reduced from eight to six aircraft in 1977 at the direction of the Department of Defense as a cost-reduction measure. An HS squadron is assigned to 10 carrier air wings, with those

wings on the MIDWAY (CV 41) and CORAL SEA (CV 43) flying only SH-3G Sea Kings in the utility role (from HC-1).

Readiness training for these squadrons is provided by HS-1 on the East Coast and HS-10 on the West Coast. Atlantic squadrons report to Helicopter Antisubmarine Wing 1 and the Pacific squadrons to ASW Wing Pacific.

LIGHT HELICOPTER ANTISUBMARINE SQUADRONS

Squadron	Code	Name	Squadron	Code	Name
HSL-30	HT	Neptune's Horsemen	HSL-34	HX	Green Checkers
			HSL-35	TG	Magicians
HSL-31	TD	Archangels	HSL-36	HY	Lamp Lighters
HSL-32	HV	Tridents	HSL-37	TH	Easy Riders
HSL-33	TF	Sea Snakes			

The HSL squadrons provide detachments of SH-2F LAMPS helicopters for deployments aboard cruisers, destroyers, and frigates. The first LAMPS were assigned to helicopter combat support squadrons, HC-4 and HC-5, which were reclassified as HSL-30 and HSL-31, respectively, on 1 March 1972. Those two squadrons now provide readiness training for their respective fleets.

The SH-60B Seahawk will be delivered to the Fleet for the LAMPS role from the mid-1980s onward. Additional squadrons will be formed to operate the aircraft, designated in the 40-series (HSL-40, HSL-41, etc.).

Atlantic HSL and HC squadrons have the initial letter H in their codes and report to Helicopter Sea Control Wing 1. The Pacific HSL squadrons are part of ASW Wing Pacific.

HELICOPTER TRAINING SQUADRONS

Squadron	Code	Name	Aircraft	Training
HT-8	E	(none)	TH-57A	Basic Helicopter
HT-18	E	(none)	UH-1E/L, TH-1L	Advanced Helicopter

These squadrons provide basic and advanced helicopter training, respectively. Students first fly fixed-wing T-28 or T-34 aircraft. These squadrons are numbered in the same series as VT squadrons and are part of Training Wing 5.

NAVAL AIR RESERVE

The Naval Air Reserve provides a combat force of two carrier air wings (CVWR) and 13 maritime patrol squadrons (VP), plus several support squadrons and units. All of these units are described here, although the Navy was decommissioning 12 squadrons during 1980–1981: 4 VR, 2 VC, 2 HAL, and 4 HS squadrons.

The Commander, Naval Air Reserve is based at New Orleans, La.; the support units are under the Reserve Tactical Support Air Wing at NAS New Orleans.

The Naval Air Reserve's carrier-type aircraft are organized into two carrier air wings, similar although not identical to active CVWs. Note the numerical sequence of the squadrons, expanded from the wing designations, except for the two AEW squadrons. CVWR-20 and -30 were previously Attack Carrier Air Wings—Reserve; changed on 1 April 1976.

RESERVE CARRIER AIR WINGS

CVWR	Code	VF	VA	VAK	VFP	VAQ	VAW
20	AF	201	203	208	206	209	78
		202	204				
			205				
30	ND	301	303	308	306	309	88
		302	304				
			305				

ATTACK SQUADRONS

Squadron	Code	Location	Squadron	Code	Location
VA-203	AF	NAS Jacksonville, Fla.	VA-303	ND	NAS Alameda, Calif.
VA-204	AF	NAS New Orleans, La.	VA-303	ND	NAS Alameda, Calif.
VA-205	AF	NAS Atlanta, Ga.	VA-305	ND	NAS Point Mugu, Calif.

All of these squadrons fly the A-7B Corsair light attack aircraft.

TANKER SQUADRONS

Squadron	Code	Location
VAK-208	AF	NAS Alameda, Calif.
VAK-308	ND	NAS Alameda, Calif.

Both squadrons fly the EKA-3B Skywarrior in the in-flight refueling role.

ELECTRONIC WARFARE SQUADRONS

Squadron	Code	Location
VAQ-209	AF	NAS Norfolk, Va.
VAQ-309	ND	NAS Whidbey Island, Wash.

These squadrons have EA-6A Intruder aircraft. VAQ-33 (active) and VAQ-209 are the only Navy EW squadrons not based at NAS Whidbey Island.

AIRBORNE EARLY WARNING SQUADRONS

Squadron	Code	Location
VAW-78	AF	NAS Norfolk, Va.
VAW-88	ND	NAS Miramar, Calif.

The E-2B Hawkeye is flown by both reserve AEW squadrons.

FIGHTER SQUADRONS

Squadron	Code	Location	Squadron	Code	Location
VF-201	AF	NAS Dallas, Texas	VF-301	ND	NAS Miramar, Calif.
VF-202	AF	NAS Dallas, Texas	VF-302	ND	NAS Miramar, Calif.

All reserve fighter squadrons fly the F-4N Phantom.

LIGHT PHOTOGRAPHIC SQUADRONS

Squadron	Code	Location
VFP-206	AF	NAF Andrews, Washington, D.C.
VFP-306	ND	NAF Andrews, Washington, D.C.

These squadrons provide photographic reconnaissance with RF-8G Crusaders, with both squadrons flying four aircraft each and VFP-306 three aircraft.

COMPOSITE SQUADRONS

Squadron	Code	Location
VC-12	JY	NAF Detroit, Mich.
VC-13	UX	NAS New Orleans, La.

Each VC squadron flies 12 TA-4J Skyhawk. The reserve VC squadrons do not use the term "fleet" in their designation as do active squadrons.

PATROL SQUADRONS

Squadron	Code	Location
VP-60	LS	NAS Glenview, Ill.
VP-62	LT	NAS Jacksonville, Fla.
VP-64	LU	NAS Willow Grove, Penna.
VP-65	PG	NAS Point Mugu, Calif.
VP-66	LV	NAS Willow Grove, Penna.
VP-67	PL	NAS Millington, Tenn.
VP-68	LW	NAS Patuxent River, Md.
VP-69	PJ	NAS Whidbey Island, Wash.
VP-90	LX	NAS Glenview, Ill.
VP-91	PM	NAS Moffett, Calif.
VP-92	LY	NAS South Weymouth, Mass.
VP-93	LH	NAF Detroit, Mich.
VP-94	LZ	NAS New Orleans, La.

These squadrons fly the P-3A/B Orion. VP-67 completed transition from the SP-2H Neptune to the Orion in 1979, the last U.S. Navy patrol squadron to fly that venerable aircraft

FLEET LOGISTICS SUPPORT SQUADRONS

Squadron	Code	Location	Squadron	Code	Location
VR-48		NAF Andrews	VR-55	RU	NAS Alameda, Calif.
VR-51	RV	NAS Glenview, Ill.			
			VR-56	JU	NAS Norfolk, Va.
VR-52	JT	NAS Willow Grove, Penna.	VR-57	RX	NAS North Island, Calif.
VR-53	RT	NAS Memphis, Tenn.			
			VR-58	JV	NAS Jacksonville, Fla.
VR-54	JS	NAS New Orleans, La.			

The VR squadrons provide logistics support for active Navy activities as well as the Naval Reserve. The squadrons fly the C-9B Skytrain II and C-118B Liftmaster; VR-48, established 1 October 1980, flies the C-131H Samaritan.

HELICOPTER COMBAT SUPPORT SQUADRONS

Squadron	Code	Location
HC-9	NW	NAS North Island, Calif.

The squadron flies HH-3A helicopters that are armed and armored for combat search-and-rescue operations.

LIGHT ATTACK HELICOPTER SQUADRONS

Squadron	Code	Location
HAL-4		NAS Norfolk, Va.
HAL-5		NAS Point Mugu, Calif.

These squadrons have HH-1K Huey helicopters for the support of riverine forces. The Navy's only active helicopter gunship squadron, HAL-3, was commissioned in April 1967 and decommissioned in 1972 after service in Vietnam.

HELICOPTER ANTISUBMARINE SQUADRONS

Squadron	Code	Location	Squadron	Code	Location
HS-74	NW	NAS South Weymouth, Mass.	HS-84	NW	NAS North Island, Calif.
HS-75	NW	NAEC Lakehurst, N.J.	HS-85	NW	NAS Alameda, Calif.

SH-3A/D Sea King ASW helicopters are flown by these squadrons. For administrative purposes they are assigned (with all other reserve helicopter units) to the Reserve Helicopter Wing, and are assigned the letter code NW (formerly used by Reserve ASW Air Group 80).

NAVAL AIR RESERVE TRAINING UNITS (NARU)

Code	Location	Code	Location
6A	NARU Andrews, Washington, D.C.	6M	NARU Memphis, Tenn.
6F	NARU Jacksonville, Fla.	6S	NARU Norfolk, Va.
6G	NARU Alameda, Calif.	6T/RU	NARU Whidbey Island, Wash.
6H	NARU North Island, Calif.	6U	NARU Point Mugu, Calif.

Aircraft assigned to Naval Air Reserve Units and Naval Air Stations have number-letter identification codes (except for RU). These are mostly administrative and transport aircraft.

NAVAL AIR STATIONS

Code	Location	Code	Location
7B	NAS Atlanta, Ga.	7W	NAS Willow Grove, Penna.
7D	NAS Dallas, Texas	7X	NAS New Orleans, La.
7V	NAS Glenview, Ill.	7Z	NAS South Weymouth, Mass.

NAVAL AIR FACILITIES

Code	Location
7Y	NAF Detroit, Mich.

MARINE CORPS AVIATION

There are three Marine Aircraft Wings (MAW), with one wing nominally assigned to support each of the three active Marine divisions. Headquarters for the First MAW is at Kadena on Okinawa, with one air group at Kaneohe Bay (Oahu), Hawaii, supporting the 1st Marine Brigade; headquarters for the Second MAW is at Cherry Point, N.C., and for the Third MAW at El Toro, Calif. The Fourth MAW is a reserve wing.

Operationally the Marine air wings are subordinate to their respective Fleet Marine Forces (FMFLant and FMFPac) and, additionally, are under the technical direction of NavAirLant and NavAirPac.

Marine helicopters regularly operate from amphibious ships, and Marine fighter and attack squadrons, as well as detachments of special-purpose aircraft, periodically are deployed aboard aircraft carriers. Marine squadrons all have two-letter identification codes. Aircraft are also assigned to Headquarters and Maintenance Squadrons (H&MS).

MARINE AIRCRAFT WINGS

MAW	VMFA	VMA	VMO	VMGR	HMA	HMH	HML	HMM
1st Brig.	212 232						463	262 265
1st	235 312	211 332		152		361	367	163 165
2nd	115 122 251 451	223 224 231 331 533 542	1	252	269	362 461	167	162 261 263 264
3rd	314 323 531	121 214 242 513	2	352	169 369	363 462	267	161 164 268 365

MARINE AIRCRAFT WINGS (cont.)

MAW	VMFA	VMA	VMO	VMGR	HMA	HMH	HML	HMM
4th (Res.)	112	124	4	234	773	769	770	764
	321	131				772		767
		133				777		774
		134						
		142						
		322						

MARINE LIGHT ATTACK SQUADRONS

Squadron	Code	Squadron	Code	Squadron	Code
VMA-211	CF	VMA-231	CG	VMA-513	WF
VMA-214	WE	VMA-311	WL	VMA-542	CR
VMA-223	WP	VMA-331	VL		

VMA-211, 214, 223, and 331 each fly 19 A-4M Skyhawks; VMA-231 and 542 each have 15 AV-8A Harriers, while VMA-513 has nine of the VSTOL aircraft; and VMA-311 does not have any aircraft assigned.

The future of Marine light attack squadrons is not clear. The Department of Defense plans to replace the Skyhawks with the F/A-18 Hornet, while the Marine Corps is seeking the AV-8B improved Harrier.

MARINE ALL-WEATHER MEDIUM ATTACK SQUADRONS

Squadron	Code	Squadron	Code	Squadron	Code
VMA(AW)-121	VK	VMA(AW)-242	DT	VMA(AW)-533	ED
VMA(AW)-224	WK	VMA(AW)-332	EA		

Each Marine Corps all-weather medium attack squadron flies ten A-6E Intruders, a reduction of two aircraft per squadron during 1980.

MARINE ELECTRONIC WARFARE SQUADRONS

Squadron	Code
VMAQ-2	CY

The Marine Corps' three composite reconnaissance squadrons (VMCJ) were decommissioned in 1975, and their aircraft were allocated to VMAQ-2 and VMFP-3. VMAQ-2, based at the MCAS Cherry Point, N.C., flies 15 EW aircraft, primarily the two-seat EA-6A Intruder with the more-capable four-seat EA-6B Prowler entering service since March 1977. Detachments from VMAQ-2 serve with various Marine aircraft wings and periodically go aboard forward-deployed carriers to compensate for the Navy's EA-6B shortfall.

MARINE FIGHTER ATTACK SQUADRONS

Squadron	Code	Squadron	Code	Squadron	Code
VMFA-115	VE	VMFA-235	DB	VMFA-323	WS
VMFA-122	DC	VMFA-251	DW	VMFA-333	DN
VMFA-212	WD	VMFA-312	DR	VMFA-451	VM
VMFA-232	WT	VMFA-314	VW	VMFA-531	EC

Each Marine fighter squadron flies 12 F-4J/N/S Phantom aircraft. All are scheduled to transition to the F/A-18 Hornet beginning in the mid-1980s. A reduction to nine VMFA squadrons by 1985 is tentatively planned to help fund the acquisition of F/A-18 and AV-8B aircraft.

MARINE PHOTORECONNAISSANCE SQUADRONS

Squadron	Code
VMFP-3	RF

The Marines fly 21 RF-4B Phantoms in the photo "recce" role, with the single VMFP squadron established in 1975 providing detachments to the aircraft wings. The recce version of the Phantom is one of the few aircraft flown by the Marine Corps but not by the Navy. (The RF-4C is flown by the U.S. Air Force and the RF-4E by foreign air forces.)

MARINE REFUELLER-TRANSPORT SQUADRONS

Squadron	Code	Squadron	Code
VMGR-152	QD	VMGR-352	QB
VMGR-252	BH		

These squadrons, each with 12 KC-130F Hercules, provide tactical logistical lift and in-flight refuelling for Marine air wings and divisions. One Marine KC-130F is assigned to support the Navy's Blue Angels flight demonstration team.

MARINE OBSERVATION SQUADRONS

Squadron	Code
VMO-1	ER
VMO-2	UV

These observation squadrons fly the nimble OV-10A Bronco, with the OV-10D night-flying variant being provided in limited numbers. Unlike previous VO-type aircraft, the Bronco can be heavily armed. Eighteen aircraft are assigned to each squadron. The Navy's light attack squadron (VAL-4) that flew Broncos during the Vietnam War has been decommissioned.

MARINE ATTACK HELICOPTER SQUADRONS

Squadron	Code	Squadron	Code	Squadron	Code
HMA-169	SN	HMA-269	HF	HMA-369	SM

These squadrons are each assigned 24 AH-1J/T SeaCobra gunships for the close air support of ground troops.

MARINE HEAVY HELICOPTER SQUADRONS

Squadron	Code	Squadron	Code	Squadron	Code
HMH-361	YN	HMH-363	YZ	HMH-462	YF
HMH-362	YL	HMH-461	CJ	HMH-463	YH

The six heavy helicopter squadrons are each assigned 21 CH-53A/D helicopters. HMH-464 was to be activated in March 1981 at New River, N.C., to fly the CH-53E. Fifteen helicopters are scheduled for assignment to the squadron.

MARINE LIGHT HELICOPTER SQUADRONS

Squadron	Code	Squadron	Code	Squadron	Code
HML-167	TV	HML-267	UV	HML-367	VT

Twenty-four UH-1N Huey helicopters are flown by each HML squadron.

MARINE MEDIUM HELICOPTER SQUADRONS

Squadron	Code	Squadron	Code	Squadron	Code
HMM-161	YR	HMM-165	YW	HMM-264	EH
HMM-162	YS	HMM-261	EM	HMM-268	YQ
HMM-163	YP	HMM-262	ET	HMM-265	EP
HMM-164	YT	HMM-263	EG	HMM-365	YM

Six HMM squadrons fly 12 and six fly 18 CH-46D/E/F Sea Knight helicopters.

MARINE HELICOPTER SQUADRONS

Squadron	Code
HMX-1	MX

This squadron—sometimes incorrectly called Marine Helicopter Experimental Squadron 1 or Marine Helicopter Development Squadron 1—was commissioned on 3 December 1947 to develop helicopter assault tactics and doctrine for the Marine Corps. The squadron fulfills a variety of functions, including providing helicopter transport for the President. For that role the squadron flies the VH-3D version of the Sea King. With the President embarked, a heli-

copter is designated *Marine One.* Informally, these helicopters are called "white tops" because of their paint scheme. The squadron also flies CH-53D Sea Stallion, CH-46F Sea Knight, and UH-1N Huey helicopters. Based at MCAF Quantico (changed from MCAS on 15 November 1976).

MARINE TRAINING SQUADRONS

Squadron	Code	Aircraft	Squadron	Code	Aircraft
VMFAT-101	SH	F-4J/S	HMT-204	GX	CH-46E
VMAT-102	SC	A-4M	HMLTE-267		UH-1N
HMLTE-167		UH-1N	HMATE-269		AH-1J
VMAT(AW)-202	KC	A-6E	HMT-301	SU	CH-46F
VMAT-203	KD	AV-8A, TAV-8A	HMATE-369		AH-1J

These squadrons provide "readiness" or transition training for Marine aviators.

MARINE AIR RESERVE

The small Marine Air Reserve forms the Fourth Marine Aircraft Wing, assigned to support the 4th Marine Division. Approximately 200 aircraft are assigned to the Wing's 20 squadrons.

MARINE ATTACK SQUADRONS

Squadron	Code	Location	Squadron	Code	Location
VMA-124	QP	NAS Memphis, Tenn.	VMA-134	MF	MCAS El Toro, Calif.
VMA-131	QG	NAS Willow Grove, Penna.	VMA-142	MB	NAS Jacksonville, Fla.
VMA-133	ME	NAS Alameda, Calif.	VMA-322	QR	NAS South Weymouth, Mass.

Both reserve fighter squadrons fly the F-4N Phantom.

MARINE FIGHTER-ATTACK SQUADRONS

Squadron	Code	Location
VMFA-112	MA	NAS Dallas, Texas
VMFA-321	MG	NAF Andrews (Washington, D.C.)

These squadrons fly the A-4 Skyhawk.

MARINE OBSERVATION SQUADRONS

Squadron	Code	Location
VMO-4	MU	NAS Atlanta, Ga.

This squadron flies the OV-10A Bronco.

MARINE REFUELLER-TRANSPORT SQUADRONS

Squadron	Code	Location
VMGR-234	QH	NAS Glenview, Ill.

KC-130F Hercules transports are flown by this squadron.

MARINE ATTACK HELICOPTER SQUADRONS

Squadron	Code	Location
HMA-773	MP	NAS Atlanta, Ga.

This squadron flies the AH-1G SeaCobra gunship.

MARINE HEAVY HELICOPTER SQUADRONS

Squadron	Code	Location
HMH-769	MS	NAS Alameda, Calif.
HMH-772	MT	NAS Willow Grove, Penna.
HMH-777	QM	NAS Dallas, Texas

These heavy helicopter squadrons fly the CH-53A Sea Stallion.

MARINE LIGHT HELICOPTER SQUADRONS

Squadron	Code	Location
HML-770	MN	NAS Whidbey Island, Wash.
HML-771	QK	NAS South Weymouth, Mass.
HML-776	QL	NAS Glenview, Ill.

These squadrons operate UH-1E Huey helicopters.

MARINE MEDIUM HELICOPTER SQUADRONS

Squadron	Code	Location
HMM-764	ML	MCAS Santa Ana, Calif.
HMM-767	MM	NAS New Orleans, La.
HMM-774	MQ	NAS Norfolk, Va.

These squadrons all fly CH-46D helicopters.

An S-3A Viking from VS-32 and an EA-6B Prowler from VAQ-133 are prepared for launching from the two waist catapults of the JOHN F. KENNEDY (CV 67). Note the jet blast deflectors being raised from the deck behind both aircraft; flight deck personnel, having directed the planes onto the catapults and hooked them up, are now clearing away. (1978, N. Polmar)

22 Naval Aircraft

This chapter describes the principal aircraft now flown by the U.S. Navy, Marine Corps, and Coast Guard.

All naval aircraft are assigned designations under a standard Department of Defense system adopted on 18 September 1962. This system replaced the Navy scheme that had been in use for naval aircraft since 29 March 1922. The older scheme identified the aircraft's mission, the manufacturer, and the model of that type by the manufacturer. The current mission and sequence designation system used for naval aircraft is similar to that long used by the U.S. Air Force and its predecessors. Where appropriate, the older aircrafts' former (pre-1962) designations are shown in parentheses.

Explanation of symbols:

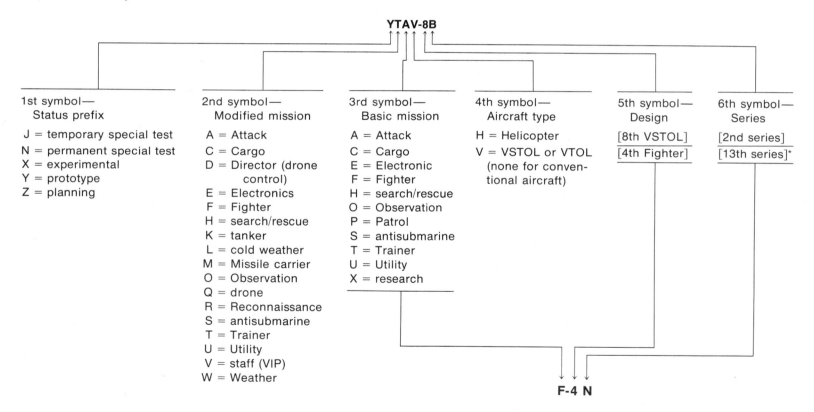

YTAV-8B

1st symbol— Status prefix	2nd symbol— Modified mission	3rd symbol— Basic mission	4th symbol— Aircraft type	5th symbol— Design	6th symbol— Series
J = temporary special test N = permanent special test X = experimental Y = prototype Z = planning	A = Attack C = Cargo D = Director (drone control) E = Electronics F = Fighter H = search/rescue K = tanker L = cold weather M = Missile carrier O = Observation Q = drone R = Reconnaissance S = antisubmarine T = Trainer U = Utility V = staff (VIP) W = Weather	A = Attack C = Cargo E = Electronic F = Fighter H = search/rescue O = Observation P = Patrol S = antisubmarine T = Trainer U = Utility X = research	H = Helicopter V = VSTOL or VTOL (none for conventional aircraft)	[8th VSTOL] [4th Fighter]	[2nd series] [13th series]*

F-4 N

NOTE: Letters I and O are not used to avoid confusion with numerals.

AIRCRAFT TYPES

The following Navy, Marine Corps, and Coast Guard aircraft are described in this chapter. In instances where only specialized variants remain in service, the aircraft are listed by their modified mission (e.g., EP-2H, RF-8G).

Mission/Type	Basic Designation	Popular Name	Status[a]	Type[b]
Fighter	F-4	Phantom II	N-NR-MC-MR	CV
	F-5	Tiger II	N	L
	F-14	Tomcat	N	CV
Fighter/Attack	F/A-18	Hornet	development	CV
Attack	A-4	Skyhawk	N-NR-MC-MR	CV
	A-6	Intruder	N-MC	CV
	A-7	Corsair II	N-NR	CV
	AV-8A	Harrier	MC	VSTOL
	AV-8B	Harrier	development	VSTOL
Antisubmarine	S-3	Viking	N	CV
Patrol	P-3	Orion	N-NR-NOAA	L
Electronic	E-2	Hawkeye	N-NR	CV
	EA-3	Skywarrior	N-NR	CV
	EA-6	Intruder	MC-NR	CV
	EA-6B	Prowler	N-MC	CV
	NC-121	Warning Star	N	L
	NKC-135	Stratotanker	N	L
	EP-2H	Neptune	N	L
Reconnaissance	RF-8	Crusader	N-NR	CV
Observation	OV-10	Bronco	MC-MR	STOL
Utility	HU-16	Albatross	CG	A
	HU-25	Falcon	CG	L
Cargo/Transport	C-1	Trader	N	CV
	C-2	Greyhound	N	CV
	C-4	Academe	N-MC-CG	L
	C-9	Skytrain II	MC-NR	L
	VC-11	Gulfstream II	CG	L
	C-12	—	N-MC	L
	C-118	—	NR	L
	C-130	Hercules	N-NR-MC-MR-CG-NOAA	L
	C-131	Samaritan	N-NR-CG	L
Trainer	T-2	Buckeye	N	CV
	T-28	Trojan	N	CV
	T-34	Mentor	N	L
	T-38	Talon	N	L
	T-39	Sabreliner	N-MC	L
	T-44	King Air	N	L
Helicopters	AH-1	SeaCobra	MC-MR	
	UH-1	Huey (Iroquois)	N-NR-MC-MR	
	SH-2	LAMPS	N	
	SH-3	Sea King	N-NR-MC	
	HH-3	Pelican	CG	
	H-46	Sea Knight	N-MC-MR	
	HH-52	Sea Guard	CG	
	H-53	Sea Stallion	N-MC-MR	
	H-53E	Super Stallion	N-MC	
	TH-57	Sea Ranger	N	
	SH-60	Seahawk (LAMPS III)	development	
	HH-65	Dolphin	CG	
Experimental	XFV-12	—	development	VSTOL
	XV-15	—	development	VSTOL
	QSRA	—	development	STOL

[a] N = Navy; NR = Naval Reserve; MC = Marine Corps; MR = Marine Corps Reserve; CG = Coast Guard; NOAA = National Oceanographic and Atmospheric Administration.
[b] CV = carrier-based; L = land-based; VSTOL = Vertical/Short Take-Off and Landing; STOL = Short Take-Off and Landing; A = amphibious.

AIRCRAFT MARKINGS

Unit markings—indicating fleet, wing, or squadron—consist of letters or letter-number combinations on the tail or afterbody; see Chapter 21 for codes.

Side numbers on fuselage and generally upper right and lower left wings indicate aircraft in squadron or other unit. The following is the side number sequence for Navy carrier wings:

Side number	Squadron	Squadron color code
100 series	fighter	insignia red
200 series	fighter	orange-yellow
300 series	light attack	light blue
400 series	light attack	international orange
500 series	medium attack	light green
600 series	ASW-photo	black
700 series	ASW-EW-AEW	
800 series	EW	
900 series	photo	

Wing commanders fly aircraft from various squadrons. Known as the CAG—from the outdated Commander, Air Group—the wing commander's aircraft are identified by double zero ("double nuts") instead of the squadrons' normal side numbers.

Bureau numbers are assigned to all Navy and Marine Corps aircraft in sequence of procurement. These numbers are used on the aircraft's after fuselage or tail, and on transports the last three digits are often used as side numbers (generally on the nose). "Bureau" recalls the Bureau of Aeronautics, which directed naval aircraft procurement from 1921–1959 (subsequently becoming the Bureau of Naval Ordnance and then the Naval Air Systems Command).

Coast Guard aircraft wear the service's wide red and narrow blue stripe insignia on the forward fuselage (with the Coast Guard crest on the former), a four-digit procurement-sequence number, and the name of the aircraft's home station. The two Coast Guard executive aircraft, a VC-11A and a VC-4A, have the side numbers 01 and 02 and carry the marking "Washington" for Washington, D.C.

National insignia for U.S. naval and Coast Guard aircraft consists of a white star on a blue circle, with white rectangles to either side of the blue circle, the panels having a red horizontal stripe and blue border. All naval aircraft have the national insignia on both sides of the fuselage, with fixed-wing aircraft also having it on the upper left and lower right wings. (Coast Guard aircraft have the national insignia or American flag on their rudder fin and the Coast Guard insignia on their orange fuselage stripe.) U.S. naval COD and some transport aircraft additionally have the American flag on their rudder fin.

A-7E Corsairs from VA-27 and VA-97 are surrounded by other CVW-14 (NK) aircraft aboard the carrier ENTERPRISE (CVN 65). The wing has since shifted to the smaller CORAL SEA (CV 43). (U.S. Navy, PH1 Ralph W. Hoffman)

FIGHTER AIRCRAFT

F-4 PHANTOM (McDonnell Douglas)

The Phantom is an all-weather, multi-purpose fighter that has served as the first-line fighter of the U.S. Navy, Marine Corps, and Air Force since the early 1960s. It has been partially replaced in the Navy by the F-14 Tomcat. (McDonnell Douglas has produced 5,073 Phantoms for U.S. and foreign use, and Japan has built 138 F-4EJ variants, including 11 from parts produced by McDonnell Douglas; all production ended in 1979.)

Navy and Marine squadrons fly the F-4J/N/S variants, with 12 aircraft assigned to each squadron. The Marine Corps also has one reconnaissance squadron that is assigned 21 RF-4B photo aircraft. (These are unarmed, two-seat aircraft that have been lengthened to $62^{5}/_{6}$ feet to accommodate cameras, infrared detector, and side-looking radar.)

From 1966–1972, 552 improved F-4J Phantoms were produced for naval air, fitted with leading-edge wing slats, the improved AWG-10 missile control system, and other features. Subsequently, 265 of these aircraft are being further updated to the F-4S configuration. In addition, from 1972–1978 228 of the F-4B aircraft were upgraded to the F-4N configuration. Beginning in the mid-1980s the Navy and Marine Phantoms are scheduled to be replaced by the F/A-18 Hornet.

Electronics: The F-4J variant has the AWG-10 system, which includes the APG-59 radar (the improved AWG-10A is fitted in the F-4N/S aircraft). Also fitted in the F-4J are ALE-29 chaff/IR decoy dispenser, ALQ-126A jamming system (coverage through I-band), ALR-45F threat-warning receiver, and APR-43 (Compass Sail/Clockwise) missile launch warning system. The F-4S has the improved ALQ-162 (Clockwise) jamming system.

(F-4J)

Crew:	1 pilot, 1 radar intercept officer
Weights:	28,000 lbs empty; 46,000 lbs loaded clean; 54,600 lbs maximum
Dimensions:	length $58^{1}/_{4}$ ft (17.76 m), span $38^{5}/_{12}$ ft (11.71 m), height $16^{1}/_{4}$ ft (4.96 m)
Engines:	2 GE J79-GE-10 turbojet; 17,900 lbst each with afterburner
Speeds:	1,450 mph clean at 36,000 ft (Mach 2.2)
Ranges:	300-n.mile radius with 8 AAMs + 6 500-lb bombs; 525-n. mile radius with 1 Mk 28; 400-n. mile radius with 8 500-lb bombs; 2,300-n. mile ferry range[a]
Ceiling:	71,000 ft
Guns:	no internal guns
Payload:	4 Sparrow AAM + 6 500-lb bombs
	or 4 Sparrow AAM + 24 250-lb bombs
	or 4 Sparrow AAM + 8 1,000-lb bombs
	or 4 Sparrow AAM + 4 Sidewinder AAM + 6 500-lb bombs
	or 1 Mk 28/43/57 nuclear weapon

[a] Combat ranges are based on hi-lo-hi mission. External drop tanks may be carried in addition to weapon stores. Ranges vary with flight profile and weather conditions.

F-4J Phantom—VF 96/CONSTELLATION (U.S. Navy, Robert L. Lawson)

The Navy has taken delivery of 17 F-5E and six two-seat F-5F fighters to simulate Soviet fighter aircraft for combat training. These planes are flown by the Navy Fighter Weapons School (called Top Gun) at Miramar, Calif., and two fighter squadrons. (The T-38A Talon and A-4E/F Skyhawk are also flown in this role.)

Electronics: The F-5E and F-5F have APQ-159 lightweight micro-miniature X-band pulse fire-control radar.

(F-5E)

Crew:	1 pilot (2 in F-5F)
Weights:	9,588 lbs empty; 24,080 lbs maximum
Dimensions:	length $48\frac{1}{3}$ feet (14.73 m), span $26\frac{2}{3}$ ft (8.13 m), height $13\frac{5}{12}$ ft (4.08 m); F-5F length $51\frac{3}{4}$ ft (15.78 m)
Engines:	2 GE J85-GE-21 turbojet; 5,000 lbst each
Speeds:	Mach 1.6 clean at 36,000 ft
Ranges:	190-n.mile radius with maximum payload; 875-n.mile radius with 2 AAMs
Ceiling:	54,000 ft
Guns:	2 20-mm M39A2 (1 in F-5F)
Payload:	no bombs carried in Navy training role

F-4N Phantom—VMFA-323/Coral Sea (LT Pete Clayton)

F-4J Phantom with six Sparrow III AAMs and three fuel tanks (U.S. Navy)

F-5E/F TIGER II (Northrop)

The F-5E and F-5F are the latest aircraft in a long series of Northrop lightweight fighter and trainer aircraft of similar design, the F-5 Freedom Fighter and T-38 Talon, respectively. More than 3,000 of these aircraft have been built for the U.S. Air Force and 25 foreign air forces, with several hundred additional F-5E/F/G aircraft on order.

F-5E Tiger—Navy Fighter Weapons School (U.S. Navy)

F-5E Tiger—Navy Fighter Weapons School (U.S. Navy)

F-14 TOMCAT (Grumman)

The F-14 was developed specifically for fleet air defense, carrying the AWG-9 missile control system and the Phoenix long-range AAM. The AWG-9 provides radar detection of aircraft at more than 100 miles, the ability to simultaneously track up to 24 targets, and to guide as many as six Phoenix missiles against targets more than 60 miles distant. The aircraft has computer-controlled variable-sweep wings that extend for slow-speed landings and long-range flight, and retract for high-speed flight and maneuvering. Pallets for carrying bombs and air-to-ground missiles have been developed but not deployed with the aircraft.

The aircraft originally was intended for U.S. Navy and Marine use, but Marine procurement was canceled in 1975. The Iranian Air Force subsequently purchased 78 aircraft. U.S. Navy planned production is for 491 aircraft through the early 1980s, sufficient to provide 18 carrier-based squadrons of 12 aircraft each, plus 12 three-plane reconnaissance detachments, and pipeline requirements. The 49 RF-14A aircraft will replace the RF-8G Crusader aircraft from 1981 on, carrying a Tactical Air Reconnaissance Pod System (TARPS). Those aircraft are convertible to the "straight" fighter role aboard ship. The pod contains a KS-87 frame camera, a KA-99 panoramic camera, and an AAD-5 infrared line scanner.

A planned F-14B version with improved engine was not procured. Delays with the F/A-18 Hornet could lead to continued production of the F-14.

Electronics: AWG-9 missile control system with pulse-doppler radar, ALE-39 chaff/IR decoy dispenser, ALQ-100 jamming system, and ALR-67 threat warning receiver.

Crew:	1 pilot, 1 radar intercept officer
Weights:	37,500 lbs empty; 72,000 lbs maximum
Dimensions:	length 61⅚ ft (18.86 m), span swept back 64¹/₁₂ ft (19.54 m), span extended 38⅙ ft (11.63 m), height 16 ft (4.88 m)
Engines:	2 P&W TF30-P-412A turbofan; 20,900 lbst each with afterburner
Speeds:	Mach 2.34
Ranges:	
Ceiling:	60,000 ft
Guns:	1 20-mm M61A1 rotary-barrel (676 rounds)
Payload:	4 Sidewinder AAMs + 4 Sparrow AAMs or 4 Sidewinder AAMs + 6 Phoenix AAMs

F-14A Tomcat with Phoenix AAM and Sparrow III AAM; wings extended—VF-111/KITTY HAWK (U.S. Navy, LCDR David P. Erickson)

F-14A Tomcat with TARPS pod between nacelles (Grumman)

F-14A Tomcat—VF-1/ENTERPRISE (U.S. Navy)

F-14A Tomcat—VF-1/ENTERPRISE (U.S. Navy)

F/A-18 HORNET (Northrop/McDonnell Douglas)

The F/A-18 is a lightweight fighter/attack aircraft planned for extensive use by the Navy and Marine Corps. The aircraft evolved from the YF-17, which was developed in competition with the General Dynamics F-16 as a lightweight fighter aircraft. The F-16 was selected by the U.S. Air Force, while the YF-17 was modified and redesignated F/A-18 for naval use. Beginning in 1984 the aircraft is scheduled to replace the F-4 Phantom in 6 Navy and 12 active Marine fighter squadrons, the A-7 Corsair in 24 Navy attack squadrons, and the A-4 Skyhawk and AV-8A/C Harrier in 8 Marine attack squadrons. Pipeline and reserve requirements aggregate a planned F/A-18 procurement of 1,377 aircraft, including several TF-18A variants. The Marine Corps, however, prefers to procure the AV-8B Harrier in place of the F/A-18 for the attack role; that move would reduce F/A-18 production by 322 aircraft.

The F/A-18 is a single-place, twin-engine multi-purpose aircraft designed for carrier operation. Special emphasis has been given to simplify maintenance, a critical factor for carrier-based aircraft. The TF-18A provides transition training. The only difference between the F and A versions will be computer software and bomb racks. An RF-18 is planned for production to replace the RF-14A.

Electronics: APG-65 multi-mode digital radar, ALR-67 threat warning receiver, and ALE-39 chaff/IR decoy dispenser.

An F/A-18 assigned to VFA-125, the Hornet readiness squadron at NAS Lemoore, California. The approval of Marine procurement of 336 AV-8B Harriers and shortfalls in the F/A-18's range and other factors will probably lead to a significant reduction in the planned 1,366-plane Hornet program. (U.S. Navy, PH1 Richard J. Boyle)

Crew:	1 pilot (2 in TF-18A)
Weights:	33,585 lbs loaded in fighter role; 47,000 lbs loaded in attack role
Dimensions:	length 56 ft (17.1 m), span 37½ ft (11.4 m), height 15⅓ ft (4.7 m)
Engines:	2 GE F404-GE-400 turbofan; 16,000 lbst each
Speeds:	Mach 1.8
Ranges:	~400-n.mile radius with AAMs; up to 550-n.mile radius with bombs or air-to-surface missiles
Ceiling:	~50,000 ft
Guns:	1 20-mm M61A1 rotary-barrel (540 rounds)
Payload:	2 Sidewinder AAM + 7 Sparrow AAM in fighter role
	2 Sidewinder AAM + ~17,000 lbs bombs or missiles in attack role

An F/A-18 Hornet—VX-4 (McDonnell Douglas)

F/A-18 Hornet taking off from AMERICA (U.S. Navy)

TF-18A Hornet with mock Sidewinder AAMs (McDonnell Douglas)

ATTACK AIRCRAFT

A-4 SKYHAWK

The A-4 (originally A4D) was developed in the early 1950s as a lightweight, daylight-only nuclear strike aircraft for use in large numbers from aircraft carriers. The aircraft has subsequently evolved into a highly versatile aircraft, with 2,960 being delivered between the first Navy squadron acceptance in 1956 and the final aircraft, which went to the Marine Corps, in 1979. This probably represents the longest production run of any combat aircraft in history.

The U.S. Navy flies the Skyhawk only in the utility and training roles; the Marine Corps has attack squadrons flying the A-4M variant as does the Marine Air Reserve. The last Navy VA squadrons with A-4s were disbanded in 1975 when the carrier HANCOCK (CVA 19) was decommissioned. A few A-4E/Fs have been stripped down and are used to simulate Soviet fighter aircraft in advanced air combat training. Those aircraft are named "Mongoose" as a play on the system of designating Soviet training aircraft with M-letter names. The Navy's Blue Angels flight demonstration team flies the A-4F, the first nonfighter aircraft to be flown by that group. Finally, the Marine Corps also flies numerous TA-4F/J aircraft for tactical air control; these are designated OA-4 and assigned to Marine Aircraft Wings and not to the tactical squadrons listed in Chapter 21. Several foreign nations fly the Skyhawk.

Electronics: The A-4M has APG-53A radar, ALE-39 chaff/IR decoy dispenser, ALQ-126A jammer, APR-43 threat warning receiver; to be fitted with ALQ-162.

A-4M Skyhawk—VMA-331 (U.S. Navy)

(A-4M)

Crew:	1 pilot (2 in EA-4/TA-4)
Weights:	10,465 lbs empty; 24,500 lbs maximum
Dimensions:	length 41$^{1}/_{3}$ ft (12.5 m), span 27$^{1}/_{2}$ ft (8.38 m), height 15 ft (4.57 m); length EA-4/TA-4 42$^{7}/_{12}$ ft (12.99 m)
Engines:	1 P&W J52-P-408A turbojet; 11,200 lbst
Speeds:	670 mph clean at sea level (Mach 0.94); 645 mph with 4,000 lbs weapons
Ranges:	335-n.mile radius with 4,000 lbs weapons; 2,055-n.mile ferry range
Ceiling:	42,250 ft
Guns:	2 20-mm Mk 12 (100 rounds each)
Payload:	20 250-lb bombs
	or 3 1,000-lb bombs
	or 1 2,000-lb bomb
	or 4 Shrike ASMs
	or 1 Mk 28/43/57 nuclear weapon

EA-4F Skyhawk—VAQ-33 (U.S. Navy)

A-4E Skyhawk with in-flight refueling tanks—VC-1 (U.S. Navy)

TA-4J Skyhawk—VF-126 (U.S. Navy)

A-6 INTRUDER (Grumman)

The A-6 (originally A2F) is an all-weather and night attack aircraft developed for conventional ground attack.

The Navy flies the A-6E in 12 carrier-based attack squadrons (10 aircraft each), and the Marines have five attack squadrons (12 aircraft each). In addition, four KA-6D tankers are assigned to all Navy carrier air wings. (Listed separately in this volume are the electronic warfare variants, the EA-6A Intruder and EA-6B Prowler.) The Navy-Marine Corps procured 159 A-6Es and upgraded 240 from the A-6A to -E configuration.

The standard attack variant now in service, the A-6E is being fitted with the TRAM package (Target Recognition Attack Multisensors), which includes a 20-inch diameter "turret" under the forward fuselage with infrared and laser targeting devices.

Electronics: The A-6E is fitted with the APQ-148 or -156 search radar, APQ-112 track radar, APN-153 doppler navigation radar, ALE-39 chaff/IR decoy dispenser, ALQ-126A jammer, and ALR-67 threat warning receiver.

A-6 Intruder landing aboard ENTERPRISE (U.S. Navy)

(A-6E)

Crew:	1 pilot, 1 bombardier/navigator
Weights:	25,630 lbs empty; 60,400 lbs maximum
Dimensions:	length $54^7/_{12}$ ft (16.67 m), span 53 ft (16.15 m), height $16^1/_6$ ft (4.92 m)
Engines:	2 P&W J52-P-8A/-8B turbojet; 9,300 lbst each
Speeds:	685 mph at sea level (Mach 0.9); 482 mph cruise
Ranges:	775-n.mile radius with 8,000 lbs weapons; 920-n.mile radius with 6,000 lbs weapons; 2,860-n.mile ferry range
Ceiling:	44,600 ft
Guns:	none
Payload:	28 500-lb bombs
	or 10 1,000-lb bombs
	or 5 2,000-lb bombs
	or 3 Mk 28/43/57 nuclear weapons

A-6E Intruder with TRAM dome under nose (Grumman)

A-6E Intruder—VA-65/EISENHOWER (U.S. Navy)

KA-6D Intruder tanker from VA-75; note refueling drogue housing under the after fuselage. The 521 number indicates the tanker is assigned to the fifth (A-6) squadron of CVW-3 (AC) aboard the SARATOGA (CV 60). (U.S. Navy, PH2 John W. Howard)

A-7 CORSAIR (LTV-Vought)

The A-7 is a carrier-based, light attack aircraft. Originally developed as a replacement for the A-4 Skyhawk in the visual, daylight attack role, succeeding variants of the A-7 have incorporated improvements in navigation and sensors to provide a limited all-weather and night capability.

There are 24 carrier-based A-7 squadrons, each flying 12 A-7E aircraft, plus 4 reserve squadrons with older A-7 aircraft. Forty A-7B and 41 A-7C single-seat aircraft are being converted to the two-seat TA-7C variant for the training and weapon test roles. The two-seat aircraft have the same electronics and weapons capabilities of the A-7E. Plans to procure an RA-7E carrying reconnaissance pods have been dropped in favor of using the RF-14 in the carrier-based "recce" role. The A-7E is similar to the U.S. Air Force A-7D variant, with the principal difference being the engine.

The F/A-18 is scheduled to replace the A-7E in Navy attack squadrons beginning in the mid-1980s.

Electronics: The A-7E has APQ-126 radar, APN-190 doppler navigation radar, ALE-39 chaff-IR decoy dispenser, ALQ-162 jammer, ALR-45F and APR-43 threat warning receivers.

(A-7E)

Crew:	1 pilot (2 in TA-7C)
Weights:	19,781 lbs empty; 42,000 lbs maximum
Dimensions:	length 46^{1}/$_{6}$ ft (14.06 m), span 38^{3}/$_{4}$ ft (11.8 m), height 16^{1}/$_{12}$ ft (4.9 m)
Engines:	1 Allison TF41-A-2 (Spey) turbofan; 15,000 lbst
Speeds:	690 mph at sea level (Mach 0.9)
Ranges:	~700-n.mile radius with 4,000 lbs ordnance; 2,800-n.mile ferry range
Ceiling:	42,600 ft
Guns:	1 20-mm M61A1 rotary-barrel (500 rounds)
Payload:	2 Sidewinder AAMs (all configurations) + 32 500-lb bombs
	or 16 1,000-lb bombs
	or 6 2,000-lb bombs
	or 6 Walleye I missiles
	or 4 Walleye II missiles
	or 2 Mk 43/57/61 nuclear weapons

A-7 Corsair—VA-122

A-7E Corsair—VA-83/FORRESTAL (U.S. Navy)

A-7E Corsairs—VA-147/CONSTELLATION (U.S. Navy, Robert L. Lawson)

AV-8A/C HARRIER (Hawker Siddeley/McDonnell Douglas)

The AV-8A was the first VSTOL aircraft to enter service with the U.S. armed forces. The British-developed Harrier and its experimental predecessor, the P.1127 Kestrel (U.S. designation (XV-6A), flew test flights from several U.S. and foreign ships prior to acceptance by the U.S. Marine Corps. The AV-8A variant, manufactured by McDonnell Douglas, entered Marine squadrons in 1971 (two years after squadron deliveries to the Royal Air Force). In addition to the 108 single-seat Harriers procured by the Marines, eight TAV-8A two-seat training aircraft were acquired. (British designation was Harrier Mk 50.)

The Harrier is powered by a vectored-thrust turbofan engine that exhausts through rotating nozzles. The nozzles are rotated for vertical and short takeoffs and landings. The wings do not fold, but the aircraft is fully carrier capable, as demonstrated during successful deployments aboard the helicopter carrier GUAM (LPH 7) in 1972 and 1974, and the attack carrier FRANKLIN D. ROOSEVELT (CV 42) in 1977.

In service the aircraft has suffered a high accident loss rate, although almost all of the losses have occurred during conventional flight and not in the vertical flight mode. The surviving aircraft are being upgraded and redesignated AV-8C. The improved AV-8B is listed separately. Payload data is for 1,000-foot takeoff roll.

Electronics: No radar; AV-8C being fitted with ALE-39 chaff/IR dispenser, APR-43 and ALR-45F threat warning receivers.

(AV-8A)

Crew:	1 pilot (2 in TAV-8A)
Weights:	12,200 lbs empty; 17,500 lbs gross for VTO; 21,489 lbs gross for STO; 25,000+ lbs maximum with conventional takeoff
Dimensions:	length 45$\frac{1}{2}$ ft (13.87 m), span 25$\frac{1}{4}$ ft (7.7 m), height 11$\frac{1}{4}$ ft (3.43 m)
Engines:	1 Rolls-Royce Pegasus Mk 103 vectored-thrust turbofan; 21,500 lbst
Speeds:	737 mph at 1,000 ft (Mach 0.95)
Ranges:	200-n.mile radius with 2,500 lbs ordnance; 400-n.mile radius with 2 AAMs and 1 hour loiter
Ceiling:	50,000+ ft
Guns:	none
Payload:	2 Sidewinder AAMs + 3 1,000-lb bombs + 2 30-mm Aden gun pods or 2 Sidewinder AAMs + 5 500-lb bombs + 2 30-mm Aden gun pods

AV-8A Harriers—VMA-231/F. D. ROOSEVELT (U.S. Navy, PH3 Greg Haas)

AV-8A Harrier—VMA-231/F. D. ROOSEVELT (U.S. Navy, PH3 Greg Haas)

AV-8A Harrier—VMA-231/F.D. ROOSEVELT (U.S. Navy, PH3 Greg Haas)

AV-8A Harrier—VMA-513/GUAM (U.S. Navy, PH1 L. M. MacKay)

AV-8B HARRIER (McDonnell Douglas)

The AV-8B is an improved VSTOL light attack aircraft based on the AV-8A Harrier. Two AV-8As were modified to the YAV-8B prototypes, the first one flying on 9 November 1978. Subsequently, the Marine Corps developed a requirement for 322 of the improved aircraft to replace the A-4M Skyhawks and AV-8A/C Harriers in eight attack squadrons, plus pipeline and training aircraft. However, the Carter Administration opposed development of the AV-8B, in part to ensure maximum production of the F/A-18 Hornet. The Congress has continued to fund full-scale development of the AV-8B with initial squadron delivery planned for 1984–1985.

The improved Harrier differs from the AV-8A variant, in having a supercritical wing shape, larger trailing-edge flaps, drooped ailerons, strakes under the gun pods, redesigned engine intakes, and strengthened landing gear. Original plans for an improved engine were dropped in favor of the above refinements in the aircraft's aerodynamic lift. The Advanced Harrier (AV-16) project was canceled in 1975, with some of the features of this joint British-American project being incorporated in the AV-8B. A two-seat TAV-8B has also been developed.

An AV-8B+ aircraft has also been proposed for Navy shipboard use. This aircraft would differ from the basic AV-8B by having increased engine thrust (22,600 lbst), an APG-65-derivative radar, autopilot, improved navigation and all-weather landing equipment. The AV-8B+ would have an empty operating weight of 13,475 pounds and a maximum weight of 31,000 pounds.

Crew:	1 pilot
Weights:	12,550 lbs empty; 29,550 lbs. maximum for STO; 18,850 lbs maximum for VTO
Dimensions:	length: 46¼ ft (14.1 m), span 30¼ ft (9.2 m), height 11⁷/₁₂ ft
Engines:	1 Rolls-Royce Pegasus F402-RR-404 vectored-thrust turbofan; 21,500 lbst
Speeds:	Approx. 750 mph (Mach 0.95)
Ranges:	100-n.mile radius with 7,800 lbs weapons in VTO mode; 150-n.mile radius with 6,000 lbs weapons in STO mode (1,000-ft takeoff run) and 1 hour on station; 650-n.mile radius with 3,500 lbs weapons in STO mode (no loiter time); 2,000-n.mile ferry range
Ceiling:	50,000+ ft
Guns:	none internal
Payload:	2 Sidewinder AAMs + 14 500-lb bombs + 2 20-mm/30-mm gun pods or 2 Sidewinder AAMs + 6 1,000-lb bombs + 2 20-mm/30-mm gun pods or 2 Sidewinder AAMs + 4 Maverick ASMs + 2 20-mm/30-mm gun pods

YAV-8B Harrier (McDonnell Douglas)

YAV-8B Harrier taking off from ski-jump ramp (McDonnell Douglas)

The Harrier's predecessor was the Hawker Siddeley P 1127, later named Kestrel in British service. The world's first truly combat-capable VSTOL aircraft, it was evaluated by U.S. services as the XV-6A, and is shown landing here aboard the RALEIGH (LPD 1) in 1966. The tail-fin markings are "Tri-Service" and the Air Force serial 64-18266 in shortened form. (U.S. Navy)

YAV-8B Harrier with 12 Mk 82 500-lb bombs (McDonnell Douglas)

ANTISUBMARINE AIRCRAFT

S-3 VIKING (Lockheed)

The S-3 is the Navy's carrier-based ASW aircraft, with one ten-plane squadron planned for each of the 12 carrier air wings. By 1978, the Viking had fully replaced the venerable S-2 Tracker in Navy first-line service (although Trackers continued to serve briefly in the utility and training roles, as well as in foreign air arms).

The aircraft carries a variety of ASW sensors with an on-board 65,000-word AYK-30 digital computer to process data for the sensors, communications, and navigation systems. The sensors include APS-116 high-resolution radar, ASQ-81 Magnetic Anomaly Detection (MAD), Forward-Looking Infrared (FLIR), Electronic Countermeasures (ECM), and fuselage tube launchers for 60 sonobuoys. The Viking's endurance is over nine hours.

Three variants of the S-3 are being proposed: The US-3A COD (Carrier On-Board Delivery), ES-3A TASES (Tactical Airborne Signal Exploitation System), and KS-3A tanker. These variants would be converted from stored S-3A aircraft or from additional production.

The COD variant would be able to carry up to 23 passengers or 8 to 10,000 pounds of cargo in the fuselage and two large, underwing pods. Four non-ASW aircraft prototypes have been modified to the US-3A COD configuration.

The TASES aircraft would perform surveillance in direct support of fleet operations, using radar and electro-optical, electronic, and hydroacoustic (sonobuoy) systems. Each aircraft would have two pilots and three equipment operators.

The fifth production S-3A has been modified to a tanker demonstration aircraft that lacks certain ASW systems and is fitted with additional fuel tanks in the weapons bay and with a hose, reel, and drogue in the after fuselage. Two external fuel tanks could also be fitted. The aircraft would thus have twice the fuel/time-on-station as the KA-6D tanker.

Electronics: APS-116 radar, ASQ-147 armament control system, APN-200 doppler navigation radar, and ALR-47 threat warning receiver.

(S-3A)

Crew:	2 pilots, 1 tactical coordinator, 1 systems operator
Weights:	26,783 lbs empty; 52,539 lbs maximum
Dimensions:	length 53^1/$_3$ ft (16.26 m), span 68^2/$_3$ ft (20.93 m), height 22^3/$_4$ ft (6.94 m)
Engines:	2 GE TF34-GE-400 high by-pass ratio turbofan; 9,275 lbst each
Speeds:	506 mph at sea level; 400+ mph cruise; 240 mph loiter at 20,000 ft
Ranges:	2,300+ n.mile patrol range; 3,000+ n.mile ferry range
Ceiling:	40,000 ft
Guns:	none
Payload:	4 Mk 46 torpedoes (weapons bay) + 6 500-lb bombs (wing pylons) or 4 500-lb bombs (weapons bay) + 6 500-lb bombs (wing pylons)

S-3A Vikings; openings in after fuselage are sonobuoy launch tubes—VS-28/INDEPENDENCE (Robert L. Lawson)

S-3A Viking with MAD boom extended—VS-41/SARATOGA (U.S. Navy)

S-3A Viking taking off from FORRESTAL with practice mines (U.S. Navy, PH3 Terry C. Mitchell)

PATROL AIRCRAFT

P-3 ORION (Lockheed)

The P-3 (formerly P3V) serves in all 24 Navy patrol squadrons and 13 Naval Reserve VP squadrons. Several foreign navies and air forces also fly the Orion (called Aurora in Canadian service).

The aircraft was adopted from the commercial Electra airliner, with a succession of ASW/maritime-patrol variants being produced for the U.S. Navy. Most active Navy squadrons now fly the P-3C variant. The P-3C in its basic configuration has the ASQ-114 digital computer for ASW tactical calculations, APS-115 search radar, ASQ-10A MAD, Electronic Countermeasures (ECM), and other sensors, and 48 external sonobuoy tubes plus one reloadable internal sonobuoy tube. Patrol endurance is up to 16 hours.

There are three major variants of the P-3C: The UPDATE I with Omega navigation, DIFAR sonobuoys (see Chapter 24), and improved computer memory; UPDATE II with the above features plus infrared sensor, sonobuoy reference system, and Harpoon ASM (fitted from 1979 on); and UPDATE III with the addition of an advanced signal processor, sonobuoy communication link, and digital magnetic tape system.

Specialized P-3 variants in U.S. service include DP-3A drone control aircraft, EP-3B/E electronic reconnaissance aircraft, RP-3D research aircraft, and WP-3D weather research planes. Beginning in 1980, Lockheed has modified older Orions to the DP-3A configuration to carry aerial target drones and provide limited EW training for fleet units. The 12 EP-3B/Es have radar pods faired into their upper and lower fuselage plus electronic surveillance equipment. They are assigned to VQ-1 and VQ-2 and have 15-man crews. The RP-3D aircraft are flown by VXN-8. The WP-3D aircraft are flown by the National Oceanic and Atmospheric Administration; they carry a crew of four plus 12 scientists. Some aircraft have been modified to a VP-3 configuration.

Total P-3 production for all nations passed the 500 number during 1980 with manufacture continuing. The P-3C entered U.S. Navy service in 1970 with an all P-3C force planned for the active 24 squadrons by 1988.

Electronics: APS-80 search radar in the P-3B, APS-115 in the P-3C, APS-120 in the EP-3E; AQS-10 MAD in the P-3B and early P-3C aircraft, with AQS-81 being subsequently installed. The EP-3E additionally has ALQ-76, ALQ-78, ALQ-108, ALQ-132, ALR-52, and ALR-60 EW systems.

(P-3C)

Crew:	1 command pilot, 2 pilots, 1 flight engineer, 1 navigator, 1 radio operator, 1 tactical coordinator, 3 systems operators; provisions for 2 additional observers
Weights:	61,491 lbs empty; 135,000 lbs loaded; 142,000 lbs maximum
Dimensions:	lenght 116⅚ ft (35.61 m), span 99⅔ ft (30.37 m), height 33¾ ft (10.28 m)
Engines:	4 Allison T56-A-14 turboprop; 4,910 shp each
Speeds:	473 mph at 15,000 ft; 378 mph cruise at 25,000 ft; 237 mph patrol at 1,500 ft.
Ranges:	2,380-n.mile patrol range; 4,500-n.mile ferry range
Ceiling:	28,300 ft
Guns:	none
Payload:	8 Mk 46 torpedoes (weapons bay) + 4 Mk 46 torpedoes (wing pylons) or 2 2,000-lb mines (weapons bay) + 4 Mk 46 torpedoes (wing pylons) or 4 1,000-lb mines (weapons bay) + 4 Mk 46 torpedoes (wing pylons) or 8 Mk 46 torpedoes (weapons bay) + 16 5-inch rockets (wing pylons)

P-3B Orion—VP-4 (U.S. Navy, PH1 L.B. Foster)

MAD boom on P-3A Orion—VP-64 (U.S. Navy)

EP-3E Orion; note fuselage electronics fairing and radome under fuselage; there is also a dorsal electronics fairing; there are no squadron markings —VQ-2 (U.S. Navy)

P-3 Orion (U.S. Navy)

ELECTRONIC AIRCRAFT

E-2 HAWKEYE (Grumman)

The Hawkeye (formerly W2F) is a carrier-based Airborne Early Warning (AEW) aircraft that in its E-2C variant is generally considered the most capable electronic warning and control aircraft yet produced. (The E-2C had been offered as an alternative to the larger, land-based E-3 AWACS aircraft.) The Navy plans to procure enough E-2C aircraft to provide a four-plane detachment for each of 12 carrier air wings, with a total of 85 aircraft (including two prototype aircraft) planned for funding through FY 1982. One of the prototype aircraft was an E-2A modified to a YE-2C configuration, and now used as a trainer (designated TE-2C). Several E-2B aircraft (all updated E-2A) remain in service pending the availability of sufficient E-2C aircraft. The E-2B entered service in 1960 and the E-2C in 1973.

Israel and Japan also fly the E-2C aircraft.

Electronics: The E-2C has a 24-foot diameter, saucer-shaped radome housing an APS-125 UHF radar. The dome revolves in the free airstream at the rate of six revolutions per minute. The radome can be retracted to reduce aircraft height to 16 feet for carrier stowage. The aircraft has an on-board computer, ALR-59 passive detection system, and secure UHF and HF data links. (The E-2A/B had APS-96 radar; the early E-2C aircraft had APS-120 radar.) The APS-125 provides an effective radar coverage out to some 240 n.miles.

(E-2C)

Crew:	2 pilots, 1 combat information center (CIC) officer, 1 air controller, 1 radar operator or technician
Weights:	37,678 lbs empty; 51,569 lbs maximum
Dimensions:	length 57$^7/_{12}$ ft (17.56 m), span 80$^7/_{12}$ ft (24.58 m), height 18$^1/_3$ ft (5.59 m)
Engines:	2 Allison T56-A-422 turboprop; 4,591 shp each
Speeds:	375 mph; 310 mph cruise
Ranges:	200-n.mile radius with up to six hours on station; 1,525-n.mile ferry range
Ceiling:	30,800 ft
Guns:	none
Payload:	none

E-2C Hawkeye—VAW-116/Constellation (Grumman)

E-2B Hawkeye—VAW-116/Constellation (U.S. Navy)

E-2C Hawkeye—VAW-123/Saratoga (U.S. Navy)

E-2C Hawkeye—VAW-116/Constellation (Grumman)

EA-3B SKYWARRIOR (Douglas)

The Navy flies the EA-3B (formerly A3D-2Q) in the TASES (Tactical Airborne Signal Exploitation System) role in squadrons VQ-1 and -2. These aircraft are based ashore, but regularly go aboard carriers deployed in the Mediterranean and Western Pacific. The EA-3B began flying in the TASES role in 1960 and is expected to continue until about 1985, when it may be replaced by converted ES-3 Viking. The TASES variant was developed from the basic A-3 (A3D) carrier-based heavy attack aircraft built in the late 1940s for the nuclear strike role.

The EA-3B is fitted with several electronic and communications-intercept systems, forward-looking and side-looking radars, infra-red sensors, and other specialized equipment. Fully loaded, the EA-3B is the heaviest carrier-based aircraft in service with any navy. In addition, ERA-3B aircraft with cameras removed are flown by VAQ-33 for EW training in fleet exercises. Two Naval Reserve squadrons fly the EKA-3B in the tanker role.

Electronics: These aircraft have ASB-1B search radar plus a variety of EW systems.

(EA-3B)

Crew:	1 pilot, 1 navigator/assistant pilot, 4 electronic systems operators, 1 additional crewman (optional); 4 crew in ERA-3B
Weights:	41,193 lbs empty; 61,593 lbs loaded; 78,000 lbs maximum
Dimensions:	length 76⅓ ft (23.28 m), span 72½ ft (22.11 m), height 22⅚ ft (6.94 m)
Engines:	2 P&W J57-P-10 turbojet; 12,400 lbst each
Speeds:	640 mph at sea level (mach 0.84); 610 mph at 10,000 ft (Mach 0.83) 459 mph cruise
Ranges:	1,100-n.mile radius
Ceiling:	41,300 ft
Guns:	removed (2 20-mm guns originally mounted in tail turret)
Payload:	none

ERA-3B Skywarrior (VAQ-33) and TA-4J Skyhawk (VC-1) (U.S. Navy, PH3, T.J. Perang)

EA-3B Skywarrior; there are no squadron markings—VQ-2 (U.S. Navy)

EA-6A INTRUDER (Grumman)

The EA-6A (formerly A2F-1H) is a tactical Electronic Countermeasures (ECM) variant of the A-6A Intruder attack aircraft. The aircraft was developed specifically for the Marine Corps, and squadron VMAQ-2 was assigned 15 of the aircraft to provide detachments to the three Marine air wings. Subsequently, two Naval Reserve squadrons have received EA-6A Intruders. In 1977 the Marines took delivery of the first of the more capable EA-6B Prowlers, which will completely replace the EA-6A aircraft in the early 1980s.

Removal of the EA-6A jamming pods from the wing pylons permits the aircraft to operate in a limited attack mode.

Electronics: The EA-6A has APQ-92 search radar and APN-122 navigation radar. In its original configuration the EA-6B could carry up to five ALQ-31B jamming pods. An ALQ-31A self-protection pod could also be carried. Other equipment includes an ALQ-29 chaff dispenser and an ALQ-100 jammer.

(EA-6A)

Crew:	1 pilot, 1 electronic systems operator
Weights:	27,769 lbs empty; 41,715 lbs loaded; 54,571 lbs maximum
Dimensions:	length 55½ ft (16.92 m), span 53 ft (16.15 m), height 15½ ft (4.72 m)
Engines:	2 P&W J52-P-6 turbojet; 8,500 lbst each
Speeds:	630 mph at sea level (Mach 0.83); 595 mph at sea level with five ECM pods
Ranges:	825-n.mile radius with one ECM pod; 600-n.mile radius with three pods; 345-n.mile radius with five pods
Ceiling:	37,800 ft
Guns:	none
Payload:	5 jamming pods or up to 18,000 lbs of weapons (see A-6 listing)

EA-6A Intruder—VMAQ-2 (Stephen H. Miller)

EA-6A Intruder aboard FORRESTAL-class carrier (U.S. Navy)

EA-6B Prowler—VAQ-133/J. F. KENNEDY (Norman Polmar)

EA-6B PROWLER (Grumman)

The EA-6B is an ECM variant of the A-6 Intruder attack aircraft that was developed for carrier operation. The aircraft differs from the EA-6A in having two more systems operators and more sophisticated jamming equipment. The name was changed from Intruder to Prowler in February 1972. The aircraft entered service in 1971.

The Navy has nine operational EA-6B "squadrons," with four aircraft each. The Navy plans to assign one such squadron to each of 12 carrier air wings. In addition, the Marine Corps has one squadron with EA-6B and EA-6A aircraft. Total EA-6B deliveries through 1981 were to total 84 aircraft.

The basic EA-6B aircraft has been updated with the EXCAP (Expanded Capability) and ICAP (Improved Capability) modifications to provide increased jamming capability. Total payload for the EA-6B is 8,000 pounds of internal avionic/EW equipment plus 950 pounds on each of four wing pylons and the centerline attachment point. Drop tanks can be substituted for jamming pods to increase range.

A KA-6H tanker variant based on the EA-6B has been proposed as a successor to the KA-6D Intruder.

Electronics: APQ-129 search radar, APN-153 doppler navigation radar, up to five ALQ-99 tactical jamming pods, ALE-39 chaff-infrared dispenser, ALR-67 threat warning receiver, and ALQ-126 jammer. Each ALQ-99 pod has a tracking receiver, power generator, and two noise jammers, permitting one aircraft to cover several frequencies simultaneously.

EA-6B Prowler—VAQ-129 (Grumman)

(EA-6B)

Crew:	1 pilot, 3 electronic systems operators
Weights:	34,581 lbs empty; 58,500 lbs maximum
Dimensions:	length $59^5/_{12}$ ft (18.11 m), span 53 ft (16.15 m), height $16^1/_4$ ft (4.95 m)
Engines:	2 P&W J52-P-408 turbojet; 11,200 lbst
Speeds:	660 mph at sea level; 477 mph cruise
Ranges:	710-n.mile radius with four ECM pods
Ceiling:	
Guns:	none
Payload:	5 ALQ-99 jamming pods

EA-6B Prowler—VAQ-129 (now code NJ)

NC-121K WARNING STAR (Lockheed)

An NC-121K aircraft is flown by VAQ-33 for fleet electronic warfare training. The aircraft, originally designated WV-2, was initially acquired as part of the Navy's seaward extension of the Distant Early Warning (DEW) line established in the early 1950s to provide warning of a Soviet bomber attack against the United States. The Navy's patrol barrier of AEW aircraft and surface ships was abolished late in 1965.

The EC-121 airframe was a military adoption of the commercial Lockheed model 1049 Super Constellation, also flown by the U.S. Air Force. Several transport versions were also flown (Navy R7V).

The following characteristics reflect the aircraft's original EC-121K (WV-2) configuration; it has subsequently been modified with additional jamming equipment. Fewer crewmen are carried in the VAQ-33 operations (beyond the 16 active crew stations, there were accommodations for 12–14 relief personnel).

Electronics: APS-20 search radar mounted in lower fuselage dome and APS-45 height-finding radar in dorsal fin.

Crew:	2 pilots, 1 flight engineer, 1 navigator, 1 radio operator, 1 CIC officer, 5 controllers, 1 track operator, 2 ECM operators, 2 radar operators
Weights:	83,671 lbs empty; 116,000 lbs loaded; 156,500 lbs maximum
Dimensions:	length 116 1/6 ft (35.39 m), span 123 5/12 ft (37.62 m), height 27 ft (8.23 m)
Engines:	4 Wright R-3350-34 piston with supercharger; 3,250 hp each maximum (T/O only); 2,650 hp each continuous
Speeds:	328 mph at 19,300 ft
Ranges:	2,580-n.mile normal search range; 3,590-n.mile search range in overload condition; 3,850-n.mile ferry range
Ceiling:	21,900 ft
Guns:	none
Payload:	none

EF-4B Phantom (now discarded), NC-121K Warning Star, EA-4F Skyhawk —VAQ-33 (U.S. Navy)

NKC-135A STRATOTANKER (Boeing)

The Navy operates two of these aircraft in the electronic warfare simulation/jamming role. They are the largest aircraft currently in service with Navy markings but are flown by McDonnell Douglas personnel. They are used in support of research, development, test and evaluation programs, and in support of Fleet training, tactics development, and readiness exercises. Each aircraft has some 12,500 pounds of electronic equipment on board. They have been described as having a greater jamming capability than any other aircraft now flying.

Both were produced for the Air Force as KC-135A tanker aircraft with standard boom refueling equipment. They were modified by the Air Force, including removal of the air-refueling equipment, for use in various R&D programs. Further modifications by the Navy include removal of some of the body fuel cells for equipment bays, replacement of the weather radar with a sea search unit, installation of pod pylons on the wings and a new EWO/navigator station in the cargo cabin. These aircraft replace two Navy-owned EB-47E Stratofortresses that were previously flown in this role. The NKC-135s retain their Air Force serial numbers in Navy service with No. 563596 entering naval service on 9 December 1977 and No. 553134 on 15 May 1978.

Crew:	2 pilots, 1 navigator/electronic warfare operator
Weights:	123,000 lbs empty; 270,000 lbs maximum
Dimensions:	length 134 1/2 ft (41.0 m), span 130 5/6 ft (40.0 m), height 41 3/4 ft (12.7 m)
Engines:	4 P&W J57-P-59W turbojet; 13,750 lbst each maximum (T/O only); 9,500 lbst each continuous
Speeds:	530 mph at 25,000 feet
Ranges:	~4,400 n.miles
Ceiling:	~41,000 ft
Payload:	~12,500 lbs EW equipment internal and pods on 2 wing pylons

NKC-135A Stratotanker (McDonnell Douglas)

EP-2H NEPTUNE (Lockheed)

The P-2 Neptune (originally P2V) was the most advanced maritime patrol aircraft developed during World War II. It entered U.S. Navy squadron service in 1947 and was the Navy's first-line VP aircraft well into the 1960s, when it was displaced in service by the P-3 Orion. It is still flown by several foreign air forces in the patrol role. The U.S. Navy has only three Neptunes in service, all EP-2H aircraft assigned to VC-8 at NAS Roosevelt Roads, Puerto Rico, for data-link control of aerial target drones. VC-8 disposed of its last DP-2H drone-launch aircraft in 1980.

Lockheed built a total of 1,099 aircraft, and Kawasaki in Japan produced another 89 P-2J variants (forty-eight of the Lockheed-manufactured P-2H aircraft were assembled in Japan). The following data is for the basic P-2H aircraft.

Electronics: Principal ASW sensors for the SP-2H ASW aircraft were APS-20E search radar, ASQ-8 MAD, plus 72 sonobuoys.

(P-2H)

Crew:	2 pilots, 1 navigator, 1 flight engineer, 3 observers/systems operators
Weights:	49,935 lbs empty; 79,895 lbs maximum
Dimensions:	length $91^2/_3$ ft (27.94 m), span $103^{11}/_{12}$ ft (31.65 m), height $29^1/_3$ ft (8.94 m)
Engines:	2 Wright R-3550-32W radial piston; 3,500 hp each + 2 Westinghouse J34-WE-32W turbojet pods 3,400 lbst each
Speeds:	356 mph at 10,000 ft (piston engines only); 173 mph patrol at 980 ft
Ranges:	2,200-n.mile patrol range; 3,685-n.mile maximun range
Ceiling:	22,000 ft
Guns:	none
Payload:	4 2,000-lb bombs (weapons bay) + 16 5-inch rockets (wing pylons) or 8 8 Mk 46 torpedoes (weapons bay) + 16 5-inch rockets (wing pylons)

EP-2H Neptune—VC-8 (U.S. Navy)

RF-8G Crusader—VFP-63/F.D. ROOSEVELT (U.S. Navy)

RECONNAISSANCE AIRCRAFT

RF-8G CRUSADER (LTV)

The Crusaders that remain in first-line U.S. Navy service are all RF-8G-photo-reconnaissance aircraft. From the mid-1950s into the late 1960s the F-8 (formerly F8U) was the standard U.S. carrier-based day fighter. Ling-Temco-Vought (now Vought) built a total of 1,266 Crusaders of all marks, including 42 specifically for French carrier service (designated F-8E (FN)).

One active Navy squadron and two reserve squadrons fly the RF-8G variant. Seventy-three RF-8A (formerly F8U-1P) photo planes were "remanufactured" in the late 1960s to extend their service life. The active squadron, VFP-63, provides five detachments of three planes each to forward deployed carriers. Under current plans the last RF-8G detachment will be disbanded in the early 1980s when sufficient RF-14 Tomcats with TARPS reconnaissance pods become available.

The RF-8G carries several cameras fitted in the forward fuselage. No other reconnaissance sensors are provided.

Crew:	1 pilot
Weights:	16,796 lbs empty; 23,752 lbs loaded; 27,822 lbs maximum
Dimensions:	length $54^1/_2$ ft (16.61 m), span $35^2/_3$ ft (10.87 m), height $15^3/_4$ ft (4.8 m)
Engines:	1 P&W J57-P420 turbojet; 11,440 lbst; 18,000 lbst with afterburner
Speeds:	983 mph at 35,000 ft; 673 mph at sea level
Ranges:	640-n.mile radius
Ceiling:	51,800 ft
Guns:	none
Payload:	no ordnance capability

An RF-8G Crusader from VFP-63 is catapulted from a waist "cat" of the KITTY HAWK (CV 63). Note the aircraft's wing in the "raised" position. The wing retracts flush with the fuselage after takeoff. Crusader fighters are still flown by the French Navy from two aircraft carriers. The photo Crusaders of the U.S. Navy will be replaced by RF-14A pod-carrying aircraft in the early 1980s. (1979, U.S. Navy, PH1 John C. Borovoy)

OBSERVATION AIRCRAFT

OV-10 BRONCO (Rockwell International)

The OV-10 is a multi-purpose light attack aircraft developed by the Navy and Marine Corps for the counterinsurgency role. It is designed for rough field operation, and has operated in the STOL mode from LHA/LPH-type amphibious ships (without the use of arresting wires or catapults). The aircraft was flown by the U.S. Navy in the Vietnam War; it is now flown by two Marine VMO squadrons, each with 18 aircraft, and one Marine Reserve squadron. The aircraft is also flown by several foreign air forces.

With the removal of the second seat, the OV-10 can carry 3,200 pounds of cargo, or five paratroopers, or two litter patients and an attendant.

Nineteen aircraft have been modified to the OV-10D Night Observation Gunship System (NOGS) configuration for evaluation by the Marines. They have Forward-Looking Infrared (FLIR) and laser target designator systems, and two M-97 20-mm cannon mounted in an under-fuselage turret. The aircraft has been lengthened $2^1/_2$ feet.

(OV-10A)

Crew:	1 pilot, 1 observer
Weights:	6,969 lbs empty; 9,908 lbs loaded; 14,466 lbs maximum
Dimensions:	length $41^7/_{12}$ ft (12.67 m), span 40 ft (12.19 m), height $15^1/_6$ ft (4.63 m)
Engines:	2 Garrett AiResearch T76-G-10/10A/12/12A turboprop; 715 shp each
Speeds:	281 mph clean at sea level
Ranges:	228-n.mile radius in attack role; 1,430-n.mile ferry range
Ceiling:	
Guns:	2 7.62-mm MG
Payload:	bombs, rocket pods, fuel tanks on 5 wing and fuselage stations (7 on OV-10D)

OV-10A Broncos—VAL-4 (now disbanded) (U.S. Navy)

An OV-10A Bronco takes off from the amphibious assault ship SAIPAN (LHA 2) during NATO operations off Scotland in September 1980. These STOL aircraft can easily operate from LHAs and LPHs. Note squared-off wings and center-line fuel tank. (1980, U.S. Navy, PHC John Francavillo)

UTILITY AIRCRAFT

HU-16 ALBATROSS (Grumman)

The HU-16E (formerly designated UF-2G) is flown by the U.S. Coast Guard in the Search And Rescue (SAR) role. The U.S. Navy retired its last HU-16D Albatross in 1977. A number of foreign nations continue to fly the aircraft, some of which may still retain a limited ASW configuration. The Coast Guard has flown the Albatross since 1951, with almost one hundred having been acquired. At the end of 1980 the Coast Guard had only six HU-16E aircraft in service, with another three in storage. The plane is nicknamed ''Goat'' in Coast Guard service.

The HU-25A Falcon was to have replaced the Albatross, but the newer plane's entry into service has been delayed (see below).

On an SAR mission the HU-16E has a 17-hour endurance.

A closeup of one of the Marines' YOV-10D Broncos modified for Night Observation Surveillance (NOS). There is a Forward-Looking Infrared (FLIR) sensor and laser target designator in the ball-turret under the nose and a 20-mm M-97 gun turret under the fuselage. The gun turret can be replaced by five weapon attachment stations for gun pods, rockets, bombs, or fuel tanks; there are also two outboard weapon stations on the wings. This view shows one of two YOV-10Ds that preceded the 17 OV-10A-to-OV-10D conversions. (U.S. Marine Corps)

(HU-16E)

Crew:	2 pilots, 1 navigator, 1 radio operator
Weights:	23,025 lbs empty; 34,000 lbs maximum water takeoff; 37,500 lbs maximum runway takeoff
Dimensions:	length 62⁵/₆ ft (19.17 m), span 96²/₃ ft (29.48 m), height 25¹¹/₁₂ ft (7.9 m)
Engines:	2 Wright R-1820-76A/B radial pistons; 1,425 hp each
Speeds:	204 mph at 3,700 ft; 150 mph at 10,000 ft cruise; 135 mph at 1,500 ft search
Ranges:	1,130-n.mile radius for SAR; 1,090-n.mile radius as transport
Ceiling	24,000 ft
Guns:	none
Payload:	10 passengers or 12 litter patients

HU-16E Albatross (U.S. Coast Guard)

HU-25 FALCON (Falcon Jet)

The Coast Guard is procuring the HU-25A as an all-weather, medium-range search aircraft. The aircraft is a modified commercial Falcon 20G business transport. Forty-one aircraft are being produced for the Coast Guard by the Falcon Jet Corporation, which is a jointly owned subsidiary of Dassault Breguet and Pan American. Deliveries were to have begun in mid-1979 at the rate of one aircraft per month; however, engine development problems delayed the first aircraft delivery until 1981, with a delivery rate of 1¹/₂ per month.

The aircraft is also being produced in the maritime reconnaissance mode for the French Navy and the Japanese Maritime Safety Agency.

In addition to the flight crew, the HU-25A can carry three passengers and four litters, plus 3,200 pounds of rescue supplies that can be parachuted from a large drop-hatch. A galley and toilet are provided to facilitate long-endurance flights.

Electronics: APS-127 radar with provision for installation of APS-94D SLAR (Side-Looking Aircraft Radar).

Crew:	2 pilots, 2 observers, 1 surveillance systems operator
Weights:	19,000 lbs empty; 20,890 lbs loaded; 32,000 lbs maximum
Dimensions:	length 56¹/₄ ft (17,15 m), span 53¹/₂ ft (16.3 m), height 17⁵/₁₂ ft (5.32 m)
Engines:	2 Garrett AiResearch. ATF3-6-2C turbofan; 5,538 lbst each
Speeds:	531 mph at 40,000 ft; 173 mph slow search at low altitude
Ranges:	2,250-n.mile maximum range with 30 minutes on station
Ceiling:	
Guns:	none
Payload:	3 passengers + 4 litter patients

Artist's concept of HU-25A Falcon (Falcon Jet)

CARGO/TRANSPORT AIRCRAFT

CARRIER ON-BOARD DELIVERY AIRCRAFT (VCX)

The Navy plans to procure 24 COD-type cargo aircraft beginning in FY 1983 to replace the existing C-1A and C-2A aircraft. The new COD may be a variant of the S-3A Viking ASW aircraft (with one aircraft configured as a US-3A for COD evaluation and subsequently flown operationally; three more were later modified to US-3As).

C-1A TRADER (Grumman)

The Trader is a Carrier On-board Delivery (COD) aircraft developed to carry high-priority freight and passengers to and from carriers at sea. The aircraft was developed from the S-2(S2F) Tracker ASW aircraft. Formerly designated TF-1, a small number of C-1As remain in Navy service. A few were configured as electronic training aircraft (EC-1A formerly TF-1Q). Fifty C-1A aircraft were procured with just over 30 remaining in service.

The aircraft's internal cargo capacity is 90 cubic feet or 3,500 pounds of cargo.

Crew:	2 pilots
Weights:	27,000 lbs loaded
Dimensions:	length 42 ft (12.8 m), span 69²/₃ ft (21.23 m), height 16¹/₃ ft (4.98 m)
Engines:	2 Wright R1820-82 radial piston; 1,525 hp each
Speeds:	334 mph
Ranges:	1,200-n.mile range
Ceiling:	
Guns:	none
Payload:	9 passengers or 3,500 lbs cargo

C-1A Trader—CONSTELLATION (U.S. Navy, PHCS Robert L. Lawson)

C-2 GREYHOUND (Grumman)

The Greyhound is a second-generation COD aircraft derived from the E-2 Hawkeye AEW aircraft, using that aircraft's wings, power plant, and tail, but having a larger fuselage and a rear-loading ramp. The last feature permits the loading of high-cube cargo, including some aircraft engines. The cargo capacity is 675 cubic feet or 8,200 pounds. In-flight refueling capability is being provided to all C-2s from 1980 on.

Twelve C-2A aircraft were procured, all of which remain in service after extensive updating. Whereas C-1A aircraft are assigned to carriers, all C-2A Greyhounds are based ashore with the remaining Traders in VR/VRC squadrons.

Crew:	2 pilots, 1 flight engineer
Weights:	31,250 lbs empty; 54,382 lbs loaded
Dimensions:	length 56^2/$_3$ ft (17.27 m), span 80^7/$_{12}$ ft (24.57 m), height 15^{11}/$_{12}$ ft (4.85 m)
Engines:	2 Allison T56-A-8A turboprop; 4,050 shp each
Speeds:	352 mph at 30,000 ft; 296 mph cruise at 30,000 ft
Ranges:	1,440-n.mile range
Ceiling:	28,800 ft
Guns:	none
Payload:	39 passengers
	or 20 litter patients
	or 8,200 lbs cargo

C-2A Greyhound (U.S. Navy)

C-2A Greyhound—VRC-50 (U.S. Navy)

C-4 ACADEME (Grumman)

The Coast Guard operates one VC-4A as an executive (VIP) transport, and the Navy and Marine Corps fly several TC-4C trainers. The latter have the after cabin configured as an A-6 cockpit for training bombardier/navigators for that aircraft. Although officially named Academe in military service, the Coast Guard uses the commercial name Gulfstream I for its Washington-based VIP aircraft.

(VC-4A)

Crew:	2 pilots, 1 crewman
Weights:	36,000 lbs loaded
Dimensions:	length 63^3/$_4$ ft (19.34 m), span 78^1/$_3$ ft (23.87 m), height 23^1/$_2$ ft (7.11 m)
Engines:	2 Rolls-Royce Dart Mk 529-8 turboprop; 2,210 shp each
Speeds:	403 mph
Ranges:	2,621-n.mile range
Ceiling:	
Guns:	none
Payload:	

VC-4A Gulfstream I (U.S. Coast Guard)

TC-4C Academe configured for training bombardier/navigators in the A-6 Intruder weapon system; the nose houses an A-6 radome and there are three student positions aft—VA-128 (U.S. Navy)

C-9 SKYTRAIN II (McDonnell Douglas)

The C-9B is a military version of the DC-9 Series 32 commercial transport, which is convertible to the cargo or transport role. The aircraft is flown by the Naval Reserve and Marine Corps. (The U.S. Air Force flies the C-9A named Nightingale for aeromedical airlift.) The Navy has shifted all C-9s from active to reserve squadrons.

Crew:	2 pilots, 1 crew chief, 2 attendants
Weights:	59,706 lbs empty in cargo configuration; 65,283 lbs empty in transport configuration; 110,000 lbs maximum
Dimensions:	length 119 1/3 ft (36.37 m), span 93 5/12 ft (28.47 m), height 27 1/2 ft (8.38 m)
Engines:	2 P&W JT8D-9 turbofan; 14,500 lbst each
Speeds:	576 mph; 504 mph cruise
Ranges:	2,538-n.mile range with 10,000 lbs cargo
Ceiling:	37,000 ft
Guns:	none
Payload:	90 passengers or 32,444 lbs cargo (8 standard type 463L cargo pallets)

C-9B Skytrain II (U.S. Navy)

C-9B Skytrain II—VR-1 (now disbanded) (U.S. Navy)

VC-11 GULFSTREAM II (Grumman)

The Coast Guard flies one Gulfstream II in the executive transport role, based in Washington, D.C. Note that the Coast Guard uses the commercial name for this, the only C-11 aircraft in U.S. government service.

Crew:	2 pilots, 2 crewmen
Weights:	59,500 lbs loaded
Dimensions:	length 79 11/12 ft (24.35 m), span 68 5/6 ft (21 m), height 24 1/2 ft (7.47 m)
Engines:	2 Rolls-Royce Mk 511-8 turbofan; 11,400 lbst each
Speeds:	588 mph
Ranges:	2,930-n.mile range
Ceiling:	
Payload:	12 passengers

VC-11A Gulfstream II (foreground) and VC-4A Gulfstream I (U.S. Coast Guard, PA2 T. Nakata)

UC-12 (Beech)

The Navy and Marine Corps are acquiring 66 UC-12B transports derived from the Super King Air 200 to replace older C-117 and C-118 transports used in the cargo, passenger, and utility roles. The C-12 is the only aircraft currently in use by the U.S. Army, Navy, Air Force, and Marine Corps. Navy-Marine deliveries began in September 1979 and were scheduled to continue over a three-year period. The T-44A King Air is a smaller version of the same basic design.

Crew:	2 pilots
Weights:	7,869 lbs empty; 12,500 lbs loaded
Dimensions:	length 43 3/4 ft (13.34 m), span 54 1/2 ft (16.61 m), height 14 1/2 ft (4.42 m)
Engines:	2 P&W PT6A-41 turboprop; 850 shp each
Speeds:	310 mph maximum cruise; 261 mph cruise
Ranges:	1,760-n.miles
Ceiling:	31,000 ft
Payload:	8 passengers

UC-12B—NAS New Orleans, La. (U.S. Navy)

C-118 LIFTMASTER (Douglas)

Four Naval Air Reserve squadrons continue to fly the C-118B (formerly R6D-1) transport. The Navy has sought to dispose of these aircraft because of their high operating and support costs. However, Congress has ordered them retained in reserve VR squadrons pending the acquisition of sufficient C-9B Skytrains for those units. The C-118/R6D is the militarized version of the DC-6A commercial transport.

Crew:	2 pilots, 1 navigator, 1 flight engineer, 1 crewman
Weights:	54,995 lbs empty; 103,000 lbs loaded; 112,000 lbs maximum
Dimensions:	length 107 ft (32.61 m), span 117½ ft (35.81 m), height 28⅔ ft (8.74 m)
Engines:	4 P&W R-2800-52W radial piston; 2,500 hp each
Speeds:	303 mph at 16,700 ft
Ranges:	2,000-n.mile range with maximum cargo
Ceiling:	21,900 ft
Payload:	76 passengers
	or 60 litter patients and 6 attendants
	or 31,611 lbs cargo

C-118B Liftmaster from VR-52 photographed at NAF Andrews. Transport aircraft are normally identified by the last three digits of their "bureau" number, in this instance 257 having the bureau number 128257. The Bureau of Aeronautics, established in July 1921, directed naval air development until December 1959 when BuAer merged with the Bureau of Ordnance to form the Bureau of Naval Weapons, and subsequently changed on 1 May 1966 to the current Naval Air Systems Command. (Peter B. Mersky)

C-130 HERCULES (Lockheed)

The Navy, Marine Corps, and Coast Guard all fly several variants of the C-130 (formerly designated GV) in a variety of mission configurations. This cargo aircraft, capable of rough-field operations, has carried out landing and takeoff trials from the aircraft carrier FORRESTAL (CV 59) without arresting gear or rocket/catapult assistance.

The Navy flies "straight" C-130 cargo aircraft, LC-130 cargo aircraft fitted with skis for Arctic or Antarctic operations, DC-130 drone-control aircraft, and EC-130 strategic communications aircraft. The last are flown by squadrons VQ-3 and -4 and provide a communications relay to strategic missile submarines at sea under a program known as TACAMO (Take Charge And Move Out). These planes have powerful VLF transmitters and can remain aloft up to 13 hours. TACAMO transmits a 200-kilowatt, highly jam-resistant VLF signal. The aircraft have 15-man crews.

The Marine Corps has KC-130 squadron of 12 aircraft assigned to each air wing to provide tactical transport and in-flight refueling services.

The Coast Guard flies 25 HC-130B/E/H Hercules in the long-range search role. They can be employed as personnel transports, cargo aircraft, or for search and rescue. In SAR operations they drop rescue and salvage gear.

The Hercules aircraft is also flown by Navy and Marine reserve squadrons. As a transport, it can carry up to 92 passengers or 74 litter patients. (More than 40 nations fly the Hercules in military and civil service.)

(KC-130R)

Crew:	2 pilots, 1 navigator, 1 flight engineer, 1 radio operator/loadmaster
Weights:	75,368 lbs empty; 109,744 lbs loaded; 155,000 lbs maximum; 175,000 lbs maximum overload
Dimensions:	length 99⁵/₁₂ ft (30.32 m), span 132⁷/₁₂ ft (40.42 m), height 38¼ ft (11.66 m)
Engines:	4 Allison T56-A-15 turboprop; 4,591 shp each maximum (T/O only); 4,061 shp each continuous
Speeds:	348 mph at 19,000 ft; 331 mph cruise
Ranges:	2,564-n.mile range with maximum payload; 3,734-n.mile range with maximum fuel; 1,000-n.mile radius in tanker mission with 32,140 lbs fuel transferred
Ceiling:	25,000 ft
Guns:	none
Payload:	92 troops or 64 paratroopers or 26,913 lbs cargo (for 155,000 lbs T/O weight)

HC-130B Hercules (U.S. Coast Guard, CWO Neil D. Ruenzel)

HC-130B Hercules (U.S. Coast Guard)

C-130F (VR-24) at Cairo, Egypt, with Soviet-built An-12 Cub aircraft of Egyptian Air force behind it (U.S. Navy)

C-131 SAMARITAN (Convair)

The Navy flies a small number of C-131F/G (formerly R4Y) aircraft in the transport role. A few are configured as VIP transports (VC-131). The Coast Guard flies 17 HC-131A for medium-range search with three additional aircraft in reserve.

(C-131G)

Crew:	2 pilots, 1 flight engineer
Weights:	53,200 lbs loaded
Dimensions:	length 79¹/₆ ft (24.14 m), span 105¹/₃ ft (32.08 m), height 28 ft (8.53 m)
Engines:	2 P&W R-2800-52W radial piston; 2,500 hp each
Speeds:	316 mph
Ranges:	2,000-n.mile range
Ceiling:	
Guns:	none
Payload:	44 passengers or 21 litter patients and 3 attendants

HC-131A Samaritan (U.S. Coast Guard)

TRAINING AIRCRAFT

ADVANCED TRAINER AIRCRAFT (VTXTS)

The Navy is seeking an advanced trainer aircraft for procurement in the late 1980s as a replacement for the T-2C Buckeye and venerable TA-4 Skyhawk. The aircraft would be carrier capable. Several existing U.S. and foreign aircraft are being considered for this role, including the A-7 Corsair modified to a TA-7 configuration after the plane is replaced in the attack role by the A-18 Hornet. The Navy will require an estimated 275–350 VTXTS aircraft.

T-2 BUCKEYE (North American Rockwell)

The T-2 (formerly T2J) is a carrier-capable jet trainer. Wing-tip fuel tanks are normally fitted. A few are flown by readiness squadrons for spin recovery training.

(T-2C)

Crew:	1 pilot + 1 student
Weights:	8,115 lbs empty; 13,179 lbs maximum
Dimensions:	length 38¹/₃ ft (11.67 m), span 38¹/₆ ft (11.62 m), height 14⁵/₆ ft (4.51 m)
Engines:	2 GE J85-GE-4 turbojet; 2,950 lbst each
Speeds:	522 mph at 25,000 ft
Ranges:	909-n.mile range
Ceiling:	40,400 ft
Guns:	none
Payload:	up to 640 lbs of bombs or rockets (wing pylons)

T-2C Buckeyes—VT-23 (U.S. Navy, PHCS Leon B. Ramage)

T-28 TROJAN (North American Rockwell)

The T-28 is a widely used piston-engine training aircraft. The Navy's T-28B/C variants are carrier-capable.

(T-28B)

Crew:	1 pilot + 1 student
Weights:	6,424 lbs empty; 8,500 lbs loaded
Dimensions:	length 33 ft (10.06 m), span 40¹/₁₂ ft (12.22 m), height 12²/₃ ft (3.86 m)
Engines:	1 Wright R-1820-86 radial piston; 1,425 hp
Speeds:	343 mph; 310 mph cruise at 30,000 ft
Ranges:	922-n.mile range
Ceiling:	35,500 ft
Guns:	none
Payload:	

T-28 Trojan—VT-5 (U.S. Navy)

T-34 MENTOR (Beech)

The T-34C now flown in the naval air training role is the successor to previous T-34 piston-engine light trainers. Used for primary training, the aircraft was introduced into the Navy early in 1978 with 179 having been acquired. An additional 45 aircraft were included in the FY 1981 program.

Crew:	1 pilot + 1 student
Weights:	2,630 lbs empty; 4,274 lbs maximum
Dimensions:	length 28³/4 ft (8.75 m), span 33¹/3 ft (10.16 m), height 9¹¹/12 ft (3.02 m)
Engines:	1 P&W of Canada PT6A-25 turboprop; 400 shp
Speeds:	257 mph at 5,335 ft; 247 mph cruise at 5,335 ft
Ranges:	700 n.miles
Ceiling:	30,000 ft
Guns:	none
Payload:	no ordnance capability

T-34C Mentor (Beech)

T-38A TALON (Northrop)

The T-38 is a standard U.S. Air Force jet trainer used in limited numbers by the Navy for test-pilot proficiency flying and air combat maneuver training. The T-38 is closely related in design and flight characteristics to Northrop's F-5 Freedom Fighter/Tiger II aircraft. (From 1958–1972, 1,187 T-38s were built; the aircraft is flown by the U.S. Air Force Thunderbirds flight demonstration team.)

Crew:	1 pilot + 1 student or pilot
Weights:	7,594 lbs empty; 12,000 lbs maximum
Dimensions:	length 46⁵/12 (14.13 m), span 25¹/4 ft (7.7 m), height 12¹¹/12 ft (3.92 m)
Engines:	2 GE J85-GE-5A/J turbojets; 2,680 lbst each; 3,850 lbst each with afterburner
Speeds:	~Mach 1.3 at 36,000 ft
Ranges:	1,140-n.mile range
Ceiling:	53,500 ft
Guns:	none
Payload:	no ordnance capability

T-38A Talon; note absence of squadron and wing markings on aircraft used for air combat maneuvering—VF-43 (Robert L. Lawson)

T-39D SABRELINER (North American Rockwell)

The T-39D (formerly T3J-1) is fitted with APQ-94 for radar training of naval flight officers (i.e. bombardier/navigators and radar intercept officers). In addition, 18 CT-39E/G aircraft remain in use as light transports for carrying high-priority cargo and passengers. The CT-39 aircraft have a crew of three and carry seven passengers. (The -E variants were seven commercial Sabreliner Series 40 aircraft purchased by the Navy; the -G variants were modified commercial Series 60 aircraft; all designated CT-39 when acquired and never used in the training role.)

(T-39D)

Crew:	1 pilot, 1 pilot/instructor + 4 students
Weights:	17,760 lbs loaded
Dimensions:	length 44 ft (13.41 m), span 44¹/2 ft (13.59 m), height 16 ft (4.88 m)
Engines:	2 P&W J60-P-3A turbojet; 3,000 lbst each
Speeds:	432 mph
Ranges:	2,500-n.mile range
Ceiling:	
Guns:	none
Payload:	no ordnance capability

CT-39G Sabreliner (U.S. Navy, PHAN B.R. Trombecky)

T-39D Sabreliner fitted as test bed for the F/A-18 Hornet's APG-65 radar (McDonnell Douglas)

T-44A AIR KING (Beechcraft)

The T-44A was procured as a replacement for the TS-2/US-2 Tracker aircraft employed in the training role. The T-44A is a military training version of the commercial Air King Model 90. It is also flown by the Air Force as the VC-6B executive transport. Sixty-one T-44A aircraft were delivered to Training Wing 4 between 1977 and 1980.

Crew:	1 pilot + 2 students
Weights:	5,640 lbs empty; 9,650 lbs maximum
Dimensions:	length 35½ ft (10.82 m), span 50¼ ft (15.32 m), height 14¼ ft (4.33 m)
Engines:	2 P&W of Canada PT6A-34B turboprop; 550 shp each
Speeds:	256 mph at 12,000 ft
Ranges:	1,200 + n.mile range
Ceiling:	31,000 ft
Guns:	none
Payload:	no ordnance capability; can be configured in transport role for 2 pilots + 3 passengers

T-44A Air King—TraWing-4 (Beech)

HELICOPTERS

AH-1 SEACOBRA (Bell)

The SeaCobra is a specialized gunship helicopter that evolved from the widely used Huey series. The SeaCobra has a narrow (38-inch) fuselage providing a minimal cross section, stub wings for carrying rocket packs or gun pods, and a nose gun turret.

The Marines have three 18-helicopter SeaCobra squadrons with a total inventory of some 20 AH-1G and 60 AH-1J variants. The former have a single engine. (They are also flown by the U.S. Army as the HueyCobra.) Fifty-seven AH-1T gunships are being procured for the Marines to replace the AH-1G helicopters and increase squadron strength to 24 units. The AH-1T will have structural provisions for carrying the TOW (Tube-launched, Optically guided, Wire-controlled) anti-tank missile, although only the last 23 helicopters procured by the Marines will have the missile fitted upon delivery.

(AH-1J)

Crew:	1 pilot, 1 gunner
Weights:	6,816 lbs loaded; 10,000 lbs maximum
Dimensions:	fuselage length 44 7/12 ft (13.6 m), overall length 53⅓ ft (16.27 m), height 13⅔ ft (4.17 m), main rotor diameter 44 ft (13.42 m)
Engines:	2 United Aircraft of Canada T-400-CP-400 turboshaft; 1,800 shp each
Speeds:	207 mph
Ranges:	360-n.mile range
Ceilings:	10,550 ft; 9,900 ft hovering in ground effect
Guns:	1 20-mm XM-197
Payload:	4 XM-159 rocket packs (19 2.75-inch rockets per pack) or 2 7.62-mm XM-18E1 minigun pods

AH-1J SeaCobra—Marine Headquarters and Maintenance Squadron 24 (code EW) (U.S. Navy, PH1 Eugene L. Goligoski)

AH-1J SeaCobra—HMM-165 (U.S. Navy, Daniel A. Fort)

UH-1 HUEY (IROQUOIS) (Bell)

The Huey series (formerly HU-1, with the name being derived from the sound of the HU-1E designation), is the most widely used helicopter in the world, with more than 9,000 produced from the late 1950s onward. It was extensively used in the Vietnam War. Its official name is Iroquois (from the U.S. Army scheme of Indian names for helicopters). UH-1 variants are today flown by about 40 nations.

The U.S. Marine Corps has four squadrons with an assigned strength of 21 helicopters each. These are being replaced by the improved UH-1N version, with a planned strength of three 24-helicopter squadrons. The Navy, Naval Reserve, and Marine Reserve fly the Huey in utility, transport, training, and rescue roles; UH-1 and TH-1 variants are used for training, and the HH-1K is an armed rescue helicopter that can be armed with guns and rockets to provide covering fire for men being recovered.

(UH-1N)

Crew:	1 pilot
Weights:	5,549 lbs empty; 10,500 lbs maximum
Dimensions:	fuselage length $42^5/_{12}$ ft (12.93 m), overall length $57^1/_4$ ft (17.47 m) height $14^5/_{12}$ ft (4.39 m), main rotor diameter $48^1/_6$ ft (14.7 m)
Engines:	2 United Aircraft of Canada PT6 turboshaft; 900 shp each
Speeds:	126 mph
Ranges:	250-n.mile range
Ceilings:	15,000 ft; 12,900 ft hovering in ground effect
Guns:	(see payload)
Payload:	16 troops or various combinations of troops, guns, and rockets

UH-1E Huey—Marine Headquarters and Maintenance Squadron 24 (code EW) (U.S. Navy, PH1 Eugene L. Goligoski)

TH-1L Huey—HT-8 (U.S. Navy)

UH-1N Huey of Antarctic Development Squadron 6 at NAS North Island (U.S. Navy, PHCS Robert Lawson)

SH-2 LAMPS (Kaman)

The LAMPS (Light Airborne Multi-Purpose System) is a ship-based antisubmarine helicopter converted from the UH-2 (formerly HU2K) Seasprite utility helicopter. The U.S. Navy's need for a ship-based ASW helicopter in the early 1970s led to the conversion of 20 utility helicopters to the SH-2D configuration and another 85 to the SH-2F variant. (Subsequently, the surviving -2D aircraft were modified to the -2F configuration.) Two additional Seasprites were experimentally converted to the YSH-2E configuration.

The Navy has six light ASW squadrons (HSL) that deploy SH-2F LAMPS detachments aboard cruisers, destroyers, and frigates, plus two readiness training squadrons. The SH-2 LAMPS will be supplemented in service during the early 1980s by the improved SH-60 Seahawk LAMPS III helicopter. The SH-2 will be retained indefinitely for use aboard older ships that cannot accommodate the SH-60. Additional SH-2F production has been proposed (although no ASW variant was previously built, as all existing SH-2s are conversions).

The SH-2 LAMPS are used to localize and attack submarine contacts detected by shipboard sonar. The helicopters are fitted with surface search radar, ASQ-81 MAD (Magnetic Anomaly Detection), and sonobuoys.

(SH-2F)

Crew:	2 pilots, 1 systems operator
Weights:	6,953 lbs empty; 12,800 lbs maximum
Dimensions:	fuselage length $38^1/_3$ ft (11,69 m), overall length $52^7/_{12}$ ft (16.04 m), height $15^1/_2$ ft (4.73 m), main rotor diameter 44 ft (13.42 m)
Engines:	2 GE T58-GE-8F turboshaft; 1,350 shp each
Speeds:	165 mph; 150 mph cruise
Ranges:	420-n.mile
Ceilings:	22,500 ft; 18,600 ft hovering in ground effect
Guns:	none
Payload:	2 Mk 46 ASW torpedoes

SH-2D LAMPS hovering over cruiser WAINWRIGHT; main landing gear is lowered—HC-4 (subsequently redesignated HSL-30) (U.S. Navy)

SH-2F LAMPS with ASW torpedo on port side—HSL-32 (Giorgio Arra)

SH-2D LAMPS streaming MAD gear; a Mk 44 practice torpedo is fitted on the portside, above which is a sonobuoy dispenser; SH-2F variant has tail wheel six feet farther forward and improved transmission—HSL-32/W.H. STANDLEY (U.S. Navy)

SH-3 SEA KING (Sikorsky)

The SH-3 (formerly HSS-2) has been the U.S. Navy's standard carrier-based ASW helicopter since entering service in 1961. It is also flown by the Air Force and several foreign services in the transport role, and other navies employ it for ASW. The Marine Corps uses the VH-3D as a presidential transport helicopter, and the Coast Guard has 37 HH-3F Pelicans for medium-range recovery (listed separately).

The Navy currently has 11 carrier-based ASW squadrons, each with six SH-3D/H helicopters, plus two readiness training squadrons. Other SH-3 helicopters are flown in the utility and rescue role, with SH-3G non-ASW helicopters being flown from the carrier MIDWAY (CV 41) and CORAL SEA (CV 43).

Two Sea Kings were modified to the YSH-3J configuration in the 1970s to test sensors and weapons for the LAMPS III helicopter (now SH-60B). In turn, the SH-60 with dipping sonar is the most likely candidate to replace the SH-3D in the carrier-based ASW role, probably beginning sometime in the late 1980s.

The SH-3D/H have surface search radar, AQS-13 dipping sonar, sonobuoys, ALE-37 chaff dispenser, ALR-66 threat warning system, and AQS-81 MAD.

(SH-3D)

Crew:	2 pilots, 2 systems operators
Weights:	11,865 lbs empty; 20,500 lbs maximum
Dimensions:	fuselage length 54¾ ft (16.7 m), overall length 72⅔ ft (22.16 m), height 16⅚ ft (5.13 m), main rotor diameter 62 ft (18.91 m)
Engines:	2 GE T58-GE-10 turboshaft; 1,400 shp each
Speeds:	166 mph; 136 mph cruise
Ranges:	625-n.mile range
Ceilings:	14,700 ft; 10,500 ft hovering in ground effect
Guns:	none
Payload:	2 Mk 46 ASW torpedoes

SH-3D Sea King hovering with dipping sonar being lowered—HS-5/INDEPENDENCE (U.S. Navy, JOCS Richard Benjamin)

HH-3F PELICAN (Sikorsky)

The HH-3F is a transport/Search and Rescue (SAR) derivative of the SH-3 Sea King ASW helicopter flown by the Coast Guard. The CH-3C/E cargo and HH-3E Jolly Green Giant rescue helicopters flown by the U.S. Air Force are of the same design as the HH-3F.

Forty HH-3F variants were delivered to the Coast Guard from 1968 onward with 37 remaining in service. They are fitted with surface-search radar and carry droppable rescue supplies.

Crew:	2 pilots, 1 crewman
Weights:	22,050 lbs maximum
Dimensions:	fuselage length 57$\frac{1}{4}$ ft (17.45 m), overall length 73 ft (22.25 m), height 18$\frac{1}{12}$ ft (5.51 m), main rotor diameter 62 ft (18.9 m)
Engines:	2 GE T58-GE-5 turboshaft; 1,500 shp each
Speeds:	162 mph; 125 mph cruise
Ranges:	400-n. mile range
Ceilings:	11,100 ft; 4,100 ft hovering in ground effect
Guns:	none
Payload:	15 passengers or 8 litter patients

HH-3F Pelican (U.S. Coast Guard)

HH-3F Pelican (U.S. Coast Guard, CWO Joseph Greco, Jr.)

SH-3D Sea King refueling in flight from frigate ELMER MONTGOMERY—HS-5/D.D. EISENHOWER (U.S. Navy, JOCS Richard Benjamin)

VH-3A Sea King over Washington, D.C.—HMX-1 (U.S. Navy)

H-46 SEA KNIGHT (Boeing Vertol)

The CH-46 (formerly HRB) is the principal assault helicopter of the U.S. Marine Corps, while the Navy flies the UH-46 in the Vertical Replenishment (VERTREP) role to carry cargo from Underway Replenishment (UNREP) ships to warships. Personnel, spare parts, and munitions are transferred by VERTREP, alleviating the need for the replenishing ship and warship to steam together, or supplementing conventional transfer methods when they are fueling alongside.

The Marine Corps has 12 squadrons, each with a nominal strength of 12 or 18 CH-46A/D/E helicopters. All will be updated to the CH-46E configuration. The Navy has four helicopter combat support squadrons flying the UH-46A/D in the VERTREP role plus one readiness squadron with UH-46 and HH-46 helicopters. A rear-loading ramp is fitted. The first CH-46E entered squadron service in October 1977.

CH-46F Sea Knight aboard assault ship Tarawa—HMT-301 (U.S. Navy, PH2 G.A. Davis)

(CH-46D)

Crew:	2 pilots, 1 crewman
Weights:	13,112 lbs empty; 23,000 lbs maximum
Dimensions:	fuselage length $44^5/_6$ ft (13.67 m), overall length $84^1/_3$ ft (25.72 m), height $16^2/_3$ ft (5.08 m), main rotor diameter 51 ft (15.56 m)
Engines:	2 GE T58-GE-10 turboshaft; 1,400 shp each
Speeds:	166 mph; 140 mph cruise
Ranges:	206-n.mile range; 774-n.mile ferry range (with external tanks)
Ceilings:	14,000 ft; 9,500 ft hovering in ground effect
Guns:	none
Payload:	17 troops or 15 litter patients + 2 attendants or 4,200 lbs cargo

UH-46A Sea Knight—HC-3 (U.S. Navy, PH1 A.E. Legare)

CH-46D Sea Knight—HMM-764 (U.S. Navy, PH1 W.J. Galligan)

CH-46D Sea Knight—HC-3 (U.S. Navy, PHCS Robert L. Lawson)

HH-52A SEA GUARD (Sikorsky)

The HH-52A (former HU2S-1G) is a commercial helicopter adopted for Coast Guard SAR missions. Although flown by several foreign nations as well as commercial operators, the helicopter (Sikorsky S-62 design) is not flown by any U.S. service except the Coast Guard. Ninety-nine were built for the Coast Guard with 79 remaining in service. Because it is a single-engine aircraft, the HH-52 requires an aircraft escort for long-range rescue operations.

First entering Coast Guard service in 1963, the HH-52A has been retained with very high maintenance costs and will be replaced in the 1980s by the HH-65A Dolphin.

Crew:	2 pilots, 1 crewman
Weights:	5,083 lbs empty; 8,100 lbs maximum
Dimensions:	fuselage length $44^7/_{12}$ ft (13.59 m), overall length $45^1/_2$ ft (13.87 m), height 16 ft (4.88 m), main rotor diameter 53 ft (16.17 m)
Engines:	1 GE T58-GE-8B turboshaft; 1,250 shp
Speeds:	109 mph; 98 mph cruise
Ranges:	150-n.mile radius with 20-minute hover over target; 475-n.mile range
Ceilings:	11,200 ft; 12,200 ft hovering in ground effect
Guns:	none
Payload:	6 passengers

HH-52A Sea Guard (U.S. Coast Guard, Dan Boyd)

HH-52A Sea Guard (U.S. Coast Guard)

H-53 SEA STALLION (Sikorsky)

The CH-53 is a heavy assault helicopter developed specifically for use by the U.S. Marine Corps. The helicopter is a hybrid combining an enlarged CH-53 Sea King fuselage and the six-bladed rotor and power train systems from the Army's CH-54 Skytrain (Tarhe) helicopter. (The CH-53E heavy-lift development of the helicopter is described separately.)

The Marine Corps and Marine Air Reserve fly CH-53A/D helicopters for amphibious assault and the Navy has three mine countermeasures squadrons with RH-53D helicopters.

The Navy's RH-53D aerial minesweepers are basic CH-53A/D helicopters with upgraded engines (T64-GE-415), strengthened fuselage, automatic flight control system, fittings for two swivel .50-cal MG, and attachment points for streaming minesweeping devices. The latter include the Mk 103 cutters for countering contact mines, the Mk 104 acoustic countermeasures, the Mk 105 hydrofoil sled for countering magnetic mines, the Mk 106 (which is the Mk 105 sled with acoustic sweep equipment added), and the SPU-1 "Magnetic Orange Pipe" (MOP) for countering shallow-water mines. The sled weighs about 6,000 pounds and is 27-feet long and 13-feet wide; the MOP is about 33-feet long and 10 inches in diameter, weighing 1,000 pounds (filled with polystyrene). An AQS-14 dipping/towed sonar is also available for the RH-53D. The helicopter is fitted with a rear-loading ramp, cargo winches, and roller conveyors.

RH-53D helicopters from Navy squadrons HM-14 and -16, flown by Marine pilots, were used on the ill-fated attempt to rescue American hostages in Iran in 1980. (Thirty RH-53D variants were built for the U.S. Navy in 1973–1975, and six others were delivered to Iran in 1976.

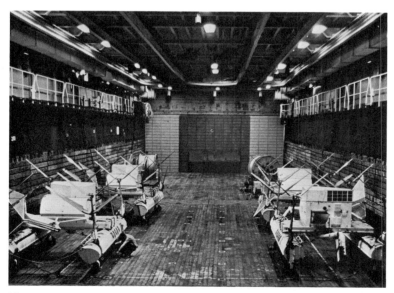

Mine countermeasure sleds and reels of towing cable for use by AMCM helicopters in well deck of amphibious transport dock DUBUQUE. (U.S. Navy, JOC Warren Grass)

(CH-53D)

Crew:	2 pilots, 1 crewman (7 in RH-53D)
Weights:	23,628 lbs empty; 34,958 lbs loaded; 42,000 lbs maximum
Dimensions:	fuselage length $67\frac{1}{6}$ ft (20.48 m), overall length $88\frac{1}{4}$ ft (26.92 m), height $24\frac{11}{12}$ ft (7.59 m), main rotor diameter $72\frac{1}{4}$ ft (22.04 m)
Engines:	2 GE T64-GE413 turboshaft; 3,925 shp each
Speeds:	196 mph; 173 mph cruise
Ranges:	540-n.mile range; 886-n.mile ferry range
Ceilings:	21,000 ft; 13,400 ft hovering in ground effect
Guns:	none
Payload:	38 troops or 24 litter patients + 4 attendants or 8,000 lbs cargo internal or external (an additional 4,000 lbs can be carried in overload condition)

CH-53 Sea Stallion lifting cargo from assault ship TARAWA—HMH-361 (U.S. Navy, PHC E.L. Goligoski)

RH-53D Sea Stallion about to lift Mk 105 mine countermeasures sled—HM-12 (U.S. Navy, PH2 E.L. Hawkins)

The surviving RH-53D Sea Stallion from the ill-fated Tehran hostage rescue mission waits at Ascension Island for further transit to the United States. While aboard the carrier NIMITZ the RH-53Ds had 600-series numbers and carried the HM-16 tail code GC. Their paint scheme was modified just before the flight into Iran. (Department of Defense, LCDR Gordon I. Peterson)

CH-53A Sea Stallion aboard assault ship TRIPOLI (U.S. Navy)

CH-53E SUPER STALLION (Sikorsky)

The CH-53E, developed for Navy and Marine Corps use, is a three-engine, heavy-lift derivative of the CH-53 Sea Stallion helicopter. Previously the most capable lift helicopter in U.S. production was the Army's CH-47 Chinook, which can carry 11 tons of cargo; the CH-53E is rated at 16 tons of lift. The Soviet Union currently has over 500 Mi-10 Harke and Mi-6 Hook helicopters with a lift capability approaching or similar to that of the CH-53E.

The U.S. Navy and Marine Corps each have a requirement for a minimum of 35 of the CH-53E helicopters. The Navy helicopters will be used for Vertical Replenishment (VERTREP) and mine countermeasures (MH-53E), with their equipment being interchangeable. The CH-53E can lift 93 percent of all heavy equipment in a Marine division, compared to 38 percent for the CH-53D helicopter. In the aircraft recovery role the CH-53E can lift all Navy and Marine fighter, attack, and electronic warfare aircraft (with engines removed from the F-14 and partial disassembly of the E-2).

In the mine countermeasures role the HM-53E will operate the equipment used by the RH-53D (see previous listing) plus the ALQ-166 Lightweight Magnetic Sweep (LMS).

The H-53E differs from the earlier H-53 variants in having a third engine, a seven-blade main rotor (instead of six), larger rotor blades, improved transmission, in-flight refueling probe, provisions for 650-gallon fuel tanks on both landing-gear sponsons, and different tail configuration.

CH-53E Super Stallion (Sikorsky)

Crew:	2 pilots, 1 crewman
Weights:	31,915 lbs empty; 70,000+ lbs maximum
Dimensions:	fuselage length $91^7/_{12}$ ft (27.94 m), overall length $99^1/_2$ ft (30.35 m), height $27^2/_3$ ft (8.44 m), main rotor diameter 79 ft (24.08 m)
Engines:	3 GE T64-GE-415 turboshaft; 4,380 shp each
Speeds:	196 mph
Ranges:	50-n.mile radius with 32,000 lbs of cargo; 500-n.mile radius with 16,000 lbs cargo; 1,000+ n.mile ferry range
Ceilings:	
Guns:	none
Payload:	56 troops or 32,000 lbs cargo

CH-53E Super Stallion lifting light tank (Sikorsky)

CH-53E Super Stallion (Sikorsky)

TH-57A SEA RANGER (Bell)

The TH-57A is the Navy's training version of the U.S. Army's OH-58 Kiowa light observation helicopter. It is flown in large numbers by the U.S. Army and several foreign nations (more than 2,500 of this craft have been produced).

The TH-57A has dual controls. The Navy purchased 40 units for basic helicopter training, all delivered in 1968. Seven additional TH-57s were provided in the FY 1981 program.

Crew:	1 pilot + 1–4 students
Weights:	1,464 lbs empty; 3,000 lbs maximum
Dimensions:	fuselage length $32^{7}/_{12}$ ft (9.94 m), overall length 41 ft (12,5 m), height $9^{7}/_{12}$ ft (2.91 m), main rotor diameter $35^{1}/_{3}$ ft (10.78 m)
Engines:	1 Allison T63-A-700 turboshaft; 317 shp
Speeds:	138 mph; 117 mph cruise
Ranges:	300-n.mile range
Ceilings:	18,900 ft; 13,600 ft hovering in ground effect
Guns:	none
Payload:	none

TH-57A SeaRanger—HT-8 (U.S. Navy)

SH-60B SEAHAWK (Sikorsky)

The SH-60 LAMPS III (Light Airborne Multi-Purpose System) is primarily an antisubmarine helicopter being developed to operate from cruisers, destroyers, and frigates. The helicopter also will be fitted with EW equipment for threat detection and possibly jamming or decoying antiship cruise missiles. Six prototype aircraft were built by Sikorsky, with just over 200 service helicopters planned for delivery during the 1980s. The SH-60B design is based on the UH-60A, the U.S. Army's Utility Tactical Transport Aircraft System (UTTAS) now being produced by Sikorsky. The Army plans to procure over 1,100 of these helicopters.

(The LAMPS I helicopters were 105 UH-2 Seasprites converted to the SH-2D/F configurations. The LAMPS II, a proposed built-for-the-purpose light ASW helicopter, did not reach the advanced design stage.)

The SH-60B has APS-124 search radar, APN-217 doppler navigation radar, ASQ-81 MAD, ALQ-142 jammer, and a stowage-ejector panel for 25 sonobuoys. No dipping sonar is provided; however, a modified SH-60 will probably be developed as a successor to the SH-3D/H for carrier-based ASW operation. FLIR is fitted.

The prototype SH-60B flew on 12 December 1979, and squadron deliveries are planned to begin in 1984–1985.

Crew:	1 pilot, 1 copilot tactical officer, 1 sensor operator
Weights:	13,648 lbs empty; 19,804 lbs loaded; 21,844 lbs maximum
Dimensions:	fuselage length 50 ft (15.26 m), overall length $64^{5}/_{6}$ ft (19.76 m), height $17^{1}/_{6}$ ft (5.23 m), main rotor diameter $53^{2}/_{3}$ ft (16.36 m)
Engines:	2 GE T700-GE-401 turboshaft; 1,713 shp maximum ($2^{1}/_{2}$ minutes); 1,284 shp each continuous
Speeds:	155 mph maximum cruise
Ranges:	50-n.mile radius with 3 hrs on station; 150-n.mile radius with 1 hr on station
Ceilings:	
Guns:	none
Payload:	2 Mk 46 ASW torpedoes

SH-60B Seahawk prototype (Sikorsky)

SH-60B Seahawk and SH-3 Sea King (Sikorsky)

HH-65A DOLPHIN (Aérospatiale)

The Aérospatiale SA366G Dauphin was selected by the Coast Guard in 1979 for its short-range recovery mission. The helicopter was selected over two U.S. helicopter proposals, the Bell 222 and Sikorsky S-76. The Coast Guard plans to procure 90 of these helicopters, with deliveries scheduled for 1982–1986.

Crew:	2 pilots, 1 crewman
Weights:	4,188 lbs; 8,400 lbs maximum
Dimensions:	fuselage length $37^1/_3$ ft (11.37 m), overall length $43^3/_4$ ft (13.33 m), height $12^1/_3$ ft (3.77 m), main rotor diameter $38^1/_3$ ft (11.68 m)
Engines:	2 Avco Lycoming LTS 101–750 turboshaft
Speeds:	145 mph cruise; 175 mph maximum
Ranges:	~165-n.mile radius with 15 minutes hover at target, maximum 420 n.miles
Ceilings:	
Guns:	none
Payload:	3 passengers

HH-65A Dolphin (U.S. Coast Guard)

EXPERIMENTAL AIRCRAFT

XFV-12A (Rockwell International)

The XFV-12A was conceived as a high-performance VSTOL fighter for shipboard operation. The prototype XFV-12A was to begin flying in 1978 in an extensive NASA-Navy test program. However, the prototype aircraft was delayed and has not proved successful. No procurement is planned.

The aircraft has a thrust-augmented wing design to allow vertical and short take-offs and landings. The unusual configuration features a delta wing aft with vertical stabilizers and small canards forward. Engine exhaust is diverted through nozzles in the wing and canards to achieve vertical flight. To reduce cost and lead times, the prototype aircraft makes extensive use of F-4 Phantom and A-4 Skyhawk components, while the engine design is based on the F-14 Tomcat.

The following were the XFV-12A design characteristics for an operational VSTOL fighter.

Crew:	1 pilot
Weights:	19,500 lbs maximum VTOL; 24,250 lbs maximum STOL
Dimensions:	length $43^5/_6$ ft (13.3 m), span $28^5/_6$ ft (8.8 m), height $10^5/_{12}$ ft (3.19 m)
Engines:	1 P&W F401-PW-400 turbofan; 14,070 lbst; 21,800 lbst in lift configuration
Speeds:	Mach 2.2–2.4
Ranges:	575-n.mile radius with AAMs
Ceiling:	
Guns:	1 20-mm M61A1 rotary-barrel
Payload:	AAMs plus limited bomb and missile capacity

XFV-12A (Rockwell International)

XFV-12A (Rockwell International)

The XV-15 has twin rotor-engine nacelles that rotate to a horizontal position for conventional aircraft flight. The large rotor diameters necessitate that the aircraft take off and land with the nacelles in a vertical position. Short-run takeoffs and landings are also possible to obtain maximum payload. Bell efforts on tilt-rotor aircraft date to the mid-1950s when an XV-3 prototype successfully demonstrated this technology.

The following characteristics are for the two XV-15 aircraft. Mission-capable naval aircraft would have a mission weight of about 30,000 pounds. First XV-15 flight was on 3 May 1977.

Crew:	2 pilots
Weights:	9,670 lbs empty; 13,000 lbs loaded; 15,000 lbs maximum
Dimensions:	length 42$^1/_6$ ft (12.83 m), span (over engine nacelles) 35$^1/_6$ ft (10.72 m), height 15$^1/_3$ ft (4.67 m), rotor diameter 25 ft (7.62 m), aircraft width (including rotors) 57$^1/_6$ ft (17.4 m)
Engines:	2 Avco Lycoming LTC1K-4K turboshaft; 1,800 shp each for 2 min contingency; 1,550 shp each continuous
Speeds:	382 mph at 17,000 ft maximum; 230–350 mph cruise
Ranges:	
Ceiling:	29,000 ft
Guns:	none

The XFV-12A being "flight tested" while tethered at the NASA Langley, Va., research center. The aircraft has not yet flown and after these tests was returned to the Rockwell factory for further modification. (National Aeronautics and Space Administration)

XV-15 (Bell)

Under contract to the U.S. Army and NASA, Bell has built two XV-15 tilt-rotor VSTOl aircraft to demonstrate the potential role of this concept for military aircraft. Subsequently, the XV-15 has become the leading candidate for a Navy-Marine Corps VSTOL aircraft for deployment in the early 1990s. Potential Navy roles are AEW and ASW, as successors to the E-2 Hawkeye, S-3 Viking, and SH-3 Sea King; Marine interest is primarily in its role as partial successor to the CH-46 medium assault helicopter with a 23-troop capacity. An anti-gunship and other roles have also been proposed.

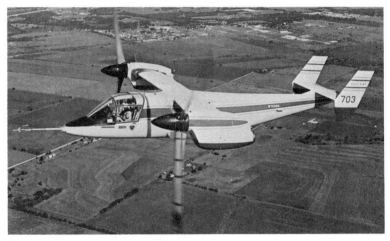

XV-15; note engine nacelle position for horizontal flight (Bell)

XV-15 in vertical flight; note engine nacelle position (Bell)

QSRA (de Havilland Canada-Boeing)

The Quiet Short-haul Research Aircraft (QSRA) is a de Havilland of Canada C-8A Buffalo aircraft converted by the Boeing Company under a NASA contract to develop technology for a quiet, short-haul transport aircraft. The Navy has supported the QSRA project, and during 1980 the test aircraft made 37 touch-and-go landings and 16 full-stop landings and deck-run takeoffs from the carrier KITTY HAWK (CV 63).

The Buffalo is a high-wing, T-tail STOL transport aircraft flown by the U.S. Army, several foreign military services, and numerous commercial users. Boeing has removed the aircraft's twin turbo-prop engines, fitted new wings, four turbofan engines in leading-edge wing pods, an improved undercarriage, and other features. Thus modified, the aircraft made its first QSRA test flight on 6 July 1978. Subsequent flight tests have demonstrated the aircraft's ability to shut down and restart all four engines in flight, the reduced operating noise, and the STOL characteristics.

During the KITTY HAWK operations the QSRA had a landing approach speed of only 65 knots, was able to come to a full stop with a deck run of about 300 feet, and make noncatapult takeoffs without encountering any problems. (The C-130 Hercules is the only other four-engine aircraft ever to land aboard an aircraft carrier.)

Crew:	2 pilots
Weights:	36,800 lbs empty; 50,000 lbs loaded; 60,000 lbs maximum
Dimensions:	length 93¼ ft (28.42 m), span 73½ ft (22.4 m), height 27⅔ ft (8.43 m)
Engines:	4 Avco Lycoming YF102 turbofan; 7,500 lbst each
Speeds:	~185 mph maximum cruise
Ranges:	
Ceiling:	
Guns:	none

NASA's Quiet Short-Haul Research Aircraft during recent carrier landing tests aboard the USS KITTY HAWK off San Diego. (NASA)

NASA/Navy QSRA landing aboard the KITTY HAWK. (NASA)

NASA/Navy Quiet Short-Haul Research Aircraft (QSRA). (NASA)

23 Weapons

GUNS

The principal guns now being installed in U.S. Navy ships are the 5-inch Mk 45 lightweight (CG 47 class), the 76-mm Mk 75 OTO Melara (FFG 7, PHM 1 classes), and the 20-mm Phalanx CIWS "Gatling" gun (warships, amphibious ships, and major underway replenishment ships). The Navy's next-generation surface combatant ship, now designated DDGX, has only a 76-mm gun proposed in preliminary planning, plus the CIWS.

Thus, the Navy's shipboard gun firepower will continue to decline during the 1980s as the FORREST SHERMAN (DD 931)-class destroyers are retired (18 ships with 38 5-inch guns). This represents almost 20 percent of the Navy's 5-inch gun inventory in the active fleet. The situation will be exacerbated in the 1990s, when some 50 cruisers and destroyers with more than 40 5-inch guns reach the 30-year mark.

The 5-inch gun is the largest caliber now in the active U.S. Fleet. The last active ship with 6-inch guns, the cruiser-flagship OKLAHOMA CITY (CG 5) was retired in December 1979, while the last ship with 8-inch guns, the NEWPORT NEWS (CA 148), was decommissioned and stricken in July 1978. The only operational warships in the world today with guns larger than 5-inch caliber are ten Soviet SVERDLOV-class cruisers (111 6-inch guns) and the World War II-built KOMSOMOLETS (12 6-inch guns).

The U.S. Navy's plan to install the 8-inch Mk 71 MCLWG (Major Caliber Lightweight Gun) in the SPRUANCE (DD 963)-class destroyers as well as possibly in some existing and future cruiser classes died with the cancellation of that project by the Secretary of Defense in July 1978. A prototype gun had been successfully evaluated in the SHERMAN-class destroyer HULL (DD 945) from 1975–1979. (Characteristics of the 8-inch Mk 71 MCLWG are provided here for historical interest.)

The large number of 3-inch antiaircraft guns deployed from the early 1950s onward in warships, amphibious ships, and auxiliaries have been removed entirely from the warships and reduced to a minimal number in the other types of ships. These weapons have a limited effectiveness and are too difficult to maintain, especially with current Navy manpower problems. A few are being retained in amphibious and auxiliary ships for defense against small craft.

The Italian-designed OTO Melara 76-mm gun is an automatic weapon, firing a larger round considerably farther than the U.S. 3-inch guns, and it requires considerably fewer crewmen. This weapon is also used in several foreign warship classes and the Coast Guard's new BEAR (WMEC 901)-class cutters.

Belated installation of the 20-mm "Gatling" gun CIWS (Close-In Weapon System) began during 1980. The six-barrel, rotary gun is intended for defense against antiship cruise missiles and is scheduled for installation in some 250 ships. Up to three mounts will be provided in aircraft carriers, two in cruisers and destroyers, one in the PERRY (FFG 7)-class frigates, two in amphibious ships, and two in the AE 26/AGF 3/AO 177/AOE 1/AOR 1 classes of auxiliary ships.

The Mk 15 CIWS has built-in search and fire control radars, and can be operated in a fully automatic mode to react to short-warning attacks. The gun has a theoretical rate of fire of some 3,000 rounds per minute and fires a "heavy" depleted uranium bullet of 12.75-mm diameter that is encased in a plastic "sabot" (to provide an overall diameter of 20 mm). Bursts of several hundred rounds are fired against incoming missiles, with the fire control radar tracking both the target and "bullet stream" to make rapid corrections in aim.

The Mk 15 CIWS underwent initial at-sea test and evaluation in the destroyer KING (then-DLG 10) from August 1973 to March 1974, and operational suitability tests in the destroyer BIGELOW (DD 942) from November 1976 to 1978.

Ammunition: Armor Piercing (AP) rounds are used against heavily armored ships and strengthened shore installations; High Capacity (HC) rounds are used against surface ships and other shore targets. Rocket Assisted Projectiles (RAP) and Laser-Guided Projectiles (LGP) have been developed for 5-inch guns. Advanced-technology ammunition has not been developed for the 76-mm Mk 75 gun, which will be the principal gun of the U.S. Fleet in the 1990s and beyond.

Classification: Guns are classified by inside barrel diameter and gun-barrel length. Diameters traditionally were listed in inches for weapons larger than one-inch diameter, and in millimeters for smaller weapons. Thus, a 5-inch/38-caliber gun has a barrel 190 inches long. The Italian-designed OTO Melara 76-mm gun retains its metric measurement in U.S. naval service.

Nomenclature: According to the *Bureau of Ordnance Manual,* "A mount is an assembled unit which includes the gun barrel (or barrels), housing(s), slide(s), carriage, stand, sight, elevating and training drives, ammunition hoists, and associated equipment. Mounts include guns from 20-mm caliber up to but not including 6-inch caliber. . . . A mount differs from a turret in that a mount does not have a barbette structure. . . .

"Mounts may be open (without shield), enclosed (with shield), or partially enclosed. Generally, the shields for mounts provide weather or splinter protection, but not protection from direct hits, although mounts on vessels such as battleships and cruisers have armored shields. . . .

"Turrets differ from mounts primarily in that turrets are heavily armored. In addition to the armor plate on the gun house of a turret, a fixed cylinder of heavy armor surrounds the rotating structure below the gun house. This cylinder, called a barbette, extends to the armored decks of the ship. The lower spaces of the turret are protected by the side armor belt and armored decks."

Turret/Mount	Gun Barrel(s)	In Service[a]	Crew	Turret/Mount Weight	Rate of Fire[b]	Maximum Ranges[c]	Ammunition Weights[d]	Ships/Class
16"/50 cal (406 mm) triple turret	Mk 7 Mod 0	1943	79	1,700 tons	2 rpm	40,185 yds AP 41,622 yds HC	2,700 lbs AP 1,900 lbs HC	BB 61
8"/55 cal (203 mm) triple turret	Mk 16 Mod 0	1948	45	451 tons	10 rpm	30,100 yds AP 31,350 yds HC @ 41° elevation	335 lbs AP 260 lbs HC	CA 134
8"/55 cal (203 mm) Mk 71 single mount (MCLWG)	Mk 39 Mod 2	1975	6	172,895 lbs	12 rpm; guided projectiles 6 rpm	31,408 yds	260 lbs HC	(program canceled)
6"/47 cal (152 mm) triple turret	Mk 16 Mod 1	1942	40	165–173 tons	10–18 rpm	26,118 yds AP 22,992 yds HC @ 47° elevation	130 lbs AP 105 lbs HC	CG 5
5"/38 cal (127 mm) Mk 24 single mount	Mk 12 Mod 1		15	33,100 lbs	18 rpm	17,306 yds @ 45° 32,250 ft @ 85°	55 lbs	CV 9, 16, CG 10
5"/38 cal (127 mm) Mk 28 twin mount	Mk 12 Mod 1		27	153,000–169,000 lbs	18 rpm	17,306 yds @ 45° 32,250 ft @ 85°	55 lbs	BB 61
5"/38 cal (127 mm) Mk 30 single mount	Mk 12 Mod 1		17	~45,000 lbs	20 rpm	17,306 yds @ 45° 32,250 ft @ 85°	55 lbs	CGN 9, FFG 1, FF 1040, FF 1098, AS 15, AS 17
5"/38 cal (127 mm) Mk 32 twin mount	Mk 12 Mod 1		27	~120,000 lbs	18 rpm	17,306 yds @ 45° 32,250 ft @ 85°	55 lbs	CG 5, CA 134
5"/38 cal (127 mm) Mk 38 twin mount	Mk 12 Mod 1		27	95,700–105,600 lbs	18 rpm	17,306 yds @ 45° 32,250 ft @ 85°	55 lbs	DD 710
5"/54 cal (127 mm) Mk 42 single mount	Mk 18 Mod 0	1953	14	Mod 1–6 ~145,000 lbs Mod 10 139,000 lbs	20 rpm	25,909 yds @ 47° 48,700 ft @ 85°	70 lbs	Mod 7 and 10 in DD 931; Mod 10 in CGN 35, CG 26, DDG 37, 31, 2, FF 1952
5"/54 cal (127 mm) Mk 45 single mount		1974	6	47,820 lbs	16–20 rpm	25,909 yds @ 47° 48,700 ft @ 85°	70 lbs	CGN 38, CGN 36, CG 47, DD 963, LHA
3"/50 cal (76 mm) Mk 22 single mount	Mk 21 Mod 0		11	7,510–8,310 lbs	20 rpm	14,041 yds @ 45° 29,367 ft @ 85°	7 lbs	auxiliaries
3"/50 cal (76 mm) Mk 26 single mount	Mk 21/22		11	9,210–10,130 lbs	20 rpm	14,041 yds @ 45° 29,367 ft @ 85°	7 lbs	auxiliaries
3"/50 cal (76 mm) Mk 27 twin mount	Mk 22		12	30,960–31,700 lbs	50 rpm	14,041 yds @ 45° 29,367 ft @ 85°	7 lbs	CA 134
3"/50 cal (76 mm) Mk 33 twin mount	Mk 22		12	~33,000 lbs	50 rpm	14,041 yds @ 45° 29,367 ft @ 85°	7 lbs	CA 134, DD 931, FF 1037, AGF 3, amphibious ships, auxiliaries
3"/50 cal (76 mm) Mk 34 single mount	Mk 22		8		50 rpm	14,041 yds @ 45° 29,367 ft @ 85°	7 lbs	PG 84
76 mm/62 cal Mk 75 single mount	Mk 75	1974 (FFG 4)	4	13,680 lbs	75–85 rpm	~21,000 yds @ 45° ~39,000 ft @ 85°	14 lbs	FFG 7
40 mm/60 cal Mk 1 twin mount	Mk 1 Mod 0		5–9	13,000 lbs	160 rpm	11,000 yds @ 42° 22,800 ft @ 90°	1.5 lbs 1.9 lbs	LST
40 mm/60 cal Mk 2 quad mount	Mk 1 Mod 0		11	23,800–25,500 lbs	160 rpm	11,000 yds @ 42° 22,800 ft @ 90°	1.5 lbs 1.9 lbs	BB 61, LSD, auxiliaries
40 mm/60 cal Mk 3/M3 single mount	M1		4–5	2,264 lbs	160 rpm	11,000 yds @ 42° 22,800 ft @ 90°	1.5 lbs 1.9 lbs	LST, MSO, ARS

Turret/Mount	Gun Barrel(s)	In Service[a]	Crew	Turret/Mount Weight	Rate of Fire[b]	Maximum Ranges[c]	Ammunition Weights[d]	Ships/Class
40 mm Mk 19 single mount								auxiliaries
20 mm/70 cal Mk 10 single mount	Mk 2/4		2	700–1,100 lbs	450 rpm	4,800 yds @ 35° 10,000 ft @ 90°	0.2 lbs	MSO, auxiliaries
20 mm Mk 67 single mount	Mk 16 Mod 5		1		800 rpm	3,300 yds	0.75 lbs	CGN 25, LHA, auxiliaries
20 mm Mk 68 single mount	Mk 16 Mod 5		1		800 rpm	3,300 yds	0.75 lbs	MSO, auxiliaries
20 mm/76 cal Mk 15 CIWS six-barrel Phalanx "Gatling" gun	M61A1	1973 (DDG 41)	—	~12,000 lbs	3,000 rpm	1,625 yds		planned for ~250 ships
81-mm mortar Mk 2[e]			2		10 rpm trigger mode; 18 rpm drop-fire mode	3,940 yds		PCF
60-mm mortar Mk 4			2		10 rpm trigger mode; 18 rpm drop-fire mode	2,000 yds		PBR

[a] Date installed in combat ship for evaluation or service.
[b] Rounds-per-minute per barrel.
[c] Maximum range at 45° elevation unless otherwise indicated.
[d] AP = Armor Piercing; HC = High Capacity.
[e] Mk 2 Mod 0 mounted "piggy-back" with .50-cal MG.

The NEW JERSEY (BB 62) rearms prior to the last deployment of a battleship. Photographed in Hampton Roads, Va., the ship has her forward guns at full elevation and rotated aft to expose magazine loading chutes. Small mobile cranes are on her deck forward; a large floating crane and munition barges are alongside. (N. Polmar)

The NEW JERSEY (BB 62) trains her 16-inch battery to port during firing exercises off the Virginia Capes. (U.S. Navy)

The 8-inch Mk 71 MCLWG in the HULL (DD 945) was the last gun of that caliber in active U.S. service; subsequently removed. (Giorgio Arra)

Triple 6-inch gun turret and twin 5-inch Mk 32 gun mount in the cruiser SPRINGFIELD (CG 7) (U.S. Navy)

Triple 6-inch gun turret and twin 5-inch Mk 32 gun mount in the LITTLE ROCK (CG 4) (U.S. Navy, CDR J. P. Mathews)

Triple 8-inch gun turrets and twin 5-inch Mk 32 gun mounts in the NEWPORT NEWS (CA 148) (U.S. Navy)

Single 5-inch Mk 30 gun mounts on the submarine tender FULTON (AS 11). World War II-era large auxiliaries often had gun batteries equal to a destroyer's firepower. Of all the auxiliary ships on the Naval Register, only two laid up submarine tenders survive with 5-inch gun batteries, the BUSHNELL (AS 15) and NEREUS (AS 17). (U.S. Navy)

Twin 5-inch Mk 38 Mod 12 gun mount in the HENDERSON (DD 785) with SH-3A Sea King overhead (U.S. Navy)

Single 5-inch Mk 45 gun mount in the SPRUANCE (DD 963) (Litton/Ingalls)

Single 5-inch Mk 42 Mod 10 gun mounts in the HULL (DD 945) (Giorgio Arra)

Single 5-inch Mk 45 gun mount in the SOUTH CAROLINA (CGN 37) (Newport News)

Single 5-inch Mk 42 Mod 9 gun mount in the WHIPPLE (FF 1062) (Giorgio Arra)

Single 5-inch Mk 30 Mod 94 gun mount in the BROOKE (FFG 1) (U.S. Navy, PH3 J.A. Austin)

Single 76-mm Mod 0 gun mount in the PEGASUS (PHM 1) (U.S. Navy)

Twin 3-inch Mk 33 Mod 0 gun mount in the CANBERRA (CAG 2/CA 70) (U.S. Navy)

Twin 3-inch Mk 33 Mod 0 gun mount in the TRUCKEE (AO 147) (N. Polmar)

Single 76-mm Mod 0 gun mount in the PERRY (FFG 7) (Bath Iron Works)

Single 40-mm Mk 3 gun mount in the HARNETT COUNTY (LST 821) (U.S. Navy)

Quad 40-mm Mk 2 gun mount (U.S. Navy)

Single 20-mm Mk 67 Mod 1 gun mount in the BAINBRIDGE (CGN 25) (N. Polmar)

Phalanx 20–mm Mk 15 CIWS on New Jersey (BB 62) (U.S. Navy)

Phalanx 20-mm Mk 15 CIWS (U.S. Navy)

81-mm Mk 2 mortar mounted with .50-caliber MG (U.S. Navy)

MINES

During the past few years, the U.S. Navy has demonstrated an increasing interest in offensive mine warfare. A large number of conventional aircraft bombs have been modified for use as shallow-water mines, production of the Mk 60 CAPTOR (Encapsulated Torpedo) was begun, while the SLMM (Submarine-Launched Mobile Mine), and IWD (Intermediate Water Depth) mine are in development.

A number of bomb types have been converted to the destructor series of mines, and a new 2,000-pound Quickstrike-type mine is being developed. These weapons are intended for use in rivers and shallow coastal areas and would be planted by aircraft.

The IWD—called Continental Shelf Mine by NATO—was formerly referred to as the Propelled Ascent Mine (PRAM) by the U.S. Navy. This weapon is intended for use against surface ships and submarines, and upon detection of a target would fire the explosive portion of the mine at the target. The IWD is being developed under competitive contracts awarded to McDonnell Douglas and General Electric in September 1979.

The Mk 60 CAPTOR became operational in 1979. It is considered the Navy's principal antisubmarine mine and is classified as a deep-water mine. Laid by aircraft or submarine, the CAPTOR is anchored to the sea floor and acoustically detects passing submarines. Surface targets are ignored. When a hostile submarine is detected, the CAPTOR launches a Mk 46 Mod 4 torpedo.

The mine, produced by Goodyear Aerospace, has experienced significant development and operational problems. Another concern is the small warhead size which, according to Navy statements, consists of 96 pounds of explosive. After limited production, the FY 1978 budget funded 550 mines, FY 1979 1,000 mines, and FY 1980 an additional 260. Additional production is planned. However, no procurement funds were provided in the FY 1981–1982 budgets because of technical problems.

The SLMM is a torpedo-like mine that will permit covert mining by submarines of waters that are inaccessible to other means of delivery. Some Mk 37 torpedoes have been modified to an SLMM configuration for test and evaluation pruposes.

Several older mines are being discarded from the U.S. Navy's mine inventory. These are primarily the World War II-developed, 1,110-pound Mk 36, the 2,025-pound Mk 25, and the 500-pound Mk 50 and Mk 53, all of which were aircraft-laid mines. Beyond the newer mines described above, the Navy has large stores of three mines developed in the 1950s, the Mk 52 and Mk 55 bottom mines, and the Mk 56 moored mine. All three are air-laid, antisubmarine weapons.

Most mines can be set with several influence combinations (e.g., magnetic acoustic) and with counters to allow a certain number of ships or submarines to pass before detonating. Timers allow a delay in activating the mines, possibly to allow the planting submarine to depart or to neutralize the mine after a certain period of time.

The principal U.S. minelaying vehicle is the aircraft. There are approximately 80 Air Force B-52D Stratofortress strategic bombers in service that are configured to carry mines (as well as conventional or nuclear bombs). Navy A-6, A-7, and S-3 carrier-based aircraft, and land-based P-3 patrol aircraft are configured for minelaying. The Department of Defense is also investigating the possibility of employing C-130, C-141, and C-5 aircraft in the minelaying role under a program called CAML (Cargo Aircraft Minelaying). The Japanese Maritime Self-Defense Force has expressed interest in forming a squadron of 12 C-130 Hercules aircraft for this role, each to carry 16 2,000-pound mines.

U.S. submarines are configured to launch Mk 57, SLMM, and CAPTOR mines. However, mines can be carried by submarines only at the expense of torpedoes. Submarines at sea when a mining decision is made would have to return to port, unload some or all of their torpedoes, load mines, and then undertake the mining mission. Depending upon how many mines were embarked, they might then have to return to port to rearm before undertaking antisubmarine or antishipping operations.

The only major U.S. mining operation since World War II was in the Vietnam War, when A-6 and A-7 aircraft laid some 8,000 mines in Vietnamese coastal waters and 3,000 in inland waterways from May to December 1972.

Designation	Launch Platform	Class	Weight	Length	Diameter	Notes
Mk 52	aircraft	1,000 lb	1,190 lbs	7⁵/₁₂ ft (2.3 m)	13¹/₃ in (337 mm)	625-lb explosive charge
Mk 55	aircraft	2,000 lb	2,120 lbs	9½ ft (2.9 m)	23¹/₃ in (591 mm)	1,290-lb explosive charge
Mk 56	aircraft	2,000 lb	2,055 lbs	11½ ft (3.5 m)	23¹/₃ in (591 mm)	350-lb explosive charge
Mk 57	submarines	2,000 lb	2,059 lbs	10¹/₁₂ ft (3.1 m)	21¹/₃ in (540 mm)	340-lb explosive charge
Mk 60 CAPTOR	aircraft, submarines	2,000 lb		12¹/₆ ft (3.7 m)	21 in (533 mm)	96-lb explosive charge; Mk 46 Mod 4 ASW torpedo
Mk 67 SLMM	submarines	1,600 lb	1,660 lbs	13⁵/₁₂ ft (4.1 m)	19 in (481 mm)	converted Mk 37 torpedo
DST Mk 36	aircraft	500 lb	531 lbs CF[a] / 570 lbs LD[a]			modified Mk 82 bomb
DST Mk 40	aircraft	1,000 lb	985 lbs CF[a] / 1,105 lbs LD[a]			modified Mk 83 bomb
DST Mk 41	aircraft	2,000 lb	2,093 lbs CF[a]			modified Mk 84 bomb
QST Ex 64	aircraft	2,000 lb	2,000 lbs	12½ ft (3.8 m)	25 in (633 mm)	modified Mk 84 bomb
QST Mk 65	aircraft	2,500 lb	2,390 lbs	10²/₃ ft (3.3 m)	29 in (734 mm)	new concept; thin-walled case
IWD	aircraft, submarines	2,500 lb				under development

[a]CF = fixed Conical Fin; LD = extending-fin Low Drag.

AIRCRAFT MINE CAPACITIES

Aircraft	Wing Pylons		Weapons Bay
A-6 Intruder	5 2,000-lb		—
A-7 Corsair II	6 2,000-lb		—
S-3 Viking	2 2,000-lb	+	4 500-lb
P-3 Orion	10 500-lb	+	8 500-lb
		or	
	8 1,000-lb	+	3 1,000-lb
		or	
	6 2,000-lb	+	1 2,000-lb
B-52D Stratofortress	12 2,000-lb	+	60 500-lb
		or	
	12 2,000-lb	+	18 1,000-lb
		or	
	10 CAPTOR	+	8 CAPTOR

Mk 55 mine (left) and Mk 52 (fins not fitted; HBX 3 is the explosive used) (U.S. Navy, PH1 G.F. Bryant, Jr.)

Mk 56 mine fitted on an A-4 Skyhawk attack aircraft (U.S. Navy)

Mk 60 Captor mine fitted with parachute pack (U.S. Navy)

MISSILES

The missiles currently in use and under development by the Navy and Marine Corps for use from aircraft, surface ships, and submarines are listed in this section. They are arranged alphabetically by popular name.

Guided missiles generally are powered through most of their flight and have aerodynamic surfaces (wings and fins) for maneuvering control during flight. Ballistic missiles generally are powered only in the initial phase of their flight and rely on a ballistic trajectory (like a bullet) to reach a preselected target. Controllable nozzles and specific engine burn times provide proper direction and thrust for ballistic missiles.

The following list covers the missiles described on the following pages, arranging them by role. All missiles in U.S. service or advanced development have letter-number designations explained below. There is a single series for missiles and a different designation series for rockets. Of the weapons described herein, the RUR-5A ASROC is the only one from the latter designation series.

Role	Designation	Name	Notes
Strategic	UGM-27	Polaris A-3	phasing out
	UGM-73	Poseidon C-3	operational
	UGM-93A	Trident C-4	operational
		Trident D-5	limited development
Air-to-Air	AIM-7	Sparrow III	medium-range; operational
	AIM-9	Sidewinder	short-range; operational
	AIM-54	Phoenix	long-range; operational
		AMRAAM	development
Surface-to-Air (including submarine launch)	RIM-2	Terrier	only nuclear version retained
	RIM-7	Sea Sparrow	operational
	RIM-24	Tartar	phasing out
	RIM-66	Standard-MR	operational
	RIM-67	Standard-ER	operational
	RIM-116A	RAM	development
		LRDMM	development
		SIAM	development

Role	Designation	Name	Notes
Air-to-Surface	AGM-45	Shrike	antiradiation; phasing out
	AGM-62	Walleye	glide bomb; operational
	AGM-78	Standard-ARM	antiradiation; phasing out
	AGM-84	Harpoon	antiship; operational
	AGM-88	HARM	antiradiation; operational
	BGM-109	Tomahawk	multi-purpose; advanced development
Surface-to-Surface (including submarine launch)	RGM-84	Harpoon	antiship; operational
	BGM-109	Tomahawk	multi-purpose; advanced development
		Penguin	short-range antiship; evaluation
Antisubmarine	RUR-5A	ASROC	operational
	UUM-44A	SUBROC	operational
		ASW SOW	development
Antitank	AGM-65E	Maverick	developments
	MGM-71	TOW	operational

AMRAAM (Northrop)

The Advanced Medium-Range Air-To-Air Missile is being developed jointly by the Navy and Air Force to provide a new generation of missiles to arm the F-14 Tomcat and F-18 Hornet plus several Air Force fighters. In naval service the AMRAAM would replace the Sparrow and Phoenix in some roles. The missile is planned to have high resistance to enemy ECM and a ''snap-down'' capability to engage low-flying aircraft. The following characteristics are design specifications.

Weight:	200 lbs (with 350 lbs upper limit)
Length:	
Span:	
Diameter:	
Propulsion:	soild-fuel rocket
Range:	
Guidance:	inertial mid-course; active radar homing
Warhead:	30–50 lbs conventional
IOC:	

Explanation of symbols:

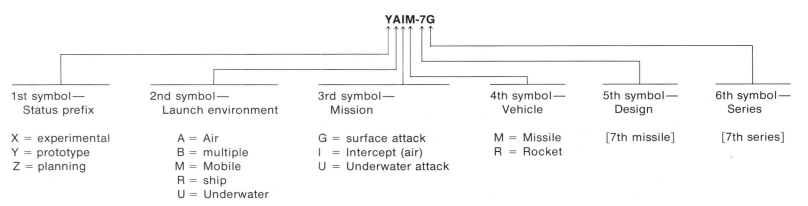

YAIM-7G

1st symbol— Status prefix	2nd symbol— Launch environment	3rd symbol— Mission	4th symbol— Vehicle	5th symbol— Design	6th symbol— Series
X = experimental	A = Air	G = surface attack	M = Missile	[7th missile]	[7th series]
Y = prototype	B = multiple	I = Intercept (air)	R = Rocket		
Z = planning	M = Mobile	U = Underwater attack			
	R = ship				
	U = Underwater				

RUR-5A ASROC (Honeywell)

The ASROC—Antisubmarine Rocket—is a ship-launched antisub-marine weapon that can be fitted with a conventional homing torpedo or nuclear depth bomb. From the early 1960s onward it was fitted to all the U.S. Navy cruisers, destroyers, and frigates until the PERRY (FFG 7)-class frigates. The ASROC is a relatively short-range weapon and will be phased out of service by the late 1980s. It is used in the conventional version by six foreign navies. Over 20,000 ASROCs were produced.

ASROC fired from BROOKE (FFG 1) (U.S. Navy)

Weight:	1,000 lbs
Length:	15 ft (4.6 m)
Span:	(ballistic missile)
Diameter:	12³/₄ in (324 mm)
Range:	6 miles
Guidance:	none (acoustic homing in Mk 46 torpedo)
Warhead:	conventional torpedo (Mk 46 Mod 1) or nuclear depth bomb (Mk 17)
Platforms:	CG CGN DDG DD FFG FF
IOC:	1961

ASROC fired by frigate BOWEN (FF 1097) (U.S. Navy)

ASROC fired from PAUL F. FOSTER (DD 964) (U.S. Navy)

ASW STAND-OFF WEAPON

The ASW Stand-Off Weapon (SOW)—earlier referred to as ASW²—is intended to replace the UUM-44A submarine-launched SUBROC when that weapon is phased out of service in the late 1980s. Whereas the SUBROC is a nuclear weapon, the ASW SOW may have both conventional and nuclear warhead options (as the Soviet SS-N-15/16 missiles). The new weapon would be compatible with standard 21-inch submarine torpedo tubes.

A variant of the Tomahawk cruise missile has been proposed for the ASW SOW. In this concept, the missile would be fired in the direction of an enemy submarine and release one or more sonobuoys; the missile would then circle the area with an on-board computer evaluating the sonobuoy signals; a weapon would be released (possibly a homing torpedo) at the target.

AGM-88 HARM (Texas Instruments)

The HARM—High-speed Anti-Radiation Missile—was developed by the Naval Weapons Center at China Lake, Calif., for attacking hostile radars. It is faster and more maneuverable than the smaller Shrike and Standard-ARM missiles now in use. It is a joint Navy-Air Force program with production scheduled to begin in 1982; a production run of some 5,000 missiles is planned for the U.S. services.

Weight:	796 lbs
Length:	13²/₃ ft (4.2 m)
Span:	3³/₄ ft (1.1 m)
Diameter:	10 in (253 mm)
Propulsion:	solid-fuel rocket
Range:	
Guidance:	passive radar homing
Warhead:	conventional
Platforms:	F/A-18 A-4 A-6 A-7
IOC:	1982 (est.)

HARM antiradiation missile launched from an A-7E Corsair is about to strike a target ship on the Pacific Missile Range, Point Mugu, Calif. (U.S. Navy)

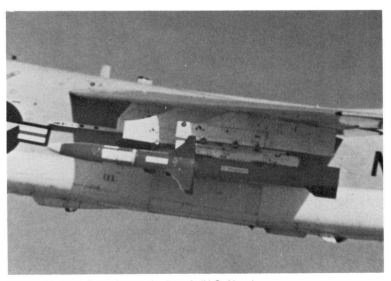

HARM on A-7E Corsair attack aircraft (U.S. Navy)

AGM/RGM-84 HARPOON (McDonnell Douglas)

The Harpoon is the first U.S. Navy weapon designed for shipboard launch in the surface-to-surface role since the Regulus I, which was developed and deployed in the 1950s. The Harpoon was designed for launch from a variety of surface ships down to missile craft, from conventional torpedo tubes in submarines, and—without the rocket booster—from aircraft. The submarine-launched Harpoon is loaded in an encasing capsule that is fired from the torpedo tube. The canister rises to the surface where the missile ignites and leaves the canister. The ship-launched version is used by nine foreign nations. Although only U.S. Navy P-3 aircraft are currently being fitted to carry the Harpoon, it is compatible with the A-6.

Weight:	1,168 lbs for air launch
	1,470 lbs for launch from Mk 11 or Mk 13 launcher
	1,530 lbs for launch from Mk 140 or Mk 141 launcher or SSN
Length:	12½ ft (3.8 m) for air launch
	15⅙ ft (4.6 m) for surface/submarine launch
Span:	3 ft (0.9 m)
Diameter:	13⅓ in (338 mm)
Propulsion:	turbojet (+ solid fuel booster for surface/submarine launch)
Range:	60 n.miles
Guidance:	active radar homing
Warhead:	510 lbs conventional
Platforms:	CG CGN DDG DD FFG FF PHM SSN P-3
IOC:	1977 surface
	1979 air

Harpoon underwater launch from HMS CHURCHILL (McDonnell Douglas)

Harpoon launch from ASROC launcher in the KNOX (FF 1052). (U.S. Navy)

Harpoon on P-3 Orion from VP-23. (McDonnell Douglas)

LRDMM

The Long-Range Dual-Mode Missile is envisioned as a long-range (over 100-mile) weapon for launching from Aegis surface ships. It would be used against incoming missiles, attacking bomber aircraft, and electronic jamming aircraft. The weapon would supplement the Standard-ER/MR missiles and would be fired from Mk 26 magazines and vertical launchers.

The same airframe might also be used for the ASW Stand-Off Weapon (SOW).

AGM-65E MAVERICK (Hughes)

The Maverick, developed and deployed by the U.S. Air Force, is being adopted in the AGM-65E version as the Navy Infrared Attack Weapon Systems (IRAWS) for use from Marine aircraft. It is an air-to-surface weapon intended primarily for use against tanks. The other versions of the missile have electro-optical or laser guidance. Several foreign air forces also use the Maverick.

Weight:	460 lbs
Length:	8 1/12 ft (2.5 m)
Span:	2 1/3 ft (0.7 m)
Diameter:	12 in (300 mm)
Propulsion:	solid-fuel rocket
Range:	~50 miles
Guidance:	imaging infrared homing
Warhead:	conventional
Platforms:	
IOC:	AGM-65E, 1985 (est.)

AIM-54 PHOENIX (Hughes)

The Phoenix missile was developed for long-range, fleet air defense to intercept attacking Soviet bomber aircraft. It is the most sophisticated air-to-air missile in the world and is carried only by the F-14 with the AWG-9 radar/fire control system, which is capable of track-while-scan while simultaneously guiding six Phoenix missiles. The improved AIM-54C is under development; it has enhanced resistance to defensive countermeasures in enemy aircraft, and is fitted with digital electronics rather than the analog system in AIM-54A. First AIM-54C airborne test launch occurred in mid-1980; production missiles are to be delivered in 1982. The AIM-54B was similar to the -54A without the earlier missile's liquid cooling system; it did not go into production. Approximately 2,500 missiles are planned to support a Navy force level of 18 F-14 squadrons. A ship-launched Phoenix system has been considered but not developed.

Weight:	985 lbs
Length:	13 ft (4.0 m)
Span:	3 ft (0.9 m)
Diameter:	15 in (380 mm)
Propulsion:	solid-fuel rocket
Range:	60+ miles (up to 126 miles in trials)
Guidance:	semiactive radar homing in cruise phase; active terminal radar homing
Warhead:	135 lbs conventional
Platforms:	F-14
IOC:	1974

Maverick AGM-65E wtih laser guidance on an A-4M Skyhawk (Hughes)

Phoenix AIM-54C being launched from an F-14A Tomcat (Hughes)

PENGUIN II (Kongsberg Vaapenfabrikk, Norway)

The Penguin II is a surface-to-surface missile developed for the Norwegian Navy's small missile craft. It is being evaluated by the U.S. Navy. The Penguin is fired from a storage/launcher container that weighs 1,100 lbs. Many Penguin components are American made.

Weight:	726 lbs
Length:	9⁴/₅ ft (3.0 m)
Span:	4⁷/₁₂ ft (1.4 m)
Diameter:	11 in (280 mm)
Propulsion:	solid-fuel rocket + solid-fuel booster
Range:	17 miles
Guidance:	inertial mid-course; infrared terminal
Warhead:	264 lbs conventional (as Bullpup-A missile)
Platform:	PB (in U.S. Navy for trials)
IOC:	undetermined

UGM-27 POLARIS A-3 (Lockheed)

The Polaris A-3 is a Submarine-Launched Ballistic Missile (SLBM) carried in the U.S. Navy's ten oldest strategic missile submarines, which were not judged suitable for conversion to the Poseidon SLBM. The missile is similar to the previous Polaris A-1 and A-2 missiles, but with a Multiple Re-entry Vehicle (MRV) warhead and significantly increased range. The MRV warhead delivers a cluster of three nuclear weapons against the same target to increase destructive effects and compensate for limited accuracy. Polaris production ended in June 1968 after the delivery of 1,409 missiles of all three versions. The missile will probably be phased out of U.S. Navy service in 1981.

Weight:	36,000 lbs
Length:	32¹/₃ ft (9.85 m)
Span:	(ballistic missile)
Diameter:	54 in (1.37 m)
Propulsion:	2-stage solid-fuel rocket
Range:	2,500 n.miles
Guidance:	inertial
Warhead:	nuclear MRV (3 re-entry vehicles)
Platforms:	SSBN 608 class
IOC:	1964

A Polaris A-3 missile is being loaded in the submarine STONEWALL JACKSON (SSBN 634) at the Polaris loading facility in Bremerton, Wash. The missiles are stored, transported, and loaded in the large cannisters shown here. The cannister is lowered to the top of an open missile hatch and the missile is winched down into the tube. The missile cannister on the pier has just been raised (by crane) to a vertical position after being transported in the horizontal position to the pier by truck. The JACKSON has since been modified to launch the Poseidon missile. (U.S. Navy)

UGM-73 POSEIDON C-3 (Lockheed)

The Poseidon SLBM was derived from the Polaris missile, with increased strike capability in a Multiple Independently targeted Re-entry Vehicle (MIRV) warhead, the first U.S. missile to have a MIRV. The weapon was designed to replace Polaris in all 41 existing SLBM submarines but only the 31 submarines of the LAFAYETTE (SSBN 616) class were converted. Each missile was designed to carry up to 14 re-entry vehicles, but only 8 to 10 are normally installed. The increase in re-entry vehicles causes a reduction of the missile's nominal 2,500-n.mile range. Procurement of the Poseidon missile has been completed.

Weight:	65,000 lbs
Length:	34 ft (10.4 m)
Span:	(ballistic missile)
Diameter:	74 in (1.9 m)
Propulsion:	2-stage solid-fuel rocket
Range:	~2,500 n.miles (nominal; reduced in actual service)
Warhead:	nuclear MIRV (8 to 10 re-entry vehicles W-68; being replaced by W-76; ~40 kilotons each)
Platforms:	SSBN 616 class
IOC:	1971

Poseidon SLBM being launched from the submerged submarine JAMES MADISON (SSBN 627). (U.S. Navy)

Polaris A-3 missile launched from underwater. (U.S. Navy)

RIM-116A RAM (General Dynamics)

The Rolling Airframe Missile (RAM) is being developed to provide a rapid-reaction, short-range missile for shipboard defense using off-the-shelf components. It was formally called the Antiship Missile Defense (ASMD) weapon. It makes use of the Stinger infrared terminal guidance, and Sidewinder/Chaparral fuze, warhead, and rocket motor. No fire control system is required. Proposed launchers include the Sea Sparrow launchers (with ten RAMs filling two of the eight Sea Sparrow tubes) or the Ex-31, a planned stand-alone launcher that would fire 24 missiles. The latter would use the Phalanx CIWS pedestal. The RAM is being developed in conjunction with West Germany and Denmark.

Weight:	156 lbs
Length:	9$^1/_6$ ft (2.8 m)
Span:	
Diameter:	5 in (127 mm)
Propulsion:	solid-fuel rocket
Range:	
Guidance:	passive dual mode radar homing for acquisition and mid-course guidance/infrared terminal
Warhead:	conventional
Platforms:	(Proposed) CV LCC LHA LPH AOE AOR
IOC:	undetermined

RIM-7H SEA SPARROW (Raytheon)

The Sea Sparrow is an adaptation of the Sparrow air-to-air missile for shipboard launching. It was developed in the 1960s as a defense against Soviet antiship missiles and is fired from the eight-tube launchers of Basic Point Defense Missile System (BPDMS) Mk 25 or the NATO Sea Sparrow Missile (NSSM) Mk 29 launcher. The Sea Sparrow is not fitted in ships that have Tartar/Terrier/Standard missile capabilities. Several foreign navies have the Sea Sparrow BPDMS and NATO Sea Sparrow.

The AIM-7M and RIM-7M are under development, the principal differences being that the latter has folding wings, clipped fins, and a remote arming capability for shipboard use.

(RIM-7H)

Weight:	450 lbs
Length:	12 ft (3.7 m)
Span:	3$^1/_3$ ft (1.0 m)
Diameter:	8 in (203 mm)
Propulsion:	solid-fuel rocket
Range:	~10 miles
Guidance:	radar homing
Warhead:	90 lbs conventional
Platforms:	CV CVN DD FF LCC LHA LPH AOE AOR
IOC:	1969

Loading Sea Sparrow in test launcher. Note that the missile fins are fixed and do not fold or retract within the launcher. (U.S. Navy)

Sea Sparrow launcher from the GUADALCANAL (LPH 7); the debris is from the break-through covering on the launch. Note the "E" for missile excellence award. (U.S. Navy)

Sea Sparrow on loading rail aboard frigate ROARK (FF 1053) (Giorgio Arra)

NATO Sea Sparrow launcher and two director/illuminators aboard the aircraft carrier KITTY HAWK (CV 63). (Giorgio Arra)

AGM-45 SHRIKE (Texas Instrument)

The Shrike is an antiradiation missile designed to home in on hostile antiaircraft radars. Used by U.S. and Israeli air forces.

Weight:	390 lbs
Length:	10 ft (3.0 m)
Span:	3 ft (0.9 m)
Diameter:	8 in (203 mm)
Propulsion:	solid-fuel rocket
Range:	~10 miles
Guidance:	passive radar homing
Warhead:	conventional
Platforms:	A-4 A-6 A-7 F/A-18
IOC:	1963

Shrike on outboard pylon and Walleye on inboard pylon of JA-4M Skyhawk aircraft (U.S. Navy, PHAN Randall Phillips)

SIAM (Ford Aerospace)

The Self-Initiating Antiaircraft Missile is designed for use from a submerged submarine against an attacking ASW fixed-wing aircraft or helicopter. The weapon would be launched in salvos from special tubes in the submarine and then home in on the aircraft. The concept is not new, with one earlier experiment using variants of the Sidewinder missile being dubbed "Subwinder." SIAM succeeds a more-recent Submarine Air-Defense (SUBAD) missile project.

The first SIAM test flight of a technology demonstration missile occurred in mid-1980 against a tethered QH-50 drone helicopter flying at 1,500 feet. The missile was ground-launched.

The following characteristics are preliminary.

(The Royal Navy-Vickers Submarine-Launched Air Missile or SLAM was a different concept, with the submarine coming to the surface or at least broaching the sail structure and extending a six-tube Blowpipe missile launcher. While details of the SIAM acoustic aircraft detection method are not yet revealed, the missile will be fired while the submarine remains completely submerged.)

Weight:	~150 lbs
Length:	~100 in (2.5 m)
Span:	5.8 in (147 mm)
Diameter:	5.7 in (144 mm)
Propulsion:	solid-fuel rocket
Range:	
Guidance:	radar homing and infrared (initial acoustic detection by submarine)
Warhead:	conventional
Platforms:	SSBN SSN
IOC:	undetermined

This photo shows the first flight test of a SIAM technology demonstration missile, being fired against flares mounted on a QH-50C drone helicopter hovering at 1,500 feet on the White Sands Missile Range, New Mexico. The SIAM is planned to have a dual radar-homing/infrared autonomous guidance system to provide autonomous search, lock-on, and track of a fixed-wing aircraft or helicopter operating above a submerged submarine. This 1980 ground-launched test flight was nondestructive, with the flares mounted on a rack extending away from the helicopter. (U.S. Army)

AIM-9 SIDEWINDER (Raytheon and Ford)

The Sidewinder is a short-range air-to-air missile. The AIM-9L is an improvement of the -9H version with an active optical fuze, enhanced warhead, and guidance that permits all-angle attacks. The motor, wings, and other components are similar to the -9H. The Sidewinder is the most widely used air-to-air missile in the West, with over 110,000 missiles produced for 27 nations in addition to the United States. The AIM-9L will be replaced in production by the -9M in 1981. The later missile has improved infrared countermeasure capability and increased capabilities against targets with "hot" backgrounds (e.g., desert).

(AIM-9L)

Weight:	186 lbs
Length:	9½ ft (2.9 m)
Span:	2 ft (0.6 m)
Diameter:	5 in (127 mm)
Propulsion:	solid-fuel rocket
Range:	~12 miles
Guidance:	infrared homing
Warhead:	conventional
Platforms:	F-4 F-14 F/A-18 A-7
IOC:	1956 (AIM-9H in 1973, AIM-9L in 1978)

Sidewinder AAM being attached to the "cheek" fuselage pylon of an F-8 Crusader fighter (U.S. Navy)

AIM-7 SPARROW III (Raytheon and General Dynamics)

The Sparrow III is an all-weather, medium-range air-to-air missile. The AIM-7F has greater range, lethality, and reliability than its predecessors, with solid-state electronics. It is also used by the USAF and eight foreign air forces. Over 40,000 Sparrow missiles of all variants have been produced to date. The AIM-7M (also RIM-7M) now under development has a new active fuze and an improved target seeker to improve missile guidance in ECM and clutter environments. The AIM-7M was to become operational in 1981.

Sparrow III AAM experimentally fitted to a UH-2C Sea Sprite helicopter (U.S. Navy)

(AIM-7F)

Weight:	500 lbs
Length:	12 ft (3.7 m)
Span:	3¹⁄₃ ft (1.1 m)
Diameter:	8 in (203 mm)
Propulsion:	solid-fuel rocket
Range:	~25 miles
Guidance:	semiactive radar homing
Warhead:	90 lbs conventional
Platforms:	F-4 F-14 F/A-18
IOC:	1958 (AIM-7F in 1976, AIM-7M in 1982)

AGM-78 STANDARD-ARM (General Dynamics)

The Standard-ARM is an aircraft-launched, antiradiation missile that evolved from the Standard surface-to-air missiles. In the 1970s it was used for an interim period as a surface-to-surface (antiship) missile pending development of the Harpoon (designated RGM-66D). It is also used by the U.S. Air Force.

Weight:	1,375 lbs
Length:	15 ft (4.6 m)
Span:	3¹⁄₂ ft (1.1 m)
Diameter:	13 in (330 mm)
Propulsion:	solid-fuel rocket
Range:	~60 miles
Guidance:	passive radar homing
Warhead:	215 lbs conventional
Platforms:	A4 A6 A7
IOC:	1968

Standard-ARM being launched from the ASROC launcher aboard the JOHN PAUL JONES (DDG 32) (U.S. Navy)

RIM-67 STANDARD-ER/SM-2 (General Dynamics)

The Standard-ER (Extended Range) was developed as a replacement for the Terrier surface-to-air missile. It has mid-course guidance, an inertial reference system, and ECCM improvements over earlier missiles. A nuclear warhead is under consideration for the SM-2. The SM-1 (ER) has been out of production since 1974. At-sea tests of the SM-2 (ER) were conducted in late 1976 from the cruiser WAINWRIGHT (CG 28). A nuclear version of the missile was approved for development in late 1979.

Weight:	2,900 lbs
Length:	26$\frac{1}{6}$ ft (7.9 m)
Span:	5$\frac{1}{4}$ ft (1.6 m)
Diameter:	13$\frac{1}{2}$ in (342 mm)
Propulsion:	solid-fuel rocket + solid-fuel booster
Range:	~40 miles for SM-1
	~75 miles for SM-2 (to be increased to 90 miles in later missiles)
Guidance:	inertial with semiactive radar homing
Warhead:	conventional
Platforms:	CG CGN DDG
IOC:	

Standard-ER SAM being launched from cruiser WAINWRIGHT (CG 28) (U.S. Navy)

RIM-66B STANDARD-MR/SM-1 (General Dynamics)

The Standard-MR (Medium Range) is the successor to the Tartar surface-to-air missile.

Weight:	1,100 lbs
Length:	14$\frac{2}{3}$ ft (4.5 m)
Span:	3$\frac{1}{2}$ ft (1.1 m)
Diameter:	13$\frac{1}{2}$ in (324 mm)
Propulsion:	solid-fuel rocket
Range:	15–20 miles
Guidance:	semiactive radar homing
Warhead:	conventional
Platforms:	CG CGN DDG FFG
IOC:	1970

RIM-66 STANDARD-MR/SM-2 (General Dynamics)

The SM-2 version of the Standard-MR is intended for use aboard Aegis missile cruisers. Initial at-sea tests of the SM-2 (MR) were conducted in 1976–1977 aboard the NORTON SOUND (AVM 1).

Weight:	1,400 lbs
Length:	14 ft (4.3 m)
Span:	3$\frac{1}{2}$ ft (1.1 m)
Diameter:	13$\frac{1}{2}$ in (342 mm)
Propulsion:	solid-fuel rocket
Range:	~40 miles; to be increased to ~90 miles in later missiles
Guidance:	semiactive radar homing
Warhead:	conventional
Platforms:	CG 47 class
IOC:	1981

Standard-MR SM-2 launch from the guided missile ship NORTON SOUND (AVM 1) (U.S. Navy, Perry Dick)

UUM-44A SUBROC (Goodyear)

The SUBROC—Submarine Rocket—is an antisubmarine missile launched from standard 21-inch torpedo tubes in the PERMIT (SSN 594) and later classes of attack submarines. It has a ballistic trajectory and is only fitted with a nuclear warhead. The weapon is scheduled to be phased out in the late 1980s.

Weight: 4,000 lbs
Length: 21 ft (6.4 m)
Span: (ballistic missile)
Diameter: 21 in (533 mm)
Propulsion: 2-stage solid-fuel rocket
Range: 25–30 n.miles
Guidance: inertial
Warhead: nuclear
Platforms: SSN 594 class and later SSN
IOC: 1965

SUBROC firing from submerged submarine (U.S. Navy)

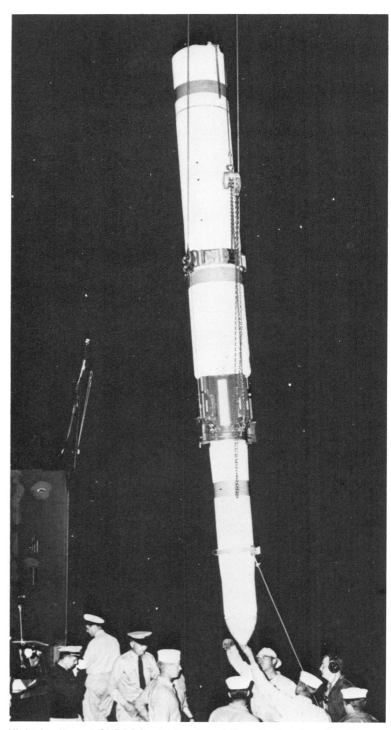

Night loading of SUBROC missile aboard the attack submarine PERMIT (SSN 594) (Goodyear)

RIM-24 TARTAR (General Dynamics)

The Tartar (along with Terrier and Talos) was evolved from the Bumblebee Program of World War II to provide a surface-to-air missile for destroyer-size ships. The RIM-24B and -24C versions are in service in the U.S. and several foreign navies. They are being replaced in the U.S. Fleet by the Standard-MR missile.

Weight:	1,300 lbs
Length:	15 ft (4.6 m)
Span:	3 1/2 ft (1.1 m)
Diameter:	13 1/2 in (342 mm)
Propulsion:	solid-fuel rocket
Range:	10+ miles
Guidance:	semiactive radar homing
Warhead:	conventional
Platforms:	CG CGN DDG FFG
IOC:	1960

Tartar SAMs on ROBISON (DDG 12) (Giorgio Arra)

RIM-2 TERRIER (General Dynamics)

The Terrier is a surface-to-air missile developed by the Bumblebee Project of World War II. It is being replaced in the Fleet by the Standard-ER missile. The BTN (Beam-riding, Terrier, Nuclear) variant is the only surface-to-air weapon now in Navy service with a nuclear warhead. (A nuclear warhead is being considered for the Standard-ER.) Conventional versions of the Terrier remain in service with the Dutch and Italian navies.

Weight:	3,000 lbs
Length:	26 1/6 ft (7.9 m)
Span:	3 1/2 ft (1.1 m)
Diameter:	13 1/2 in (342 mm); booster 18 in (456 mm)
Propulsion:	solid-fuel rocket + solid-fuel booster
Range:	20–40 miles (varies with version)
Guidance:	radar homing
Warhead:	conventional or nuclear
Platforms:	CV 64 CGN CG DDG
IOC:	1955

Terrier SAM being fired from the cruiser LEAHY (CG 16) (U.S. Navy)

BGM-109 TOMAHAWK (General Dynamics)

The Tomahawk is a long-range cruise missile for use against surface ships and land targets. Initially the Tomahawk was known as the Sea-Launched Cruise Missile (SLCM); in 1979 the Navy began using the terms Tomahawk Land Attack Missile (T-LAM) and Tomahawk Anti-ship Missile (T-ASM) to indicate the principal versions. The Missile can be aircraft-launched and was a competitor with the Boeing Air-Launched Cruise Missile (ALCM) for use in B-52 strategic bombers.

Weight:	3,200 lbs for surface launch
	4,000 lbs for submarine launch
Length:	18 1/4 ft (5.6 m) for T-ASM + 2 ft (0.6 m) booster
	18 1/2 ft (5.6 m) for T-LAM + 2 ft (0.6 m) booster
Span:	8 2/5 ft (2.6 m)
Diameter:	21 in (533 mm)
Propulsion:	turbofan + solid-rocket booster
Range:	300-500 n.miles in T-ASM version
	1,000 + n.miles in T-LAM version
Guidance:	active radar homing in T-ASM version (*same as Harpoon*)
	inertial and contour matching in T-LAM version
Warhead:	1,000 lbs conventional (Bullpup-B warhead) in T-ASM version
	W-80 nuclear in T-LAM version
Platforms:	surface ships SSN
IOC:	T-ASM in submarines 1982
	T-ASM in surface ships in 1983

Tomahawk cruise missile with fins and engine air intake scoop extended (U.S. Navy)

A Tomahawk T-ASM streaks skyward after being launched from the amidships torpedo tubes of the attack submarine GUITARRO (SSN 665) (U.S. Navy)

Tomahawk cruise missile with fins and engine air intake scoop extended (U.S. Navy)

A Tomahawk is launched from an armored box launcher being evaluated aboard the destroyer MERRILL (DD 976). (U.S. Navy)

UGM-93A TRIDENT C-4 (Lockheed)

The Trident SLBM evolved from the Department of Defense's STRAT-X study of the late 1960s that proposed an advanced SLBM with a range of some 6,000 n.miles to be carried in a new class of strategic submarines. Subsequently, the Navy proposed a two-phase program: the Trident C-5 (also called Trident I) based on an improved Poseidon design with a range of some 4,000 n.miles, and the Trident D-4 (Trident II) to be developed at a later date with the longer range. The C-5 missile was designed to be refitted into the Poseidon tubes of the later LAFAYETTE (SSBN 616)-class submarines and carried in the later OHIO (SSBN 726) class.

Weight:	65,000 lbs
Length:	34 ft (10.4 m)
Span:	(ballistic missile)
Diameter:	74 in (1.9 m)
Propulsion:	3-stage solid-fuel rocket
Range:	~4,000 n.miles
Guidance:	inertial
Warhead:	nuclear MIRV (8 Mk 4 re-entry vehicles); can be fitted with MaRV (Maneuvering Re-entry Vehicle) MK-500 Evader warhead
Platforms:	SSBN 616 class (last 12 submarines) SSBN 726 class
IOC:	1979

Tomahawk with fins and engine air intake scoop deploying after vertical launch

MGM-71 TOW (Hughes and Emerson Electric)

The TOW—Tube-launched, Optically guided, Wire-controlled—missile is an antitank weapon carried in Marine helicopters and ground vehicles. It is fired from a fiber-glass launch tube. Six tubes can be fitted to the Marine AH-1T helicopter. The missile is used by the U.S. Army and several foreign nations, with some 220,000 having been produced.

Weight:	43 lbs
Length:	3²/₃ ft (1.1 m)
Span:	3³/₄ ft (1.1 m)
Diameter:	6 in (152 mm)
Propulsion:	solid-fuel rocket + solid-fuel booster
Range:	2.6 miles
Guidance:	wire-guided
Warhead:	8 lb conventional (shaped-charge)
Platforms:	AH-1
IOC:	

Trident SLBM launch from FRANCIS SCOTT KEY (SSBN 657) (U.S. Air Force)

TRIDENT D-5 (Lockheed)

The so-called Trident II SLBM is in development but with no sched-uled operational date. The weapon is designed to be carried in the OHIO (SSBN 726)-class submarines. It will have a MIRV warhead similar to the Trident C-4, with the principal difference being in-creased range. The following are preliminary characteristics.

Weight:	~126,000 lbs
Length:	44 ft (13.4 m)
Span:	(ballistic missile)
Diameter:	83 in (2.1 m)
Propulsion:	3-stage solid-fuel rocket
Range:	~6,000 n.miles
Guidance:	inertial
Warhead:	nuclear MIRV
Platforms:	SSBN 726 class
IOC:	undetermined

AGM-62 WALLEYE (Martin and Hughes)

The Walleye is an unpowered glide bomb. However, it is listed in the missile designation series and is operationally considered as such in contrast to other guided bombs. The missile is intended for use against surface ships and hardened ground targets. It is locked on to the target before launch by the pilot or bombardier/navigator who aligns the target on a television display in the cockpit. The aircraft can immediately depart the area after launch with the missile glid-ing toward the preselected TV target image. The missile is also used by the U.S. and Israeli air forces. The Walleye I is no longer in pro-duction.

Weight:	1,100 lbs for Walleye I
	2,000 lbs for Walleye II
Length:	11¼ ft (3.4 m) for Walleye I
	13 ft (4.0 m) for Walleye II
Span:	3¾ ft (1.1 m) for Walleye I
	4¼ ft (1.3 m) for Walleye II
Diameter:	15 in (380 mm) for Walleye I
	18 in (456 mm) for Walleye II
Propulsion:	none (a ram air turbine is provided for electrical supply for guidance and control)
Range:	14 n. miles for Walleye I
	30 n. miles for Walleye II
Guidance:	electro-optical (television)
Warhead:	nuclear (W-72) or
	850 lbs conventional in Walleye I
	2,000 lbs conventional in Walleye II
Platforms:	F-4 A-4 A-7
IOC:	Walleye I in 1967

Walleye ASM on A-4 Skyhawk light attack aircraft (U.S. Navy)

Walleye I ASM on A-7 Corsair; the pod on the outer wing pylon is for the missile data link. The Walleye has a cover on the optical seeker in the nose. (U.S. Navy)

MISSILE LAUNCHING SYSTEMS

Designation	Missiles	Type	Operational	System Weight[a]	Ships
Mk 9 Mod 1	60 Terrier	twin	1959	~500,000 lbs	CG 6–7
Mk 10 Mod 0	40 Terrier/Standard-ER	twin	1960	275,875 lbs	DDG 37–46
Mk 10 Mod 1	40 Terrier/Standard-ER	twin	1961	277,436 lbs	CGN 9 (forward)
Mk 10 Mod 2	80 Terrier/Standard-ER	twin	1961	450,857 lbs	CGN 9 (forward)
Mk 10 Mod 3	40 Terrier/Standard-ER	twin	1961	284,665 lbs	CV 63, 64, 66 (starboard)
Mk 10 Mod 4	40 Terrier/Standard-ER	twin	1961	284,665 lbs	CV 63, 64, 66 (port)
Mk 10 Mod 5	40 Terrier/Standard-ER	twin	1962	287,516 lbs	CG 16–24, CGN 25 (forward)
Mk 10 Mod 6	40 Terrier/Standard-ER	twin	1962	274,938 lbs	CG 16–24, CGN 25 (aft)
Mk 10 Mod 7	60 Terrier/Standard-ER/ASROC	twin	1964	361,994 lbs	CG 26–34, CGN 35
Mk 10 Mod 8	60 Terrier/Standard-ER/ASROC	twin	1967	364,197 lbs	CGN 35
Mk 11 Mod 0	42 Tartar/Standard-MR/Harpoon	twin	1962	165,240 lbs	DDG 2–14
Mk 11 Mod 1	42 Tartar/Standard-MR	twin	1962	165,240 lbs	CG 10–11 (starboard)
Mk 12 Mod 0	42 Tartar/Standard-MR	twin	1962	165,240 lbs	CG 10–11 (port)
Mk 12 Mod 1	52 Talos	twin	1962	~700,000 lbs	CG 10–11 (forward and aft)
Mk 13 Mod 0	40 Tartar/Standard-MR	single	1962	132,561 lbs	DDG 15–24
Mk 13 Mod 1	40 Tartar/Standard-MR	single	1967	135,079 lbs	DDG 31–34
Mk 13 Mod 2	40 Tartar/Standard-MR	single	1968	135,079 lbs	DDG 35–36
Mk 13 Mod 3	40 Tartar/Standard-MR	single	1974	135,012 lbs	CGN 36–37
Mk 13 Mod 4	40 Tartar/Standard-MR/Harpoon	single	1978	134,704 lbs	FFG 7
Mk 16 Mods 1 to 6	8 ASROC[b]	8-tube		47,782 lbs	cruisers, destroyers, frigates; some modified to launch Harpoon or Standard-ARM missiles (Mk 112 launcher "box")
Mk 22 Mod 0	16 Tartar/Standard-MR	single	1966	92,395 lbs	FFG 1–6
Mk 25 Mod 1	8 Sea Sparrow BPDMS	8-tube	1967	32,081 lbs	carriers, frigates, amphibious ships
Mk 26 Mod 0	24 Standard-MR/ASROC	twin	1976	162,028 lbs	CGN 38–41, AVM 1
Mk 26 Mod 1	44 Standard-MR/ASROC	twin	1976	208,373 lbs	CGN 38–41, CG 47
Mk 26 Mod 2	64 Standard-MR/ASROC	twin		254,797 lbs	CGN 42 design
Mk 29 Mod 0	8 NATO Sea Sparrow	8-tube	1974	24,000 or 28,000 lbs[c]	carriers, destroyers, frigates, amphibious ships, auxiliaries; NATO Sea Sparrow (Mk 132 launcher "box")
Ex-41	61 Standard/Harpoon/Tomahawk/ASROC	vertical	development	~188,000 lbs	later CG 47, DDGX, DD 963 (?)
Ex-41	29 Standard/Harpoon/Tomahawk/ASROC	vertical	development	~94,000 lbs	DDGX
Mk 140 Mod 0[d]	4 Harpoon	4-tube	1976	9,000 lbs	PHM 1–6
Mk 141 Mod 1[d]	4 Harpoon	4-tube	1977	13,000 lbs	cruisers, destroyers
Ex-31	24 RAM	24-tube	development	11,700 lbs	undetermined

[a] Does not include missiles and hydraulic fluids; missiles are included for Mk 16, 25, 29, 140, and 141.
[b] Does not include reloads available in some ships.
[c] One-director and two-director systems, respectively.
[d] These are launcher and not system designations.

Sea Sparrow launcher Mk 25 in the frigate STEIN (FF 1065) (N. Polmar)

Terrier/Standard-ER launcher Mk 10 Mod 5 in the cruiser LEAHY (CG 16) (U.S. Navy, PHCS Virgil McColley)

Artist's concept of Vertical Launch System (VLS) Ex 41 on TICONDEROGA (CG 47)-class cruiser (Martin Marietta)

Tartar/Standard-MR launcher Mk 13 Mod 4 in the cruiser CALIFORNIA (CGN 36) (U.S. Navy, PH2 James Brown)

TORPEDOES

The U.S. Navy has three torpedoes in service use: the Mk 37 and Mk 46 antisubmarine torpedoes, and the Mk 48, which can be used against submarines and surface targets.

The Mk 37 is a medium-length torpedo that is being retained in the Navy as a submarine-launched, ASW weapon because of a shortfall in the procurement of the Mk 48. (The original Navy requirement objective was over 4,000 Mk 48 torpedoes based on SSN/SSBN "shipfills" plus resupply and test-training; the Department of Defense has reduced this goal to about 2,700. Some 1,200 Mk 37 torpedoes are available.)

The Mk 46 is a short torpedo that can be launched from surface warships (Mk 32 torpedo tubes or ASROC) or aircraft, and is also used in the Mk 60 CAPTOR mine. The Mk 46 has fully replaced its predecessor, the Mk 44, in U.S. service. The Mk 46 Mod 3 torpedo is being improved under the NEARTIP (Near Term Improvement Program) with improved acoustic guidance and countermeasure resistance features being fitted to 2,700 torpedoes. Thus upgraded, the torpedoes are designated Mk 46 Mod 5. The Mk 46 Mod 4 torpedo is used in the CAPTOR mine.

The Mk 48 is a long or heavy torpedo, developed as a replacement for the Mk 14 torpedo in the antiship role, and the Mk 37 and Mk 45 ASTOR (Antisubmarine Torpedo) in the ASW role.

In several respects the Mk 48 is probably the most capable torpedo in service with any navy. A number of advanced guidance features are provided, including a sophisticated passive-active acous-

tic search as well as wire guidance. The identification of advanced Soviet submarines in the 1970s, especially the high-speed, deep-diving Alfa-class SSN, has led to the ADCAP (Additional Capability) modification program for the Mk 48. Under ADCAP the weapon is being refitted with improved acoustic guidance and counter-countermeasures.

The availability of the Mk 48 has led to the phasing out of the Mk 45 ASTOR, the U.S. Navy's only torpedo with a nuclear warhead. The discarded Mk 37 torpedoes are being fitted with improved engines and guidance and are being provided to foreign navies as the NT-37C. Only the Mk 46 and Mk 48 are now in production for the U.S. Navy.

An Advanced Lightweight Torpedo (ALWT), currently designated Mk XX, is being developed as a replacement for the Mk 46 during the mid- to late-1980s. The ALWT will be designed to counter Soviet submarine threats anticipated through the year 2000, and be compatible with fixed-wing patrol/ASW aircraft, the SH-2 and SH-60 LAMPS helicopters, and the Mk 32 torpedo tubes. It may also become the payload for the ASW Stand-Off Weapon, planned as the successor to SUBROC.

Although not technically a torpedo, the SUBROC (Submarine Rocket) must be mentioned in this section. This antisubmarine weapon is fired from standard 21-inch submarine torpedo tubes. It projects a nuclear depth charge to a distance of 25–30 miles from the launching submarine.

Designation	Launch Platforms	Operational	Weight	Length	Diameter	Propulsion	Guidance	Notes
Mk 37 Mod 2	submarines	1967	1,690 lbs	13½ ft (4.1 m)	19 in (481 mm)	electric	wire; active-passive acoustic	range ~5 miles
Mk 37 Mod 3	submarines	1967	1,430 lbs	11¼ ft (3.4 m)	19 in (481 mm)	electric	active-passive acoustic	range ~5 miles
Mk 46 Mod 0	aircraft	1966	568 lbs	8½ ft (2.6 m)	12¾ in (324 mm)	solid-propellant	active-passive acoustic	
Mk 46 Mod 1/2	surface ships (Mk 32 tubes and ASROC); aircraft	1967	508 lbs	8½ ft (2.6 m)	12¾ in (324 mm)	liquid mono-propellant (OTTO fuel)	active-passive acoustic	Mod 4 in CAPTOR mine; mod 5 is NEARTIP
Mk 48 Mod 1/3	submarines	1972	3,450 lbs	19¹/₁₂ ft (5.8 m)	21 in (533 mm)	liquid mono-propellant	wire; active-passive acoustic	range ~25 miles
Mk XX	surface ships (Mk 32 tubes and ASROC: aircraft	mid-1980s	500 lbs	8 ft (2.4 m)	9⅜ in (240 mm)		active-passive acoustic	ASW Advanced Light-weight Torpedo (ALWT)

Mk 48 Mod 1 torpedoes are readied for loading aboard an attack submarine at Port Canaveral, Fla. (U.S. Air Force)

Loading a Mk 48 torpedo in a SKIPJACK (SSN 585)-class submarine. Note that torpedo is being loaded or "shipped" forward, directly into the bow torpedo room. In later SSNs, with amidships torpedo tubes, the torpedoes and tube-launched missiles are loaded through a weapons hatch-and-chute system abaft the sail structure. (U.S. Navy)

A Mk 46 torpedo fitted on an SH-3 Sea King helicopter (U.S. Navy, Lorin Miller)

A P-3C Orion from VP-47 releases a Mk 46 torpedo. Note the parachute deploying and the restraining bands breaking away from the chute. (U.S. Navy, Lorin Miller)

Four Mk 46 Mod 1 torpedoes in the weapons bay of a P-3 Orion aircraft. Parachute packs are fitted to the tails of the torpedoes. (U.S. Navy)

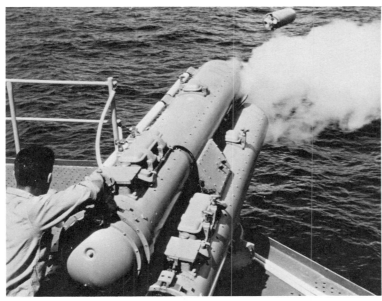

A Mk 46 torpedo is launched from the Mk 32 triple tubes aboard the destroyer NEWMAN K. PERRY (DD 863). (U.S. Navy)

Crewmen of the attack submarine PARGO (SSN 650) load a Mk 48 Mod 1 torpedo at Port Canaveral. (U.S. Navy)

24 Electronics

Explanation of symbols:

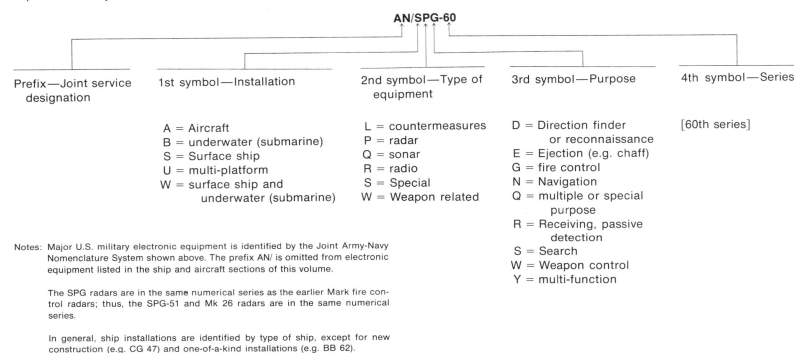

AN/SPG-60

| Prefix—Joint service designation | 1st symbol—Installation | 2nd symbol—Type of equipment | 3rd symbol—Purpose | 4th symbol—Series |

1st symbol—Installation

A = Aircraft
B = underwater (submarine)
S = Surface ship
U = multi-platform
W = surface ship and underwater (submarine)

2nd symbol—Type of equipment

L = countermeasures
P = radar
Q = sonar
R = radio
S = Special
W = Weapon related

3rd symbol—Purpose

D = Direction finder or reconnaissance
E = Ejection (e.g. chaff)
G = fire control
N = Navigation
Q = multiple or special purpose
R = Receiving, passive detection
S = Search
W = Weapon control
Y = multi-function

4th symbol—Series

[60th series]

Notes: Major U.S. military electronic equipment is identified by the Joint Army-Navy Nomenclature System shown above. The prefix AN/ is omitted from electronic equipment listed in the ship and aircraft sections of this volume.

The SPG radars are in the same numerical series as the earlier Mark fire control radars; thus, the SPG-51 and Mk 26 radars are in the same numerical series.

In general, ship installations are identified by type of ship, except for new construction (e.g. CG 47) and one-of-a-kind installations (e.g. BB 62).

ELECTRONIC WARFARE SYSTEMS[a]

Designation	Purpose	Manufacturer	Platforms
ALR-600	radar warning	General Instrument	65-ft PB
BLQ-3/4/5	acoustic jammer	General Electric	submarines
BLQ-8	acoustic system	Bendix, Aerojet (various)	submarines
BLR-1/10	acoustic warning		submarines
BLR-13	ECM receiver	Kollmorgan	submarines
BLR-14 SAWS[b]	threat warning, processor, countermeasure launcher	Sperry	submarines
BLR-15	ESM receiver	Kollmorgan	submarines
BRD-6/7	radio direction finder	Sanders	submarines
SLQ-17	jammer	Hughes	surface ships
SLQ-25 NIXIE	torpedo countermeasure[d] (towed)	Aerojet	surface ships
SLQ-29	SLQ-17 plus WLR-8 installation	Hughes	surface ships
SLQ-32(V)1	radar warning (H/I/J bands)	Raytheon	AE, AF, AFS, LST, LSD, LKA

Designation	Purpose	Manufacturer	Platforms
SLQ-32(V)2	radar warning (B through J bands)	Raytheon	DDG 2, 31; DD 963; FFG 1, 7; FF 1052
SLQ-32(V)3	radar warning (B through J bands); ECM (H/I/J)	Raytheon	CG, CGN, DDG 37, LCC, LHA, LPH, AOE, AOR
SSQ-74 OUT-BOARD[c]	electronic warfare system	ITT Avionics	surface ships
SSQ-82 MUTE	shipboard emitter monitor and control		surface ships
SRD-19 DIAMOND	radio direction finder	Sanders	surface ships
ULQ-6	deception repeater	General Instrument	surface ships
WLR-1	radar warning	(various)	surface ships
WLR-6 WATER-BOY	radar warning, signal collection	GTE-Sylvania	surface ships, submarines
WLR-8	radar warning	GTE-Sylvania	carriers (WLR-8(V)4, in submarines)

ELECTRONIC WARFARE SYSTEMS[a] (cont.)

Designation	Purpose	Manufacturer	Platforms
WLR-9	sonar detection	Norden	submarines
WLR-10	ECM receiver	Astro Labs	submarines
WLR-11	radar warning	ARGO Systems	surface ships
T-Mk 6 fanfare	torpedo counter-measure[d]		surface ships
Mk 70 MOSS	Mobile Submarine Simulator	Gould	SSBNs

[a] Aircraft EW systems are listed in Chapter 22 under the specific aircraft.
[b] Submarine Acoustic Warfare System.
[c] Also designated SSES (Ships Signal Exploitation System).
[d] Towed system; T-Mk 6 being replaced in older ships by SLQ-25.

RADAR BANDS

NATO Band Designations
Megahertz

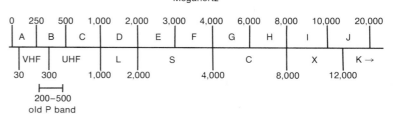

200–500
old P band

Conventional Band Designations

RADARS[a]

Designation	Purpose	Operational[b]	Band	Manufacturer	Ships	Notes
Mk 13	radar for Mk 31 and Mk 38 gun directors (range and bearing)		X	Western Electric	BB, CA, CG	Mod 0; none in active ships
Mk 25	radar for Mk 37 GFCS (conical scanning)		X	Western Electric	BB, CA, CG, DD	Mod 3
Mk 34/SPG-34	radar for Mk 57 gun director and Mk 63 GFCS (conical scanning)		X	Western Electric	BB, CA	Mod 2/4/16; none in active ships
Mk 35	radar for Mk 56 GFCS		X	General Electric	BB, CA, CG, CGN, DD, FFG, FF, LPD, LSD	Mod 2
BPS-5	surface search	1953	X	Lockheed	submarines	
BPS-11	surface search		X	Western Electric	submarines	
BPS-12/14	surface search		X	Fairchild	submarines	modified BPS-5
BPS-15	surface search		X	Sperry	submarines	
SG-6	surface search				CA	none in active ships
SPG-49	Talos illumination and tracking		C	Sperry	CG	Mods A/B; none in active ships
SPG-51	Tartar/Standard-MR illumination and tracking	1960	C/X	Raytheon	CG, CGN, DDG, FFG	Mods B/C/D; pulse-doppler
SPG-53	radar for Mk 68 GFCS		X	Western Electric	DDG, DD, FF	Mods A/D/F; modified SPG-48
SPG-55	Terrier/Standard-ER illumination and guidance		C	Sperry	CV, CG, CGN, DDG	Mods A/B; replaces SPQ-5
SPG-60	Standard-MR/gun tracking and illuminator for Mk 86 GFCS		X	Lockheed	CGN, DD, LHA	see STIR (below); pulse-doppler
SPG-62	Standard SM-2 illuminator (Aegis)		X	Raytheon	CG 47, AVM 1	Mk 99 Missile FCS component; slaved to SPY-1 radar
SPQ-5	Terrier illumination		X	Raytheon	CG	Mod A; replaced by SPG-55
SPQ-9A	surface search and weapons control for Mk 86 GFCS	1970	X	Lockheed	CG 47, CGN, DD 963, LHA	Mod A; high-resolution, short-range, track-while-scan; pulse-doppler
SPS-6	air search	1950	L	Bendix Westinghouse	BB 62, CA, LSD 28, AOE 3–4	Mods B/C/E; Mod C in active ships
SPS-8	height-finding	1955	S	General Electric	BB, CA	Mod A; none in active ships
SPS-10	surface search	1953	C	Raytheon GTE-Sylvania	most combatant, amphibious, auxiliary ships	Mods B–F
SPS-12	air search	1953	L	RCA	CVT 16, CA 139	Mod C
SPS-29	air search[c]	1958	P	Westinghouse	DDG, DD	Mods B/C/E
SPS-30	long-range height-finding	1962	S	General Electric	CV, CG	
SPS-37	long-range air search[c]	1960	P	Westinghouse	CV, CG, CGN, CA, DDG, DD	antenna identical to SPS-29
SPS-39	3-D search	1960	S	Hughes	CGN 25, DDG	Mod A
SPS-40	air search	1961	UHF	Lockheed	CGN, DDG, DD, FF, LCC, LHA, LPH	Mods A–D
SPS-43	long-range air search[c]	1962	P	Hughes Westinghouse	CVN, CV, CG, CA	Mod A
SPS-48	3-D search	1962	S	ITT-Gilfillan	CVN, CV, CG, CGN, DDG, LCC	Mods A–E; Frequency Scan (FRES-CAN) in elevation and mechanical scan in azimuth
SPS-49	long-range air search	1965[d]		Raytheon	CVN, CV, CG 47, CG 19, FFG 7	narrow-beam, very long-range

RADARS[a] (cont.)

Designation	Purpose	Operational[b]	Band	Manufacturer	Ships	Notes
SPS-52	3-D search	1963	S	Hughes	DDG, FFG, LHA	Mods A–C; improved SPS-39A; FRESCAN
SPS-53	surface search	1967	X	Sperry Marine	BB 62, PG, MSO, auxiliary ships	navigation radar
SPS-55	surface search		X	Cordion	BB 62, CG 47, DD, FFG 7	slotted array; SPS-10 replacement
SPS-58/65	low-level threat detection		L	Westinghouse	CVN, CV, FF, LCC, LHA, LPH, AOE, AOR	can use SPS-10 antenna; fed directly to NTDS; pulse-doppler
SPW-2	Talos guidance		C	Sperry	CG	Mods A/B; none in active ships
SPY-1	Aegis multi-function, long-range radar		S	RCA	CG 47, AVM 1	Mod A; fixed array; 4 12 × 12-ft array with 4,080 radiating elements each; integrated with fire control
STIR	Separate Target Illumination Radar	1974	X		FFG 7	modified SPG-60

[a] Aircraft radars are listed in Chapter 22 with specific aircraft.
[b] Includes installation in ship for at-sea evaluation.
[c] The SPS-29/37/43 use the same antenna; the SPS-37A and SPS-43A use a larger antenna. The SPS-37A has an effective range of 300 miles vice approximately 230 for the SPS-37.
[d] Original version tested aboard GYATT (DD 712) in 1965; current version first went to sea in the DALE (CG 19) in 1976.

SONARS

Designation	Purpose	Operational[a]	Manufacturer	Platforms	Notes
AQS-13	helicopter dipping sonar			SH-3D/H	
AQS-14	mine countermeasures	1979	Westinghouse	RH-53D	
BQG-4 PUFFS	passive fire control	1963	Sperry	SS 574, SS 576, SSAG 567, SSN 597	three fin domes; Passive Underwater Fire control System
BQQ-2	active/passive sonar system	1960	Raytheon	SSN 594, 597, 637, 671, 686	includes BQR-7 and BQS-6; being upgraded to BQQ-5
BQQ-5	active/passive sonar system	1976	IBM	SSN 688 plus BQQ-2 updates	improved BQQ-2
BQQ-6	passive sonar system	1981	IBM	SSBN 726	passive BQQ-5
BQR-2B	passive detection	1955	EDO	see BQS-4	component of BQS-4
BQR-7	passive detection	1955	Raytheon / EDO	see BQQ-2	conformal hydrophone array
BQR-15	passive detection	1974	Western Electric	SSBN 608, 616	towed array; includes BQR-23 signal processor
BQR-19	short-range, rapid-scanning	1970	Raytheon	SSBN	
BQR-21	passive detection		Honeywell	SSBN	
BQR-23	passive detection			SSBN	
BQS-4	active/passive sonar system	1955	EDO	SS, older SSN	
BQS-8/14/20	mine/under ice detection	1960	EDO / Hazeltine	newer SSN	replaces BQS-6; component of BQQ-2/5; spherical array in bow dome
BQS-15					
SQQ-14	mine detection-classification		EDO	MSO, MCM	cable-lowered sonar; retracts into hull
SQQ-23 PAIR	active/passive detection	1972	Sperry	DDG 2, DDG 37, CG 16, CGN 9 mod.	modified SQS-23; Passive/Active Integration Retrofit[b]
SQR-15	passive towed array			FF	
SQR-17	acoustic processor for LAMPS helicopters	1975	DRS	CG, DDG, DD, FFG, FF with LAMPS	
SQR-18 TACTAS	passive long-range detection	1978	EDO	FF 1052	Tactical Towed Array Sonar; employs winch, cable, towing body of SQS-35
SQR-19	passive long-range detection		General Electric	CG 47, DD 963, FFG 7	improved TACTAS
SQS-23	active/passive detection	1958	Sangamo	CV 66, CGN, CG, DDG, DD 931 ASW Mod.	
SQS-26	active/passive detection	1962	General Electric	AXR in CG 26, FFG 1, FF 1098, FF 1040, FF 1037 CX in CGN 36, FF 1052	
SQS-35 IVDS	Independent Variable Depth Sonar	1968	EDO	FF 1052	
SQS-53	active/passive detection	1975	General Electric	CGN 38, CG 47, DD 963	SQS-26CX with digital interface for Mk 116 underwater FCS
SQS-56	active/passive detection	1977	Raytheon	FFG 7	
SURTASS	long-range passive detection			T-AGOS	Surveillance Towed Array System

[a] Includes first installation in combat ship for at-sea evaluation.
[b] Designation subsequently changed to Performance and Integration Retrofit; two hull-mounted domes.

SONOBUOYS[a]

Designation	Type	Manufacturer	Notes
SQQ-36	bathythermograph (water temperature profile)	Sparton	profile from surface to 1,000 ft
SQQ-41 OMNI	omnidirectional passive	Magnavox Sparton Hermes	large-area search; 41B in production
SQQ-47	active explosive echo ranging		mini-"Julie"
SQQ-50 CASS	Command Active Sonobuoy System		
SQQ-53 DIFAR	passive directional	Sparton Magnavox	used for accurate localization after initial detection; 53A in production
SQQ-57	passive	Sparton Hermes Raytheon	for restricted waters; 57A in production
SQQ-62 DICASS	Directional Command Active Sonobuoy System		
SQQ-77 VLAD	passive Vertical Line Array DIFAR	Sparton	

[a] Carried by fixed-wing aircraft and helicopters.

SLQ-17A(V) ECM antenna on ENTERPRISE (CVN 65) (Hughes)

WLR-6 ECM antenna (N. Polmar)

Electronics have a vital place in modern naval warfare, with contemporary U.S. warships covered with antennas as is the super carrier NIMITZ (CVN 68), shown here at Norfolk, Va., with the guided missile cruiser SOUTH CAROLINA (CGN 37) just visible at far right. The mast in the foreground, immediately abaft the carrier's island, mounts an SPS-43A long-range air search radar. This radar will be replaced in modern U.S. warships with the SPS-49. (U.S. Navy, JO2 Jerry A. Chison)

SLQ-32(V)3 antennas (port and starboard) in missile cruiser VIRGINIA (CGN 38); the radar antenna at center is an SPG-60. (Raytheon)

A seagull casts a shadow on the SPY-1 antenna aboard the NORTON SOUND (AVM 1). The ship has only one SPY-1 antenna; the TICONDEROGA (CG 47)-class missile cruisers will have four such "faces," each with 4,480 separate radiating elements in an octagonal face some 12½ feet across.

SLQ-32(V)2 antenna in SPRUANCE (DD 963)-class destroyer (N. Polmar)

Mk 25 radar atop Mk 37 GFCS (right) and Mk 13 radar atop Mk 38 gun director aboard battleship NEW JERSEY (BB 62). (U.S. Navy)

A technician inserts a block of radiating elements in a SPY-1A antenna. The SPY-1A antenna "face" and its associated equipment have improved its capabilities compared to the prototype sea-going SPY-1 radar in the NORTON SOUND (AVM 1), and it is some 30 percent lighter. A modified SPY-1 system for the DDGX would be still lighter. (RCA)

The reverse side of a SPY-1A antenna during assembly (RCA)

BPS-15 radar on HAWKBILL (SSN 666) (Giorgio Arra)

SPG-49B "searchlight" Talos illuminating and tracking radars in the CHICAGO (CG 11) are installed below the cruiser's diminutive SPW-2 radar. (Giorgio Arra)

Mk 35 radar affixed to the Mk 56 GFCS aboard the aircraft carrier MIDWAY (CV 41). The 48-inch-diameter dish provides acquisition and tracking for the Mk 56, which is used for 3-inch and 5-inch gun control. All guns have been removed from aircraft carriers with the Phalanx CIWS soon to be installed in all active aircraft carriers except possibly the CORAL SEA (CV 43). (U.S. Navy)

Twin SPG-55B radars in missile cruiser HALSEY (CG 23). The twin 3-inch/50 caliber mount shown here has been removed. (Giorgio Arra)

Twin SPG-51C radars, part of the Mk 74 missile FCS, face aft aboard the guided missile destroyer HENRY B. WILSON (DDG 7). The SPS-39A three dimensional air search radar is mounted on the ship's after stack. (G. Arra)

Mk 25 radar atop Mk 37 GFCS. The 60-inch-diameter dish antenna was found aboard most World War II-built U.S. carriers, cruisers, battleships, and destroyers armed with 5-inch guns. (U.S. Navy)

SPG-53A radar atop Mk 68 GFCS (N. Polmar)

SPS-6 air search radar atop SPS-10 surface search radar in THOMASTON (LSD 28) (N. Polmar)

SPS-48A radar in JOHN PAUL JONES (DDG 32) (Giorgio Arra)

SPS-29E radar in JOHN PAUL JONES (DDG 32) (Giorgio Arra)

SPS-43A (left) and SPS-30 antennas in MIDWAY (CV 41) (Giorgio Arra)

SPS-43 air search radar in the missile cruiser WAINWRIGHT (CG 28) (U.S. Navy)

SPS-40 air search radar in the destroyer MORTON (DD 948) (Giorgio Arra)

SPS-49 air search radar in the missile destroyer PREBLE (DDG 46) (Giorgio Arra)

SPS-52 three-dimensional search radar in missile frigate BROOKE (FFG 1) (Giorgio Arra)

SPS-48 three-dimensional search radar in WILLIAM H. STANDLEY (CG 32) (Giorgio Arra)

SPS-48 three-dimensional search radar in CHICAGO (CG 11) (Giorgio Arra)

STIR (left) and SPS-49 radar in the missile frigate OLIVER HAZARD PERRY (FFG 7) (Bath Iron Works)

SPG-62 illuminator for Aegis system at Navy-RCA test and training facility in Moorestown, N.J. (N. Polmar)

This is a rare view of a submarine sonar dome—in this view a 15-foot-diameter BQS-6 sphere that was subsequently fitted with transducers and installed in an SSN. The complementary BQR-7 passive sonar consists of hydrophones in a conformal array along the bow of the submarine. (U.S. Navy)

SH-3D Sea King ASW helicopter lowering AQS-13 dipping sonar (U.S. Navy)

The structure immediately abaft the sail of the DARTER (SS 576) is the amidships sonar dome for the BQG-4 PUFFS. Submarines equipped with PUFFS have a similar dome forward and aft, the latter as widely separated as possible. (Giorgio Arra)

An uncovered SQS-53 sonar dome during installation in a SPRUANCE (DD 963)-class destroyer. Transducers are not yet fitted. (Litton/Ingalls)

Large bow-mounted sonar domes have become a key feature of major U.S. antisubmarine ships since the 1950s. The destroyer SPRUANCE (DD 963), shown here while fitting out, has the SQS-53 active sonar. The SQS-53 and its predecessor, the SQS-26, are the largest ship sonars in service with any navy. (Litton/Ingalls)

An overhead view of the SQS-35 "fish" being deployed from the frigate VALDEZ (FF 1096) (U.S. Navy)

The SQS-35 Variable Depth Sonar (VDS) "fish" is lowered from the frigate FRANCIS HAMMOND (FF 1067) during dockside tests. The hoisting gear and "fish" retract into the open stern compartment. Towed arrays are larger and more complex. (U.S. Navy)

A sailor loads SSQ-41 sonobuoys in the engine nacelle dispensers of an S-2E Tracker ASW aircraft. Contemporary Navy ASW aircraft—the S-3, P-3, Sh-2, and SH-60 have fuselage dispensers. Only the SH-3H of the Sea King series has sonobuoys. Retardation fins (a "rotochute") extend in flight to slow the descent of sonobuoys; upon entering the water the hydrophone is released and sinks to a predetermined depth, connecting by wire to the floating buoy that then transmits signals to the aircraft. (U.S. Navy)

The McCLOY (FF 1038) is the smallest ship to have SQS-26 bow-mounted sonar. The dome partially floods when at sea and has some dampening effects on ship motion. Unofficial sources credit the SQS-26/53 sonars with an effective range of about 35 miles using "convergence zone" techniques in the active mode. Passive "listening" use of these sonars can provide greater detection ranges against some targets. (U.S. Navy, Ed Dowling)

Navy technicians maintain the AWG-10/APG-59 radar of an F-4 Phantom fighter aboard the aircraft carrier NIMITZ (CVN 68). (U.S. Navy, JO1 Chris Christensen)

25 Coast Guard

The U.S. Coast Guard is a separate military service under the Department of Transportation and is responsible for the enforcement of U.S. laws in coastal waters and on the high seas, subject to the jurisdiction of the United States.

At the direction of the President, the Coast Guard can become a part of the Navy (as it did during both World Wars) or operate in a war zone while remaining an independent service (as during the Korean and Vietnam Wars).

The Coast Guard was established on 4 August 1790 as the Revenue Marine of the Department of Treasury. Subsequently renamed Revenue Cutter Service and, from 1915, the Coast Guard, the service incorporated the Lighthouse Service in 1939. In 1967 the Coast Guard was transferred to the newly established Department of Transportation.

OPERATIONS

The principal peacetime missions of the Coast Guard are: (1) recreational boating safety, (2) search and rescue, (3) aids to navigation (maintaining almost 400 lighthouses and some 13,000 minor navigational lights), (4) merchant marine safety, (5) environmental protection, (6) port safety, and (7) enforcement of laws and treaties.

The last mission comprises the enforcement of the nation's customs and immigration laws, including the prevention of smuggling and narcotics, and also the enforcement of fisheries laws, including international treaties related to the 200-mile national economic zone. This mission in particular, aggravated by the mass exodus of Cubans in May-June 1980, has created major operational problems for the Coast Guard.

In 1981 three former Navy tug-type auxiliary ships were placed in service with the Coast Guard as medium endurance cutters (WMEC). See Addenda.

Current and predicted Coast Guard missions, especially the maritime law enforcement mission, have led Coast Guard officials to calculate that an additional 57 cutters will be required by the mid-1980s if the service is to fulfill all assigned missions. Then, in the 1990s an additional 174 cutters would reach the end of their useful service life and require replacement.

VESSELS

The Coast Guard uses the term *vessels* for all watercraft operated by the service. Within that classification, the term *cutter* is used for ships that have "an assigned personnel allowance and that [have] installed habitability features for the extended support of a permanently assigned crew." In practice, this includes 65-foot tugs and larger vessels, except ferries. Cutters are generally identified by their length (e.g., the HAMILTON-class cutters are 378-feet long).

All smaller Coast Guard vessels are referred to as *boats,* including barges, yachts, and ferryboats.

The Coast Guard vessel designation scheme is derived from that of the U.S. Navy (see Appendix A). All Coast Guard designations are prefixed by the letter W (*unofficially* for White-painted ships). The larger cutters are numbered in a single, sequential series that was initiated in 1941–1942. Cutters less than 100 feet in length and boats have hull numbers with the first two digits indicating the vessel's length overall.

The cutter designations currently in use for ocean-going vessels and other major types are:

WAGB	Icebreaker
WAGO	Oceanographic cutter
WHEC	High Endurance Cutter (multi-mission; 30 to 45 days at sea without support)
WIX	Training cutter
WLB	Offshore buoy tender (full sea-keeping capability; medium endurance)
WLI	Inshore buoy tender (short endurance)
WLIC	Inland construction tender (short endurance)
WLM	Coastal buoy tender (medium endurance)
WLR	River buoy tender (short endurance)
WLV	Light Vessel
WMEC	Medium Endurance Cutter (multi-mission; 10 to 30 days at sea without support)
WPB	Patrol Boat (multi-mission; 1 to 7 days at sea without support)

The Coast Guard also uses the term "icebreaker" for a variety of vessels with the following categories:

Type A	GLACIER	(WAGB 4)
Type B	MACKINAW (WAGB 83) and "Wind" class (WAGB 281)	
Type C	"Bay" class (WTGB 140)	
Type D	medium harbor tugs (WYTM)	
Type E	small harbor tugs (WYTL)	
Type P	POLAR (WAGB 10) class	

Cutter names are prefixed by USCGC for U.S. Coast Guard Cutter.

The Coast Guard also operates several hundred small lifeboats and patrol boats. These are mostly 44-, 40-, 30-, and 22-foot unnamed craft.

Most cutters are painted white, with the larger icebreakers painted red and buoy tenders and harbor tugs painted black (superstructures remain white).

The Coast Guard insignia, a narrow blue and wide red stripe with the Coast Guard shield superimposed on the latter, is carried on the bows of all vessels except lightships.

Type	Class/Ship	Active	Building	Reserve	Commissioned	Notes
WHEC 715	HAMILTON	12	—	—	1967–1972	
WHEC 379	CASCO	1	—	—	1943	ex-U.S. Navy
WHEC 41	OWASCO	—	—	5	1945–1946	
WHEC 31	"Secretary"	5	—	1	1936–1937	
WMEC 901	BEAR	—	9	—	1981–	
WMEC 615	RELIANCE	16	—	—	1964–1969	1 ship is WTR
WMEC 167	ACUSHNET	2	—	—	1944	ex-U.S. Navy
WMEC 153	CHILULA	3	—	—	1940–1945	ex-U.S. Navy
WMEC 194	MODOC	2	—	—	1944–1945	ex-U.S. Navy
WMEC 38	STORIS	1	—	—	1942	
WPB	"Cape"	26	—	—	1953–1959	95-foot cutters
WPB	"Point"	53	—	—	1960–1970	82-foot cutters
WAGB 10	"Polar"	2	—	—	1976–1978	
WAGB 4	GLACIER	1	—	—	1955	ex-U.S. Navy
WAGB 281	"Wind"	2	—	—	1943–1945	
WAGB 83	MACKINAW	1	—	—	1944	
WIX 327	EAGLE	1	—	—	1936	sailing bark
WLB	seagoing buoy tenders	35	—	—	1942–1944	1 ship WAGO
WLM	coastal buoy tenders	15	—	—		
WLI	inland buoy tenders	6	—	—		
WLIC	inland construction tenders	18	—	—		
WLR	river buoy tenders	18				
WTGB	icebreaking tugs	6	3	—		
WYTM	medium harbor tugs	13	—	1		1 is training tug
WYTL	small harbor tugs	15	—	—		
WLV	lightships	3	—	—		
—	ferries	3	—	—		2 ex-U.S. Army

An HH-52A Sea Guard rests on the water near the Coast Guard Air Station, Miami, Fla. Coast Guard aircraft are based at 27 airfields in the United States (including Alaska, Hawaii, and Puerto Rico). (U.S. Coast Guard)

AVIATION

The Coast Guard air arm operates some 170 aircraft based at 27 air stations in the United States and overseas. In addition, the service's high-endurance cutters and icebreakers regularly operate helicopters, while some smaller cutters have landing decks but can not support helicopters.

Coast Guard aviators are Navy-trained, with their specialized Coast Guard aircraft training being given at the Coast Guard Aviation Training Center in Mobile, Ala.

Two major Coast Guard aircraft procurement programs are under way: forty-one HU-25A Falcon Medium-Range Search (MRS) aircraft are being acquired to replace the HU-16 Albatross amphibians (most of which have already been retired) and the HC-131 Samaritan land-based aircraft; 90 HH-65A Dolphin Short-Range Recovery (SRR) helicopters will be put in service to take the place of the currently flown HH-52A Sea Guard helicopters. (See Chapter 22.)

The following aircraft are currently in Coast Guard inventory. The numbers in parenthesis indicate additional aircraft in reserve or storage.

Number	Type	Mission
12	HC-130B Hercules	Long-Range Search (LRS)
1	HC-130E Hercules	Long-Range Search (LRS)
12	HC-130H Hercules	Long-Range Search (LRS)
17 (3)	HC-131A Samaritan	Medium-Range Search (MRS)
6 (3)	HU-16E Albatross	Medium-Range Search (MRS)
1	VC-4A Gulfstream I	executive transport
1	VC-11A Gulfstream II	executive transport
37	HH-3F Pelican	Medium-Range Recovery (MRR)
70	HH-52A Sea Guard	Short-Range Recovery (SRR)

PERSONNEL

Uniformed Coast Guard personnel operate all cutters and boats. Medical personnel are provided by the U.S. Public Health Service on assignment to the Coast Guard.

Coast Guard strength at the end of 1980 was 4,800 commissioned officers, 1,400 warrant officers, and 32,000 enlisted personnel. In addition, there is a Coast Guard Reserve with some 11,700 men and women.

Women have served at sea in the Coast Guard since the fall of 1977 when the cutters GALLANTIN and MORGENTHAU each embarked two female officers and ten enlisted women. These were the first U.S. combat ships to have regular female crewmen assigned. Subsequently, other women were assigned to cutters, and in 1979 two 95-foot "Cape"-class patrol boats were assigned female commanding officers.

With reference to the above-described increase in Coast Guard cutters required to undertake all missions predicted for the mid-1980s onward, the Coast Guard would require an estimated 81,150 personnel, an increase of almost 80 percent above its current strength.

On the following pages the vessel's allowance is given and, if significantly different, the actual on-board manning is also provided.

12 HIGH ENDURANCE CUTTERS: "HAMILTON" CLASS

Number	Name	Builder	Laid down	Launched	Commissioned	Status
WHEC 715	HAMILTON	Avondale Shipyards	4 Jan 1965	18 Dec 1965	20 Feb 1967	**AA**
WHEC 716	DALLAS	Avondale Shipyards	7 Feb 1966	1 Oct 1966	1 Oct 1967	**AA**
WHEC 717	MELLON	Avondale Shipyards	25 July 1966	11 Feb 1967	22 Dec 1967	**PA**
WHEC 718	CHASE	Avondale Shipyards	15 Oct 1966	20 May 1967	1 Mar 1968	**AA**
WHEC 719	BOUTWELL	Avondale Shipyards	12 Dec 1966	17 June 1967	14 June 1968	**PA**
WHEC 720	SHERMAN	Avondale Shipyards	13 Feb 1967	23 Sep 1967	23 Aug 1968	**PA**
WHEC 721	GALLANTIN	Avondale Shipyards	17 Apr 1967	18 Nov 1967	20 Dec 1968	**AA**
WHEC 722	MORGENTHAU	Avondale Shipyards	17 July 1967	10 Feb 1968	14 Feb 1969	**PA**
WHEC 723	RUSH	Avondale Shipyards	23 Oct 1967	16 Nov 1968	3 July 1969	**PA**
WHEC 724	MUNRO	Avondale Shipyards	18 Feb 1970	5 Dec 1970	10 Sep 1971	**PA**
WHEC 725	JARVIS	Avondale Shipyards	9 Sep 1970	24 Apr 1971	30 Dec 1971	**PA**
WHEC 726	MIDGETT	Avondale Shipyards	5 Apr 1971	4 Sep 1971	17 Mar 1972	**PA**

Displacement:	2,716 tons standard
	3,050 tons full load
Length:	350 feet (106.7 m) wl
	378 feet (115.2 m) oa
Beam:	42¾ feet (13.0 m)
Draft:	20 feet (6.1 m)
Propulsion:	CODOG: 2 gas turbines (Pratt & Whitney), 28,000 shp; 2 diesels (Fairbanks Morse), 7,200 shp; 2 shafts
Speed:	29 knots
Range:	14,000 n.miles at 11 knots; 2,400 n.miles at 29 knots
Allowance:	153–155 (15 O + 138–140 enlisted)
Manning:	148–165 (13–16 O + 132–151 enlisted)
Helicopters:	1 HH-3F Pelican or HH-52A Sea Guard
Guns:	1 5-inch (127-mm) 38 cal DP Mk 30 (1 × 1)
	2 40-mm Mk 19 (2 × 1)
	2 20-mm Mk 67 (2 × 1)
ASW weapons:	6 12.75-inch (324-mm) torpedo tubes Mk 32 (2 × 3)
Radar:	SPS 29 air search
	SPS 64 surface search
Sonars:	SQS 38 keel-mounted
Fire control:	1 Mk 1 target designation system
	1 Mk 56 gun FCS
	1 Mk 309 torpedo control panel
	1 Mk 35 radar

Electronics: The original keel-mounted SQS-36 sonar has been replaced by the SQS-38, a hull-mounted version of the SQS-35 variable-depth sonar.

Engineering: These were the largest U.S. combat ships to have gas-turbine propulsion until completion of the SPRUANCE (DD 963) in 1975. The gas turbines are FT-4A, marine versions of the J75 aircraft engine. The propulsion machinery is CODOG (Combination Diesel Or Gas turbine). Fitted with a 350-hp bow propeller pod.

Names: The first nine ships are named for Secretaries of the Treasury; the three other ships honor heroes of the Coast Guard.

These are the largest cutters in Coast Guard service except for the Polar-class icebreakers. They are the only cutters other than icebreakers that can support helicopters, and are the only Coast Guard ships with on-board ASW weapons.

Antisubmarine: As completed, the earlier ships of this class were fitted with two ahead-firing hedgehogs. They have been removed.

Class: Originally 36 ships of this class were proposed. Planning for additional ships was deferred in favor of retaining older cutters and then was dropped with construction of the smaller BEAR-class cutters.

Design: The superstructures of these ships are fabricated largely of aluminum. They are fitted with oceanographic and meteorological facilities.

CHASE (1976, Giorgio Arra)

The high endurance cutter GALLATIN (WHEC 721) in the Atlantic during the Cadet Practice Squadron Cruise to Europe, in company with another WHEC and the training barque EAGLE (WIX 327). Like the Navy, the Coast Guard continuously fulfills operational missions in peace as well as in war. The WHEC and WMEC type cutters have a wartime ASW role, but lack of exercises and training, and limited ASW equipment make their potential effectiveness in that role doubtful. (1977, U.S. Coast Guard, PA2 Rod Kirby)

MIDGETT (1972, U.S. Coast Guard)

1 HIGH ENDURANCE CUTTER: "CASCO" CLASS

Number	Name	Builder	Laid down	Launched	AVP Comm.	Status
WHEC 379 (ex-AVP 31)	Unimak	Associated Shipbuilders, Seattle, Wash.	15 Feb 1942	27 May 1942	31 Dec 1943	**AA**

Displacement:	1,766 tons standard
	2,800 tons full load
Length:	300 feet (91.4 m) wl
	310¾ feet (94.7 m) oa
Beam:	41 feet (12.5 m)
Draft:	13½ feet (4.1 m)
Propulsion:	diesels (Fairbanks Morse); 6,080 shp; 2 shafts
Speed:	18 knots
Range:	20,000 n.miles at 10 knots
Allowance:	127 (12 O + 115 enlisted)
Manning:	132 (12 O + 120 enlisted)
Helicopters:	no facilities
Guns:	1 5-inch (127-mm) 38 cal DP Mk 30 (1 × 1)
	2 40-mm Mk 19 (2 × 1)
ASW weapons:	removed
Fire control:	removed

The Unimak is the only survivor in U.S. service of 34 Barnegat (AVP 10)-class seaplane tenders built during World War II (four were completed as torpedo-boat tenders and one as an amphibious force flagship). The Unimak and 17 sister ships were transferred to the Coast Guard in 1946–1948 (WAVP/WHEC 370–387). She operated as a training cutter (WTR) from 1969 until her decommissioning in 1975. The ship had been scheduled for transfer to South Vietnam (as had other ships of this class), but with the fall of the Saigon government she was laid up in reserve; she was recommissioned as a WHEC in 1977 to support the 200-mile U.S. offshore resource zone.

Armament: The Unimak has carried a variety of armament during her Navy and Coast Guard service. An ASW hedgehog and two Mk 32 triple tubes had been removed prior to her decommissioning in 1975.

Classification: The ship was built as the Navy AVP 31. Her classification was changed to WAVP 31 upon transfer to the Coast Guard and to WHEC 379 on 1 May 1966. Subsequently, she was changed to WTR 379 on 28 November 1969, but was recommissioned in 1977 as WHEC.

The Unimak and the Navy's Norton Sound (AVM 1) are the last seaplane tender-type ships in U.S. service. Note the weather balloon hangar aft; the cluttered fantail is not suitable for helicopter operations. The hedgehog shown abaft the 5-inch gun (B position) in this photo has since been removed. (1970, U.S. Coast Guard)

5 HIGH ENDURANCE CUTTERS: "OWASCO" CLASS

Designation	Name	Builder	Laid down	Launched	Commissioned	Status
WHEC 41	CHAUTAUQUA	Western Pipe & Steel, San Pedro, Calif.	22 Dec 1943	14 May 1944	4 Aug 1945	CGR
WHEC 65	WINONA	Western Pipe & Steel, San Pedro, Calif.	8 Nov 1944	22 Apr 1945	15 Aug 1946	CGR
WHEC 67	MINNETONKA	Western Pipe & Steel, San Pedro, Calif.	26 Dec 1944	21 Nov 1945	20 Sep 1946	CGR
WHEC 69	MENDOTA	Coast Guard Yard, Curtis Bay, Md.	1 June 1943	29 Feb 1944	2 June 1946	CGR
WHEC 70	PONTCHARTRAIN	Coast Guard Yard, Curtis Bay, Md.	1 July 1943	29 Apr 1944	28 July 1945	CGR

Displacement:	1,563 tons standard
	1,913 tons full load
Length:	254 feet (77.4 m) oa
Beam:	43 feet (13.1 m)
Draft:	17 feet (5.2 m)
Propulsion:	turbo-electric (Westinghouse turbines); 4,000 shp; 2 shafts
Boilers:	2
Speed:	18.4 knots
Range:	12,000 n.miles at 10 knots; 6,000 n.miles at 18.4 knots
Allowance:	139 (13 O + 126 enlisted)
Helicopter:	no facilities
Guns:	1 5-inch (127-mm) 38 cal DP Mk 30 (1 × 1)
ASW weapons:	removed
Fire control:	1 Mk 52 gun FCS
	1 Mk 26 radar

The CHAUTAUQUA, MENDOTA, and PONTCHARTRAIN were decommissioned in 1973, and the WINONA and MINNETONKA in 1974. They were to be stricken but were instead laid up in reserve. The WINONA and MINNETONKA are at Alameda, Calif., the others at Curtis Bay.

Armament: Into the 1960s these ships each had an ASW armament of one ahead-throwing hedgehog and two Mk 32 triple torpedo tubes; they were subsequently removed from all ships.

As built, these cutters each mounted four 5-inch guns in twin mounts, four 40-mm AA guns in twin mounts, and four 20-mm AA guns. Depth-charge racks were also fitted.

Class: There were originally 13 ships in this class: WPG 39–44 and WPG 64–70.

Classification: All built as gunboats (WPG); all 13 were changed to high endurance cutters (WHEC) on 1 May 1966.

Names: Names changed during construction were WHEC 67 ex-SUNAPEE and WHEC 70 ex-OKEECHOBEE.

MINNETONKA (1970, U.S. Coast Guard)

CHAUTAUQUA with Hedgehog abaft 5-inch gun in "B" position (U.S. Coast Guard)

6 HIGH ENDURANCE CUTTERS: "SECRETARY" CLASS

Number	Name	Builder	Laid down	Launched	Commissioned	Status
WHEC 31	BIBB	Charleston Navy Yard	15 Aug 1935	14 Jan 1937	19 Mar 1937	**AA**
WHEC 32	CAMPBELL	Philadelphia Navy Yard	1 May 1935	3 June 1936	22 Oct 1936	**PA**
WHEC 33	DUANE	Philadelphia Navy Yard	1 May 1935	3 June 1936	16 Oct 1936	**AA**
WHEC 34	INGHAM	Philadelphia Navy Yard	1 May 1935	3 June 1936	6 Nov 1936	**AA**
WHEC 36	SPENCER	New York Navy Yard	11 Sep 1935	6 Jan 1936	13 May 1937	CGR
WHEC 37	TANEY	Philadelphia Navy Yard	1 May 1935	3 June 1936	24 Oct 1936	**AA**

Displacement:	2,216 tons standard
	2,656 tons full load
Length:	308 feet (93.9 m) wl
	327 feet (99.7 m) oa
Beam:	41 feet (12.5 m)
Draft:	15 feet (4.6 m)
Propulsion:	steam turbines (Westinghouse); 6,200 shp; 2 shafts
Boilers:	2 (Babcock & Wilcox)
Speed:	19.8 knots
Range:	8,000 n.miles at 10.5 knots; 4,000 n.miles at 19.8 knots
Allowance:	128 (12 O + 116 enlisted)
Manning:	124–136 (13–15 O + 110–121 enlisted)
Helicopters:	no facilities
Guns:	1 5-inch (127-mm) 38 cal DP Mk 30 (1 × 1)
	2 40-mm Mk 19 (2 × 1)
ASW weapons:	removed
Fire control:	removed

These are large cruising cutters, the largest ships in Coast Guard service prior to the HAMILTON class. The DUANE and INGHAM were built in the same dry dock at the Philadelphia Navy Yard. The SPENCER was decommissioned on 23 January 1974; she is now used as a stationary steam-propulsion training ship at the Coast Guard Yard, Curtis Bay, Md.

Armament: These ships carried a variety of armament during their long service lives. During World War II their main battery was three 5-inch/51 cal guns. Into the 1960s they carried an ASW armament of one hedgehog and two Mk 32 triple torpedo tubes.

Class: Seven ships of this class were built; one ship, the ALEXANDER HAMILTON (WPG 34), was sunk by a German submarine in 1942. Three additional ships were authorized, but their construction was deferred in 1941 in favor of the OWASCO (WPG 39) class.

Classification: Early in World War II these ships were classified as gunboats (WPG 31–37). In 1944–1945 six ships were reclassified as amphibious force flagships and carried an AGC prefix with their Coast Guard hull numbers, except that the DUANE was changed to AGC 6 in the Navy designation sequence. All were retained on the Coast Guard roles and were not transferred to the Navy.

After the war all reverted to their WPG classifications. All were changed to high endurance cutters (WHEC) on 1 May 1968.

Names: These ships were named for Secretaries of the Treasury. Originally full names were used, but in 1942 they were shortened to surnames only; these ships were formerly GEORGE M. BIBB, GEORGE W. CAMPBELL, WILLIAM J. DUANE, SAMUEL D. INGHAM, JOHN C. SPENCER, and ROGER B. TANEY.

CAMPBELL; note hangar abaft funnel for weather research balloons. (1977, Giorgio Arra)

INGHAM (1976, Giorgio Arra)

CAMPBELL (*Ships of the World*)

INGHAM (1980, Robert L. Scheina)

(13) MEDIUM ENDURANCE CUTTERS: "BEAR" CLASS

Number	Name	FY	Launched	Commission	Status
WMEC 901	BEAR	77	25 Sep 1980	1981	Bldg.
WMEC 902	TAMPA	77		1981	Bldg.
WMEC 903	HARRIET LANE	78		1982	Bldg.
WMEC 904	NORTHLAND	78		1982	Bldg.
WMEC 905	SENECA	79		1983	Bldg.
WMEC 906	PICKERING	79		1983	Bldg.
WMEC 907	ESCANABA	80		1984	Bldg.
WMEC 908	LEGARE	80		1984	Bldg.
WMEC 909	ARGUS	80			Auth.
WMEC 910	TAHOMA				Planned
WMEC 911	ERIE				Planned
WMEC 912	McCULLOCH				Planned
WMEC 913	EWING				Planned

Builders:	Tacoma Boatbuilding Co, Wash. (see Addenda)
Displacement:	1,730 tons full load
Length:	270 feet (82.3 m) oa
Beam:	38$^1/_3$ feet (11.7 m)
Draft:	13$^1/_2$ feet (4.2 m)
Propulsion:	diesels; 7,000 shp; 2 shafts
Speed:	19.5 knots
Range:	8,400 n.miles at 14 knots; 4,500 n.miles at 19 knots
Manning:	96 (10 O + 86 enlisted)
Helicopters:	1 HH-3F Pelican or HH-52A Sea Guard
Guns:	1 76-mm 62 cal AA Mk 75 (1 × 1)
ASW weapons:	(helicopter-delivered torpedoes; see notes)
Radar:	SPS 64 surface search
Sonars:	none
Fire control:	1 Mk 92 gun FCS

This class of medium endurance cutters was intended to replace the "Secretary"-class ships and complement the HAMILTON class. However, the anticipated shortfall of cutters in the 1980s make these ships more likely to be additions rather than replacements to the Coast Guard fleet.

The Carter Administration held back approval for contracting of the third ship (WMEC 909) authorized in FY 1980. The WMEC 910–913 are planned for authorization in FY 1981–1982 and completion in 1985–1986.

ASW weapons: Although considered to be ASW-capable, these ships will have no ship-launched weapons, but are intended to embark Navy LAMPS helicopters.

Design: These ships will be the only patrol cutters other than the HAMILTONS to have helicopter hangars. Fin stabilizers will be provided.

Electronics: The Mk 92 weapons control system will be fitted, as will an automated command and control center to enhance these ships' combat capabilities.

Guns: These ships will have the 76-mm OTO Melara rapid-fire gun, which is also fitted in the PERRY (FFG 7)-class frigates and PEGASUS (PHM 1)-class patrol hydrofoils. Space and weight are reserved for provision of the 20-mm Phalanx Mk 15 gun during wartime.

Sonars: No hull-mounted sonar is provided. A containerized SQR-19 towed acoustic array can be embarked for ASW operations.

BEAR (U.S. Coast Guard)

Artist's concept of BEAR

COURAGEOUS (1980, Robert L. Scheina)

16 MEDIUM ENDURANCE CUTTERS: "RELIANCE" CLASS

Number	Name	Launched	Commissioned	Status
WTR 615	RELIANCE	25 May 1963	20 June 1964	AA
WMEC 616	DILIGENCE	20 July 1963	26 Aug 1964	AA
WMEC 617	VIGILANT	24 Dec 1963	3 Oct 1964	AA
WMEC 618	ACTIVE	21 July 1965	17 Sep 1966	AA
WMEC 619	CONFIDENCE	8 May 1965	19 Feb 1966	PA
WMEC 620	RESOLUTE	30 Apr 1966	8 Dec 1966	PA
WMEC 621	VALIANT	14 Jan 1967	28 Oct 1967	AA
WMEC 622	COURAGEOUS	18 Mar 1967	19 Apr 1968	AA
WMEC 623	STEADFAST	24 June 1967	25 Sep 1968	AA
WMEC 624	DAUNTLESS	21 Oct 1967	10 June 1968	AA
WMEC 625	VENTUROUS	11 Nov 1967	16 Aug 1968	PA
WMEC 626	DEPENDABLE	16 Mar 1968	22 Nov 1968	AA
WMEC 627	VIGOROUS	4 May 1968	2 May 1969	AA
WMEC 628	DURABLE	29 Apr 1967	8 Dec 1967	AA
WMEC 629	DECISIVE	14 Dec 1967	23 Aug 1968	AA
WMEC 630	ALERT	19 Oct 1968	4 Aug 1969	AA

Builders:	WTR/WMEC 615–617	Todd Shipyards, Houston, Texas
	WMEC 618	Christy Corp, Sturgeon Bay, Wisc.
	WMEC 619, 625, 628–629	Coast Guard Yard, Curtis Bay, Md.
	WMEC 620–624, 626–627, 630	American Shipbuilding Co, Lorain, Ohio
Displacement:	950 tons standard	
	1,007 tons full load except WTR/WMEC 616–619 970 tons	
Length:	210½ feet (64.2 m) oa	
Beam:	34 feet (10.4 m)	
Draft:	10½ feet (3.2 m)	
Propulsion:	2 turbo-charged diesels (Alco); 5,000 shp; WTR/WMEC 615–619 additionally have 2 gas turbines (see notes); 4,000 shp; 2 shafts	
Speed:	18 knots	
Range:	6,100 n.miles at 14 knots (WTR/WMEC 615–619 at 13 knots); 2,700 n.miles at 18 knots (WTR/WMEC 615–619 2,100 n.miles)	
Allowance:	66–70 (8 O + 58–62 enlisted)	
Manning:	64–76 (8–10 O + 54–66 enlisted)	
Helicopters:	none assigned	
Guns:	1 3-inch (76-mm) 50 cal Mk 22 (1 × 1)	
	2 40-mm Mk 19 (2 × 1)	
ASW weapons:	none	

These are search-and-rescue ships. They can land helicopters but have no hangar. The RELIANCE is a reserve training ship since 1975, assigned to Yorktown, Va.

Classification: These ships were originally classified as patrol craft (WPC); changed to WMEC with same hull numbers on 1 May 1966. The RELIANCE was changed to WTR on 27 June 1975 (the TR indicating Training of Reserves).

Design: The RELIANCE design has a small "island" superstructure with 360° visibility from the bridge to facilitate helicopter operations and towing.

Engineering: The first five cutters were built with CODAG (Combination Diesel And Gas turbine) plants to provide experience in operating mixed propulsion plants. Those cutters have a high acceleration rate from all stop, or with their engines shut down can be at full speed in a few minutes; they can make 15.25 knots on gas turbines alone. The cost factor influenced the decision to make the remaining ships all-diesel.

RELIANCE (1979, Giorgio Arra)

DILIGENCE with HH-52A Sea Guard landing aboard (1979, U.S. Coast Guard)

2 MEDIUM ENDURANCE CUTTERS: FORMER SALVAGE SHIPS

Number	Name	Launched	Navy ARS Comm.	Status
WMEC 167 (ex-ARS 9)	ACUSHNET	1 Apr 1943	5 Feb 1944	**AA**
WMEC 168 (ex-ARS 26)	YOCONA	8 Apr 1944	3 Nov 1944	**PA**

Builders:	Basalt Rock Co, Napa, Calif.
Displacement:	1,557 tons standard
	1,745 tons full load
Length:	213½ feet (70.0 m) oa
Beam:	39 feet (12.8 m)
Draft:	15 feet (4.9 m)
Propulsion:	diesels; 3,000 shp; 2 shafts
Speed:	15.5 knots
Range:	20,000 n.miles at 7 knots; 9,000 n.miles at 15.5 knots
Allowance:	72 (7 O + 65 enlisted)
Manning:	77 (9 O + 68 enlisted)
Helicopters:	no facilities
Guns:	2 40-mm Mk 19 (2 × 1)

These are former Navy salvage ships transferred to the Coast Guard after World War II.

Classification: Upon transfer to the Coast Guard, these ships were classified as tugs (WAT 167 and WAT 168, respectively). Changed to WMEC on 1 May 1966, with the ACUSHNET subsequently modified to handle environmental data buoys and changed to oceanographic cutter (WAGO 167) in 1969; she has been redesignated as WMEC.

Names: Renamed in Coast Guard service; former Navy names were SHACKLE and SEIZE, respectively.

3 MEDIUM ENDURANCE CUTTERS: FORMER FLEET TUGS

Number	Name	Launched	Navy ATF Comm.	Status
WMEC 153 (ex-ATF 153)	CHILULA	1 Dec 1944	5 Apr 1945	**AA**
WMEC 165 (ex-ATF 66)	CHEROKEE	10 Nov 1939	26 Apr 1940	**AA**
WMEC 166 (ex-ATF 95)	TAMAROA	13 July 1943	9 Oct 1943	**AA**

Builders:	WMEC 153 Charleston Shipbuilding and Dry Dock Co, S.C.
	WMEC 165 Bethlehem Steel, Staten Island, N.Y.
	WMEC 166 Commercial Iron Works, Portland, Ore.
Displacement:	1,731 tons full load
Length:	205 feet (62.5 m) oa
Beam:	38½ feet (11.7 m)
Draft:	17 feet (5.2 m)
Propulsion:	diesel-electric (General Motors diesels); 3,000 shp; 1 shaft
Speed:	16.2 knots
Range:	15,000 n.miles at 8 knots; 6,500 n.miles at 16.2 knots
Allowance:	74 (7 O + 67 enlisted)
Manning:	76 (6 O + 70 enlisted)
Helicopters:	no facilities
Guns:	1 3-inch (76-mm) 50 cal Mk 22 (1 × 1)
	2 40-mm Mk 19 (2 × 1)

These are former Navy fleet tugs transferred to the Coast Guard after World War II.

Classification: These ships were classified ATF by the Navy; upon transfer to the Coast Guard they became WAT 153, 165, 166, respectively; all changed to WMEC on 1 May 1966.

Names: The TAMAROA was named ZUNI in Navy service. The others retained their Navy names.

CHEROKEE (1975, Giorgio Arra)

YOCONA (1970, U.S. Coast Guard)

2 MEDIUM ENDURANCE CUTTERS: FORMER AUXILIARY TUGS

Number	Name	Launched	Navy ATA Comm.	Status
WMEC 194 (ex-ATA 194)	MODOC	4 Dec 1944	14 Feb 1945	**PA**
WMEC 202 (ex-ATA 202)	COMANCHE	10 Oct 1944	8 Dec 1944	**PA**

Builders:	WMEC 194 Levingston Shipbuilding and Drydock, Orange, Texas
	WMEC 202 Gulfport Boiler & Welding Works, Port Arthur, Texas
Displacement:	534 tons standard
	860 tons full load
Length:	143 feet (43.6 m) oa
Beam:	33⅚ feet (10.3 m)
Draft:	14 feet (4.3 m)
Propulsion:	diesel-electric (General Motors diesels); 1,500 shp; 1 shaft
Speed:	13.5 knots
Range:	12,000 n.miles at 8.5 knots; 7,300 n.miles at 13.5 knots
Allowance:	
Manning:	
Helicopters:	no facilities
Guns:	2 40-mm Mk 19 (2 × 1)

These are former U.S. Navy tugs. They are the smallest medium endurance cutters in Coast Guard service. The MODOC was stricken from the Naval Register after World War II and transferred to the Maritime Administration; she was acquired by the Coast Guard on 15 April 1959. The COMANCHE was transferred from the Navy to the Coast Guard on 25 February 1959 on loan; she was subsequently transferred on permanent status on 1 June 1969.

Classification: As Navy tugs, these ships were ATA 194 and 202, respectively. As acquired by the Coast Guard they were classified as WATA with the same hull numbers; changed to WMEC in 1968.

Names: These ships were assigned the Navy names BAGADUCE (ATA 194) and WAMPANOAG (ATA 202) in 1948; they were renamed when transferred to the Coast Guard.

MODOC (1970, U.S. Coast Guard)

1 MEDIUM ENDURANCE CUTTER: "STORIS" TYPE

Number	Name	Launched	Commissioned	Status
WMEC 38	STORIS	4 Apr 1942	30 Sep 1942	**PA**

Builders:	Toledo Shipbuilding Co, Ohio
Displacement:	1,715 tons standard
	1,925 tons full load
Length:	230 feet (70.1 m) oa
Beam:	43 feet (13.1 m)
Draft:	15 feet (4.6 m)
Propulsion:	diesel-electric (Cooper Bessemer diesels); 1,800 shp; 2 shafts
Speed:	14 knots
Range:	22,000 n.miles at 8 knots; 12,000 n.miles at 14 knots
Allowance:	76 (8 O + 68 enlisted)
Manning:	72 (9 O + 63 enlisted)
Helicopters:	no facilities
Guns:	1 3-inch (76-mm) 50 cal Mk 22 (1 × 1)
	2 40-mm Mk 19 (2 × 1)

The STORIS was built specifically for offshore icebreaking and patrol. She has been employed in Alaskan service for search, rescue, and law enforcement since 1949.

Classification: The STORIS originally was classified WAG 38; she was changed to WAGB 38 on 1 May 1966. Subsequently she was reclassified as a medium endurance cutter (WMEC) on 1 July 1972 to emphasize her role in law enforcement off the Alaskan fishing grounds.

Guns: As built, the STORIS carried two 3-inch guns and four 20-mm guns.

Names: The ship was initially named the ESKIMO.

STORIS (1979, U.S. Coast Guard)

PATROL BOATS

26 PATROL BOATS: "CAPE" CLASS

Number	Name	Number	Name
(A Series)			
WPB 95300	Cape Small	WPB 95313	Cape Morgan
WPB 95301	Cape Coral	WPB 95314	Cape Fairweather
WPB 95302	Cape Higgon	WPB 95316	Cape Fox
WPB 95303	Cape Upright	WPB 95317	Cape Jellison
WPB 95304	Cape Gull	WPB 95318	Cape Newagen
WPB 95305	Cape Hatteras	WPB 95319	Cape Romain
WPB 95306	Cape George	WPB 95320	Cape Starr
WPB 95307	Cape Current	(C Series)	
WPB 95308	Cape Strait	WPB 95321	Cape Cross
WPB 95309	Cape Carter	WPB 95322	Cape Horn
WPB 95310	Cape Wash	WPB 95324	Cape Shoalwater
WPB 95311	Cape Hedge	WPB 95326	Cape Corwin
(B Series)		WPB 95328	Cape Henlopen
WPB 95312	Cape Knox	WPB 95332	Cape York

Builders:	Coast Guard Yard, Curtis Bay, Md.
Displacement:	105 tons full load
Length:	95 feet (29.0 m) oa
Beam:	19 feet (5.8 m)
Draft:	6 feet (1.8 m)
Propulsion:	diesels (Cummins); 2,300 shp; 2 shafts
Speed:	A and B series 20 knots
	C series 21 knots
Range:	A series 2,600 n.miles at 9 knots; 460 n.miles at 20 knots
	B series 3,000 n.miles at 9 knots; 460 n.miles at 20 knots
	C series 2,800 n.miles at 9 knots; 500 n.miles at 21 knots
Allowance:	14 (1 O + 13 enlisted)
Manning:	14–17 (1 O + 13–16 enlisted)
Guns:	removed (see notes)

These are 95-foot cutters employed for port security, search and rescue, and patrol functions. The A series was constructed in 1953, the B series in 1955–1956, and the C series in 1958–1959. (Nine additional C-series cutters were transferred to South Korea in 1968.)

Plans to discard this class in favor of new construction were dropped and they were modernized instead. All are active.

Design: These are steel-hulled cutters. As built, the principal difference in the series was that the last group had less electronic equipment.

Guns: During the 1970s these cutters each carried two .50-cal MG or an 81-mm mortar mounted "piggyback" with a .50-cal MG. Only small arms are now carried.

Modernization: All modernized from 1977 through 1981. They have been fitted with new engines, improved electronics, and their superstructures have been modified; their accommodations also have been upgraded.

Cape Starr with .50-cal machine gun/81-mm mortar on forecastle (since removed) (1969, U.S. Coast Guard)

Point Stuart (1979, Giorgio Arra)

Cape Knox (top) and Point Barnes; these two classes can be readily distinguished by their superstructures and the first two digits of their hull numbers. (1972, U.S. Coast Guard)

53 PATROL BOATS: "POINT" CLASS

Number	Name	Number	Name
	(A Series)	WPB 82353	POINT MONROE
WPB 82302	POINT HOPE	WPB 82354	POINT EVANS
WPB 82311	POINT VERDE	WPB 82355	POINT HANNON
WPB 82312	POINT SWIFT	WPB 82356	POINT FRANCIS
WPB 82314	POINT THATCHER	WPB 82357	POINT HURON
	(C Series)	WPB 82358	POINT STUART
WPB 82318	POINT HERRON	WPB 82359	POINT STEELE
WPB 82332	POINT ROBERTS	WPB 82360	POINT WINSLOW
WPB 82333	POINT HIGHLAND	WPB 82361	POINT CHARLES
WPB 82334	POINT LEDGE	WPB 82362	POINT BROWN
WPB 82335	POINT COUNTESS	WPB 82363	POINT NOWELL
WPB 82336	POINT GLASS	WPB 82364	POINT WHITEHORN
WPB 82337	POINT DIVIDE	WPB 82365	POINT TURNER
WPB 82338	POINT BRIDGE	WPB 82366	POINT LOBOS
WPB 82339	POINT CHICO	WPB 82367	POINT KNOLL
WPB 82340	POINT BATAN	WPB 82368	POINT WARDE
WPB 82341	POINT LOOKOUT	WPB 82369	POINT HEYER
WPB 82342	POINT BAKER	WPB 82370	POINT RICHMOND
WPB 82343	POINT WELLS		(D Series)
WPB 82344	POINT ESTERO	WPB 82371	POINT BARNES
WPB 82345	POINT JUDITH	WPB 82372	POINT BROWER
WPB 82346	POINT ARENA	WPB 82373	POINT CAMDEN
WPB 82347	POINT BONITA	WPB 82374	POINT CARREW
WPB 82348	POINT BARROW	WPB 82375	POINT DORAN
WPB 82349	POINT SPENCER	WPB 82376	POINT HARRIS
WPB 82350	POINT FRANKLIN	WPB 82377	POINT HOBART
WPB 82351	POINT BENNETT	WPB 82378	POINT JACKSON
WPB 82352	POINT SAL	WPB 82379	POINT MARTIN

Builders:	Coast Guard Yard, Curtis Bay, Md.
Displacement:	A series 67 tons full load
	C series 66 tons full load
	D series 69 tons full load
Length:	83 feet (25.3 m) oa
Beam:	17$\frac{1}{6}$ feet (5.2 m)
Draft:	5¾ feet (1.8 m)
Propulsion:	diesel; 1,600 shp; 2 shafts
Speed:	A series 23.5 knots
	C series 23.7 knots
	D series 22.6 knots
Range:	A and C series 1,500 n.miles at 8 knots
	D series 1,200 n.miles at 8 knots
Allowance:	9–10 (0–1 O + 8–10 enlisted)
Manning:	8–10 (0–2 O + 8–10 enlisted)
Guns:	2 .50-cal MG (2 × 1)
	or 1 81-mm mortar Mk 2/1 .50-cal MG (1 × 1/1)
	removed from some cutters

These are 82-foot cutters used for port security, search and rescue. The A series was constructed in 1960–1961, the C series in 1961–1967, and D series in 1970. (Twenty-six Point-class cutters were transferred to South Vietnam in 1969–1970.) All Coast Guard units are active.

Design: These are steel-hulled cutters with aluminum superstructures. There are no noticeable differences among the various series of the Point class.

Guns: The mortars and MGs are being replaced by small arms.

Names: The WPB 82301–82344 were assigned geographical point names in January 1964; later cutters were named as built.

ICEBREAKERS

2 ICEBREAKERS: "POLAR" CLASS

Number	Name	Launched	Commissioned	Status
WAGB 10	POLAR STAR	17 Nov 1973	17 Jan 1976	**PA**
WAGB 11	POLAR SEA	24 June 1975	23 Feb 1978	**PA**

Builders:	Lockheed Shipbuilding Co, Seattle, Wash.
Displacement:	13,190 tons full load
Length:	399 feet (121.6 m) oa
Beam:	83½ feet (25.5 m)
Draft:	33½ feet (10.2 m)
Propulsion:	CODOG: 6 diesels (Alco), 18,000 shp; 3 gas turbines (Pratt & Whitney), 60,000 shp; 3 shafts
Speed:	18 knots
Range:	28,000 n.miles at 13 knots; 16,000 n.miles at 18 knots
Allowance:	139 (14 O + 125 enlisted) + 10 scientists
Helicopters:	2 HH-52A Sea Guard
Guns:	2 40-mm Mk 19 (2 × 1)

These are the largest icebreakers in service outside of the Soviet Union. Several ships were originally planned in this class as replacements for the Wind-class icebreakers. No additional ships are planned, in part because of the higher-than-anticipated costs.

Design: These ships have conventional icebreaker hull forms. A hangar and flight deck are fitted aft and two 15-ton-capacity cranes are abaft the hangar. Artic and oceanographic laboratories are provided.

Engineering: CODOG (Combination Diesel Or Gas turbine) propulsion is provided, with diesel engines for cruising and rapid-reaction gas turbines available for surge-power requirements. The gas turbines are FT-4A-12s. Controllable-pitch propellers allow propeller thrust to be reversed without reversing the direction of shaft rotation.

The original design provided for a speed of 21 knots; not reached.

POLAR STAR (1976, U.S. Coast Guard)

The POLAR SEA (foreground) and POLAR STAR steam together in the Strait of Juan de Fuca between Canada and the United States. An HH-52A Sea Guard sits on the helicopter deck of the POLAR STAR. Earlier "Polar" designs provided for a single amidships funnel. (1978, U.S. Coast Guard, PA1 L. M. Parris)

1 ICEBREAKER: "GLACIER"

Number	Name	Launched	AGB Comm.	WAGB Comm.	Status
WAGB 4	GLACIER	27 Aug 1954	27 May 1955	30 June 1966	**PA**

Builders:	Ingalls Shipbuilding Corp, Pascagoula, Miss.
Displacement:	8,449 tons full load
Length:	309½ feet (94.4 m) oa
Beam:	74 feet (6.9 m)
Draft:	29 feet (8.8 m)
Propulsion:	diesel-electric (10 Fairbanks-Morse diesels, 2 Westinghouse electric motors); 21,000 shp; 2 shafts
Speed:	17.5 knots
Range:	29,000 n.miles at 12 knots; 12,000 n.miles at 17.5 knots
Allowance:	229 (14 O + 215 enlisted)
Helicopters:	2 HH-52A Sea Guard
Guns:	2 40-mm Mk 19 (2 × 1)

The GLACIER was the largest icebreaker constructed in the United States until completion of the POLAR STAR. She was active in the U.S. Navy as AGB 4 from 1955 until she was transferred to the Coast Guard in 1966 (stricken from the Navy on 1 July 1966, the day after transfer to the Coast Guard).

Guns: As built, the GLACIER mounted two 5-inch DP guns, six 3-inch AA guns, and four 20-mm AA guns. The lighter weapons were removed prior to transfer to the Coast Guard, and the 5-inch guns were removed in 1969.

GLACIER (top) and BURTON ISLAND (1975, U.S. Coast Guard)

2 ICEBREAKERS: "WIND" CLASS

Number	Name	Launched	Commissioned	Status
WAGB 281 (ex-AGB 6)	WESTWIND	31 Mar 1943	18 Sep 1944	**GL**
WAGB 282	NORTHWIND	25 Feb 1945	28 July 1945	**AA**

Builders:	Western Pipe and Steel, San Pedro, Calif.
Displacement:	3,500 tons standard
	6,515 tons full load
Length:	269 feet (82.0 m) oa
Beam:	63½ feet (19.4 m)
Draft:	29 feet (8.8 m)
Propulsion:	diesel-electric (Enterprise diesels); 10,000 shp; 2 shafts
Speed:	16 knots
Range:	38,000 n.miles at 10.5 knots; 16,000 n.miles at 12.5 knots
Manning:	131 (14 O + 117 enlisted) in WAGB 281
	157 (15 O + 142 enlisted) in WAGB 282
Helicopters:	1 or 2 HH-52A Sea Guard
Guns:	2 40-mm Mk 19 (2 × 1)

The "Wind"-class icebreakers were the principal U.S. icebreakers for more than three decades. Originally seven ships were in this class, with two built for the Navy and the remaining five to Coast Guard specifications. Three of the latter ships served with the Soviet Navy after World War II.

Class: The accompanying table lists all seven "Wind"-class ships and their service.

Design: The two Navy-sponsored ships had reduced armament (guns and ASW weapons) as originally built compared to the Coast Guard ships. The Navy ships were also among the first constructed with a helicopter platform.

Engineering: As built, these ships had a third propeller shaft forward capable of delivering 3,300 shp for backing down in heavy ice. The bow shafts were removed because of continued propeller losses in heavy ice operations. Both ships were built with Fairbanks Morse diesels; the WESTWIND was re-engined in 1973–1974 and the NORTHWIND in 1974–1975, both with Enterprise diesels. (Funnel heightened.)

Guns: As built, some of the Coast Guard design ships had up to four 5-inch DP guns, 12 40-mm AA guns, and several 20-mm AA guns. The postwar-built Navy ships were equipped with one 5-inch gun and lighter weapons. Into the 1960s the NORTHWIND had two 5-inch guns and the other ships each had one 5-inch gun; all were removed 1969–1970.

The WESTWIND is one of two survivors of a class of highly versatile and capable icebreakers that served in the U.S. and Soviet navies as well as in the Coast Guard. As built, they carried up to four 5-inch guns in twin mounts plus a dozen 40-mm guns in quad mounts; the survivors have only a pair of 40-mm guns that can be shipped in time of war. An HH-52A Sea Guard rests on the WESTWIND's helicopter deck. She and the NORTHWIND were re-engined in 1973–1974 and 1974–1975, respectively; taller funnels were fitted, distinguishing them from other ships of the class. (U.S. Coast Guard)

Original No./Name	USSR Name	Postwar U.S. Navy	Coast Guard No./Name	Stricken
AG 88 BURTON ISLAND	. . . .	AGB 1 BURTON ISLAND (1946–1966)	WAGB 283 BURTON ISLAND	1978
AG 89 EDISTO	. . . .	AGB 2 EDISTO (1947–1965)	WAGB 284 EDISTO	1976
WAG 278 NORTHWIND	SEVERNI VETER (1945–1951)	AGB 5 STATEN ISLAND (1951–1966)	WAGB 278 STATEN ISLAND	1976
WAG 279 EASTWIND	. . . .	—	WAGB 279 EASTWIND	1972
WAG 280 SOUTHWIND	KAPITAN BELUSOV (1945–1950)	AGB 3 ATKA (1950–1966)	WAGB 280 SOUTHWIND	1974
WAG 281 WESTWIND	SEVERNI POLIUS (1945–1951)	(AGB 6 WESTWIND)[a]	WAGB 281 WESTWIND	(active)
WAG 282 NORTHWIND (II)	. . . .	—	WAGB 282 NORTHWIND	(active)

[a] The WESTWIND was assigned a U.S. Navy hull number but was actually transferred directly from the USSR to the Coast Guard.

1 ICEBREAKER: "MACKINAW"

Number	Name	Launched	Commissioned	Status
WAGB 83	MACKINAW	4 Mar 1944	20 Dec 1944	**GL**

Builders:	Toledo Shipbuilding Co, Ohio
Displacement:	5,252 tons full load
Length:	290 feet (88.4 m) oa
Beam:	75 feet (22.9 m)
Draft:	19 feet (5.8 m)
Propulsion:	diesel-electric (Fairbanks Morse diesels. Westinghouse electric motors); 10,000 shp aft + 3,000 shp forward; 2 shafts aft + 1 shaft forward
Speed:	18.7 knots
Range:	41,000 n.miles at 9 knots; 10,000 n.miles at 18.7 knots
Allowance:	127 (10 O + 117 enlisted)
Helicopters:	none assigned
Guns:	none

The MACKINAW was designed and constructed specifically for Coast Guard use on the Great Lakes.

Classification: The ship originally was classified WAG 83; she was changed to WAGB on 1 May 1966.

Design: The MACKINAW has many of the features of the "Wind" class; however, being designed for the Great Lakes, the ship is longer and wider than the oceangoing ships, but has significantly less draft. Two 12-ton-capacity cranes are fitted. The ship has a clear deck aft for a helicopter, but no hangar is provided.

TRAINING CUTTERS

In addition to the EAGLE, listed below, the former medium endurance cutter RELIANCE and medium harbor tug OJIBWA are employed as training ships. They are both listed in this volume under their original classes.

MACKINAW (U.S. Coast Guard)

The EAGLE off the U.S. naval base at Guantanamo Bay, Cuba, with most of her sails spread. When the Coast Guard hull stripes and letters "Coast Guard" were applied to cutters, the EAGLE was exempted; they were finally applied in 1976 in preparation for the U.S. bicentenial celebration and Operation Sail 1976 in New York Harbor. (1978, U.S. Navy, PH1 L.L. Sallions)

1 TRAINING BARK: "EAGLE"

Number	Name	Launched	Coast Guard Comm.	Status
WIX 327	EAGLE	13 June 1936	1946	**TRA-A**

Builders:	Blohm and Voss, Hamburg, Germany
Displacement:	1,816 tons full load
Length:	231 feet (90 m) wl
	295 feet (89.9 m) over bowsprit
Beam:	39¹/₆ feet (11.9 m)
Draft:	17 feet (5.2 m)
Masts:	fore and main 150¹/₃ feet (45.7 m)
	mizzen 132 feet (40.2 m)
Propulsion:	auxiliary diesels (M.A.N.); 700 shp; 1 shaft
Speed:	up to 18 knots under sail; 10.5 knots on auxiliary diesels
Allowance:	65 (19 O + 46 enlisted) + 195 cadets
Guns:	Some are unarmed

The EAGLE is the former German naval training bark HORST WESSEL. Taken by the United States as a war reparation, she was acquired in January 1946 at Bremerhaven and assigned to the Coast Guard. Based at New London, Conn., she has been employed to carry Coast Guard Academy cadets on summer practice cruises.

Class: The ALBERT LEO SCHLAGETER (launched 1937) was also taken over by the United States in 1945, but was sold to Brazil in 1948 and re-sold to Portugal in 1962; a third ship of this basic design, the GORCH FOCK (1933), was taken over by the Soviet Union in 1946, and renamed the TOVARISH. A later ship of the same general design, also named the GORCH FOCK, was built at the same German yard for the West German Navy (launched 1958).

Design: The EAGLE is steel-hulled. She carries up to 21,350 square feet of sail.

Coast Guard buoy tenders are painted black except for the EVERGREEN, modified for use as an oceanographic research ship. She has a built-up amidships structure, laboratories, a stern hoist, and additional electronic equipment. (1973, U.S. Coast Guard)

BUOY TENDERS

34 SEAGOING BUOY TENDERS AND 1 OCEANOGRAPHIC CUTTER— "BALSAM" CLASS

Number	Name	Number	Name
WLB 62	BALSAM	WLB 389	BITTERSWEET
WLB 277	COWSLIP	WLB 390	BLACKHAW
WLB 290	GENTIAN	WLB 392	BRAMBLE
WLB 291	LAUREL	WLB 393	FIREBRUSH
WLB 292	CLOVER	WLB 394	HORNBEAM
WAGO 295	EVERGREEN	WLB 395	IRIS
WLB 296	SORREL	WLB 396	MALLOW
WLB 297	IRONWOOD	WLB 397	MARIPOSA
WLB 300	CITRUS	WLB 399	SAGEBRUSH
WLB 301	CONIFER	WLB 400	SALVIA
WLB 302	MADRONA	WLB 401	SASSAFRAS
WLB 303	TUPELO	WLB 402	SEDGE
WLB 305	MESQUITE	WLB 403	SPAR
WLB 306	BUTTONWOOD	WLB 404	SUNDEW
WLB 307	PLANETREE	WLB 405	SWEETBRIER
WLB 308	PAPAW	WLB 406	ACACIA
WLB 309	SWEETGUM	WLB 407	WOODRUSH
WLB 388	BASSWOOD		

Builders:	WLB 62, 290–291, 296, 302–303, 389, 392–393, 395–397, 399–400, 406–407 Zenith Dredge Co, Duluth, Minn.
	WLB 277, 292, 295, 300–301, 305–309, 388, 390, 394, 401–405 Marine Iron and Shipbuilding Co, Duluth, Minn.
	WLB 297 Coast Guard Yard, Curtis Bay, Md.
Displacement:	935 tons standard
	1,025 tons full load
Length:	180 feet (54.9 m) oa
Beam:	37 feet (11.3 m)
Draft:	13 feet (4.0 m)
Propulsion:	diesel-electric; 1,000 shp in WLB 62–303 series except WLB 297, others 1,200 shp; 1 shaft
Speed:	WLB 62–303 series (except WLB 297) 12.8 knots; others 15 knots
Allowance:	WAGO 61 (6 O + 55 enlisted)
	WLB 46–48 (5–6 O + 41–42 enlisted)
Manning:	WAGO 66 (7 O + 59 enlisted)
	WLB 49–57 (6–7 O + 43–50 enlisted)
Guns:	2 40-mm Mk 19 (2 × 1) in most tenders; others are unarmed

These tenders service navigation buoys and other aids to navigation in coastal waters. They were completed in 1942–1945 with several sub-types. All are active or are undergoing modernization.

Class: The EVERGREEN was refitted as an oceanographic cutter in 1973 and reclassified WAGO.

Design: The WLB 62, 296, 300, 390, 392, 402–404 have strengthened hulls for icebreaking.

Engineering: The WLB 277, 389, 394, and WAGO 295 are fitted with controllable-pitch, bow-thrust propellers.

Guns: As completed, these tenders had one 3-inch AA gun and two or four 40-mm AA guns.

Names: The ACACIA originally was named the THISTLE.

3 COASTAL BUOY TENDERS: "HOLLYHOCK" CLASS

Number	Name	Number	Name
WLM 212	Fir	WLM 252	Walnut
WLM 220	Hollyhock		

Builders:	
Displacement:	989 tons full load
Length:	175 feet (53.3 m) oa
Beam:	34 feet (10.4 m)
Draft:	12 feet (3.7 m)
Propulsion:	diesels; 1,350 shp; 2 shafts
Speed:	12 knots
Allowance:	40 (5 O + 35 enlisted)

These tenders were originally classified WAGL; they were changed to coastal tenders (WLM) on 1 January 1965. WLM 220 was launched in 1937; WLM 212 and 252 in 1939.

Fir (1969, U.S. Coast Guard)

5 COASTAL BUOY TENDERS: "RED" CLASS

Number	Name	Number	Name
WLM 685	Red Wood	WLM 688	Red Cedar
WLM 686	Red Beech	WLM 689	Red Oak
WLM 687	Red Birch		

Builders:	Coast Guard Yard, Curtis Bay, Md.
Displacement:	471 tons standard
	512 tons full load
Length:	157 feet (47.8 m) oa
Beam:	33 feet (10.1 m)
Draft:	6 feet (1.8 m)
Propulsion:	diesels; 1,800 shp; 2 shafts
Speed:	12.8 knots
Allowance:	31 (4 O + 27 enlisted)
Manning:	33–35 (4–5 O + 29–32 enlisted)

These buoy and navigation aid tenders have strengthened steel hulls for light icebreaking and are fitted with bow thrusters. WLM 685–686 were launched in 1964, WLM 687 in 1965, WLM 688 in 1970, and WLM 689 in 1971.

Armament: No coastal or small buoy tenders are armed.

Red Cedar (1975, Giorgio Arra)

7 COASTAL BUOY TENDERS: "WHITE" CLASS

Number	Name	Number	Name
WLM 540	White Sumac	WLM 545	White Heath
WLM 542	White Bush	WLM 546	White Lupine
WLM 543	White Holly	WLM 547	White Pine
WLM 544	White Sage		

Builders:	
Displacement:	435 tons standard
	600 tons full load
Length:	133 feet (40.5 m) oa
Beam:	31 feet (9.4 m)
Draft:	9 feet (2.7 m)
Propulsion:	diesels (Union); 600 shp; 2 shafts
Speed:	9.8 knots
Allowance:	21 (1 O + 20 enlisted)
Manning:	19–22 (1–2 O + 18–21 enlisted)

All of these tenders are converted Navy self-propelled lighters (YF). All were launched in 1943.

White Bush (1969, U.S. Coast Guard)

1 INLAND BUOY TENDER
4 INLAND CONSTRUCTION TENDERS—["COSMOS" CLASS]

Number	Name	Number	Name
WLIC 293	COSMOS	WLIC 315	SMILAX
WLIC 298	RAMBLER	WLIC 316	PRIMROSE
WLI 313	BLUEBELL		

Builders:	
Displacement:	178 tons full load
Length:	100 feet (30.5 m) oa
Beam:	24 feet (7.3 m)
Draft:	5 feet (1.5 m)
Propulsion:	diesels; 600 shp; 2 shafts
Speed:	10.5 knots
Allowance:	13 (1 O + 12 enlisted)
Manning:	14 (1 O + 13 enlisted)

All formerly WLI; 4 changed to inland construction tenders (WLIC) on 1 October 1979. COSMOS launched in 1942, others in 1944, except BLUEBELL in 1945.

1 INLAND BUOY TENDER: "BUCKTHORN" TYPE

Number	Name
WLI 642	BUCKTHORN

Builders:	Mobile Ship Repair, Ala.
Displacement:	200 tons full load
Length:	100 feet (30.5 m) oa
Beam:	24 feet (7.3 m)
Draft:	4 feet (1.2 m)
Propulsion:	diesels; 600 shp; 2 shafts
Speed:	11.9 knots
Allowance:	14 (1 O + 13 enlisted)
Manning:	17 (1 O + 16 enlisted)

The BUCKTHORN was launched in 1963.

BUCKTHORN (1970, U.S. Coast Guard)

2 INLAND BUOY TENDERS: "BERRY" CLASS

Number	Name
WLI 65303	BLACKBERRY
WLI 65304	CHOKEBERRY

Builders:	Dubuque Boat and Boiler, Iowa
Displacement:	68 tons full load
Length:	65 feet (19.8 m) oa
Beam:	17 feet (5.2 m)
Draft:	4 feet (1.2 m)
Propulsion:	diesel; 220 shp; 1 shaft
Speed:	9 knots
Allowance:	5 (enlisted)

These tenders were launched in 1946.

2 INLAND BUOY TENDERS: IMPROVED "BERRY" CLASS

Number	Name
WLI 65400	BAYBERRY
WLI 65401	ELDERBERRY

Builders:	
Displacement:	68 tons full load
Length:	65 feet (19.8 m) oa
Beam:	17 feet (5.2 m)
Draft:	4 feet (1.2 m)
Propulsion:	diesels; 400 shp; 2 shafts
Speed:	11.3 knots
Allowance:	8 (enlisted)
Manning:	10 (enlisted)

Both tenders were launched in 1954.

BAYBERRY (1968, U.S. Coast Guard)

10 INLAND CONSTRUCTION TENDERS: "ANVIL" CLASS

Number	Name	Number	Name
(A series)		(C series)	
WLIC 75301	ANVIL	WLIC 75306	CLAMP
WLIC 75302	HAMMER	WLIC 75307	WEDGE
(B series)		WLIC 75308	SPIKE
WLIC 75303	SLEDGE	WLIC 75309	HATCHET
WLIC 75304	MALLET	WLIC 75310	AXE
WLIC 75305	VISE		

Builders:	
Displacement:	145 tons
Length:	75 feet (22.9 m) oa, except C series 76 feet (23.2 m) oa
Beam:	22 feet (6.7 m)
Draft:	4 feet (1.2 m)
Propulsion:	diesels; 600 shp; 2 shafts
Speed:	A series 8.6 knots
	B series 9.1 knots
	C series 9.4 knots
Allowance:	9–10 (1 O in some tenders + 9 enlisted)

These tenders were launched in 1962–1965.

WEDGE with crane barge (1971, U.S. Coast Guard)

1 RIVER BUOY TENDER: "SUMAC" TYPE

Number	Name
WLR 311	SUMAC

Builders:	Peterson and Haecker, Blair, Neb.
Displacement:	478 tons full load
Length:	115 feet (35.0 m) oa
Beam:	30 feet (9.1 m)
Draft:	6 feet (1.8 m)
Propulsion:	diesels; 2,250 shp; 3 shafts
Speed:	10.6 knots
Allowance:	22 (1 O + 21 enlisted)
Manning:	23 (1 O + 22 enlisted)

The SUMAC was launched in 1943.

1 RIVER BUOY TENDER: "DOGWOOD" CLASS

Number	Name
WLR 259	DOGWOOD

Builders:	
Displacement:	310 tons
Length:	114 feet (34.7 m) oa
Beam:	26 feet (7.9 m)
Draft:	5 feet (1.5 m)
Propulsion:	diesels; 2,800 shp; 2 shafts
Speed:	11 knots
Allowance:	17 (1 O + 16 enlisted)
Manning:	19 (enlisted)

The DOGWOOD was launched in 1940.

1 RIVER BUOY TENDER: "LANTANA" TYPE

Number	Name
WLR 80310	LANTANA

Builders:	Peterson and Haecker, Blair, Neb.
Displacement:	235 tons full load
Length:	80 feet (24.4 m) oa
Beam:	30 feet (9.1 m)
Draft:	6 feet (1.8 m)
Propulsion:	diesels; 945 shp; 3 shafts
Speed:	10 knots
Allowance:	20 (1 O + 19 enlisted)

The LANTANA was launched in 1943.

CHEYENNE with buoy barge (1971, U.S. Coast Guard)

9 RIVER BUOY TENDERS: "GASCONADE" CLASS

Number	Name	Number	Name
WLR 75401	GASCONADE	WLR 75406	KICKAPOO
WLR 75402	MUSKINGUM	WLR 75407	KANAWHA
WLR 75403	WYACONDA	WLR 75408	PATOKA
WLR 75404	CHIPPEWA	WLR 75409	CHENA
WLR 75405	CHEYENNE		

Builders:
Displacement:	141 tons full load
Length:	75 feet (22.9 m) oa
Beam:	22 feet (6.7 m)
Draft:	4 feet (1.2 m)
Propulsion:	diesels; 600 shp; 2 shafts
Speed:	7.6–8.7 knots
Allowance:	19 (enlisted)
Manning:	18–20 (enlisted)

These tenders were launched in 1964–1971.

6 RIVER BUOY TENDERS: "OUACHITA" CLASS

Number	Name	Number	Name
WLR 65501	OUACHITA	WLR 65504	SCIOTO
WLR 65502	CIMARRON	WLR 65505	OSAGE
WLR 65503	OBION	WLR 65506	SANGAMON

Builders:
Displacement:	143 tons
Length:	65½ feet (20.0 m) oa
Beam:	21 feet (6.4 m)
Draft:	5 feet (1.5 m)
Propulsion:	diesels; 600 shp; 2 shafts
Speed:	10.5 knots
Allowance:	19 (enlisted)
Manning:	19–23 (enlisted)

These tenders were launched in 1960–1962.

OSAGE with buoy barge; note the square bow and stern common to most river and inland buoy tenders. The 65-foot class tenders have twin funnels. (1971, U.S. Coast Guard)

4 INLAND CONSTRUCTION TENDERS: "PAMLICO" CLASS

Number	Name	Number	Name
WLIC 800	PAMLICO	WLIC 802	KENNEBEC
WLIC 801	HUDSON	WLIC 803	SAGINAW

Builders:	Coast Guard Yard, Curtis Bay, Md.
Displacement:	416 tons
Length:	160 feet (48.8 m) oa
Beam:	30 feet (9.1 m)
Draft:	4 feet (1.2 m)
Propulsion:	diesels; 1,000 shp; 2 shafts
Speed:	10 knots
Allowance:	13 (enlisted)

These tenders were all launched in 1976.

TUGS

6 + 3 ICEBREAKING TUGS: "BAY" CLASS

Number	Name	Number	Name
WTGB 101	KATMAI BAY	WTGB 104	BISCAYNE BAY
WTGB 102	BRISTOL BAY	WTGB 105	NEAH BAY
WTGB 103	MOBILE BAY	WTGB 106	MORRO BAY

Builders:	Tacoma Boat Building, Wash.
Displacement:	662 tons full load
Length:	140 feet (42.7 m) oa
Beam:	37 feet (11.3 m)
Draft:	12 feet (3.7 m)
Propulsion:	diesel-electric; 2,500 shp; 1 shaft
Speed:	14.7 knots
Allowance:	17 (3 O + 14 enlisted)

These are the largest tugs to be specifically constructed for the Coast Guard. Three additional tugs are being built: PENOBSCOT BAY (107), THUNDER BAY (108), and STURGEON BAY (109). Launched from 1978 on.

Classification: These tugs were originally designated WYTM; redesignated upon completion as icebreaking tugs (WTGB).

The BRISTOL BAY on trials. As completed, the early ships of this class were black hulled; repainted white upon entry into service. (U.S. Coast Guard)

BISCAYNE (1979, U.S. Coast Guard, Mike Kelley)

13 MEDIUM HARBOR TUGS: "MANITOU" CLASS

Number	Name	Number	Name
WYTM 60	MANITOU	WYTM 92	NAUGATUCK
WYTM 61	KAW	WYTM 93	RARITAN
WYTM 71	APALACHEE	WYTM 96	CHINOOK
WYTM 72	YANKTON	WYTM 97	OJIBWA
WYTM 73	MOHICAN	WYTM 98	SNOHOMISH
WYTM 90	ARUNDEL	WYTM 99	SAUK
WYTM 91	MAHONING		

Builders:
Displacement: 370 tons full load
Length: 110 feet (33.5 m) oa
Beam: 27 feet (8.2 m)
Draft: 11 feet (3.3 m)
Propulsion: diesel-electric; 1,000 shp; 1 shaft
Speed: 11.2 knots
Allowance: 20 (1 O + 19 enlisted)

The YTM 90–93 were launched in 1939; the others in 1943. The OJIBWA has been used as a training ship at Yorktown, Va., since the loss of the CUYAHOGA (WIX 157) in late 1978. The NAUGATUCK is in reserve.

CHINOOK testing fire-fighting water guns (1980, U.S. Coast Guard)

1 MEDIUM HARBOR TUG: 85-FT CLASS

Number	Name
WYTM 85009	MESSENGER

Builders:
Displacement: 230 tons full load
Length: 85 feet (25.9 m) oa
Beam: 23 feet (7.0 m)
Draft: 9 feet (2.7 m)
Propulsion: diesel; 700 shp; 1 shaft
Speed: 9.5 knots
Allowance: 10 (enlisted)

The MESSENGER was launched in 1944.

MESSENGER (1969, U.S. Coast Guard)

15 SMALL HARBOR TUGS: 65-FT CLASS

Number	Name	Number	Name
WYTL 65601	CAPSTAN	WYTL 65609	SHACKLE
WYTL 65602	CHOCK	WYTL 65610	HAWSER
WYTL 65603	SWIVEL	WYTL 65611	LINE
WYTL 65604	TACKLE	WYTL 65612	WIRE
WYTL 65605	TOWLINE	WYTL 65613	BITT
WYTL 65606	CATENARY	WYTL 65614	BOLLARD
WYTL 65607	BRIDLE	WYTL 65615	CLEAT
WYTL 65608	PENDANT		

Builders:
Displacement: 72 tons full load
Length: 65 feet (19.8 m) oa
Beam: 19 feet (5.8 m)
Draft: 7 feet (2.1 m)
Propulsion: diesel; 400 shp; 1 shaft
Speed: 9.8–10.5 knots
Allowance: 10 (enlisted)

These tugs were launched in 1961–1967.

LINE (1976, Stefan Terzibaschitsch)

LIGHTSHIPS

2 LIGHTSHIPS

Number	Name (Station)
WLV 612	LIGHTSHIP NANTUCKET
WLV 613	LIGHTSHIP RELIEF

Builders:	Coast Guard Yard, Curtis Bay, Md.
Displacement:	WLV 612–613 607 tons full load
Length:	128 feet (39.0 m) oa
Beam:	30 feet (9.1 m)
Draft:	11 feet (3.4 m)
Propulsion:	diesel; 550 shp; 1 shaft
Speed:	11 knots
Allowance:	18 (1 O + 17 enlisted)

The WLV 612 launched in 1950; WLV 613 in 1952. Coast Guard lightships exchange names according to location, but their hull numbers remain constant. Both of these ships are home-ported at Boston, Mass., the WLV 612 being on station off Nantucket Island.

Design: These are steel-hull ships with two 55-foot masts.

LIGHTSHIP NANTUCKET (U.S. Coast Guard)

FERRIES

2 FERRIES

Number	Name
(ex-FB 812)	LT. SAMUEL S. COURSEN
(ex-FB 813)	PVT. NICHOLAS MINUE

Builders:	John H. Mathis, Camden, N.J.
Displacement:	869 tons full load
Length:	172 feet (52.4 m) oa
Beam:	48 feet (14.6 m)
Draft:	14 feet (4.3 m)
Propulsion:	diesel-electric; 1,000 shp
Speed:	12 knots
Allowance:	(civilian)

These ferries are used to transport personnel and vehicles between lower Manhattan and Governors Island, N.Y. Both are former U.S. Army ferries built in 1955. They do not have Coast Guard hull numbers.

LT. SAMUEL S. COURSEN (1974, U.S. Coast Guard)

1 FERRY

Number	Name
(none)	TIDES

Builders:	
Displacement:	744 tons full load
Length:	185 feet (56.3 m) oa
Beam:	55 feet (16.8 m)
Draft:	9 feet (2.7 m)
Propulsion:	diesel-electric; 1,350 shp
Speed:	12 knots
Allowance:	(civilian)

The TIDES is assigned to Governors Island, N.Y. She is a former commercial ferry, launched in 1946.

26 National Oceanic and Atmospheric Administration

The National Oceanic and Atmospheric Administration (NOAA) conducts ocean surveys and other research and surveying activities for the U.S. government. These activities are of a nonmilitary nature. However, NOAA maps and charts are used by the armed forces, and during time of war or national crisis the NOAA oceanographic and hydrographic research ships can be expected to operate with the Navy, either as a separate service or integrated into the Navy.

NOAA is an agency of the Department of Commerce with the ships operated by the National Ocean Survey. Prior to the establishment of NOAA in 1970, the National Ocean Survey was a division of the Environmental Services Science Administration from 1965. Before that the ships were operated by the Coast and Geodetic Survery (since 1878, and the Coast Survey from 1834, and the Survey of the Coast from 1807).

SHIPS

Oceanographic and hydrographic research and survey ships are listed on the following pages. In addition, the National Marine Fisheries Service of NOAA operates a dozen fisheries research ships.

NOAA ships are classified by their "Horsepower Tonnage," the numerical sum of the vessel's shaft horsepower plus gross tonnage. Class I ships are 5501-9000 HPT, Class II are 3501-5500 HPT, Class III are 2001-3500 HPT, Class IV are 1001-2000 HPT, Class V are 501-1000 HPT, and Class VI are up to 500 HPT.

These ships are designated by a three-digit number preceded by the letter R for Research and S for Survey, with the first digit indicating the HPT class.

The following table lists the NOAA research and survey ships, their HPT class, current hull number, and previous designation.

Armament: NOAA ships are unarmed.

Class	No.	Name	Former No.
I	R101	OCEANOGRAPHER	OSS 01
I	R102	DISCOVERER	OSS 02
I	R103	RESEARCHER	OSS 03
I	S132	SURVEYOR	OSS 32
II	S220	FAIRWEATHER	MSS 20
II	S221	RAINIER	MSS 21
II	S222	MT. MITCHELL	MSS 22
III	S328	PEIRCE	CSS 28
III	S329	WHITING	CSS 29
III	S330	McARTHUR	CSS 30
III	S331	DAVIDSON	CSS 31
IV	S492	FERREL	ASV 92
V	S590	RUDE	ASV 90
V	S591	HECK	ASV 91

Research and survey ships at NOAA Pacific Marine Center at Seattle, Wash. (NOAA)

AVIATION

The Research Flight Facility of NOAA's Environmental Research Laboratories operates three atmospheric research aircraft: one WC-130B Hercules and two WP-3D Orions. Their basic characteristics are described in Chapter 22.

The WC-130B has a 10-man flight crew: 2 pilots, 1 flight engineer, 1 navigator, 1 mission scientist, 1 flight director, 1 photo-optical operator, 1 dropsonde operator, and 2 crewmen. Several passenger scientists can also be carried. The WP-3D aircraft have 8-man crews: 2 pilots, 1 flight engineer, 1 navigator, 1 mission scientist, 1 camera operator, 1 flight director, and 1 chief scientist; passenger scientists can also be embarked in these aircraft.

PERSONNEL

NOAA has some 375 commissioned officers, of whom approximately 265 are assigned to the National Ocean Survey, which operates the Administration's ships. One hundred and sixty officers are assigned to research and survey ships (listed on the following pages), and another ten commissioned officers are assigned to fisheries research ships.

One hundred licensed civil service personnel and about 700 unlicensed personnel are assigned to NOAA ships.

2 RESEARCH SHIPS: "OCEANOGRAPHER" CLASS

Number	Name	Launched	Commissioned	Status
R101	OCEANOGRAPHER	18 Apr 1964	13 July 1966	**PA**
R102	DISCOVERER	29 Oct 1964	29 Apr 1967	**PA**

Builders: Aerojet-General Corp, Jacksonville, Fla.
Displacement: 3,959 tons light
Length: 303⅓ feet (92.4 m) oa
Beam: 52 feet (15.8 m)
Draft: 18½ feet (5.6 m)
Propulsion: diesel-electric (4 diesels); 5,000 shp; 2 shafts
Speed: 18 knots
Manning: R101 14 O + 63 civilians + 30 scientists
R102 13 O + 66 civilians + 24 scientists

Design: Maritime Administration S2-MET-MA62a design.
Engineering: These ships have a 400-hp through-bow thruster.

DISCOVERER (1978, NOAA)

OCEANOGRAPHER; note radar dome abaft the funnel. (1978, NOAA)

1 RESEARCH SHIP: "RESEARCHER" TYPE

Number	Name	Launched	Commissioned	Status
R103	RESEARCHER	5 Oct 1968	8 Oct 1970	**AA**

Builders:	American Shipbuilding Co, Lorain, Ohio
Displacement:	2,875 tons light
Length:	278¼ feet (84.8 m) oa
Beam:	51 feet (15.5 m)
Draft:	16¼ feet (5.0 m)
Propulsion:	2 diesels; 3,200 shp; 2 shafts
Speed:	16 knots
Manning:	13 O + 55 civilians + 14 scientists

Design: Maritime Administration S2-MT-MA74a design.

Engineering: The RESEARCHER is fitted with a 450-hp, 360° retractable bow thruster for precise maneuvering and "creeping" speeds up to seven knots.

RESEARCHER; note helicopter platform aft. (NOAA)

1 SURVEY SHIP: "SURVEYOR" TYPE

Number	Name	Launched	Commissioned	Status
S132	SURVEYOR	25 Apr 1959	30 Apr 1960	**PA**

Builders:	National Steel Co, San Diego, Calif.
Displacement:	3,150 tons light
Length:	292⅓ feet (88.8 m) oa
Beam:	46 feet (14.0 m)
Draft:	18 feet (5.5 m)
Propulsion:	steam turbine (De Laval); 3,200 shp; 1 shaft
Boilers:	2 (Combustion Engineering)
Speed:	16 knots
Manning:	12 O + 64 civilians + 16 scientists

Design: Maritime Administration S2-S-RM28a design. A helicopter platform has been fitted aft.

Engineering: The SURVEYOR is the only steam-powered ship in NOAA service.

SURVEYOR; note helicopter platform aft. (1977, NOAA)

3 SURVEY SHIPS: "FAIRWEATHER" CLASS

Number	Name	Launched	Commissioned	Status
S220	FAIRWEATHER	15 Mar 1967	2 Oct 1968	**PA**
S221	RAINIER	15 Mar 1967	2 Oct 1968	**PA**
S222	MT. MITCHELL	29 Nov 1966	23 Mar 1968	**AA**

Builders:	Aerojet-General Corp, Jacksonville, Fla.
Displacement:	1,798 tons light
Length:	231 feet (70.4 m) oa
Beam:	42 feet (12.8 m)
Draft:	13⅚ feet (4.2 m)
Propulsion:	2 diesels; 2,400 shp; 2 shafts
Speed:	14.5 knots
Manning:	12 O + 57 civilians + 4 scientists

Design: Maritime Administration S1-MT-MA72a design.

Engineering: These ships have a 200-shp diesel through-bow thruster.

FAIRWEATHER (1978, NOAA)

2 SURVEY SHIPS: "PEIRCE" CLASS

Number	Name	Launched	Commissioned	Status
S328	PEIRCE	15 Oct 1962	6 May 1963	**AA**
S329	WHITING	20 Nov 1962	8 July 1963	**AA**

Builders:	Marietta Manufacturing Co, Point Pleasant, W.Va.
Displacement:	760 tons light
Length:	164 feet (50.0 m) oa
Beam:	33 feet (10.1 m)
Draft:	10 feet (3.0 m)
Propulsion:	diesels; 1,600 shp; 2 shafts
Speed:	12.5 knots
Manning:	8 O + 33 civilians + 2 scientists

Design: Maritime Administration S1-MT-59a design.

PEIRCE (NOAA)

WHITING (NOAA)

WHITING (1977, NOAA)

2 SURVEY SHIPS: "McARTHUR" CLASS

Number	Name	Launched	Commissioned	Status
S330	McARTHUR	15 Nov 1965	15 Dec 1966	**PA**
S331	DAVIDSON	7 May 1966	10 Mar 1967	**PA**

Builders:	Norfolk Shipbuilding and Dry Dock Co, Va.
Displacement:	995 tons light
Length:	175 feet (53.3 m) oa
Beam:	38 feet (11.5 m)
Draft:	11½ feet (3.5 m)
Propulsion:	diesels; 1,600 shp; 2 shafts
Speed:	13 knots
Manning:	8 O + 30 civilians + 2 scientists

Design: Maritime Administration S1-MT-MA70a design.

McARTHUR (1977, NOAA)

1 SURVEY SHIP: "FERREL" TYPE

Number	Name	Launched	Commissioned	Status
S492	FERREL	4 Apr 1968	4 June 1968	**AA**

Builders:	Zigler Shipyard, Jennings, La.
Displacement:	363 tons light
Length:	133¼ feet (40.5 m) oa
Beam:	32 feet (9.7 m)
Draft:	7 feet (2.1 m)
Propulsion:	diesels; 750 shp; 2 shafts
Speed:	10.6 knots
Manning:	5 O + 14 civilians

The FERREL conducts near-shore and estuarine-current surveys. She employs data collection buoys in her work; there is a large open buoy stowage area aft as well as a comprehensive workshop.

Design: Maritime Administration S1-MT-MA83a design.

Engineering: Fitted with a 100-hp through-bow thruster.

FERREL with mast removed. (NOAA)

2 SURVEY SHIPS: "RUDE" CLASS

Number	Name	Launched	Commissioned	Status
S590	RUDE	17 Aug 1966	29 Mar 1967	**AA**
S591	HECK	1 Nov 1966	29 Mar 1967	**AA**

Builders:	Jacobson Shipyard, Oyster Bay, N.Y.
Displacement:	214 tons light
Length:	90 feet (27.4 m) oa
Beam:	22 feet (6.7 m)
Draft:	7 feet (2.1 m)
Propulsion:	diesels; 800 shp; 2 shafts
Speed:	11.5 knots
Manning:	S590 3 O + 8 civilians
	S591 2 O + 8 civilians

These ships work as a pair using wire drags to locate underwater navigational hazards. One commanding officer is assigned to the two vessels; he normally rides one ship and the executive officer the other.

Design: Maritime Administration S1-MT-MA71a design.

Engineering: The propellers on these ships are protected by shrouds, similar to Kort nozzles. Auxiliary propulsion provides 70 hp to each propeller for slow-speed dragging operations.

HECK (1977, NOAA)

A Ship Classifications

U.S. Navy ships and small craft, with a few specific exceptions, are classified by type, and by sequence within that type. The list of classifications (Secretary of the Navy Instruction 5030.1) is issued periodically, updating a system that was begun in 1922. The current list, based on a format developed in 1977, seeks to better define ship types and missions, and facilitate comparisons with Soviet ship types.

The following are those classifications on the current list, dated 5 November 1979.

Letter prefixes to the basic symbols are used to indicate: E—prototype ship or craft in an experimental or developmental status; F—ship or craft being constructed for a foreign government; T—ship assigned to the Military Sealift Command (formerly Military Sea Transportation Service); W—Coast Guard ship.

The suffix letter N is used to denote nuclear-propelled ships. For service craft the suffix N indicates a non-self-propelled version of a similar self-propelled unit. The letter X is used as a suffix to indicate new designs or classes (e.g., SSNX, ARX, DDGX), but does not appear in the official list of classifications.

Warships

Aircraft Carriers

CV	Multi-purpose Aircraft Carrier
CVN	Multi-purpose Aircraft Carrier (nuclear)
CVS	ASW Aircraft Carrier

Surface Combatants

BB	Battleship
CA	Gun Cruiser
CG	Guided Missile Cruiser
CGN	Guided Missile Cruiser (nuclear)
DD	Destroyer
DDG	Guided Missile Destroyer
FF	Frigate
FFG	Guided Missile Frigate

Submarines

SS	Submarine
SSG	Guided Missile Submarine
SSN	Submarine (nuclear)
SSBN	Ballistic Missile Submarine (nuclear)
SSAG	Auxiliary Submarine

Other Combatants

Patrol

PG	Patrol Combatant
PHM	Guided Missile Patrol Combatant (hydrofoil)

Amphibious Warfare

LHA	Amphibious Assault Ship (general purpose)
LPH	Amphibious Assault Ship (helicopter)
LPD	Amphibious Transport Dock
LKA	Amphibious Cargo Ship
LPA	Amphibious Transport
LSD	Dock Landing Ship
LST	Tank Landing Ship
LCC	Amphibious Command Ship

Mine Warfare

MSO	Minesweeper—Ocean
MCM	Mine Countermeasures

Auxiliary Ships

Mobile Logistics Ships

AE	Ammunition Ship
AF	Store Ship
AFS	Combat Store Ship
AO	Oiler
AOE	Fast Combat Support Ship
AOR	Replenishment Oiler
AD	Destroyer Tender
AR	Repair Ship
AS	Submarine Tender

Support Ships

ARS	Salvage Ship
ASR	Submarine Rescue Ship
ATA	Auxiliary Ocean Tug
ATF	Fleet Ocean Tug
ATS	Salvage and Rescue Ship
AG	Miscellaneous
AGDS	Deep Submergence Support Ship
AGEH	Hydrofoil Research Ship
AGF	Miscellaneous Command Ship
AGFF	Frigate Research Ship

AGM	Missile Range Instrumentation Ship
AGOR	Oceanographic Research Ship
AGOS	Ocean Surveillance Ship
AGP	Patrol Craft Tender
AGS	Surveying Ship
AGSS	Auxiliary Research Submarine
AH	Hospital Ship
AK	Cargo Ship
AKR	Vehicle Cargo Ship
AOG	Gasoline Tanker
AOT	Transport Oiler
AP	Transport
APB	Self-Propelled Barracks Ship
ARC	Cable Repairing Ship
ARL	Repair Ship, Small
AVM	Guided Missile Ship
AVT	Auxiliary Aircraft Landing Training Ship

Combatant Craft

Patrol Craft

PB	Patrol Boat
PCF	Patrol Craft (fast)
PGH	Patrol Gunboat (hydrofoil)
PTF	Fast Patrol Craft
ATC	Mini-Armored Troop Carrier
PBR	River Patrol Boat

Amphibious Warfare Craft

AALC	Amphibious Assault Landing Craft
LCAC	Landing Craft, Air Cushion
LCM	Landing Craft, Mechanized
LCPL	Landing Craft, Personnel, Large
LCU	Landing Craft, Utility
LCVP	Landing Craft, Vehicle, Personnel
LWT	Amphibious Warping Tug
SLWT	Side Loading Warping Tug
LSSC	Light Seal Support Craft
MSSC	Medium Seal Support Craft
SDV	Swimmer Delivery Vehicle
SWCL	Special Warfare Craft, Light
SWCM	Special Warfare Craft, Medium

Mine Warfare Craft

MSB	Minesweeping Boat
MSD	Minesweeping Drone
MSI	Minesweeper, Inshore
MSM	Minesweeper, River (converted LCM-6)
MSR	Minesweeper, Patrol

Service Craft

AFDB	Large Auxiliary Floating Dry Dock
AFDL	Small Auxiliary Floating Dry Dock

AFDM	Medium Auxiliary Floating Dry Dock
ARD	Auxiliary Repair Dry Dock
ARDM	Medium Auxiliary Repair Dry Dock
YBD	Bowdock
YFD	Yard Floating Dry Dock
YTB	Large Harbor Tug
YTL	Small Harbor Tug
YTM	Medium Harbor Tug
YO	Fuel Oil Barge
YOG	Gasoline Barge
YW	Water Barge
YC	Open Lighter
YCF	Car Float
YCV	Aircraft Transportation Lighter
YF	Covered Lighter
YFN	Covered Lighter
YFNB	Large Covered Lighter
YFNX	Lighter (Special Purpose)
YFR	Refrigerated Covered Lighter
YFRN	Refrigerated Covered Lighter
YFU	Harbor Utility Craft
YG	Garbage Lighter
YGN	Garbage Lighter
YOGN	Gasoline Barge
YON	Fuel Oil Barge
YOS	Oil Storage Barge
YSR	Sludge Removal Barge
YWN	Water Barge
APL	Barracks Craft
DSRV	Deep Submergence Rescue Vehicle
DSV	Deep Submergence Vehicle
IX	Unclassified Miscellaneous
NR	Submersible Research Vehicle (nuclear)
YAG	Miscellaneous Auxiliary
YD	Floating Crane
YDT	Diving Tender
YFB	Ferry Boat or Launch
YFND	Dry Dock Companion Craft
YFP	Floating Power Barge
YFRT	Covered Lighter (Range Tender)
YHLC	Salvage Lift Craft, Heavy
YM	Dredge
YNG	Gate Craft
YP	Patrol Craft
YPD	Floating Pile Driver
YR	Floating Workshop
YRB	Repair and Berthing Barge
YRBM	Repair, Berthing, and Messing Barge
YRDH	Floating Dry Dock Workshop (Hull)
YRDM	Floating Dry Dock Workshop (Machine)
YRR	Radiological Repair Barge
YRST	Salvage Craft Tender
YSD	Seaplane Wrecking Derrick

MARITIME ADMINISTRATION CLASSIFICATIONS

The U.S. Maritime Administration classifies its ships by their design characteristics. This classifiction scheme is included in *Ships and Aircraft* because of the large number of Maritime Administration (previously Maritime Commission) ships that remain on the Naval Register in the amphibious warfare and auxiliary ship categories. (During World War II escort aircraft carriers and patrol frigates also were built to Maritime Commission designs.) NOAA ships are also built to MarAd design.

Explanation of symbols:

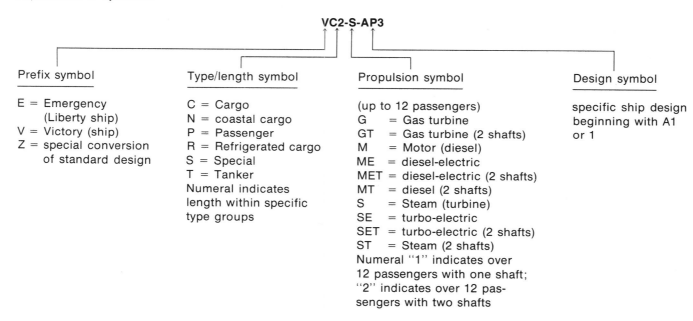

VC2-S-AP3

Prefix symbol

E = Emergency
    (Liberty ship)
V = Victory (ship)
Z = special conversion
    of standard design

Type/length symbol

C = Cargo
N = coastal cargo
P = Passenger
R = Refrigerated cargo
S = Special
T = Tanker
Numeral indicates
length within specific
type groups

Propulsion symbol

(up to 12 passengers)
G   = Gas turbine
GT = Gas turbine (2 shafts)
M   = Motor (diesel)
ME = diesel-electric
MET = diesel-electric (2 shafts)
MT = diesel (2 shafts)
S   = Steam (turbine)
SE = turbo-electric
SET = turbo-electric (2 shafts)
ST = Steam (2 shafts)
Numeral "1" indicates over
12 passengers with one shaft;
"2" indicates over 12 pas-
sengers with two shafts

Design symbol

specific ship design
beginning with A1
or 1

B Shipyards

There are some 200 shipyards and ship-repair facilities in the United States. Of these, 19 qualify as major shipyards and have recent experience building or performing major overhaul or modernization work on naval ships. Since 1972 all U.S. Navy ship construction has been done in private (commercial) shipyards, with government-owned (naval) and private yards doing ship overhaul, conversion, and maintenance. By dollar value of work, about one-third of the overhaul, conversion, and maintenance is done in private yards.

There are eight naval shipyards in operation. The yards, their current employment and areas of specialization, are listed in the following table. Naval shipyard activities reached a post–World War II peak in 1961 when there were 11 active shipyards with 101,000 employees. No longer active are the Boston, New York (Brooklyn), and San Francisco naval shipyards. The last new ship deliveries by naval shipyards were the Drum (SSN 677) by Mare Island, Sand Lance (SSN 660) by Portsmouth, Blue Ridge (LCC 19) by Philadelphia, and Detroit (AOE 4) by Puget Sound, all delivered in 1970–1972. The Mare Island and Puget Sound yards are credited with being able to resume construction activities in the near term if necessary.

Shipyard	Employment	Specialization
Charleston Naval Shipyard South Carolina	7,200	SSN, SSBN, guided missile ships, ASW ships
Long Beach Naval Shipyard California	7,000	CV, guided missile ships, ASW ships
Norfolk Naval Shipyard Virginia	10,900	SSN, CVN, CGN, guided missile ships, ASW ships
Mare Island Naval Shipyard Vallejo, California	9,050	SSBN, SSN, CGN
Pearl Harbor Naval Shipyard Oahu, Hawaii	5,850	SSN, guided missile ships, ASW ships
Philadelphia Naval Shipyard Pennsylvania	9,250	SS, CV, guided missile ships, ASW ships
Portsmouth Naval Shipyard Kittery, Maine	7,450	SSBN, SSN
Puget Sound Naval Shipyard Bremerton, Washington	10,015	SSBN, SSN, CVN, CGN, guided missile ships, ASW ships

There are 11 private shipyards with recent major naval construction experience. These yards account for about 60 percent of the total civilian shipbuilding industry employment. All of the yards are below their postwar employment peaks except for Bath Iron Works and Todd Shipyards, Seattle, which currently have more employees than at any time since World War II. Electric Boat builds only submarines, while Ingalls builds destroyers and guided missile cruisers and is seeking other naval construction. The other nine major private yards build merchant ships as well as naval units. Asterisks indicate ship classes currently under construction.

Shipyard	Employment	Specialization	
Avondale Shipyards, Inc. New Orleans, Louisiana	7,500	*AO 177 DDG	FF
Bath Iron Works Corp. Bath, Maine	4,950	*FFG 7 CG	DDG FF
Bethlehem Steel Sparrows Point, Maryland	2,800	AE	ARDM
Electric Boat Division, General Dynamics Corp. Groton, Connecticut	22,100	*SSBN 726	*SSN 688
General Dynamics Corp. Quincy, Massachusetts	5,600	SSN CGN DDG LSD	AE AOR AS
Ingalls Shipbuilding Div. Litton Industries, Pascagoula, Mississippi	19,150	*CG 47 *DDG 993 *DD 963 SSN	LPH LPD LSD AO AS
Lockheed Shipbuilding & Construction Co. Seattle, Washington	3,270	*AS 39 FFG	FF LPD
National Steel & Shipbuilding Co. San Diego, California	6,400	*AD 41 LST	AFS AOR
Newport News Shipbuilding & Dry Dock Co. Virginia	22,500	*SSN 688 *CVN 68 CGN 38	CV LCC LKA
Todd Shipyards Corp. San Pedro, California	2,650	*FFG 7 CG	FF AO
Todd Shipyards Corp. Seattle, Washington	2,425	*FFG 7 DDG	FF AGOR

Smaller yards that are currently constructing Navy ships are: Marinette Corp. (Wis.), building ATF 166-class fleet tugs; Tacoma Boatbuilding Co. (Wash.) and Peterson Builders (Sturgeon Bay, Wis.), building small combatants for foreign transfer and service craft; and Boeing Airplane Co. (Seattle, Wash.), producing PHM 1-class missile combatants.

The old and the new joining the U.S. Fleet in the 1980s: the USNS APACHE (T–ATF 172), a civilian-manned tug of the Military Sealift Command, tows the 39-year-old battleship IOWA (BB 61) from her resting place at the Philadelphia Naval Shipyard to New Orleans for the first stage in her reactivation; and the TICONDEROGA (CG 47) at high speed. Her Aegis radar/fire control system makes her the most effective antiair warfare ship afloat. (1982; U.S. Navy and Ingalls Shipbuilding)

C   Ship Disposals, 1970–1980

The following ships were stricken from 1970 through 1980. Former designations are indicated in parentheses; where no hull number appears it was the same as indicated in the first column. Transfer dates are listed for ships going to other nations; actual strike dates may differ, as most ships were transferred on loan or lease until the mid-1970s and stricken at a later date.

Destroyer Tenders

AD 16 CASCADE	stricken 23 Nov 1974
AD 23 ARCADIA	stricken 1 July 1973
AD 25 FRONTIER	stricken 1 Dec 1972
AD 26 SHENANDOAH	stricken 1 Apr 1980
AD 27 YELLOWSTONE	stricken 12 Sep 1974
AD 29 ISLE ROYALE	stricken 1 Sep 1971
AD 31 TIDEWATER	to Indonesia 14 Mar 1980

Degaussing Ships

ADG 8 LODESTONE	stricken 21 Feb 1975(PCE 876)
ADG 9 MAGNET	stricken 21 Feb 1975(PCE 879)
ADG 10 DEPERM	stricken 21 Feb 1975(PCE 883)
ADG 383 SURFBIRD	stricken 21 Feb 1975(AM/MSF)

Ammunition Ships

AE 5 RAINIER	stricken 7 Aug 1970
AE 8 MAUNA LOA	stricken 1 Sep 1971
AE 9 MAZAMA	stricken 1 Sep 1970
AE 12 WRANGELL	stricken 1 Oct 1976
AE 14 FIREDRAKE	stricken 15 July 1976
AE 15 VESUVIUS	stricken 14 Aug 1973
AE 16 MOUNT KATMAI	stricken 14 Aug 1973
AE 17 GREAT SITKIN	stricken 2 July 1973
AE 18 PARICUTIN	stricken 1 June 1973
AE 19 DIAMOND HEAD	stricken 1 Mar 1973
AE 30 VIRGO	stricken 18 Feb 1971
AE 31 CHARA	stricken 10 Mar 1972(AKA 58)

Store Ships

AF 10 ALDEBARAN	stricken 1 June 1973
AF 28 HYADES	stricken 1 Sep 1971
AF 30 ADRIA	stricken 1 July 1974
AF 37 MALABAR	stricken 1 July 1974
AF 42 BONDIA	stricken 1 May 1973
AF 44 LAURENTIA	stricken 28 Apr 1970

AF 49 ZELIMA	stricken 1 Sep 1971
AF 50 BALD EAGLE	stricken 19 Oct 1971
AF 51 BLUE JACKET	stricken 19 Oct 1971
AF 52 ARCTURUS	stricken 1 Oct 1976
AF 54 PICTOR	stricken 1 June 1976
AF 55 ALUDRA	stricken 1 June 1976
AF 56 DENEBOLA	stricken 30 Apr 1976
AF 57 REGULUS	stricken 10 Sep 1971
AF 59 VEGA	stricken 29 Apr 1977
AF 60 SIRIUS	stricken 30 June 1974
AF 61 PROCYON	stricken 1 June 1976
AF 63 ASTERION	stricken 15 June 1973
AF 64 PERSEUS	stricken 15 June 1973

Floating Dry Docks, Large

AFDB 1 (Sections A, G, J)	stricken 1 June 1977
AFDB 6	stricken 1 Jan 1974

Floating Dry Docks, Small

AFDL 11	to Khmer Republic 20 June 1972(AFD)
AFDL 22	to South Vietnam 30 Sep 1971(AFD)
AFDL 26	stricken 1 Sep 1977(AFD)
AFDL 28	to Mexico 23 Jan 1973(AFD)
AFDL 29	stricken 1 Dec 1977(AFD)
AFDL 30	stricken 15 Nov 1977(AFD)
AFDL 35	stricken 1 Aug 1973(ARDC 2)
AFDL 42	stricken 1 May 1974(ARDC 9)
AFDL 43	stricken 17 Feb 1978(ARDC 10)

Miscellaneous Auxiliaries

AG 162 MISSION CAPISTRANO	stricken 19 Oct 1971(AO 112)
AG 169 PVT. JOSE E. VALDEZ	stricken 1 Sep 1971(APC 119)
AG 172 PHOENIX	stricken 15 June 1973
AG 173 PROVO	stricken 15 June 1973
AG 174 CHEYENNE	stricken 15 June 1973
AG 175 SGT. CURTIS F. SHOUP	stricken 28 Apr 1970
AG 178 FLYER	stricken 17 July 1975
AG 179–190	not used; reserved for floating depot ships
AG 191 SPOKANE	stricken 15 Apr 1972(CLAA 120)
AG 192 S. P. LEE	leased to U.S. Coast and Geodetic Survey Feb 1974(AGS 31)
AG 193 GLOMAR EXPLORER	stricken 17 June 1977
AG 335 (unnamed)	stricken 21 Dec 1970(LSM)
AG 520 ALACRITY	stricken 30 Sep 1977(MSO)
AG 521 ASSURANCE	stricken 30 Sep 1977(MSO)

Auxiliary Deep Submergence Support Ships

AGDS 1 WHITE SANDS   stricken 1 Apr 1974(ARD 20)

Hydrofoil Research Ships

AGEH 1 PLANVIEW   stricken 30 Sep 1978

Miscellaneous Flagships

AGF 1 VALCOUR   stricken 15 Jan 1973(AVP 55)
AGF 2 not used

Missile Range Instrumentation Ships

AGM 1 RANGE TRACKER   stricken 28 Apr 1970(AG 160)
AGM 2 RANGE RECOVERER   changed to service craft YFRT 524 16 May 1972 (AG 161/FS 278)
AGM 3 LONGVIEW   stricken 1 Nov 1974(AK 238)
AGM 5 SUNNYVALE   stricken 15 Dec 1974(AK 256)
AGM 6 WATERTOWN   stricken 16 Feb 1973
AGM 7 HUNTSVILLE   stricken 8 Nov 1974
AGM 11 TWIN FALLS   stricken 1 Sep 1972
AGM 13 SWORD KNOT   stricken 1 Apr 1971
AGM 15 COASTAL SENTRY   stricken 1 Apr 1971
AGM 21 MERCURY   stricken 28 Apr 1976(AO 126)

Major Communications Relay Ships

AGMR 1 ANNAPOLIS   stricken 15 Oct 1976(AKV 39/CVE 107)
AGMR 2 ARLINGTON   stricken 15 Aug 1975(CC 3/AVT 6/CVL 48)

Oceanographic Research Ships

AGOR 1 JOSIAH WILLARD GIBBS   to Greece 7 Dec 1971 (AVP 51)
AGOR 4 JAMES M. GILLISS   to Mexico 1981
AGOR 5 CHARLES H. DAVIS   to New Zealand 28 July 1970
AGOR 6 SANDS   to Brazil 1 July 1974
AGOR 8 ELTANIN   to Argentina 19 Feb 1974 (returned to U.S. Navy)
AGOR 17 CHAIN   stricken 30 Dec 1977(ARS 20)
AGOR 18 SNATCH   stricken 1 May 1970(ARS 27)

Patrol Craft Tenders

AGP 786 GARRETT COUNTY   to Philippines Apr 1976(LST)
AGP 821 HARNETT COUNTY   to Philippines Apr 1976(LST)
AGP 838 HUNTERDON COUNTY   to Malaysia 1 July 1971(LST)
AGP 1176 GRAHAM COUNTY   stricken 1 Mar 1977(LST)

Surveying Ships

AGS 23 MICHELSON   stricken 15 Apr 1975
AGS 24 SERRANO   stricken 2 Jan 1970 (ATF 112)
AGS 25 KELLAR   to Portugal 21 Jan 1972
AGS 35 SGT. GEORGE D. KEATHLEY   to Taiwan 29 Mar 1972
AGS 36 COASTAL CRUSADER   stricken 30 Apr 1976(AGM 16)
AGS 37 TWIN FALLS   stricken 6 Nov 1972(AGM 11)
AGS 50 REHOBOTH   stricken 15 Apr 1970(AVP)

Auxiliary Submarines

See Submarines
AGSS 569 ALBACORE   stricken 1 May 1980

Technical Research Ships

AGTR 4 BELMONT   stricken 16 Jan 1970(AG 167)
AGTR 5 LIBERTY   stricken 1 June 1970(AG 168)

Hospital Ships

AH 15 CONSOLATION   stricken 16 Sep 1974
AH 16 REPOSE   stricken 15 Mar 1974

Cargo Ships

AK 180 FENTRESS   stricken 15 Oct 1973; to Department of Interior 1974
AK 188 HERKIMER   stricken 15 June 1973; to Department of Interior 1973
AK 198 MUSKINGUM   stricken 10 June 1973; to Department of Interior 1973
AK 241 PVT. FRANCIS X. MCGRAW   stricken 15 May 1974
AK 243 SGT. ARCHER T. GAMMON   stricken 1 May 1973
AK 244 SGT. MORRIS E. CRAIN   stricken 1 Apr 1975
AK 246 COL. WILLIAM J. O'BRIEN   stricken 1 Sep 1973
AK 249 SHORT SPLICE   stricken 15 June 1973
AK 250 PVT. FRANK J. PETRARCA   stricken 15 Oct 1973
AK 251 LT. GEORGE W. G. BOYCE   stricken 15 July 1973
AK 252 LT. ROBERT CRAIG   stricken 10 July 1973
AK 260 BETELGEUSE   stricken 1 Feb 1974
AK 275 PVT. JOSEPH E. MERRELL   stricken 31 Jan 1974(AKV 4)
AK 276 SGT. JACK J. PENDLETON   stricken 15 Feb 1974
AK 277 SCHUYLER OTIS BLAND   stricken 15 Aug 1979
AK 279 NORWALK   stricken 1 Aug 1979

Light Cargo Ships

AKL 10 SHARPS   to South Korea 15 Nov 1974
AKL 12 MARK   to Taiwan 1 July 1971(AG 143/FS 214)
AKL 28 BRULE   to South Korea 1 Nov 1971(FS 370)

AKL 31 (unnamed)	stricken 21 Dec 1970; to Dept. of Interior
AKL 170 TRILLIUM	stricken 20 Aug 1974; to South Korea 15 Nov 1974(WAK/FS 397)
AKL 398 REDBUD	stricken 20 Nov 1970; to Philippines May 1972(WAGL)

Vehicle Cargo Ships

AKR 8 TAURUS	stricken 22 June 1971*(AK 273/LSD 23)

Stores-Issue Ships

AKS 32 ALTAIR	stricken 1 June 1973(AK 257)

Cargo Ship and Aircraft Ferries

AKV 8 KULA GULF	stricken 15 Sep 1970(CVE 108)
AKV 9 CAPE GLOUCESTER	stricken 1 Apr 1971(CVE 109)
AKV 11 VELLA GULF	stricken 1 Dec 1970(CVE 111)
AKV 12 SIBONEY	stricken 1 June 1970(CVE 112)
AKV 14 RENDOVA	stricken 1 Apr 1971(CVE 114)
AKV 16 BADOENG STRAIT	stricken 1 Dec 1970(CVE 116)
AKV 17 SAIDOR	stricken 1 Dec 1970(CVHE/CVE 117)
AKV 19 POINT CRUZ	stricken 15 Sep 1970(CVE 119)
AKV 21 RABAUL	stricken 1 Sep 1971(CVHE/CVE 121)
AKV 23 TINIAN	stricken 1 June 1970(CVHE/CVE 123)
AKV 37 COMMENCEMENT BAY	stricken 1 Apr 1971(CVHE/CVE 105)
AKV 40 CARD	stricken 15 Sep 1970(CVHE/CVE 11)
AKV 41 CORE	stricken 15 Sep 1970(CVHE/CVE 13)
AKV 42 BRETON	stricken 6 Aug 1971(CVHE/CVE 23)
AKV 43 CROATAN	stricken 15 Sep 1970(CVHE/CVE 25)

Net Laying Ships (all formerly AN)

ANL 78 COHOES	stricken 30 June 1972
ANL 89 TONAWANDA	stricken 15 Apr 1977

Oilers

AO 24 PLATTE	stricken 25 Sep 1970
AO 25 SABINE	stricken 1 Sep 1971
AO 30 CHEMUNG	stricken 18 Sep 1970
AO 32 GUADALUPE	stricken 15 May 1975
AO 36 KENNEBEC	stricken 1 June 1973
AO 39 KANKAKEE	stricken 1 June 1973
AO 41 MATTAPONI	stricken 15 Oct 1970
AO 43 TAPPAHANNOCK	stricken 1 Sep 1971; to Taiwan 1981
AO 47 NECHES	stricken 1 Oct 1970
AO 49 SUAMICO	stricken 15 Nov 1974

AO 50 TALLULAH	stricken 29 May 1975*
AO 52 CACAPON	stricken 14 Aug 1973
AO 53 CALIENTE	stricken 1 Dec 1973
AO 54 CHIKASKIA	stricken 1 Dec 1977
AO 55 ELOKOMIN	stricken 17 Mar 1970
AO 56 AUCILLA	stricken 1 Dec 1976
AO 58 MANATEE	stricken 14 Aug 1973
AO 60 NANTAHALA	stricken 2 July 1973
AO 61 SEVERN	stricken 1 July 1974
AO 63 CHIPOLA	stricken 14 Aug 1973
AO 64 TOLOVANA	stricken 15 Apr 1975
AO 65 PECOS	stricken 1 Oct 1974
AO 67 CACHE	stricken 6 May 1972*
AO 77 COSSATOT	stricken 18 Sep 1974
AO 78 CHEPACHET	stricken 13 Mar 1972*
AO 79 COWANESQUE	stricken 1 June 1972
AO 97 ALLAGASH	stricken 1 June 1973
AO 100 CHUKAWAN	stricken 1 July 1972
AO 111 MISSION BUENAVENTURA	stricken 31 Mar 1972
AO 116 MISSION LORETO	stricken 1 Feb 1972
AO 128 MISSION SAN LUIS REY	stricken 1 Feb 1972
AO 130 MISSION SAN RAFAEL	stricken 28 Apr 1976
AO 133 MISSION SANTA CRUZ	stricken 15 Sep 1970
AO 137 MISSION SANTA ANA	stricken 1 Aug 1974
AO 138 CEDAR CREEK	stricken 1 Feb 1972
AO 140 PIONEER VALLEY	stricken 15 Aug 1972
AO 142 SHAWNEE TRAIL	stricken 29 Feb 1972

Gasoline Tankers

AOG 1 PATAPSCO	stricken 1 Aug 1974
AOG 7 ELKHORN	to Taiwan 1 July 1972
AOG 8 GENESEE	to Chile 5 July 1972
AOG 9 KISHWAUKEE	stricken 1 Aug 1974
AOG 11 TOMBIGBEE	to Greece 7 July 1972
AOG 50 CHEWAUCAN	stricken 1 July 1971; to Colombia 1 July 1971
AOG 53 NAMAKAGON	to Taiwan 29 June 1971†
AOG 55 NESPELEN	stricken 1 July 1975
AOG 56 NOXUBEE	stricken 1 July 1975
AOG 57 PECATONICA	stricken 15 Apr 1976; to Taiwan May 1976
AOG 80 PISCATAQUA	stricken 1 Aug 1974

Transports

AP 116 GEN. G. C. MEIGS	stricken 9 Jan 1972

Self-Propelled Barracks Ships

APB 36 COLLETON	stricken 1 June 1973(APL 36)
APB 46 DORCHESTER	stricken 1 June 1973(AKS 17/LST 1112)

*Scrapped two years earlier (!).

*Retained for Navy in National Defense Reserve Fleet.
† Formerly on loan to New Zealand.

| APB 47 KINGMAN | stricken 1 Oct 1977(AKS 18/LST 1113) |
| APB 48 VANDERBURGH | stricken 1 Apr 1972(AKS 19(LST 1114) |

Coastal Transports

| APC 116 SGT. JONAH E. KELLEY | stricken 28 Apr 1970 |

Repair Ships

AR 9 DELTA	stricken 1 Oct 1977(AK 29)
AR 12 BRIAREUS	stricken 1 Jan 1977
AR 13 AMPHION	to Iran 1 Oct 1971
AR 14 CADMUS	to Taiwan 15 Jan 1973
AR 21 DIONYSUS	stricken 1 Sep 1971
AR 22 KLONDIKE	stricken 15 Sep 1974(AD 22)
AR 23 MARKAB	stricken 1 Sep 1976(AK 31/AD 21)
AR 28 GRAND CANYON	stricken 1 Sep 1978(AD)

Battle Damage Repair Ships

ARB 4 ZEUS	stricken 1 June 1973(LST 132)
ARB 5 MIDAS	stricken 15 Apr 1976(LST 514)
ARB 7 SARPEDON	stricken 15 Apr 1976(LST 956)
ARB 8 TELAMON	stricken 1 June 1973(LST 976)

Cable Repairing Ships

| ARC 4 THOR | stricken 1 Mar 1978(AKA 49) |

Auxiliary Repair Docks

ARD 9 (unnamed)	to Taiwan 12 Jan 1977
ARD 10 (unnamed)	stricken 1 July 1971
ARD 11 (unnamed)	to Mexico 17 June 1974
ARD 12 (unnamed)	to Turkey 18 Nov 1971
ARD 16 (unnamed)	stricken 1 Oct 1972
ARD 22 WINDSOR	to Taiwan 1981
ARD 24 (unnamed)	to Ecuador 1981
ARD 25 (unnamed)	to Chile 20 Aug 1973
ARD 27 (unnamed)	stricken 1 Apr 1973
ARD 29 ARCO	to Iran 1 Nov 1971

Internal Combustion Engine Repair Ships

| ARG 4 TUTUILA | to Taiwan 21 Feb 1972 |

Landing Craft Repair Ships

ARL 1 ACHELOUS	stricken 1 June 1973(LST 10)
ARL 2 AMYCUS	stricken 1 June 1970(LST 489)
ARL 7 ATLAS	stricken 1 June 1972(LST 231)
ARL 8 EGERIA	stricken 1 Oct 1977(LST 136)
ARL 9 ENDYMION	stricken 1 June 1972(LST 513)
ARL 23 SATYR	to South Vietnam 30 Sep 1971; to Philippines 1975(LST 852)
ARL 30 ASKARI	to Indonesia 31 Aug 1971(LST 1131)
ARL 31 BELLEROPHON	stricken 1 Oct 1977(LST 1132)
ARL 37 INDRA	stricken 31 Dec 1977(LST 1147)
ARL 38 KRISHNA	to Philippines 31 Oct 1971(LST 1149)

Salvage Ships

ARS 6 ESCAPE	stricken 1 Sep 1978
ARS 7 GRAPPLE	to Taiwan 1 Dec 1977
ARS 19 CABLE	stricken 15 Apr 1977
ARS 22 CURRENT	stricken 1 June 1973
ARS 23 DELIVER	stricken 15 Aug 1979
ARS 24 GRASP	to South Korea 31 Mar 1978
ARS 25 SAFEGUARD	stricken 30 Sep 1979

Salvage Lifting Ships

ARSD 1 GYPSY	stricken 1 June 1973(LSM 549)
ARSD 2 MENDER	stricken 1 June 1973(LSM 550)
ARSD 3 SALVAGER	stricken 1 Aug 1972(LSM 551)
ARSD 4 WINDLASS	stricken 1 Aug 1972(LSM 552)

Salvage Craft Tenders

| ARST 1 LAYSAN ISLAND | stricken 1 June 1973(LST 1098) |
| ARST 3 PALMYRA | stricken 1 June 1973(LST 1100) |

Aircraft Repair Ships (Aircraft)

| ARVA 5 FABIUS | stricken 1 June 1973(LST 1093) |
| ARVA 6 MEGARA | to Mexico 1 Oct 1973(LST 1094) |

Aircraft Repair Ships (Engine)

| ARVE 4 CHLORIS | stricken 1 June 1973(LST 1095) |

Aircraft Repair Ships (Helicopter)

| ARVH 1 CORPUS CHRISTI BAY | stricken 31 Dec 1974(AV 5) |

Submarine Tenders

AS 13 GRIFFIN	stricken 1 Aug 1972
AS 14 PELIAS	stricken 1 Aug 1971
AS 22 EURYALE	stricken 1 Dec 1971
AS 23 AEGIR	stricken 1 June 1971

Submarine Rescue Ships

ASR 7	CHANTICLEER	stricken 9 June 1973
ASR 8	COUCAL	stricken 15 Sep 1977
ASR 10	GREENLET	to Turkey 12 June 1970
ASR 12	PENGUIN	stricken 30 June 1970(ATF 99)
ASR 16	TRINGA	stricken 30 Sep 1977; to Turkey
ASR 20	SKYLARK	to Brazil 30 June 1973(ATF 165)

Auxiliary Tugs

ATA 184	KALMIA	to Colombia 1 July 1971(ATR 111)
ATA 185	KOKA	to Samoa 3 Dec 1973(ATR 112)
ATA 186	CAHOKIA	to Taiwan 14 Apr 1972(ATR 113)
ATA 187	SALISH	to Argentina 10 Feb 1972(ATR 114)
ATA 188	PENOBSCOT	stricken 28 Feb 1975(ATR 115)
ATA 190	SAMOSET	stricken 1 July 1978; to Haiti 16 Oct 1978(ATR 117)
ATA 192	TILLAMOOK	to South Korea 9 Aug 1971(ATR 119)
ATA 195	TATNUCK	stricken 1 Oct 1977(ATR 122)
ATA 196	MAHOPAC	to Taiwan 1 July 1971(ATR 123)
ATA 204	WANDANK	stricken 1 Aug 1973(ATR 131)
ATA 208	SAGAMORE	to Dominican Republic 1 Feb 1972(ATR 135)
ATA 209	UMPQUA	to Colombia 1 July 1971(ATR 136)
ATA 210	CATAWBA	to Argentina 10 Feb 1972(ATR 137)
ATA 240	(unnamed)	stricken 4 Aug 1971(LT 455)

Fleet Tugs

ATF 67	APACHE	to Taiwan 30 June 1974
ATF 72	KIOWA	to Dominican Republic 16 Oct 1972
ATF 75	SIOUX	to Turkey 30 Oct 1972
ATF 84	CREE	stricken 21 Apr 1978
ATF 86	MATACO	stricken 1 Oct 1977
ATF 92	TAWASA	stricken 1 Apr 1975
ATF 96	ABNAKI	to Mexico 30 Sep 1978
ATF 98	ARIKARA	to Chile 1 July 1971
ATF 100	CHOWANOC	to Ecuador 1 Oct 1977
ATF 101	COCOPA	to Mexico 30 Sep 1978
ATF 103	HITCHITI	to Mexico 30 Sep 1978
ATF 106	MOLALA	to Mexico 1 Aug 1978
ATF 114	TAWAKONI	to Taiwan 1 June 1978
ATF 156	BUISENO	to Argentina 1 July 1975
ATF 157	NIPMUC	to Venezuela 1 Sep 1978
ATF 161	SALINAN	to Venezuela 1 Sep 1978
ATF 162	SHAKORI	to Taiwan 29 Aug 1980
ATF 163	UTINA	to Venezuela 3 Sep 1971

Seaplane Tenders

AV 7	CURRITUCK	stricken 1 Apr 1971
AV 10	CHANDELEUR	stricken 1 May 1971
AV 12	PINE ISLAND	stricken 1 Feb 1971
AV 13	SALISBURY SOUND	stricken 1 Feb 1971

Advanced Base Support Ships

AVB 2	TALLAHATCHEE COUNTY	stricken 15 Jan 1970(LST 1154)

Aircraft Transports

AVT 2	MONTEREY	stricken 1 June 1970(CVL 26/CL 78)
AVT 3	CABOT	stricken 1 Aug 1972(CVL 28/CL 79)
AVT 5	SAN JACINTO	stricken 1 June 1970(CVL 30/CL 100)

Water Carriers

AW 4	ABATAN	stricken 1 May 1970(AO 92)

Cruisers

CA 68	BALTIMORE	stricken 15 Feb 1971
CA 69	BOSTON	stricken 4 Jan 1974(CAG 1)
CA 70	CANBERRA	stricken 31 July 1978(CAG 2)
CA 71	QUINCY	stricken 1 Oct 1973
CA 72	PITTSBURGH	stricken 1 July 1973
CA 73	ST. PAUL	stricken 31 July 1978
CA 75	HELENA	stricken 1 Jan 1974
CA 122	OREGON CITY	stricken 1 Nov 1970
CA 124	ROCHESTER	stricken 1 Oct 1973
CA 130	BREMERTON	stricken 1 Oct 1973
CA 131	FALL RIVER	stricken 19 Feb 1971
CA 133	TOLEDO	stricken 1 Jan 1974
CA 135	LOS ANGELES	stricken 1 Jan 1974
CA 148	NEWPORT NEWS	stricken 31 July 1978

Command Ships

CC 1	NORTHAMPTON	stricken 31 Dec 1977(CA 125/CLC 1)
CC 2	WRIGHT	stricken 31 Dec 1977(CVL 49/AVT 7)
CC 3	changed to AGMR 2	

Guided Missile Cruisers

CG 12	COLUMBUS	stricken 9 Aug 1976(CA 74)

Light Cruisers

CL 65	PASADENA	stricken 1 Dec 1970
CL 101	AMSTERDAM	stricken 2 Jan 1971
CL 102	PORTSMOUTH	stricken 1 Dec 1970
CL 103	WILKES-BARRE	stricken 15 Jan 1971
CL 106	FARGO	stricken 1 Mar 1970
CL 144	WORCESTER	stricken 1 Dec 1970
CL 145	ROANOKE	stricken 1 Dec 1970

Guided Missile Light Cruisers

CLG 3	GALVESTON	stricken 21 Dec 1973(CL 93)
CG 4	LITTLE ROCK	stricken 22 Nov 1976(CL 92/CLG)
CG 5	OKLAHOMA CITY	stricken 15 Dec 1979 (CL 91/CLG); see Addenda
CG 6	PROVIDENCE	stricken 30 Sep 1978(CL 82/CLG)
CG 7	SPRINGFIELD	stricken 30 Sep 1978(CL 66/CLG)
CLG 8	TOPEKA	stricken 1 Dec 1973(CL 67)

Coastal Patrol and Interdiction Craft

CPIC 1	(unnamed)	to South Korea 1 Aug 1975 (returned to U.S. Navy)

Aircraft Carriers

CVS 9	ESSEX	stricken 1 June 1973(CV/CVA)
CVS 10	YORKTOWN	stricken 1 June 1973(CV/CVA)
CVS 14	TICONDEROGA	stricken 16 Nov 1973(CV/CVA)
CVS 15	RANDOLPH	stricken 1 June 1973(CV/CVA)
CVS 18	WASP	stricken 1 July 1972(CV/CVA)
CVS 19	HANCOCK	stricken 31 Jan 1976(CV/CVA)
CVS 33	KEARSARGE	stricken 13 Feb 1970(CV/CVA)
CVS 36	ANTIETAM	stricken 1 May 1973(CV/CVA)
CV 42	FRANKLIN D. ROOSEVELT	stricken 30 Sep 1977(CVB/CVA)

Destroyers

DD 422	MAYO	stricken 1 Dec 1970
DD 432	KEARNY	stricken 1 June 1971
DD 435	GRAYSON	stricken 1 June 1971
DD 437	WOOLSEY	stricken 1 July 1971
DD 440	ERICSSON	stricken 1 June 1970
DD 441	WILKES	stricken 1 Mar 1971
DD 443	SWANSON	stricken 1 Mar 1971
DD 448	LA VALLETTE	to Peru 26 July 1974
DD 449	NICHOLAS	stricken 30 Jan 1970(DDE)
DD 450	O'BANNON	stricken 30 Jan 1970(DDE)
DD 454	ELLYSON	stricken 1 Feb 1970; to Taiwan 6 Aug 1970(DMS 19)
DD 455	HAMBLETON	stricken 1 June 1971(DMS 20)
DD 462	FITCH	stricken 1 July 1971(DMS 25)
DD 475	HUDSON	stricken 1 Dec 1972
DD 478	STANLEY	stricken 1 Dec 1970
DD 479	STEVENS	stricken 1 Dec 1972
DD 490	QUICK	stricken 15 Jan 1972(DMS 32)
DD 491	FARENHOLT	stricken 1 June 1971
DD 493	CARMICK	stricken 1 July 1971(DMS 33)
DD 494	DOYLE	stricken 1 July 1971(DMS 34)
DD 496	McCOOK	stricken 15 Jan 1972(DMS 36)
DD 497	FRANKFORD	stricken 1 June 1971
DD 499	RENSHAW	stricken 14 Feb 1970(DDE)
DD 501	SCHROEDER	stricken 1 Oct 1972
DD 502	SIGSBEE	stricken 1 Dec 1974
DD 511	FOOTE	stricken 1 Oct 1972
DD 513	TERRY	to Peru 26 July 1974
DD 519	DALY	stricken 1 Dec 1974
DD 528	MULLANY	to Taiwan 6 Oct 1971
DD 530	TRATHEN	stricken 1 Nov 1972
DD 531	HAZELWOOD	stricken 1 Dec 1974
DD 534	McCORD	stricken 1 Oct 1972
DD 535	JAMES MILLER	stricken 1 Dec 1974
DD 536	OWEN	stricken 15 Apr 1973
DD 537	THE SULLIVANS	stricken 1 Dec 1974
DD 538	STEPHEN POTTER	stricken 1 Dec 1972
DD 540	TWINING	to Taiwan 16 Aug 1971
DD 547	COWELL	to Argentina 17 Aug 1971
DD 554	FRANKS	stricken 1 Dec 1972
DD 558	LAWS	stricken 15 Apr 1973
DD 562	ROBINSON	stricken 1 Dec 1974
DD 563	ROSS	stricken 1 Dec 1974
DD 564	ROWE	stricken 1 Dec 1974
DD 566	STODDARD	stricken 1 June 1975
DD 567	WATTS	stricken 1 Feb 1974
DD 568	WREN	stricken 1 Dec 1974
DD 573	HARRISON	to Mexico 19 Aug 1970
DD 574	JOHN RODGERS	to Mexico 19 Aug 1970
DD 575	McKEE	stricken 1 Oct 1972
DD 578	WICKES	stricken 1 Nov 1972
DD 585	HARADEN	stricken 15 Apr 1973
DD 587	BELL	stricken 1 Nov 1972
DD 588	BURNS	to Brazil 1 July 1972
DD 594	HART	stricken 15 Apr 1973
DD 595	METCALF	stricken 2 Jan 1971
DD 596	SHIELDS	to Brazil 1 July 1972
DD 598	BANCROFT	stricken 1 June 1971
DD 600	BOYLE	stricken 1 June 1971
DD 601	CHAMPLIN	stricken 2 Jan 1971
DD 602	MEADE	stricken 1 June 1972
DD 603	MURPHY	stricken 1 Nov 1970
DD 604	PARKER	stricken 1 July 1971
DD 606	COGHLAN	stricken 1 July 1971
DD 607	FRAZIER	stricken 1 July 1971
DD 608	GANSEVOORT	stricken 1 July 1971
DD 609	GILLESPIE	stricken 1 July 1971
DD 610	HOBBY	stricken 1 July 1971
DD 613	LAUB	stricken 1 July 1971
DD 614	MacKENZIE	stricken 1 July 1971
DD 615	McLANAHAN	stricken 1 July 1971
DD 616	NIELDS	stricken 15 Sep 1970
DD 617	ORDRONAUX	stricken 1 July 1971
DD 618	DAVISON	stricken 15 Jan 1972(DMS 37)
DD 619	EDWARDS	stricken 1 July 1971
DD 621	JEFFERS	stricken 1 July 1971(DMS 27)
DD 626	SATTERLEE	stricken 1 Dec 1970
DD 627	THOMPSON	stricken 1 July 1971(DMS 38)
DD 629	ABBOT	stricken 1 Dec 1974
DD 630	BRAINE	to Argentina 17 Aug 1971
DD 632	COWIE	stricken 1 Dec 1970(DMS 39)
DD 634	DORAN	stricken 15 Jan 1972(DMS 41)
DD 637	GHERARDI	stricken 1 June 1971(DMS 30)
DD 638	HERNDON	stricken 1 July 1971
DD 640	BEATTY	to Venezuela 14 July 1972

DD 641 TILLMAN	stricken 1 June 1970	
DD 643 SIGOURNEY	stricken 1 Dec 1974	
DD 644 STEMBEL	stricken 1 Sep 1975	
DD 646 STOCKTON	stricken 1 July 1971	
DD 647 THORN	stricken 1 July 1971	
DD 649 ALBERT W. GRANT	stricken 14 Apr 1971	
DD 650 CAPERTON	stricken 1 Dec 1974	
DD 652 INGERSOLL	stricken 20 Jan 1970	
DD 653 KNAPP	stricken 6 Mar 1972	
DD 654 BEARSS	stricken 1 Dec 1974	
DD 655 JOHN HOOD	stricken 1 Dec 1974	
DD 657 CHARLES J. BADGER	to Chile 17 May 1974	
DD 659 DASHIELL	stricken 1 Dec 1974	
DD 660 BULLARD	stricken 1 Dec 1972	
DD 661 KIDD	stricken 1 Dec 1974	
DD 662 BENNION	stricken 15 Apr 1971	
DD 667 CHAUNCEY	stricken 1 Oct 1972	
DD 669 COTTEN	stricken 1 Dec 1974	
DD 671 GATLING	stricken 1 Dec 1974	
DD 672 HEALY	stricken 1 Dec 1974	
DD 674 HUNT	stricken 1 Dec 1974	
DD 679 MCNAIR	stricken 1 Dec 1974	
DD 680 MELVIN	stricken 1 Dec 1974	
DD 681 HOPEWELL	stricken 2 Jan 1970	
DD 682 PORTERFIELD	stricken 1 Mar 1975	
DD 683 STOCKHAM	stricken 1 Dec 1974	
DD 685 PICKING	stricken 1 Mar 1975	
DD 687 UHLMANN	stricken 15 July 1972	
DD 688 REMEY	stricken 1 Dec 1974	
DD 690 NORMAN SCOTT	stricken 15 Apr 1973	
DD 691 MERTZ	stricken 1 Oct 1970	
DD 692 ALLEN M. SUMNER	stricken 15 Aug 1973	
DD 693 MOALE	stricken 2 July 1973	
DD 694 INGRAHAM	to Greece 16 July 1971	
DD 697 CHARLES S. SPERRY	to Chile 8 Jan 1974	
DD 698 AULT	stricken 16 July 1973	
DD 699 WALDRON	to Colombia 30 Oct 1973	
DD 700 HAYNSWORTH	stricken 30 Jan 1970; to Taiwan 12 May 1970	
DD 701 JOHN W. WEEKS	stricken 12 Aug 1970	
DD 702 HANK	to Argentina 1 July 1972	
DD 703 WALLACE L. LIND	to South Korea 4 Dec 1973	
DD 704 BORIE	to Argentina 1 July 1972	
DD 705 COMPTON	to Brazil 27 Sep 1972	
DD 706 GAINARD	stricken 26 Feb 1971; to Iran Mar 1971	
DD 707 SOLEY	stricken 13 Feb 1970	
DD 708 HARLAN R. DICKSON	stricken 1 July 1972	
DD 709 HUGH PURVIS	to Turkey 1 July 1972	
DD 710 GEARING	stricken 1 July 1973	
DD 711 EUGENE A. GREENE	to Spain 31 Aug 1972	
DD 713 KENNETH D. BAILEY	to Iran 13 Jan 1975(DDR)	
DD 714 WILLIAM R. RUSH	to South Korea July 1978(DDR)	
DD 715 WILLIAM M. WOOD	stricken 1 Dec 1974	
DD 716 WILTSIE	stricken 23 Jan 1976; to Pakistan 29 Apr 1977	
DD 717 THEODORE E. CHANDLER	stricken 1 Apr 75	
DD 718 HAMNER	to Taiwan 1 Oct 1979	
DD 719 EPPERSON	stricken 30 Jan 1976; to Pakistan 29 Apr 1977(DDE)	
DD 723 WALKE	stricken 1 Feb 1974	
DD 724 LAFFEY	stricken 29 Mar 1975	
DD 725 O'BRIEN	stricken 18 Feb 1972	
DD 727 DE HAVEN	to South Korea 5 Dec 1973	
DD 728 MANSFIELD	to Argentina 4 June 1974	
DD 729 LYMAN K. SWENSON	to Taiwan 6 May 1974	
DD 730 COLLETT	to Argentina 4 June 1974	
DD 731 MADDOX	to Taiwan 6 July 1972	
DD 734 PURDY	stricken 2 July 1973	
DD 735 ROBERT H. SMITH	stricken 26 Feb 1971(DM/MMD 23)	
DD 736 THOMAS E. FRASER	stricken 1 Nov 1970(DM/MMD 24)	
DD 737 SHANNON	stricken 1 Nov 1970(DM/MMD 25)	
DD 739 ADAMS	stricken 1 Dec 1970(DM/MMD 27)	
DD 740 TOLMAN	stricken 1 Dec 1970(DM/MMD 28)	
DD 742 FRANK KNOX	to Greece 30 Jan 1971(DDR)	
DD 744 BLUE	stricken 1 Feb 1974	
DD 746 TAUSSIG	to Taiwan 6 May 1974	
DD 749 HENRY A. WILEY	stricken 15 Oct 1970(DM/MMD 29)	
DD 752 ALFRED A. CUNNINGHAM	stricken 1 Feb 1974	
DD 753 JOHN R. PIERCE	stricken 2 July 1974	
DD 755 JOHN A. BOLE	to Taiwan 6 May 1974	
DD 756 BEATTY	to Venezuela 14 July 1972	
DD 757 PUTNAM	stricken 6 Aug 1973	
DD 758 STRONG	to Brazil 31 Oct 1973	
DD 759 LOFBERG	to Taiwan 6 May 1974	
DD 760 JOHN W. THOMASON	to Taiwan 6 May 1974	
DD 761 BUCK	to Brazil 16 July 1973	
DD 762 HENLEY	stricken 2 July 1973	
DD 764 LLOYD THOMAS	to Taiwan 12 Oct 1972(DDE)	
DD 765 KEPPLER	to Turkey 1 July 1972(DDE)	
DD 770 LOWRY	to Brazil 29 Oct 1973	
DD 771 LINDSEY	stricken 1 Oct 1970(DM/MMD 32)	
DD 775 WILLARD KEITH	to Colombia 1 July 1972	
DD 776 JAMES C. OWENS	to Brazil 16 July 1973	
DD 777 ZELLARS	to Iran 19 Mar 1971	
DD 778 MASSEY	stricken 19 Sep 1973	
DD 779 DOUGLAS H. FOX	to Chile 8 Jan 1974	
DD 780 STORMES	to Iran 16 Feb 1972	
DD 781 ROBERT K. HUNTINGTON	to Venezuela 31 Oct 1973	
DD 782 ROWAN	to Taiwan June 1977	
DD 783 GURKE	to Greece 17 Mar 1977	
DD 785 HENDERSON	stricken 1 Oct 1980; to Pakistan 30 Sep 1980	
DD 786 RICHARD B. ANDERSON	to Taiwan 10 June 1977	
DD 787 JAMES E. KYES	to Taiwan 18 Apr 1973	
DD 788 HOLLISTER	stricken 1 Oct 1979	
DD 789 EVERSOLE	to Turkey 11 July 1973	
DD 790 SHELTON	to Taiwan 18 Apr 1973	
DD 793 CASSIN YOUNG	stricken 1 Dec 1974	
DD 800 PORTER	stricken 1 Oct 1972	
DD 805 CHEVALIER	to South Korea 5 July 1972(DDR)	
DD 806 HIGBEE	stricken 15 July 1979(DDR)	

DD 807	BENNER	stricken 1 Feb 1974(DDR)
DD 808	DENNIS J. BUCKLEY	stricken 2 July 1973(DDR)
DD 818	NEW	stricken 1 July 1976; to South Korea 23 Feb 1977(DDE)
DD 819	HOLDER	stricken 1 Oct 1976
DD 820	RICH	stricken 15 Dec 1977(DDE)
DD 822	ROBERT H. McCARD	to Turkey 5 June 1980
DD 823	SAMUEL B. ROBERTS	stricken 2 Nov 1970
DD 824	BASILONE	stricken 1 Nov 1977(DDE)
DD 826	AGERHOLM	stricken 1 Dec 1978
DD 829	MYLES C. FOX	stricken 1 Oct 1979; to Greece 2 Aug 1980 (DDR)
DD 830	EVERETT F. LARSON	to South Korea 30 Oct 1972(DDR)
DD 831	GOODRICH	stricken 1 Feb 1974
DD 832	HANSON	to Taiwan 18 Apr 1973(DDR)
DD 833	HERBERT J. THOMAS	to Taiwan 6 May 1974(DDR)
DD 835	CHARLES P. CECIL	stricken 1 Oct 1979; to Greece 2 Aug 1980 (DDR)
DD 836	GEORGE K. MACKENZIE	stricken 1 Oct 1976
DD 837	SARSFIELD	to Taiwan 1 Oct 1977
DD 838	ERNEST G. SMALL	stricken 13 Nov 1970; to Taiwan 19 Feb 1971(DDR)
DD 839	POWER	to Taiwan 1 Oct 1977
DD 840	GLENNON	stricken 1 Oct 1976
DD 841	NOA	to Spain 31 Oct 1973
DD 842	FISKE	to Turkey 5 June 1980
DD 843	WARRINGTON	to Taiwan 24 Apr 1973 (hulk)
DD 844	PERRY	stricken 2 July 1973
DD 845	BAUSSELL	stricken 30 May 1978
DD 846	OZBOURN	stricken 1 June 1975
DD 847	ROBERT L. WILSON	stricken 30 Sep 1974(DDE)
DD 849	RICHARD E. KRAUS	to South Korea 1 July 1972(AG 151)
DD 850	JOSEPH P. KENNEDY JR.	stricken 2 July 1973
DD 851	RUPERTUS	to Greece 10 July 1973
DD 852	LEONARD F. MASON	to Taiwan Jan 1978
DD 853	CHARLES H. ROAN	to Turkey 21 Sep 1973
DD 858	FRED T. BERRY	stricken 15 Sep 1970(DDE)
DD 859	NORRIS	stricken 1 Feb 1974; to Turkey 7 July 1974(DDE)
DD 860	McCAFFERY	stricken 30 Sep 1973(DDE)
DD 861	HARWOOD	to Turkey 17 Dec 1971
DD 865	CHARLES R. WARE	stricken 12 Dec 1974
DD 867	STRIBLING	stricken 1 July 1976
DD 868	BROWNSON	stricken 30 Sep 1976
DD 869	ARNOLD J. ISBELL	to Greece 4 Dec 1973
DD 870	FECHTELER	stricken 11 Sep 1970(DDR)
DD 871	DAMATO	stricken 1 Oct 1980; to Pakistan 30 Sep 1980 (DDE)
DD 872	FORREST ROYAL	to Turkey 27 Mar 1971
DD 873	HAWKINS	stricken 1 Oct 1979(DDR)
DD 874	DUNCAN	stricken 1 Sep 1973(DDR)
DD 875	HENRY W. TUCKER	stricken 3 Dec 1973(DDR)
DD 877	PERKINS	to Argentina 15 Jan 1973(DDR)
DD 878	VESOLE	stricken 1 Dec 1976(DDR)
DD 879	LEARY	to Spain 31 Oct 1973(DDR)
DD 880	DYESS	stricken 1 Oct 1980(DDR)

DD 881	BORDELON	to Iran 1 Feb 1977(DDR)
DD 882	FURSE	to Spain 31 Aug 1972(DDR)
DD 884	FLOYD B. PARKS	stricken 2 July 1972
DD 885	JOHN R. CRAIG	stricken 27 July 1979
DD 887	BRINKLEY BASS	to Brazil 3 Dec 1973
DD 888	STICKELL	to Greece 1 July 1972(DDR)
DD 889	O'HARE	to Spain 31 Oct 1973(DDR)
DD 890	MEREDITH	to Turkey 7 Dec 1979

Guided Missile Destroyers

DDG 35	MITSCHER	stricken 1 June 1978(DL 2/DD 927)
DDG 36	JOHN S. McCAIN	stricken 29 Apr 1978(DL 3/DD 928)

Destroyer Escorts

DE 130	JACOB JONES	stricken 2 Jan 1971
DE 131	HAMMANN	stricken 1 Oct 1972
DE 134	POPE	stricken 2 Jan 1971
DE 137	HERBERT C. JONES	stricken 1 July 1972
DE 138	DOUGLAS L. HOWARD	stricken 1 Oct 1972
DE 139	FARQUHAR	stricken 1 Oct 1972
DE 140	J. R. Y. BLAKELEY	stricken 2 Jan 1971
DE 141	HILL	stricken 1 Oct 1972
DE 145	HUSE	stricken 1 Aug 1973
DE 146	INCH	stricken 1 Oct 1972
DER 147	BLAIR	stricken 1 Dec 1972(DE)
DE 149	CHATELAIN	stricken 1 Aug 1973
DE 150	NEUNZER	stricken 1 July 1972
DE 151	POOLE	stricken 2 Jan 1971
DE 152	PETERSON	stricken 1 Aug 1973
DE 162	LEVY	stricken 1 Aug 1973
DE 163	McCONNELL	stricken 1 Oct 1972
DE 164	OSTERHAUS	stricken 1 Nov 1972
DE 165	PARKS	stricken 1 July 1972
DE 167	ACREE	stricken 1 July 1972
DE 172	COONER	stricken 1 July 1972
DE 180	TRUMPETER	stricken 1 Aug 1973
DE 181	STRAUB	stricken 1 Aug 1973
DE 191	COFFMAN	stricken 1 July 1972
DE 202	EICHENBERGER	stricken 1 Dec 1972
DE 217	COOLBAUGH	stricken 1 July 1972
DE 219	J. DOUGLAS BLACKWOOD	stricken 30 Jan 1970
DE 220	FRANCIS M. ROBINSON	stricken 1 July 1972
DE 231	HODGES	stricken 1 Dec 1972
DE 238	STEWART	stricken 1 Oct 1972
DER 239	STURTEVANT	stricken 1 Dec 1972 (DE)
DE 240	MOORE	stricken 1 Aug 1973
DE 241	KEITH	stricken 1 Nov 1972
DE 242	TOMICH	stricken 1 Nov 1972
DE 243	J. RICHARD WARD	stricken 2 Jan 1971
DER 244	OTTERSTETTER	stricken 1 Aug 1974 (DE)

DE	245	SLOAT	stricken 2 Jan 1971	DE	398	COCKRILL	stricken 1 Aug 1973
DE	247	STANTON	stricken 1 Dec 1970	DE	399	STOCKDALE	stricken 1 July 1972
DE	248	SWASEY	stricken 1 Nov 1972	DER	400	HISSEM	stricken 1 June 1975(DE)
DE	249	MARCHAND	stricken 2 Jan 1971	DE	405	DENNIS	stricken 1 Dec 1972
DE	250	HURST	stricken 1 Dec 1972; to Mexico 1 Oct 1973	DE	406	EDMONDS	stricken 15 May 1972
				DE	409	LA PRADE	stricken 15 Jan 1972
DER	251	CAMP	to South Vietnam 6 Feb 1971; to Philippines 1975(DE)	DE	411	STAFFORD	stricken 15 Mar 1972
				DE	414	LERAY WILSON	stricken 15 May 1972
DE	253	PETTIT	stricken 1 Aug 1973	DE	415	LAWRENCE C. TAYLOR	stricken 1 Dec 1972
DE	254	RICKETTS	stricken 1 Nov 1972	DE	416	MELVIN R. NAWMAN	stricken 1 July 1972
DER	317	JOYCE	stricken 1 Dec 1972 (DE)	DE	417	OLIVER MITCHELL	stricken 15 Mar 1972
DER	318	KIRKPATRICK	stricken 1 Aug 1974 (DE)	DE	418	TABBERER	stricken 1 July 1972
DE	320	MENGES	stricken 2 Jan 1971	DE	419	ROBERT F. KELLER	stricken 1 July 1972
DE	321	MOSLEY	stricken 2 Jan 1971	DE	420	LELAND E. THOMAS	stricken 1 Dec 1972
DE	323	PRIDE	stricken 2 Jan 1971	DE	421	CHESTER T. O'BRIEN	stricken 1 Dec 1972
DER	324	FALGOUT	stricken 1 June 1975 (DE)	DE	423	DUFILHO	stricken 1 Dec 1972
DER	326	THOMAS J. GARY	to Tunisia 27 Oct 1973 (DE)	DE	438	CORBESIER	stricken 1 Dec 1972
DER	328	FINCH	stricken 1 Feb 1974 (DE)	DE	439	CONKLIN	stricken 1 Oct 1970
DER	329	KRETCHMER	stricken 30 Sep 1973 (DE)	DE	441	WILLIAM SEIVERLING	stricken 1 Dec 1972
DE	330	O'REILLY	stricken 15 Jan 1971 (DE)	DE	443	KENDALL C. CAMPBELL	stricken 15 Jan 1972
DER	332	PRICE	stricken 1 Aug 1974(DE)	DE	444	GOSS	stricken 1 Mar 1972
DER	333	STRICKLAND	stricken 1 Dec 1972(DE)	DE	449	HANNA	stricken 1 Dec 1972
DER	334	FORSTER	to South Vietnam 25 Sep 1971(DE)	DE	450	JOSEPH E. CONNOLLY	stricken 1 June 1970
				DE	508	GILLIGAN	stricken 1 Mar 1972
DE	335	DANIEL	stricken 15 Jan 1971	DE	531	EDWARD H. ALLEN	stricken 1 July 1972
DER	336	ROY O. HALE	stricken 1 Aug 1974(DE)	DE	533	HOWARD F. CLARK	stricken 15 May 1972
DE	337	DALE W. PETERSON	stricken 2 Jan 1971	DE	534	SILVERSTEIN	stricken 1 Dec 1972
DE	339	JOHN C. BUTLER	stricken 1 June 1970	DE	537	RIZZI	stricken 1 Aug 1972
DE	340	O'FLAHERTY	stricken 1 Dec 1972	DE	538	OSBERG	stricken 30 June 1974
DE	341	RAYMOND	stricken 1 July 1972	DER	539	WAGNER	stricken 1 Nov 1974(DE)
DE	342	RICHARD A. SUESENS	stricken 15 Mar 1972	DER	540	VANDIVIER	stricken 1 Nov 1974(DE)
DE	346	EDWIN A. HOWARD	stricken 1 Dec 1972	DE	577	ALEXANDER J. LUKE	stricken 1 May 1970
DE	348	KEY	stricken 1 Mar 1972	DE	580	LESLIE L. B. KNOX	stricken 15 Jan 1972
DE	349	GENTRY	stricken 15 Jan 1972	DE	581	MCNULTY	stricken 1 Mar 1972
DE	353	DOYLE C. BARNES	stricken 1 Dec 1972	DE	587	THOMAS F. NICKEL	stricken 1 Dec 1972
DE	354	KENNETH M. WILLETT	stricken 1 July 1972	DE	589	TINSMAN	stricken 15 May 1972
DE	356	LLOYD E. ACREE	stricken 15 Jan 1972	DE	639	GENDREAU	stricken 1 Dec 1972
DE	357	GEORGE E. DAVIS	stricken 1 Dec 1972	DE	640	FIEBERLING	stricken 1 Mar 1972
DE	358	MACK	stricken 15 Mar 1972	DE	641	WILLIAM C. COLE	stricken 1 Mar 1972
DE	360	JOHNNIE HUTCHINS	stricken 1 July 1972	DE	643	DAMON M. CUMMINGS	stricken 1 Mar 1972
DE	362	ROLF	stricken 1 Dec 1972	DE	667	WISEMAN	stricken 15 Apr 1973
DE	363	PRATT	stricken 15 Mar 1972	DE	681	GILLETTE	stricken 1 Dec 1972
DE	364	ROMBACH	stricken 1 Mar 1972	DE	685	COATES	stricken 30 Jan 1970
DE	367	FRENCH	stricken 15 May 1972	DE	696	SPANGLER	stricken 1 Mar 1972
DE	370	JOHN L. WILLIAMSON	stricken 15 Sep 1970	DE	699	MARSH	stricken 15 Apr 1973
DER	382	RAMSDEN	stricken 1 Aug 1974(DE)	DE	700	JOBB	stricken 15 Nov 1974
DER	383	MILLS	stricken 1 Aug 1974(DE)	DE	701	OSMUS	stricken 1 Dec 1972
DER	384	RHODES	stricken 1 Aug 1974(DE)	DE	703	HOLTON	stricken 1 Nov 1972
DER	386	SAVAGE	stricken 1 June 1975(DE)	DE	704	CRONIN	stricken 1 June 1970
DER	387	VANCE	stricken 1 June 1975(DE)	DE	705	FRYBARGER	stricken 1 Dec 1972(DEC)
DER	388	LANSING	stricken 1 Feb 1975(DE)	DE	708	PARLE	stricken 1 July 1970
DER	389	DURANT	stricken 1 Apr 1974(DE)	DE	742	HILBERT	stricken 1 Aug 1972
DER	390	CALCATERRA	stricken 2 July 1973(DE)	DE	743	LAMONS	stricken 1 Aug 1972
DER	391	CHAMBERS	stricken 1 Mar 1975(DE)	DE	744	KYNE	stricken 1 Aug 1972
DE	392	MERRILL	stricken 2 Apr 1972	DE	745	SNYDER	stricken 1 Aug 1972
DE	394	SWENNING	stricken 1 July 1972	DE	750	MCCLELLAND	stricken 1 Aug 1972
DE	395	WILLIS	stricken 1 July 1972	DE	765	EARL K. OLSEN	stricken 1 Aug 1972
DE	396	JANSSEN	stricken 1 July 1972	DE	767	OSWALD	stricken 1 Aug 1972

DE	795	GUNASON

DE 795 GUNASON — stricken 1 Sep 1972
DE 796 MAJOR — stricken 1 Dec 1972
DE 798 VARIAN — stricken 1 Dec 1972
DE 800 JACK W. WILKE — stricken 1 Aug 1972
DE 1006 DEALEY — to Uruguay 28 July 1972
DE 1014 CROMWELL — stricken 5 July 1972
DE 1015 HAMMERBERG — stricken 31 Jan 1974
DE 1021 COURTNEY — stricken 14 Dec 1973
DE 1022 LESTER — stricken 31 Jan 1974
DE 1023 EVANS — stricken 3 Dec 1973
DE 1024 BRIDGET — stricken 12 Nov 1973
DE 1025 BAUER — stricken 3 Dec 1973
DE 1026 HOOPER — stricken 6 July 1973
DE 1027 JOHN WILLIS — stricken 14 July 1972
DE 1028 VAN VOORHIS — stricken 1 July 1972
DE 1029 HARTLEY — to Colombia 8 July 1972
DE 1030 JOSEPH K. TAUSSIG — stricken 1 July 1972
DE 1033 CLAUD JONES — to Indonesia 16 Dec 1974
DE 1034 JOHN R. PERRY — to Indonesia 20 Feb 1973
DE 1035 CHARLES BERRY — to Indonesia 31 Jan 1974
DE 1036 MCMORRIS — to Indonesia 16 Dec 1974

Frigates

DL 1 NORFOLK — stricken 1 Nov 1973(CLK 1)
DL 4 WILLIS A. LEE — stricken 15 May 1972(DD 929)
DL 5 WILKINSON — stricken 1 May 1974(DD 930)

Unclassified Miscellaneous

IX 304 ATLANTA — stricken 1 Jan 1970*(CL 104)
IX 305 PROWESS — to South Vietnam 3 June 1970(MSF 280)
IX 311 BENEWAH — stricken 1 Sep 1973; to Philippines 22 May 1974 (APB 35)†
IX 505 (unnamed) — stricken 1 Dec 1977(YTM 759/LT 2077)

Amphibious Command Ships (all formerly AGC)

LCC 7 MOUNT MCKINLEY — stricken 30 July 1976
LCC 11 ELDORADO — stricken 16 Nov 1972
LCC 12 ESTES — stricken 30 July 1976
LCC 16 POCONO — stricken 1 Dec 1976
LCC 17 TACONIC — stricken 1 Dec 1976

Inshore Fire Support Ships (all formerly LSMR except CARRONADE)

LFR 1 CARRONADE — stricken 1 May 1973(IFS 1)
LFR 401 BIG BLACK RIVER — stricken 1 May 1973
LFR 405 BROADKILL RIVER — stricken 1 May 1973

*Originally stricken as CL on 1 Oct 1962; reinstated as IX 304 on 15 May 1964.
†For civilian use.

LFR 409 CLARION RIVER — stricken 8 May 1970
LFR 412 DES PLAINES RIVER — stricken 1 Sep 1972
LFR 512 LAMOILLE RIVER — stricken 1 May 1973
LFR 513 LARAMIE RIVER — stricken 1 May 1973
LFR 515 OWYHEE RIVER — stricken 1 May 1973
LFR 522 RED RIVER — stricken 1 May 1973
LFR 525 ST. FRANCIS RIVER — stricken 17 Apr 1970
LFR 531 SMOKEY HILL RIVER — stricken 1 May 1973
LFR 536 WHITE RIVER — stricken 22 May 1970

Amphibious Cargo Ships (all formerly AKA)

LKA 12 LIBRA — stricken 1 Jan 1977
LKA 19 THUBAN — stricken 1 Jan 1977
LKA 54 ALGOL — stricken 1 Jan 1977
LKA 56 ARNEB — stricken 13 Aug 1971
LKA 57 CAPRICORNUS — stricken 1 Jan 1977
LKA 61 MULIPHEN — stricken 1 Jan 1977
LKA 88 UVALDE
LKA 93 YANCEY — stricken 1 Jan 1977
LKA 94 WINSTONE — stricken 1 Sep 1976
LKA 97 MERRICK — stricken 1 Sep 1976
LKA 103 RANKIN — stricken 1 Jan 1977
LKA 104 SEMINOLE — stricken 1 Sep 1976
LKA 106 UNION — stricken 1 Sep 1976
LKA 107 VERMILION — stricken 1 Jan 1977
LKA 108 WASHBURN — stricken 1 Sep 1976

Amphibious Transports (all formerly APA)

LPA 36 CAMBRIA — stricken 14 Sep 1970
LPA 38 CHILTON — stricken 1 July 1972
LPA 44 FREMONT — stricken 1 June 1973
LPA 45 HENRICO — stricken 1 June 1973
LPA 194 SANDOVAL — stricken 1 Dec 1976
LPA 199 MAGOFFIN — stricken 1 Sep 1976
LPA 208 TALLADEGA — stricken 1 Sep 1976
LPA 209 TAZEWELL — stricken 1 Aug 1972
LPA 213 MOUNTRAIL — stricken 1 Dec 1976
LPA 215 NAVARRO — stricken 1 Sep 1976
LPA 220 OKANOGAN — stricken 1 June 1973
LPA 222 PICKAWAY — stricken 1 Sep 1976
LPA 227 RENVILLE — stricken 1 Sep 1976
LPA 234 BOLLINGER — stricken 15 Dec 1974
LPA 237 BEXAR — stricken 1 Sep 1976
LPA 248 PAUL REVERE — to Spain 17 Jan 1980
LPA 249 FRANCIS MARION — to Spain 11 July 1980

Amphibious Assault Ships

LPH 5 PRINCETON — stricken 30 Jan 1970(CV/CVA/CVS 37)
LPH 8 VALLEY FORGE — stricken 15 Jan 1970(CV/CVA/CVS 45)

Amphibious Transports (Small) (all formerly APD)

LPR 55	LANING	stricken 1 Mar 1975(DE 159)
LPR 86	HOLLIS	stricken 15 Sep 1974(DE 794)
LPR 90	KIRWIN	stricken 15 Sep 1974(DE 229)
LPR 100	RINGNESS	stricken 15 Sep 1974(DE 590)
LPR 101	KNUDSON	stricken 15 July 1972(DE 591)
LPR 119	BEVERLY W. REID	stricken 15 Sep 1974(DE 722)
LPR 123	DIACHENKO	stricken 15 Sep 1974(DE 690)
LPR 124	HORACE A. BASS	stricken 15 Sep 1974(DE 691)
LPR 127	BEGOR	stricken 15 May 1975(DE 711)
LPR 132	BALDUCK	stricken 15 July 1975(DE 716)
LPR 135	WEISS	stricken 15 Sep 1974(DE 719)

Amphibious Transport Submarines

LPSS 315	SEALION	stricken 15 Mar 1977(SS/APSS)

Dock Landing Ships

LSD 5	GUNSTON HALL	to Argentina 1 May 1970
LSD 13	CASA GRANDE	stricken 1 Nov 1976
LSD 14	RUSHMORE	stricken 1 Nov 1976; to Brazil 1981
LSD 15	SHADWELL	stricken 1 Nov 1976
LSD 16	CABILDO	stricken 9 July 1970
LSD 17	CATAMOUNT	stricken 31 Oct 1974
LSD 18	COLONIAL	stricken 4 Sep 1970
LSD 19	COMSTOCK	stricken 30 June 1976
LSD 20	DONNER	stricken 1 Nov 1976; to Brazil 1981
LSD 21	FORT MANDAN	to Greece Jan 1971
LSD 22	FORT MARION	to Taiwan 15 Apr 1977
LSD 25	SAN MARCOS	to Spain 1 July 1971
LSD 26	TORTUGA	stricken 1 Sep 1971
LSD 27	WHETSTONE	stricken 1 Sep 1971

Tank Landing Ships

LST 47	(unnamed)	to Philippines 13 Sep 1976
LST 117	(unnamed)	to Singapore 27 June 1974
LST 176	(unnamed)	stricken 1 Nov 1973
LST 222	(unnamed)	to Philippines 15 July 1972
LST 276	(unnamed)	to Singapore 27 June 1974
LST 277	(unnamed)	to Chile 2 Feb 1973
LST 287	(unnamed)	to Philippines 13 Sep 1976
LST 288	BERKSHIRE COUNTY	to South Korea Nov 1974
LST 344	BLANCO COUNTY	stricken 15 Sep 1974
LST 448	(unnamed)	to Philippines 15 July 1972
LST 456	(unnamed)	stricken 15 June 1973
LST 491	(unnamed)	to Philippines 13 Sep 1976
LST 525	CAROLINE COUNTY	stricken 15 Sep 1974
LST 530	(unnamed)	stricken 15 June 1973
LST 532	CHASE COUNTY	to Singapore June 1974
LST 533	CHEBOYGAN COUNTY	stricken 15 Sep 1974
LST 546	(unnamed)	to Philippines 15 July 1972
LST 550	(unnamed)	stricken 1 Nov 1973
LST 551	CHESTERFIELD COUNTY	stricken 1 June 1970

LST 566	(unnamed)	to Philippines 13 Sep 1976
LST 572	(unnamed)	stricken 15 June 1973
LST 579	(unnamed)	to Singapore 4 June 1976
LST 581	(unnamed)	stricken 1 June 1972
LST 583	CHURCHILL COUNTY	stricken 15 Sep 1974
LST 587	(unnamed)	stricken 15 June 1973
LST 590	(unnamed)	stricken 15 June 1973
LST 602	CLEARWATER COUNTY	to Mexico 30 May 1972
LST 607	(unnamed)	to Philippines 13 Sep 1976
LST 613	(unnamed)	to Singapore 4 June 1976
LST 623	(unnamed)	to Singapore 4 June 1976
LST 626	(unnamed)	stricken 1 June 1972
LST 629	(unnamed)	to Singapore 4 June 1976
LST 630	(unnamed)	stricken 15 June 1973
LST 643	(unnamed)	stricken 15 June 1973
LST 649	(unnamed)	to Singapore 4 June 1976
LST 664	(unnamed)	stricken 15 June 1973
LST 692	DAVIESS COUNTY	to Philippines Sep 1976
LST 722	DODGE COUNTY	to Thailand 17 Nov 1975
LST 758	DUVAL COUNTY	stricken 15 Sep 1974
LST 762	FLOYD COUNTY	stricken 1 Apr 1975
LST 822	HARRIS COUNTY	to Philippines Sep 1976
LST 824	HENRY COUNTY	to Malaysia 7 Oct 1976
LST 836	HOLMES COUNTY	to Singapore 1 July 1971
LST 846	JENNINGS COUNTY	stricken 25 Sep 1970
LST 848	JEROME COUNTY	to South Vietnam 1 Apr 1970; to Philippines 1976
LST 854	KEMPER COUNTY	to Barbados 6 Jan 1976
LST 901	LITCHFIELD COUNTY	stricken 1 Apr 1975
LST 902	LUZERNE COUNTY	stricken 12 Aug 1970
LST 980	MEEKER COUNTY	stricken 1 Apr 1975
LST 983	MIDDLESEX COUNTY	stricken 15 Sep 1974
LST 1032	MONMOUTH COUNTY	stricken 12 Aug 1970
LST 1066	NEW LONDON COUNTY	to Chile 29 Aug 1973
LST 1067	NYE COUNTY	to Chile 29 Aug 1973
LST 1069	ORLEANS PARISH	to Philippines Oct 1976(MSC 6)
LST 1072	(unnamed)	to Philippines Sep 1976
LST 1073	OUTAGAMIE COUNTY	to Brazil 21 May 1971
LST 1076	PAGE COUNTY	to Greece 5 Mar 1971
LST 1077	PARK COUNTY	to Mexico 20 Sep 1971
LST 1082	PITKIN COUNTY	stricken 1 Apr 1975
LST 1083	PLUMAS COUNTY	stricken 1 June 1972
LST 1084	POLK COUNTY	stricken 15 Sep 1974
LST 1088	PULASKI COUNTY	stricken 1 Nov 1973
LST 1096	ST. CLAIR COUNTY	stricken 1 Apr 1975
LST 1122	SAN JOAQUIN COUNTY	stricken 1 May 1972
LST 1123	SEDGEWICK COUNTY	to Malaysia 7 Oct 1976
LST 1126	SNOHOMISH COUNTY	stricken 1 July 1970
LST 1141	STONE COUNTY	to Thailand 12 Mar 1970
LST 1146	SUMMIT COUNTY	to Ecuador 14 Feb 1977
LST 1148	SUMNER COUNTY	stricken 15 Sep 1974
LST 1150	SUTTER COUNTY	stricken 15 Sep 1974
LST 1153	TALBOT COUNTY	stricken 1 June 1973
LST 1156	TERREBONNE PARISH	to Spain 29 Oct 1971
LST 1157	TERRELL COUNTY	to Greece 17 March 1977
LST 1159	TOM GREEN COUNTY	to Spain 5 Jan 1972
LST 1160	TRAVERSE COUNTY	to Spain 6 Jan 1972
LST 1161	VERNON COUNTY	to Venezuela 29 June 1973

LST 1166	WASHTENAW COUNTY	stricken 30 Aug 1973(MSS 2)
LST 1167	WESTCHESTER COUNTY	to Turkey 27 Aug 1974
LST 1168	WEXFORD COUNTY	to Spain 29 Oct 1971
LST 1169	WHITFIELD COUNTY	to Greece 17 Mar 1977
LST 1170	WINDHAM COUNTY	to Turkey 1 June 1973
LST 1171	DE SOTO COUNTY	to Italy 17 July 1972
LST 1173	SUFFOLK COUNTY	to Greece 1981
LST 1174	GRANT COUNTY	to Brazil 15 Jan 1973
LST 1175	YORK COUNTY	to Italy 1 July 1972
LST 1177	LORAIN COUNTY	to Mexico 1981
LST 1178	WOOD COUNTY	to Greece 1981

Mine Countermeasures Support Ships

MCS 1	CATSKILL	stricken 20 Nov 1970(CM 6/AP 106 /LSV 1)
MCS 2	OZARK	stricken 1 Apr 1974(CM 7/AP 107 /LSV 2)

Coastal Minehunters

MHC 43	BITTERN	stricken 1 Feb 1972(AMCU 57)

Destroyer Minelayers

MMD 26	HARRY F. BAUER	stricken 15 Aug 1971(DM/DD 738)
MMD 30	SHEA	stricken 1 Sep 1973 (DM/DD 750)
MMD 33	GWIN	to Turkey 22 Oct 1971(DM/DD 772)

Coastal Minesweepers (formerly AMS)

MSC 121	BLUEBIRD	stricken 2 Jan 1975
MSC 122	CORMORANT	stricken 15 Mar 1974
MSC 190	FALCON	to Indonesia June 1971
MSC 191	FRIGATE BIRD	to Indonesia 11 Aug 1971
MSC 192	HUMMINGBIRD	to Indonesia June 1971
MSC 193	JACANA	to Indonesia Apr 1971
MSC 194	KINGBIRD	stricken 1 July 1972
MSC 195	LIMPKIN	to Indonesia June 1971
MSC 196	MEADOWLARK	to Indonesia Apr 1971
MSC 197	PARROT	stricken 1 Aug 1972
MSC 198	PEACOCK	stricken 1 July 1975
MSC 199	PHOEBE	stricken 1 July 1975
MSC 201	SHRIKE	stricken 1 July 1975
MSC 203	THRASHER	to Singapore 5 Dec 1975
MSC 204	THRUSH	stricken 1 Aug 1977
MSC 205	VIREO	to Fiji 14 Oct 1975
MSC 206	WARBLER	to Fiji 14 Oct 1975
MSC 207	WHIPPOORWILL	to Singapore 5 Dec 1975
MSC 208	WIDGEON	stricken 2 July 1973
MSC 209	WOODPECKER	to Fiji 17 June 1976
MSC 289	ALBATROSS	stricken 1 Apr 1970
MSC 290	GANNET	stricken 1 Apr 1970

Ocean Minesweepers (formerly AM)

MSO 421	AGILE	stricken 1 Sep 1977
MSO 422	AGGRESSIVE	stricken 28 Feb 1975
MSO 423	AVENGE	stricken 1 Feb 1970
MSO 424	BOLD	stricken 28 Feb 1975
MSO 425	BULWARK	stricken 28 Feb 1975
MSO 426	CONFLICT	stricken 1 June 1972
MSO 432	DYNAMIC	to Spain 1 Aug 1974
MSO 434	EMBATTLE	stricken 15 May 1976
MSO 435	ENDURANCE	stricken 1 July 1972
MSO 436	ENERGY	to Philippines 5 July 1972
MSO 444	FIRM	to Philippines 5 July 1972
MSO 445	FORCE	sunk 24 Apr 1973
MSO 447	GUIDE	stricken 1 June 1972
MSO 451	(no U.S. name)	to Uruguay 16 Oct 1979*
MSO 457	LOYALTY	stricken 1 July 1972
MSO 458	LUCID	stricken 15 May 1976
MSO 459	NIMBLE	stricken 1 Nov 1976
MSO 460	NOTABLE	stricken 1 Feb 1971
MSO 461	OBSERVER	stricken 1 Sep 1977
MSO 462	PINNACLE	stricken 1 Sep 1977
MSO 463	PIVOT	to Spain 1 July 1971
MSO 466	PRIME	stricken 28 Feb 1975
MSO 467	REAPER	stricken 28 Feb 1975
MSO 468	RIVAL	stricken 1 Feb 1971
MSO 469	SAGACITY	stricken 1 Oct 1970
MSO 470	SALUTE	stricken 1 Feb 1971
MSO 471	SKILL	stricken 1 Sep 1977
MSO 472	VALOR	stricken 1 Feb 1971
MSO 473	VIGOR	to Spain 5 Apr 1972
MSO 474	VITAL	stricken 1 Sep 1977
MSO 491	PERSISTENT	to Spain 1 July 1971
MSO 494	STURDY	stricken 1 Sep 1977
MSO 495	SWERVE	stricken 1 Sep 1977
MSO 496	VENTURE	stricken 1 Sep 1977
MSO 508	ACME	stricken 15 May 1976
MSO 510	ADVANCE	stricken 15 May 1976
MSO 519	ABILITY	stricken 1 Feb 1971

Submarine Chasers

PCER 853	AMHERST	to South Vietnam 3 June 1970; to Philippines 1975(PCE)
PCER 855	REXBURG	stricken 2 Mar 1970(PCE)
PCE 856	WHITEHALL	stricken 1 July 1970(PCER)
PCER 857	MARYSVILLE	stricken 15 July 1970(PCE)
PCE 877	HAVRE	stricken 1 July 1970 (training hulk)
PCE 880	ELY	stricken 1 July 1970
PCE 902	PORTAGE	stricken 1 July 1970
PCS 1385	HOLLIDAYSBURG	stricken 1 July 1976

*Formerly transferred to France.

Patrol Gunboats (all formerly PGM)

PG 84	ASHEVILLE	stricken 31 Jan 1977
PG 85	GALLUP	stricken 15 Dec 1976; to Taiwan 1981
PG 86	ANTELOPE	stricken 1 Oct 1977; to Environmental Protection Agency 17 Jan 1978
PG 87	READY	stricken 1 Oct 1977
PG 88	CROCKETT	stricken 31 Jan 1977; to Environmental Protection Agency Apr 1977
PG 89	MARATHON	stricken 31 Jan 1977
PG 90	CANON	stricken 31 Jan 1977; to Taiwan 1981
PG 95	DEFIANCE	to Turkey 11 June 1973
PG 96	BENICIA	to South Korea 2 Oct 1971
PG 97	SURPRISE	to Turkey 28 Feb 1973
PG 99	BEACON	to Colombia 1981
PG 100	DOUGLAS	stricken 1 Oct 1977 (assigned to Naval Ship Research and Development Center 1979; see Chapter 18)
PG 101	GREEN BAY	to Colombia 1981

Hydrofoil Submarine Chasers

PCH 1	HIGH POINT	stricken (WMEH 1)

Hydrofoil Gunboats

PGH 1	FLAGSTAFF	see Coast Guard WPGB 1
PGH 2	TUCUMCARI	wrecked 16 Nov 1972; scrapped Oct 1973

Fast Patrol Boats (all unnamed)

PTF 3	stricken 1977
PTF 6	stricken 1977
PTF 7	stricken 1977
PTF 12	stricken 1977
PTF 18	stricken 1980
PTF 19	stricken 1980

Submarines

SS 224	COD	stricken 15 Dec 1971(AGSS/IXSS)
SS 240	ANGLER	stricken 15 Dec 1971 (SSK/AGSS/IXSS)
SS 245	COBIA	stricken 1 July 1970(AGSS)
SS 246	CROAKER	stricken 20 Dec 1971 (SSK/AGSS/IXSS)
SS 269	RASHER	stricken 20 Dec 1971 (SSR/AGSS/IXSS)
SS 272	REDFIN	stricken 1 July 1970(SSR/AGSS)
SS 287	BOWFIN	stricken 1 Dec 1971(AGSS/IXSS)
SS 297	LING	stricken 1 Dec 1971(AGSS/IXSS)
SS 298	LIONFISH	stricken 20 Dec 1971(AGSS/IXSS)
SS 301	RONCADOR	stricken 1 Dec 1971(AGSS/IXSS)
SS 313	PERCH	stricken 1 Dec 1971 (ASSP/APSS/LPSS/IXSS)
SS 315	SEALION	stricken 15 Mar 1977 (ASSP/APSS/LPSS)
SS 318	BAYA	stricken 30 Oct 1972(AGSS)
SS 319	BECUNA	stricken 15 Aug 1973(AGSS)
SS 322	BLACKFIN	stricken 15 Sep 1972
SS 323	CAIMAN	to Turkey 30 June 1972
SS 324	BLENNY	stricken 15 Aug 1973(AGSS)
SS 328	CHARR	stricken 20 Dec 1971(AGSS/IXSS)
SS 331	BUGARA	stricken 1 Oct 1970(AGSS)
SS 334	CABEZON	stricken 15 May 1970(AGSS)
SS 338	CARP	stricken 20 Dec 1971(AGSS/IXSS)
SS 339	CATFISH	to Argentina 1 July 1971
SS 340	ENTEMEDOR	to Turkey 31 July 1972
SS 341	CHIVO	to Argentina 1 July 1972
SS 342	CHOPPER	stricken 1 Oct 1971(AGSS/IXSS)
SS 343	CLAMAGORE	stricken 27 June 1975
SS 344	COBBLER	to Turkey 21 Nov 1973
SS 346	CORPORAL	to Turkey 21 Nov 1973
SS 347	CUBERA	to Venezuela 5 Jan 1972
SS 349	DIODON	stricken 15 Jan 1971
SS 350	DOGFISH	to Brazil 28 July 1972
SS 351	GREENFISH	to Brazil 19 Dec 1973
SS 352	HALFBEAK	stricken 1 July 1971
SS 365	HARDHEAD	to Greece 26 July 1972
SS 368	JALLAO	to Spain 26 June 1974
SS 370	KRAKEN	stricken 18 Nov 1974
SS 382	PICUDA	to Spain 1 Oct 1972
SS 383	PAMPANITO	stricken 20 Dec 1971(AGSS/IXSS)
SS 385	BANG	to Spain 1 Oct 1972
SS 391	POMFRET	to Turkey 1 July 1971
SS 394	RAZORBACK	to Turkey 30 Nov 1970
SS 396	RONQUIL	to Spain 1 July 1971
SS 398	SEGUNDO	stricken 8 Aug 1970
SS 402	SEA FOX	to Turkey 14 Dec 1970
SS 403	ATULE	to Peru 31 July 1974(AGSS)
SS 406	SEA POACHER	to Peru 1 July 1974(AGSS)
SS 407	SEA ROBIN	stricken 10 Oct 1970
SS 409	PIPER	stricken 1 July 1970(AGSS)
SS 410	THREADFIN	to Turkey 18 Aug 1972
SS 416	TIRU	stricken 1 July 1975
SS 417	TENCH	stricken 15 Aug 1973(AGSS)
SS 418	THORNBACK	to Turkey 1 July 1971
SS 419	TIGRONE	stricken 27 June 1975(SSR/AGSS)
SS 420	TIRANTE	stricken 1 Oct 1973
SS 421	TRUTTA	to Turkey 1 July 1972
SS 423	TORSK	stricken 15 Dec 1971(AGSS/IXSS)
SS 425	TRUMPETFISH	to Brazil 15 Oct 1973
SS 426	TUSK	to Taiwan 18 Oct 1973
SS 476	RUNNER	stricken 15 Dec 1971(AGSS/IXSS)
SS 478	CUTLASS	to Taiwan 12 Apr 1973
SS 480	MEDREGAL	stricken 1 Aug 1970(AGSS)
SS 481	REQUIN	stricken 20 Dec 1971 (SSR/AGSS/IXSS)
SS 483	SEA LEOPARD	to Brazil 27 Mar 1973
SS 484	ODAX	to Brazil 8 July 1972
SS 485	SIRAGO	stricken 1 June 1972
SS 486	POMODON	stricken 1 Aug 1970
SS 487	REMORA	to Greece 29 Oct 1973

SS 490	VOLADOR	to Italy 18 Aug 1972
SS 522	AMBERJACK	to Brazil 17 Oct 1973
SS 523	GRAMPUS	to Brazil 13 May 1972
SS 524	PICKEREL	to Italy 18 Aug 1972
SS 525	GRENADIER	to Venezuela 15 May 1973
SS 563	TANG	to Turkey 8 Feb 1980*(AGSS)
SS 564	TRIGGER	to Italy 10 July 1973
SS 565	WAHOO	stricken 30 June 1980*
SS 566	TROUT	stricken 19 Dec 1978*
SS 568	HARDER	to Italy 15 Mar 1974
SS 572	SAILFISH	stricken 30 Sep 1978(SSR)
SS 573	SALMON	stricken 1 Oct 1977(SSR/AGSS)

Training Submarines

SST 1	MACKEREL	stricken 31 Jan 1973(SS 570)
SST 2	MARLIN	stricken 31 Jan 1973
SST 3	BARRACUDA	stricken 1 Oct 1973(SSK 1)

COAST GUARD

Icebreakers

WAGB 278	STATEN ISLAND	sold 14 May 1975(AGB 5)
WAGB 279	EASTWIND	sold 31 July 1972
WAGB 280	SOUTHWIND	stricken 1974(AGB 3)
WAGB 283	BURTON ISLAND	sold 9 May 1978(AGB 1/AG 88)
WAGB 284	EDISTO	stricken 15 Nov 1974(AGB 2/AG 89)

Oceanographic Cutters

WAGO 377	ROCKAWAY	sold 25 Oct 1973(WAVP/AVP 29)

Weather Cutters

WAGW 387	GRESHAM	sold 25 Oct 1973(WHEC/AGP 9/AVP 57)

Supply Ships

WAK 186	KUKUI	to Philippines 1 Mar 1972(AK 174)

High Endurance Cutters

WHEC 39	OWASCO	sold 7 Oct 1974(WPG)
WHEC 40	WINNEBAGO	sold 7 Oct 1974(WPG)
WHEC 42	SEBAGO	to MarAd 14 Apr 1972(WPG)
WHEC 44	WACHUSETT	sold Sep 1974(WPG)
WHEC 64	ESCANABA	decommissioned 16 Jan 1974 (WPG)

WHEC 66	KLAMATH	sold Sep 1974(WPG)
WHEC 68	ANDROSCOGGIN	sold 7 Oct 1974(WPG)
WHEC 372	HUMBOLDT	sold 22 May 1970(AVP 21)
WHEC 374	ABSECON	to South Vietnam 15 July 1972(AVP 23)
WHEC 375	CHINCOTEAGUE	to South Vietnam 21 June 1972; to Philippines 1975(AVP 24)
WHEC 378	HALF MOON	sold 18 June 1970(AVP 26)
WHEC 380	YAKUTAT	to South Vietnam 1 Jan 1971(AVP 32)
WHEC 381	BARATARIA	stricken 12 Nov 1970(AVP 33)
WHEC 382	BERING STRAIT	to South Vietnam 1 Jan 1971; to Philippines 1975(AVP 34)
WHEC 383	CASTLE ROCK	to South Vietnam 21 Dec 1971; to Philippines 1975(AVP 35)
WHEC 384	COOK INLET	to South Vietnam 21 Dec 1971(AVP 36)
WHEC 386	MCCULLOCH	to South Vietnam 21 June 1972; to Philippines 1975(AGP 8/AVP 56)

Training Cutters

WIX 157	CUYAHOGA	sunk 20 Oct 1978 (collision; 11 killed)(WMEC/WSC/WPC/AG 26)

Seagoing Buoy Tenders

WLB 270	CACTUS	sold 9 Oct 1973
WLB 289	WOODBINE	stricken 9 June 1972
WLB 328	MAGNOLIA	sold 15 Nov 1972
WLB 329	IVY	sold 28 Nov 1971
WLB 330	JONQUIL	sold 6 May 1970(WAGL/ACM 6)
WLB 332	WILLOW	sold 28 Aug 1971
WLB 391	BLACKTHORN	sunk 28 June 1980 (collision; 17 killed)
WLB 398	REDBUD	to Philippines 1 Mar 1972 (WAGL/AKL)

Inland Buoy Tenders

WLI 228	LINDEN	sold 22 May 1970
WLI 234	MAPLE	stricken 8 Aug 1973
WLI 238	NARCISSUS	stricken 5 May 1971; to Guiana
WLI 248	TAMARACK	sold 2 Aug 1971
WLI 255	ZINNIA	stricken 1 Mar 1972; to USAF
WLI 294	BARBERRY	stricken 23 Feb 1971
WLI 317	VERBENA	sold 19 Feb 1978
WLI 641	AZALEA	stricken Apr 1979
WLI 65302	BLUEBERRY	sold Jan 1976
WLI 65305	LOGANBERRY	sold July 1977
WLI 72260	ELM	sold 19 June 1972
WLI 74286	CLEMATIS	stricken Feb 1977
WLI 74287	SHADBUSH	sold Oct 1976
WLI 80801	TERN	sold 30 Jan 1977

*Three submarines were scheduled to be transferred to Iran: TROUT in 1978 (actually transferred but not delivered), WAHOO in 1980, and TANG in 1982.

Coastal Buoy Tenders

WLM 224	JUNIPER	sold Dec 1975
WLM 227	LILAC	stricken 6 June 1972

River Buoy Tenders

WLR 63	FORSYTHIA	sold 12 Aug 1977
WLR 213	GOLDENROD	stricken 26 Sep 1973; to National Science Foundation
WLR 241	POPLAR	stricken 26 Sep 1973; to National Science Foundation
WLR 268	SYCAMORE	sold 30 June 1977
WLR 285	FOXGLOVE	sold 8 July 1977
WLR 304	FERN	sold 19 June 1972
WLR 73264	OLEANDER	sold 1 June 1977

Lightships

WLV 189	NEW ORLEANS	stricken 6 June 1975
WLV 196	UMATILLA REEF	stricken 20 May 1972
WLV 523	SAN FRANCISCO	to South Vietnam Sep 1971
WLV 526	LAKE HURON	stricken 25 Aug 1970
WLV 530	FIVE FATHOM	stricken 29 Dec 1971
WLV 534	(unnamed)	stricken 28 May 1975
WLV 536	PORTLAND	stricken 9 Aug 1973
WLV 538	DELAWARE	stricken 25 Aug 1971
WLV 539	BOSTON	stricken 9 Aug 1976
WLV 604	COLUMBIA RIVER	decommissioned 13 Dec 1979
WLV 605	RELIEF	sold 1 Aug 1976

Medium Endurance Cutters

WMEC 143	KIMBALL	sold 24 Feb 1970(WSC/WPC)
WMEC 147	MORRIS	stricken 5 Nov 1971(WSC/WPC)
WMEC 156	YEATON	sold 16 July 1970(WSC/WPC)

Patrol Boats

WPB 82301	POINT CAUTION	to South Vietnam 29 Apr 1970
WPB 82303	POINT YOUNG	to South Vietnam 16 Mar 1970
WPB 82305	POINT PARTRIDGE	to South Vietnam 27 Mar 1970
WPB 82306	POINT JEFFERSON	to South Vietnam 21 Feb 1970
WPB 82307	POINT GLOVER	to South Vietnam 14 Feb 1970
WPB 82308	POINT WHITE	to South Vietnam 12 Jan 1970
WPB 82309	POINT ARDEN	to South Vietnam 14 Feb 1970
WPB 82316	POINT MAST	to South Vietnam 16 June 1970
WPB 82319	POINT ORIENT	to South Vietnam 14 July 1970
WPB 82320	POINT KENNEDY	to South Vietnam 16 Mar 1970
WPB 82321	POINT LOMAS	to South Vietnam 26 May 1970
WPB 82323	POINT GRACE	to South Vietnam 16 June 1970
WPB 82324	POINT GREY	to South Vietnam 14 July 1970
WPB 82325	POINT DUME	to South Vietnam 14 Feb 1970
WPB 82326	POINT CYPRESS	to South Vietnam 15 Aug 1970
WPB 82327	POINT BANKS	to South Vietnam 26 May 1970
WPB 82329	POINT WELCOME	to South Vietnam 29 Apr 1970
WPB 82331	POINT MARONE	to South Vietnam 15 Aug 1970
WPB 82373	POINT CAMDEN	to South Vietnam 4 May 1970

Hydrofoil Patrol Boats

WPGB 1	FLAGSTAFF	sold 18 Sep 1978(PGH 1)

Reserve Training Cutters

WTR 379	UNIMAK	stricken 29 May 1975(AVP 31)
WTR 410	COURIER	stricken 31 Jan 1973; to MarAd (WAGR/AK 176)
WTR 885	TANAGER	sold 3 Nov 1972(MSF 385)
WTR 899	LAMAR	sold 8 Nov 1971(PCE)

A pair of Mk 70 MOSS decoys are loaded aboard a nuclear attack submarine. (See Chapter 24.) (U.S. Navy)

Ship Names Index

(Service craft, yard craft, and buoy tenders are not listed)
* Also see Addenda

Ship Designation Index

Addenda

STATE OF THE FLEET
The following is the five-year shipbuilding program put forward by the Carter Administration in late January 1981. A total of 80 new construction ships were proposed; this was an average of five ships less per year than Mr. Carter had previously proposed for the period FY 1982–1986 (see page 3).

Class	FY 1982	FY 1983	FY 1984	FY 1985	FY 1986	Total
SSBN 726	1	1	1	2	1	6
SSN 688	1	1	1	1	2	6
FA-SSN				1		1
CG 47	2	2	4	4	4	16
DDGX				1		1
FFG 7	1					1
FFX			1	2	3	6
MCM	1		4	4	4	13
T-AGOS	4	3	3			10
T-AKX	1	1	2	2	2	8
T-AO	1		2	2	2	7
T-ARC					1	1
ARS	2	1	1			4
	(14)	(9)	(19)	(18)	(20)	(80)

SHIP ACQUISITIONS

Class	FY 1982	FY 1983	FY 1984	FY 1985	Note
T-AFS	1				Note: RFA Lyness
T-AKR	2	3	3		Note: SL-7 commercial ships
T-AKR	1	2		1	Note: Maine-class commercial ships
	(4)	(5)	(3)	(1)	

As this edition of *Ships and Aircraft* went to press, the Reagan Administration was developing a FY 1982–1986 shipbuilding program to provide significantly more ships, including one or more Nimitz (CVN 68)-class carriers and probably a nuclear-propelled cruiser.

FLEET ORGANIZATION
Submarine Squadron 17 established 5 January 1981 at Bremerton, Wash., to support Trident SSBNs; initially assigned Ethan Allen (SSN 608), Thomas A. Edison (SSN 610), and Sam Houston (SSN 609).

SUBMARINES
The Navy has begun phasing the Polaris-armed SSBNs out of service because of their age and in some cases their refueling requirements. Because of the delays in the Trident program, the SSBN force will probably decline to 31 or 32 submarines in 1982. The following is the schedule for the ten Polaris SSBNs. The use of some in the attack role with missile tubes inactivated is planned but subject to reappraisal.

George Washington (SSBN 598) to SSN in FY 1982
Patrick Henry (SSBN 559) to SSN in FY 1982
Theodore Roosevelt (SSBN 600) laid up 1980
Robert E. Lee (SSBN 601) to SSN FY 1982
Abraham Lincoln (SSBN 602) laid up 1980
Ethan Allen (SSBN 608) to SSN 1 Sep 1980
Sam Houston (SSBN 609) to SSN 10 Nov 1980
Thomas A. Edison (SSBN 610) to SSN 6 Oct 1980
John Marshall (SSBN 611) to SSN 1 May 1981
Thomas Jefferson (SSBN 618) to SSN 13 Mar 1981
Florida (SSBN 728) named Jan 1981
Rhode Island (SSBN 730) named Jan 1981
Nautilus (SSN 571) to be emplaced as a memorial in early 1982. The Navy originally selected Annapolis, Md., as the site for the submarine. However, a comprehensive Navy analysis subsequently determined the Navy Yard in Washington, D.C., was the optimum location. President Carter, without consulting with the Navy, later changed the site of the Nautilus to New London, Conn.
Albacore (AGSS 569) stricken 1 May 1980

AIRCRAFT CARRIERS
Coral Sea (CV 43) fitted with Phalanx CIWS in 1980.

CRUISERS
Oklahoma City (CG 5) stricken 15 Dec 1979; however, as of January 1981 the Navy had no plans to dispose of the ship.
Correction: CA 134, 139, and 148 officially Salem class, the Des Moines (CA 134) having originally been considered a unit of the Baltimore class.

DESTROYERS

The Navy had planned to decommission all Naval Reserve Force destroyers by late 1980 except for five ships (DD 827, 862, 863, 886, and 946), with all except the Edson (DD 946). However, the Congress halted further reductions in the NRF destroyer force and the issue is being reconsidered in 1981. DDGX design is being reconsidered with a single 5-inch/54 Mk 45 lightweight gun in place of the 76-mm OTO Melara. Note in the above table the further delay of the DDGX to FY 1986 in the final Carter shipbuilding plan.

FRIGATES

Estocin (FFG 15) commissioned 10 Jan 1981 (AA)
McInerney (FFG 8) lengthened to 454 feet with installation of RAST (Recovery Assist and Secure and Traversing) system to support the SH-60B Seahawk LAMPS III helicopter.

An SH-60B Seahawk hovers off the frigate McInerney (FFG 8) during evaluation of the LAMPS III recovery system, designated RAST. (1980, IBM)

AUXILIARY SHIPS

Pvt. John R. Towle (T-AK 240) laid up in National Defense Reserve Fleet 1980
Pvt. Leonard C. Brostrom (T-AK 255) laid up in National Defense Reserve Fleet 1980
Hospital ships: In addition to the Sanctuary (AH 17), the super liner United States was under consideration for use as a hospital ship in support of the Rapid Deployment Force. The United States, designed to carry 1,982 passengers plus a crew of 1,000, was completed in 1952 and operated as a commercial liner until laid up in 1969. She achieved a record 38.32 knots on trials. (See page 202.)
Ponchatoula (AO 148) to Military Sealift Command 5 Sep 1980 (now T-AO 148)
Cimarron (AO 177) commissioned 10 Jan 1981
Monongahela (AO 178) commissioned Feb 1981
Escape (ARS 6) to Coast Guard 30 Sep 1980 (see below)
Ute (T-ATF 76) to Coast Guard 30 Sep 1980 (see below)
Lipan (T-ATF 85) to Coast Guard 30 Sep 1980 (see below)
Catawba (T-ATF 168) in service 28 May 1980
Navajo (T-ATF 169) in service 13 June 1980
Mohawk (T-ATF 170) in service 16 Oct 1980

The USNS Sirius (T-AFS 8) as RFA Lyness. The ship will operate in the Mediterranean, replacing the USNS Rigel (T-AF 58), which will shift to the Pacific area. (Royal Navy)

SURFACE EFFECTS SHIPS

The Navy purchased a Bell-Halter BH-110 surface effects ship late in 1980 for evaluation in certain Navy and Coast Guard roles. During 1981 the craft will be evaluated by the Coast Guard for six months after which she will be lengthened 50 feet for evaluation by the Navy with the designation SES 200; the following characteristics reflect the Navy modifications:

Displacement:	150 tons light
	216 tons loaded
Length:	159 feet (48.46 m) oa
Beam:	39 feet (11.9 m)
Draft:	8¼ feet (2.5 m) hullborne
	5¼ feet (1.7 m) on air cushion
Propulsion:	2 diesels (Detroit 16V-149TI); 2 fixed-pitch propellers in rigid sidewalls
Lift:	2 diesels (Detroit 8V-92TI); 2 lift fans
Speed:	19 knots hullborne (15 knots in sea state 3)
	40 knots on cushion (33 knots in sea state 3)
Manning:	14 (in naval evaluation)

Bell-Halter BH-110 under way (1980, Bell Aerospace Textron)

A P-3C Orion conducts simulated in-flight refueling from a Boeing KC-135A over Edwards Air Force Base. An actual in-flight refueling capability will be available in prototype configuration about mid-1981. Indian Ocean operations have emphasized the need for extended ranges for patrol aircraft and COD aircraft, with the Navy's C-2 Greyhounds now being fitted with similar gear. (U.S. Navy)

COAST GUARD

Four BEAR-class cutters (WMEC 901-904) are under construction at Tacoma Boatbuilding Co. A contract for the construction of nine additional cutters (WMEC 905-913) was awarded in 1980. However, in December 1980 that award was declared invalid by a federal judge. The Coast Guard had disqualified two lower bids from Robert E. Derector of Middletown, R.I., and Marine Power & Equipment Co. of Seattle, Wash. Neither firm has previously built ships. The Coast Guard is appealing to have the entire class built by the Tacoma firm.

Three former Navy tug-type ships are being modified for use as cutters to help alleviate the shortfall of Coast Guard patrol vessels. They were scheduled to be operational by mid-1981. The cutters and their new hull numbers and location of conversion to Coast Guard configuration are:

USCGC ESCAPE (WMEC 6), formerly ARS 6, Portsmouth Naval Shipyard

USCGC UTE (WMEC 76), formerly T-ATF 76, Coast Guard Yard Curtis Bay

USCGC LIPAN (WMEC 85), formerly T-ATF 85, Coast Guard Yard Curtis Bay